CELTIC FROM THE WEST

CELTIC STUDIES PUBLICATIONS
series editor: John T. Koch

CELTIC STUDIES PUBLICATIONS I

The Celtic Heroic Age: Literary Sources for Ancient Celtic Europe and Early Ireland and Wales, ed. John T. Koch with John Carey (Fourth Edition, revised and expanded, 2003) Pp. x + 440

ISBN 1–891271–09–1

CELTIC STUDIES PUBLICATIONS II

A Celtic Florilegium: Studies in Memory of Brendan O Hehir, ed. Kathryn Klar, Eve Sweetser, and †Claire Thomas (1996) Pp. xxxvi + 227

ISBN *hc* 0–9642446–3–2 *pb* 0–9642446–6–7

CELTIC STUDIES PUBLICATIONS IV

Ildánach Ildírech. A Festschrift for Proinsias Mac Cana, ed. John Carey, John T. Koch, and Pierre-Yves Lambert (1999) Pp. xvii + 312

ISBN 1–891271–01–6

CELTIC STUDIES PUBLICATIONS VII

Yr Hen Iaith: Studies in Early Welsh, ed. Paul Russell (2003) Pp. viii + 224

ISBN 1–891271–10–5

CELTIC STUDIES PUBLICATIONS VIII

Landscape Perception in Early Celtic Literature, Francesco Benozzo (2004) Pp. xvi + 272

ISBN 1–891271–11–3

CELTIC STUDIES PUBLICATIONS IX

Cín Chille Cúile—Texts, Saints and Places: Essays in Honour of Pádraig Ó Riain, ed. John Carey, Máire Herbert, and Kevin Murray (2004) Pp. xxiv + 405

ISBN 1–891271–13–X

CELTIC STUDIES PUBLICATIONS X

Archæologia Britannica: Texts and Translations, Edward Lhwyd, ed. Dewi W. Evans and Brynley F. Roberts (2009) Pp. xii + 262

ISBN 978–1–891271–14–4

CELTIC STUDIES PUBLICATIONS XI

Ireland and the Grail, John Carey (2007) Pp. xxii + 421   ISBN 978–1–891271–15–1

CELTIC STUDIES PUBLICATIONS XII

An Atlas for Celtic Studies: Archaeology and Names in Ancient Europe and Early Medieval Ireland, Britain, and Brittany, John T. Koch with Raimund Karl, Antone Minard, and Simon Ó Faoláin (2007) Pp. viii + 216

ISBN 978–1–84217–309–1

CELTIC STUDIES PUBLICATIONS XIII

Tartessian: Celtic in the South-west at the Dawn of History, John T. Koch (2009) Pp. viii + 184

ISBN 978–1–891271–17–5

CELTIC STUDIES PUBLICATIONS XIV

Moment of Earth: Poems & Essays in Honour of Jeremy Hooker, ed. Christopher Meredith (2007) Pp. xvi + 313

ISBN 978–1–891271–16–8

CELTIC STUDIES PUBLICATIONS XV

Celtic from the West: Alternative Approaches from Archaeology, Genetics, Language and Literature, ed. Barry Cunliffe and John T. Koch (2010) Pp. xii + 383

ISBN 978–1–84217–410–4

Editorial correspondence: CSP-Cymru Cyf., Centre for Advanced Welsh and Celtic Studies,
National Library of Wales, Aberystwyth, Ceredigion, SY23 3HH Wales

CELTIC FROM THE WEST

Alternative Perspectives from Archaeology, Genetics, Language and Literature

edited by

Barry Cunliffe and John T. Koch

OXBOW BOOKS
OXFORD

2010

Published by
Oxbow Books, Oxford, UK

ISBN: 978–1–84217–410–4

This book is available direct from
Oxbow Books, Oxford
(Phone: 01865-241249; Fax: 01865-794449)
and

The David Brown Book Company
PO Box 511, Oakville, CT 06779, USA
(Phone: 860-945-9329; Fax: 860-945-9468)

or from our website
www.oxbowbooks.com

A CIP record for this book is available from the British Library.

Library of Congress Cataloging-in-Publication Data

Celtic from the West : alternative perspectives from archaeology, genetics, language, and literature / edited by Barry Cunliffe and John T. Koch.
    p. cm.
Includes bibliographical references and index.
ISBN 978-1-84217-410-4
  1. Civilization, Celtic--Congresses. 2. Celts--Origin--Congresses. 3. Ethnoarchaeology--Europe--Atlantic Coast Region--Congresses. 4. Celtic antiquities--Congresses. 5. Celtic languages--History--Congresses. 6. Language and culture--Europe--Atlantic Coast Region--Congresses. I. Cunliffe, Barry W. II. Koch, John T.
  CB206.C443 2010
  936.1--dc22
                                    2010013075

Text typeset in the Cynrhan type family by CSP-Cymru Cyf.
Cover design by CSP-Cymru Cyf.

Printed in Wales by
Cambrian Printers, Aberystwyth

CONTENTS

MAPS AND ILLUSTRATIONS

INTRODUCTION

THIS book, and the conference on which it is based, came about because one archaeologist and one linguist, following separate lines of inquiry, arrived at the same novel hypothesis: **Celtic probably evolved in the Atlantic Zone during the Bronze Age** (Cunliffe 2008, 258).[1] This 'Celticization from the West' proposal contrasts with the more familiar accounts of Celtic origins, in which the core narrative is tightly entwined with the La Tène and Hallstatt cultures of Iron Age west-central Europe (also called the 'North Alpine Zone'). The limitations of the standard Hallstatt–La Tène scenario have become increasingly evident in recent years, accounting poorly for how Celtic languages ever became established in Ireland or the Iberian Peninsula, for example (cf. Raftery 2006). Therefore, we were eager to explore this Atlantic Bronze Age alternative further from various perspectives to see whether it might now provide a more robust multidisciplinary foundation for Celtic studies.

To make clear what is being considered here, some terms should be defined. For present purposes, the Atlantic Zone comprises Ireland, Britain, Armorica, and the north and west of the Iberian Peninsula. Across this region, bronze as a standardized alloy of copper with more than 5% tin became the usual material of tools, personal ornaments, and weapons by *c.* 2000 BC in Britain and Ireland, later in the Iberian Peninsula (Pare 2000). Western Europe's Beaker Copper Age began in the first half of the 3rd millennium BC. Though extensive use of iron probably came earlier in Iberia and last in Ireland, the Bronze–Iron Transition was, generally speaking, underway within the relevant region at *c.* 750 BC. 'Celtic' is used here primarily in the linguistic sense, meaning the language family (and ancestral proto-language) represented by the four continuously surviving members Breton, Irish, Scottish Gaelic, and Welsh. The recognized Ancient Celtic languages are Goidelic (or Primitive Irish), British (or Brittonic), Gaulish, Galatian (attested in central Asia Minor), Celtiberian in east-central Spain, and Lepontic in the Italian Lakes District and nearby Switzerland. To these, a case is presented here for adding Tartessian (known from inscriptions in southern Portugal and south-west Spain) as the earliest attested Celtic language. Of the

---

[1] This idea was first elaborated by Cunliffe (2001, 293–7) then restated (2003, 54–5). Apparently independently and with a distinct argument, Brun (2006) has come to similar conclusions, focusing on networks in the aftermath of the Beaker period. Koch (1986; 1991) proposed that Ireland and Britain had become Celtic speaking during the Bronze Age; however, those papers did not exclude the prior emergence of Celtic in central Europe. More recently, Koch (2009) concludes that the Celticity of Tartessian tips the balance in favour of an Atlantic Bronze Age homeland. The precocious proposal of Kalb (1979), that the north-western Iberian Peninsula's Atlantic Bronze Age had been Celtic speaking, received little attention at the time.

various possible definitions of Celtic, *a proven affiliation with the Celtic languages or (for non-linguistic evidence) a demonstrable close connection with them* holds the advantages of detailed scientific precision and a remarkable theoretical stability since the Celtic linguistic family was discovered by the Oxford Welshman Edward Lhuyd over 300 years ago. In saying that Celtic must have existed by the end of the Bronze Age, this does not take us far back into the text-free archaeological record. We are not leaping over, and disregarding, a sequence of intervening developments. Lepontic (attested from the 6th century BC) and Tartessian (from the earlier 7th) are but slightly past the cusp of the Late Bronze Age themselves. They are already significantly differentiated from reconstructed Proto-Celtic, and each other, to put their common ancestor well back into the preceding period.

Refocusing on an earlier date and more westerly location can be viewed as an incremental adjustment, responding to the implications of particular details of linguistic and archaeological discoveries. But beyond a refinement of details, the shift places Proto-Celtic in a world fundamentally different in its social patterns and dominant cultural themes (cf. Kristiansen & Larsson 2005). The Europe that preceded the fragmentation and regionalization of the Bronze–Iron Transition saw the maintenance over many centuries of geographically extensive exchange networks, through which complex beliefs and values were transmitted along with scarce raw materials and standardized artefacts of increasing sophistication. Rising mobility was not merely one of the technological achievements defining the Bronze Age, but also a widely adopted feature of the era's value system, as reflected in recurrent images of horses, wheels, vehicles, and sea-going vessels. In contemplating the restricted compass of the world as known to Herodotus (pp. 18–20, 192), it may now be worth asking whether the horizons of 'the Father of History's' Bronze Age forebears had in fact been broader. There are also unconsidered linguistic implications to the declining mobility of the Early Iron Age: the observable break-up into cultural regionalism would have naturally led to geographically smaller linguistic communities. Therefore, although there were probably fewer Indo-European languages in the mid 2nd millennium BC than a thousand years later, it does not necessarily follow that Indo-European had occupied far less territory in the Bronze Age than in the Iron Age.

Not to overemphasize the radicalism of the present departure, the 'Celtic Atlantic Bronze Age' hypothesis (1) does not involve a re-evaluation of Indo-European as the language from which Celtic evolved (despite Meid 2008), (2) does not require a relocation of the Indo-European homeland itself to the west (nor favour a particular proposed homeland, such as Early Neolithic Anatolia or the Copper Age Pontic–Caspian steppe), and (3) continues to regard the La Tène culture as predominantly Celtic speaking from its beginnings in the 5th century BC and most probably also its Hallstatt predecessor, especially the western Hallstatt D of the 6th century BC. In other words, there is no dispute here about Indo-European coming originally from the east or that it had already appeared, as Celtic, along the entire Atlantic seaboard from Sagres to

Orkney *by* pre-Roman proto-historical times, the later 1st millennium BC. The question is rather whether Indo-European became Celtic before or after it reached the ocean.

To frame such a question meaningfully requires agreed linguistic criteria for the stage at which we define Celtic emerging from Late Indo-European. The traditional diagnostic of the loss of Indo-European *p* (in most positions) was formulated in ignorance of the pre-Roman languages of the Iberian Peninsula. This is the territory where the burgeoning evidence for indigenous Indo-European languages now shows *p* sometimes lost (as in the Celtiberian and Tartessian preverb **ro** from Indo-European **pro*), sometimes retained (in languages otherwise resembling Celtic), and sometimes appearing as *b*, as in *Bletisama* 'Broadest', an ancient place-name from the Peninsula's interior, today *p*-less, and *b*-less, *Ledesma* (Villar 2004). The affinities and affiliation of the Lusitanian language, now attested in six inscriptions of Roman date from the lower Tagus vicinity, are pivotal in this connection, as tackled in the present study by Dagmar Wodtko. Though laden with apparently Celtic names, the Lusitanian inscriptions' word for 'pig' is (accusative) PORCOM retaining Indo-European *p*, thus contrasting with the ancient Insular place-name Ὀρκαδες 'Orkney', for example. Interpretations of Lusitanian thus far range from Untermann (1985–6), who sees it as a Celtic dialect conservatively retaining *p*, to Prósper (2008) for whom it is more akin to Italic. The reflexes of Indo-European *p* on the Peninsula are as yet far from well understood. However, given that such a bewildering pattern is uniquely Hispanic in the ancient Celtic world, that pattern itself is at least consistent with the possibility that this is where *p* was lost and Celtic first emerged alongside its nearest kin.

A second key issue in reconsidering the setting of the emergence of Celtic is the possibility of regional sub-groupings among the principal Indo-European languages. There are long-established ideas placing Celtic, largely on the basis of shared vocabulary, in a western subgroup, together with Germanic and Italic (Mallory & Adams 2006). For many linguists (e.g. Cowgill 1970; Hamp 1998; Kortlandt 2006; Schrijver 2006), shared phonological and morphological features still support the concept of Italo-Celtic as a coherent proto-language between Indo-European and Celtic on the branching family tree, situated geographically somewhere on the west or south-west of an expanding cluster of ancient Indo-European dialects. An alternative theory of Schmidt (1996) and Graham Isaac (this volume) sees special and early affinities between Celtic and a configuration of Indo-European languages that make their appearance to the east, including Greek, Indo-Iranian, Baltic, Slavic, and Albanian. Under the usual understanding of the family-tree model applied to the Indo-European sub-families, such a special connection between Celtic and Indo-Iranian, Greek, &c., would be mutually exclusive with an Italo-Celtic (or an Italic–Celtic–Germanic) proto-language. While Isaac understandably raises this 'Celtic as eastern Indo-European' theory as evidence against the western genesis of Celtic, the two are not a priori incompatible. Absolute dating remains the elusive key, and Isaac's very approximate 2000 BC (for the eastern location of the forerunner of Celtic) is a frank admission that most historical linguists distrust dating proto-languages by statistical formulae applied to word lists and prefer to grope intuitively for the chronological implications of suggestively uncommon shared innovations among related languages. An eastern pre-Celtic leading to an Atlantic Proto-Celtic could be reconciled under an appealingly tightened chronology in which a community of Late Indo-European speakers from eastern Europe (or Anatolia) relocated to the west during the Chalcolithic or Early Bronze Age. We may consider together with such a possibility Stephen Oppenheimer's evidence for gene-flow from the western Balkans to the British Isles (possibly by way of Galicia) at roughly this time. Even so, a single genetic or archaeological proxy, or even a single piece of linguistic evidence, can probably not be decisive, by itself, in tracing the prehistoric diffusion of a language. Nevertheless, this Albanian gene is not the only pointer to the Indo-European east at this period. For example, the two-wheeled chariots represented on the Late Bronze Age 'warrior stelae' of the south-western Iberian Peninsula (25 recognized in Harrison 2004; cf. Celestino 2001) have close analogues in Mycenaean and Scandinavian relief carvings. These can now be traced back directly to the first chariots and chariot burials of the Sintashta–Arkaim culture east of the southern Urals from *c.* 2000 BC (cf. Kuznetsov 2006), a society widely regarded as Indo-European speaking and often as specifically Proto-Indo-Iranian (Anthony 2007).

Thus far, research in molecular population genetics has fallen somewhat short of a straightforward confirmation of the Celtic Atlantic Bronze Age hypothesis from a third discipline. As made plain in the chapters on genetics here (especially Ellen Røyrvik's), this might be too much to ask at present, unless Celticization had come about as the result of a massive influx of new people. Nonetheless, recent research, including work by present contributors Brian McEvoy, Daniel Bradley, and Stephen Oppenheimer, has consistently pointed to extensive and early genetic links between the populations of the British Isles and of the Iberian Peninsula. The disparity or gap to be bridged between various categories of evidence for Insular–Iberian connections has thus far been primarily chronological, with the geneticists drawing most attention to the immediately post-glacial repeopling of northern Europe, as opposed to the later horizons usually seen as more relevant to the spread of Indo-European languages. However, the genetic methods do not permit, as yet, tight chronological precision on their own and therefore tend to be used to reinterpret events already known and dated through archaeology or some other discipline. In other words, it is not genetics that tells us when the glaciers retreated from northern Europe or that people arrived to occupy empty land shortly afterwards, but genetics can help to determine where those people came from. (As Røyrvik's chapter here emphasizes, there is a potential danger of circularity in this, basing conclusions on the hypothesis being tested.) The negative testimony of the geneticists is clearer: any evidence for gene-flow from the prehistoric North Alpine Zone to Britain or Ireland—as we would anticipate if early Celtic speakers had taken their expected route—has been conspicuously absent. A possible minor exception, discussed by McEvoy and Bradley here, appears as Y chromosome evidence linked with a few Ulster Gaelic surnames which could suggest continental background at an Iron Age date. However, the geographical distribution would correlate more nearly with the La Tène style in Ireland than with Celtic/Gaelic speech. In short, then, genetics can be included within a convergence of lines of inquiry calling into question the standard central-European explanation of the origin of the Celtic languages, but has thus far focused mainly on Iberian connections at a date too early to throw direct light on questions of the expansion of the Indo-European languages by the usually accepted chronology.

Twelve years ago, Patrick Sims-Williams concluded: 'A convincing synthesis of genetics, linguistics and prehistoric archaeology is still some way off' (1998, 524). The present book is not intended to refute that assessment, either as having been too pessimistic in the first place or by claiming that all the obstacles to multidisciplinary research have been surmounted in the meantime. Rather, the formidable challenge is faced because the goal is compellingly worthwhile, as Sims-Williams recognized, quoting Sir Walter Bodmer's evocation of 'the enormous power of combining humanistic studies of human populations with the scientific investigation of genetic differences' (1993, 57). It should also then be worthwhile enough for us to brave the pitfalls in the nearer term, rather than leaving them to resolve themselves over an indeterminate length of ripening time.

As well as what we actually do not yet know, and in some cases may never know, there is a great deal that is already known but not yet understood, or been made understandable, outside of one specialism. This will require understanding in considerable depth of detail what lies behind labels like 'Celtic' or 'Urnfield', because it is by now overwhelmingly obvious that language groups and archaeological cultures are not equivalent phenomena from different perspectives (i.e. parallel reflections of 'peoples') nor can they be adequate proxies for one another. In large part the challenge to be taken up—sailing against the tide of 21st-century academic habit—is for workers in one field to engage seriously with the others, to learn to a high degree of competence the methods, limitations, concepts, jargon, modes of criticism, &c. This recommendation should not be taken simply as a quixotic exhortation—long live jargon! However, we can probably not achieve our goals if we interpret the task as providing interdisciplinary colleagues with concise and intelligible answers to their questions while keeping the hideous complexity and uncertainties of our respective sausage factories concealed. Historical linguistics is especially notorious as impenetrable to non-specialists, and, whether as cause or effect, there have been few attempts to present the subject through 'trade books' or mass media. 'Linguistic hegemony' within Celtic studies presents obvious barriers to the sort of multidisciplinary interchange of evidence and ideas sought here, especially for the archaeologists and geneticists, as well as for general readers. Despairing at the inaccessibility of the primary evidence, experts of the various disciplines often cross frontiers travelling light with redacted simplifications only, interpretations that will probably prove more short-lived than the datasets on which they are based.

One unfortunate side-effect of the laudable aim of accessibility across disciplines has been the repeated revivification of a simplistic concept of a people called Celts. Of course, there were groups referred to as Κελτοί by the Greeks and *Celtae* by the Romans—Celts they were, fair enough—and Kim McCone (2008) has now emphasized that *Keltoi* was one name that the speakers of Ancient Celtic languages called themselves. However, as Raimund Karl argues here, the concept of the Celts (or of any other people, as should follow), as something coherent, continuous, and essential is fallacious. As well as having tragic consequences, the notion of race is unscientific nonsense. When what we are actually investigating is the relationship between languages, the material remains of ancient societies, and human DNA, 'Celts' may seem unavoidable as the least long-winded term for the populations where these categories intersect. However, once this genie is out of the bottle, it achieves a life of its own, becomes what we are talking about (or a straw man to be deconstructed, once again) and the Celts' more substantial components can then be subserviently reinterpreted to maintain the integrity of this more familiar and accessible concept. Along these lines, Sims-Williams cautions against 'primitivism', the unexamined expectation that the world had once been inherently simpler, so that national group labels had once designated unities of genes, languages, and material cultures with a high degree of stable integrity over long periods of time. A contemporary New World—specifically US—perspective might assist as an antidote to such foggy thinking about ancient European tribes: it is perfectly possible to have an ethnogenesis resulting in a society in which the expected norm is for an individual's language, genetic background, and national identity to have distinct histories, all of which are well known through both the living memory of the family and a documentary record.

The 'alternative perspectives' of the subtitle refers to both the range of disciplines and differences of opinion. The intention is to stimulate a breadth of original thinking, rather than to launch an Atlantic Celtic thesis as a manifesto. Accordingly, Graham Isaac's ideas about the eastern affinities of Celtic are here restated and extended from Isaac 2004, a critique of the hypothesis as first expressed in Cunliffe 2001.

Raimund Karl's contribution reflects the influential 'Celtosceptic' thinking of archaeologists, such as Simon James (2000) and, especially, John Collis (2003). For Karl, the fallacy of an essentialist concept of 'the Celts' is so grievous and so pervasive as to invalidate from the outset any inquiry into the region and period of origin of the Celtic languages. Despite emphatically deconstructing Celts as a folk, Karl is unwilling to release the study of the languages from their traditional associations with Celtic archaeology (i.e. La Tène and Hallstatt), druids, and so on. Most of these non-linguistic Celtic attributes do not occur in the Iberian Peninsula or during the Bronze Age, which would thus remain perpetually marginal to, if not wholly outside, the scope of Celtic studies. Pushing the argument on from Celtic to language in general, Karl concludes that no language has a time and place of origin. At least Celtic isn't being singled out. In our view, if the proposition that Celtic necessarily emerged somewhere and at some time can only be denied by also denying all such propositions as 'Latin originated in central Italy in the 1st millennium BC', the present quest can continue. After repeated debunking of all things Celtic over the last twenty years, it probably *is* now necessary to confirm that the scientific reality of the Celtic family of languages has never been seriously in doubt since Lhuyd first propounded his discovery in 1707. Certainly the editors agree that it can be a stumbling block when precisely definable languages share their name with desperately elusive peoples or imagined nations. A quest for vaguely defined, or undefined, 'Celtic origins' will not do. We accept the basic linguistic principal that all languages, as attributes of specific human communities, have locations in time and space. However, the well-documented and intelligible analogue of the descent of the Romance languages from Latin may have been overworked and misapplied to the Indo-European and Celtic questions in the past; that is, we require sociolinguistic models in which a speech community takes shape and spreads within a geographically and politically diffuse pre-urban network as opposed to a state expanding around a single literate urban elite centre.

Drawing on her work as a researcher in Sir Walter Bodmer's 'People of the British Isles' Project, Ellen Røyrvik sets out the theoretical and methodological considerations for interpreting the genetic structure of the British population. She enumerates problems that molecular population genetics must overcome before becoming, on its own, a useful tool in historical anthropology. These include (1) obtaining sufficiently large and representative samples to be statistically meaningful; (2) defining human populations according to some combination of often difficult to determine criteria—nation (i.e. political-geography/citizenship), language, and ethnicity (?= cultural self-definition); (3) finding modes of analysis that can accurately represent complex relationships between human populations to reveal significant patterns extracted from thousands of variables; and (4) moving from such recognizable patterns to their correct historical explanations.

David Parsons considers how place-names might be used to determine where a language had originated and in which direction it spread. Comparing the Celtic situation with the more recent and at least notionally historical migration and settlement of the Anglo-Saxons, he soberingly concludes that without an accepted historical framework the place-names would probably not be enough to trace the direction that a preliterate language spread across the land. Against this background, the newly re-collected continent-wide distributions of names in Celtic *-brigā* and *-dūnon* may have less certain testimony than we once thought. That leaves the microcosm of *Noviodunum* 'the new fortified settlement' and *Aliobrix* 'the other hillfort', referring to one another across the lower Danube, as an intriguing 'chicken and egg' problem. The broader implications are potentially unsettling in suggesting that even as our grasp of the data increases exponentially we have only a finite stock of venerable historical models to fall back on to interpret it. Some of the most crucial of these, including the story of the Anglo-Saxon Conquest going back to Gildas, could be myths.

This book brings together the papers that were presented at the one-day Forum on the theme 'Celticization from the West' organized by the University of Wales Centre for Advanced Welsh and Celtic Studies and held at the National Library of Wales in Aberystwyth on 6 December 2008. The collection's publication is supported by the British Academy with a grant which enabled Martin Crampin to prepare the maps, charts, and other illustrations during the period December 2008 to July 2009. As the Iberian Peninsula has remained distinctly marginal to Celtic studies in the English-speaking world, we have invited three scholars who did not present papers at the Forum to contribute 'ancillary studies' providing useful and up-to-date background in this field. As mentioned above, the resolution of 'The problem of Lusitanian', as canvassed here by Dagmar Wodtko, will be essential to understanding the story of Indo-European in the pre-Roman west. The testimony of the Greek and Roman authors on the Κελτοί and *Celtae* is by now fairly well known in Celtic studies, thanks to such publications as Tierney 1959–60, Rankin 1996, Freeman 1996, Freeman et al. in Koch & Carey 2003, and Collis 2003. By contrast, Tartessos has played only a minor and marginal role in modern Celtology, as the semi-legendary portal to the west through which the Phoenicians and Greeks became aware of Armorica and the British Isles. The collection of ancient texts presented here by Philip Freeman redresses the balance, affording primary access to the breadth and detail of sources referring to the place beyond (or near) the Pillars of Hercules called Tartessos. The corpus of south-western or Tartessian inscriptions, the primary subject of Koch's chapter, continues to grow with new and exciting discoveries. What is now the longest extant inscription (with a text of 82 signs), the stone from Mesas do Castelinho, Almodôvar, Portugal, was unearthed in September 2008. An account of this momentous find is published here by its discoverer, Amílcar Guerra. He establishes a reading for this long text together with those of the shorter recently discovered inscriptions from Corte Pinheiro and Vale de Águia.

Barry Cunliffe, Oxford
John T. Koch, Aberystwyth
September 2009

BIBLIOGRAPHY

Anthony, D. 2007 *The Horse, the Wheel, and Language: How Bronze-Age Riders from the Eurasian Steppes Shaped the Modern World*. Princeton, Princeton University Press.

Bodmer, W. 1993 'The Genetics of Celtic Populations', *Proceedings of the British Academy* 82, 37–57.

Brun, P. 2006 'L'origine des Celtes: Communautés linguistiques et réseaux sociaux', *Celtes et Gaulois, l'Archéologie face à l'Histoire, 2: la Préhistoire des Celtes*, dir. D. Vitali. Bibracte 12/2, 29–44.

Celestino Pérez, S. 2001 *Estelas de guerrero y estelas diademadas: La precolonización y formación del mundo tartésico*. Barcelona, Edicions Bellaterra.

Collis, J. 2003 *The Celts: Origins, Myths & Inventions*. Stroud, Tempus.

Cowgill, W. 1970 'Italic and Celtic Superlatives and the Dialects of Indo-European', *Indo-European and Indo-Europeans*, 113–53. Philadelphia, University of Pennsylvania Press.

Cunliffe, B. 2001 *Facing the Ocean: The Atlantic and its Peoples 8000 BC–AD 1500*. Oxford, Oxford University Press.

Cunliffe, B. 2003 *The Celts, A Very Short Introduction*. Oxford, Oxford University Press.

Cunliffe, B. 2008 *Europe between the Oceans, 9000 BC–AD 1000*. New Haven, Yale University Press.

Freeman, P. 1996 'The Earliest Greek Sources on the Celts', *Études Celtiques* 32, 11–48.

Hamp, E. P. 1998 'Whose were the Tocharians?' *The Bronze Age and Early Iron Age Peoples of Eastern Central Asia*, ed. V. H. Mair, vol 1, 307–46. Journal of Indo-European Studies Monograph 26. Washington DC, Institute of the Study of Man.

Harrison, R. J. 2004 *Symbols and Warriors: Images of the European Bronze Age*. Bristol, Western Academic & Specialist Press.

Isaac, G. R. 2004 'The Nature and Origins of the Celtic Languages: Atlantic Seaways, Italo-Celtic and Other Paralinguistic Misapprehensions', *Studia Celtica* 38.49–58.

James, S. 2000 *The Atlantic Celts: Ancient People or Modern Invention?* London, British Museum Press.

Kalb, Ph. 1979 'Die Kelten in Portugal', *Actas del II Coloquio sobre lenguas y culturas prerromanas de la Península Ibérica (Tübingen 1976)*, eds. A. Tovar et al., 209–23. Salamanca.

Koch, J. T. 1986 'New Thoughts on Albion, Ierne, and the "Pretanic" Isles', *Proc. Harvard Celtic Colloquium* 6/7, 1–28.

Koch, J. T. 1991 '*Ériu, Alba*, and *Letha*: When was a Language Ancestral to Gaelic First Spoken in Ireland?', *Emania* 9, 17–27.

Koch, J. T. 2009 *Tartessian: Celtic in the South-west at the Dawn of History*, Celtic Studies 13. Aberystwyth.

Koch, J. T., & J. Carey, eds. 2003 *The Celtic Heroic Age: Literary Sources for Ancient Celtic Europe & Early Ireland & Wales*. 4th ed. Celtic Studies 1. Aberystwyth.

Kortlandt, F. 2006 *Italo-Celtic Origins and Prehistoric Development of the Irish Language*, Leiden Studies in Indo-European 14. Amsterdam–New York, Rodopi.

Kristiansen, K., & T. Larsson 2005 *The Rise of the Bronze Age: Travels, Transmissions, and Transformations*. Cambridge, Cambridge University Press.

Kuznetsov, P. F. 2006 'The Emergence of Bronze Age Chariots in Eastern Europe', *Antiquity* 80, 638–45.

Lhuyd, E. 1707 *Archaeologia Britannica, Giving some Account . . . of the Languages, Histories and Customs of the Original Inhabitants of Great Britain: from Collections and Observations in Travels through Wales, Cornwall, Bas-Bretagne, Ireland and Scotland. Vol. I. Glossography*. Oxford, The Theater.

McCone, K. R. 2008 *The Celtic Question: Modern Constructs and Ancient Realities*. Myles Dillon Memorial Lecture, April 2008. Dublin, Dublin Institute for Advanced Studies.

Mallory, J. P., & D. Q. Adams 2006 *The Oxford Introduction to Proto-Indo-European and the Proto-Indo-European World*. Oxford, Oxford University Press.

Meid, W. 2008 'Celtic Origins, the Western and the Eastern Celts', Sir John Rhŷs Memorial Lecture, *Proceedings of the British Academy* 154, 177–99.

Pare, C. F. E. 2000 'Bronze and the Bronze Age', *Metals Make the World Go Round: Supply and Circulation of Metals in Bronze Age Europe*, ed. C. F. E. Pare, 1–37. Oxford, Oxbow.

Prósper Pérez, B. 2008 'Lusitanian. A Non-Celtic Indo-European Language from Western Hispania', *Celtic and Other Languages in Ancient Europe*, ed. J. L.

García Alonso, 53–64. Salamanca, Ediciones Universidad de Salamanca.

Raftery, B. 2006 'The Insular Celts', *Celtes et Gaulois, l'Archéologie face à l'Histoire, 2: la Préhistoire des Celtes*, dir. D. Vitali. Bibracte 12/2, 107–29.

Rankin, D. 1996 *Celts and the Classical World.* 2nd ed. Routledge, London & New York.

Schmidt, K. H. 1996 *Celtic: A Western Indo-European Language?* Innsbruck, Innsbrucker Beiträge zur Sprachwissenschaft.

Schrijver, P. 2006 Review of G. Meiser, *Veni Vidi Vici: Die Vorgeschichte des lateinischen Perfektsystems* in *Kratylos* 51, 46–64.

Sims-Williams, P. 1998 'Genetics, Linguistics, and Prehistory: Thinking Big and Thinking Straight', *Antiquity* 72, 505–27.

Tierney, J. J. 1959–60 'The Celtic Ethnography of Posidonius', *Proceedings of the Royal Irish Academy* C 60, 189–275.

Untermann, J. 1985–6 'Lusitanisch, Keltiberisch, Keltisch', *Studia Palaeohispanica. Actas del IV Coloquio sobre lenguas y culturas paleohispánicas*, Vitoria/Gasteiz 1985 = *Veleia* 2–3, 57–76.

Villar, F. 2004 'The Celtic Language of the Iberian Peninsula', *Studies in Baltic and Indo-European Linguistics in Honor of William R. Schmalstieg*, eds. P. Baldi & P. U. Dini, 243–74. Amsterdam, John Benjamins.

PART ONE

ARCHAEOLOGY

CHAPTER ONE

CELTICIZATION FROM THE WEST
THE CONTRIBUTION OF ARCHAEOLOGY

Barry Cunliffe

A TRADITIONAL belief, still widely held, is that the Celts originated somewhere in western central Europe, to the north of the Alps, and from there, in a succession of movements over many centuries, spread westwards into Iberia, Britain and Ireland, southwards to the Po valley and the Italian peninsula and eastwards to the Carpathian Basin, Transylvania, the Ukraine, the Balkans eventually reaching Anatolia. The southern and eastern migrations are not in contention. Ample Classical sources attest the movements of peoples from west and north of the Alps impinging on the Classical world in the Hellenistic period in the 4th to 2nd centuries (Rankin 1987, *passim*). These peoples were referred to by the later Greek and Roman writers variously as *Keltoi* (Κελτοί), *Celtae, Galli* and *Galatae* (Γαλάται)—a terminology used rather loosely for invaders from the north.

But what of the supposed movements to Atlantic Europe? The presence of Keltoi is mentioned by early Greek writers describing Iberia as early as the 5th or 6th century (below, pp. 18–20) while the language group identified as Celtic is attested in Iberia, France, Britain and Ireland by the early Roman period at the latest and survives as a spoken language in Brittany, Wales, Scotland and Ireland today. It was not illogical, therefore, for antiquarians to suppose that westerly movements of Celts had taken place starting as early as the 6th century or even before. By the middle of the last century this was widely believed to be so and recent accounts are broadly agreed on the subject (Hubert 1934; Powell 1958; Piggott 1965; Filip 1977). But in the last 40 years or so, as knowledge of the archaeological record has dramatically increased and interpretations have become more nuanced, doubts about this westerly movement have begun to be expressed particularly among British archaeologists.

In the early 1960s the publication of Christopher Hawkes' scheme for the British Iron Age (Hawkes 1959), which was based on the traditional paradigm, was roundly criticized by Roy Hodson on the grounds that the theoretical construct was not supported by the archaeological data (Hodson 1960; 1962; 1964). Then followed Grahame Clark's devastating attack on invasionist hypotheses (Clark 1966) in which he argued that the archaeological evidence from the British Isles offered no support for the then widely held views that British prehistory was punctuated by waves of immigrants flowing in from Continental Europe. He did, however, allow that the Beaker phenomenon may have been an exception. This straw was grasped by Myles Dillon and Nora Chadwick in their book *The Celtic Realms* when they reluctantly accepted that 'the Celtic settlement of the British Isles' might have to be dated to the Beaker period. They concluded that 'There is no reason why so early a date for the coming of the Celts should be impossible' (Dillon and Chadwick 1967, 18–19). In *Iron Age Communities in Britain* (1st edn 1974) I took the position that invasion hypotheses were best relegated to a chapter on the history of the discipline allowing the data for the British Iron Age to be presented with the minimum of preconceptions. For this I was roundly chastised by Pierre-Roland Giot who asked how could one discuss the British Iron Age without mentioning the Celtic language: he was right.

The question of Celtic ethnogenesis was explored at some length by Colin Renfrew in his book *Archaeology and Language* (1987) in a careful analysis that distinguished between the evidence presented in historical texts, material culture and language. Renfrew agreed with Myles Dillon that it is language that distinguishes the Celt and went on to conclude: 'I would prefer to see the development of the Celtic languages, in the sense that they are Celtic as distinct from generalized Indo-European, as taking place essentially in those areas where their speech is later attested' (Renfrew 1987, 245). This was a bold contention and serves as a starting point for the present debate.

But before we can enter the discussion it is necessary to sketch out how the traditional model came into being and why it has survived for so long.

Celts from the east: the traditional paradigm

It was the Scottish antiquary George Buchanan (1506–82) who, in his book *Rerum Scoticarum Historia* published in 1582, first put forward the view that Celts from the Continent settled in the British Isles (Collis 1999). Buchanan had at his disposal a number of Classical sources that were becoming available for the first time in the 16th century and used them selectively to modify traditional mythologies. His model proposed three separate incursions into Britain: Gauls and Belgae from northern Gaul moved into southern Britain, Picts from the shores of the Baltic made their way into eastern Scotland, while the west of Scotland and Ireland were settled by Celts who had sailed along the Atlantic seaways from north-western Iberia having arrived there earlier from central Gaul. It was a model built on scraps gleaned from the Classical sources moulded into a narrative still relying heavily on Irish mythologies. It was also motivated by a desire to give the Scots a respectable pedigree separate from that of the English. Buchanan's account was innovative but had surprisingly little effect on British or European scholarship.

A far more influential work was Paul-Yves Pezron's *Antiquité de la nation et de la langue des Celtes* published in 1703 (and in English as *The antiquities of nations; more particularly of the Celtae or Gauls* in 1706). Pezron (1639–1706) was a Breton theologian (Morgan 1965) and it was natural that he should attempt to link his people's origins to Biblical history. Thus, he persuaded himself that the Celts were descended from Gomer, the grandson of Noah, and that they spread eastwards across Europe, conquering Greece and Rome en route, eventually settling in Brittany and Wales where they continued to speak the Celtic language.

Edward Lhuyd, Keeper of the Ashmolean Museum, became aware of Pezron's studies as early as 1698 (Gunther 1945, 400–1) though the two men never seem to have corresponded. Lhuyd was at this time already at work on his *Archaeologia Britannica* and had begun a period of extensive travels in Cornwall, Wales, the Scottish Islands, Ireland and Brittany to collect material for his great enterprise. The first volume, subtitled *Glossography*, was eventually published in 1707. In it Lhuyd presented vocabularies and grammars of Irish, Breton, Cornish, Welsh and Gaulish. He recognized them to be one language group for which he chose the name 'Celtic', whether in deference to Pezron or to distinguish them from Britons—a term which was beginning to be used to include all the inhabitants of the British Isles (James 1999, 44–52).

Lhuyd's work was a philological study of outstanding value, quite unlike the rambling speculations of Buchanan and Pezron. It was based on first-hand research and careful methodological analysis and set the standards of the discipline. How he might have built on this first volume we will never know: he died in 1709 before the work could be completed but there are some hints of how his thoughts were developing. In letters to his friends and in the preface to the Welsh edition of the *Glossography* he began to speculate on how the Celtic language reached Britain and Ireland (Roberts 1986, 7). He envisaged two waves of invaders arriving from Gaul. The first were the C Britons who settled in the south-east of Britain but were forced out by a second Gaulish wave—P Britons—into the far north of Britain and into Ireland. In Ireland these C Britons constituted a distinct nation alongside another group, the Scots, some of whom migrated to the Scottish Highlands. The Scots, he believed, originally came from Spain. Although he says that this sketch was based solely on linguistic arguments it is tempting to suggest that he was trying to find some accord with the theories of Buchanan and with those of Pezron by integrating them into a single narrative. Lhuyd had been writing at a time when little was known of the archaeology of western Europe—a situation which prevailed until the last decades of the 19th century by which time the archaeological record was beginning to be assembled in a coherent way. It is hardly surprising, therefore, that linguistic models continued to form the framework for interpretation.

The next milestone was the publication, in 1882, of *Early Britain: Celtic Britain* by John Rhŷs, the Jesus Professor of Celtic at Oxford. In it Rhŷs sets out with great clarity his views on the coming of the Celts—views which clearly owe much to Lhuyd. Goidelic Celts were first to arrive in southern Britain from the Continent whence they spread westwards eventually reaching Ireland. Later another Continental group, the Brythonic Celts, arrived in the south exacerbating the westward migration of the Goidels. *Early*

Britain: Celtic Britain was a persuasive book easy of access. Although Rhŷs's theories came under criticism from some philologists they were readily accepted by prehistorians eager to make sense of the fast expanding archaeological record. T. Rice Holmes makes extensive use of the theory in his popular but influential *Ancient Britain and the Invasion of Julius Caesar* (1907), and in later, more detailed, studies, Abercromby (1912), Crawford (1922) and Peake (1922) debate the relationship between the successive Goidelic and Brythonic invasions and assemblages of Bronze and Iron Age material culture. Such beliefs were explicit (or implicit) in most writing on British prehistory in the first half of the 20th century. The most succinct examination of the theme was that offered by Gordon Childe in his *Prehistoric Communities of the British Isles* (1940, 258–63), a book which remained the standard text into the 1960s. But by that time, as we have seen, a new generation of archaeologists was becoming vociferously critical.

The hypothesis of Britain's Celtic migrations, first propounded in cohesive form by Edward Lhuyd at the beginning of the 18th century, is, by any standards, a remarkable survival. Few 18th-century hypotheses can have lasted so long. But longevity does not necessarily mean that it is correct. It was, at best, a simple model deeply rooted in mythology put forward to help explain the few known facts. For nearly two hundred years little new was added by philologists, historians or antiquarians and when at last the rate of archaeological discoveries began dramatically to increase the evidence-base, archaeologists remained content to pay homage to the senior discipline. Thus the discussion spun on into a comforting, self-supporting, circularity. In the more critical atmosphere of the 1960s the old underlying hypothesis was found to be wanting but it was now deeply embedded in scholarship. As Maynard Keynes observed of innovation in 1935, 'The difficulty lies, not in new ideas, but in escaping from the old ones which ramify . . . into every corner of our minds.'

The last 40 years has seen the discipline of archaeology come of age: an exponential growth of data has run parallel with a deep critique of the methods and theories employed to interrogate and explain it. The time is now right for a new model of 'Celtic origins' to be offered, based on archaeological evidence, in the hope that we can engage in a fresh debate with kindred disciplines free from the perceptions of the past.

Mapping the early Celts

Any attempt to consider the origins of the Celts must begin with a mapping exercise. Since language is our prime determinant we begin with a map of Celtic names using here Patrick Sims-Williams' (2006) data remapped by Stephen Oppenheimer (2006, fig. 2.1b). The map (Fig. 1.1), we should remind ourselves, shows the density of Celtic names that have survived in various sources mostly of the Hellenistic or Roman period: blank areas cannot be taken to mean that Celtic was not spoken there but only that it has not survived. Another constraint is that the map is achronic to the extent that it represents all

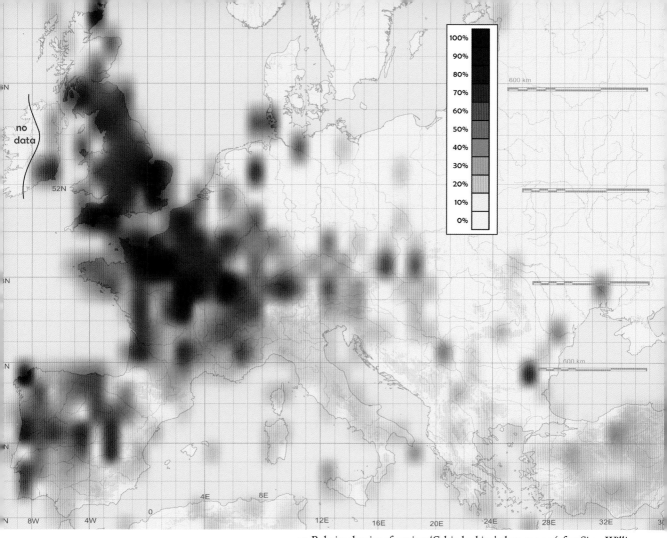

1.1. Relative density of ancient 'Celtic-looking' place-names (after Sims-Williams 2006, Map 5.2); cf. Figure 6.1 drawn from same data, Oppenheimer, p. 124 below.

periods during which Celtic was spoken in pre-medieval Europe. Thus the distribution of Celtic words in the Carpathian Basin and lands to the east in all probability reflects a late situation following the historic 'Celtic migrations' of the 4th and 3rd centuries. At best, then, the map shows us that Celtic was widely spoken in the Atlantic Zone of Europe and along the great rivers flowing into the Atlantic and was resilient enough to survive in place-name evidence. John Koch's recent demonstration that Tartessian was a Celtic language (Koch 2009) adds further substance to this distribution.

The next map offered here (Fig. 1.2) is Stuart Piggott's famous plot of the extent of La Tène material culture (Piggott 1965, fig. 134). Since no one would now argue that La Tène material culture can be taken as a surrogate for the extent of the Celts and since it maps a late phase of European connectivity in the 2nd–1st century BC it is largely irrelevant to our consideration of Celtic origins. Its inclusion here is simply to enable these negative points to be made because there is still, lingering in the work of some writers, the belief that La Tène culture = Celts. It is true that many late Celtic speakers adopted La Tène material culture but that is an entirely different matter.

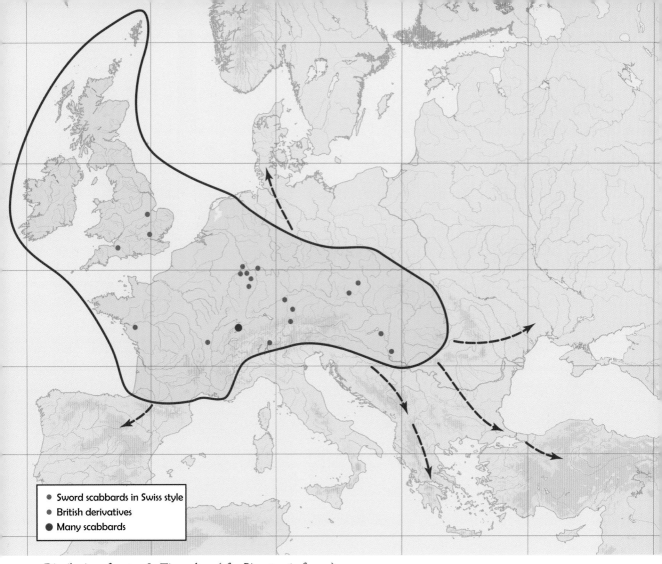

- Sword scabbards in Swiss style
- British derivatives
- Many scabbards

1.2. Distribution of mature La Tène culture (after Piggott 1965, fig. 134)

Finally let us consider the early Greek knowledge of the Barbarian world (Fig. 1.3) since it is in the 6th and 5th centuries BC that the Celts are first mentioned. The earliest source is Hecataeus of Miletus who, in the late 6th century, wrote a *Periegesis* based on a coastal voyage around the Mediterranean and the Black Sea. Three of the surviving fragments mention Celts in the context of coastal towns:

Narbon: trading centre and Celtic city

Massalia: a Ligurian city near Celtica

Nyrax: a Celtic city.

Narbon and Massalia can be directly located and thus confirm the existence of Celts around the Golfe du Lion. Nyrax is more problematical and cannot be located with certainty though it is quite possible that it was a coastal settlement in the same region.

The second source is Herodotus, who wrote his famous *Histories c.* 430–425 BC. Celts are mentioned in two similar passages:

For the Ister, beginning in the land of the Celts and the city of Pyrene flows through the middle of Europe. The Celts live beyond the Pillars of Hercules and border the Cynesii [Κυνησιοι], who are the westernmost inhabitants of Europe (*Hist.* 2.33).

For the Ister flows through all of Europe rising among the Celts who are the westernmost inhabitants of Europe, except for the Cynetes [Κυνητες] (*Hist.* 4.41).

The source of Herodotus' information is unknown. It is quite possible that he took the information from Hecataeus while knowledge of the inland tribes of Iberia would have been widely available among the western Greek maritime fraternity by the end of the 5th century. Greek colonists had begun to settle around the Golfe du Lion as early as 600 BC and there is ample archaeological evidence to show that they had explored the east and south coasts of Iberia and were trading with the Tartessians at the port city, now Huelva, which may have been ancient Tartessos.

1.3. Greek knowledge of the Celts in the age of Hecataeus and Herodotus

The first scrap of information which Herodotus offers is straightforward—the Celts were one of the tribes living in the extreme west of the Iberian Peninsula. The second is more confused—the Ister (Danube) rose in the land of the Celts near the city of Pyrene. If, as seems likely, Pyrene may be identified as Emporion or at least relates to the Pyrenees (Domínguez 2004, 164), then the simplest explanation is that Herodotus must have been misinformed about the source of the Ister.

Finally there is the 4th-century writer Ephorus. According to the incredulous Strabo:

> Ephorus describes Celtica as of excessive size so that most of what we now call Iberia he assigns to it as far as Gades (*Geog.* IV, IV, 6).

Our earliest Classical sources, then, leave little doubt that they understood that the Celts—presumably identifiable in that they were Celtic speakers—were spread across a wide swathe of land bordering the Greek colonies around the Golfe du Lion and extending west to the Atlantic. That said, it is as well to remember that beyond the littoral zone the world remained largely unknown.

This brief review of the spatial extent of the early Celts has emphasized the tenuous and limited nature of the evidence. At best we can say that the Classical sources demonstrate the presence of Celts in the far west as early as the 6th century BC while John Koch's study of Tartessian indicates that the Celtic language may have been spoken in the southern extremity of this Atlantic Zone up to two centuries earlier (Koch 2009). Moreover, the density of surviving Celtic place-names is sufficient to demonstrate that the Celtic language was widely spoken along the entire Atlantic Zone. Given these observations it is not unreasonable to put forward the hypothesis that the Celtic language may have developed somewhere along the Atlantic façade of Europe.

It is now time to turn to the archaeological record to see what evidence there is of systems of connectivity and mobility which might be expected to have some bearing on the question.

The Atlantic Zone: its beginnings

The physical characteristics of the Atlantic Zone have been discussed elsewhere in some detail (Cunliffe 2001a, 19–63). Suffice it to say that the Atlantic face of Europe from the Straits of Gibraltar to the Shetland Islands was bound by a complex series of maritime networks which served to link communities together. For the most part it is likely that the maritime networks were short haul with boat crews making journeys only to neighbouring coastal communities but the aggregate of these movements was to create a continuous network along which goods and ideas were transmitted. At times no doubt longer journeys—perhaps initially journeys of exploration—were undertaken and some of these might have been repeated at intervals in the interests of maintaining social

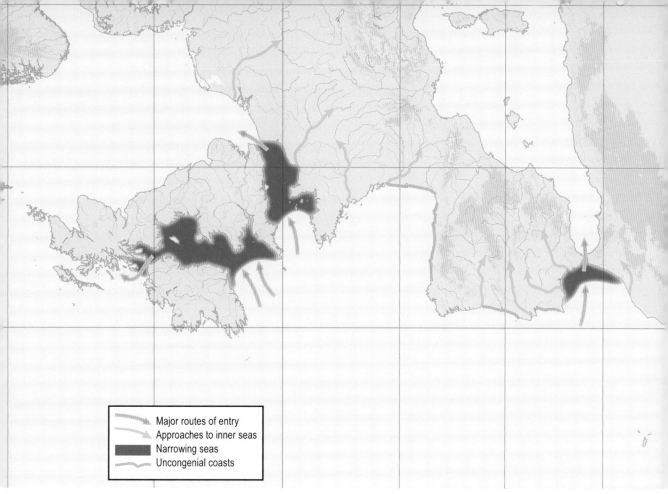

1.4. A cognitive geography of the Atlantic Zone as it might have been viewed by an Atlantic mariner

Legend:
Major routes of entry
Approaches to inner seas
Narrowing seas
Uncongenial coasts

obligations. Along the north-west coast of North America, for example, sea journeys of up to 500 km were made for ceremonial purposes to reaffirm allegiances between distant communities. The sea, far from being a barrier to mobility actually facilitated it: journeys by land were far slower and could be more dangerous.

The Atlantic coast was not uniformly welcoming (Fig. 1.4). Long stretches were fringed with sand bars backed by marshland while other sectors were rocky and sheer. But between these inhospitable coasts there were more congenial zones most notably the ria coastlines of north-western Iberia, Armorica, south-west Britain and southern Ireland where a general rise in sea-level has drowned river valleys creating wide, sheltered waterways thrusting deep inland. The estuaries of the major rivers also presented highly congenial points of entry and the rivers themselves provided routes leading deep inland. The west-flowing rivers of Europe from the Guadalquivir to the Rhine allowed the cultural impact of the Atlantic maritime zone to extend far inland.

Maritime networks presuppose the technical skills to build boats and to navigate (Cunliffe 2001a, 64–71). When humans first took to the sea is uncertain but one possibility is that it was during the time that the Atlantic littoral was used as a migration route for hunter-gatherer groups moving northwards as the climate improved following the retreat of the last ice sheets. Certainly by the Mesolithic period dug-out log boats powered with oars are known and it remains a strong possibility that hide boats, built of skins stretched over a light wooden framework, were in operation. Such vessels would have been well within the technical competence of the hunter-gatherer groups and, because of their light construction, provided a highly flexible mode of travel since they could be carried overland with comparative ease.

The earliest reference we have to hide boats in Atlantic waters is a mention by Pliny in the first century AD but he is quoting a much earlier source, most probably Pytheas who travelled along the Atlantic coasts at the end of the 4th century BC (Cunliffe 2001b, 74–7). The not infrequent references to hide boats by later Classical writers and their persistence in some areas, such as the west coast of Ireland, up to the present day, are an indication of their value, and most likely their predominance, along the Atlantic Zone throughout prehistory.

Already, by the beginning of the 5th millennium BC, there is ample evidence of the small-scale exchange of commodities among coastal hunter-gatherer communities. These early networks, conditioned by the need to maintain systems of social interdependence, set in train the much more vigorous and extensive systems of connectivity that were to dominate the next five millennia of prehistory.

Standing back from the detail of Atlantic prehistory it is possible to distinguish in the changing rhythms of connectivity four broad phases which may be characterized as:

establishing connectivity	5000–2700 BC
escalating mobility	2700–2200 BC
consolidation	2200–800 BC
dislocation and isolation	800–400 BC

Each of these phases will be considered in turn.

Establishing connectivity 5000–2700 BC
The introduction of food-producing economies to the European peninsula is a well-studied phenomenon and the outline of the process is not in doubt. In summary, after the initial introduction of the Neolithic package to Greece in the 7th millennium BC the economic system spread rapidly across middle Europe reaching north-western France *c.* 5300 BC and throughout the Mediterranean, as the result of a number of swift seaborne movements (Fig. 1.5). By the second half of the 6th millennium this Mediterranean advance had led to the establishment of two Neolithic enclaves on the Atlantic coast of Iberia, one in the south-western Algarve and one between the Tagus and Mondego estuaries: by about 4800 BC most of the coastal zone between the two enclaves had adopted food-producing economies. While the nature of this early Neolithic settlement of the Atlantic Zone has been much debated (Zilhão 1993; 2000; Arias 1999), the

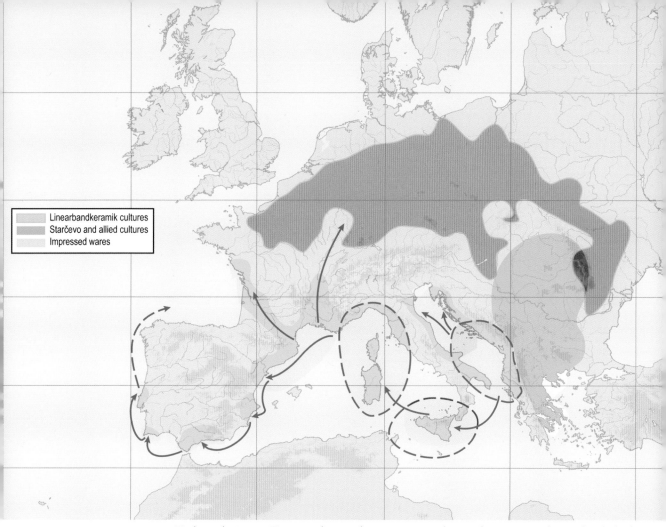

1.5. Enclave colonization. Europe in the period *c.* 5500–4100 BC, showing the two principal routes by which the Neolithic way of life spread through Europe from the southern Balkans, the overland spread via the Danube and North European Plain and the Mediterranean route by sea ultimately to the Atlantic coast of Iberia

simplest explanation is that it resulted from the intrusion of new people coming from the Mediterranean. Barely 500 years separated the earliest colonists setting out from the eastern coasts of the Greek peninsula and the arrival of settlers in Portugal.

The spread of the Neolithic system into the Atlantic coastal regions of France is less well understood. One route was from the Mediterranean along the Garonne–Gironde to the Atlantic, the other led via the middle European route to Normandy and the Channel Islands. There remains the possibility that the Atlantic coastal zone may also have received settlers from the Portuguese enclaves but there is no conclusive evidence of this. Britain and Ireland received Neolithic influences from both the east and the west. The eastern route across the Channel brought people from the northwestern French region (Sheridan 2007) while the western (Atlantic) route saw first the arrival of domesticated animals, quite possibly in the context of gift exchange (Tresset 2003; Woodman & McCarthy 2003) followed by more specific cultural characteristics

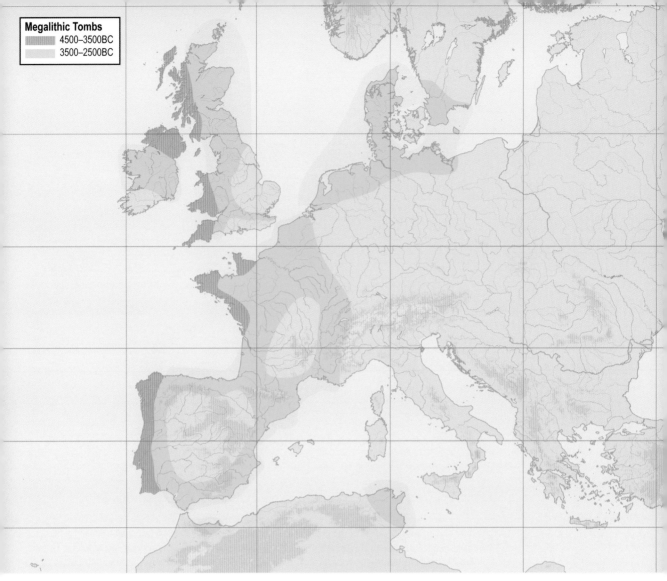

1.6. The distribution of megalithic tombs shows them to be essentially an Atlantic phenomenon. The earliest tombs—passage graves dating c. 4500–3500 BC—have a maritime distribution, suggesting that the beliefs and technologies behind their construction were communicated along the Atlantic seaways.

such as pottery styles and burial rites (Sheridan 2003a; 2003b). Thus, in a comparatively brief period, from 5500–3800 BC, the entire Atlantic coastal region had moved from a hunter-gatherer economy to one of settled food production. The processes of that transition were complex and varied but there can be no reasonable doubt that they involved the movement of people as well as livestock and seed corn and that the sea played a significant role in the rapidity of the transformation.

The continued significance of the seaways in maintaining social and cultural contact is evident in the archaeological record. The most dramatic example is that offered by the spread of passage graves along the Atlantic façade (Fig. 1.6). The concept of the stone-built passage grave probably originated in the Tagus region in the early centuries of the 5th millennium and spread rapidly to Armorica and later further north to Ireland

and western Britain, reaching the Orkney Isles by 3000 BC. Each region developed its own interpretation of the basic concept but all shared in common an underlying belief system and cosmology as well as adopting similar architectural and artistic styles. While the old idea of 'megalithic missionaries' plying the Atlantic coasts is no longer in favour, the evidence suggests that the Atlantic maritime networks were sufficiently active in the 5th and 4th millennia for ideas and beliefs to flow freely creating a degree of cultural cohesion over considerable distances.

Superimposed on these broader systems of maritime connectivity it is possible to identify a number of regional systems recognizable through the distribution of characteristic artefacts, most notably polished axes. Polished stone axes made from distinctive stone sources were frequently distributed over wide areas implying that the axe had a social value which greatly exceeded its practical utility. Axes made from a dolerite from quarries identified at Sélédin, Plussulien in central Brittany seem to have been particularly valued (Le Roux 1999). They account for more than 40 per cent of the known axes in Brittany and were distributed widely across north-western France particularly along the Loire valley and into the river systems of the Seine. Another Breton axe type—this time a shaft-hole axe made of hornblendite from quarries at Pleuven, Quimper—shows a very similar distribution pattern though the actual number of specimens is fewer (Giot & Cogné 1955). Since the axes are likely to have passed from hand to hand as valued items within systems of gift exchange, the distribution patterns reflect the social networks which bound communities together. While the sea was evidently important it is clear from these examples that, already by 3000 BC, the major Atlantic-flowing rivers had become an intimate part of the system.

The extent of the western European networks is no better demonstrated than by the distribution of the magnificent axes made from jadeite coming from a limited number of sources in the eastern Alps (Pétrequin et al. 2008). Axes were manufactured here between 4700 and 3800 and were distributed widely throughout western Europe reaching northern Spain, Scotland and Ireland (Fig. 1.7). The fact that it was the larger and more finely finished versions that travelled the furthest is a sure indication that they were transmitted as items of high prestige. What is significant from our point of view is that the distribution pattern of the axes shows up in stark relief the networks of connectivity which bound the disparate western European communities together. Some of the routes are those along which the Breton axes passed, though in the reverse direction.

It would have been possible to multiply examples of distribution networks, distinguishable through artefact distributions, across the whole face of western Europe but the main point has been well made by the selected examples. In the period from about 5000 BC to about 2700 BC, during which time a food-producing economy was established throughout the region, social networks binding communities continued to expand. The Atlantic seaways provided a major channel of communication but so too did the major rivers flowing into the ocean. These offered routes that led deep into Europe eventually joining with the Rhône, the Po, the Rhine and the Elbe. The maximum extent

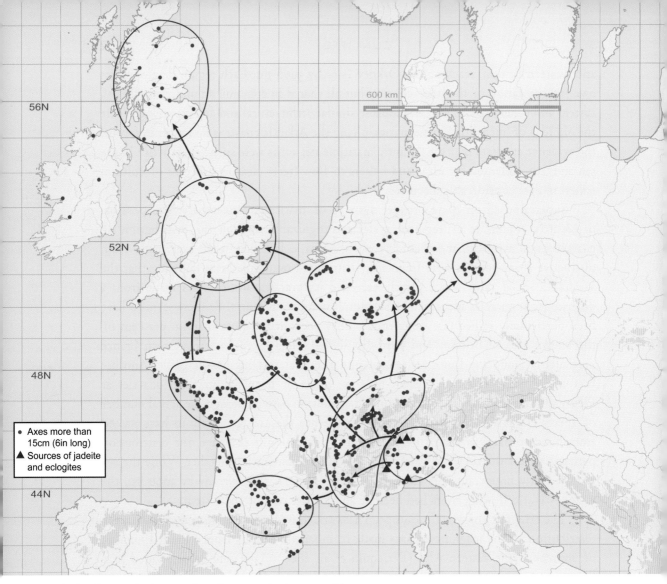

1.7. The distribution of jadeite axes from their source in the western Alps across Europe. The distribution vividly displays the exchange networks then in operation.

of the northern part of this network is vividly demonstrated by the distribution of jadeite axes but similar riverine networks also drew much of the Iberian Peninsula into the Atlantic system.

Systems of connectivity of this kind do not necessarily imply extensive mobility: beliefs, values and commodities can easily pass over considerable distances through the social mechanisms that had come into being to maintain harmony between neighbouring communities. What is important is that the networks allowed cultural characteristics to be shared over considerable distances, between peoples who may have had no direct knowledge of each other, leading to convergences in culture over extensive areas. This *longue durée* of connectivity, coming into being over several millennia, created a structure which was to influence developments in the next period when the mobility of people and commodities was to increase dramatically.

Escalating mobility: 2700–2200 BC

In the 3rd millennium much of the western part of Europe was caught up in what has been referred to as the 'Beaker phenomenon' which saw the appearance of a distinctive type of pottery beaker often associated with recurring sets of grave goods including copper knives and archers' equipment in some regions accompanying single burials. The phenomenon has been variously interpreted (e.g. Clarke 1976; Lanting & Van der Waals 1976; Harrison 1980) but now, with the availability of high precision radiocarbon dates and a more nuanced study of the associated material culture, a new consensus is beginning to emerge.

The earliest form of Bell Beaker—the so-called Maritime Bell Beaker—probably originated in the vibrant copper-using communities of the Tagus estuary around 2800–2700 BC and spread from there to many parts of western Europe (Case 2007). As the map (Fig. 1.8) indicates the initial movements were maritime. A southern move led to the Mediterranean where 'enclaves' were established in south-western Spain and southern France around the Golfe du Lion and into the Po valley. A northern move incorporated the southern coast of Armorica with further, less well defined, contacts extending to Ireland and possibly to central southern Britain. What these archaeological distributions mean in terms of the physical movement of people it is difficult to say, but such are the distances involved that it is difficult to see how the transference of such distinctive sets of cultural values and beliefs could have taken place without significant degree of human mobility and perhaps some element of enclave settlement. This is quite different from the simple down-the-line exchanges we have considered earlier.

One possible context for the increased mobility may lie in the development of a copper technology which was becoming established at this time in the west. The earliest copper production took place in the Tagus region and spread from there to the other areas. The earliest copper production in Ireland, identified at Ross Island in the period 2400–2200, was associated with early Beaker pottery (O'Brien 2004, 451–78). Here the local sulpharsenide ores were smelted to produce the first copper axes used in Britain and Ireland. The same technologies were used in the Tagus region and in the west and south of France (Ambert 2001). The evidence is sufficient to support the suggestion that the initial spread of Maritime Bell Beakers along the Atlantic and into the Mediterranean, using the sea routes that had long been in operation, was directly associated with the quest for copper and other rare raw materials.

The enclave established in southern Brittany was linked closely to the riverine and landward route via the Loire and across the Gâtinais to the Seine valley and thence to the Lower Rhine. This, as we have seen, was a long-established route reflected in early stone axe distributions and it was via this network that Maritime Bell Beakers first reached the Lower Rhine in about 2700–2500. Other materials passing along the exchange networks at this time were the honey-coloured Grand Pressigny flint mined not far from Poitiers and, in reverse direction, amber from the coast of Jutland. Grand Pressigny flint also found its way to the western Alps in the period 2800–2400 BC. It was probably along

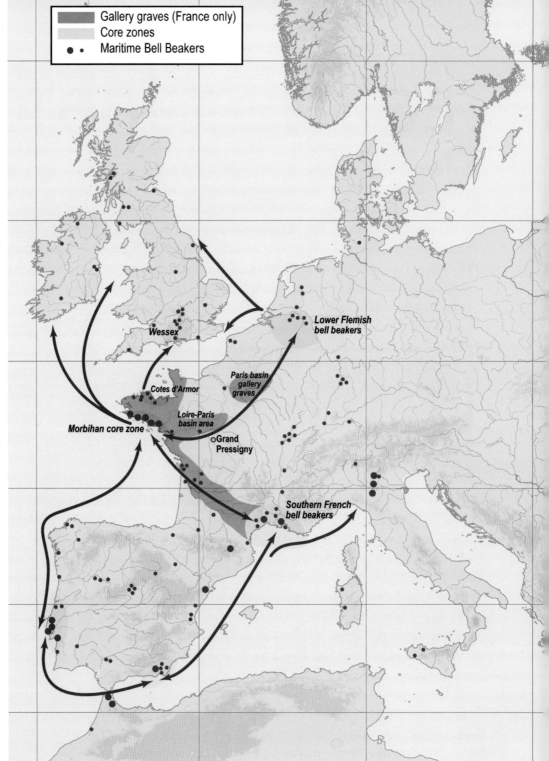

1.8. The distribution of Maritime Bell Beakers in Atlantic Europe during the 3rd millennium: the crucial nodes in this network were the Tagus estuary and the Morbihan, while major hinterland routes followed the navigable rivers.

Legend:
- Gallery graves (France only)
- Core zones
- Maritime Bell Beakers

Map labels:
Lower Flemish bell beakers
Wessex
Paris basin gallery graves
Cotes d'Armor
Loire-Paris basin area
Morbihan core zone
○Grand Pressigny
Southern French bell beakers

the ancient western Alpine routes, used to distribute jadeite axes in the 4th millennium, that Maritime Bell Beakers were transmitted to the Po valley.

The Lower Rhine region had, by 3000 BC, adopted a burial rite characterized by single inhumation accompanied by a beaker decorated with cord zone impressions and, frequently, by a perforated stone battle-axe. This cultural package was characteristic of belief systems which extended across the North European Plain into Russia. The arrival of the Maritime Bell Beaker from the west a century or two later initiated a period of borrowing and experimentation in what has been called the Primary Bell Beaker/Corded Ware contact zone and cultural traits developed here, such as single burial and the shaft-hole axe, were transmitted westwards along the exchange networks from the Rhine to the Loire (Salinova 2000). It was from this *fusion zone* that the modified Beaker package spread northwards across the Channel to Britain (Needham 2005).

The maximum extent of the Bell Beaker complex in the period 2700–2200 BC is shown in sketch form in Figure 9. It extends northwards to the Elbe, eastwards as far as the Danube Bend and into northern Italy and western Sicily but it was by no means uniform and there were tracts where the Beaker package was totally unknown and indigenous culture continued uninterrupted (Heyd 2007): the dense Bell Beaker distributions tend to favour the major corridors of communication by sea and by river.

What all this means in terms of population mobility is a fraught but fascinating question. Archaeologists are reluctant to return to old models of 'Beaker Folk' rampaging across Europe, but that there was a high level of human mobility at this time is not in doubt as numerous studies of stable isotopes in human bones are beginning to demonstrate. The now-famous Amesbury Archer, buried with all his finery within sight of Stonehenge around 2200 BC, was a specialist coppersmith who, according to the percentage of stable isotopes in his teeth, had probably spent his childhood in the western Alps before making the long journey to Wessex (Fitzpatrick 2002). Other studies have shown that surprisingly high percentages of people buried in Beaker-period cemeteries were not born in the region of their death (Price et al. 1998; 2004). It will be some time before the many analyses of this kind, now under way, are published and assessed but the evidence is increasingly pointing to a much higher degree of mobility than had previously been allowed.

Mobility of this kind need not be surprising. We have already seen how, over a period of some two thousand years, complex networks of connectivity had already grown up binding distant communities in western Europe together in loose systems involving socially embedded exchange. The flow of commodities through trade networks was probably on a modest scale and actual movements of people circumscribed. What we see in the Bell Beaker phenomenon of the period 2700–2200 BC is a rapid escalation of these processes. The volume of commodities on the move was now considerable, greatly exacerbated by the new demand for metals—copper, gold and tin—much of which was extracted in the metal-rich Atlantic Zone. This was also a period of fast-developing technologies. The extraction of metal required expertise, so too did its successful alloying. It is worth remembering that the first regular tin-bronze in western Europe is found in the Atlantic Zone where the two components, copper and tin, were found in close proximity (Pare 2000, fig. 1.1). Metalworkers were the new men whose skills were revered and whose presence was worth soliciting. In a fast-changing world of this kind

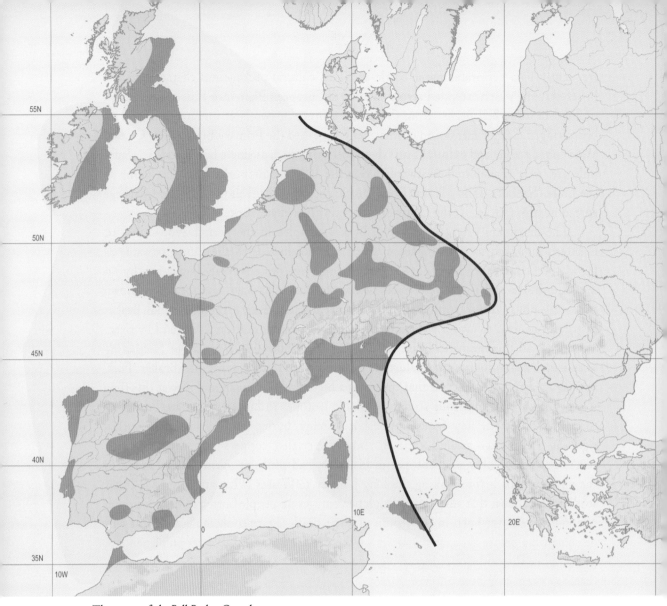

1.9. The extent of the Bell-Beaker Complex 2700–2200 BC

population mobility would have greatly increased.

One further point deserves consideration. The 3rd millennium also saw considerable changes in eastern European society, perhaps the most notable being the intrusion of nomadic horse-riding peoples coming from the Pontic steppe to settle along the Lower Danube valley and on the Great Hungarian Plain within the Carpathian Basin. The Late Yamnaya culture, as it is known, appeared in Hungary around 2700 BC bringing well-trained riding horses from the steppe and a technology of vehicle building to confront the Single Grave/Corded Ware culture of the North European Plain and the Bell Beaker communities of the west (Harrison & Heyd 2007, 193–203). The interactions which must have taken place on the interfaces of these different worlds (Fig. 1.10) would have brought lasting changes to all those involved. It is no exaggeration to say that the middle

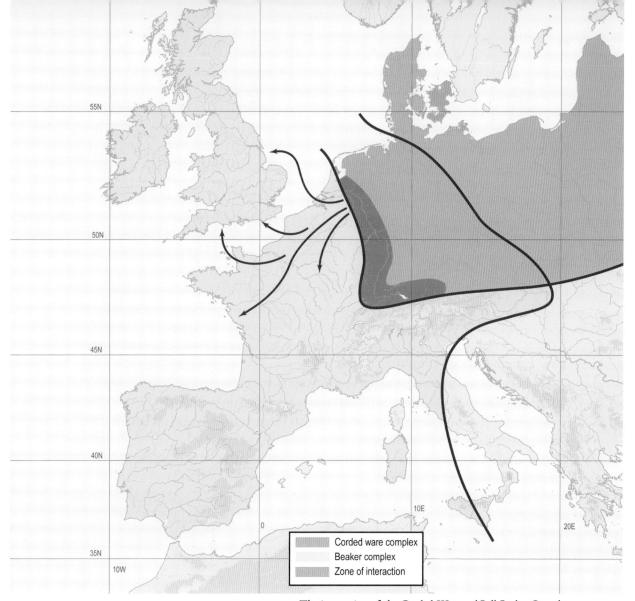

1.10. The interaction of the Corded-Ware and Bell-Beaker Complexes *c.* 2500 BC

of the 3rd millennium was a period of movement and interchange quite unlike anything that had gone before or was to come for another two millennia.

Consolidation: 2200–800 BC

For western Europe the period after about 2200 BC was one of consolidation. There is little evidence of large-scale population mobility but regional networks continued to operate, often on a more intensified scale, leading to the development of distinct regional cultural zones. One good example of this is the English Channel and southern North Sea zone. At the end of the 3rd millennium interaction between the Continent and Britain introduced various elements of the evolved Beaker package to the island, no doubt using the existing maritime networks (Needham 2005). Stuart Needham has further developed his study of these activities by arguing that the mastery of the sea at this time became a mark of elite status and that the surprisingly large numbers of cups made of precious materials, which concentrate in these maritime regions, may have been a symbol of these elites in the early centuries of the 2nd millennium BC. If this is so then the sea itself, rather than being a space between territories, becomes a territory in its own right—in Needham's phrase a *maritory*—over which the elite demonstrate their command (Needham 2009). The hypothesis, though difficult to prove, has distinct attractions.

Throughout the 2nd millennium BC and into the 1st millennium, the maritime connectivity between the south-east of Britain and the adjacent Continent, from Lower Normandy to the Low Countries, intensifies. This is shown by the exchange of bronze implements between the two regions (O'Connor 1980) and also by very close similarities which develop in material cultures, particularly pottery, and in settlement form and layout (Cunliffe 2009). Cyril Marcigny, who has recently surveyed the Continental evidence, writes of a *composante culturelle Manche–Mer du Nord* embracing both sides of the Channel (Marcigny et al. 2002; 2007).

Cultural similarities of this kind, which are now becoming apparent as the French archaeological record continues to be explored and published, imply far more than simple networks maintaining stable relationships through the exchange of material gifts. What we are seeing here are communities creating much closer social ties, involving the movement of people, through marriage and other bonds of obligation which hold lineages together.

This one small study focusing on the English Channel may well be typical of the intensification that was going on throughout the Atlantic Zone in the 2nd and early 1st millennia. It has long been recognized that the Atlantic Bronze Age reflects a time when communities along the entire Atlantic face of Europe were engaged in the exchange of bronze metalwork on a large scale with items being exported over considerable distances. Sicilian shaft-hole axes found their way to Armorica and the Solent coast while lunate spearheads of Irish manufacture were found in collections of bronze-work deposited in the sea off Huelva in south-western Iberia. Viewed overall the Atlantic Bronze Age has the appearance of being a vigorous system of exchange binding maritime Europe from Iberia to Shetland (Chevillot & Coffyn (eds.) 1991; Jorge (ed.) 1998).

But we are looking at far more than just the bulk movement of metal. Embedded within this system lies the sharing of social values and belief systems. The armaments of the warrior, so vividly represented on the carved stelae found in south-western Iberia, depicting the long slashing sword, the spear and the circular shield (Harrison 2004), recur throughout the entire Atlantic Zone while the accoutrements of the hearth—the bronze cauldron, the flesh hook and the roasting spit—are equally widely dispersed. These items are the physical manifestation of the feast which would have played a central role in the display of hospitality expected of the elite. While the bronzes found in quantity in the hundreds of hoards buried or dumped in watery locations throughout the length of Atlantic Europe can, at one level, be regarded as scrap metal dedicated to the deities, at another they reflect the very being of Bronze Age society—its values and its practices.

Dislocation and isolation 800–400 BC

The networks of exchange which developed along the Atlantic seaways during the Late Bronze Age (*c.* 1300–800 BC), and extended deep into the Continent along the river valleys, intensified as time progressed but in the 8th century BC the old system seems to have collapsed. The disposal of bronze in large 'hoards', which had characterized the system for centuries, came to a complete end. Many reasons have been suggested for this comparatively sudden transformation. The matter is complex and cannot be considered in detail here but the likelihood is that a number of factors converged to exacerbate the change. One, of relevance to the present discussion, is the expansion of Phoenician commercial interests into the Atlantic following the establishment of a permanent colonial port-of-trade at Gadir (modern Cádiz) (Aubet 1993). The 8th and 7th centuries saw the creation of Phoenician enclaves down the west coast of Africa as far south as Essaouira and northwards along the coast of Iberia at least as far as the Mondego estuary. The intention clearly was to command control of the wide range of commodities that were available along these coasts, most particularly gold, silver, copper, tin, ivory and ostrich shell, and to draw them, through Gadir, into the Mediterranean trading systems. Such a development cannot have failed to have dislocated the old Atlantic system by appropriating the whole of its southern sector. As a result western Iberia was now drawn into the Mediterranean sphere.

For a while north-western France, Britain and Ireland remained in close contact, but after about 500 BC Ireland seems to have fallen out of the network and remained isolated until probably as late as the 1st century BC. Southern Britain and the adjacent Continent maintained contact but even that seems to have decreased in intensity after the 4th century and Britain remained in comparative isolation until the 1st century BC when the bow wave effects of the approaching Roman Empire began to make themselves felt (Cunliffe 2009).

Some generalizations and some questions

This very rapid and highly selective overview of Atlantic European prehistory has been offered to try to redress the still deeply ingrained prejudices—based on the old *ex oriente lux* hypothesis—that all things good and innovative flowed from east to west and that the poor benighted communities of the Atlantic façade lived in a peripheral gutter into which benefits from 'higher' cultures were occasionally flushed. As the rich archaeological record now shows, nothing could be further from the truth. Throughout much of prehistory the Atlantic communities were highly innovative and relatively self-contained—though not unreceptive of influences from the Mediterranean. The western ocean provided the resources, the stimulus and the networks of communication that allowed the littoral and its deep hinterland to serve as a cohesive system in its own right.

Our sketch has emphasized the broad rhythms of change: the arrival of farming communities from the Mediterranean settling in Portugal in the 5th millennium and the development of networks of connectivity that allowed beliefs and technologies to spread along the entire Atlantic littoral; the dramatic increase in mobility in the 3rd millennium possibly exacerbated by the search for raw materials which saw an eastward flow of people from the Atlantic confront a westward flow from the Pontic steppe; the long period of consolidation throughout the 2nd millennium as the Atlantic systems brought communities into ever closer relationships; and the gradual fragmentation of the system during the course of the 1st millennium leaving communities in comparative isolation.

Through these transformations people communicated with language. Given the extent and intensity of the connectivity, and the complexity of the technological knowledge and belief systems communicated, there must have been a lingua franca and possibly pidgins and creoles, and there must have been times of language convergence and language divergence. The one thing we can be reasonably sure about is that over the five thousand years with which we are concerned, language development is likely to have been complex. So the challenge is, given what is now known of the period based on the rapidly growing archaeological record, can we begin to bring our knowledge of European philology into some form of creative juxtaposition with it? This is a question for philologists. But perhaps an archaeologist can help by breaking the overarching enquiry down into a series of more limited questions.

— is it possible that the Indo-European language reached the Atlantic Zone *c.* 5000 BC as the result of enclave colonization bringing the Neolithic lifestyle from the Mediterranean?

— if so, is it possible that *Celtic* began to develop in the Atlantic Zone between 5000 and 3000 BC during the period when extensive connectivity was established along the Atlantic façade? It may be worth noting here that three attempts made to 'date' the branching of the Indo-European tree using phylogenetic methods hint at the early appearance of Celtic (Foster and Toth 2003; Gray and Atkinson 2003; Ringe, Warnow and Taylor 2002) though the uncertainties inherent in the method have to be recognized (McMahon and McMahon 2003).

— if a distinct Celtic language had emerged by the 3rd millennium then could the period of rapid mobility, reflected in the Beaker phenomenon, have provided the context for the language to spread across much of western Europe?

— if the period of the Atlantic Bronze Age (*c.* 1300–800 BC) saw the Celtic language firmly established as the lingua franca along the entire Atlantic façade, does the subsequent period of dislocation provide a context that could have led to the emergence of the different 'dialects' evident in the remnants that survive in the texts and place-names, and in the Insular languages?

All these questions arise from what would seem to be the simplest scenario based on the archaeological evidence but there is an alternative that might be worth considering. In the period *c.* 2800–2200 we can recognize a phase of exceptional mobility throughout Europe when very different cultural traditions came into contact and learned much from each other. Is it possible that this brief phase of interaction—between the Bell Beaker communities from the west, the Single Grave/Corded Ware Complex from the north and the Late Yamnaya horse riders from the east—was the time when Celtic emerged, somewhere in the broad zone of interaction in middle Europe? But if so, from which of the component cultures did the main contribution come?

By asking this torrent of questions I hope we may begin to open a new debate about the origins of the Celtic language and of the Celts. Though philology and archaeology are different disciplines with their own very distinctive methodologies they are both concerned with human communities and the way in which people interact through culture and language. It may be that it is too much to expect a single consistent narrative to emerge but there is much to be gained in trying to discover one.

BIBLIOGRAPHY

Abercromby, J. 1912 *A Study of the Bronze Age Pottery of Great Britain and Ireland and its Associated Grave-goods*, 2 vols. Oxford, Clarendon Press.

Ambert, P. 2001 'La place de la métallurgie campaniforme dans la première métallurgie française', *Bell Beakers Today*, Proceedings of the Riva del Garda conference May 1998, 2 vols. ed. F. Nicolis, II, 577–88. Trento, Provincia autonoma di Trento.

Arias, P. 1999 'The Origins of the Neolithic Along the Atlantic Coast of Continental Europe: a survey', *Journal of World Prehistory* 13, 403–66.

Aubet, M. E. 1993 *The Phoenicians in the West*. Cambridge, Cambridge University Press.

Buchanan, G. 1582 *Rerum Scoticarum Historia*. Edinburgh.

Case, H. 2007 'Beakers and Beaker Culture'. *Beyond Stonehenge: Essays on the Bronze Age in honour of Colin Burgess*, eds. C. Burgess, P. Topping, & F. Leach, 237–54. Oxford, Oxbow.

Chevillot, C., & A. Coffyn, eds. 1991 *L'Age du Bronze Atlantique*. Beynac, Association des Musées du Sarladais.

Childe, V. G. 1940 *Prehistoric Communities of the British Isles*. London, Chambers.

Clark, G. 1966 'The Invasion Hypothesis in British Archaeology', *Antiquity* 40, 172–89.

Clarke, D. L. 1976 'The Beaker Network—Social and Economic Models', *Glockenbechersymposion: Oberried 1974*, eds. J. N. Lanting, & J. D. Van der Waals, 459–76. Bussum, Fibula-Van Dishoeck.

Collis, J. 1999 'George Buchanan and the Celts in Britain', *Celtic Connections. Proceedings of the 10th International Congress of Celtic Studies. Vol. 1. Language, Literature, History, Culture*, eds. R. Black, W. Gillies, & R. Ó Maolalaigh, 91–107. East Linton, Tuckwell Press.

Crawford, O. G. S. 1922 'A Prehistoric Invasion of England', *Antiquaries Journal* 2, 27–35.

Cunliffe, B. 1974 (2005) *Iron Age Communities in*

Britain (1st edn. 1974, 4th edn. 2005). London, Routledge & Kegan Paul.

Cunliffe, B. 2001a *Facing the Ocean: The Atlantic and its Peoples.* Oxford, Oxford University Press.

Cunliffe, B. 2001b *The Extraordinary Voyage of Pytheas the Greek.* London, Allen Lane.

Cunliffe, B. 2009 'Looking Forward: Maritime Contacts in the First Millennium BC', *Bronze Age Connections: Cultural Contact in Prehistoric Europe*, ed. P. Clark, 80–93. Oxford, Oxbow.

Dillon, M., & N. Chadwick 1967 *The Celtic Realms.* London, Weidenfeld & Nicolson.

Domínguez, A. I. 2004 'Spain and France (including Corsica)', *An Inventory of Archaic and Classical Poleis*, eds. M. H. Hansen, & T. H. Nielsen, 157–71. Oxford, Oxford University Press.

Filip, J. 1977 *Celtic Civilization and its Heritage*, trans. R. F. Samsour. 2nd rev. edn. Wellingborough, Collet.

Fitzpatrick, A. P. 2002 '"The Amesbury Archer": a well-furnished Early Bronze Age burial in southern England', *Antiquity* 76, 629–30.

Foster, P., & A. Toth 2003 'Towards a Phylogenetic Chronology of Ancient Gaulish, Celtic and Indo-European', *Proceedings of the National Academy of Science USA* 100, 9079–84.

Giot, P.-R., & J. Cogné 1955 'Étude petrographique des haches polies de Bretagne IV—Les haches de combat en métahornblendite', *Bulletin de la Société préhistorique française* 52, 402–9.

Gray, R., & Q. Atkinson 2003 'Language-Tree Divergence Times Support the Anatolian Theory of Indo-European Origins', *Nature* 405, 1052–5.

Gunther, R. T. 1945 *Life and Letters of Edward Lhwyd.* Early Science in Oxford 14. Oxford, Oxford University Press.

Harrison, R. J. 1980 *The Beaker Folk: Copper Age Archaeology in Western Europe.* London, Thames & Hudson.

Harrison, R. J. 2004 *Symbols and Warriors: Images of the European Bronze Age.* Bristol, Western Academic & Specialist Press.

Harrison, R., & V. Heyd 2007 'The Transformation of Europe in the Third Millennium BC: The Example of "Le Petit-Chasseur I and III" (Sion, Valais, Switzerland)', *Praehistorische Zeitschrift* 82, 129–214.

Hawkes, C. F. C. 1959 'The ABC of the British Iron Age', *Antiquity* 33, 170–82.

Heyd, V. 2007 'Families, Prestige Goods, Warriors and Complex Societies: Beaker Groups and the 3rd Millennium cal BC', *Proceedings of the Prehistoric Society* 73, 327–79.

Hodson, F. R. 1960 'Reflections on the "ABC" of the British Iron Age', *Antiquity* 34, 138–40.

Hodson, F. R. 1962 'Some Pottery from Eastbourne, the "Marnians" and the Pre-Roman Iron Age in Southern England', *Proceedings of the Prehistoric Society* 28, 140–55.

Hodson, F. R. 1964 'Cultural Groupings within the British Pre-Roman Iron Age', *Proceedings of the Prehistoric Society* 30, 99–110.

Holmes, T. R. 1907 *Ancient Britain and the Invasions of Julius Caesar.* Oxford, Clarendon Press.

Hubert, H. 1934 *The Rise of the Celts.* London, K. Paul, Trench, Trubner.

James, S. 1999 *The Atlantic Celts.* London, British Museum Press.

Jorge, S. O., ed. 1998 *Existe uma Idade do Bronze Atlântico?* Trabalhos de Arqueologia 10. Lisboa, Instituto Português de Arqueologia.

Koch, J. T. 2009 *Tartessian: Celtic in the South-west at the Dawn of History.* Celtic Studies Publications XIII. Aberystwyth.

Lanting, J. N., & J. D. Van der Waals 1976 'Beaker Culture Relations in the Lower Rhine Basin', *Glockenbechersymposion: Oberried 1974*, eds. J. N. Lanting, & J. D. Van der Waals, 1–80. Bussum, Fibula-Van Dishoeck.

Le Roux, C. T. 1999 *L'outillage de pierre polie en métadolérite du type A. Les ateliers de Plussulien (Côtes-d'Armor): Production et diffusion au Néolithique dans la France de l'ouest et au delà.* Rennes, Travaux du Laboratoire Anthropologie, Préhistoire et Quarternaire Armoricains, Université de Rennes.

Lhuyd, E. 1707 *Archaeologia Britannica, giving some account Additional to what has been hitherto Publish'd, of the Languages, Histories and Customs of the Original Inhabitants of Great Britain: From Collections and Observations in Travels Through Wales, Cornwall, Bas-Bretagne, Ireland and Scotland. Vol. I. Glossography.* Oxford, The Theater.

McMahon, A., & R. McMahon 2003 'Finding Families: Quantitative Methods in Language Classification', *Trans. of the Philological Society* 101, 7–55.

Marcigny, C., B. Aubry, A. Verney, S. Vacher, & C. Thooris 2002 'Découvertes récentes de l'Age du Bronze moyen dans le département de la Sarthe (Pays-de-la-Loire)', *Revue archéologique de l'Ouest* 19, 7–23.

Marcigny, C., E. Ghesquiere, & I. Kinnes 2007 'Bronze Age Cross Channel Relations. The Lower Normandy (France) Example: Ceramic Chronology and First Reflections', *Beyond Stonehenge: Essays on the Bronze Age in Honour of Colin Burgess*, eds. C. Burgess, P. Topping, & F. Lynch, 255–67. Oxford, Oxbow.

Morgan, P. T. J. 1965 'The Abbé Pezron and the Celts', *Trans. of the Honourable Society of Cymmrodorion 1965*, 286–95.

Needham, S. 2005 'Transforming Beaker Culture in North-West Europe; Processes of Fusion and Fission', *Proceedings of the Prehistoric Society* 71, 171–217.

Needham, S. 2009 'Encompassing the Sea: "Maritories" and Bronze Age Maritime Interactions', *Bronze Age Connections: Cultural Contact in Prehistoric Europe*, ed. P. Clark, 12–37. Oxford, Oxbow.

O'Brien, W. 2004 *Ross Island: Mining, Metal and Society in Early Ireland*. Galway, Dept. of Archaeology, National University of Ireland.

O'Connor, B. 1980 *Cross-Channel Relations in the Later Bronze Age*. BAR Int. Ser. 91. Oxford, British Archaeological Reports.

Oppenheimer, S. 2006 *The Origins of the British: A Genetic Detective Story*. London, Constable.

Pare, C. F. E. 2000 'Bronze and the Bronze Age', *Metals Make the World Go Round: The Supply and Circulation of Metals in Bronze Age Europe*, ed. C. F. E. Pare, 1–38. Oxford, Oxbow.

Peake, H. 1922 *The Bronze Age and the Celtic World*. London, Benn Brothers Ltd.

Pétrequin, P., A. Sheridan, S. Cassen, M. Errera, E. Gauthier, L. Klassen, N. Le Maux, & Y. Pailler 2008 'Neolithic Alpine Axeheads, from the Continent to Great Britain, the Isle of Man and Ireland', *Between Foraging and Farming* (= *Analecta Praehistorica Leidensia* 40), eds. H. Fokkens, B. J. Coles, A. L. Van Gijn, J. P. Kleijne, H. P. Hedwig, & C. G. Slappendel, 261–79. Leiden, Faculty of Archaeology, Leiden University.

Pezron, P.-Y. 1703 *Antiquité de la nation et de la langue des Celtes autrement appellez Gaulois*. Paris, Prosper Marchand et Gabriel Martin.

Pezron, P.-Y. 1706 *The Antiquities of Nations; More Particularly of the Celtae or Gauls*. London, printed by R. Janeway for S. Ballard and R. Burrough.

Piggott, S. 1965 *Ancient Europe*. Edinburgh, Edinburgh University Press.

Powell, T. G. E. 1958 *The Celts*. London, Thames & Hudson.

Price, T. D., G. Grupe, & P. Schröter 1998 'Migration and Mobility in the Bell Beaker Period in Central Europe', *Antiquity* 72, 405–11.

Price, T. D., C. Knipper, G. Grupe, & V. Smrcka 2004 'Strontium Isotopes and Prehistoric Human Migration: The Bell Beaker Period in Central Europe', *European Journal of Archaeology* 7(1), 9–40.

Rankin, H. D. 1987 *Celts and the Classical World*. London, Croom Helm.

Renfrew, C. 1987 *Archaeology and Language: The Puzzle of Indo-European Origins*. London, Jonathan Cape.

Rhŷs, J. 1882 *Celtic Britain*. London, SPCK.

Ringe, D., T. Warnow, & A. Taylor 2002 'Indo-European and Computational Cladistics', *Trans. of the Philological Society* 100, 59–129.

Roberts, B. F. 1986 'Edward Lhuyd and Celtic Linguistics', *Proceedings of the 7th International Congress of Celtic Studies*, eds. D. E. Evans, J. G. Griffith, & E. M. Jope, 1–9. Oxford, D. E. Evans.

Salinova, L. 2000 *La question du campaniforme en France et dans les Îles Anglo-Normandes*. Paris, Éditions du Comité des travaux historiques et scientifiques, Société préhistorique française.

Sheridan, A. 2003a 'French Connections I: Spreading the *Marmites* Thinly', *Neolithic Settlement in Ireland and Western Britain*, eds. I. Armit, E. Murphy, E. Nelis, & D. Simpson, 3–17. Oxford, Oxbow.

Sheridan, A. 2003b 'Ireland's Earliest "Passage" Tombs: A French Connection?' *Stones and Bones: Formal Disposal of the Dead in Atlantic Europe during the Mesolithic–Neolithic Interface, 6000–3000 BC*, ed. G. Burenhult, 9–25. BAR Int. Ser. 1201. Oxford, Archaeopress.

Sheridan, A. 2007 'From Picardie to Pickering and Pencraig Hill? New Information on the "Carinated Bowl Neolithic" in Northern Britain', *Going Over: the Mesolithic–Neolithic Transition in North West Europe* (= *Proceedings of the British Academy* 144), eds. A. W. R. Whittle, &

V. Cummings, 441–92. Oxford, British Academy.

Sims-Williams, P. 2006 *Ancient Celtic Place-Names in Europe and Asia Minor*. Publications of the Philological Society 39. Oxford, Blackwell Publishing.

Tresset, A. 2003 'French Connections II: Of Cows and Men', *Neolithic Settlement in Ireland and Western Britain*, eds. I. Armit, E. Murphy, E. Nelis, & D. Simpson, 18–30. Oxford, Oxbow.

Woodman, P., & M. McCarthy 2003 'Contemplating Some Awful(ly Interesting) Vistas: Importing Cattle and Red Deer into Prehistoric Ireland', *Neolithic Settlement in Ireland and Western Britain*, eds. I. Armit, E. Murphy, E. Nelis, & D. Simpson, 31–9. Oxford, Oxbow.

Zilhão, J. 1993 'The Spread of Agro-Pastoral Economies Across Mediterranean Europe', *Journal of Mediterranean Archaeology* 6, 5–63.

Zilhão, J. 2000 'From Mesolithic to the Neolithic in the Iberian Peninsula', *Europe's First Farmers*, ed. T. D. Price, 144–82. Cambridge, Cambridge University Press.

CHAPTER TWO

THE CELTS FROM EVERYWHERE AND NOWHERE
A RE-EVALUATION OF THE ORIGINS OF THE CELTS
AND THE EMERGENCE OF CELTIC CULTURES

Raimund Karl

I N his *Antiquité de la nation et de la langue des Celtes*, probably the founding study of the discipline of Celtic Studies, published in 1703, Abbé Paul-Yves Pezron (1639–1706) argued that the Celtic language had been one of the 'original languages' spoken at the time of the Tower of Babel. He tried to trace 'the Celts' from that time to their first attestation in historical sources from antiquity (Collis 2003, 48–9). Since then, the search for their origins has occupied many scholars. For much of the last *c.* 150 years, following Henri d'Arbois de Jubainville (1827–1910), a 'central European origin' of Celtic culture, at *c.* 1000 BC, has been the dominant view. Only relatively recently, two new views have been emerging. One argues for an 'origin' of the Celtic languages in the West, with Barry Cunliffe and John Koch being the main proponents of this theory. The other one, dominant at least in British archaeology and increasingly gaining support on the Continent, is that there were no Celts in antiquity, at least not in the British Isles (cf. James 2000), but perhaps even not at all (cf. Collis 2003).

I believe in neither of these theories. If anything, I am closer to the last, but think the term 'Celts' is not only still useful as a classificatory term in Europe, but also in the British Isles, and that it does (usefully) describe something. I am also relatively close to Christopher Hawkes' (1973) concept of 'cumulative Celticity', and Colin Renfrew (1989, 211–49), even though I also differ from their views in some regards. Following Ludwig Pauli (1980; 2007) in a significant but mostly unnoticed German contribution, I think the search for the 'origins' of 'the Celts' is ultimately meaningless. This 300-year search for the 'origins' of something that in my opinion cannot have 'an origin' has hampered our understanding of (later) European prehistory and thus should be stopped, so that we can finally start to concentrate on more important questions.

The 'traditional' model

This model assumed an 'origin' of 'the Celts' in central Europe, between eastern France, southern Germany, western Bohemia, parts of Austria, and Switzerland. Dates given for this 'origin' vary between the Late Bronze Age to the beginning of the later Iron Age or

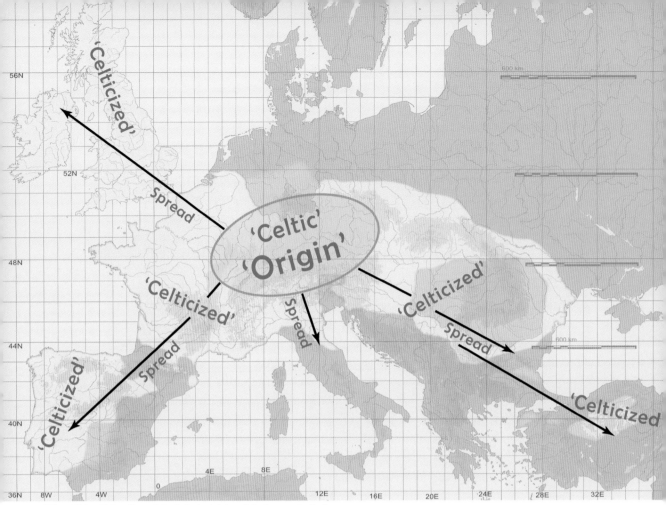

2.1: The old 'traditional' model of the 'origin' and the 'expansion' of 'the Celts', superimposed on a distribution of attested Celtic-looking place-names in antiquity (base map adapted Koch et al. 2007; cf. Sims-Williams 2006, maps 5.2, 11.1, and 11.2).

La Tène period, with a tendency towards the latter half of that period as the most likely time when 'the Celts' emerged as a distinct entity, with the term 'Celt' first attested in Hecataeus in the late 6th century BC (Tomaschitz 2002, 15).

Arguments for a 'central European origin' were found in the two archaeological cultures dominating much of the area assigned by historical references to 'the Celts' in antiquity, the Hallstatt and the La Tène 'culture'. Of these, particularly the latter has a spatial distribution that—at least roughly—matches well with the distribution of attested Celtic place-names in antiquity (cf. Koch et al. 2007; Sims-Williams 2006). The first attestation of the earliest attested 'Celtic' language, Lepontic, in the 6th century BC in an area immediately south of this 'central European' area of 'origin', seemed to confirm that the Celtic languages also emerged in a 'central European heartland' of 'Celtic culture'.

From this 'origin', 'the Celts' were seen spreading over much of Europe, mainly by migration—several 'Celtic' migrations are historically attested (cf. Tomaschitz

2002)—'Celticizing' other, originally 'non-Celtic' populations, as they went along (Fig. 2.1).

This model has been strongly criticized in the last decades (cf. Pauli 1980; Collis 2003, to give but two examples). It has been argued that the 'traditional' model is based on nationalist agenda of early scholarship, that the term 'Celts' has too many different meanings, that cultural features considered to be 'Celtic' emerge in different times and places, that changes through time fundamentally change what is 'Celtic', and that any connection between the distant past of the 'original Celts' and later 'Celts' is at best tenuous. As such, this model is widely rejected today.

The 'new' (but still 'traditional') 'Celticization from the West' model

More recently, a 'new' model has been proposed, mainly by Barry Cunliffe (2001, 293–7 and this volume) and John Koch (2009 and this volume). This 'Celticization from the West' model differs from the 'traditional' model in the proposed area and time of 'origin' for 'the Celts', putting it firmly along the 'Atlantic fringe' of the European continent. Communication networks in this area provide evidence for substantial exchange of ideas between the communities inhabiting the Atlantic coasts of Europe, from the south-western corner of the Iberian Peninsula to Ireland in the north-west. On the linguistic side, John Koch's new reading of the Tartessian inscriptions, first attested in the 8th or 7th century BC as written in a Celtic language (2009 and this volume) seems to confirm a much earlier presence of Celtic in the far south-west of Europe. The new model now proposes that 'the Celtic languages' emerged along the Atlantic coasts of Europe, as a 'lingua franca' (Cunliffe 2001, 293), and spread to the east from there (Fig. 2.2). John Koch has even referred to this as an emerging 'new paradigm'.

Without question, this model has some advantages over the old model, particularly where the attestations of Celtic-looking place-names in antiquity are concerned: they are clearly attested more densely in the 'Atlantic' west and Gaul than anywhere further east (cf. Sims-Williams 2006, maps 5.2, 11.1, and 11.2). This would fit much better with an 'expansion' of the Celtic languages from the west to the east, rather than from central Europe to both the west and the east.

Yet, this 'new' model has already been criticized, not least on linguistic grounds (see Isaac 2005 and this volume). Also it hardly constitutes a 'new paradigm' (cf. Kuhn 1976 for the definition of what constitutes a 'paradigm'). Rather, it retains all the problems of the 'traditional' model: it still assumes an 'original' co-location of cultural features—shared material culture indicating shared language. It still 'locates' the 'original' language in prehistory, and it leaves the 'origin' and 'spread' of 'the Celtic' unexplained—is the area of the 'origin' of 'the Celtic' as large as the 'Atlantic fringe'? If less, how does it spread within the 'Atlantic fringe' zone? And how does it spread beyond the 'Atlantic fringe'? Nor does it address the criticisms that the term 'Celts' has too many different meanings, that cultural features considered to be 'Celtic' emerge in different times and places, that changes through time fundamentally alter what is and what is not 'Celtic', and that any connection between the distant past of the 'original Celts' and later 'Celts' is at best tenuous. All the new model seems to do is to replace one location with another, and one set of 'essential' features with another, without any changes to the logic underlying the 'traditional' model. It thus should be rejected for the very same reasons.

The flawed prevailing ideas about who 'the Celts' are

Much of the problem of the 'origins' of 'the Celts' depends on who we think 'the Celts' are (or were). Quite interestingly, for a long time most of us have behaved as if that were self-evident, and many of us still do. It is virtually impossible to find a sensible definition of what we—as a scholarly community—mean when we use the word 'Celt'. Even though, in response to 'Celtoscepticism', scholars have become more careful in specifying what they mean when they are talking about 'the Celts' (e.g. Koch et al. 2007,

2.2: The new 'Celticization from the West' model of the 'origin' and 'expansion' of 'the Celts', superimposed on a distribution of attested Celtic-looking place-names in antiquity (base map adapted Koch et al. 2007; cf. Sims-Williams 2006, maps 5.2, 11.1, and 11.2).

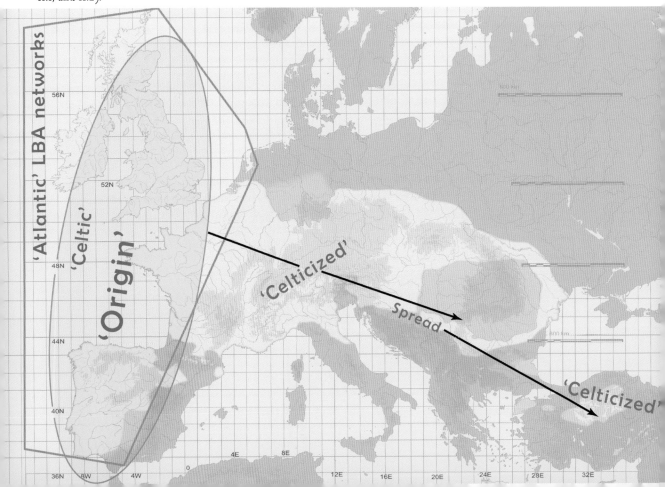

1–17, specifically 2–4), 'universally applicable' definitions of who or what 'the Celts' are (supposed to be) are still conspicuously absent.

There are seemingly uncontentious definitions and it is those which appear in print most frequently. Let me critically examine the one John Koch gives: 'Therefore, the following scrupulously linguistic definition is adopted here: belonging to the subfamily of Indo-European languages that is represented by the four continuously surviving languages—Breton, Irish, Scottish Gaelic, and Welsh' (Koch et al. 2007, 3). Against the distribution of this language subfamily, and place-names, are then mapped various kinds of things—mostly archaeological finds and features. Yet, which archaeological finds and features were mapped, and which not? While Koch gives numerous further explanations about the extent of the subject, and what has been called 'Celtic' by archaeologists and historians (Koch et al. 2007, 1, 7), none of what he discusses fully explains what 'things' were mapped against 'words', let alone providing us with a universal definition of 'the Celtic'.

The Atlas (Koch et al. 2007) is not unique in not coming up with a 'universal' definition—such a definition is generally missing, because we have been assuming that it was self-evident who or what 'the Celts' were or are. Celtosceptics (e.g. Collis 2003, 224) have argued that this is due to an unacceptable application of the discredited theories of the German nationalist scholar Gustaf Kossinna (1920), and that 'the Celts' were created as a nationalist myth. 'Celtic' thus obviously was a reference to a 'people' or 'nation' and its cultural expressions, 'national' territory, spirit, &c. While this cannot be denied completely—such nationalist Celticists existed and probably still do—the charge that all modern Celticists are either 'nationalist Celtomaniacs' or too stubborn (or too stupid) to realize that their discipline is based exclusively on 'nationalist Celtomaniac' myths is too simplistic.

Rather, I think that our problem is that Celtic Studies is still mostly dominated by a logical positivist mindset (Wittgenstein 1963). We thus have assumed that our subject, 'the Celts', is (or was) an existing entity, a 'thing' (die 'Sache') for which 'the Celts' is the name (das 'Wort') (Wittgenstein 1963, 19–59). From a logical positivist perspective, the thing and its name are the same (Wittgenstein 1963, 22). The name cannot be further analysed or dissected by definitions: it is an 'Urzeichen' (Wittgenstein 1963, 23), a signifier for the one specific, real thing that is the signified it signifies. In a way, it is like a table, with the word 'table' defined by the thing it stands for, i.e. the real table; with any definition necessarily having to be a description of the thing the word stands for.

It thus is also an essentialist view: 'the Celts' as a positivist entity must have had a set of characteristics or properties that make them 'Celtic'. Whether this is a 'Celtic spirit', 'ethnicity', 'speaking a Celtic language', or whatever else, only matters in specific details, in what (specifically) we see as 'Celtic', and what not. As such, someone like John Koch, who sees the property 'they speak a Celtic language' as the essential one for being 'Celtic' (Koch et al. 2007, 2–4), will necessarily conclude that 'the ancient Britons' indisputably were 'Celts', while someone like Simon James, who sees the property 'self-identifying as Celtic' as the essential characteristic for being 'Celtic' (James 2000, 67–81), will equally necessarily conclude that 'the ancient Britons' cannot have been 'Celts'. James even explicitly rejects the view of Koch as 'unacceptable', as the name 'Celt', in his opinion, 'was originally a group name applied to one or more peoples, *not* a linguistic description, and is still understood as an ethnonym by most people today' (James 2000, 81, emphasis as in original). On a more fundamental level, however, this does not matter: both Koch and James are looking for a 'Celtic essence', they just cannot agree on what the essence is that they should be looking for. But neither seems to see a need to define what the Celtic is: it is sufficient to describe whether a certain characteristic or property is present or not. If it is, the 'thing', the real entity under examination, is 'Celtic'; if it is not, the 'thing' is not 'Celtic'.

As long as this logical positivist, essentialist approach to Celtic Studies prevails, establishing the 'origins' of 'the Celts' is an essential task. In this approach, when- and wherever the 'essentially Celtic' characteristics first appear, 'the Celts' as an entity, and thus as a subject that can be studied, come into being. And it is equally essential to establish their precise geographical distribution at any given time, as this defines what can meaningfully be studied by 'Celtic Studies'. After all, under this paradigm, only if the presence of the thing can be confirmed can it be meaningfully studied. Also, as long as we think of 'the Celts' as a 'real' thing, we tend to perceive it as akin to the 'normal' physical things we know. Physical things not only have an origin and clear physical boundaries (i.e. a clearly 'limited' spatial distribution), they are also mutually exclusive and uniform (i.e. only the characteristic combination of their constituent parts makes them 'the thing'). This results in the assumption that something can either be Celtic or something else, but not both at the same time, and in the assumption that if something is 'Celtic', it must have the characteristic 'form'.

In my opinion, this logical positivist, essentialist approach is fundamentally flawed, the root of the problems in finding the 'origins of the Celts', and at the heart of the 'Celticity' debate. And as long as we continue to search for 'the essential Celts', they will never go away. Yet, I do think that, in practice, we have been doing something quite different for a long time, perhaps even since the first time anybody identified anything as 'Celtic'—and only because in reality, the 'essentialist' approach simply does not work.

What we have been (and what we should be) doing: Celtic by association

In reality, what we arguably have done since the first identification of something or someone as 'Celtic' is not simply to describe a 'thing' that exists independently of us as observers. Rather, what we have been doing is to define what, to us as observers, 'the Celtic' is, as based on our observations of reality (which include the perceptions of others, i.e. Greeks and Romans and 'Celts' themselves). And that, in a sense, is what we should be doing as scholarly (or scientific, if you prefer,) researchers: our theories and definitions should match our observations of reality.

Let us return to John Koch's 'narrow' definition of 'the Celtic' for *An Atlas for Celtic Studies*: 'Therefore, the following scrupulously linguistic definition is adopted here: belonging to the subfamily of Indo-European languages that is represented by the four continuously surviving languages—Breton, Irish, Scottish Gaelic, and Welsh.' In other words, a 'Celt' is somebody who speaks a 'Celtic language'.[1] The Celtic languages, in turn, are defined by a set of observable linguistic features (cf. Fife 2002; Eska & Evans 2002; Schmidt 2002).

Quite similarly, 'Celtic art' has been defined by a set of observable features in artistic decoration, as has 'Celtic archaeology' by a set of observable features in the archaeological record (cf. Megaw & Megaw 2001, 12–23; Collis 2003, 71–92). 'Celtic ancient history' has been defined by observable features, the references to Κελτοί, *Celtae*, *Galli* and Γαλάται in the sources from antiquity (cf. Koch et al. 2007, 1). And 'Celtic ethnicity' has been defined by observable features, in the historical record and by interviewing people in the present. Following the same logic as John Koch did for his 'linguistic Celts',[2] we could see as an 'artistic Celt' anyone who makes or uses 'Celtic art', as an 'archaeological Celt' anyone who makes or uses 'Celtic archaeology' (i.e. artefacts), as an 'ancient historical Celt' anyone who was called such in texts from antiquity, and as an 'ethnic Celt' anyone who considered or considers himself or was or is considered 'a Celt' by somebody else.

Seen independently of each other, neither one of these definitions is problematic: each basically states 'we call something X which has the observable features x, y and z'. Neither of them is problematic even if they are seen as related, loosely coupled definitions in parallel to each other, as long as no essentialist approach is taken. If seen as non-essentialist parallel definitions, they, taken together, would say: 'We call something X if it *either* shows the observable features x, y and z *or* the observable features a, b, and c'. X would be no different from any other polysemous term, e.g. the term 'chair', which can, among other things, *either* mean a thing on which one can sit *or* a professorship at a university.

For 'the Celts', we could thus come up with the following general definition: 'A Celt is someone who *either* speaks a Celtic language *or* produces or uses Celtic art *or* archaeology *or* has been referred to as one in written records *or* has identified himself *or* been identified by others as such'. This definition could even easily be expanded if further parallel definitions of the term 'Celts' existed, e.g. that of a 'biological Celt', based e.g. on the observable feature of the presence of a characteristic mutation in a person's genome (cf. McEvoy & Bradley this volume; Oppenheimer this volume; Røyrvik this volume). The expanded definition would then be: 'A Celt is someone who *either* is characterized by any

---

1　[This is not the intended meaning of the passage cited, which has instead to do with a scientifically valid definition of 'Celtic' rather than any essential characteristic of an imagined coherent people called 'the Celts'. — editors]

2　[The inverted commas are throughout those supplied by this chapter's author and not to be misunderstood as implying that 'linguistic Celts' is the editors' phrase or concept. — editors]

of the above features *or* has a specific mutation as observable in his genome'.

The issue only becomes problematic when we take an essentialist approach: if we think that there are some universally characteristic properties that necessarily must be present for someone to *truly be* 'a Celt'. If we do, our above definition changes: 'X is something that *necessarily* has the properties m, n and o, which are essential for it to be X, *and* may also have additional properties, which are inconsequential'. Our different 'linguistic', 'artistic', 'archaeological', 'historical', 'ethnic', &c. 'Celts' from above can now only be reconciled with each other if the features we have chosen to be 'essential' for *truly being* 'a Celt' perfectly overlap in both their spatial and temporal distribution (i.e. everyone who speaks a 'Celtic' language also necessarily uses 'Celtic' art, archaeology, is necessarily referred to as a Celt in written sources and by others and identifies himself as such, &c.)—which they, of course, in reality never do. As a result of taking an essentialist approach, we arrive at incommensurable views (Kuhn 1976, 209–16), which—as neither is more correct than the other—can be debated endlessly without ever arriving at a resolution.

As such, any definition for our subject that starts out with a preface stating anything like 'In a narrow sense, Celtic Studies can be restricted in its meaning to philology, the study of language and literature' (Koch et al. 2007, 2) is fundamentally flawed and has to be rejected. After all, the subject that studies Celtic languages and literature is not Celtic Studies, it already has a different name: Celtic philology. Only a wider, more inclusive definition, that also takes in 'the study of material culture, historical records, religion, mythology and folklore, music, law and politics—all cultural domains, in fact' (Koch et al. 2007, 2–3), and for what it's worth, probably also a number of 'natural sciences' like physical anthropology, can rightfully claim to be Celtic Studies. And that requires a definition that satisfies the needs of all disciplines involved, that allows them to collaborate without creating incommensurable points of view or the submission of all other sub-disciplines in the field under the primacy of just one. After all, we need to cooperate (cf. Karl 2004; 2007).

A (new) definition of 'the Celts'
The easiest way to achieve this cooperative approach is by abandoning the essentialist approach and replacing it with a more practical and useful one. And the easiest way of doing so is by starting out from the assumption that 'the Celts' never existed as a real thing, but only as a construct, as the object of our study. If 'the Celts' do not and never did exist, we cannot take them to be self-evident. Rather, it forces us to define 'the Celts', as there is nothing we can talk about without a definition. We are, by our definition, creating the object of our study, which only exists because we as observers say so.

If we completely abandon the 'Celtic essence', if there are and were no 'Celts',[3] we can

---

3   Please note that this is not to say that 'the Celts', whether in the past or in the present, did not exist as a real entity—they may very well have (at least from some points of view). Their non-existence, as argued here, is simply an assumption to remove an obstacle in understanding the past and the present, not a statement about

easily combine the above observation-based definitions, which can exist in parallel, into an inclusive, associative definition that makes perfect sense and can work for all disciplines involved in Celtic Studies. According to this new, inclusive and associative definition, '**a Celt is someone who *either* speaks a Celtic language *or* produces or uses Celtic art *or* material culture *or* has been referred to as one in historical records *or* has identified himself *or* been identified by others as such &c.**' For each individual discipline, this results in no change to current practice: for Celtic philology, a Celt continues to be somebody who was or is speaking a Celtic language as defined by agreed observable linguistic features; for Celtic archaeology, a Celt continues to be somebody who uses or produces Celtic material culture as defined by observable archaeological features; for Celtic ancient history, a Celt continues to be somebody who has been identified as one in ancient writings; and for those who want to stick with a purely *emic* ethnic definition, a Celt continues to be someone who identifies himself as being a Celt. So, for those engaging in practical work within their own discipline exclusively, nothing much changes.

For Celtic Studies as a whole, however, pretty much everything changes. Firstly, such an associative definition removes all problems with the lack of precise spatial and temporal overlap in the distribution of such features that have been previously proposed to be 'essentially Celtic'—and as will be demonstrated below, they do not precisely overlap. If the 'linguistic Celt' and the 'archaeological Celt' no longer are necessarily (referring to) the same one 'real' thing (i.e. the 'essential Celt'), but are parallel definitions of observable features (whose spatial and temporal distributions partially overlap), there is no problem that there are 'linguistic Celts' who do not use e.g. La Tène (i.e. one 'archaeologically Celtic') material culture, and 'archaeological Celts' (e.g. those who do use La Tène material culture) who did not speak a Celtic language. Secondly, it removes the ridiculous problem of necessary 'uniformity' and all its consequences: if the properties **a**, **b**, **c**, &c., are part of our new inclusive and associative definition, it no longer matters if feature **a** is not present, if feature **b** or feature **c**, &c., is. Nor is there any reason any more to assume that just because feature **a** is present, so must be feature **b** and feature **c**, &c., because—as was the old assumption—all of them are required to make something 'a Celt', implying that as soon as we have, on the balance of probabilities, decided that something must have been 'a Celt', all 'essential' Celtic features must be assumed to have been present in it. Thus, a Galatian of the 3rd century BC in Asia Minor can be as much a Celt as a modern inhabitant of Ireland, without the two sharing any single observable feature between them. And thirdly, it removes all debate about whether something is 'really Celtic' or not, because we no longer need to look for that, we just need to check our observations: if a feature that is part of our definition of 'the Celtic' is observable, it is part of our object of study, regardless of all

---

the reality of that past or present. But as removing this obstacle, the 'essential Celt' if you like, makes no difference at all in actual scholarly practice, but can be immensely useful in furthering our understanding of 'the Celtic'—whatever that was or is, if it had or has any reality to it—this is a justified and necessary step.

other considerations.

In other words, we will be working with a set of observable features or characteristics to which we have ascribed Celticity, not trying to identify features or characteristics that are, independent of what we think, 'Celtic' in their own right.

The observable reality

To demonstrate what this means, let us now take a look at the reality that underlies our research, and the sets of features and characteristics observable in it. Sets of observable features are something that we can very well deal with as scholars, and as such should pose no problems. Yet, the features we are looking at depend upon which sub-discipline (linguistics, history, archaeology, &c.) we are in, and their nature and composition differ depending on what sets of features we are interested in. Yet, there are commonalities as well, which also need to be recognized.

Archaeology and Language

To illustrate this point, let us take a very short look at archaeology and language. Sets of features are characteristic for both archaeology and linguistics, and while they share several similarities, they differ in other regards, with consequences for how to understand and to deal with them.

Language, as systems to codify and transport meaning, is based on a **simple** set of rules (a grammar), which allow people to associate meaningfully **many** words (a vocabulary), which themselves comprise (arbitrarily) associated individual features (sounds/letters). Language is mostly self-referential, and in this sense is a 'closed' system, and is internally consistent to fulfil its purpose, meaning that a language is usually relatively clearly bounded, both in terms of competence (you either can speak it or not, with little in between) and of geographical distribution (since it needs to be practised reasonably regularly to remain competent in it; particularly in historical periods when much of the population was not very mobile).

Material culture (archaeology), on the other hand, also often transports meaning, but is not codified, and thus consists of many coexisting **complex** sets of rules allowing people to associate (meaningfully) comparatively **few** things (types) comprising of associated individual features (characteristics). Material culture is mainly physically referenced, and in this sense is an 'open' system, and thus is internally very diverse, meaning that it is usually not clearly bounded (it can easily move around, since the thing references itself and is not necessarily part of an integrated system of meaningful associations).

Archaeology and language thus differ in the nature of the associations between features in each separate field, which makes it necessary to treat them somewhat differently, and especially makes them behave differently in reality—language behaves according to definable laws, while archaeology doesn't, or if it does, it does so to a much

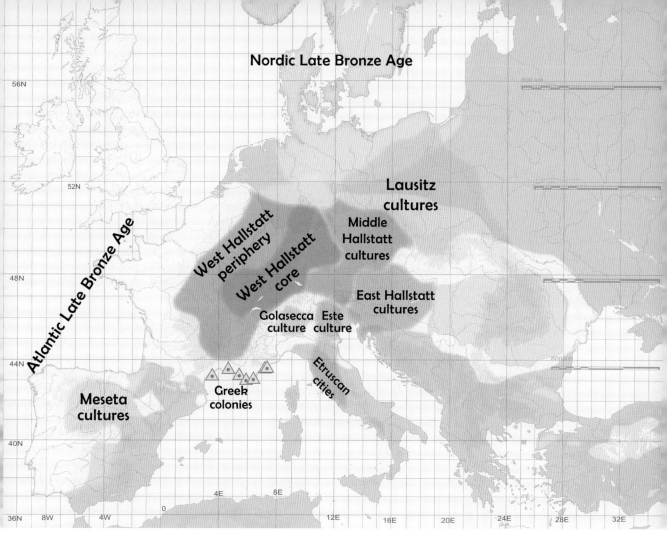

2.3: The Hallstatt 'culture' and some of its rough contemporaries in LBA/EIA Europe

lesser degree. Yet, both work with associated features, features that are observable and can be assigned names.

The archaeological reality

Archaeological reality is exceedingly complex. In the past, archaeologists have tried to reduce this complexity by creating 'cultures', each of which is characterized by a set of features or, as Gordon Childe has expressed it: 'We find certain types of remains—pots, implements, ornaments, burial rites and house forms—constantly recurring together. Such a complex of associated traits we shall term a "cultural group" or just a "culture".' (Childe 1929: v–vi). But this is, in many regards, treating archaeology as if it were a language—which is hardly surprising, since the concept as expressed by Childe draws strongly on the ideas of Gustaf Kossinna (1920), who was originally trained as a linguist (Veit 2000, 41–4). As such, the clear boundedness and (reasonable) internal homogeneity of 'cultures' featured quite strongly in his 'settlement-archaeological method'.

As a result, archaeological cultures are usually presented as having a relatively clearly 'bounded' area of distribution, which may slightly or even considerably change over time, but which is seen as internally reasonably uniform across both space and time. In 'Celtic archaeology', this has led to 'culture' distribution maps having been drawn depicting archaeological cultures as clearly bounded. As an example to demonstrate this, the archaeological culture most closely associated with the 'original Celts' will be used here, the Hallstatt culture (Fig. 2.3).

Of course, archaeologists realized pretty quickly that this didn't work as well in reality as the distribution maps seemed to show, since the features recognized as 'characteristically Hallstatt' were by no means distributed evenly across the whole 'Hallstatt culture', in fact, they did not even all appear across the whole area of the 'Hallstatt culture'. But instead of abandoning the concept altogether, they simply developed smaller 'regional variants' of what, on the larger scale, continued to be seen as the 'Hallstatt culture': a western and an eastern Hallstatt culture or 'circle' was defined, some also saw a 'middle' Hallstatt 'circle', the Lusitan (Lausitz) culture may perhaps be considered a north-eastern 'variant' of the Hallstatt culture, a west Hallstatt periphery was suggested, and the strongly Hallstatt-influenced Golasecca culture in north-western Italy, the area in which Lepontic inscriptions are found, may also be seen as somehow connected to this larger Hallstatt 'culture group'. Some also wanted to see the Meseta cultures on the Iberian Peninsula as the emerging 'Celtiberians', possibly remotely related to the 'Hallstatt Celts'.

Yet, if one looks in greater detail at the actual distribution of the features that allegedly make up all of these regional variants of the 'Hallstatt culture' (cf. Müller-Scheeßel 2000), one quickly realizes that the idea of the clear and sharp boundedness of the features does not exist. Regardless of how much more detailed the examination of material culture becomes, how many smaller and ever smaller 'variants' and 'sub-variants' &c. are created, the archaeological record stays messy. If mapped even only very roughly against each other, all the different features that have been used to define different 'Hallstatt cultures' can clearly be shown to partially overlap, but never precisely overlap (Fig. 2.4). In fact, in most cases, the distributions of different features are not even nicely nested within each other, which would perhaps have allowed defining a 'core zone' as opposed to a 'periphery', but the overlaps are largely chaotic. What is more, had different features been chosen, similar 'overlaps' would continue in pretty much all directions across the map of Europe—perhaps not as densely as at the 'core' of the 'Hallstatt zone', but overlapping nonetheless.

In fact, the reasons for the original 'creation' of the Hallstatt culture lie very much in the site of Hallstatt, the date when it was discovered (in the middle of the 19th century), and especially its famous cemetery itself: this cemetery contains items from over almost the entire 'Hallstatt culture' (and in fact also from beyond that; cf. Hodson 1990, Kern et al. 2008), and thus is the 'sticky glue' that keeps the 'Hallstatt culture' together. Had the sequence of archaeological discoveries been different, and the Hochdorf burial and some 'east Hallstatt' cemeteries been discovered first, and the Hallstatt cemetery only

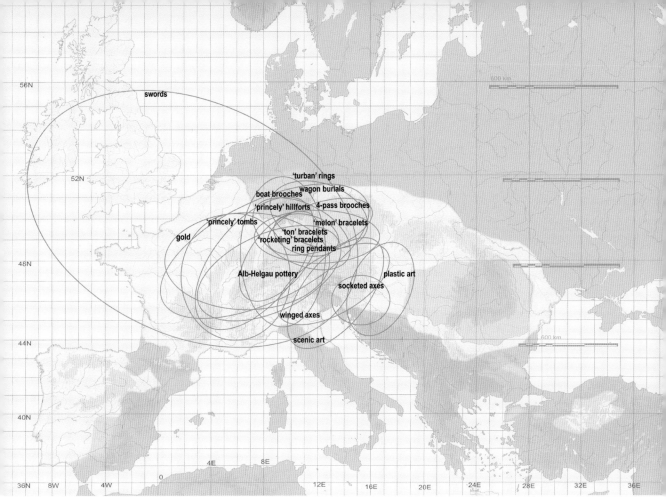

2.4: The messy reality behind the 'characteristic features' allegedly characterizing the 'Hallstatt culture' (adapted from Müller-Scheeßel 2000, maps 1–4).

much later, we would now most probably be talking about two separate 'Hochdorf' and 'Sopron' cultures, with a wealthy mining community at Hallstatt somewhere halfway between them and trading with both.

This problem—that the archaeological record is messy—not only applies to the spatial distribution of material culture, but also to its chronological distribution, as John Collis has admirably demonstrated in a recent paper (Collis 2009). The chronological ranges of different types, while clearly overlapping, are never the same, but only partially overlapping. Also, any two features A and B may very well appear contemporary in different places, and only later be adopted in the respective other place, resulting in a chronological sequence of A followed by B in one and B followed by A in the other. Putting observable features in 'stages' or 'phases', each characterized by a typical association of different 'type fossils', which in turn are associated with 'cultures' is therefore at best an unsustainable simplification, and at worst seriously hampers our attempts to understand the past. As a consequence, Collis has suggested that we abandon the concept of the 'phase' or 'stage' altogether (much as he has argued for abandoning the term 'Celts', Collis 2003), and instead construct our chronologies based on the (order of) appearance of individual observable features in the local sequence (Collis 2009).

Archaeological reality thus does not lend itself to drawing lines: both spatial and chronological boundaries are always and necessarily unclear, fuzzy, and by no means clean cut. As I will argue below, boundaries are nonetheless necessary for classificatory reasons, but we must realize that all such boundaries, at least in archaeology, are more or less arbitrarily imposed on the archaeological data and do not reflect any realities. They are tools, used by archaeologists, to simplify the chaos that is ever present in our data, to reduce complexity to a level where we can reasonably talk to each other.

That, however, also means that the search for the 'origins' of 'archaeological cultures' is ultimately meaningless, since they do not 'originate'—in any meaningful sense of the word—in the past, but in the present. There is no such 'thing' as an 'archaeological culture', or a 'chronological phase', there is only archaeological chaos, which has no 'origins' (except for individual features) or 'ends'. Looking for the 'origins' of an archaeological culture in the (distant) past (rather than in the more recent past of modern scholarly definitions) thus necessarily will never lead to any useful results, and we thus should abandon it.

The emergence of culture(s) in prehistory (and the present)
This is not to say that the chaos that is archaeology is an entirely random chaos, and that all patterns that we might see in it are just imaginary (cf. James 2007, 23). Quite to the contrary, many, if not most, of the patterns we are able to observe are 'real', in the sense that they not only exist (as do random patterns), but are also there for a reason. Rather, these patterns are what is expected to emerge in complex systems (cf. Ruelle 1992; Kauffman 1996; Prigogine 1997; Marion 1999; Buchanan 2001; Sawyer 2005), something that cultural interaction quite clearly is.

Cultural activities, as found in the material (archaeological) record, can be described as a structured continuum that has come about through interaction and associations created by humans. Underlying the formation of the archaeological record that we can observe were—and still are—complex exchange networks, networks in which cultural ideas, knowledge, and practices can be expressed through practice, both material and immaterial (Bourdieu 1977; Latour 2005), can be learnt by other human beings, and thus perpetuated in constantly changing, but nonetheless non-random, ways (Ruelle 1992; Kauffman 1996; Prigogine 1997; Marion 1999; Buchanan 2001; Sawyer 2005).

Particularly in prehistory, but even up to today, most of these networks are locally constituted, and are mostly small-scale: human actors are interlinked with other actors mostly at the local level, where the density of associations between individuals is by far the highest, and where usually many people in a group are mainly interlinked with many other people in the same group (Watts 1999; Buchanan 2003; Karl forthcoming; also see Figs. 2.5, 2.6). Medium- or even long-distance links are comparatively rare, and in much of prehistory probably also rare in absolute terms (Buchanan 2003). As such, information can flow very quickly at a local level, and homogenizing factors dominate within such localities in the cultural exchange networks, but much less so where long distances are concerned, where diversifying factors dominate, resulting in 'real' patterning of the archaeological record in both spatial and chronological terms.

The structure of these cultural exchange networks is also scale invariant (Buchanan 2001; 2003): there will be many more short links than there will be medium-distance links, and there will be many more medium-distance links than there will be long-distance links. But there will be, at any rate, longer and shorter links, which result in information being able to flow—albeit usually more slowly and less regularly—over longer distances as well. This medium- and long-distance connectedness leads to some degree of spatial

2.5: A random model of complex associations in a network of human actors (Karl forthcoming), resulting in different, more closely 'interlinked' clusters.

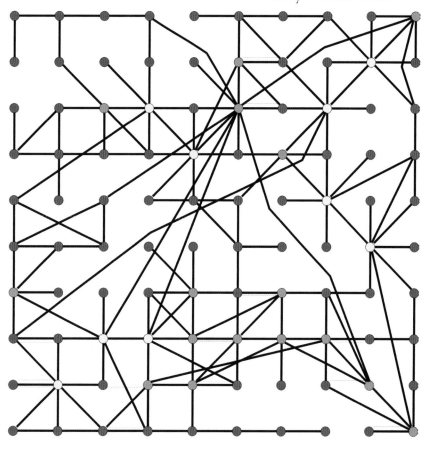

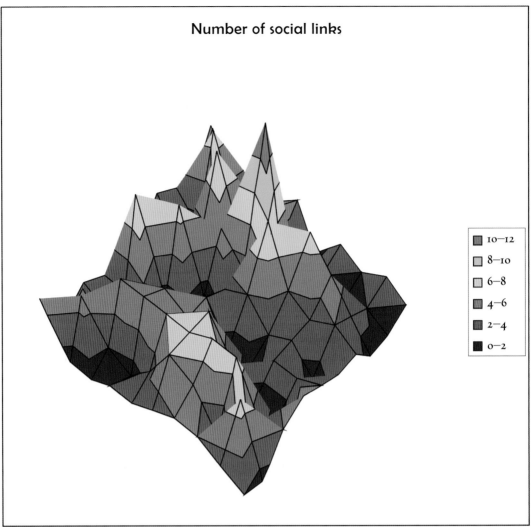

Number of social links

■	10–12
▢	8–10
▢	6–8
▨	4–6
▨	2–4
■	0–2

2.6: The same model, shown as a 3D surface (Karl forthcoming). High elevations (light shading) are strongly linked with other actors, low elevations (dark shading) are only linked with few other actors. 'Mountains' show highly interlinked clusters, which are more likely to be subject to homogenization, while 'valleys' constitute boundaries and inhibit information flow.

and chronological continuity, resulting in both spatial and chronological overlaps, with hardly any radical breaks and only relatively few rapid ones, which could be identified as 'boundaries'.

Where we can identify such comparatively 'sudden' breaks, like e.g. at the Hallstatt-to-La Tène transition, or at the 'borders' between 'Roman' influence and that of neighbouring 'cultures', we have traditionally drawn our 'major' chronological and cultural boundaries. But since the underlying cultural exchange networks are scale invariant, every time we take a closer, more detailed look at the evidence, we find additional 'internal' divisions: the 'stages' or 'phases' of our chronologies (and their sub-phases, sub-sub-phases &c., e.g. La Tène B, La Tène BI, La Tène BIa, &c.), and the 'variants' or 'sub-groups' of our 'cultures' (and their sub-variants, &c., e.g. Hallstatt, east Hallstatt, Kalenderberg Culture &c.).

Yet, all actors in these networks are reasonably equal, especially where their 'creativity' is concerned, and thus can (and do) regularly 'invent' new cultural information, which will then be either picked up by others, and thus be distributed through the network, or will not be picked up and thus quickly disappear from the network. Of course, some will be more creative than others, and have skills better suited to turn their creative ideas into reality than others, and thus may have more ideas, which are more likely to be picked up than those of others. Similarly, some actors will be 'better connected', both on a local and a longer distance scale, and as such, ideas that they might have, or might pick up in their locality from less well-connected actors, are more likely to be distributed more widely through the network. But in general terms, everybody is always 'inventing' new ideas, and such inventions spread pretty much randomly through the network, or die out. Individual tastes and 'cultural' fashions of course influence, to a certain extent, what spreads in what directions, but since particularly medium- and even more so long-distance links are rare, and probably also only rarely actually activated (they are 'weak links' in terms of complexity and small worlds theory; Buchanan 2001; 2003), every single invention, even if made by the same actor, will spread somewhat differently through the network. This results in partly, but not perfectly, overlapping patterns of distribution of different 'types', different associations of different features, depending on historical accidents of what is picked up, by whom, and when, or in other words, in the mess that archaeology is. But since all human actors are creative (to some extent, at least), and all 'invent' information which is then randomly distributed, it is exceedingly unlikely that any archaeological 'culture', or any classificatory concept that we can come up with in archaeology, will have a clear point of 'origin' in space and time, or a distribution perfectly overlapping with the distribution of any other idea. While we may find an item which is actually the first ever made of a type that later comes to dominate a sizeable area for considerable time, and thus may be able to identify the 'origin' of that particular type, any association of several types, features, traits, &c., that we can think of will almost never have originated in the same place in the same time. 'Culture' emerges, from multiple different 'origins', which may perhaps all individually be localized, but never localize the emergence of the 'culture' itself.

Of course, this is not only true in archaeology, but in many regards also of the emergence of languages, which works slightly differently, but nonetheless follows the same principles. Modern 'wave models' of language families, like Antilla's (1972) wave model of the Indo-European language family, can be seen as an example for this, with innovations 'rippling' through systems and resulting in the emergence of new systems, which can only be understood if the associations and the process of how innovations became associated with each other are taken into account, and thus do not allow us to establish an 'origin' of a language, because there simply is none.

How to deal with this mess: the practical solution

It is impossible to deal with this mess, this incredibly complex network of associations and information exchanges, by just focusing on the details, even though looking at and discussing these details is of course necessary, too. But if we were to describe, in all possible detail, all the individual observations available to us, every time we want to discuss something, we would never be able to discuss anything, since the necessary description alone would be a never-ending sermon. Thus, we need to simplify, to reduce this complexity to a level where we can reasonably talk about 'things', even if they are not 'real things'.

This simplification we achieve by creating artificial boundaries for classificatory purposes, which we impose on our data. And while it can, in each case, of course be discussed whether a specific imposition is justified or not, whether it is helpful or not, there can be no doubt that any such imposed boundary will essentially be, at least to some degree, arbitrary. We create these artificial boundaries between things, areas, chronological periods and between 'cultures' (most commonly a combination of spatial and chronological dimension, a 4D-description of sorts), each of which is characterized by 'typical' associations. And while in some areas of research we may already have reached, or are attempting to reach, such a fine resolution in our analysis of our data that, for detailed studies, such classificatory 'crutches' may become more of a hindrance rather than a help (cf. Collis forthcoming), for most subjects we research, and for some more general discussions, they still are and most probably always will remain necessary.

The groups we create by these artificially and at least somewhat arbitrarily imposed boundaries we then name with equally artificial and arbitrary signifiers, with (more or less randomly chosen) terms that are convenient to us, or have been convenient for earlier scholars for some reasons: e.g. 'Celtic' for pretty much all observable cultural features found in an area (and beyond that area) which was inhabited in antiquity by populations classical historians chose to refer to as Κελτοί or *Celtae*, and all cultural features descendent from or genetically closely related to these observable features; 'Hallstatt' for certain similarities in material culture because some particularly good exemplars were found early in the sequence of discoveries near the Upper Austrian town of that name; 'La Tène' for a different set of similarities with early finds at the site La Tène on Lake Neuchâtel in Switzerland, &c. Of course, any other name would also do, but at some point scholarship decided to use these, and there is no particularly strong reason for changing any of these labels, even if—like the term 'Celtic'—it occasionally may cause some confusion (cf. Karl 2008).

The question now remains how we best do this for the 'Celtic', and what consequences that has for the search for the 'origins' of 'the Celts'. I have suggested above that, in practice, we are defining the 'Celtic' by associations, so what we now must do is to create a model of how we can imagine these features to become associated with each other in the first place.

An Ontogenetic Model of the 'Origin(s) of Celtic Culture(s)' or Associative 'Celticity'

How this process of features becoming associated with each other happens, and how this creates the associations we consider as 'Celtic', can be shown in a simplified model (Fig. 2.7). For this, a virtual space is assumed, in which different points can carry different cultural information (features). These points are connected to each other by more or less random connections (they have been chosen non-randomly for the illustration on Fig. 2.7, to demonstrate a certain evolution), along which cultural information can flow in one or both directions. Some of the cultural features present are considered 'Celtic' by the observer, but only if they are associated with other features which are also considered to be 'Celtic', while other features are not considered to be 'Celtic' at all. A cultural feature, however, which would be considered to be 'Celtic' once it is associated with other such features, can be considered to be 'pre-Celtic' before it becomes associated with other 'Celtic' features. The model develops in linear time, the amount of time that passes between any two points shown in Fig. 2.7 is arbitrary. In other words, t2 is an indeterminate amount of time after t1, t3 an indeterminate time after t2, &c. For the sake of simplicity, only 10 points in time are being shown.

At time t1 a cultural feature is invented at some point in the cultural contact network, which can be considered to be 'pre-Celtic' as defined above. In the time that passes between t1 and t2, some of the contacts between different points in the network change.

2.7: An ontogenetic model of the 'origin(s) of Celtic culture(s)' (Karl 2008, 211).

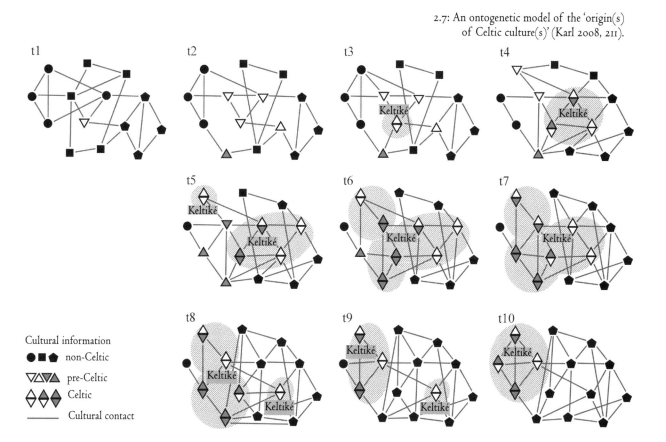

At t2, the 'pre-Celtic' feature invented at t1 has been adopted by two other points, and two more 'pre-Celtic' features have been invented independently of each other at two different points in the communication network. However, none of these 'pre-Celtic' features are yet associated with each other, so the 'Celtic' has not yet emerged. It is only at t3 that the first association of two cultural features, now considered to be 'Celtic' by the observer, appears. With this, the 'Celtic' has emerged, even if it only has a very limited distribution.

At t4, associations between different 'Celtic' features already exist in several places. The spatial distribution of the 'Celtic' has thus increased. At the same time, however, since each associative process has happened independently, several different 'variants' of 'Celtic' culture ('Celtic' cultures, if you will), have emerged: 'Celtic' culture isn't internally homogeneous and uniform, but rather the patterned chaos we would expect. Also, an 'originally Celtic' feature has appeared at t4 by innovation or variation (white inverted triangle which changes to grey inverted triangle) and association with another 'Celtic' feature within the Keltiké.

At t5, not only has the distribution of the already existing Keltiké spread more widely, but a new local association of features considered to be 'Celtic' by the observer has independently emerged in a different locality. In other words, a second, independent Keltiké has emerged, which has no genetic relationship with the previously existing Keltiké whatsoever. As such, there are not just several cultural features that have independent origins in this model, that only have become 'Celtic' by association with each other, there are also several spatially and chronologically independent 'origins of Celtic culture(s)'.

At t6, the areas of distribution of the different Keltikés merge, and 'Celtic' culture reaches its maximum distribution within the model. However, at that point as at any other point in time, it is not internally homogeneous or uniform, but at different localities within the Keltiké, there are different associations of different features, some of which can possibly even be established as regional sub-groups (e.g. a 'pure white triangular culture' at the far right, and a 'pure grey triangular culture' at the bottom left).

At t7, the 'non-Celtic' pentagonal culture starts to gain increasing influence in the cultural exchange network. 'Celtic' cultural features go out of fashion in peripheral areas, and the Keltiké starts to shrink. At t8, the pentagonal culture has started to gain a foothold in formerly 'core' areas of the Keltiké. The formerly contiguous area of the Keltiké now again splits into separate zones. Much like at earlier stages of the ontogenesis of Celtic culture(s), several Keltikés exist parallel to each other. At t9, the Keltiké has shrunk even further, even though an enclave still continues to exist within the now considerably expanded area of the pentagonal culture. At t10, the Keltiké has shrunk to the far top left of the virtual space—but still isn't homogeneous or uniform.

For the ontogenesis of the 'Celtic', this means that any feature that, by association with other 'Celtic' features, will at some point become a 'Celtic' feature, emerges independently at a specific, but largely irrelevant, point in the space-time continuum. Since features that, by their association, become 'Celtic' at some point, can be and will become associated with each other at different places and different times, the ontogenesis of the 'Celtic' is a poly-local, drawn-out process. And since new cultural features, which by association with other 'Celtic' features become 'Celtic' themselves, are still being invented in the present, e.g. by speakers of modern 'Celtic' languages, or are adopted into their cultural repertoire even if they have been invented in different, non-'Celtic' contexts, this process has not ended as of yet. So unless one wants to assume that earlier features are more essentially or more originally 'Celtic' than recently invented or adopted features, the 'Celtic' is still originating, even in the present.

Associative 'Celticity' in practice

If we look back at the past and take three sets of cultural features that are usually considered to be 'Celtic' by us as present-day observers, like the epigraphically attested 'Celtic' languages, historically attested 'Celtic' druidism and archaeologically 'Celtic' La Tène culture, we can get an idea what such a model might mean in 'real' terms. We can take these different sets of cultural features to be 'Celtic' cultural features independently of each other, since we, as discussed above, don't consider any cultural feature to be essentially 'Celtic' any more. Rather, each of these features can reasonably be considered to be 'Celtic' based on modern-day observations: in antiquity, historical sources consider much of what today is France to be inhabited by 'Celtic' populations (e.g. *De Bello Gallico* 1,1,1; but see Collis 2003, 98–103 for some problems associated with definitions of 'the Celts' in antiquity). In this area, in the Late Iron Age, we can observe attested 'Celtic' languages, found both in epigraphic inscriptions and in historical sources, mainly in the form of place-, group and personal names. Equally, we can observe the presence of La Tène material culture in this area, though its distribution, even in modern-day France, does not exactly match with that of its contemporary 'Celtic' languages. Finally, 'druidism' is observable in this area, attested in historical sources (e.g. *De Bello Gallico* 6,13–18), though the distribution of this set of cultural features (druidism probably not just consisting of the existence of a social role called 'druid', but also of a belief system of some kind or form) again is unlikely to have been perfectly matched with the distribution of both the 'Celtic' languages and the 'La Tène' culture, even within the area of modern-day France. Yet, since we consider none of these cultural features to be essential for something or someone to be 'Celtic' any more, and since scholarship has long considered each of them 'Celtic'—if perhaps for no other reason than that each of these sets of features are attested in an area and time when historical sources refer to at least parts of that very area as 'Celtic'—we are entirely justified in continuing to call each of them 'Celtic'. Since they are associated with each other, and are associated with populations considered 'Celtic' in a time when and an area where all these features are attested, the label 'Celtic' can be attached to them by association.

In fact, it would be ridiculous, unless we reject the use of the label 'Celtic' altogether, not to call each of these sets of features 'Celtic' in their own right, or to insist on seeing one of them as 'essentially Celtic', but not the others: none of them matches, exactly, the distribution of any of the respective other features (not even in France), nor does the distribution of any of them match, exactly, the use of the word 'Celtic' for populations in antiquity. Their association with the word 'Celtic' is exactly the same: their distribution partly overlaps with that of populations that have, in antiquity, been referred to as 'Celts'. Thus, the languages associated with populations referred to as 'Celts' in antiquity, and also the material culture(s) used by these populations, can be referred to as 'Celtic'—even if technically, in archaeological terms, one of them is called 'La Tène'. Similarly, neither is the language nor the material culture more 'essential' than the other: the 'Celtic' languages of Gaul in antiquity, the material culture(s) used there and 'druidism' as practised there can equally justly be referred to as 'Celtic'.

So what about their respective origins (Fig. 2.8)? If we are to follow John Koch's proposal, the 'Celtic' languages originated somewhere along the 'Atlantic fringe', perhaps even in the south-west of the Iberian Peninsula, where we hardly have any observable evidence for La Tène culture nor for 'druidism', let alone for this area being their respective area of 'origin'. Nor does e.g. La Tène culture exist at all at the time when the first Tartessian inscriptions appear in the 8th or 7th century BC, and no observable evidence can be found for 'druidism' until at least several centuries later. If we look at the emergence of the La Tène culture, its area of origin is somewhere far to the east of south-western Iberia, traditionally located somewhere in an area between eastern France and western Austria, middle Germany and the Alps, in the 5th century BC. And 'druidism', at least if we were to take Caesar literally (and we have no other evidence as to its area of origin), allegedly originated in the British Isles (*De Bello Gallico* 6,13.10–12), possibly as late as the 3rd or even early 2nd century BC. So if, as demonstrated above, each of these sets of cultural features, with equal justification, can be called 'Celtic', where does 'the Celtic' originate?

The Celts from everywhere and nowhere

If we accept (1) that 'Celticity' is not an inherent quality that something either has, or has not; (2) that 'Celtic' is a label stuck to our scholarly observations, based on observable features in reality, which are not 'real' as such, but constructed by us as a classificatory tool to make sense of the mess that the evidence for the past (and also for the present) presents to us; (3) that logical positivist approaches to studying the past are fundamentally flawed, and that no label, definition or even description we can attach to any observations we can make can ever really reflect 'how it really', 'how it essentially' was, the quest for the 'origins of the Celts' is clearly exposed for the folly that it is. If we take a realistic look at what we really do to make sense of the chaos that we can observe, if we take a serious look at what we actually do, rather than what we would like to be able to do, any attempt at locating the 'origins' and the 'direction' in which 'Celticization' happened is clearly exposed as ultimately meaningless.

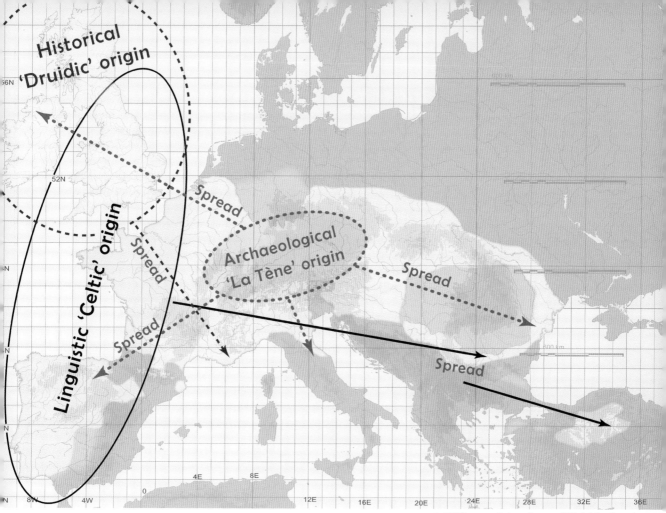

2.8: Different origins of sets of 'Celtic' cultural features (base map adapted Koch et al. 2007; cf. Sims-Williams 2006, maps 5.2, 11.1, and 11.2).

Attempting to track 'Celticization' can, in reality, be little more than tracking individual cultural features that, at different places and in different times, merge into sets of features, which again merge with each other in yet different places and different times, which we decide to call 'Celtic' once the patterns that become observable in the record meet certain criteria that we have more or less arbitrarily chosen as allegedly 'representative'. Since none of these individual features, and even none of these sets of cultural features, can reasonably be given primacy over the others, since none of them is necessarily 'essential', let alone more 'essential' than many, if any, others, there can be no 'origin' of 'the Celts', nor can 'Celticization' be described in simple terms like 'from the west', 'from central Europe', &c. The 'Celtic' thus originates everywhere and nowhere, then and now, and 'spreads' by partly similar, partly different means in different directions.

Any specific attempt to locate and track the 'real' 'origin and spread of the Celts' thus is bound to fail: if we base this search on a linguistic definition of 'the Celtic', we are talking about prehistoric periods in which there is no direct evidence for languages, where archaeological evidence does not map onto language distributions, and where no archaeology dates or allows to locate languages. Thus, there is no evidence allowing to identify their place or time of 'origin', nor the direction of their 'spread', and we are looking at a question that cannot seriously be answered. If, on the other hand, we base our search on an archaeological definition of the 'Celtic', there can be no 'origin', or at best many different 'origins' of different aspects of the 'Celtic', and thus again, we face an unanswerable question.

The meaninglessness of 'origins', and relevant questions to ask

Indeed, not only is the question where and when 'the Celts' came into being impossible to answer, it is, ultimately, also perfectly meaningless. Because knowing the 'origin of the Celts', whatever that should be and however we want to define it, would not really help us with anything at all, since it does not answer any relevant questions. How did 'the Celtic' come into being? How did it spread later on? Why did it become dominant in large areas of prehistoric western and central Europe? It also does not open up any relevant 'new' questions: we already know that the 'Celtic', whatever that may be, must have emerged, whether we can put any specific time and place to this or not. Thus, where it actually emerged (if it did at all, and as I have argued, I think it did not 'really' emerge at all, but only emerged 'virtually' in our classificatory labelling) does not tell us anything new beyond the location itself, without any apparent additional questions emerging from this.

Thus, knowing where and when 'the Celts' originated does not answer any relevant questions, nor do we need to know the answer to the particular question of when and where 'the Celts' originated to examine the really significant questions underlying those specific questions. These much more relevant, but much less obvious, questions exist aplenty, and I will name but a few, which might be worth following up in the immediate future, since they may very well be much more answerable, and are much more meaningful for understanding the past, than the one about the 'origins of the Celts' that has distracted us from real work for the better part of almost three centuries:

Why could the features we now define as 'Celtic' spread in the area of their distribution?

What facilitated this high degree of information exchange between what essentially seem to be small-scale, locally constituted societies?

Can what we learn from archaeological formation processes also be applied to linguistic ones, or do they work completely differently?

How do languages emerge in prehistory at all?

Answering even only some of them, even only partially and perhaps only speculatively, would take us much further than trying to pinpoint, on a time-slice map, where 'the Celts' originally came from, and would open up many more relevant questions that we should look at if we want to gain a better understanding and an improved knowledge of the past, whether the 'Celtic', or more generally of the human condition. Thus, it is my opinion that we should focus on such questions, questions for which that which we have decided to call the 'Celtic' may well be suited to provide some, if only tentative, answers, rather than wasting more time on squabbling about whether 'the Celts' came from the east, the middle, or the west, whether it is the languages, the art, the material culture, the historical identifications, the religious beliefs, the ethnic identification or anything else that is of the essence for something to be truly 'Celtic', or whether the term 'Celtic' is useful at all. That, rather than a new proposal for a new spot of the 'origin of the Celts' on a map, or a 'new' direction of their spread, would really constitute the paradigmatic shift (Kuhn 1976) that is long overdue.

BIBLIOGRAPHY

Antilla, R. 1972 *An Introduction to Historical and Comparative Linguistics*. New York, Macmillan.

Bourdieu, P. 1977 *Outline of a Theory of Practice*. Cambridge Studies in Social Anthropology 16, Cambridge, Cambridge University Press.

Buchanan, M. 2001 *Ubiquity: The new science that is changing the world*. London, Phoenix Press.

Buchanan, M. 2003 *Small World: Uncovering Nature's Hidden Networks*. London, Phoenix Press.

Childe, V. G. 1929 *The Danube in Prehistory*. Oxford, Oxford University Press.

Collis, J. R. 2003. *The Celts. Origins, Myths & Inventions*. Stroud, Tempus.

Collis, J. R. 2009 'Die Konstruktion von Chronologien', *Interpretierte Eisenzeiten 3*, R. Karl & J. Leskovar (eds.), 373–420. Studien zur Kulturgeschichte von Oberösterreich, Linz, Oberösterreichische Landesmuseen.

Cunliffe, B. 2001 *Facing the Ocean. The Atlantic and its Peoples 8000 BC–AD 1500*. Oxford, Oxford University Press.

De Bello Gallico from Deissmann, M. L. (ed. & trans.) 1980. *Gaius Iulius Caesar. De Bello Gallico/Der Gallische Krieg* (Lateinisch/Deutsch). Stuttgart, Reclam.

Eska, J. F. & D. E. Evans 2002 'Continental Celtic', *The Celtic Languages*, M. J. Ball with J. Fife (eds.), 26–63. Routledge Language Family Descriptions, pbk. ed., London & New York, Routledge.

Fife, J. 2002 'Introduction', *The Celtic Languages*, M. J. Ball with J. Fife (eds.), 3–25. Routledge Language Family Descriptions, pbk. ed., London & New York, Routledge.

Hawkes, C. F. C. 1973 'Cumulative Celticity in Pre-Roman Britain', *Études Celtiques* 13/2, 607–28.

Hodson, F. R. 1990 *Hallstatt: The Ramsauer Graves*. Bonn, Habelt.

Isaac, G. R. 2005 'The nature and origins of the Celtic languages: Atlantic seaways, Italo-Celtic and other paralinguistic misapprehensions', *Studia Celtica* 38, 49–58.

James, S. 2000 *The Atlantic Celts. Ancient People or Modern Invention?* London, British Museum Press.

James, S. 2007 'Iron Age Paradigms and the Celtic Metanarrative: A Case Study in Conceptualising the Past, and Writing Histories', *The Grand "Celtic" story?*, G. Anthoons & H. Clerinx (eds.), 11–31. Memoires de la Société Belge d'Études Celtiques 28, Bruxelles, Société Belge d'Études Celtiques.

Karl, R. 2004 'Erwachen aus dem langen Schlaf der Theorie? Ansätze zu einer keltologischen Wissenschaftstheorie', *Keltologie heute. Themen und Fragestellungen*, E. Poppe (ed.), 291–303. Studien und Texte zur Keltologie 6, Münster, Nodus.

Karl, R. 2007 'Awaking from the Long Sleep of Theory? Approaches to theory in Celtic Studies', *The Celtic World. Vol. I—Theory in Celtic Studies*, R. Karl & D. Stifter (eds.), 333–46. Critical Concepts in Historical Studies, London & New York, Routledge.

Karl, R. 2008 'Feine Unterschiede. Zu "Keltengenese" und ethnogenetischen Prozessen in der Keltiké', *Mitteilungen der Anthropologischen Gesellschaft in Wien* 138, 205–23.

Karl, R. forthcoming 'Becoming Welsh. Modelling 1st millennium BC Societies in Wales and the Celtic Context', *Atlantic Europe in the First millennium BC: Crossing the Divide*, T. Moore & L. Armada (eds.). Oxford, Oxford University Press.

Kauffman, S. 1996 *At Home in the Universe. The Search for Laws of Self-Organization and Complexity*. London, Penguin.

Kern, A., K. Kowarik, A. W. Rausch, H. Reschreiter 2008 *Salz–Reich. 7000 Jahre Hallstatt*. Veröffentlichungen der prähistorischen Abteilung 2. Wien, Verlag des Naturhistorischen Museums.

Koch, J. T. 2009 *Tartessian: Celtic in the South-west at the Dawn of History*. Celtic Studies Publications 13. Aberystwyth, Celtic Studies Publications.

Koch, J. T., R. Karl, A. Minard, & S. Ó Faoláin 2007 *An Atlas for Celtic Studies. Archaeology and Names in Ancient Europe and Early Medieval Ireland, Britain and Brittany*. Celtic Studies Publications 12. Oxford, Oxbow.

Kossinna, G. 1920 *Die Herkunft der Germanen. Zur Methode der Siedlungsarchäologie*. 2nd ext. ed., Leipzig, Verlag C. Kabitzsch.

Kuhn, T. S. 1976 *Die Struktur wissenschaftlicher Revolutionen. Zweite revidierte und um das Postskriptum von 1969 ergänzte Auflage*. Frankfurt am Main, suhrkamp.

Latour, B. 2005 *Reassembling the Social. An Introduction to Actor-Network-Theory*. Oxford, Oxford University Press.

Marion, R. 1999 *The Edge of Organization. Chaos and Complexity Theories of Formal Social Systems*. Thousand Oaks, Sage.

Megaw, M. R. & J. V. S. Megaw 2001 *Celtic Art from its beginnings to the Book of Kells*. Rev. & exp. ed., London, Thames and Hudson.

Müller-Scheeßel, N. 2000 *Die Hallstattkultur und ihre räumliche Differenzierung. Der West- und Osthallstattkreis aus forschungsgeschichtlich-methodischer Sicht*. Tübinger Texte 3. Rahden/Westf., Verlag Marie Leidorf.

Pauli, L. 1980 'Die Herkunft der Kelten—Sinn und Unsinn einer alten Frage', *Die Kelten in Mitteleuropa. Kultur—Kunst—Wirtschaft*, L. Pauli (ed.), 16–24. Salzburg, Amt der Salzburger Landesregierung.

Pauli, L. 2007 'The Origin of the Celts: Sense and Nonsense of an Old Question', *The Celtic World. Vol. II—Celtic Archaeology*, R. Karl & D. Stifter (eds.), 9–24. Critical Concepts in Historical Studies. London & New York, Routledge.

Prigogine, I. 1997 *The End of Certainty. Time, Chaos and the New Laws of Nature*. New York, Free Press.

Renfrew, C. 1989 *Archaeology and Language. The Puzzle of Indo-European Origins*. Pbk. ed. London, Penguin.

Ruelle, D. 1992 *Zufall und Chaos*. Berlin, Springer.

Sawyer, R. K. 2005 *Social Emergence. Societies As Complex Systems*. Cambridge, Cambridge University Press.

Schmidt, K. H. 2002 'Insular Celtic, P- and Q-Celtic', *The Celtic Languages*, M. J. Ball with J. Fife (eds.), 64–98. Routledge Language Family Descriptions, pbk. ed. London & New York, Routledge.

Sims-Williams, P. 2006 *Ancient Celtic Place-Names in Europe and Asia Minor*. Publications of the Philological Society 39. Oxford, Blackwell.

Tomaschitz, K. 2002 *Die Wanderungen der Kelten in der antiken literarischen Überlieferung*. Mitteilungen der prähistorischen Kommission 47, Wien, Österreichische Akademie der Wissenschaften.

Veit, U. 2000 'Gustaf Kossinna and his concept of a national archaeology', *Archaeology, Ideology and Society. The German Experience*, H. Härke (ed.), 40–64. Gesellschaften und Staaten im Epochenwandel 7. Frankfurt am Main, Peter Lang.

Watts, D. J. 1999 *Small Worlds. The Dynamics of Networks between Order and Randomness*. Princeton Studies in Complexity. Princeton, Princeton University Press.

Wittgenstein, L. 1963 *Tractatus logico-philosophicus. Logisch-philosophische Abhandlung*. Frankfurt am Main, Suhrkamp [originally published 1921].

NEWLY DISCOVERED INSCRIPTIONS FROM THE SOUTH-WEST OF THE IBERIAN PENINSULA

Amílcar Guerra

Introduction

THIS is a synopsis of the most recent finds of monuments inscribed with the Palaeohispanic script called 'Tartessian' or south-western. Particular emphasis is given to the discovery of an important inscription on stone recently found in the southern Alentejo, an area where there is a major concentration of Tartessian inscribed stones. The stela was identified during excavations at the site of Mesas do Castelinho, in an archaeological context relating to the Roman Republic, as part of a pavement dating to the end of the 2nd century BC. Most of the stone and its inscription were in good condition, and the writing constitutes the most extensive Tartessian text currently known, with more than 80 characters. In this respect the stela is of particular importance within the extant corpus in which very few long sequences of text are well preserved. This paper also discusses a new stela discovered in 2008 at the site Corte Pinheiro (Loulé) as part of the research undertaken by the ESTELA Project. Finally, the paper will reanalyse the Tartessian inscribed stone from Vale de Águia (Silves), which has been published recently.

A team from the University of Lisbon, under the direction of Carlos Fabião and myself, has undertaken research in the southern Alentejo province, which has produced a range of significant results. This project was initiated by the archaeological survey of the site of Mesas do Castelinho, which has been known in the specialist literature since the end of the 19th century and was first described in the mid 20th century. Despite this, the site had not been subject to major intervention until the end of 1986, when an unauthorized visit caused considerable destruction. Following this unfortunate episode, the managing body of Cultural Heritage at that time instructed a team from Lisbon to begin, in 1988, a project to study and evaluate the importance of this settlement site (Fabião & Guerra 1991, 305–11). From that time till the present, those responsible for the project have regularly undertaken archaeological fieldwork and excavation, following the original objectives. The fieldwork of 2008 was carried out in September, as the 20th campaign, during which excavation was continued in the area called 'Platform B', which is the most extensive and best preserved of all the areas within the settlement, and in particular was focused on the zone known as Sector B–3.

While the research team was especially focused on the settlement, their presence in the district stimulated interest on a variety of types of archaeological remains there, most notably the south-western inscriptions. Already in 1997 the team had been alerted to the consequences of reforesting activities on the site of the Monte Novo do Castelinho. A late Roman cemetery was discovered and investigated, in association with an ancient agricultural site and a nearby dam, which were already known in the specialist literature (Fabião et al. 1998, 199–200).

Despite its late date, excavation of one of the graves in the Monte Novo cemetery revealed a stela inscribed with the south-western script, which had been re-used during the late Roman period. It is likely that this was the second re-use of the stone, as it had previously been used as a door jamb, which had unfortunately seriously damaged part of the inscription. Consequently, it is possible to make a near complete reading of only a single line of text, to be read right-to-left (Guerra et al. 1999; see below Koch, p. 254, for the reading).

Afterwards Rui Cortes, archaeology officer of the Almodôvar council district, learned that another Tartessian inscribed stone had been identified at São Martinho, in the municipality of Silves near its boundary with Almodôvar. At that time this important piece constituted one of the two most extensive texts then known (for the text, see below Koch, p. 255). However, it took some time before it was published together with the fragmentary text of the stela from Corte do Freixo, which had been identified some years before, but not yet published (Guerra 2002; see below Koch, p. 254).

This aspect of the investigation did not figure among the initial objectives of the project, but the ongoing presence of the research team in the neighbourhood continued to attract local information leading to the recovery of Tartessian inscribed stones. The same sort of fortuitous circumstances subsequently led to the discovery of the great inscription of Mesas do Castelinho during the excavation work carried out at the site. Although this find was not found as part of a pavement of Republican Roman date and not in the chronological context normally associated with south-western inscriptions (First Iron Age), its discovery was not a complete surprise. The first years of archaeological intervention in this vicinity had come across a local account of an inscription of the south-western type which had been seen near the same settlement. Mr José Mestre of Monte do Farranhão was the source of this information, and he had previously collected remains of inscriptions known to the investigators; therefore, his testimony was deemed highly credible. Even so, we did not expect to be so lucky as to turn up Tartessian inscriptions while excavating the settlement.

In the last decade, however, we have had the opportunity to publish the discovery of five previously undocumented inscribed stones, substantially adding to the region's inventory of this category of artefact. Recognizing the importance of these finds, a team came together for the purpose of disseminating these discoveries.

In September 2008, a new museum specifically dedicated to the south-western (or

Tartessian) script, namely MESA ('Museu da Escrita do Sudoeste, Almodôvar') was opened in the town of Almodôvar. MESA is the fruit of an initiative, begun some three years before, by the council of that municipality, with the aim of making the oldest writing in the Iberian Peninsula better known in order to promote the cultural heritage in this region. This initiative naturally received the support of the investigators who had over the years conducted the excavations at Mesas do Castelinho. The research team then collaborated with the Almodôvar council concerning how best to present and disseminate the archaeological material. Thus, MESA is closely linked, as an institutional partner, with the long-term programme of fieldwork carried out in the district. It is also the place where the two Tartessian inscribed stones published in this chapter can be seen.

1.) The stela of Mesas do Castelinho, Almodôvar (Figs. 3.1–3.4)

Towards the end of the 2007 campaign, in the area of the site known as 'Street 1' which is part of a settlement complex excavated in Sector B-3, a block of local schist of considerable dimensions was uncovered in layer 726. It showed some signs of wear on the face that was visible (Fig. 3.1). However, keeping to the excavation plan, that campaign was concluded without raising the stone. When excavation resumed the following year, it was decided that the block should be lifted. What we found when it was raised surpassed the most optimistic expectations about its suspected importance. Not only was an inscription revealed, but it is the most extensive and best preserved Tartessian text known at present.

The stela has maximum dimensions of 112 cm in height, 51 cm in width, and 9 cm in thickness. The inscribed text has been inserted in a carved frame that covered around two-thirds of the front surface of the schist block. The part of the stone that was intended to be set in the ground is defined by a carved line that neatly separates the above- and under-ground sections. However, as a result of serious surface deterioration, this separation line was only well preserved in the right-hand side of the stela (Figs. 3.2–3.4).

Above this line, the writing zone followed a ruled layout, generally rectangular in shape, although it is narrower in the upper part, in order to conform to the shape of the schist block.

In keeping with a recurring feature of the south-western inscribed stones, the text is placed within a box bound by two lines, which, in general, are approximately parallel, though sometimes having a tendency to deviate from geometric regularity. This tendency is particularly clear in the outer set of lines, especially the two longer, lateral ones. The outer pair of 'parallel' lines between which the text is written on the right-hand side widens out towards the top of the stone. On the contrary, the corresponding lines on the left become much narrower towards the top. The interior lines show more regularity in their layout, but the differences in width between the top and base of the epigraphic field force the upper ends of the lines to be more irregular.

3.1. View of the excavation of Mesas do Castelinho: some
of the work carried in 'Rua 1', corresponding to the
beginning of layer 726, showing the location of the stela

In terms of general organization, the text is continued anti-clockwise around four outer lines, each of which forms one of four sides of a rectangle which delimits the epigraphic field. From there, the text continues over three vertical lines in the middle of the rectangle, whose boustrophedon orientation alternates, the first and second are placed in a left-to-right order, while the third is ascending right-to-left (Figs. 3.3–3.4). Thus, the direction in which the sequence of letters flows follows principles which can be paralleled in other south-western inscriptions. In general, the complex epigraphy has been laid out so that the different blocks of letters placed within ruled frames can be read continuously, with each sequence beginning where the previous one ends. Taken as a whole, we see that the organizing principles of the structure are mixed, in that a linear pattern alternates with a concentric one. This mixed structure is not usual for the south-western inscriptions, which most often favour right-to-left linear orientation or anti-clockwise concentric orientation. It can be noticed that the person responsible for the organization of the main body of the text applied these principles to the four external lines and the two which were initially placed in the internal space. The strategy used for these lines made it necessary that the last line assume left-to-right orientation. The organization of the concluding lines in the interior of the layout may have been undertaken by an engraver who preferred the less common, but attested, left-to-right orientation. In any event, the seventh line breaks with the usual orientation in order to avoid the beginning of a line of text being placed opposite the end of the previous line. Naturally, those responsible for the engraving would have been preoccupied in following some of the most distinctive norms of south-western epigraphy, which, having an internal logic and common-sensical appeal, were easily learned.

The orientation of the individual letters is as in most examples in which a Tartessian text is arranged to flow around a continuous concentric circuit: i.e. they are in an 'extroverse' position, so that the top of the sign is oriented towards the outside of the stone. Thus, we can think of the signs with their stems converging at, or emerging out of, an imagined point at the centre of the rectangle, and their tops radiating outward. Taking this into account, the start of the text is in the lower right-hand corner, where an oblique line separates the inscription's opening character (Φ **t^{i}**) and closes the first long sequence of signs that goes around the whole external rectangle (ending with Ч **u**).

The engraving was made by a process of incision, using a pointed object, which in general produced a fine line of medium depth. The exceptional length of the engraved text, compared to the space available in the 'epigraphic field', imposed a layout requiring letters of only medium size that might nonetheless be visible and readable from some distance. Moreover, the tight arrangement of the lines of letters gives the impression of an exuberance, tightly bunched together, but a respect for principles of symmetry is also clearly conveyed in the overall visual effect.

The original block had a smooth surface, which was a result of natural fractures in the schist. Yet the raw material had suffered from some weathering, leading to deterioration of the first compact layer and to its total degradation in some areas. Fortunately this occurred only in small places, and it is possible to reconstruct it almost entirely.

From the palaeographic point of view, the inscription shows some peculiarities which deserve a special reference. Most significantly, there are uncertainties relating to the form of three of the letters which are traditionally transcribed **k^{u}**, **t^{e}**, and **b^{o}**, and are similar to one another in shape. This similarity can make them hard to distinguish, an ambiguity which is then resolved by the vowel sign that follows it.[1] Analysis of the inscription, however, shows a total of four instances where we can see formal features which distinguish these three consonant signs without relying on the following vowel. Two of the signs preceding the vowel sign **u** (Ч) are substantially different in palaeographic detail, most notably in the first example, where the horizontal lines do not continue completely to the vertical strokes, thus contrasting with the normal style. On the other hand, it is not possible to understand the significance of the formal distinction between the second character preceding a **u** (Ч), from the earlier one immediately following **e** (O) on the same line, i.e. the outer left-hand sequence opening the inscription. According to the principle of redundancy (**k^{u}** before **u**, &c.) which operates in the stop consonants

1 With regard to this question, see in particular Untermann 1997, 148–9.

3.3. Detail of the inscribed area of the
stela of Mesas do Castelinho

3.2. The inscribed stone of
Mesas do Castelinho

in the south-western writing system, we should probably conclude that these signs have
the same phonetic value on the basis of the vowel (**u** ५) that follows, however, the two
letters are quite different formally. Conversely, the third sign of this type, part of the
sequence of letters at the top of the stone, precedes an **e** (O) and, therefore, though
formally similar to the second example, which precedes **u** (५), should be transcribed as
t^e. Comparison of these three signs would allow us to infer that **b°** is presented by the
presence of only two horizontal lines (□) as its distinguishing feature. Nevertheless, this
way of representing this sign distinctively in this inscription is not consistently applied
throughout the corpus (Untermann 1997, 171). In a significant number of counter-
examples occurring in other south-western inscriptions, these signs, which according to

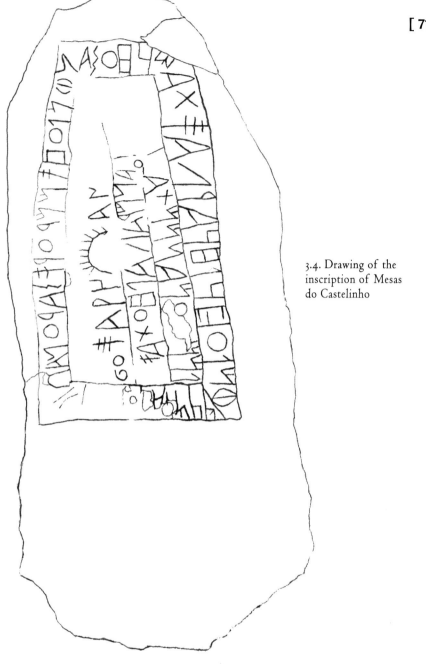

3.4. Drawing of the inscription of Mesas do Castelinho

the principle of redundancy should be followed by **e** (O), **o** (+), or **u** (4), have instead an **a** (A) following. It is possible to cite at least four such exceptional examples to this rule (J.1.1, J.1.4, J.3.1 e J.6.2).[2] It therefore appears that the practical use of the signs was subject to a significant degree of fluidity, and even when we are dealing with only a single engraver's work on one stone, as presently, we might expect a certain variation as usual, a natural feature of the engravers' technique in composing and transcribing south-

---

2   It would also be possible, I think, that these examples could also join the two occurrences of J.7.1 where a singly config-ured sign could be a variant of this association.

western texts. Therefore, it can be no simple matter to establish reliable and universal standards to describe in accurate detail the components that make up each of the signs as they were actually used.

Another issue raised by the Mesas do Castelinho inscription concerns the third to the last symbol in the final line. It is represented by a character of unique shape. Like other unique signs occurring elsewhere in the Tartessian corpus, the one here raises several unresolvable questions. The basic letter form—the representation of an approximately semi-circular line, above which there are small vertical lines—does not have a clear parallel elsewhere in the south-western script's palaeographic inventory. It is however possible that the unique character in the last line of the Mesas do Castelinho inscription can ultimately be interpreted as equivalent to the comparable symbol, also of unknown value, found in the 'Signário de Espanca' (J.25.1; see below, Fig. 9.6, p. 207), where it is represented twice in position 26, and thus figures as the penultimate element of this 'alphabet' and no. 46 of J. A. Correa's full register of south-western characters (1993, 548). The first (upper) sequence of signs on the Espanca stone reveals a much better technique of engraving, implying that this 'signary' or 'alphabet' was the work of the master. The configuration is slightly different from that of the signary as repeated below it, presumably the copy made by the apprentice. However, it is the apprentice's copy that is more similar to the third-to-last grapheme on the Mesas do Castelinho inscription. The affinities between these three representations are obvious, therefore their equation seems possible to me, taking into account the range of oscillation that many of the signs display (for a summary of variations see Untermann 1997, 171). This grapheme's occurrence on the stela of Mesas do Castelinho would be the first time in which it has been documented in a textual sequence (as opposed to the Espanca practice ab^{e}k^{e}t^u), which is not easy to explain if it represents a sound, or sequence of sounds, common in the language. We must bear in mind that it is not just in this case where variant letter forms are a factor in the corpus.

With regard to the possible phonetic value of this unusual grapheme some logical deductions are possible. There are 21 distinct signs in the entire Mesas do Castelinho inscription, which substantially limits the possible equivalences. The puzzling grapheme is followed by an a (A), which implies that it did not correspond to a sign of syllabic value, since the three characters corresponding to stop consonant + /a/ (t^a, b^a and k^a) are also found on this stela, all with their usual forms (X, }, ∧). Similarly, the stela also contains the phonemic symbols l (↑), n (ꓬ), r (ꟼ), ŕ (ꓹ), and s (≢), so we can consider it a valid and complete system using the traditional 27 Tartessian signs. We may consider the hypothesis that the unusual grapheme is an alternative form for the letter ŕ (ꓹ), with which it shows some similarity of form. But as ꓹ occurs on the stela in another, more usual, form, such a highly divergent dual representation would be unexplained. That leaves only the possibility that the grapheme corresponds to the 'standard' Tartessian signs m or ś. Weighing against the last possibility, if we retain the theoretical assumption that the south-western system of signs had been fairly fixed and consistent, a comparison with the 'Signary of Espanca' shows that the usual ś sign ᛘ is clearly present in its usual form and that the remaining unclassified signs are of distinctively problematical character, i.e. cannot be assigned a certain or probable phonetic value. That leads us to the deduction that **m** is the Mesas do Castelinho grapheme's probable value. It is, however, acknowledged that this conclusion entails a number of assumptions that must now remain unconfirmed. The argument is offered only to show one possible philological approach to establishing this grapheme's value.

In the light of the above, the transcript, following the system of MLH 4, is as follows:[3]

1) t^{i}ilek^{u}ur̲k^{u}uark^{a}ast^{a}ab̲^{u}ut^{e}eb^{a}ant^{i}ileb^{o}ooiirerob^{a}arenaŕk̲^{e}[en---]aφiuu
2) lii*eianiit^{a}a
3) eanirak^{a}alt^{e}et^{a}ao
4) b^{e}esaru?an

With a total of 82 signs, 80 of which have an identifiable phonetic value, this inscription is the longest Tartessian text known at present. Moreover, the fact that the portion of text that is damaged and lost can be seen to contain the well-known Tartessian formula b^{a}are naŕk^{e}e[n---] means that it is possible to determine the inscription's content almost completely.

However, as is normal in the majority of known Tartessian documents, the sequences of letters that can be found repeated elsewhere are largely limited to this b^{a}are naŕk^{e}e[n---] formula. It is clear that in a text of this size, it is always possible to find small segments which correspond to others that have already been identified. If we build on Untermann's work in MLH, we inevitably find something which may correspond to the inventory of forms already defined by him, but this affinity is limited in the main. Some of the segments that can be paralleled there are quite small. Recurring sequences of two or three characters cannot be assumed to be meaningful.

Following similar methods, we may consider proposals for onomastic identification, namely some previously documented personal names of Indo-European origin. It would be possible, for example, to assume that the beginning of the text t^{i}ilek^{u}ur or t^{i}ilek^{u}ul corresponds to the personal name *Tillegus*, which is attested in the tablet of El Caurel, Lugo, Galicia (AE 1961, 96 = AE 1973, 289 = HEp 8, 334 = AE 2000, 748).

Similarly, a comparison of elements attested elsewhere in the corpus justifies some further observations. The sequence b^{a}ant^{i}i may be related to one already known: b^{a}ane recurs in J.11.1, J.20.1, J.26.1, and J.19.1. The last inscription shows some clear parallels with the stele of Mesas do Castelinho, if we compare their respective long sequences: t^{e}e b^{a}ant^{i}i leb^{o}ooiir ero b^{a}are naŕk^e[en---] which can be approximated to J.19.1 b^{a}ane ooŕoir e b^a[are naŕ]k^{e}enii (see further Koch below, p. 243). As a general

---

3 John Koch has been kind enough to offer pertinent comments and observations regarding this epigraphy, for which I am very grateful. These include many interpretations, some of which are shared by me and therefore included here.

rule, bᵃane occurs in sequences preceding the formula bᵃare naŕkᵉenii, and the like, almost always only brief elements intervening; thus, in the following contexts:

J.11.1 bᵃane ro bᵃare naŕkᵉenii
J.26.1. bᵃane [---]bᵃare naŕkᵉ[e---]

Jürgen Untermann also grouped these occurrences with J.21.1. bᵃan tᵉe[---bᵃ]are naŕkᵉenii. We might also now consider, although the idea is presented here only as a preliminary suggestion, that bᵃane and bᵃantⁱi could be added to two groups of Tartessian stems that appear to be inflected as verbs: naŕkᵉe, naŕkᵉen, naŕkᵉeii, naŕkᵉenii, naŕkᵉentⁱi, naŕkᵉenai and bᵃare, bᵃaren, bᵃareii, bᵃarentⁱi. Most likely, as many investigators have already pointed out, we have in these series verb forms in -ntⁱi, preserving the Indo-European third person plural active ending, also found in Tartessian lakᵉentⁱi. However, contrary to what has been proposed for bᵃarentⁱi and naŕkᵉentⁱi, which are sometimes interpreted as the past forms of their respective verbs (Untermann 1997, 166), bᵃantⁱi is possibly a third person plural present tense verb form, a category possibly not previously attested in the corpus. Therefore, bᵃane might represent the singular of the same verbal paradigm.

If we take the preceding hypotheses together, proposing tⁱilekᵘur as a personal name and the various possible verbal inflections in the Tartessian corpus, both can be linked with elements identified in the indigenous Indo-European languages of the Iberian Peninsula. Moreover, the issue of the inflected endings could have some special relevance in determining the structure and affiliation of language recorded in the south-western inscriptions. The possible personal names would not significantly alter the picture.

Apart from these two areas, the possible interpretations and any similarities with sequences already known are more problematic. Though hampered by inherent limitations in our knowledge of this language discussed above, one might still see in the sequence of characters at the end of the inscription an element related to the form saruneea, already identified in the inscriptions J.22.1 and J.22.2. This hypothesis would necessarily depend on the analysis of the system of signs with regard to the third-to-last letter of saruʔan, which may be an m, as proposed above. Anyway, these suggestions are only mere conjecture, without any basis other than graphical (and therefore presumably also phonetic) similarities of comparative groups, resemblances that could be apparent rather than real in terms of the underlying etymology.

2. The stela of Corte Pinheiro, Loulé (Figs. 3.5–3.6)

Shortly after the discovery of the Mesas do Castelinho inscription described above, another stela was identified at the site of Corte Pinheiro, located in the area of Serra Algarvia, on the border between the municipalities of Loulé and Almodôvar, in the

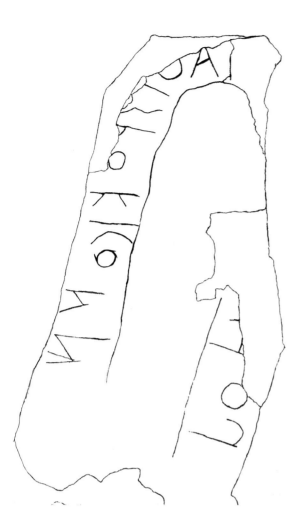

3.6. Drawing of the inscribed
area of the Corte Pinheiro stela

3.5. The Corte Pinheiro stela

administrative region belonging to the former. The discovery occurred during fieldwork undertaken by Samuel Melro and Pedro Barros, with the scientific support of Carlos Fabião and myself, as part of the first remit promoted by the ESTELA Project (Melro, Barros, & Guerra 2009). The ESTELA Project was launched following the opening of MESA in Almodôvar. Among its objectives, a key priority for ESTELA is further research into the archaeological contexts in which literacy developed in this region. Towards this goal, an initial strategy was to relocate all the sites that had produced inscribed stones, focusing on fieldwork in the hilly country around Almodôvar, where inscriptions have been found in a dense concentration.

Visits to Corte Pinheiro enabled the research team to identify this place as the find spot of an inscribed stone that had been given into the care of MESA. The stela is a block of local shale, 111 cm high, 39 cm wide, and 14 cm maximum thickness. It is generally in good condition, although it had suffered from a fracture affecting a sizeable area near its upper right corner, with the consequence of the loss of a significant section of text. The base of the stela had been designed to be placed in the ground, as there is a well-defined separation between the text and the lower uninscribed third of the stone.

The text is in a single line and adheres to the most common model, using the contour of the upper part of the stone (the part intended to be seen above ground surface level). The text follows the curve along the top and is bound by one line, which defines the frame for lettering only on the internal side, the exterior of the frame being defined by the edge of the stone itself. It was probably inscribed as a continuous text, laid out in a single line as *scripta continua*.

The letters stand outside the single looping line, and on its interior the space remains blank and lacks inscription. The orientation of the signs is extroverse, i.e. with the tops of the signs pointing to the outside of the inscribed face of stone and the text aligned from right to left, which is in accordance with the norms in this system of writing. The inscription was engraved by fairly shallow incision, but it is quite clear, since the stone has a hard smooth surface (of brownish surface colour) and resisted weathering fairly well. Therefore, it is in general quite easy to identify the different characters which may be transcribed as follows:

b^{e}eu*[ ]ae*b^{a}reŕk^{e}eni

We find here some of the more usual elements of the so-called Tartessian epigraphic formulae. Some of the manifestations are of the recurring attested form, but there are also some anomalies. First, the recognizable formulaic **b^{a}re** (without the regular redundancy of stop consonant + following vowel) occurs instead of the usual **b^{a}are** without the characteristic redundancy. Elsewhere, we find the redundancy rule disrespected similarly in one text in the case of the stela J.52.1 from Villamanrique de la Condesa, Seville, which reads]**irea b^{a}re la**[(see Koch below, p. 250). It ought to be considered as an anomaly that the two signs have been omitted at the beginning of the following word, (na)ŕk^{e}eni, which is another example (along with that of Mesas do Castelinho) of the most frequently occurring formulaic word in the corpus. Finally, it should be noted that the sign ŕ (ᴎ) in the last word has a unique form, as if turned 90° onto its side. The resulting grapheme has formal affinities with some realizations for the sign k^e)| (namely that found on J.19.1), but in the present context, where it precedes a clear k^e, this is clearly different, and does not, in my view, permit any reading other than ŕ (ᴎ).

3.7. Drawing of the stela of Vale de Águia (Silves)

Other recent finds

Two fragmentary inscriptions associated with one another have been recently reported. The first, found in Sabóia, Odemira, is still unpublished. The other comes from the Vale de Águia, in the parish of São Bartolomeu de Messines, in the municipality of Silves, and was presented at the 5th Meeting of Archaeology of the Algarve and published by H. Sauren in the minutes of that conference (Sauren 2008). The stela was given to the Museu Municipal de Silves, where it is now displayed. The author of the publication provided a photograph of the stela which is not very clear, but also a tracing (Fig. 3.7). Following an approach taken in earlier publications on the south-western script, which leads in a direction quite different from the one taken here, Sauren (2008, 56–7) proposes an analysis of the text and a corresponding translation. Taking into account the established research in such studies and their assumptions, and considering these more valid and appropriate, Sauren's interpretation should be revised. From this perspective and assuming that the published drawing is accurate, the surviving fragment corresponds to the final section of the inscription. Following the principles for transcribing Tartessian in MLH 4, the text can be transcribed as follows:

]bᵃtᵉebᵃarena[ŕkᵉe---]

Once again, this includes the most common sequence attested in the corpus (bᵃare naŕ[kᵉe...]), although the text is incomplete and it is not possible to determine its complete configuration or reading. Furthermore, it is noted that the sequence that precedes this known formula,]bᵃtᵉe, breaches the general rule of redundancy (that is, a $\wedge$ is usual after bᵃ $\}$), and redundancy is one of the most striking characteristics distinguishing the Tartessian writing system. However, as discussed above, there are several other attested examples of redundancy ignored or violated, so this instance would not be surprising.

Conclusion

This area of southern Portugal continues to represent a territory where remains of epigraphy are found in notable concentrations. Because of this, this investigation provides a significant contribution to a growing inventory of texts, which remains very small overall. However, it is precisely this gradual increase in the epigraphic corpus, particularly when a proportion of the textual sequences are long and well-preserved, that create the necessary conditions for progress in this field. Thus, it is expected that ongoing projects aimed at a systematic exploration in areas with the greatest potential will continue to provide results in several key areas: the knowledge of the writing system and the language that it embodies, its archaeological context, and its chronological and cultural associations.

BIBLIOGRAPHY

Correa, J. A. 1993 'El signario de Espanca (Castro Verde) y la escritura tartesia', *Lengua y cultura en la Hispania prerromana, Actas del V Coloquio sobre Lenguas y Culturas Prerromanas de la Península Ibérica (Colonia, 25–28 de Noviembre de 1989)* eds. J. Untermann, F. Villar, Salamanca, 521–62.

Fabião, C. & A. Guerra 1991 'O povoado fortificado de Mesas do Castelinho, Almodôvar', *Actas das IV Jornadas Arqueológicas (Lisboa, 1990)*, 305–19, Associação dos Arqueólogos Portugueses, Lisboa.

Fabião, C., A. Guerra, T. Laço, S. Melro, & A. C. Ramos 1998 'Necrópole romana do Monte Novo do Castelinho (Almodôvar)', *Revista Portuguesa de Arqueologia* 1(1), 199–220.

Guerra, A. 2002 'Novos monumentos epigrafados com escrita do Sudoeste da vertente setentrional da Serra do Caldeirão', *Revista Portuguesa de Arqueologia* 5(2), 219–31.

Guerra, A., A. C. Ramos, S. Melro, & A. Pires 1999 'Uma estela epigrafada da Idade do Ferro, proveniente do Monte Novo do Castelinho (Almodôvar)', *Revista Portuguesa de Arqueologia* 2(1), 153–62.

Melro, S., P. Barros, & A. Guerra 2009 'Projecto *ESTELA*: do museu para o território', *Almadan* nº 16 (12 Oct. 2009), 9–10. http://www.almadan.pub./último%20(geral).htm

Sauren, H. 2008 'Vale de Águia, S. B. de Messines', *Actas do 5.º Encontro de Arqueologia do Algarve (25 a 27 de Outubro de 2007), vol. II – Posters = Xelb* 8, Silves, 53–8.

Untermann, J. 1997 *Monumenta Linguarum Hispanicarum, Band IV: Die tartessischen, keltiberischen und lusitanischen Inschriften*, Dr. Ludwig Reichert Verlag, Wiesbaden (=MLH 4).

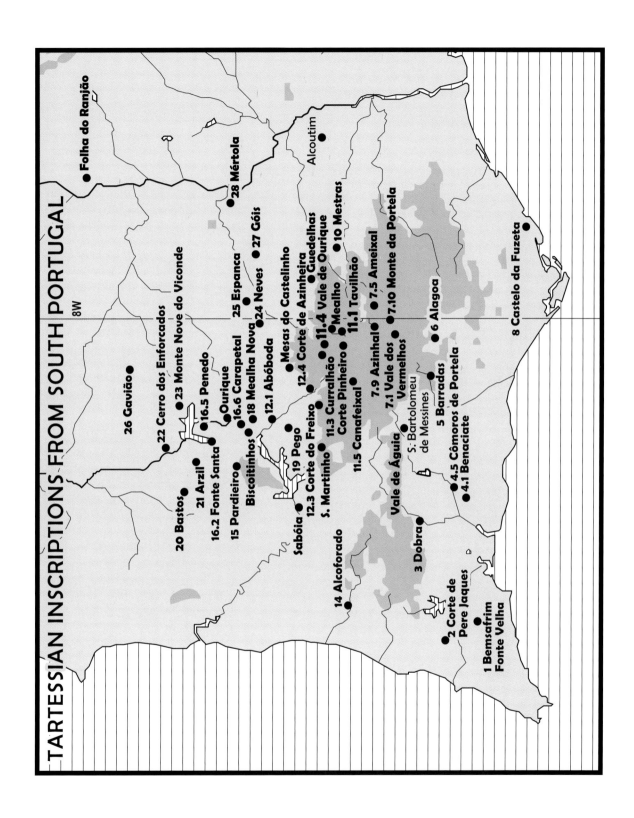

TARTESSIAN INSCRIPTIONS FROM SOUTH PORTUGAL

8W

Folha do Ranjão ●

28 Mértola ●

Alcoutim ●

27 Góis ●
25 Espanca ●
24 Neves ●

Mesas do Castelinho ●
12.4 Corte de Azinheira ●
Guedelhas ●
11.4 Vale de Ourique ●
10 Mestras ●
11.1 Tavilhão ●
7.5 Ameixal ●
7.10 Monte da Portela ●

26 Gavião ●

22 Cerro dos Enforcados ●
23 Monte Nove do Viconde ●
16.5 Penedo ●
Ourique ●
16.6 Carapetal ●
18 Mealha Nova ●
12.1 Abóboda ●

8 Castelo da Fuzeta ●

20 Bastos ●
21 Arzil ●
16.2 Fonte Santa ●
15 Pardieiro ●
Biscoitinhos ●

19 Pego ●
12.3 Corte do Freixo ●
S. Martinho ●
11.3 Curralhão ●
Corte Pinheiro ●
11.5 Canafeixal ●

7.9 Azinhal ●
7.1 Vale dos
Vermelhos ●

6 Alagoa ●

Sabóia ●

S: Bartolomeu
de Messines ●

5 Barradas ●
4.5 Cômoros de Portela ●
4.1 Benaciate ●

14 Alcoforado ●

Vale de Águia ●

3 Dobra ●

2 Corte de
Pere Jaques ●

1 Bemsafrim
Fonte Velha ●

PART TWO

GENETICS

CHAPTER FOUR

WESTERN CELTS?
A GENETIC IMPRESSION OF BRITAIN
IN ATLANTIC EUROPE

Ellen C. Røyrvik

Introduction

THE comparatively young field of molecular population genetics has of late
been heavily relied upon in the elucidation of population movements in history
and prehistory, and the idea of biological idiosyncrasies linked to culture has
led to the search for genetic signatures of culturally defined human groups. In attempting
to use the genetics of current populations to throw light on populations of the past,
one will inevitably run great risks of misinterpreting one's data or overstating one's
conclusions. Historical genetic anthropology is too new a field to have had its strengths
established. It is, however, old enough that initial enthusiasm has, for many, turned to
disillusionment as the discipline failed to answer all the questions left unanswered by
history, archaeology and historical philology. Nevertheless, the potential pitfalls should
not prove a deterrent from venturing into the field, if the genetic studies can be designed
for independent use and their conclusions are not themselves based on hypotheses they
claim to confirm or refute. In this paper I intend to give a brief introduction to the nature
of genetic variation, and certain commonly used methods of population genetics, and
to outline two potential avenues of Celticization. (In the interest of avoiding excessive
equivocation, nuance in describing these paths has been sacrificed for the sake of clarity.)
Several key points I will make are that the concept of human populations is to be
defined by local geographical criteria and not as static or discrete units, that cultural and
linguistic traits are not linked to genetic traits in any more than an ephemeral fashion,
and that population genetics, while extremely useful and suited to many settings, does
not have the power to be informative with regard to *every* historical hypothesis. Finally,
I will assess what the human genetics of Atlantic Europe, and in particular Britain, may
reveal in the matter of the development of communities speaking Celtic languages.

DNA and genetic variation

DNA is frequently called the blueprint of life, and virtually every biological trait is to some degree determined by it. Simply put, each individual inherits exactly half of his/her DNA from each parent: 23 chromosomes from each. Males inherit an X chromosome from their mothers, and the male sex chromosome (Y) from their fathers, while females inherit one X chromosome from each parent. In addition to these 46 chromosomes in the nucleus of the cell, the mitochondria—the energy producing centres of the cell—have a very small chromosome of their own. As the only mitochondria to survive in the foetus come from the initial egg cell, the mitochondrial DNA is passed down through the maternal line only.

Since chromosomes are discrete units of DNA, one would a priori assume that there was a one in 4^{23} chance that two children born of the same parents would be genetically identical, as identical twins are.[1] However, nature has a way of mixing chromosomes that increases genetic diversity further, and thereby creates new, and potentially more viable combinations. This is known as recombination, specifically as crossing over, and allows one chromosome to exchange part of itself with the corresponding part in another chromosome during meiosis (the genesis of egg and sperm cells). Another implication of meiotic crossing over is that you truly are a product of your ancestors—without this recombination, the chance of having none of a particular, fairly recent ancestor's DNA is comparatively large. With even a moderate recombination rate estimate, the figure rises significantly. Perhaps most importantly from a population genetics point of view is that the 22 autosomes (non-sex chromosomes) are effectively a patchwork of DNA pieces whose evolutionary history cannot be traced in a single line; they are not passed down inviolate—each chromosome consists of irregular chunks of its ancestral chromosomes.

In historical population genetics most of the studies to date have dealt with what are known as classical genetic markers (mostly blood groups, tissue types and enzymes), the Y chromosome and mitochondrial (mt) DNA. Classical markers are those that could be assessed without the use of the more modern molecular techniques such as DNA sequencing (see Box 4.1). The non-recombining section of the Y chromosome and mtDNA were chosen because of their non-reticulated form of descent; that is, they do not undergo recombination. Thus they can be illustrated in the manner of a 'family tree', the branches of which are known as haplogroups. Their popularity can also be attributed to their convenient telling of the 'male versus female' story—to quote a notable biological philosopher of our day 'Mitochondrial DNA is blessedly celibate' (Dawkins 1996), and the same may be said of most of the Y chromosome.

---

1   If a child only inherited one chromosome from each parent, the chance of having identical children would be one in four (4^1), as there can be only four combinations of the parents' two chromosomes in any child. With two inherited chromosomes from each parent, identical offspring would be expected 1/16, that is $1/4^2$, so for each additional chromosome, the likelihood decreases exponentially.

Molecular genetic markers are discrete differences in the DNA sequence of different individuals. The location of a marker is known as a locus, and the variants found at a given locus are known as alleles. One of the most abundant, informative and computationally tractable types of markers is called a single nucleotide polymorphism, or SNP (see Box 4.1 and Fig. 4.1), and such SNPs are rapidly becoming markers of choice for high-resolution population genetic studies.

Population genetics in humans

Most molecular variation in humans, at a frequency high enough to be detected, is old enough to occur across, rather than within, populations (Lewontin 1972; Excoffier, Smouse et al. 1992; Barbujani, Magagni et al. 1997; Seielstad, Minch et al. 1998; Jorde, Watkins et al. 2000; Romualdi, Balding et al. 2002; Sanchez-Mazas 2007), meaning that any randomly selected allele is likely to be found worldwide.[2] If any difference is to be found between populations, it is generally in the shape of differing proportions of one allele to another, rather than their absolute presence or absence. The differences in frequency in different populations or geographic areas are usually due to random effects, most notably interdependent founder effects and genetic drift (Cavalli-Sforza and Bodmer 1999). A founder effect is observed when a population has low genetic diversity due to the founding members of that population carrying a small subset of the extant global diversity, and genetic drift is the effect of fluctuations in the frequency of an allele following random differences in the reproductive success of its carriers. A key concept for the creation of genetic patterns is that of isolation by distance (Wright 1943). It is quite simply that populations that are closer geographically are likely to be more similar genetically, due to gene flow between them, while populations far enough apart to limit or preclude gene flow will dissimilate because of genetic drift. The mathematical models of isolation by distance are, as are most models in population genetics, simplified abstractions of real processes, and gene flow is usually not as uniform as they imply (Cavalli-Sforza, Menozzi et al. 1994). This fact can be attributable to, for example, geographical or cultural barriers.

The application of population genetics to anthropology and archaeology has had, and in truth is still having, numerous teething problems. These can broadly be divided into two camps: the issues of adequate sample sizes and sampling locations, and the problem of creating useful and rigorous definitions for the field. The first is conceptually simple but logistically challenging. To find the few genetic variants that may differentiate between populations (especially closely related ones) a comparatively large, and more importantly *representative*, sample of individuals from the populations in question must be available to ensure that all the genetic information within that population is taken into account. Scarcely anywhere have these requirements been fulfilled—Iceland is an exception, and has been comprehensively sampled (Helgason, Yngvadottir et al. 2004).

---

2   This is at least true of most of the currently known variation, but it could be subject to change if there has been a systematic ascertainment bias against local varieties.

BOX 4.1. DNA STRUCTURE AND SNPs

DNA is composed of four chemical compounds known as bases, attached to a sugar-phosphate backbone. The bases, known as adenine (A), guanine (G), cytosine (C) and thymine (T), are the units that encode genetic information, and they do so according to the order in which they follow each other in the human genome. Deciphering their order is known as DNA sequencing. Each human cell, except red blood cells, has a total of over 3 billion bases. The overwhelming majority of them are identical in all humans, but occasionally there are differences. One class of variation is known as SNPs—single nucleotide polymorphisms, meaning that a single nucleotide (base) is different at the same position in different individuals.

These SNPs can be 'silent', i.e. have no noticeable effect in the bearer. Most non-silent SNPs cause normal variation such as that of hair or eye colour, or they can cause genetic diseases, for example cystic fibrosis. In the context of genes, which for this purpose we will define as a specific segment of DNA, a SNP will mean the difference between different alleles, or versions, of the gene.

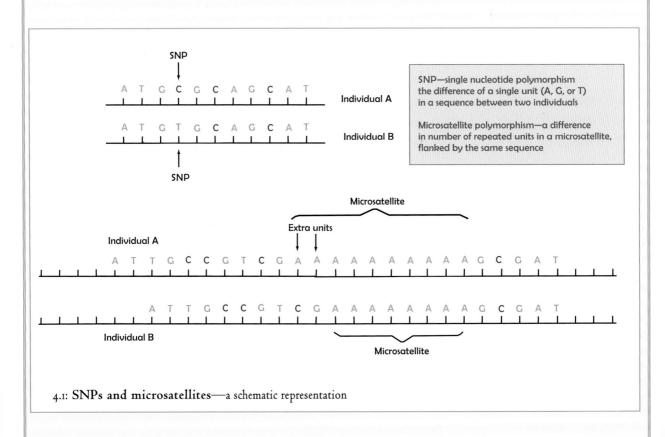

4.1: **SNPs and microsatellites**—a schematic representation

BOX 4.2. THE GENETICS OF THE FACE

While the potential for mistakes is great, it is often surprisingly easy for someone with sufficient experience to correctly guess where in Europe an individual comes from, solely based on that individual's face and colouring, so the genetics of facial features is enormously interesting when one is looking at variation that serves to stratify a given population. Hair-, skin-, and eye-colour genes have been much easier to identify, and there are SNPs known to correlate well with visible pigmentation differences. Unfortunately, the genes and alleles governing normal facial variation are almost totally unknown. Faces are particularly fascinating to the historical population geneticist in that they are one of the few instances of easily observable and highly polymorphic features where the genotype (DNA sequence) completely determines the phenotype (in this case, appearance). Barring injuries or excessive weight difference, identical twins will have the same facial features, even if they were raised separately (Bouchard 1984). This wealth of variation and capacity for peculiarly localized types raises the possibility of exceptionally fine dissection of regional population structuring.

The second troublesome area is the matter of constructing meaningful definitions for the populations involved in the analysis. What is a population? The standard biological definition, which is a group of individuals who mate randomly within the group but never or very infrequently outside it, is rarely a reasonable approximation of how human societies function. This kind of stringency being wanting, there has been a tendency to define populations in genetic studies according to modern national boundaries and in select cases more restricted 'ethnic' or 'tribal' labels (Bandelt, Macaulay et al. 2002). In this way, a situation in which 'the French' are considered a single population and can be compared to 'Basques' arises—a nation state with a patchwork of past ethnic identities versus a group *chosen* for its odd-man-out ethnicity and with a group size more than an order of magnitude smaller. The importance of sampling by geography alone rather than modern politics, while recognized (Capelli, Redhead et al. 2003; Dubut, Chollet et al. 2004), is as yet the exception rather than the norm. Once populations have been defined and the genetic type of the individuals has been determined, there are hosts of mathematical procedures that can be applied to the genetic data. A straightforward approach of this kind is simply to compare the frequencies of a given allele in the different populations.

An illustration of this approach can be taken from the intriguing area of pigmentation genetics. As opposed to the potentially difficult task of unravelling which SNPs may be involved in facial variation (see Box 4.2), the causative alleles for pigmentation—in

4.3. Map of *MC1R* 'red hair' allele frequencies White sections of
the pie charts represent *MC1R* alleles that in combination give the carrier
red or reddish hair; the magenta section represents the frequency of non-
red alleles. The frequencies do *not* indicate the number of redheads versus
other hair colours. British data is from the PoBI project, Swedish and Irish
data from Harding et al., Danish from Mengel-From et al. (Harding, Healy
et al. 2000; Mengel-From, Borsting et al. 2008).

Europe, at least—are becoming clear. The most famous of these genes is *MC1R*, the
melanocortin 1 receptor, several variants of which were early on associated with red
hair (Valverde, Healy et al. 1995). The variation in others, e.g. *OCA2*, *HERC2*, *ASIP*,
TYRP1, and *TYR*, have been shown to cumulatively affect all aspects of our outward
colouring—eye colour, hair colour, basic skin tone, freckling and tanning ability
(Sulem, Gudbjartsson et al. 2007; Han, Kraft et al. 2008; Kayser, Liu et al. 2008; Sulem,
Gudbjartsson et al. 2008). Alleles of the genes in question here are likely to be extremely
useful in the context of European population genetics, as they account for a great deal
of the easily observable geographical diversity—few would deny that blond hair and
blue eyes are more common in Holland than in Spain, and that black-haired citizens

with brown eyes are traditionally more likely to be found in Rome than in Uppsala. These facile contrasts only serve to illustrate the continuum of shadings, and so the necessarily differential geographic distribution of the aforementioned pigmentation alleles. However, Figure 4.3 illustrates how anecdotal impressions of physical traits can be misleading: the red-headed Irish Celt of popular imagination is, by this token, on average less ginger than someone from Yorkshire.

A classic, if somewhat coarse, measure of population differentiation is called F_{ST}. It is a single number, which can be defined as the amount of total genetic variation that can be explained by differences between populations/subpopulations (Wright 1969; Hudson, Slatkin et al. 1992). Given the comparatively small amount of human genetic variation, F_{ST} estimates are usually very small, globally no higher than 0.12 across many loci (International HapMap Consortium 2005). An F_{ST} value of zero indicates that there is no detectable genetic difference between subpopulations. An F_{ST} estimate can be calculated for any given SNP; for local (e.g. national) populations, discriminatory SNPs with comparatively high F_{ST} for subgroups can be identified even when the F_{ST} values across many loci/SNPs is approaching zero.

Other standard population genetics methods include trees and principal components analysis for visualizing the most pronounced trends in a given dataset, and admixture analysis. In the latter, given two genetically distinct source populations, and a third which springs from the first two, it is possible to calculate the relative contribution of each source to the daughter population. The technique, however, must rely on the ability of the researcher to identify correctly all major source populations of the group under scrutiny and on the existence genetic stability within these source populations. In the context of historical genetics one is naturally obliged to use proxies for any assumed source population, as the true one is no longer available.[3] Much care must be taken in selecting proxy source populations and, in addition to identifying the most likely location for sources, the following must be considered: the longer the time that has passed since the admixture event (assuming there has been only one), the more opportunity there has been for genetic drift to change both the admixed and parental populations, as well as for subsequent migrations to have obscured the genetic signature of the event in question.

Trees with dichotomous branching may also be used to represent relationships between populations. They can be constructed using a matrix of genetic distances between all possible pairs of populations under consideration. A high number of characters (allele frequency measures) is needed to avoid constructing trees with large

---

3 It has been proposed, e.g. by Patrick Sims-Williams (1998), that the use of DNA from categorized archaeological sites is a more scientifically stringent way to define a given historical population. Unfortunately, given the nature of human genetic variation this would frequently require much more historic and prehistoric skeletal material than can feasibly be produced for any given period and region to be statistically significant. Furthermore, there is no way to ensure that such skeletal material as may become available would be *representative* of the local population at the time.

statistical errors, and few trees will be completely free of them (Cavalli-Sforza, Menozzi et al. 1994). Representing populations as terminal branches in a strictly bifurcating tree can be double-edged sword. Such illustrations are very useful in depicting the simplest relationships between population groups, but they can also give the impression that these populations are the products of straightforward fission. This is, almost without exception, not the case, and one of the main drawbacks of the method is its general inability to incorporate reticulating events such as admixture.

Principal components analysis (PCA) is a variance maximization method, which reduces the dimensionality—this can notionally be read as 'complexity'—of the information in a dataset, while minimizing the loss of pertinent data (Manly 1986). In other words, it can find the 'patterns' in genetic data comprising hundreds or thousands of variables, which in this case are genetic markers. It creates synthetic variables, principal components, which represent the observed data and account for a maximum amount of the variance. The first principal component, PC1, accounts for more variation than PC2, PC2 for more than PC3, and so on until all the variation is accounted for. One of the most relevant features of principal components analysis is that the number of highly informative principal components is far smaller than the number of starting variables. Most principal components analyses in human population genetics literature focus on the first two principal components, which can be used to create a two-dimensional plot. Such plots are a simple way of visualizing relationships between populations, with the more similar populations occurring in closer proximity in the plot than less similar ones. While a valuable tool, PCA has been accorded something of a pre-eminent position in the field, and is perceptually endowed with powers it does not have. Firstly, it can return certain types of patterning, e.g. clinal and patterns, even with input data whose spatial variation is *solely* a function of geographical distance, not any particular population process, due to inherent features of the mathematical treatment (Novembre and Stephens 2008). This does not mean that all patterns observed are artefacts of the method, but rather that they should not be regarded uncritically. Secondly, any real patterns offer a picture of the current situation only, the 'end product' of a population history, and in most cases there are a whole host of different population histories that could lead to the observed result. Finally, PCA results are susceptible to change depending on data amount and the location of sampling sites (Novembre and Stephens 2008). Principal co-ordinates analysis, also known as multidimensional scaling, is a similar type of method, and the terminology is occasionally used interchangeably. Multidimensional scaling can be seen as a more flexible, generalized version of PCA based on distance matrices rather than variance, and likewise allows visualization of dominant trends in a dataset (Manly 1986).

Phylogeography is, strictly speaking, considered to be a discipline of its own, but it has overlapping features and goals with historical population genetics. It is seen as occupying a central position in a web of subjects including molecular genetics, palaeontology, phylogenetics, historical geography, demography and population genetics

(Avise 2000). Phylogeography attempts to explain the geographical distribution of branches of a gene tree. (A gene tree follows the evolutionary history of variants of a gene, or stretch of DNA. All variants eventually trace back to a single sequence.) This approach naturally demands a discretely inherited unit to work with—either an autosomal sequence small enough to be confidently free of recombination, or, as has proved to be most popular, mtDNA and the Y chromosome. While interesting, and potentially very revealing, proponents stress that any gene tree is just that—the descent of a single DNA segment, which may well be discordant with a population tree. Indeed, population trees, in many cases, may not even exist as such, but rather be a large reticulation of interlocking genealogies in the case of poorly isolated subpopulations (Templeton 2005). Most phylogeographers consequently urge the use of as wide a choice of different markers as possible in making historical demographic inferences (Avise 2000; Emerson and Hewitt 2005; Templeton 2005). The field has also been criticized for lacking a statistical framework for hypothesis testing, instead simply inferring causes of association and leaving it at that. However, statistical phylogeographical tests to improve rigour and reliability are being developed (Knowles 2004; Richards, Cartstens et al. 2007). Even so, it seems prudent to end this treatment of the discipline with the following: 'Achieving a joint estimate of the multiple processes that characterize a [population's] history is difficult. And no matter how appealing such an inference might be, it is simply untenable (at least at this time)' (Knowles 2008).

Briefly put, all of the above methods are possible only if different groupings of individuals have a differing, if only slightly, average genetic make-up. Recalling that most genetic variation is essentially universal, it is important to find the few genetic markers whose allele frequency differences can 'sort' an individual into one type of ancestry as opposed to another. The search for such ancestry informative markers (AIMs) is complicated by the fact that different markers, most often SNPs, will be good AIMs for different sets of populations. AIMs for distinguishing African from European ancestry, for example, are likely to be useless for telling apart Norwegians from Swedes, and vice versa. Therefore, separate sets of AIMs must be determined for use in different populations. Powerful discriminatory SNPs can, perhaps surprisingly, be found for an area as small as southern Britain (see below), and it is this type of tool that will be invaluable when we turn to discussing our principal topic—who, genetically speaking, were the Celts? Were they, in some small way, distinct? Can we know where they lived? And can we identify their descendants? It is important to remember that, however helpful a population genetics approach may turn out to be, it can rarely be considered to be hypothesis verifying. Virtually any contemporary detectable, genetic signal can be compatible with several possible historical processes, and it is best to use genetic information for generating or falsifying hypotheses, rather than seeing a lack of incongruity as confirmation of them.

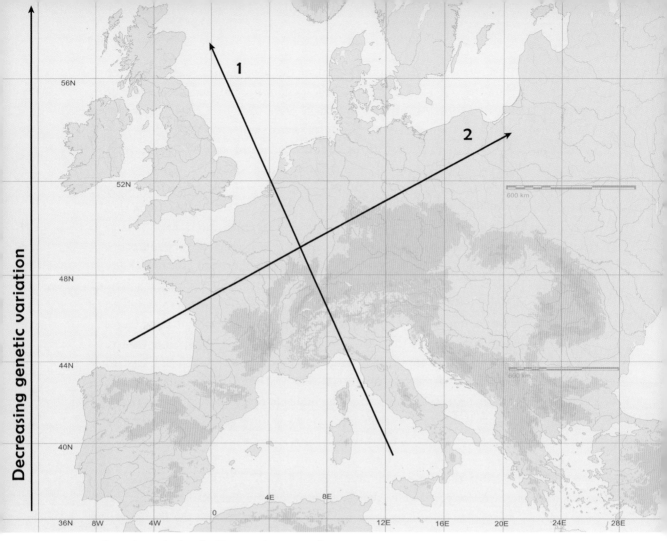

Figure 4.4. **Genetic variation in Europe** Arrows 1 and 2 represent
the two primary axes of European genetic variation as demonstrated
by autosomal SNP and Y chromosome analysis, and the south to north
arrow shows the direction of decreasing genetic diversity.

Genetics of Europe and the Atlantic Fringe

Europe is one of the areas of the globe where human genetic variation is best
characterized. Unfortunately, much of the genotyping that has been done has not been
standardized. Few studies type all of the same markers, making comparisons between
studies difficult, especially in the case of the Y chromosome and the mitochondrial
genome where one needs a fairly large set of markers for even quite coarse haplogroup
designation. Furthermore, as mentioned above, the samples are usually grouped by the
comparatively fluid notion of nationality, and the sample sizes have often been much
smaller than is needed to pick up the rarer variants. In spite of these complications
and the fact that one of the main analysis types (principal components analysis) has

considerable methodological limitations (see above), the underlying genetic structure of Europe appears to be one of broad continua, with similarities decreasing as geographic distance increases (Cavalli-Sforza, Menozzi et al. 1994; Rosser, Zerjal et al. 2000; Bauchet, McEvoy et al. 2007; Lao, Lu et al. 2008; Novembre, Johnson et al. 2008). The east-west difference may be more significant, but there is also a notable north-south gradient (Seldin, Shigeta et al. 2006). The baseline diversity in southern Europe also appears to be greater than in the north, probably as a result of a subset of southern variation going into the founding of the northern populations. Figure 4.4 illustrates the main axes of differentiation on the European subcontinent.

Atlantic Europe naturally occupies a peripheral place in this pattern, so that among the populations studied along the Atlantic Ocean there is a degree of similarity that sets them apart from the peoples of the interior, though in one dimension only. The question of whether the cultural continuum and genetic continuum have any kind of meaningful overlap is more contentious. Just as linguists famously don't do dates (McMahon and McMahon 2006), in many cases historical geneticists probably *shouldn't*: the standard errors of dating genetic splits is often so large as to be useless in respect of human history, and even if a genetic split were easily datable, this is not the same as a population split (Avise 2000). The basic genetic component of the Atlantic countries could easily have been laid down in the Palaeolithic and have remained virtually unchanged in the post-glacial period (Richards, Corte-Real et al. 1996; Currat, Ray et al. 2008). Accepted opinions on the development of Indo-European languages imply that, if this is the case, a significant language shift, perhaps several shifts, will have occurred over the ten thousand odd years that passed between the recolonization of post-glacial Europe and the first linguistic evidence in Atlantic areas. This would not be at all historically anomalous (Wardhaugh 1987; Thomason 2001), but it does further complicate the issue. Were one to implement an unadulterated population genetics approach, and treat humans like any other animal—and so essentially disregard any concept of culture or language—there is no reason to consider Europe as a whole as anything but a largely homogeneous zone, even including comparatively 'isolated' outliers such as the Basques, Finns, Saami, and Sardinians. Moreover, geographic barriers are a much better indication of such genetic differentiation as exists than linguistic borders (Dupanloup de Ceuninck, Schneider et al. 2000; Rosser, Zerjal et al. 2000), and even these borders do not delineate highly significant areas of differentiation. Is there therefore any scientific justification for including these elements (language and culture) in our analyses? To some extent, yes—certainly, when the stated goal is historical. Genetic information can, if a high degree of resolution is reached, potentially answer some questions posed by archaeology, such as how many incomers were involved at the time of a given cultural shift. In this context, more and better markers, as well as more and better-defined samples, are needed to detect structure in groups that appear to be quite closely related. Similarly, in constricting the area of study, samples should be more localized in order to ascertain whether intranational structure exists.

With autosomal SNP-based studies in the earliest of stages, and mitochondrial DNA being such a small section, beset with recurrent, and thereby confounding, mutations as well as tending to be quite homogenous across Europe (Simoni, Calafell et al. 2000; Kivisild, Shen et al. 2006), the Y chromosome is at present one of the best available guidelines to underlying structure in Europe. Briefly stated, the Atlantic seaboard excluding Norway shows some cohesion in terms of its Y chromosome diversity, largely due to the very high frequency of a haplogroup (type) called R1b in these areas. Another region of similarity, which distinguishes the north-eastern part of western Europe from the Atlantic arc, is defined by a higher frequency of haplogroup R1a and stretches across northern-central Europe into Britain (Rosser, Zerjal et al. 2000).[4] Within these areas there are also clinal variations, even though the subdivision of Y haplogroups is quite coarse-grained. One of this marker's greatest advantages, its ability to establish patterns rapidly by enhanced drift as compared to autosomes, can also be a drawback at greater time depths in that it allows these patterns to change equally rapidly, and so be overwritten. Nevertheless, the potential of the Y chromosome to distinguish older events from newer (by using stable SNPs and the more rapidly changing microsatellites) may help disentangle at least the masculine effects of separate population movements in this area.

Below, when we come to treat the Celtic matter, we will have to focus on several different areas and several different epochs. This treatment will involve trying to discount all of the subsequent population influences we know of, such as the Moors in Spain and Portugal[5] and Germanic tribes throughout western and central Europe, as well as minimizing the impact on analyses of any putative ones of whose existence we are unaware.

People of the British Isles

Even small-scale genetic substructuring in populations can potentially skew results of medical genetics association studies (Price, Patterson et al. 2006). The 'People of the British Isles' (PoBI) study was initiated to provide a correction for these false associations in British medical studies by elucidating what population structure actually exists in Britain. In essence, this involves creating a genetic atlas of the area (see Figure 4.5 for a simple schematic illustration). It will involve identifying signatures that are typical of a given area by sampling individuals who may reasonably be supposed to be descended from a long-established community in that area—our criterion being having all four grandparents from within 30–40 miles of each other. The high-density, high-resolution

---

4   Other subsequent studies tend to confirm this picture.

5   South-western Iberia has the largest mean heterozygosity in Europe (Lao, Lu et al. 2008), suggested by Adams to be due to the influence of African and Sephardic Jewish immigration (Adams, King et al. 2006).

Figure 4.5. A Genetic Atlas of Britain
This mock-up of a genetic map illustrates the rationale behind the many-markers approach. A, B and C each represent a marker; the colours of the letters indicate their allelic variants. With reference to the map of Britain, they create six broad zones, each with its own typical, but not exclusive, combination. The map is to be interpreted so that an average person from the northernmost section, for example, has the red A, green B and blue C combination, while an average Welshman has red A, orange B and yellow C—not excluding the possibility that a randomly chosen northern Scot could *not* have the latter combination. With a large array of markers, consistent if possibly faint patterns of a similar nature may be expected to emerge in the actual population.

genetic resource that is being constructed will also be useful in the matter of historical population genetics of Britain.

Previous studies of Y chromosome and blood types have already demonstrated the existence of some genetic substructuring within Britain (Watkin 1952; Bodmer 1992; Wilson, Weiss et al. 2001; Weale, Weiss et al. 2002; Capelli, Redhead et al. 2003), and preliminary results from the PoBI project point towards autosomal markers with complementary and probably increasing discriminatory powers. Of the nine regions included in the pilot study (Cornwall, Cumbria, Devon, north-eastern England, Norfolk, Orkney, Yorkshire, Oxford and the Forest of Dean), Orkney is the most clearly differentiated from all the others with average F_{ST} values of 0.0045–0.0050 and of the above populations is most different from Norfolk. Cornwall and the Forest of Dean follow. For an apparent enrichment of the very highest single F_{ST} values in the study (0.05–0.11), however, Cumbria stands out, most particularly in relation to Cornwall. The pilot study includes only *c.* 700 individuals, and *c.* 400 markers. It is to be expected that, when all the areas, the full sample size for each area and the final panel of markers (over 3,500 individuals from around 30 regions of Britain, for roughly a million and a half markers) are assessed, more subtle and statistically significant patterns of diversity will emerge.

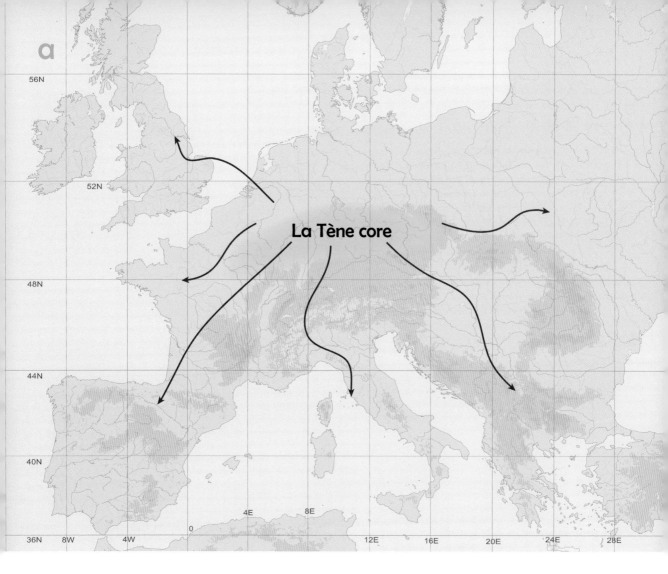

56N

52N

48N

44N

40N

36N   8W   4W   4E   8E   12E   16E   20E   24E   28E

0

La Tène core

Celts—Atlantic, Central, or Both?

The Celtic question has received more than its fair share of print space in the field of historical population genetics, much as it has in archaeology and the popular press. Numerous papers try, on the basis of DNA sequences, to define who is Celtic and how Celtic they are. The questions of appropriate population sampling and labelling, and the vexed matter of proxy parent populations, are of the utmost importance here, and all too frequently studies can become untenably tautological. Virtually all studies have used populations on the modern Celtic fringe as their baseline for what 'Celtic DNA' looks like, thus following current or recent linguistic patterns rather than the Κελτοί/ Celtae of classical antiquity. This may be a sensible approach, but it cannot be denied that it excludes huge numbers of people who are equally descended from Celtic speakers, though they themselves speak Germanic or Romance languages. For the purposes of a genetic investigation, using a linguistic rather than cultural (as in material culture) definition of Celtic is more convenient. This definition means a Celtic speaker *of any*

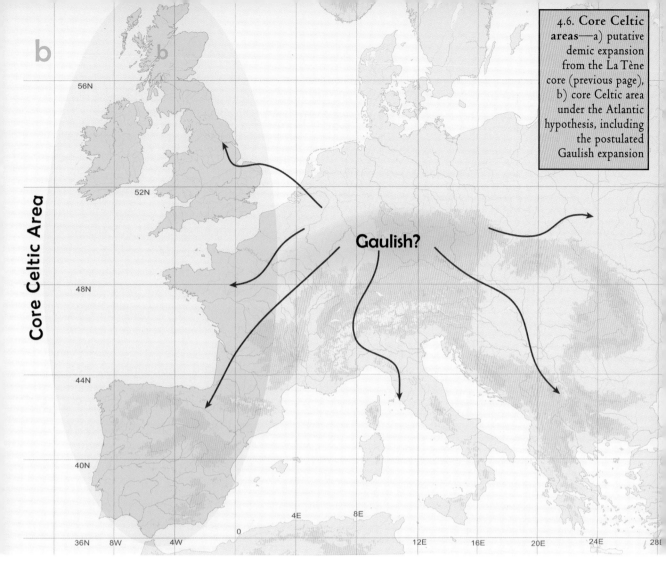

4.6. **Core Celtic areas**—a) putative demic expansion from the La Tène core (previous page), b) core Celtic area under the Atlantic hypothesis, including the postulated Gaulish expansion

given period, not just a current Irish speaker or Gaul of Caesar's time, will be considered a Celt, thus allowing our genetic Celt to adapt through cultural and linguistic shifts—though admittedly adding another layer of complexity. A cultural definition can be dismissed on the somewhat arbitrary grounds that a genetic-linguistic correlation is likely to decay less rapidly, though decay it does, than a correlation between genetic fingerprints and cultural complexes.[6]

The combined forces of archaeology and linguistics have provided us with two scenarios for the development of the Celtic world of western Europe. The first is the established view of a 'homeland' in west-central Europe out of which the Celts migrated in large numbers to conquer, in a military, cultural and/or linguistic sense, great swathes

---

6   I do not mean to imply by this that 'Celtic culture' was a meaningful concept at the time, but rather that, if faced with one area whose inhabitants speak a Celtic language and another area with material that can be identified as 'Celtic', i.e. artefacts of the La Tène style or an early medieval style derived from it, the former will be a more rational choice from which to construct a genetic identity.

of territory to the east, west and partially to the south of their core area in the latter half of the first millennium BC (Chadwick 1970; Cunliffe 1997). The second hypothesis, born of changes in dominant disciplinary paradigms as well as of evidence that can be taken as contradictory to the above proposition, posits that Celtic speech was born in the broad cultural continuum of Bronze Age Atlantic Europe (Cunliffe 2001), with the possibility of narrowing this range to the Late Bronze Age, or Atlantic Bronze Age, as the period c. 1300 to 700 BC is also known (Brun 1992). Figure 5a represents the traditional view and 5b the possibility of Celticization from the West.

In order for genetic tests of these hypotheses, henceforth called *Central* and *Atlantic*, to be designed, one must first consider what the genetic ramifications for each of them could likely be. For the Central hypothesis, the cultural impact is the essential theme—typified by a certain artistic style and luxury goods (Cunliffe 1997). In this case, the movement of people, and thereby genes, can easily be so small as to be negligible. With imitations in marginal areas of classical La Tène art, as it developed in its core region in west-central Europe, and otherwise great heterogeneity in Iron Age western/Atlantic material culture (Alvarez-Sanchis 2000; Cunliffe 2000; Lorrio & Ruiz Zapatero 2005; Raftery 2005; Henderson 2007), a plausible suggestion could be that expansion, which had a historically attested demic impact to the south and east, was nearly exclusively a cultural influence in the west. It follows that there would be no genetic signature for this event. Conversely, if this expansion event were the vehicle for the initial spreading of Celtic, one would expect there to have been a significant influx of people into the western zone. I say significant, rather than large, as language shifts can come about with comparatively few native speakers (Thomason 2001), but there must be a critical minimum to allow a language community to grow. A genetic signature would then not be implausible, but the expanding population would have to be genetically distinguishable from the natives of the Atlantic fringe, and this signal would have to be strong enough to avoid subsequent erasure. These two criteria are not independent, in that the more distinct an intrusive population is from the native population, the smaller the intrusive element can be while remaining detectable.

The Atlantic scenario presents us with a different demographic model to be tested, and a significantly greater time depth in which to operate. Following Koch and Cunliffe (chapters 1 and 9, this volume) and Almagro-Gorbea (Almagro-Gorbea 1994), Celtic was present in Iberia well before the Central Celtic expansion is supposed to have taken place, and the non-Scandinavian part of Atlantic Europe had wide cultural links throughout a good proportion of prehistory, from Mesolithic through to the Late Bronze Age (Cunliffe 2001). This idea of Celtic speech and cultural identity associated with it developing largely *in situ* on the western seaboard is, from a genetic point of view, a less clear-cut problem than the Central Celtic one. The timing is less restricted, the area is less well-defined, and written records for any related events are completely lacking. These considerations by no means imply that the Atlantic theory is inherently less tenable, simply that the framework for predicting relevant genetic patterns will be much more fluid. A gradual, autochthonous process of ethnogenesis, covering an area which there is every reason to believe was originally peopled by a genetically homogenous group, will be problematic to detect genetically, nor is there any reason to doubt that gene flow along the corridors of trade was uncommon at any time. One might term this process cumulative Celticity, though of a very different kind from that envisioned by Hawkes, with successive waves of upper-class continental invasions into Britain (Hawkes 1973). If Proto-Celtic and Proto-Celts *did* radiate from western, perhaps south-western, Europe at a slow rate, there may be no genetic component that can be correlated with the specific event or series of events. What is certain is that the coverage and resolution of genetic data that we currently have is unequal to answering the issue.

An interesting possibility, put forward by Javier de Hoz, is that though the La Tène expansion cannot be equated with the Celticization of Iberia, it is not so incongruous to correlate it with an expansion of *Gaulish* (de Hoz 1992). This theory—in the quotidian sense of the word—is worth considering as a putative confounding element for genetic analyses. If the Gaulish language and La Tène cultural complex spread concomitantly one would expect to find exactly the same kind of genetic signature for this event as postulated for an undifferentiated Celtic-La Tène expansion. Given a situation where both the Central and Atlantic hypotheses find support in genetic data, this is a potential route, though by no means the only one, towards reconciling the two.

Celtic Britain

Turning to Britain, there are some grounds for greater optimism in the matter of determining whether the Central or Atlantic hypothesis is more likely, given the genetic situation. There is a longstanding archaeological divide on the island: a line bisecting it into highland and lowland zones (Fox 1943), comprising the western and northern parts, on the one hand, and the south-east corner, on the other. While no doubt a very rough-hewn distinction, probably owing much to the landscape types themselves, it is still a useful perspective to have when attempting to determine what kinds of genetic impacts the two possibilities under investigation would have had on Britain. Firstly, the La Tène cultural complex as a whole (as opposed to local stylistic imitation) is not much in evidence in Britain. What there are of societies with stronger links to northern French La Tène are limited to East Yorkshire and the south-east, and so by and large within the lowland zone (Hodson 1964; Haselgrove 1999; Cunliffe 2001). The route across the North Sea to eastern Britain, evidenced by trade, would be a likely one for invading Central Celts to take. Though the lowland area is also expected to be heavily influenced by the later Anglo-Saxon invasion (Hunter Blair 1977), we must work on the assumption that a southern Scandinavian/northern German influence is distinguishable from a southern German/northern French one; indeed, there is some indication that modern northern and southern Germans are genetically heterogeneous (Steffens, Lamina et al. 2006). We would in either case expect to find higher genetic diversity in the lowland

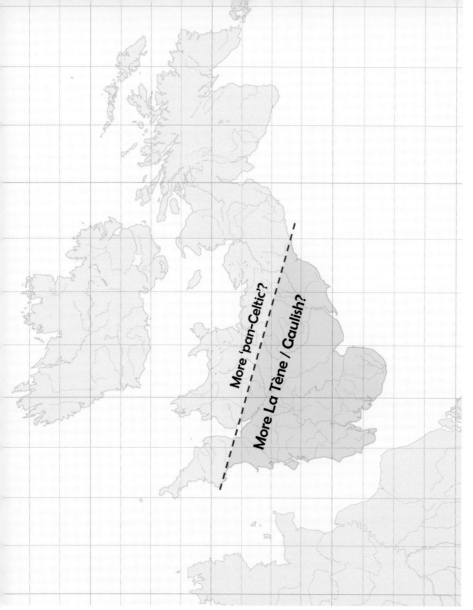

Figure 4.7.**Highland and lowland zones** This map shows the rough highland/lowland division, suggested by non-genetic disciplines, and possible genetic differences that may exist between the areas, following the Atlantic hypothesis.

More 'pan-Celtic'?

More La Tène / Gaulish?

zone—the question is rather to what extent it may be attributable to an Iron Age Celtic immigration as well as an early medieval Germanic one. However, if this putative Celtic immigration were to be responsible for the dissemination of a Celtic language in Britain, its genetic fingerprint should be diffused well beyond the domains of the La Tène-derived or -connected cultures of Arras in Yorkshire and Aylesbury in the south-east.

An Atlantic Celtic continuum from the Bronze Age, by nature not as abrupt a method of Celticization, is pleasingly consistent with the current distribution of the Celtic languages in the British Isles, but that is a very minor and misleading point—more importantly it allows more time for Celtic languages to have become spoken throughout Britain. Whether one assumes a western British or more uniform focus for this continuum, the resulting pattern of modern British genetic diversity is likely to be similar: the highland zone will have a higher proportion of 'typically Celtic' genetic types, due either to an initial distribution or to the higher levels of non-Celtic introgression in the south-east.

For Britain, as for the above discussion of Atlantic Europe as a whole, the difficulty is then the continuity itself. The Atlantic system of connections is of such antiquity (Cunliffe 2001) that the type of short-range population movements and contacts envisioned for the development and spread of Celtic are likely to make the genetic trail virtually invisible, especially if the idea of post-glacial repopulation of western Europe from a Franco-Cantabrian refuge is accepted (Achilli, Rengo et al. 2004). The best confirmation to anticipate from this approach will be consistent data that do not falsify the hypothesis, such as a longstanding pattern of similarity along the Atlantic arc demonstrated by a wide variety of genetic loci. The highland-lowland zone division of Britain seen in Figure 6 again raises the possibility of Gaulish influence separated from other variants of Celtic.

As a first step in testing the competing hypotheses, in-depth sampling of deeply rooted natives from all the presumed source and sink areas should be conducted. For this discussion, focusing on western Europe and Britain in particular, the most relevant source location is likely to be northern France for the Central Celtic option, with western France, Iberia and the British Isles as sinks. For the Atlantic scenario, a source area like that above is a less appropriate concept, and the aforementioned sink areas must be considered both source and sink, with populations lying to the east of these areas included as a control for the expected differences under this hypothesis.

Concluding Remarks

There is no doubt that determining the most likely path of Celtic population history will be no easy task. On a much simpler problem, that of the genetic impact of early Near Eastern farmers on the European gene pool, there is still much discord despite the presumed significant genetic differences between the first agriculturalists and the Palaeolithic/Mesolithic Europeans (Richards, Corte-Real et al. 1996; Semino, Passarino et al. 1996; De Benedetto, Nasidze et al. 2000; Richards, Macaulay et al. 2000; Semino, Passarino et al. 2000; Barbujani and Dupanloup 2002; Chikhi, Nichols et al. 2002; Brion, Salas et al. 2003; Dupanloup, Bertorelle et al. 2004; Currat & Excoffier 2005; Barbujani & Chikhi 2006; Battaglia, Fornarino et al. 2009), and despite the freedom to ignore virtually all cultural attributes and speculations as to the language of the infiltrating population. Of all times and places that have been put forward as the location for the emergence of the Proto-Celtic, a non-European origin has never been suggested. Therefore one must posit that the Celts, their ancestors and their descendants took part in all the myriad processes that shaped the European gene pool. Founding groups, genetic drift, and differentiation through the millennia, low-level background migration (a small trickle over a thousand years will still make sizeable impact), as well as migrations large enough to be perceivable as such by contemporary populations—all of these must be taken into account. Underlying all the above speculation on how genetic patterns could be expected to emerge following different scenarios is the requirement that wherever and by whatever criteria our Celts started to be recognizable Celts, they would have to have been—in whatever manner—on average genetically distinguishable from their neighbours for the approach to be valid. It is worthwhile to stress this initial point: when I speak of a genetic signature or distinctiveness, the intended meaning is not that of absolute traits, but on average differing ratios of alleles between populations. Considering two groups of people, descended from the splitting of an amorphous proto-European group, probably influenced both by each other and exogenous tribes throughout the course of their existence, how can a single and only possibly sizeable event be detected? This, I think, is a question it would be premature to attempt to answer in any but the vaguest manner. Given suitable high-resolution genetic data from individuals of exact, long-term geographical provenance and probably ancient DNA as well, a model may be put forward that will reliably support or refute either, both or none of the discussed hypotheses. Genetic evidence could thus far be interpreted as favouring the Atlantic over the Central hypothesis, simply on the basis of the observed Atlantic similarities (McEvoy, Richards et al. 2004), but in the absence of a specifically designed study along the lines stipulated above, with special consideration for dating estimates provided by Y chromosome microsatellites, an outright dismissal of Iron Age migrations would be closed minded.

To conclude, population genetics should be able to make a considerable contribution towards the elucidation of Celtic and British prehistory, given careful and extensive sampling of populations in western and central Europe and a well-developed, scientifically based framework for interpreting the data from these samples. Fundamentally, however, any answer will always be constrained by the phrasing of the question. In discussing Celtic—an inherently non-genetic term, as are all expressions pertaining to culture—a geneticist will invariably be forced to depend on the definitions and syntheses provided by archaeologists, historians, and linguists. To disregard any variable but those that are purely biological would arguably render an investigation less biased and more reliable, but doing so would simultaneously remove most elements of interest. While avoiding doing violence to any discipline by complete disregard or crass misinterpretation, we hope that tempering hypotheses in the light of all the evidence, whatever form it takes, will be the approach most likely to give us the truest account of all aspects of the development and spread of Celtic.

Acknowledgements

I would like to thank B. Cunliffe and W. Bodmer for their comments on the manuscript, and participants in the People of the British Isles project for data collection and analysis.

BIBLIOGRAPHY

Achilli, A., C. Rengo, et al. 2004 'The molecular dissection of mtDNA haplogroup H confirms that the Franco-Cantabrian glacial refuge was a major source for the European gene pool', *American Journal of Human Genetics* 75(5), 910–18.

Adams, S. M., T. E. King, et al. 2006 'The case of the unreliable SNP: recurrent back-mutation of Y-chromosomal marker P25 through gene conversion', *Forensic Science International* 159(1), 14–20.

Almagro-Gorbea, M. 1994 '"Proto-Celtes" et Celtes en Péninsule Iberique', *Aquitania* 12, 283–96.

Alvarez-Sanchis, J. R. 2000 'The Iron Age in western Spain (800 BC–AD 50): an overview', *Oxford Journal of Archaeology* 19(1), 65–90.

Avise, J. C. 2000 *Phylogeography: The History and Formation of Species*. Cambridge, Mass., Harvard University Press.

Bandelt, H. J., V. Macaulay, et al. 2002 'What Molecules Can't Tell Us about the Spread of Languages and the Neolithic'. *Examining the Farming/Language Dispersal Hypothesis*, eds. P. R. Bellwood & C. Renfrew, 99–107. Cambridge, McDonald Institute for Archaeological Research.

Barbujani, G., & L. Chikhi 2006 'Population genetics: DNAs from the European Neolithic', *Heredity* 97(2), 8.

Barbujani, G., & I. Dupanloup 2002 'DNA Variation in Europe: Estimating the Demographic Impact of Neolithic Dispersals'. *Examining the Farming/Language Dispersal Hypothesis*, eds. P. R. Bellwood & C. Renfrew, 421–33. Cambridge, McDonald Institute for Archaeological Research.

Barbujani, G., A. Magagni, et al. 1997 'An apportionment of human DNA diversity', *Proceedings of the National Academy of Science U S A* 94(9), 4516–19.

Battaglia, V., S. Fornarino, et al. 2009 'Y-chromosomal evidence of the cultural diffusion of agriculture in southeast Europe', *European Journal of Human Genetics* 17(6), 820–30.

Bauchet, M., B. McEvoy, et al. 2007 'Measuring European population stratification with microarray genotype data', *American Journal of Human Genetics* 80(5), 948–56.

Bodmer, W. F. 1992 'The Genetics of Celtic Populations', *Proceedings of the British Academy* 82, 37–57.

Bouchard, T. J. 1984 'Twins Reared Together and Apart: What They Tell Us About Human Diversity'. *Individuality and Determinism—Chemical and Biological Bases*, ed. S. W. Fox. New York, Plenum Press.

Brion, M., A. Salas, et al. 2003 'Insights into Iberian population origins through the construction of highly informative Y-chromosome haplotypes using biallelic markers, STRs, and the MSY1 minisatellite', *American Journal of Physical Anthropology* 122(2), 147–61.

Brun, P. 1992 'Le Bronze Atlantique: essai de definition'. *L'âge du bronze Atlantique*, eds. C. Chevillot & A. Coffyn. Beynac-et-Cazenac Association des Musées du Sarladais.

Capelli, C., N. Redhead, et al. 2003 'A Y chromosome census of the British Isles', *Current Biology* 13(11), 979–84.

Cavalli-Sforza, L. L., & W. F. Bodmer 1999 *The Genetics of Human Populations*. New York, Dover Publications, Inc.

Cavalli-Sforza, L. L., P. Menozzi, et al. 1994 *The History and Geography of Human Genes*. Princeton, NJ, Princeton University Press.

Chadwick, N. 1970 'The Celts in Europe'. *The Celts*, N. Chadwick. Harmondsworth, Pelican Books.

Chikhi, L., R. A. Nichols, et al. 2002 'Y genetic data support the Neolithic demic diffusion model', *Proceedings of the National Academy of Science U S A* 99(17), 11008–13.

Cunliffe, B. 1997 *The Ancient Celts*. London, Penguin Books Ltd.

Cunliffe, B. 2000 'Brittany and the Atlantic rim in the later first millennium BC', *Oxford Journal of Archaeology* 19(4), 367–86.

Cunliffe, B. 2001 *Facing the Ocean: The Atlantic and its Peoples 8000 BC–1500 AD*. Oxford, Oxford University Press.

Currat, M., & L. Excoffier 2005 'The effect of the

Neolithic expansion on European molecular diversity', *Proceedings of Biological Sciences* 272(1564), 679–88.

Currat, M., N. Ray, et al. 2008 'Genetic simulations of population interactions during past human expansions in Europe'. *Simulations, Genetics and Human Prehistory*, eds. S. Matsumura, P. Forster, & C. Renfrew. Cambridge, McDonald Institute for Archaeological Research.

Dawkins, R. 1996 *River Out of Eden: A Darwinian View of Life*. London, Phoenix.

De Benedetto, G., I. S. Nasidze, et al. 2000 'Mitochondrial DNA sequences in prehistoric human remains from the Alps', *European Journal of Human Genetics* 8(9), 669–77.

De Hoz, J. 1992 'Lepontic, Celtiberian, Gaulish and the Archaeological Evidence', *Études Celtiques* 29, 223–39.

Dubut, V., L. Chollet, et al. 2004 'mtDNA polymorphisms in five French groups: importance of regional sampling', *European Journal of Human Genetics* 12(4), 293–300.

Dupanloup de Ceuninck, I., S. Schneider, et al. 2000 'Inferring the Impact of Linguistic Boundaries on Population Differentiation and the Location of Genetic Barriers: A New Approach'. *Archaeogenetics: DNA and the Population Prehistory of Europe*, eds. C. Renfrew & K. V. Boyle, 325–31. Cambridge, McDonald Institute for Archaeological Research.

Dupanloup, I., G. Bertorelle, et al. 2004 'Estimating the impact of prehistoric admixture on the genome of Europeans', *Molecular Biology Evolution* 21(7), 1361–72.

Emerson, B. C., & G. M. Hewitt 2005 'Phylogeography', *Current Biology* 15(10), R367–71.

Excoffier, L., P. E. Smouse, et al. 1992 'Analysis of molecular variance inferred from metric distances among DNA haplotypes: application to human mitochondrial DNA restriction data', *Genetics* 131(2), 479–91.

Fox, C. 1943 *The Personality of Britain*. Cardiff, National Museum of Wales.

Han, J., P. Kraft, et al. 2008 'A genome-wide association study identifies novel alleles associated with hair color and skin pigmentation', *Public Library of Science Genetics* 4(5), e1000074.

Harding, R. M., E. Healy, et al. 2000 'Evidence for variable selective pressures at MC1R', *American Journal of Human Genetics* 66(4), 1351–61.

Haselgrove, C. 1999 'The Iron Age'. *The Archaeology of Britain*, eds. J. Hunter & I. Ralston. Abingdon, Routledge.

Hawkes, C. 1973 '"Cumulative Celticity" in Pre-Roman Britain', *Études Celtiques* 13(2), 607–28.

Helgason, A., B. Yngvadottir, et al. 2004 'An Icelandic example of the impact of population structure on association studies', *Nature Genetics* 37(1), 90–5.

Henderson, J. C. 2007 'The Atlantic West in the Early Iron Age'. *The Earlier Iron Age in Britain and the Near Continent*, eds. C. Haselgrove & R. Pope, 306–27. Oxford, Oxbow Books.

Hodson, F. R. 1964 'Cultural Grouping within the British pre-Roman Iron Age', *Proceedings of the Prehistoric Society* 30, 99–110.

Hudson, R. R., M. Slatkin, et al. 1992 'Estimation of levels of gene flow from DNA sequence data', *Genetics* 132(2), 583–9.

Hunter Blair, P. 1977 *Anglo-Saxon England*. Cambridge, Cambridge University Press.

International_HapMap_Consortium, T. 2005 'A haplotype map of the human genome', *Nature* 437(7063), 1299–1320.

Jorde, L. B., W. S. Watkins, et al. 2000 'The distribution of human genetic diversity: a comparison of mitochondrial, autosomal, and Y-chromosome data', *American Journal of Human Genetics* 66(3), 979–88.

Kayser, M., F. Liu, et al. 2008 'Three genome-wide association studies and a linkage analysis identify HERC2 as a human iris color gene', *American Journal of Human Genetics* 82(2), 411–23.

Kivisild, T., P. Shen, et al. 2006 'The role of selection in the evolution of human mitochondrial genomes', *Genetics* 172(1), 373–87.

Knowles, L. L. 2004 'The burgeoning field of statistical phylogeography', *Journal of Evolutionary Biology* 17(1), 1–10.

Knowles, L. L. 2008 'Why does a method that fails continue to be used?' *Evolution* 62(11), 2713–17.

Lao, O., T. T. Lu, et al. 2008 'Correlation between

genetic and geographic structure in Europe', *Current Biology* 18(16), 1241–8.

Lewontin, R. C. 1972 'The apportionment of human diversity', *Evolutionary Biology* 6, 381–98.

Lorrio, A. J., & G. Ruiz Zapatero 2005 'The Celts in Iberia: An Overview', *e-Keltoi: Journal of Interdisciplinary Celtic Studies* 6, 167–254.

McEvoy, B., M. Richards, et al. 2004 'The Longue Durée of genetic ancestry: multiple genetic marker systems and Celtic origins on the Atlantic facade of Europe', *American Journal of Human Genetics* 75(4), 693–702.

McMahon, A., & R. McMahon 2006 'Why linguists don't do dates'. *Phylogenetic Methods and the Prehistory of Languages*, eds. C. Renfrew & P. Forster. Cambridge, McDonald Institute for Archaeological Research.

Manly, B. F. J. 1986 *Multivariate Statistical Methods*. London, Chapman and Hall, Ltd.

Mengel-From, J., C. Borsting, et al. 2008 'Determination of cis/trans phase of variations in the MC1R gene with allele-specific PCR and single base extension', *Electrophoresis* 29(23), 4780–7.

Novembre, J., T. Johnson, et al. 2008 'Genes mirror geography within Europe', *Nature* 456, 98–101.

Novembre, J., & M. Stephens 2008 'Interpreting principal component analyses of spatial population genetic variation', *Nature Genetics* 40(5), 646–9.

Price, A. L., N. J. Patterson, et al. 2006 'Principal components analysis corrects for stratification in genome-wide association studies', *Nature Genetics* 38(8), 904–9.

Raftery, B. 2005 'Iron Age Ireland'. *A New History of Ireland I: Prehistoric and Early Ireland*, ed. D. O. Croinin. Oxford, Oxford University Press.

Richards, C., B. Cartstens, et al. 2007 'Distribution modelling and statistical phylogeography: an integrative framework for generating and testing alternative biogeographical hypotheses', *Journal of Biogeography* 34(11), 1833–45.

Richards, M., H. Corte-Real, et al. 1996 'Paleolithic and neolithic lineages in the European mitochondrial gene pool', *American Journal of Human Genetics* 59(1), 185–203.

Richards, M., V. Macaulay, et al. 2000 'Tracing European founder lineages in the Near Eastern mtDNA pool', *American Journal of Human Genetics* 67(5), 1251–76.

Romualdi, C., D. Balding, et al. 2002 'Patterns of human diversity, within and among continents, inferred from biallelic DNA polymorphisms', *Genome Research* 12(4), 602–12.

Rosser, Z. H., T. Zerjal, et al. 2000 'Y-chromosomal diversity in Europe is clinal and influenced primarily by geography, rather than by language', *American Journal of Human Genetics* 67(6), 1526–43.

Sanchez-Mazas, A. 2007 'An apportionment of human HLA diversity', *Tissue Antigens* 69 Suppl 1, 198–202.

Seielstad, M. T., E. Minch, et al. 1998 'Genetic evidence for a higher female migration rate in humans', *Nature Genetics* 20(3), 278–80.

Seldin, M. F., R. Shigeta, et al. 2006 'European population substructure: clustering of northern and southern populations', *Public Library of Science Genetics* 2(9), e143.

Semino, O., G. Passarino, et al. 1996 'A view of the neolithic demic diffusion in Europe through two Y chromosome-specific markers', *American Journal of Human Genetics* 59(4), 964–8.

Semino, O., G. Passarino, et al. 2000 'The genetic legacy of Paleolithic Homo sapiens sapiens in extant Europeans: a Y chromosome perspective', *Science* 290(5494), 1155–9.

Simoni, L., F. Calafell, et al. 2000 'Geographic patterns of mtDNA diversity in Europe', *American Journal of Human Genetics* 66(1), 262–78.

Sims-Williams, P. 1998 'Genetics, linguistics, and prehistory: thinking big and thinking straight', *Antiquity* 72(277), 505–27.

Steffens, M., C. Lamina, et al. 2006 'SNP-based analysis of genetic substructure in the German population', *Human Heredity* 62(1), 20–9.

Sulem, P., D. F. Gudbjartsson, et al. 2007 'Genetic determinants of hair, eye and skin pigmentation in Europeans', *Nature Genetics* 39(12), 1443–52.

Sulem, P., D. F. Gudbjartsson, et al. 2008 'Two newly identified genetic determinants of pigmentation in Europeans', *Nature Genetics* 40(7), 835–7.

Templeton, A. R. 2005 'Haplotype trees and modern human origins', *American Journal of*

Physical Anthropology Supplement 41, 33–59.

Thomason, S. G. 2001 *Language Contact—An Introduction.* Washington, D.C., Georgetown University Press.

Valverde, P., E. Healy, et al. 1995 'Variants of the melanocyte-stimulating hormone receptor gene are associated with red hair and fair skin in humans', *Nature Genetics* 11(3), 328–30.

Wardhaugh, R. 1987 *Languages in Competition.* Oxford, Basil Blackwell Ltd.

Watkin, I. 1952 'Blood Groups in Wales and the Marches', *Man* 52, 83–6.

Weale, M. E., D. A. Weiss, et al. 2002 'Y chromosome evidence for Anglo-Saxon mass migration', *Molecular Biology and Evolution* 19(7), 1008–21.

Wilson, J. F., D. A. Weiss, et al. 2001 'Genetic evidence for different male and female roles during cultural transitions in the British Isles', *Proceedings of the National Academy of Sciences USA* 98(9), 5078–83.

Wright, S. 1943 'Isolation by Distance', *Genetics* 28(2), 114–38.

Wright, S. 1969 *Evolution and the Genetics of Populations Vol 2: The Theory of Gene Frequencies.* Chicago, University of Chicago Press.

CHAPTER FIVE

IRISH GENETICS AND CELTS

Brian P. McEvoy & Daniel G. Bradley

'When I say that I am an Irishman. . . My extraction is the extraction of most Englishmen: that is, I have no trace in me of the commercially imported North Spanish strain which passes for aboriginal Irish.'

—George Bernard Shaw in the Preface for politicians (1906) of *John Bull's Other Island.*

P AST migrations and demographic processes leave an imprint in the patterns of genetic variation in modern populations. Undoubtedly, close examination of genetic diversity within western Europe can enlighten on aspects of population history—a more difficult aspiration is securely linking these patterns to other attributes of past peoples such as language or material culture. Associating Celtic languages with particular genetic signatures is no exception to this; archaeological stone may be dumb, but genes may be dumber.

Celts and genes have been juxtaposed in several senses in the genetics literature. Firstly, and most commonly from an Australian or American perspective, the term is often used to describe those genetic traits common in the portions of their mixed populations that have alternately Irish, Scottish, Welsh, or Breton ancestry. Thus freckles, fair skin, susceptibility to skin cancer and haemochromatosis and predispositions to other conditions are all a result of 'Celtic' genes (Lucotte & Dieterlen 2003; Dieterlen & Lucotte 2005; Haugarvoll et al. 2007). Secondly, but more rarely, genetic patterns may be mentioned as resonating with the archaeological evidence for the expansion of Iron Age elites from central Europe (Cashman et al. 1995). Finally, Celtic (or Briton) is often used as an oppositional term within studies of the British Isles, contrasting with the alternate proposed major strand of ancestry, Anglo-Saxon (Weale et al. 2002; Thomas, Stumpf, & Harke 2006).

Genetic Geography and the Atlantic Façade

The perception emerging from North American populations that ancestry from Ireland and other populations of the western British Isles carries a particular genetic import is borne out by direct studies of these regions. Ireland, for example, carries a remarkable series of world frequency maxima for genetic variants (alleles) that cause or predispose to important genetic diseases. Examples include cystic fibrosis, perhaps the most important single gene disease in Europe, which has a carrier frequency of 1 in 23 and its highest disease prevalence in Ireland. Another example is phenylketonuria which results from an enzyme deficiency that, whereas treatable by dietary intervention, can result in severe mental retardation. It is a disease which is sufficiently prevalent and important to be universally screened for in newborns in many countries. Of the two major variants or gene copies causing phenylketonuria, one reaches its worldwide frequency peak in the west of Ireland (Tighe et al. 2003). Thirdly, haemochromatosis is a potentially fatal disease of iron overload and is well described as having an elevated incidence in people of Irish extraction. Strikingly, about one quarter of people sampled in Ireland carry one of the two variants of the *Hfe* gene locus that are known, when homozygous, to predispose to this condition (Byrnes et al. 2001). Nowhere else matches this incidence but other 'Celtic' regions (i.e. those where currently or historically a Celtic language was predominantly spoken) such as Brittany, Scotland, and Cornwall also show high levels of predisposing variants (Lucotte & Dieterlen 2003).

While there might be a real genetic legacy to ancestry from Ireland or other 'Celtic' regions, it seems unlikely that this is substantially the legacy of mass migration to these parts from the supposed central European Celtic heartland during the Iron Age. Rather Ireland's place in at least some analyses of the overall European genetic landscape points to links due south rather than east in the continent's interior. Many genetic markers, most famously the ABO and Rhesus blood groups and the Y chromosome, link 'Celtic' regions to each other and to other Atlantic communities in south-west Europe. Mourant and Watkin (1952) noted that blood groups O and Rhesus positive were prevalent in the Basque regions either side of the Pyrenees as well as in the western British Isles. Lucotte notes the same by looking directly at DNA diversity on the Y chromosome (Dieterlen & Lucotte 2005)—a finding reinforced when Irish samples are added and SNP and microsatellite typing are employed (Hill, Jobling, & Bradley 2000; Wilson et al. 2001).

A more general survey of western European genetic affinities looked at several genetic systems that have different inheritance patterns. The small DNA genome of the mitchondrion (mtDNA)—the cell's powerhouse—is maternally inherited and thus gives a uniquely female perspective on population history. Conversely, the Y chromosome is paternally inherited while the vast majority of the remaining genome (termed the autosomal chromosomes 1–22) is derived from a mixture of both parents. Direct analysis of mtDNA and Y chromosome DNA as well as examination of around 100 autosomal 'classical' gene frequencies (which are protein polymorphisms such as the ABO blood group) demonstrated that the Atlantic Façade phylogeographical theme is one which is somewhat robust among different elements of the genome (McEvoy et al. 2004). Figure 5.1 shows a contour map charting genetic affinity among European population samples where genetic distances have been computed using Y chromosome haplotype frequencies

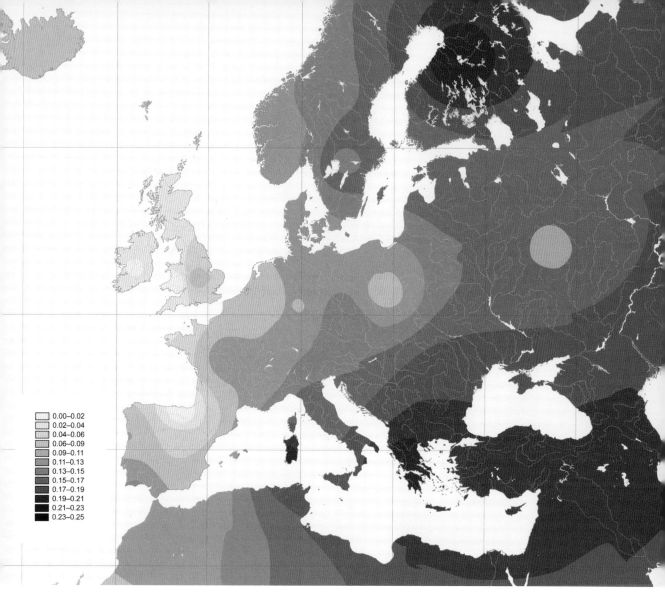

5.1. Contour map of the major pattern (or Dimension 1) derived from multidimensional scaling analysis (MDS) of Y-chromosome genetic distances between several European populations. Figure taken from McEvoy et al. 2004.

and then condensed into a small number of meaningful dimensions by multidimensional scaling. This plot of the most important of these, dimension 1, resembles that of dimension 1 of mitochondrial and dimension 2 of classical gene diversity. All suggest a shared genetic heritage along the Atlantic Façade of Western Europe.

While these types of analysis reveal what appears to be a real affinity, it is important to remember that statistical techniques like multidimensional scaling and the mathematically similar principal component analysis (PCA) are, by definition, data reduction methods, designed to reveal only major patterns or trends. Secondly, mtDNA and the Y chromosome are but single-locus systems and diversity at each independent part of the genome could have been predominantly shaped by different demographic processes. For example, western populations appear to share a stratum of pre-Neolithic ancestry but several have very strong (almost fixed) frequencies of an undoubted Neolithic genetic trait—a single letter change in the DNA sequence (termed single nucleotide polymorphisms or SNPs) of the gene encoding the enzyme lactase that confers the ability to digest raw milk into adulthood (so called 'lactose tolerance') (Bersaglieri et al. 2004). While it is interesting that Atlantic Celtic samples tend toward concordant contours in such analyses to the exclusion of inland European samples, it is difficult to assert that these two population characteristics are coterminal. Whereas language and genes are both predominantly vertically transmitted—there are known examples where rapid replacement of the former can occur with relatively little disturbance of the latter within a population.

Nonetheless, these summaries of genetic variation do not offer support for one story of Celtic genetics, the origins of the populations of the British Isles in massive Iron Age invasions within the first millennium BC from mainland Europe. Such an event would surely have left less differentiation between the heartland of the La Tène cultural package and the western periphery. However, this analysis by its nature cannot exclude the influence of minor migrations (to which we return later). The inclusion of an outlying non-Indo-European linguistic group, the Basques, in this western genetic cohort is intriguing and suggestive of some antiquity in the origins of the shared genetics. Whereas it may be fallacious to regard the Basque (and other Atlantic) genomes as primeval or Mesolithic their concordance does hint at an earlier pre-Indo-European layer to the genetics of the Atlantic Zone. Unfortunately, there is little security in assigning time depths to patterns such as these using currently available data and methods.

Interestingly, the Iberian similarity to Ireland coincides with a prevalent founding myth of the Gaels. G. B. Shaw was aware of this (and adamant that he was of different rather superior stock). This emerges from the recounting in the 11th-century *Book of Invasions* (*Lebar Gabála Érenn*) of the conquest of Ireland by the sons of the Spanish king Míl Espáine and their foundation of the Gaelic population. There are echoes of this—an ancient kinship was an aid to translocated Irish nobility in the 17th-century Spanish court. A modern version is the rather preposterous idea that enough shipwrecked sailors of the Spanish Armada survived both crown orders for summary execution plus the larcenous attentions of the native Irish and fathered enough children to give the western Irish gene pool an injection of swarthy skin and black hair.

New DNA genotyping technologies and accompanying data analyses promise to provide additional insights into patterns of European population structure and how these were crafted and formed. Whole genome population genetic analysis has recently become possible with efficient genotyping of hundreds of thousands of single nucleotide polymorphisms, the basic unit of genetic variation in each person. These data offer an enhanced ability to look at the individual histories of people in a population rather than summarizing the populations as a collective group. Europe has been the focus of such studies thus far and the major trends identified reveal a genetic space that is remarkably reflective of the geographic origin of populations and individuals (Novembre et al. 2008). While further and more detailed analysis will likely reveal greater insights into a putative Atlantic-façade heritage, it is clear again that on a whole genome level the Irish do not share a particularly close affinity with central Europeans which might have been expected if the population had been replaced or even substantially admixed with 'Celtic' invaders from continental Europe.

The genetic dissection of fine structure between European populations is ultimately based on frequency differences of alternative alleles (or genetic letters) at each SNP. Most of these frequencies' differences are due to the action of genetic drift. Genetic drift simply describes the random changes in allele frequencies that develop as time goes by and populations separate into semi-independent units. However, it is possible that some of the differences, rather than being passive, are actually driven by the active force of natural selection where a particular genetic variant confers an advantage to prevailing environmental conditions in some European populations but not others (such as the lactase tolerance trait mentioned earlier). The SNPs that show the most extreme frequency differences between populations are the most likely to have been affected by natural selection although it is important to remember that such differences are not absolute evidence of its action. Some studies have begun to examine the impact of natural selection amongst European populations and have found evidence for its general action particularly in relation to genes involved in immunity. One potential explanation is variation in the geographical extent of infectious disease epidemics which have potentially high mortality and thus strong selective power (McEvoy et al. 2009). Given this, it is possible that many of the traits, and paradoxically disease risks, associated with 'Celtic' areas are a response to the action or relaxation of geographically restricted natural selection. For example, under the specific climatic conditions of the British Isles region, exceptionally pale skin may have been an advantage in the production of Vitamin D in the skin, an environmental force that is thought to have driven the initial evolution of light skin as modern humans left Africa for higher latitudes over the past 50,000 years or so (Norton et al. 2006).

Celts as an oppositional term

Clear genetic patterns over smaller geographic regions can often be difficult to discern. Nonetheless, a general east to west/south-east to north-west gradient in blood group frequencies and Y chromosome haplotypes has long been apparent across the British Isles. The pattern corresponds roughly with the contrast between regions that until recently spoke Celtic languages (or still do to some extent) and those with a longer association with the prevalent Germanic tongue. For example, in Ireland, frequencies of blood group O and Rhesus positive decline dramatically in the north-east and south-east—regions where migration from Britain has been strongest, as evidenced for example by surname distributions in the 1659 census (Dawson 1964; Smyth 1988). Also a Y chromosome sample transect through central Britain showed a sharp step in allele frequencies in north Wales (Weale et al. 2002). This sharp dissimilarity and a similarity between central England and a sample from Friesland allowed an assertion that this pattern reflected a dichotomy between earlier Celtic/Brittonic ancestry and Anglo-Saxon replacement of patrilineages. A later study of Y chromosome diversity within Britain gave median estimates of continental introgression into a range of English samples of between 24 and 73% (Capelli et al. 2003).

Anglo-Saxon invasions as a major determinant of modern English population structure remains a disputed if well-argued assertion (Thomas, Stumpf, & Harke 2006) and in many ways mirrors the debate over Celtic origin, in trying to link mass migration to cultural and social changes. However, the genetic evidence at the very least supports two or more divergent ancestral influences within the islands. Most recently, this has been shown from whole genome polymorphism data from nearly 300,000 SNPs in British and Irish individuals. Principal component analysis (PCA) of these data has confirmed a striking ability to separate English and Irish with surprising little overlap between the two populations (Figure 5.2). Although numbers were low, Scottish and Welsh individuals had more varied positions in the genetic space, an observation consistent with the general population level gradient (McEvoy et al. 2009).

Irish mammals and colonization routes

If patterns in human genome diversity are difficult to link with linguistic attributes, those in animals are surely dumber still. However, animal population history can resonate with that of humans from the same geographical region. In Ireland, this may be because of two reasons—first, the geological history of the island may influence both in similar ways. Second, certain animals (wild as well as domestic) may have travelled along with humans and their genetic affinities with other regions may give some reflection of ancient human traversal. Often, where human and animal patterns echo each other, the phylogenetic signal may be higher in the latter. Indeed, the dichotomy in ancestral human genomes within the British Isles is more accentuated within other mammals. At the coarsest level, there are differences in the suites of species present within each island—Britain has a diminished but similar range of species to that on the mainland, but Ireland displays a more marked reduction in taxa (including some that occur otherwise in south-west Europe).

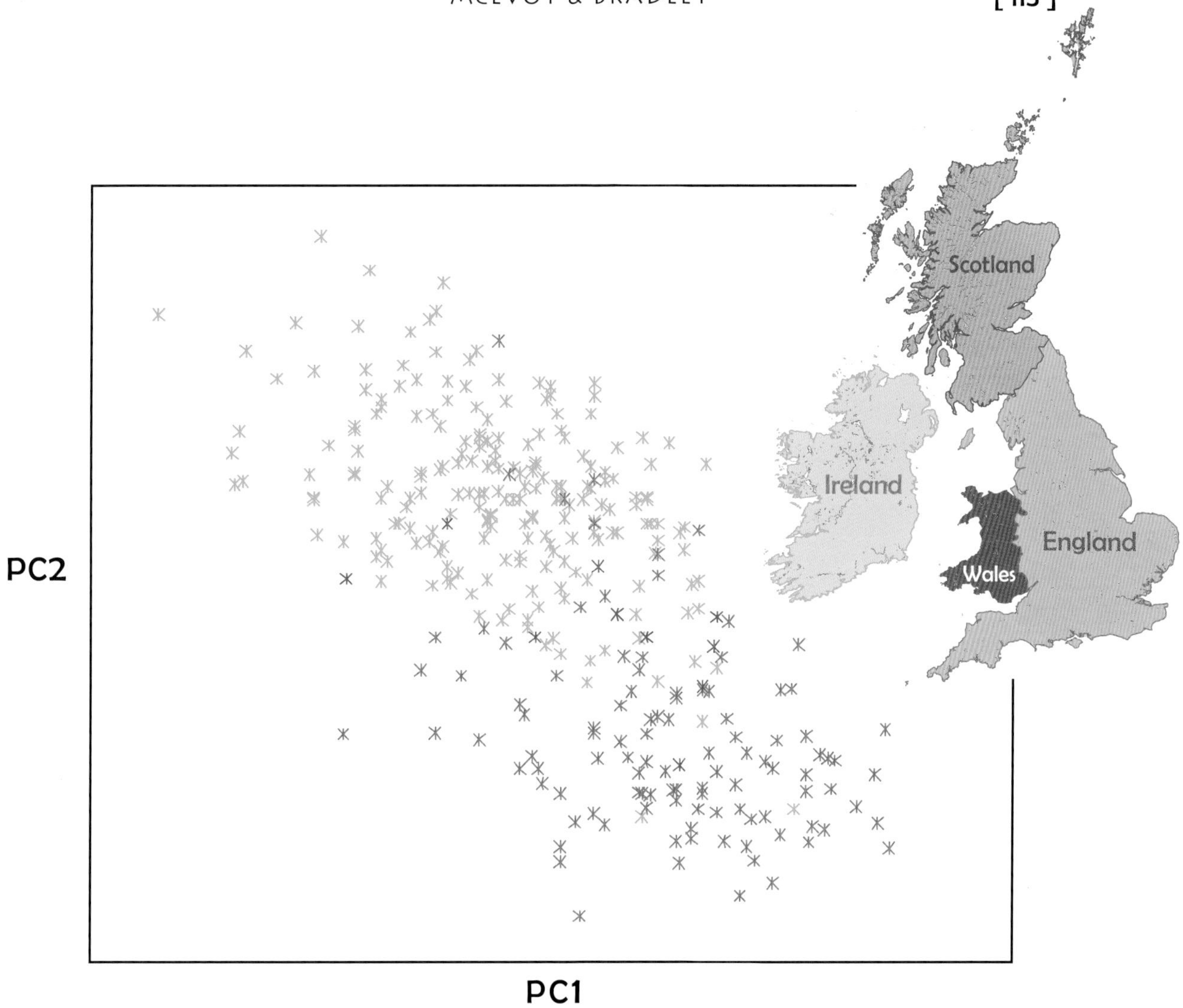

5.2. The genetic space of the British Isles. Principal Component (PC) 1 and 2 values, for each individual calculated from about 300,000 SNPs spread across the autosomal genome, are plotted against each other. Each individual is colour-coded by country of birth as shown in the accompanying map (green for Ireland, red for England, blue for Scotland and purple for Wales). Figure is adapted from McEvoy et al. 2009).

The genetic geography of several of the small mammals present in both islands has been investigated using mitochondrial DNA (mtDNA) sequencing—pygmy shrew give a strong example of patterns seen. In this mammal, mtDNA sequences from Britain cluster among a large number of samples from northern continental Europe implying an origin for the island populations in a migration from the mainland. However, those from Ireland are divergent from this cluster and instead show affinity with Iberian and southern European sequences, implying a different origin (Mascheretti et al. 2003). A sharp discontinuity in mtDNA genomes between the two islands has also been documented in pine martens, house mice, mountain hare, and stoats (Davison et al. 2001; Hamill, Doyle, & Duke 2006; Martinkova, McDonald, & Searle 2007; Searle et al. 2009). This recurring pattern strongly implies radically different postglacial colonization histories for each island. It is likely that no one history fits all species but a probable recurring factor is the persistence of a Holocene land bridge between Britain and the continent across which a majority of species migrated to that island. In contrast, it seems unlikely from these patterns that such a land connection for Ireland endured substantially beyond the Last Glacial Maximum (indeed recent geological modelling concurs with this (Edwards & Brooks 2008). It is possible that cold-adapted species such as stoat and mountain hare (argued cogently by Martinkova et al. 2007) may have migrated to the island during the glacial maximum. However, a reasonable assertion is that, whereas British mammals walked there from the Continent, many small mammal species in Ireland arrived there by boat. Pine martens, as with pygmy shrews, show closest affinity with Iberian samples and it is tempting to speculate that at least some of these western Atlantic arks came from south-western Europe, providing proxy evidence for early human connections.

Gaelic Surnames and Y Chromosomes

Genome-wide approaches promise many new insights into population history and have in some respects supplanted the traditional population genetic workhorse loci of mtDNA and Y chromosomes. However, because of their unique maternal and paternal inheritance patterns, the two should continue to enjoy niche roles. One of these roles relates to the history of surnames, since like the Y chromosome, these are paternally inherited in many European cultures. Gaelic surname nomenclature emphasizes ancestry from named individuals, reflecting the patriarchal nature of medieval Irish society c. AD 1000 when surnames began to form. By comparison, English surnames are based on professions, places of origin, physical attributes and more. Virtually all indigenous Irish surnames contain the prefix *Mac* or *Ó* meaning 'son of' or 'grandson of' respectively. It follows that if a surname is indeed founded by just one male then all modern male bearers of the surname will have his Y chromosome allowing for some degree of mutational change, non-paternities, adoptions, etc. Overall, Gaelic Irish surnames, typically, do show a substantial legacy of shared patrilineal kinship consistent with a limited number of founders about 1000 years ago (McEvoy & Bradley 2006).

The combination of surnames and Y chromosomes offers the surprising potential to explore other aspects of early (prior to AD 1000) Gaelic/Celtic society and its

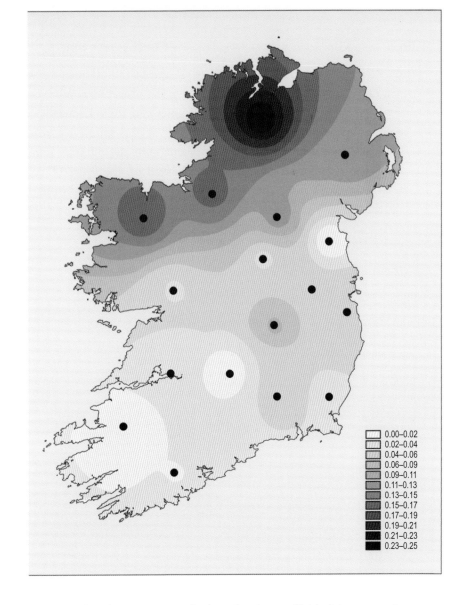

5.3. Contour map showing the geographic frequency distribution of the Irish Modal Haplotype (IMH) and closely related Y-chromosomes. Figure taken from Moore et al. 2006

	0.00–0.02
	0.02–0.04
	0.04–0.06
	0.06–0.09
	0.09–0.11
	0.11–0.13
	0.13–0.15
	0.15–0.17
	0.17–0.19
	0.19–0.21
	0.21–0.23
	0.23–0.25

organization. During this early Christian period, the island was divided into a series of hierarchical kingdoms or tribes. Like later surnames, these emphasised a paternal ancestral founding figure. The two most prominent of these were the *Uí Néill* meaning 'descendants of Niall' in the northern half of the country and the *Éoganachta* meaning 'people of Eoghan' (i.e. Éogan Taídlech, a.k.a. Mug Nuadat) in southern parts of the island. However, whether this implied a real paternal kinship between tribal members or just amongst the ruling family was an unanswerable question using scant historical records of the period.

A detailed survey of the Irish Y chromosome pool, both in terms of number of individuals and in high resolution DNA genotyping, revealed an extraordinary preponderance of one Y chromosome (and its close relatives), which was termed the Irish Modal Haplotype or IMH. Approximately 8% of Irish men had one of the IMH group of Y chromosomes. Furthermore, the IMH displayed a striking geographical specificity to the north-western part of the Island (Figure 5.3) where more than 1/5 men carried the Y chromosome. By using the observed number of mutational changes between the IMH group of Y chromosomes and some knowledge of the mutation rate it was possible to roughly date the ancestor of this group to 1,700 years before present. The dates and geography were coincident with the putative founder of the Uí Néill dynasty, the warlord Níall Noígíallach 'Niall of the Nine Hostages', a figure on the intersection of history and mythology, who putatively lived in the 5th century AD.

In order to test the circumstantial association and prove a link between the IMH

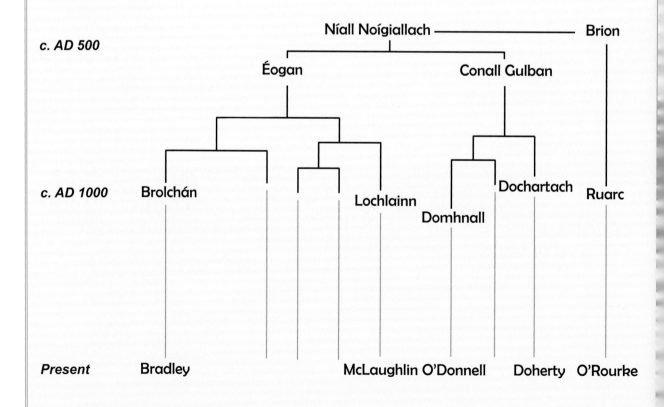

5.4. Illustrative Genealogy of the Uí Néill dynasty. Reputedly founded by the eponymous Níall Noígíallach ('Niall of the Nine Hostages') in the 5th century AD. The unique corpus of Irish genealogical records allows the tracing of his putative descendants to the 11th and 12th centuries when they in turn became the founding fathers of many modern Irish surnames. Those who bear these surnames today thus have a direct, albeit putative, patrilineal link to the early medieval dynastic founder.

and the Uí Néill's founder, modern surnames were crucial since they can be traced back to the sometimes pre-historical tribal kingdoms and their putative founders (Figure 5.4). The IMH was found to be significantly enriched in men with surnames that were genealogically linked to the Uí Néill compared to the men from the same area whose surnames were not (Moore et al. 2006). In turn this suggests that the greatest kingdom of early medieval Ireland was in fact bound together by substantial amounts of patrilineal kinship. The remarkable frequency of the IMH is consistent with the practice of polygyny with a tight link between power and profligacy. In contrast, a later but similar study of the Eóganachta provided little evidence of paternal kinship (McEvoy, Simms, & Bradley 2008), in turn suggesting strong socio-cultural differences between different parts of the Island at that time.

Finally, the Y chromosomes from another part of the island—the north-east—provide some tentative evidence of ancient flow with eastern areas that could support the idea that the La Tène cultural package was accompanied by some migration. Bearers of several surnames across this region carry a Y chromosome belonging to a family (known as haplogroup I1c) that is untypical of Ireland but relatively common in continental Europe. The fact that this Y chromosome is observed across several surnames that are Gaelic in origin, which by definition arose in Ireland about 1000 years ago, suggests that this Y chromosome arrived prior to this and is thus not a result of known recent gene flow between Britain and Ireland. For example, it is shared between McGuinness and McCartan males—groups that have a historically recorded 6th-century common ancestor. Indeed, using the observed mutational divergence between men with these haplogroup I1c Y chromosomes, its foundation in Ireland can be dated, very approximately, to 2300 years before present. While the dates and geography are circumstantially associated with Iron Age continental Europe, it is clearly impossible to ascribe its origin securely to a migration associated with the appearance of La Tène artefacts. Nonetheless, it does illustrate some potential to track small levels of gene flow through individual Y chromosome lineages which could be expanded in the future.

The shared historical trajectories of surnames and Y chromosomes provide one example where we can say that genes have a link to language and in Ireland it is one that has persisted for a thousand years. This gives us a window to the genetic landscape of the island in the first millennium AD and this reveals a vista which resonates with the modern vista. This gives some support to the veracity of studying modern genetic diversity as a means to infer aspects of deeper prehistory.

Conclusion

The study of genetic variation, first indirectly and more recently through direct DNA genetic typing, has shown intriguing patterns that are crafted by our population history.

While interpreting them can often be controversial, they offer little support for the proposition that people of areas considered Celtic today, by the continued or recent use of a Celtic language, are mainly descendent from mass Iron age invasions from central Europe. Even with current cutting-edge technology, we are still restricted to examining but a fraction of the human genome's diversity and it seems likely that further rapid advances in DNA sequencing will produce a torrent of new genetic data that will allow for the identification of finer scale genetic relationship and patterns and in turn provide further insights, as well as generating fresh debate, on the Irish past.

Acknowledgements

We wish to thank Patrick Guinness, Joseph A. Donohoe and the Wellcome Trust for their generous support of our Y-chromosome/surname research as well as the many DNA volunteers who made the described studies possible.

BIBLIOGRAPHY

Bersaglieri, T., P. C. Sabeti, N. Patterson, T. Vanderploeg, S. F. Schaffner, J. A. Drake, M. Rhodes, D. E. Reich, & J. N. Hirschhorn 2004 'Genetic Signatures of Strong Recent Positive Selection at the Lactase Gene', *American Journal of Human Genetics* 74, 1111–20.

Byrnes, V., E. Ryan, S. Barrett, P. Kenny, P. Mayne, & J. Crowe 2001 'Genetic Hemochromatosis, A Celtic Disease: Is it Now Time for Population Screening?' *Genetic Testing* 5, 127–30.

Capelli, C., N. Redhead, J. K. Abernethy, F. Gratrix, J. F. Wilson, T. Moen, T. Hervig, M. Richards, M. P. Stumpf, P. A. Underhill, P. Bradshaw, A. Shaha, M. G. Thomas, N. Bradman, & D. B. Goldstein 2003 'A Y Chromosome Census of the British Isles', *Current Biology* 13, 979–84.

Cashman, S. M., A. Patino, A. Martinez, M. Garcia-Delgado, Z. Miedzybrodzka, M. Schwarz, A. Shrimpton, C. Ferec, O. Raguenes, M. Macek, Jr., et al. 1995 'Identical Intragenic Microsatellite Haplotype Found in Cystic Fibrosis Chromosomes Bearing Mutation G551D in Irish, English, Scottish, Breton and Czech Patients', *Human Heredity* 45, 6–12.

Davison, A., J. D. Birks, R. C. Brookes, J. E. Messenger, & H. I. Griffiths 2001 'Mitochondrial Phylogeography and Population History of Pine Martens Martes Martes Compared with Polecats Mustela Putorius', *Molecular Ecology* 10, 2479–88.

Dawson, G. W. 1964 'The Frequencies of the Abo and Rh (D) Blood Groups in Ireland from a Sample of 1 in 18 of the Population', *Annals of Human Genetics* 28, 49–59.

Dieterlen, F., and G. Lucotte 2005 'Haplotype XV of the Y-Chromosome is the Main Haplotype in West-Europe', *Biomedicine & Pharmacotherapy* 59, 269–72.

Edwards, R., & A. Brooks 2008 'The Island of Ireland: Drowning the Myth of an Irish Land Bridge', *Mind the Gap: Postglacial Colonization of Ireland*, J. L. Davenport, D. P. Sleeman, & P. C. Woodman (eds.). Special supplement of the Irish

Naturalist's Journal, Dublin.

Hamill, R. M., D. Doyle, & E. J. Duke 2006 'Spatial Patterns of Genetic Diversity across European Subspecies of the Mountain Hare, Lepus timidus L.', *Heredity* 97, 355–65.

Haugarvoll, K., M. Toft, O. A. Ross, J. T. Stone, M. G. Heckman, L. R. White, T. Lynch, J. M. Gibson, Z. K. Wszolek, R. J. Uitti, J. O. Aasly, & M. J. Farrer 2007 'ELAVL4, PARK10, and the Celts', *Movement Disorders* 22, 585–7.

Hill, E. W., M. A. Jobling, & D. G. Bradley 2000 'Y-Chromosome Variation and Irish Origins', *Nature* 404, 351–2.

Lucotte, G., & F. Dieterlen 2003 'A European Allele Map of the C282Y Mutation of Hemochromatosis: Celtic Versus Viking Origin of the Mutation?' *Blood Cells, Molecules & Diseases* 31, 262–7.

Martinkova, N., R. A. McDonald, & J. B. Searle 2007 'Stoats (Mustela erminea) Provide Evidence of Natural Overland Colonization of Ireland', *Proceedings. Biological Sciences / The Royal Society* 274, 1387–93.

Mascheretti, S., M. B. Rogatcheva, I. Gunduz, K. Fredga, & J. B. Searle 2003 'How Did Pygmy Shrews Colonize Ireland? Clues from a Phylogenetic Analysis of Mitochondrial Cytochrome B Sequences', *Proceedings. Biological sciences / The Royal Society* 270, 1593–9.

McEvoy, B., & D. G. Bradley 2006 'Y-Chromosomes and the Extent of Patrilineal Ancestry in Irish Surnames', *Human Genetics* 119, 212–19.

McEvoy, B., M. Richards, P. Forster, & D. G. Bradley 2004 'The Longue Durée of Genetic Ancestry: Multiple Genetic Marker Systems and Celtic Origins on the Atlantic Façade of Europe', *American Journal of Human Genetics* 75, 693–702.

McEvoy, B., K. Simms, & D. G. Bradley 2008 'Genetic Investigation of the Patrilineal Kinship Structure of Early Medieval Ireland', *American Journal of Physical Anthropology* 136, 415–22.

McEvoy, B. P., G. W. Montgomery, A. F. McRae, S. Ripatti, M. Perola, T. D. Spector, L. Cherkas, K. R. Ahmadi, D. Boomsma, G. Willemsen, J. J. Hottenga, N. L. Pedersen, P. K. Magnusson, K. O. Kyvik, K. Christensen, J. Kaprio, K. Heikkila, A. Palotie, E. Widen, J. Muilu, A. C. Syvanen, U. Liljedahl, O. Hardiman, S. Cronin, L. Peltonen, N.

G. Martin, & P. M. Visscher 2009 'Geographical Structure and Differential Natural Selection among North European Populations', *Genome Research* 19, 804–14.

Moore, L. T., B. McEvoy, E. Cape, K. Simms, & D. G. Bradley 2006 'A Y-Chromosome Signature of Hegemony in Gaelic Ireland', *American Journal of Human Genetics* 78, 334–8.

Mourant, A. E., & I. M. Watkin 1952 'Blood Groups, Anthropology and Language in Wales and the Western Countries', *Heredity* 6, 23.

Norton, H. L., J. S. Friedlaender, D. A. Merriwether, G. Koki, C. S. Mgone, & M. D. Shriver 2006 'Skin and Hair Pigmentation Variation in Island Melanesia', *American Journal of Physical Anthropology* 130, 254–68.

Novembre, J., T. Johnson, K. Bryc, Z. Kutalik, A. R. Boyko, A. Auton, A. Indap, K. S. King, S. Bergmann, M. R. Nelson, M. Stephens, & C. D. Bustamante 2008 'Genes Mirror Geography within Europe', *Nature* 456, 98–101.

Searle, J. B., C. S. Jones, I. Gunduz, M. Scascitelli, E. P. Jones, J. S. Herman, R. V. Rambau, L. R. Noble, R. J. Berry, M. D. Gimenez, & F. Johannesdottir 2009 'Of Mice and (Viking?) Men, Phylogeography of British and Irish House Mice', *Proceedings. Biological Sciences / The Royal Society* 276, 201–7.

Smyth, W. J. 1988 'Society and Settlement in Seventeenth Century Ireland: The Evidence of the 1659 Census', *Common Ground: Essays on the Historical Geography of Ireland*, W. J. Smyth, & K. Whelan (eds.) 55–83. Cork University Press, Cork.

Thomas, M. G., M. P. Stumpf, & H. Harke 2006 'Evidence for an Apartheid-Like Social Structure in Early Anglo-Saxon England', *Proceedings. Biological Sciences / The Royal Society* 273, 2651–7.

Tighe, O., D. Dunican, C. O'Neill, G. Bertorelle, D. Beattie, C. Graham, J. Zschocke, F. Cali, V. Romano, E. Hrabincova, L. Kozak, M. Nechyporenko, L. Livshits, P. Guldberg, M. Jurkowska, C. Zekanowski, B. Perez, L. R. Desviat, M. Ugarte, V. Kucinskas, P. Knappskog, E. Treacy, E. Naughten, L. Tyfield, S. Byck, C. R. Scriver, P. D. Mayne, & D. T. Croke 2003 'Genetic Diversity within the R408W Phenylketonuria Mutation Lineages in Europe', *Human Mutation* 21, 387–93.

Weale, M. E., D. A. Weiss, R. F. Jager, N. Bradman, &

M. G. Thomas 2002 'Y Chromosome Evidence for Anglo-Saxon Mass Migration', *Molecular Biology and Evolution* 19, 1008–21.

Wilson, J. F., D. A. Weiss, M. Richards, M. G. Thomas, N. Bradman, & D. B. Goldstein 2001 'Genetic Evidence for Different Male and Female Roles During Cultural Transitions in the British Isles', *Proceedings of the National Academy of Sciences of the United States of America* 98, 5078–83.

CHAPTER SIX

A REANALYSIS OF MULTIPLE PREHISTORIC IMMIGRATIONS TO BRITAIN AND IRELAND AIMED AT IDENTIFYING THE CELTIC CONTRIBUTIONS

Stephen Oppenheimer

Introduction

THE fact that Great Britain and Ireland are islands gives the British and Irish added security in the knowledge of their unique identities and differences, when compared with the jigsaw of those countries facing us across the Channel. But do we really know who we are, where we come from and what really defines the nature of our genetic and cultural heritage? Who are and were the Scots, the Welsh, the Irish and the English? Are the English descendants of the Anglo-Saxons and recent usurpers of a formerly glorious Celtic-British aboriginal heritage?

A recent polar opposite of this view, for which Celtic linguist Sims-Williams coined the term 'Celtoscepticism' (1998), critiques over-enthusiastic linguistic-ethnic labelling and over-interpretation of historical and archaeological context, during the Celtic revivalist movement in Britain and Ireland, in the absence of any classical texts identifying anyone living in these isles as 'Celts' (Collis 2003; James 1999).

While I do not take the extreme view that the modern terms 'Celt' and 'Celtic' are irretrievably devalued by the revivalist fervour of recent centuries, it is necessary to understand the main features and problems of the current Celtic paradigm, inherited particularly from the 19th century, and examine how they came about. Three 19th-century preconceptions are in urgent need of review before even attempting to define Celts genetically: 1) Were the Celts the British aboriginals? 2) Did the Anglo-Saxons commit a genocide of the Celts, who were supposed to have completely occupied England, leaving a Celtic fringe to the west? 3) Was the Celtic homeland in central Europe?

While such a review may indeed help remove 18th-/19th-century cobwebs, sharpen questions, and even approach the issue of a Celtic linguistic homeland from an evidence-base, it may still not be possible satisfactorily to define 'Celts' genetically. After all there is no good reason to expect any source population to have homogeneous genetic labelling and in spite of conviction-based attempts to prove congruence of prehistoric proxies (e.g. Diamond and Bellwood 2003), gene flow rarely maps well on migrating languages when the evidence is examined impartially (Oppenheimer 2004).

Nearly all adults in the British Isles have heard the terms 'Celts', 'Anglo-Saxons', and 'Vikings', and most are familiar with the perceptions that the inhabitants of England are descended from Anglo-Saxons, who invaded eastern England after the Romans left, while those from the rest of the Isles derive from indigenous Celtic ancestors with a sprinkling of Viking blood around the fringes. Many would feel confident that they could answer a television quiz question on any of these ethnic terms. Millions feel proud to celebrate their Celtic heritage.

Yet, there is no general agreement, least of all among historians, on the actual meaning of the words 'Celtic' or 'Anglo-Saxon'. What is more, the new genetic evidence suggests that the Anglo-Saxons and Celts, to the extent they can be defined genetically, are and were both immigrant minorities. Neither group had much greater impact on the modern gene pools of their new homes than the Vikings, the Normans or, indeed, the immigrations of the past 50 years (Oppenheimer 2007).

How does one trace Celts and Celtic migrations or any migrations genetically? There are two general approaches to tracing migrations or demic diffusion: classical population genetics and genetic phylogeography (Oppenheimer 2008). The former method compares relative gene frequencies between different populations and by a combination of summary statistical analysis (including comparison of genetic distances e.g. principal components analysis) and admixture analysis (estimating hypothetical prehistoric admixture events) reconstructs intrusions from source regions. Admixture analysis requires making an estimate of the genetic make-up of the putative source populations in the past, so depends on knowledge of present populations in those source regions and some idea as to major founding events in their own genetic prehistory. Any locus or a combination of loci can be used in this kind of analysis, but in the principal components analysis, dates cannot be estimated, since the vectors summarize several markers/loci without respect to age and thus create a palimpsest of all migrations ancient and recent.

Genetic phylogeography concentrates on tracing movement of specific lineages from the putative source populations into target populations, by identifying and dating founder haplotypes and their derivatives, the latter form founding cluster lineages with unique new variation in the target population. The date of arrival of each novel cluster can be estimated from their derived mutational diversity. Phylogeography is much more powerful when using non-recombining loci (such as mitochondrial DNA or the Y chromosome), since detailed, mutation-defined trees can be reconstructed, and the derivative branches can be traced with surprising geographic detail. Unlike methods used in population genetics, it is not nearly as dependent on estimates of past population sizes (for an illustration of methods in the European context see Richards et al. 2000).

Ideally in each of these two genetic approaches to tracing gene flow, alternate hypotheses suggested by other prehistoric disciplines have to be tested. This means models of migration from alternative putative sources to the relevant target region also have to be tested. If there is only one suggested model of source and target, predictions from that model still have to be tested. All this means that geneticists cannot work in isolation and need to be cognizant of information and migration models derived from several disciplines, and alert to the strength of evidence and controversies, testing hypotheses rather than passively trying to fit the genes into the prevailing historical paradigm.

A third approach should be mentioned if only to dismiss it as of no real use. This method ignores the need to estimate or test models and the effects of migration past and present from specific putative sources and depends instead on accepting the current historic paradigms of migrations as correct and using that received-model to estimate the different contributions of traditional invaders. So in the instance of the British Isles, one might accept the received history of a previously uniform 'Celticity' squeezed to a western fringe first by Anglo-Saxon invasions and genocide then by the Vikings in the north and north-east. Regions like Ireland and Wales are then regarded as representative of Celtic genes while East Anglia would be the gold standard for Anglo-Saxons and York for Vikings. Now whether such self-fulfilling definitions bore any relation to real migrations, there is no doubt that they could not advance knowledge further than received wisdom (or myth), which essentially means moving backwards in a circular fashion.

Bearing the last cautionary tale in mind, how could Celts be defined genetically? Strictly it is not possible even with the first two approaches, since genes do not routinely carry ethnic signatures. So, some form of evidence-based prehistoric proxy must be used; yet that approach has pitfalls of uncertainty in this instance, mainly since there is no agreed definition of Celts, Celticity or even of a Celtic homeland, and as mentioned, using historic preconceptions to define genetic types tends to perpetuate misconceptions and circular arguments.

It should be recognized that, in spite of persuasive arguments over recent centuries, to link or conflate surviving Insular Celtic languages with classical descriptions of *Keltoi* (Κελτοί) and *Celtae* (e.g. Buchanan, Lhuyd & Pezron reviewed in Collis 2003), there is little direct evidence for such an assumption. First, as mentioned, no classical author ever referred to inhabitants of the British Isles as Celts, although commentators such as Caesar and Tacitus had every opportunity to do so. Both authors instead referred to linguistic and cultural similarities between the Belgae and the inhabitants of what is now south-east England, but neither labelled Belgae as Celts; Caesar explicitly excluded Belgae from that self-label (*De Bello Gallico* 1.1).

Second, the only direct classical link between the name *Celtae* and any language was Caesar's brief but clear comment at the beginning of his *Gallic Wars*, where he noted that the inhabitants of middle Gaul (south of the Seine and the Marne, thus specifically

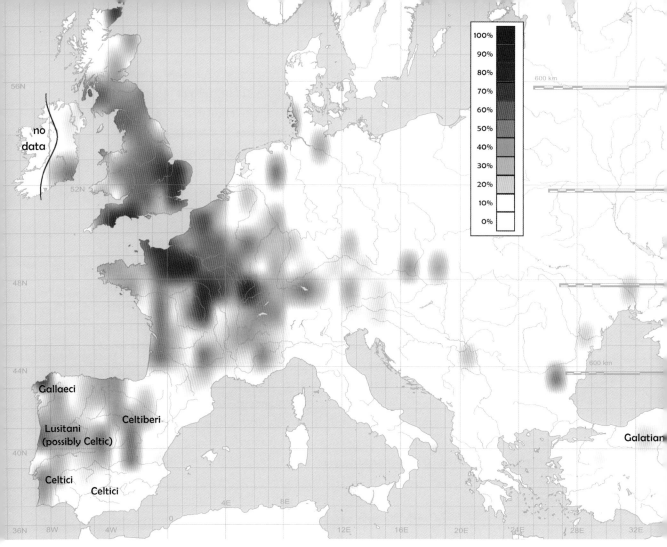

Figure 6.1. Map of Europe and Asia Minor with the frequencies of ancient place-names, which were Celtic, shown as percentage contours. The highest frequencies were in Celtica, Britannia, and Iberia. Their absence in western Ireland is due to lack of data. Data, with permission, from Sims-Williams, 2006. (Cf. Cunliffe above (Fig. 1.1) drawn from the same data.)

excluding the Belgae and excluding the Aquitani to the south-west of the Garonne), *called themselves Celts in their own language.* Caesar acknowledges implicitly that Romans had a looser definition of Gauls (*Galli*), which included others as well as Celts. Although Caesar doesn't specify it, one might add the southern Roman province of Narbonne to his Celtic Central Gaul, since other authors such as Strabo (*Geographia* 4.1.14) and Diodorus Siculus (V.32) identify the non-Greek aboriginal inhabitants of Narbonne as Celts, again emphasizing their distinction from the general Latin terms 'Galli/Galatae'.

The ancient Greek explorer Pytheas called Central Gaul 'Keltiké' (Κελτική) according to Strabo.

Given this specific regional association with some of the earliest Celtic epigraphy (Collis 2003, 121–32) and the additional significant density of Celtic place-names and personal names attested in sources of the classical period (Sims-Williams 2006, figs. 5.2, 11.1, and 11.2; Raybould & Sims-Williams 2007) within these two regions of France, the most parsimonious interpretation is that Gaulish, the local sub-branch of the Celtic branch of Indo-European, was spoken by the inhabitants of Central Gaul who self-identified as 'Celts' in their own language. This in turn is consistent with, though not proof of, the orthodox view of Celtic languages defining all the Celts of classical antiquity (i.e. groups called *Keltoi*, *Celtae*, &c.).

However, while it is reasonable on this argument to accept an association between 'Gaulish' inscriptions, and communities whom several Roman authors identified as 'Celts', it does not identify a clear source region to define genetic markers for tracing hypothetical Celtic migrations to the British Isles. For a start Central Gaul and Narbonne together constitute a huge and likely genetically non-homogeneous region. What is more, the same sort of association can be made for very early Lepontic inscriptions and Cisalpine Gaul (Collis 2003, 121–32), thus further increasing the size of the territory in which to find a possible homeland.

More importantly, there is another large western European region, identified by Herodotus in the 5th century BC as the home of the Keltoi, namely Iberia (Collis 2003, 121–32). There is again ample epigraphic (Raybould & Sims-Williams 2007), tribal and place-name evidence (Figure 6.1 here and Sims-Williams 2006, figs. 5.2, 11.1, and 11.2) to support the classical geographic association of Celts with branches of Celtic languages, here in a region comprising two-thirds of the Iberian Peninsula. While this enhances the picture in central Gaul of a more western European centre of gravity for the classical Celts, supported by the predominantly western distribution of ancient Celtic place-names, it still makes the finding of a Celtic demic/linguistic homeland even more difficult by including further multiple putative homelands.

Which of the locations, middle Gaul, Narbonne, Cisalpine Gaul or Iberia, was the original Celtic cultural or linguistic homeland and which among these regions was/were the source(s) of the several Insular Celtic languages? There is of course good epigraphic, place-name and personal-name evidence for the presence of Celtic languages in the British Isles since Roman times (and in Irish epigraphy since at least early medieval times); so they must have come from somewhere. The linguistic questions are best answered by linguists, but with such a huge potential source area for demic movements, there seems little way of using the foregoing information, as it stands, to define Celts genetically.

The cultural homeland is even more of a problem since the current orthodoxy has long placed the Celtic linguistic and cultural homeland not in south-west Europe but among the Hallstatt and La Tène cultures of central Europe, where there is a dearth of epigraphic or place-name evidence for it (Collis 2003, 120–1). In particular, ancient

Celtic place-names are hard to find east of the Rhine and north of the Danube, in central Europe (Sims-Williams 2006). Which brings us to the problem of the central European Celtic homeland.

Hallstatt and La Tène

The current orthodox view of the origins of the Celts is one of the last remaining archaeological myths left over from the 19th century. The last couple of hundred years have seen a romantic reconstruction of the Celts as a vast, culturally sophisticated but noisy and warlike people from central Europe, north of the Alps and the Danube, who invaded most of Europe, including the British Isles, during the Iron Age, around 300 BC.

Central Europe during the last millennium BC was the time and place of the exotic and fierce Hallstatt culture and, later, the La Tène culture, with their prestigious Iron Age metal jewellery wrought with beautiful, intricately woven swirls. Hoards of such weapons and jewellery, some fashioned in gold, have indeed been discovered in Ireland, seeming to confirm central Europe as the source of migration. The curvilinear style of decoration is immortalized in such cultural icons as the glorious illuminated Irish manuscript, the Book of Kells (Trinity College Library, Dublin), and the bronze Battersea shield (British Museum), evoking the British Isles as a small surviving remnant of past Celtic glory.

This view of grand Iron Age Celtic origins in the centre of the Continent and progressive westward shrinkage since Roman times is still held by some archaeologists. It is also the basis of strong perceptions of ethnic identity held by millions of the so-called *Celtic diaspora*. The problem seems to be that the homeland is wrong in time, place, genes and language, largely as a result of a too-literal 19th-century interpretation of Herodotus' poor knowledge of the course of the Danube.

If it were not a sincerely held conviction, the Iron Age, central European Celtic homeland story could be regarded as a hoax. There is no clear direct evidence, linguistic, archaeological or genetic (e.g. Oppenheimer 2007; McEvoy et al. 2004), which identifies the Hallstatt or La Tène regions and cultures as Celtic-linguistic homelands. The cultural spreads from Hallstatt and La Tène are not in doubt but could just as easily have been initially associated with another language group such as Germanic (or pre-Germanic if the date is regarded as too early by linguists), or with a range of other factors. There is a lack of adequate epigraphic, place-name or personal-name evidence east of the Rhine or north of the Danube (Sims-Williams 2006; Raybould & Sims-Williams 2007; Oppenheimer 2007) to underwrite the central European Celtic linguistic homeland theory, even if it were based on more than Herodotus' mistake.

The hypothesis of a substantial Iron Age immigration to the British Isles from central Europe has been genetically tested and found wanting; instead, a genetic influence on eastern England from the north-west of the Low Countries has been related not to Iron Age 'Celtic' nor Anglo-Saxon invasions but mainly to the Neolithic period or earlier

(McEvoy et al. 2004; Oppenheimer 2007).

Examination of the literature of the past 150 years reveals the perceived Celtic association with central Europe as based on a mistake made by the historian Herodotus nearly 2,500 years ago. In a passing remark about the Keltoi, he placed them at the source of the Danube, apparently, in his view, somewhere near the Pyrenees (Herodotus, *Histories* 2.34). Aristotle made an identical mistake (in *Meteorologica* 1.13.). Everything else about Herodotus' description located the Keltoi in the region of Iberia, in which case he was just misinformed about the source of the Danube, which of course rises in central Europe, not in the Pyrenees.

The Celtosceptic view, deriving in no small part from the long-term results of misinterpreting Herodotus, is that the term 'Celt', used by Romans and Greeks for a thousand years, is now so hopelessly corrupted in the archaeological and popular literature that it is worthless for modern use.

It is a mistake to dismiss Celts like this, since it flushes out a more likely Celtic prehistory and all the valid information from the classical historians with the bathwater of debunked modern myths. Only the central European homeland theory is unsupported, not the association of groups called Celts with the Celtic languages.

Many Celtic homelands

Putting the central European Celtic homeland hypothesis to the side as unsupported by evidence, there is still a huge area of south-west Europe with strong epigraphic, textual and place-name evidence for Celtic (Sims-Williams 2006; Raybould & Sims-Williams 2007), in several cases reaching as far back as the mid-first millennium BC or even earlier. This area includes the British Isles, Middle Gaul, Narbonne, Cisalpine Gaul, and the western 2/3 of Iberia and encompasses all the known branches of Celtic languages (Figure 6.1). Note that on the evidence of language distribution, the British Isles have to be included initially as putative linguistic homelands, although the classical texts only specify two homelands for the Celtae/Keltoi, respectively Narbonne and south-west Iberia. Furthermore, the issue of whether the two insular branches of Celtic, Brythonic and Goidelic, diverged after or before arrival in the British Isles, would affect the number and route of migrations and equally the approach to genetic hypothesis testing.

What additional information from non-genetic disciplines can be used to focus on a smaller area or areas to test? If there is any correlation between Celtic languages and movement of so-called Celts (and there may have been little demic movement or correlation with language), historical linguists using the comparative method should ideally be able to construct geographic hypotheses including putative homelands. However, there may be controversy even here. For instance, Schmidt's phylogeny (1988) reconstructs a deep split between P-Celtic—which includes Brythonic, Gaulish and Lepontic—on one branch, and a cladistically earlier Q-Celtic—which includes Gaelic and Iberian Celtic—on the other. This schema is consistent with the Iberian origins of the pre-Christian Irish, at a date corresponding to the Bronze Age in the present-day scheme, suggested long ago in the much-ridiculed *Lebar Gabála Érenn* (the 11th-century Irish 'Book of Invasions'). Brythonic and Goidelic are on opposite sides of Schmidt's Celtic tree, and the Continental Celtic languages are scattered in between.

In contrast to this, McCone's tree (1996), which may be based on more areal features, has Gaulish, Celtiberian and an Insular Celtic branch all arising directly from a Proto-Celtic root, as single branches on a garden-rake. At the risk of making an uninformed judgement on this disagreement, the Schmidt tree, being ostensibly based more on regular sound changes, rather than as features that might be explained as areal effects, should be most appropriate for identifying a homeland for the whole Celtic branch. Structurally at least, it is the only one that offers possible separate migration routes, with Goidelic and Celtiberian sharing relict status defined by conservatism and Brythonic linked to Gaulish much further down the phylogeny by shared innovation.

Given the near-root position of Celtiberian on Schmidt's tree, and the existence (based on texts, epigraphy and/or place-names) of other putatively Celtic-speaking tribal groups in Iberia (Gallaeci, Celtici and possibly the Lusitani) it might be worth focusing genetically on an even more specific region of Iberia as a potential early Celtic source region.

Portugal: Herodotus is almost the earliest classical source on Celts and, apart from the controversial reference to 'Pyrene' (possibly Portus Pyrene, as an alternative ancient name for Emporion, now Ampurias), gives a further two specific Iberian locators, that 'the Keltoi are outside the Pillars of Heracles', i.e. beyond Gibraltar—presumably on the Atlantic coast of Iberia—'and border upon the Kynesians (Κυνησιοι), who dwell furthest towards the sunset of all those who have their dwelling in Europe'. The Kynesians (referred to in other writings, including elsewhere by Herodotus, as the Kynetes (Κυνητες), another variant being *Conii*) lived at the westernmost point of Europe, in south-west Iberia. This third locator fits with other authors' statements that the Kynetes were neighbours of Tartessus, i.e. north-west of Gibraltar in the Gulf of Cádiz and in the region of the modern port of Huelva (Rankin 1996, 7).

Herodotus' 5th-century text is also consistent with John Koch's linguistic analysis of Tartessian epigraphy as Celtic (Koch, this volume), from inscriptions in modified Semitic script carved in the first half of the 1st millennium BC, that predate the oldest Lepontic 'by a century or two'. Koch notes 'the Gaulish (and Goidelic and British) affinities of Tartessian contrast with the conservative and relatively isolated character of Celtiberian'. This observation, if confirmed by linguistic consensus, strengthens western Iberia as a potential linguistic source of Insular Celtic and thus as a source for a putative Celtic-speaking demic movement towards the British Isles, although it does not exclude a separate origin of Brythonic from Gaulish.

The geographic implications of Tartessian are also consistent with Cunliffe's suggestion (2004, 296) of 'Atlantic Celtic' as a lingua franca stretched along the Atlantic seaways from Portugal to Britain by the middle of the 1st millennium BC. However,

Cunliffe (2004; and Oppenheimer 2007) goes further back in time than the late Bronze Age, when suggesting the start of this language chain and the associated Atlantic trade network.

Cunliffe (2004, 296–7, and this volume) suggests the network may have commenced as far back as the 3rd millennium BC when metals became a significant item of exchange. In connection with this trade network, Cunliffe also promotes the concept of the origin of Maritime Bell Beakers in the Tagus region of Portugal in the early 3rd millennium (and their extensive mobility), preceded in the late 4th millennium by the exploitation of copper in that region (2004, 222–8). By the time copper-exploitation reached southern Ireland in the middle of the 3rd millennium BC, it was associated with beakers.

Now the Chalcolithic is a lot earlier than most linguists would accept for the dispersal of Celtic languages and much earlier than their earliest epigraphy, even if a Celtic Tartessian is accepted at *c.* 700 BC. But many historical linguists/Celticists would not accept pre-epigraphic dates for Celtic language as meaningful anyway (i.e. 'If it is not written in stone . . . &c.'). So, that objection can only be justified on that basis and cannot exclude earlier dates.

From the point of view of identifying a putative Celtic source region for genetic phylogeography, however, this gap of 1700 years between the arrival of beakers and copper miners in Ireland by 2400 BC (Cunliffe 2004, 225) and the earliest Celtic epigraphy at Tartessos poses an equal gap of credibility to extrapolate Celtic back into the Chalcolithic. For links between language, genetics, and archaeology to be valid in the absence of epigraphy, dates for each prehistoric proxy have to be obtained independently to avoid circularity of argument (Oppenheimer 2004); furthermore, most linguists reject dates of language splits based on lexical evidence, which would be the only other way at present to extrapolate linguistic dates prior to epigraphy.

Dividing up the genetic cake in time slices; or who were British and Irish aboriginals?
There is an alternative cruder but more robust way of looking at Insular Celtic and the Neolithic that covers this gap of extrapolation. In spite of differences of opinion about homeland and the dates of arrival of 'Celts', 'Celtic' culture, and/or Celtic languages in the British Isles (ranging from Neolithic to Iron Age), virtually no linguist or archaeologist argues that Celts came *before* the first farmers. And yet several researchers, working mainly from uniparental genetic markers, suggest that the bulk of ancestors for modern Britain and Ireland *did* arrive before the first farmers and came from the region of northern Iberia (Watkin 1966; Hill et al. 2000; Wilson et al. 2001; McEvoy et al. 2004; Oppenheimer 2006/7; Sykes 2006). If these are valid conclusions, then 'Celts' could not be regarded as aboriginals, nor then could they, reliably, be genetically identified as the bulk of those present today in the western fringes of the British Isles.

So leading from this perspective, if relative contributions of the pre-Neolithic, Neolithic, Bronze Age, and Iron Age to the modern gene pool of Britain and Ireland can be identified, estimated and put to one side, then specific European migrations to

Britain and Ireland stretching from Neolithic to Iron Ages should be identifiable; and it should be possible to determine whether they derive from the Atlantic Façade or elsewhere. Failing that, this process should provide, at the least, a maximum estimate of contribution from Celtic-speaking regions to the insular gene pool and answer the initial questions: 1) Were the Celts the British aboriginals? 2) Did the Anglo-Saxons commit a genocide of the Celts who were supposed to have completely occupied England, leaving a Celtic fringe to the west?

There are a number of additional advantages of, initially, just asking when did people arrive in the British Isles and where did they come from, and individually what proportion did each in-migrating or invading ancestral group contribute to our modern gene pool? There is no presupposition of what language each incoming group spoke, nor when Celtic languages or 'Celts' arrived in the British Isles, nor what the classical authors meant by 'Celts' or any genetic definitions of Celts.

Did the 'Celts' arrive before, with, or after the first farmers, and what are the connections with Iberia?

Texts
One of the earliest suggestions of an Iberian connection with the western British Isles was perhaps Tacitus who, when referring to the Silures, inhabitants of what is now south Wales, whom he called 'a naturally fierce people', stated: 'The dark complexion of the Silures, their usually curly hair, and the fact that Spain is the opposite shore to them, are an evidence that Iberians of a former date crossed over and occupied these parts' (Tacitus, *Agricola* 11).

The collector of mythological love stories, Parthenius of Apamea (1st century BC) gave a version of the popular legend of the origins of the Celts in his *Erotica pathemata*, which preserves the Spanish connection and even hints at Ireland. Heracles was wandering through Celtic territory on his return from a labour—obtaining cattle from Geryon of Erytheia (probably Cádiz). He came before a king named Bretannos (Βρεταννός). The king had a daughter, Keltine (Κελτίνη), who hid Heracles' cattle. She insisted on sex in return for the cattle. Heracles, complied. The issue of this union was a boy and a girl. The boy, Keltos (Κελτός), was ancestor of the Celts; the girl was Iberos (Ιβηρός), presumably linking Britain and Celts to Iberia. Rankin speculates further that the homophony between 'Iberos/Iberia' and the Irish mythical ancestor, Éber, may be more than coincidence (Rankin 1996, 81, 166). A similar claim of Iberian roots for the Irish was made in the *Lebar Gabála Érenn*, as already mentioned.

Such connections also persist (or recur) in modern popular culture and literature, as we see when Evelyn Waugh has one of his characters alluding to such things in the novel *Decline and Fall* (1928) long before geneticists tried to get to grips with the issue: Dr Fagan, the proprietor of Llanabba School, makes some offensive remarks about the Welsh on meeting the hapless new teacher Paul Pennyfeather, including the statement

'The ignorant speak of them as Celts, which is of course wholly erroneous. They are of pure Iberian stock—the aboriginal inhabitants of Europe, who survive only in Portugal and the Basque district'.

Genetics

The legendary aboriginal theme persisted when first put under the scrutiny of genetic evidence. Working with blood groups. Mourant and Watkin argued in 1952 that: 'There appear to us reasonable grounds for the belief that, prior to the advent of Celtic-speaking immigrants, the British Isles were inhabited by a people whose domain had at one time extended over a considerable part of Europe and North Africa but who under ever increasing pressure from the east had been driven from their homelands. Some, no doubt, found refuge in the more isolated mountain regions, but the remainder were gradually driven westwards and finally came to occupy a limited area near the Atlantic seaboard of Europe.'

Morgan Watkin, however, later (1966) softened this migrationist-replacement view of Celts as secondary invaders to one implying language shift as a greater factor: 'One wonders, therefore, whether a large part of Britain's very early population did not arrive by the western sea routes and whether Celtic speech was acquired from later invaders . . .'

The synthetic Principal Component Analysis (PCA) maps of Cavalli-Sforza and colleagues (1994) show Irish and Basque populations falling very near one another on the first principal component axis at the end of a cline from the Near East. This suggested the possibility of a Basque–Celtic connection. Wilson and colleagues (2001) interpreted Cavalli-Sforza's PCA result as also reflecting a relatively small Neolithic component in these two populations.

Hill and colleagues (2000) noted a similar gradient of Y chromosome haplogroup 1 with the lowest rates in the Near East and highest rates in western Europe, in particular the Basque country, with haplogroup 1 rising to near fixation (98.3%) in Gaelic-surnamed men of Connacht in western Ireland. This was interpreted as haplogroup 1 (in this instance largely composed of the more recently characterized haplogroup 'R1b' (Y chromosome consortium (YCC), 2002 or 'YCC 2002') putatively characteristic of pre-Neolithic western Europe, and also identifying the earlier, indigenous Irish. It should be noted here that as more mutations characterizing further Y chromosome subgroups are rapidly discovered, the YCC nomenclature has changed progressively and this can be confusing. So, for instance, R1b (YCC 2008) effectively became R1b1 in the YCC 2008 (Karafet et al. 2008). However, since most of the data discussed here was collected, characterized and published before 2008, the simpler 2002 nomenclature will be used here where possible, including older (e.g. haplogroup 1) with newer equivalents indicated where necessary, or just the relevant mutational marker (e.g. -M12 or -V13).

Wilson and colleagues took these comparisons further (2001) by comparing specific STR haplotypes of haplogroup 1 between the Basque countries on the one hand and Orkney, Wales, Ireland and several north-west European populations on the other. They

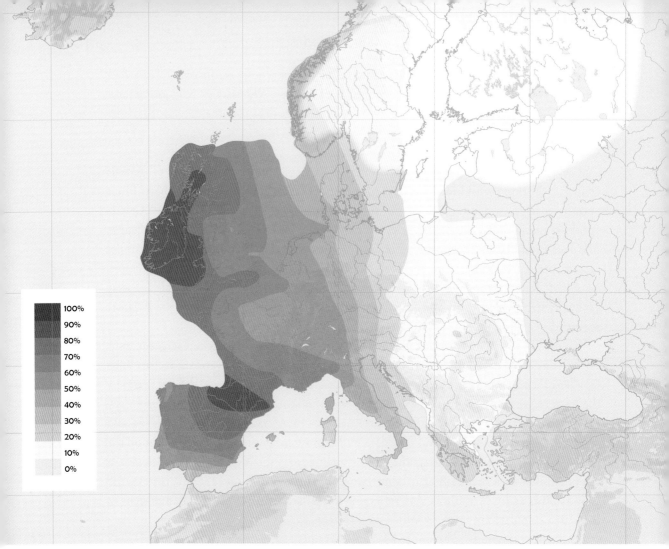

Figure 6.2. Frequency distribution of genetic haplogroup R1b. This map shows the impact of pre-Neolithic male re-expansions from the south-west European refuge in northern Iberia; R1b represents nearly the entire source gene pool from there. The densest gene flow follows the Atlantic façade, thus favouring Ireland, which was then part of the Continent. Since R1b also covers later periods, contours are shown in Scandinavia beyond the ice line (figure from Oppenheimer 2006/7).

found no significant differences on this basis between Basques, Welsh and Irish and argued that such Basque-Celtic '. . . similarity not only implies that Basque- and Celtic-speaking populations derive from common paternal ancestors, but that genetic drift in these communities has not been sufficiently great to differentiate them'. Note that Wilson et al. correctly qualify 'Celt' to Celtic-speaking. They also studied mtDNA and X chromosome and conclude overall as follows: 'Accepting the widely held view that the Basques are representative of pre-Neolithic European Y chromosomes, we have also shown that Neolithic, Iron Age, and subsequent cultural revolutions had little effect on the paternal genetic landscape of the Celtic-speaking populations (there has been continuity from the Upper Palaeolithic to the present).'

McEvoy and colleagues (2004) extended the Wilson Y chromosome PCA analysis to include the dataset of Rosser et al. (2000) using, instead, multidimensional scaling (MDS) showing, on a contour map of the first dimension, that Cornwall and western Britain, in general, additionally shared the close relationship with Basques. They attributed this relationship to expansion from an archaeologically identified glacial refuge in northern Iberia. In fact, this genetic distance pattern is already apparent in Rosser's original PCA 2D-dotplot of the first and second principal components (Rosser et al. 2000, fig. 5A), where a triangle is formed from which the three apices of the dotplot can be inferred to represent geographic sources of genetic re-expansions respectively from three putative glacial refuges (northern Iberia, Ukraine and the western Balkans with the Basque apex characterized by high haplogroup 1 frequencies—illustrated in Oppenheimer 2006/7, fig. 11.4a).

In addition to their Y chromosome analysis, McEvoy and colleagues (2004) reanalysed mitochondrial DNA (mtDNA: equivalent to the Y chromosome in non-recombining properties but maternally inherited instead) in Europe again using MDS. Lacking much of the geographic specificity of the Y chromosome, mtDNA was previously less informative due to lack of sufficient data, but is nonetheless important if the Y chromosome inferences are to be validated. Up to that point, the only clear mtDNA support for a northern Iberian 'refuge' influence on western Europe came from the phylogeography of the minor 'V' haplogroup (Torroni et al. 1998, 2001). Evidence that the major European mtDNA haplogroup H, to a certain extent, mirrored the known western European distribution of Y haplogroup 1/R1b, was first suggested on frequency evidence by Richards et al. (2002; see also figs. 3.4 & 3.5 Oppenheimer 2006/7). This was later put on a more phylogeographic footing with Late Glacial/Post Glacial expansion estimates (Achilli et al. 2004; Pereira et al. 2005; see below). McEvoy et al. (2004) also reanalysed and mapped Cavalli-Sforza's classical autosomal markers in more detail to show a similar Basque–Irish geographic pattern in the second dimension.

Capelli and colleagues (2003) made the largest systematic cluster sample survey of Y chromosomes in the British Isles to that date, using a slightly larger set of single nucleotide polymorphisms (SNPs, which are unique bi-allelic mutational markers and are stable and unambiguous compared with STRs) than Wilson et al. (2001), but using the same set of six single tandem repeat markers (STRs with much more random mutational detail but much less stability and specificity than SNPs). Unsurprisingly, their findings for the Basque Country, Ireland, and western Britain confirmed the previous Atlantic Façade pattern, albeit in much more detail, of extremely high rates of haplogroup 1 (R1xR1a1 in their analysis (effectively equivalent to R1b (YCC 2002) in this context). However, their a priori analytic assumptions, leading to the interpretation of this finding, need careful attention and review:

> To represent the indigenous population of the British Isles, we selected a site in central
> Ireland that has had no known history of contact with Anglo-Saxon or Viking invaders
> (Castlerea)... Given the demonstrated similarity of Celtic and Basque Y chromosomes
> (... using haplogroups), these sample sets provide[d] a representation of the Y
> chromosomes of the indigenous population of the British Isles. (Capelli et al. 2003)

In this choice of words, Capelli et al. appear to conflate 'Celts' and 'indigenes', in spite
of being aware (not the least from several co-authors shared with the Wilson et al. 2001
paper) that this aboriginal role could imply by default that Celts were the first settlers
in Britain and Ireland and had brought their language and themselves from the Basque
Country as a post-glacial, pre-Neolithic re-expansion. But in fact nothing is known of
the language of the first settlers apart from Venneman's Vasconic theory (2003), which
argues that the first language of post-glacial Western Europe was similar to Basque.

Giving an impression that Celts were aboriginal to the isles was almost certainly not
Capelli's or his colleagues' intention, since the foregoing reasons for Irish and British
similarity to Basques are explicit in their introduction and discussion but their focus
may have been influenced by a paper the year before, with again some shared authorship
(Weale et al. 2002), that attempted to prove that all 'Celts' had been wiped out in
England by the Anglo-Saxon invasion of the 5th century AD leaving the traditional
'Celtic fringe' in the west. The Weale paper has since been critiqued on method and
assumptions (reviewed in Oppenheimer 2006/7).

Given their 'Celtic indigenous' vs Anglo-Saxon plus Viking paradigm, Capelli and
colleagues (2003) estimated admixture due to the latter two groups. In England overall
this was 37%, rising to peaks of 70% in Norfolk and York, in other words a sizeable
but much lower Anglo-Saxon replacement than Weale's estimate of 50%–100%. They
acknowledge that, contra Weale, this would mean there is a '... clear indication of a
continuing indigenous component in the English paternal genetic makeup. Whether
the 37% continental "introgression" into England was the result of Anglo-Saxon and
Viking invasions as they claim is another matter since, in their analysis, they ignore any
possibility of previous post-founding gene flow across the Channel and North Sea from
the nearby continent, for instance during the Neolithic, Bronze and Iron Ages'.

A major problem with all such studies of Britain and Ireland up to 2004/5 was the
lack of any reliable, genetically based date estimates of the postulated recolonization
events. For statistical approaches such as PCA and MDS, this was inherent in the
methods, which packaged and conflated multiple haplogroups of different ages, thus
producing undatable palimpsests of gene flow and furthermore discarding the enormous
phylogenetic information available from the characterization. Estimates of dates of
expansion had been attempted both for Y and mtDNA lineages, but without formal
phylogeographic founder analysis, specific dated movements could not be detected.

Genetic dating and founder analysis

Richards and colleagues' major European founder analysis (2000) estimated dates and sizes of mtDNA founding events in Europe arriving from the Near East since the earliest Upper Palaeolithic. When partitioned by region, north-west Europe had its largest tranche of founding events between the LGM and the start of the Neolithic (52.7% +/− 4.5, divided between Late Upper Palaeolithic and Mesolithic), with the Neolithic accounting for 21.7% (+/− 4.5) and Bronze Age and later only 4.6% (+/− 1.5). However, because of sampling and methodological issues, nothing could be inferred specifically at the scale of Britain and Ireland, although a relevant point noted was that 'the Basque Country has the lowest [Neolithic] value of all, only 7%'. Indeed, no founder analysis has yet been published for these isles in a peer-reviewed journal.

'Origins of the British' project: an overview

With the lack of phylogeographic analysis and dating of the available Y chromosome and mtDNA data from Britain, Ireland and their putative source regions on the mainland, I decided in 2004 to combine and reanalyse the entire Y chromosome cluster data provided by Hill (2000), Wilson (2001), Weale (2002), Capelli (2003) and others in Ireland, Britain, Iberia and north-west Europe, using both summary statistical methods and founder analysis, and also to review the available mtDNA data and publications (Oppenheimer 2006/7).

Inherent in the former aim there were potential methodological problems: 1) a sample base of 3084 individuals with 31 British and Irish clusters and 14 putative European source regions might be regarded as insufficient; 2) At that time only 6 STR loci were available for all participants, which with the known instability of STRs could result in ambiguities of phylogeny; 3) The calibration of STR mutation rate is controversial.

In spite of these potential drawbacks: 1) I felt that increasing sampling was an impossible council of perfection, since there was no other similar systematically sampled database at that time; 2) The number of STR loci, although small compared to what is available today, was the standard for the dates of collection and had the advantage of being comparable across all relevant source datasets; 3) As validation, the STR calibration method used (Forster et al. 2000) consistently and appropriately dated the root of each relevant major haplogroup in the combined dataset to the Last Glacial Maximum (LGM). The caveats were also stated in the methods, added to the fact that this was intended as a preliminary analysis pending a better dataset and more secure dating methods.

Methods and results are published in detail elsewhere (Oppenheimer 2006/7), so only relevant highlights of the Y chromosome analysis are given here. Chronological partitioning of founding clusters was based on mean cluster age within the British Isles. Overall haplogroup age largely agreed with existing literature estimates. There were a number of findings, the relevant ones of which are summarized here under pre-Neolithic and Neolithic headings:

Pre-Neolithic

Nearly three quarters (73%) overall of British and Irish ancestors arrived before the first farmers. This proportion increased progressively in western Britain and Ireland: 88% of Irish, 81% of Welsh, 79% of Cornish, 70% of the people of Scotland and its associated islands and 68% (over two-thirds) of the English and their geographically associated islands. Nearly all of the founding clusters dating to the pre-Neolithic belonged, as expected, to haplogroup 1 (RxR1a1 i.e. R1b in this context (YCC 2002, confirmed on STR, Athey 2006; see Figure 6.2 this paper). The remaining four per cent was mainly contributed by haplogroup I1c (Late Glacial according to Rootsi et al. (2004); I2b in YCC 2008), and I1b2 (now I2a2 in YCC 2008). The I1b2 subclade is included in this section on the basis of Late Mesolithic estimated age in the British Isles, but is dealt with further below, since its overall European age on a larger dataset is younger (Rootsi et al. 2004), and archaeological and geographic contexts strongly suggest early Neolithic).

Using STR markers to create a phylogeny, the R1b haplotypes were broken up into 13 putative founding clusters deriving ancestry from northern Iberia. Six of these founding clusters arrived in what is now the British Isles during the Late Upper Palaeolithic prior to the Younger Dryas cold episode (assuming that lasted between 13,000–11,500 years ago), and impinged mainly on Cornwall, Ireland, Wales and Scotland, which then formed the west coast of Europe. The other seven clusters arrived during the British Mesolithic (between 11,500 BP–7,500 BP). There is some phylogenetic uncertainty for estimating the age of the main R1b sub-cluster characterizing Ireland, which is assigned here to the Late Upper Palaeolithic, but it could have arrived during the early Mesolithic. Much of the subsequent diversity of these clusters derives from local re-expansions occurring during the Late Mesolithic and in the Neolithic.

The Y chromosome pre-Neolithic colonization pattern was mirrored in size, age, and geography by inferred expansions of mtDNA haplogroups H and V out of northern Iberia (figs. 3.4 and 3.5 in Oppenheimer 2006/7), H subgroup 1 and V expanding pre-Younger Dryas and H subgroups 2, 3, 4, and 5a during the Mesolithic (Achilli et al. 2004; Pereira et al. 2005).

Neolithic

Taking the archaeological evidence for the British and Irish Neolithic to span 4500 BC to 2000 BC (Cunliffe 2004), over a dozen putative Y-founding clusters were identified as intrusive (i.e. excluding re-expansions of pre-existing lineages) over that period. These belonged to four major Y-haplogroups: R1a1, I, J and E3b (E1b1b1 in YCC 2008). Other minor paragroups in the British database most likely associated with the Neolithic included paragroups FxIJK and KxPN3, which are not discussed further here, due to dating problems, although FxIJK tends to follow the same distribution as J2, while KxPN3 follows that of E3b in these datasets.

The two haplogroups, J and E3b, are fairly well recognized in the literature as

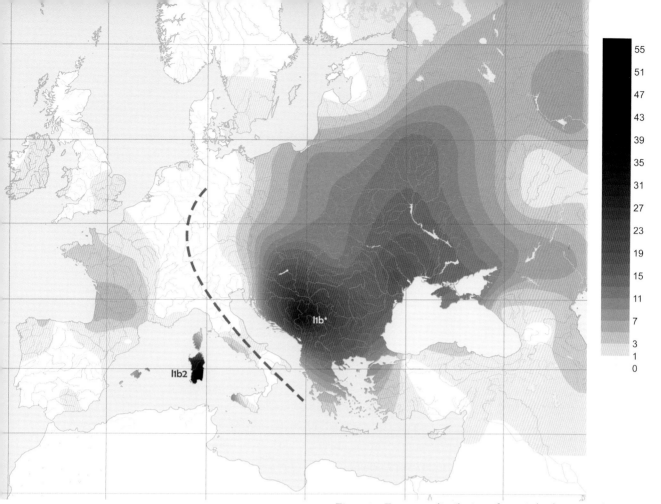

Figure 6.3. Frequency distribution of genetic haplogroups I1b2
(- M26) and I1b* (- P37.2). Frequencies are combined, but to the
east of the dashed line only I1b* is found, while to the west I1b2
predominates. Only I1b2 is found in Sardinia, with high haplotype
diversity and frequencies overall over 40% (Rootsi et al. 2004) rising
to 55.6% in Monte Ferru. I1b* coexists with I1b2 over the rest of the
latter's western distribution, but at lower frequencies. This places the
homeland of the I1b haplogroup to the east of the line, likely in the
Balkans (Rootsi et al. 2004), with spread westwards predominantly
of the derived haplogroup I1b2 [Frequency data from Rootsi et al.
2004, Scozzari et al. 2001 & Oppenheimer 2006/7].

moving westwards from the eastern Mediterranean/Near Eastern region via the north
Mediterranean coast during the Neolithic and later (Scozzari et al. 2001; Richards 2003;
Semino et al. 2004; Di Giacomo et al. 2004; Cruciani et al. 2004; 2007), with subgroups of both haplogroups expanding again and spreading westwards from the Balkans
in the Northern Mediterranean in the Early Bronze Age (Cruciani et al. 2007). These
are discussed in detail below after dealing with haplogroups R1a1 and 'I', which have a
less well-known Neolithic role in the west.

In north-west Europe, Y-haplogroup R1a1 characterizes mainly Scandinavia and north-west Germany, and its sparse presence in Britain, derived from those regions, has been presumed to signal Viking invasions, as supported by its coastal and island distribution (without supporting founder dates: Weale et al. 2002; Capelli et al. 2003). In my analysis, however, four of five R1a1 British founder clusters are dated to the Bronze Age (two) and earlier (three), with only one relating clearly to the Viking invasions (Chapter 12, Oppenheimer 2006/7). Having no relevance to the Celtic question they are not discussed further here.

Haplogroup I is not normally included in the literature as a candidate for European Neolithic gene flow (Richards 2003, but see Rootsi et al. 2004), probably because it originates within Europe rather than the Near East, the latter region tending to be more perceived as associated with Neolithic expansions. However, not all of the Neolithic gene flow need have come from outside Europe, since there was a thriving Neolithic in the Balkans prior to its spread up the Danube with Linearbandkeramik (Gronenborn 2003), and the Balkans have the highest frequencies and diversity of haplogroup I subgroups (Rootsi et al. 2004). In my analysis, subgroups of haplogroup I account for a considerable amount of westward gene flow during the Neolithic and less so in Late Mesolithic. I1a (I1 in YCC 2008) is a good candidate for association with the LBK movement up the Danube with ages of STR variation of 8,800 years ago (+/–3,200) overall in Europe (Rootsi et al. 2004, table 3), with later movement into Eastern Britain shown by five founding cluster events dating from 4,000–7,000 years ago (Oppenheimer 2006/7). The latter make up a larger proportion of the Neolithic input than R1a1, mainly to eastern Britain from north-west Europe and Scandinavia.

I1b2 (defined by M26 & P37.2) and I1b* (defined by P37.2) are also good candidates for Neolithic spread from the Balkans ultimately as far as Ireland, but by a completely different route, west via the northern Mediterranean and across southern France to the Atlantic coast. They are now classified as I2a2 and I2a* respectively in YCC 2008, but for consistency with the literature sources cited in this review, the old nomenclature is used here. They are the only putative Mediterranean Neolithic lineages to be found in Ireland, also being found in south Wales, Wessex, and the Channel Islands (Figure 6.3). Both subgroups date, by STR analysis, overall in Europe to the early Neolithic (I1b*: 7,600 yr +/– 2,700; I1b2: 8,000 +/– 4,000 Rootsi et al. 2004), but I1b* concentrates at high rates of 20–40% (40% in Bosnia) in a presumed I1b homeland in the Balkans (Rootsi et al. 2004). I1b* spreads at high rates extensively further east in Europe, but is also found scattered west of the Balkans at much lower rates of 1–2% in Western Europe, including Italy, Portugal (Rootsi et al. 2004), Catalonia and 2%–5% Ireland and western Britain (Figure 6.3; see also Oppenheimer 2006/7 chapter 5).

There is thus a sharp divide between the relative frequency distributions of I1b2 and the paragroup I1b*, running down the Italian Peninsula (dotted line in Figure 6.3). I1b2 although derived from the I1b root is absent east of Italy, i.e. from the Balkans and Eastern Europe, only being found in Italy and westwards, in particular in Sardinia

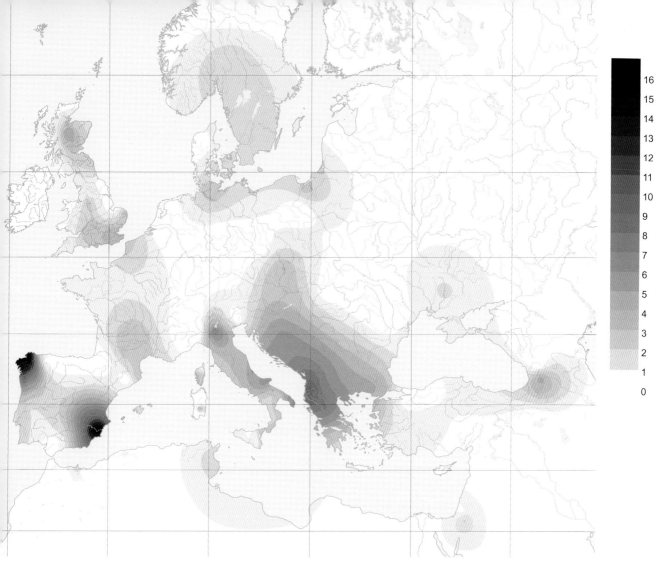

Figure 6.4. Frequency distribution of genetic haplogroup J2-M12
in Europe showing, according to Cruciani et al. 2007, a specific
European expansion event from the Balkans (epicentre Albania)
during the early Balkans Bronze Age. [Frequency data from
Cruciani et al 2007; Di Giacomo et al. 2004; Semino et al. 2004;
Scozzari et al. 2001 & Oppenheimer 2006/7. British M-12 status in
Scotland and southern England inferred from STR haplotypes]

where a frequency of 41% and a high diversity of STR haplotypes suggests an ancient
colonization event there up to 8,000 years ago (Rootsi et al. 2004; Scozzari et al. 2001).
Further west, the I1b2 frequency follows that of I1b* in Portugal, but relatively high
rates of I1b2 (6–8%) are found in the Basque Country and Bearnais in southern France
(Rootsi et al. 2004) in addition to appreciable rates of 2–3% in Ireland, Wessex, and the
Channel Islands (Figure 6.3 and see Oppenheimer 2006/7, chapter 5).

I1b2 dates as a whole in western Europe to around 8,000 years ago in the early Neolithic (Rootsi et al. 2004) with a similar founding date within the British Isles of 8,600 years (+/− 4,270 Oppenheimer 2006/7, chapter 5). I1b* has a slightly younger overall STR age (7,600 yr +/− 2,700, Rootsi et al. 2004). The only chronologically and geographically parallel archaeological signal for these ages of I1b & I1b2 is the dated spread of Cardial ware with pastoralism in the north-west Mediterranean. The distribution of these lineages and of Cardial ware further north implies a bypass of southern Spain en route to the Atlantic coast via the Aude-Garonne overland route. Such genetic dates have large errors and spread into Britain and Ireland during the later Neolithic is an alternate possibility. At any rate, I1b* and I1b2 (and KxPN3) are the only putative Mediterranean-route Neolithic migrants to reach Ireland (Figure 6.3).

The Y-haplogroup J has been argued to be a marker for the movement of Neolithic farmers into Europe (largely as J2) from the Near East, spreading a dense swathe across the northern Mediterranean from the Levant through Greece, the Balkans and Albania, and Italy, where J2 accounts for up to 30% of Y-lineages, to Iberia (Richards 2003, Semino et al. 2004 and see fig. 5.8b in Oppenheimer 2006/7). However, when a specific SNP-defined subclade of J2 originating in Albania in the Balkans was more closely examined by Cruciani and colleagues (2007), this general East–West pattern of Neolithic movement in the northern Mediterranean appears to show a secondary expansion west in a more focused way in the Early Bronze Age (Age of expansion of J2e-M12: 4.1ky (95% CI 2.8–5.4 kyr) and 4.7kyr (95% CI 3.3–6.4 kyr using two different methods). Cruciani and colleagues (2007) use this finding as evidence 'of a recent population growth in situ [i.e. from the Balkans] rather than the result of a mere flow of western Asian migrants in the early Neolithic.' In other words J2e–M12 (J2b in YCC 2008) expanded locally from the Balkans to Italy, France, and Iberia in south-western Europe during the Early Bronze Age (see also Di Giacomo et al. 2004, and data in Semino et al. 2004, Scozzari et al. 2001). This Late Chalcolithic/Bronze Age expansion scenario could even be consistent with the anomalous finding of significant frequencies (1%–8%) of J2e–M12 among Indic (Indo-European) speaking populations of south Asia (table 2, Semino et al. 2004).

In the British dataset I examined, nearly all of J belonged to the J2 subgroup; further, all the STR marker profiles of J2 were most consistent with the J2e–M12 subgroup (as inferred using both STR table 3 of SOM in Cruciani et al. 2007 and Appendix table in Di Giacomo et al. 2004), thus implying a Balkan Bronze Age source for much of J2 in Britain. J2 is found throughout Britain mainly concentrating in southern England and in central Scotland in a formerly Pictish region. In both regions it is present at rates from 2% up to 7%. It is absent from Ireland and large islands clustered near Britain such as the Isle of Man, Orkney, Shetland, and the Western Isles (Figure 6.4).

Y-haplogroup E3b accounts for a substantial proportion (10%–30%) of males in Balkans populations. This proportion is highest (32%) in the case of Albania (Cruciani et al. 2004, 2007) and is entirely made up there by the subclade E3b1 (E1b1b1 in YCC

2008 nomenclature, Karafet et al. 2008), defined by bi-allellic marker M78. Cruciani and colleagues (2007) specifically link the above-mentioned Balkan-Albanian expansion of J-M12 with a simultaneous and co-distributed expansion of an STR-defined sub-cluster of a branch of the E3b1 Y-lineage: namely E-M78α, from the same region during the Bronze Age. However, whereas J–M12 is *not* the predominant European subclade of J2 (Di Giacomo et al. 2004), E–M78, ultimately derived from north-eastern Africa (Cruciani et al. 2007), *is* the predominant European E/E3b lineage, and its derivative STR cluster E-M78α, best defined by a unique SNP 'V13' (V13/ E3b1a2* Cruciani et al. 2006) has been shown to be nearly specific for Europe and the Levant (85% of European E–M78 chromosomes Cruciani et al. 2007). Cruciani et al. have argued (2007) that the E3b–78α–V13 subgroup (E3b1a2*) originates in the Balkans (highest rate of V13: 32.29% in Albania) and dates there by two methods to 4.0–4.7 ky (95% CI 3.5–4.6 kyr and 4.1–5.3 kyr, respectively).

Apart from originating in the Balkans, E3b1a2* (AKA E1b1b1a2 in YCC 2008, Karafet et al. 2008) characterizes north-central Europe, and also most of western Europe such as western Iberia, Denmark, Germany, and France, with the notable exception of Spanish Basques (Cruciani et al. 2007). Although there is no a priori reason why Britain should differ from the rest of north-west Europe in this respect, neither the M78 nor V13 characters have been tested in British E3b haplogroup representatives, except in commercial testing, where they have indeed been found to predominate. E3b/E3b1-M35 STR-haplotypes in the systematic database used here for Britain are, in fact, consistent with the predominant presence of the E3b1a2 subgroup spread in Britain (by inference using DYS19, 391 and 393 patterns from table 1 of SOM Cruciani et al. 2007 and the absence of the DYS392 12-repeat allele (see also Semino et al. 2004; Athey 2006). Figure 6.5 shows the frequency distribution of the E-V13 in Europe and the Levant, including the British Isles as inferred from STR haplotypes.

Y-haplogroup E3b is unique among putative Neolithic/Bronze Age entrants to Britain and Ireland in that it shows a large, clear, focal founding event centred in northern Wales, with a substantial overall rate in the Abergele cluster of 39% (Figure 6.5). The low sample size in Abergele (18) might be questioned, but the diversity of STR-haplotypes is high in Abergele, and the three other nearby clusters in north Wales and England also have relatively high rates of E3b (4.5%–5.6%). The northern Midlands and East Anglia similarly have rates of 3.5%–5% E3b, with slightly lower rates along the south coast, and in northern England, none north of Cumbria and mostly absent in Ireland (Oppenheimer 2006/7). There were four separate founding clusters of E3b in Britain (n=47). It was possible to obtain a reasonable estimate of the age of one of these cluster-founding events: 4,500 years (SE 2,480; n=20; Oppenheimer 2006/7). The other three founding clusters gave similar dates with larger errors (Oppenheimer 2006/7, note 87 on p.235). This age is consistent with the Late Chalcolithic/ Early Bronze Age and with the current oldest radiocarbon date (1700 BC) in the nearby prehistoric copper mine at Great Ormes Head, Llandudno (Lewis 1996). The likely immediate origin of the north

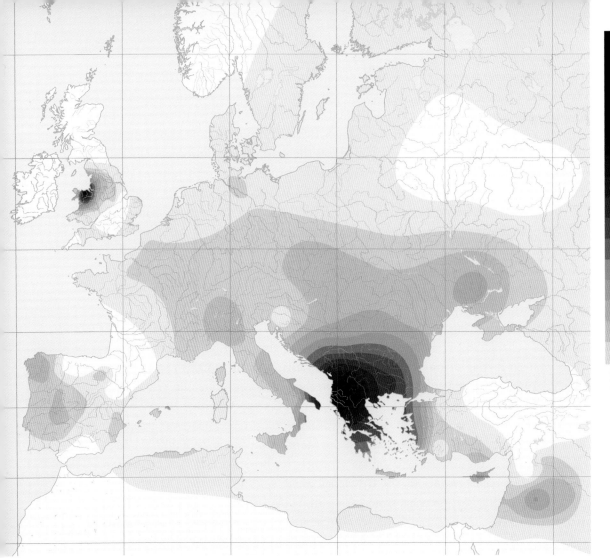

Figure 6.5. Frequency distribution of genetic haplogroup E3b1a2 in Europe showing, according to Cruciani et al. 2007, a specific European expansion event from the Balkans (epicentre Albania) during the early Balkans Bronze Age. [Frequency data from Cruciani et al. 2007; Adams et al. 2008; Di Giacomo et al. 2004; Semino et al. 2004; Scozzari et al. 2001 & Oppenheimer 2006/7.]

Wales founding event from regions such as western Iberia is further supported by a number of matched R1b haplotypes between the Abergele and Galicia cluster samples.

To test this hypothesis by another approach, I have additionally examined the entire western European part of my composite Y-dataset using Principal Component Analysis, which reveals that the Abergele cluster is an extreme outlier from the rest of the British Isles, grouping instead with the coastal Iberian clusters of Galicia and Valencia (Figure 6.6). Galicia and Valencia for their part do not group on this plot with the parts of north-eastern Iberia and south-west France that flank the Pyrenees (e.g. Catalonia and the Basque Country). As mentioned already the 'Basque refuge' region groups best with Ireland, see Figure 6.6). Recent detailed regional work on Y-SNP/STR subgroups in Iberia confirms the separation of the rest of Iberia from north-eastern Iberia (including the formerly Basque-speaking Gascony) and further shows Valencia and Galicia grouping mainly with western Iberian regions such as Portugal, north-west Castile, Asturias, Extremadura and west Andalusia, all with higher rates of E3b1a (E3b–M78) at 4%–8% (Adams et al. 2008).

Figure 6.6. Principal Components (PC) Analysis of Y chromosomes in Western Europe: PC1, largely determined by relative frequencies of R1b & R1a1, with secondary contribution respectively of I1b2 & I1a. PC2, skewed by the outliers Abergele, Galicia and Valencia, and largely determined by relative frequencies of Neolithic/Bronze Age lineages E3b, J & KxPN3. 2-D plot of first and second Principal Components, using 13 haplogroups (R1b, R1a1, *PxR1*, I1a, *I*+I1**, *I1b/I1b** I1b2, *I1c*, E3b, J, *FxIJK*, *N3*, KxPN3. Haplogroups in italics relatively non-contributary to PCA hence not indicated on Figure), [Database as in Oppenheimer 2006/7].

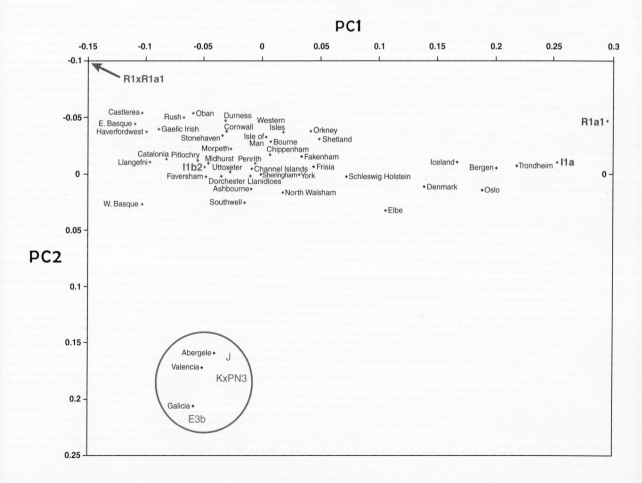

Discussion

The evidence on the age and origins of the British mtDNA and Y chromosome haplogroups, discussed above, leads to the conclusion that pre-Neolithic colonization of Britain and Ireland up the Atlantic coast from the former glacial refuge in northern Iberia contributed by far the bulk of ancestors for pre-1950s populations. This in turn makes for a low likelihood that 'Celts', defined as speakers of Celtic languages and the language that became Celtic, formed a homogeneous indigenous aboriginal population in Britain and Ireland since there is general agreement that they arrived either after or with the first farmers, but not before. Rather, by inference, Celts and their cultures were minority later arrivals whose languages replaced some or all of those spoken by the real indigenes. This perspective puts the identity of western British and Irish genes as representative of Celts on a shaky footing.

Furthermore, the pre-Neolithic Y and mtDNA genetic ancestry of two-thirds of English populations makes the claimed Anglo-Saxon genocide of the indigenous population living in the south-east of Britain a scenario unsupported by genetic evidence and more likely to be due to a small elite invasion. Additionally, the origins of the genetic differences between east and west Britain appear to be more seated in the late prehistoric period than during historic times. In fact, there is little further genetic evidence of significant inward migration after the Bronze Age and during the Iron Age until the modest contributions of the Anglo-Saxons and Vikings (Oppenheimer 2006/7).

Finding genetic evidence for Celtic invasions and homelands still depends to a great extent on testing existing historic, archaeological, and linguistic models for a credible scenario. D'Arbois Jubainville's 19th-century reconstruction of an Iron Age Celtic homeland in central Europe can be seen to have resulted from emphasizing Herodotus' obvious mistake on the source of the Danube, while ignoring his more credible pointers to western Iberia. The former has no credible historic, archaeological, linguistic, or genetic support that does not rely on circular arguments, while the latter coincides with multiple positive lines of linguistic, historic, and archaeological evidence. The main problem is that the same can be said for central and Cisalpine Gaul and Narbonne, thus leaving three to four putative Celtic homelands in south-western Europe.

For each of the three sets of candidate Y-lineages (subgroups of I1b, J2 & E3b1) moving from south-west Europe to Britain and Ireland during the Neolithic and Early Bronze Age, Galicia seems the most likely proximal source, on the multiple lines of evidence discussed above, yet southern France or Liguria are also possible sources. However, such indecision could be resolved, if the ultimate single origin of these genetic expansions is taken as the western Balkans. Curiously, this eastern Mediterranean origin, with an Iberian-staging solution is still consistent with the narrative in the *Lebar Gabála Érenn*.

The possible archaeo-linguistic counterparts of these three *north-western Mediterranean* genetic trails, all arising apparently in the Balkans, have to be highly speculative. The

I1b*/I1b2 trail differs from the other two in having a Bosnian rather than Albanian source focus in the Balkans, being possibly earlier, matching the Cardial Ware distribution and age to a certain extent and ultimately ending up uniquely in Ireland apparently as the only Neolithic founders there. This suggests a discrete early Neolithic event, partially parallel but still distinct in time and space from both J2e–M12 and E3b1a2. However, the standard error on the I1b*/I1b2 dates is very large and the difference may well be illusory.

In contrast, given the phylogeographic evidence and dating of J2–M12 and E3b–78α that dually links an early Bronze Age lineage expansion from the Balkans with western Iberia and Britain, in particular with northern Wales, Pictish Scotland and southern England, one might postulate a common factor or attraction linking this sinuous long-distance migration, rather than the more general theory of Neolithic demic-diffusion. The latter model would have less relevance during the Late Neolithic in any case.

An obvious common factor is copper exploitation and the chronological archaeological evidence of the earlier Balkans Chalcolithic with its postulated influence on the Iberian Chalcolithic (Scarre 1995, 110–11), implying focused migration of specialist copper miners. This would certainly provide an explanation or narrative for the subsequent and final dated E3b1 demic founding event near the Great Ormes Head copper mine.

Other questions remain, as to whether the language spoken by these genetic trailmakers was the same and indeed what language(s) they spoke. Leaving the 'I1b' lineages and Ireland to one side for the moment, would the suggestion for a recent new pioneer language intruding to north Wales and the rest of Britain, particularly the western part, be, by default of other candidates, Celtic? This hypothesis would be consistent with the relatively high frequencies of both J2–M12 and E3b–78α in Galicia. Indeed, excepting Valencia, the mainly western distribution of these two lineages even down to southern Portugal are consistent with Cunliffe's and Koch's hypotheses in this volume. Could these two genetic trails signal the hypothetical spread of Chalcolithic mining experts from the Balkans to Iberia and south-eastern France and thence to the British Isles? If the common single Balkan origin of these two sets of lineages had any linguistic parallels, it could provide a substrate for the uncontentious argument for an ultimately more eastern origin of the Celtic languages (Graham Isaac, this volume) as well as resolving the multiplicity of putative western European Celtic homelands. Such a hypothesis is consistent with the pattern of south-west European distribution of these lineages which coincidentally also covers the three putative Celtic homelands discussed above.

Was there any connection between the simultaneous spreads of J2e–M12 and E3b1–78α with the separate, and the apparently earlier, movement of the I1b Y-lineages from nearby homelands in the Balkans, probably via Italy, Sardinia and France, to Ireland, Wales and south-east England as well as Galicia? Speculatively, such separate parallel routes to Britain and Ireland might have been the basis of the systematic sound differences between Goidelic and Brythonic language branches. If there were parallelism with the deep and distinct ancestry of Goidelic from other western Celtic languages as implied by the Schmidt tree, could this imply a Neolithic central Mediterranean proto-Celtic homeland geographically consistent with the Italo-Celtic hypothesis and a secondary spread in the Bronze Age?

The presence of J2e–M12 in Indic-speaking populations and in Central Asia, as well as Italy, Spain, Britain and Scandinavia, could be consistent with a more general Indo-European spread at that time, though whether this was a primary (e.g. David W. Anthony's gene-free synthesis *The Horse, the Wheel, and Language: How Bronze-Age Riders from the Eurasian Steppes Shaped the Modern World*), or more-likely secondary spread, would be even more speculative.

Conclusion

In line with the title of this symposium, Celticization from the West, this genetic review is aimed at providing some perspective as to the possible relative demic contributions of the people that Romans called *Celtae* and Greeks *Keltoi* to the prehistoric colonization of the British Isles. As stated in the introduction to this paper, this may be an impossible task, since genes do not carry ethnic or linguistic labels and there is no agreement as to who the Celts were or where they came from or at what time. Given the general consensus that they did not arrive before the first farmers, it is probable on present evidence that, like other Neolithic and post-Neolithic invaders, they would have represented a minority intrusion to the gene pool, overall perhaps less than ten per cent. In other words, genetically, their descendants could not qualify as aboriginal especially in Ireland and on the Atlantic side of Britain.

Genetic analysis is best at testing hypotheses generated by other prehistoric disciplines. Given the growing rejection of the central European homeland hypothesis, an immediate south-western European homeland presents the next obvious source to test. However, there is a multiplicity of such sources including north-west Italy, south-east France, and western Iberia, hampering meaningful founder analysis.

Analysis of Y chromosomes that could have arrived in the British Isles from the south-west, during the Neolithic and onwards, reveals a limited choice of three main groups of lineages I1b*/I1b2, J2e–M12 and E3b1, which are all found in the same distribution as the three putative western Celtic homelands as well as in the British Isles. While I1b*/I1b2 appears to have expanded in the early European Neolithic, recent studies show that J2e–M12 and E3b1a2 both expanded from Albania in the Late Neolithic/Early Bronze Age. STR haplotypes of J2 and E3b1 in Britain are consistent respectively with J2–M12 and E3b1a2, and the E3b1 founding event in north Wales is close geographically and in age to the Great Ormes Head copper mine of Llandudno, consistent with it being the terminus of a rapid focused movement associated with copper exploitation during the late European Chalcolithic, and possibly with the spread of Celtic languages.

Clearly such a hypothesis is highly speculative and preliminary at this stage and would require much more detailed genetic, archaeological and linguistic research to evaluate. However, it has several parsimonious features. Firstly, it would provide a specialist mining motive for such focused long-distance migration at the end of the Neolithic; secondly, the multiplicity of putative western Celtic homelands would be resolved; and thirdly, there would no longer be a conflict between Celtic homelands in eastern and western Europe—both could exist, the former being primary. Postulated Albanian (Hamp 1998) and Italo-Celtic (Cowgill 1970) linguistic connections could also then be seen possibly as a consequence of demic spread westwards from the Balkans via Italy and northern Mediterranean seaways in the early Bronze Age.

BIBLIOGRAPHY

Achilli, A., C. Rengo, C. Magri, V. A. Battaglia, et al. 2004 'The molecular dissection of mtDNA haplogroup H confirms that the Franco-Cantabrian glacial refuge was a major source for the European gene pool', *American Journal of Human Genetics* 75, 910–18.

Adams, S. M., E. Bosch, P. L. Balaresque, S. J. Ballereau, et al. 2008 'The Genetic Legacy of Religious Diversity and Intolerance: Paternal Lineages of Christians, Jews, and Muslims in the Iberian Peninsula', *American Journal of Human Genetics* 83, 725–36.

Anthony, D. W. 2007 *The Horse, the Wheel, and Language: How Bronze-Age Riders from the Eurasian Steppes Shaped the Modern World.* Princeton, Princeton University Press.

Athey, T. W. 2006 'Haplogroup Prediction from Y-STR Values Using a Bayesian-Allele-Frequency Approach', *Journal of Genetic Genealogy* 2, 34–9.

Capelli, C., N. Redhead, J. K. Abernethy, F. Gratrix, et al. 2003 'A Y chromosome census of the British Isles', *Current Biology* 13, 979–84.

Cavalli-Sforza, L. L., P. Menozzi, & A. Piazza 1994 *The History and Geography of Human Genes.*

Princeton, Princeton University Press.

Collis, J. 2003 *The Celts: Origins, Myths, Inventions.* Stroud, Tempus.

Cowgill, W. 1970 'Italic and Celtic superlatives and the dialects of Indo-European', *Indo-European and Indo-Europeans, Papers presented at the Third Indo-European Conference*, eds. G. Cardona et al., 113–53. Philadelphia, University of Pennsylvania Press.

Cruciani, F., R. La Fratta, P. Santolamazza, et al. 2004 'Phylogeographic analysis of haplogroup E3b (E-M215) Y chromosomes reveals multiple migratory events within and out of Africa', *American Journal of Human Genetics* 74, 1014–22.

Cruciani, F., R. La Fratta, A. Torroni, P. A. Underhill, & R. Scozzari 2006 'Molecular dissection of the Y chromosome haplogroup E-M78 (E3b1a): a posteriori evaluation of a microsatellite-network-based approach through six new biallelic markers', *Human Mutation* 27, 831–2.

Cruciani, F., R. La Fratta, B. Trombetta, P. Santolamazza, et al. 2007 'Tracing Past Human Male Movements in Northern/

Eastern Africa and Western Eurasia: New Clues from Y-Chromosomal Haplogroups E-M78 and J-M12', *Molecular Biology and Evolution* 24(6), 1300–11.

Cunliffe, B. 2004 *Facing the Ocean: The Atlantic and Its Peoples*. Oxford, Oxford University Press.

Cunliffe, B. 2010 'Celticization from the West: The Contribution of Archaeology', this volume 13–37.

Di Giacomo, F., F. Luca, L. O. Popa, et al. 2004 'Y chromosomal haplogroup J as a signature of the post-neolithic colonization of Europe', *Human Genetics* 115, 357–71.

Diamond, J., & P. Bellwood 2003 'Farmers and their languages: the first expansions', *Science* 300, 597–603.

Diodorus Siculus, 5.32, trans. C. H. Oldfather 1939 *Diodorus of Sicily* III, 163. Loeb Classical Library. London, Heinemann.

Forster, P., A. Röhl, P. Lünnemann, C. Brinkmann, et al. 2000 'A short tandem repeat–based phylogeny for the human Y chromosome', *American Journal of Human Genetics* 67, 182–96.

Gronenborn, D. 2003 'Migration, acculturation and culture change in western temperate Eurasia, 6500–5000 cal BC', *Documenta Praehistorica* 30, 79–91.

Hamp, E. P. 1998 'Whose Were the Tocharians?—Linguistic subgrouping and diagnostic idiosyncrasy', *The Bronze Age and Early Iron Age Peoples of Eastern Central Asia*, ed. V. H. Mair, 307–46. Washington, DC, Institute for the Study of Man.

Hill, E. W., M. A. Jobling, & D. G. Bradley 2000 'Y-chromosome variation and Irish origins', *Nature* 404, 351–2.

Isaac, G. 2010 'The Origins of the Celtic Languages: Language Spread from East to West', this volume 152–67.

James, S. 1999 *The Atlantic Celts: Ancient People or Modern Invention?* London, British Museum Press.

Julius Caesar, *The Gallic Wars*, trans. W. A. McDevitte & W. S. Bohn 1869 *De Bello Gallico*. New York, Harper & Brothers.

Karafet, T. M., F. L. Mendez, M. B. Meilerman,

P. A. Underhill, S. L. Zegura, M. F. Hammer 2008 'New binary polymorphisms reshape and increase resolution of the human Y chromosomal haplogroup tree', *Genome Research* 18, 830–8 (= YCC 2008).

Koch, J. T. 2010 'Paradigm Shift? Interpreting Tartessian as Celtic', this volume 185–301.

Lewis, C. A. 1996 'Prehistoric mining at the Great Orme: Criteria for the identification of early mining', M.Phil Thesis, University of Wales, Bangor Agricultural and Forest Sciences.

Macalister, R. A. S., ed. & trans. 1938–56, *Lebar Gabála Érenn* (first extant recension from the Book of Leinster, *c.* 1150), vols. 34, 35, 39, 41, 44. London, Irish Texts Society.

McCone, K. R. 1996 *Towards a Relative Chronology of Ancient and Medieval Celtic Sound Change*. Maynooth, Department of Old and Middle Irish, St Patrick's College.

McEvoy, B., M. Richards, P. Forster, & D. G. Bradley 2004 'The Longue Durée of Genetic Ancestry: Multiple genetic marker systems and Celtic origins on the Atlantic facade of Europe', *American Journal of Human Genetics* 75, 693–702.

Mourant, A. E., & I. M. Watkin 1952 'Blood Groups, Anthropology and Language in Wales and the Western Countries', *Heredity* 6, 13–36.

Oppenheimer, S. 2004 'The "Express Train from Taiwan to Polynesia": on the congruence of proxy lines of evidence', *World Archaeology* 36, 591–600.

Oppenheimer, S. 2007 *The Origins of the British: The new prehistory of Britain and Ireland from Ice-Age hunter gatherers to the Vikings as revealed by DNA analysis*. London, Constable (hardcover edn. 2006).

Oppenheimer, S. 2008 'Following Populations or Molecules? Two contrasting approaches and descriptive outcomes of island colonization arising from a similar knowledge-base'. *Simulations, Genetics and Human Prehistory*, eds. S. Matsumura, P. Forster, & C. Renfrew, chapter 3, 27–34. Cambridge, McDonald Institute for Archaeology.

Pereira, L., M. Richards, A. Goios, A. Alonso, et

al. 2005 'High-resolution mtDNA evidence for the late-glacial resettlement of Europe from an Iberian refugium', *Genome Research* 15, 19–24.

Rankin, D. 1996 *Celts and the Classical World*. London, Routledge (1st edn. 1987, London, Areopagitica Press).

Raybould, M. E., & P. Sims-Williams 2007 *A Corpus of Latin Inscriptions of the Roman Empire containing Celtic Personal Names*. Aberystwyth, Cambrian Medieval Celtic Studies.

Richards, M. 2003 'The Neolithic Invasion of Europe', *Annual Review of Anthropology* 32, 135–62.

Richards, M., V. Macaulay, E. Hickey, E. Vega, et al. 2000 'Tracing European Founder Lineages in the Near Eastern Mitochondrial Gene Pool', *American Journal of Human Genetics* 67, 1251–76.

Richards M., V. Macaulay, A. Torroni, H.-J. Bandelt 2002 'In Search of Geographical Patterns in European Mitochondrial DNA', *American Journal of Human Genetics* 71, 1168–74.

Rootsi, S., C. Magri, T. Kivisild, G. Benuzzi, et al. 2004 'Phylogeography of Y Chromosome Haplogroup I Reveals Distinct Domains of Prehistoric Gene Flow in Europe', *American Journal of Human Genetics* 75, 128–37.

Rosser, Z. H., T. Zerjal, M. E. Hurles, M. Adojaan, et al. 2000 'Y-Chromosomal Diversity in Europe is Clinal and Influenced Primarily by Geography, Rather than Language', *American Journal of Human Genetics* 67, 1526–43.

Scarre, C., ed. 1995 *Past Worlds: The Times Atlas of Archaeology*. London, Times Books.

Schmidt, K. H. 1988 'On the reconstruction of Proto-Celtic'. *Proceedings of the First North American Congress of Celtic Studies*, ed. G. W. MacLennan, 231–48. Ottawa.

Scozzari, R., R. Cruciani, A. Pangrazio, et al. 2001 'Human Y-Chromosome Variation in the Western Mediterranean Area: implications for the peopling of the region', *Human Immunology* 62, 871–84.

Semino, O., C. Magri, G. Benuzzi, A. A. Lin, et al. 2004 'Origin, Diffusion, and Differentiation of Y-Chromosome Haplogroups E and J: Inferences on the Neolithization of Europe and Later Migratory Events in the Mediterranean Area', *American Journal of Human Genetics* 74, 1023–34.

Sims-Williams, P. 1998 'Celtomania and Celtoscepticism', *Cambrian Medieval Celtic Studies* 36, 1–35.

Sims-Williams, P. 2006 *Ancient Celtic Place-Names in Europe and Asia Minor*, Publications of the Philological Society, vol. 39. Oxford, Blackwell.

Strabo, *Geographia* 4.1.14, ed. & trans. H. L. Jones 1917–32 *The Geography of Strabo*, vols. 1–8, containing Books 1–17. Loeb Classical Library. London, Heinemann.

Sykes, B. 2006 *Blood of the Isles: Exploring the genetic roots of our tribal history*. London, Bantam.

Tacitus, *Agricola*, ed. & trans. A. J. Church & W. J. Brodribb 1942 *The Life of Cnæus Julius Agricola*. New York, Random House.

Torroni, A., H.-J. Bandelt, L. D'Urbano, P. Lahermo, et al. 1998 'MtDNA Analysis Reveals a Major Late Paleolithic Population Expansion from South-western to North-eastern Europe', *American Journal of Human Genetics* 62, 1137–52.

Torroni, A., H.-J. Bandelt, V. Macaulay, M. Richards, et al. 2001 'A Signal, from Human mtDNA, of Post-Glacial Recolonization in Europe', *American Journal of Human Genetics* 69, 844–52.

Vennemann, T. 2003 *Europa Vasconica—Europa Semitica*, ed. P. N. Aziz Hanna. Trends in Linguistics: Studies and Monographs 138. Berlin, Mouton de Gruyter.

Watkin, I. M. 1966 'An Anthropological Study of Eastern Shropshire and Southwestern Cheshire: ABo blood-groups', *Man NS* 1, 375–85.

Waugh, E. 1928 *Decline and Fall*. London, Chapman and Hall.

Weale, M. E., D. A. Weiss, R. F. Jager, N. Bradman, & M. Thomas 2002 'Y Chromosome Evidence for Anglo-Saxon Mass Migration', *Molecular Biology and Evolution* 19,

1008–21.

Wilson, J. F., D. A. Weiss, M. Richards, M. G. Thomas, et al. 2001 'Genetic Evidence for Different Male and Female Roles during Cultural Transitions in the British Isles', *Proceedings of the National Academy of Sciences of the USA* 98, 5078–83.

Y Chromosome Consortium 2002 'A Nomenclature System for the Tree of Human Y-Chromosomal Binary Haplogroups', *Genome Research* 12, 339–48. (= YCC 2002)

PART THREE

LANGUAGE & LITERATURE

Archæologia Britannica,

GIVING SOME ACCOUNT

Additional to what has been hitherto Publifh'd,

OF THE

LANGUAGES, HISTORIES and CUSTOMS

Of the Original Inhabitants

OF

GREAT BRITAIN:

From Collections and Obfervations in Travels through
Wales, Cornwal, Bas-Bretagne, Ireland and *Scotland.*

By EDWARD LHUYD M.A. of *Jefus College,*
Keeper of the ASHMOLEAN MUSEUM in OXFORD.

VOL. I.
GLOSSOGRAPHY.

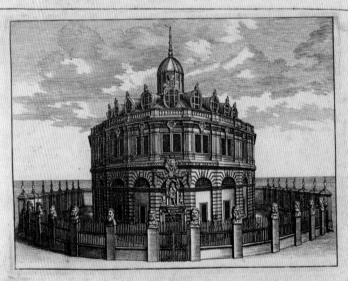

OXFORD,
Printed at the THEATER for the Author, MDCCVII.
And Sold by Mr. *Bateman* in *Pater-Nofter-Row, London*: and *Jeremiah Pepyat*
Bookfeller at *Dublin.*

CHAPTER SEVEN

THE ORIGINS OF THE CELTIC LANGUAGES
LANGUAGE SPREAD FROM EAST TO WEST

G. R. Isaac

THE basic principles at the heart of the scientific investigation of historical and prehistoric language relationships were well stated by Edward Lhuyd:

> The design of this first volume, being, The giving some account, additional to what has been hitherto publish'd, of the Ancientest Languages of *Britain* and *Ireland*, with regard to their changes or alteration into various dialects; and the Analogy they bear to those of our neighbouring Nations; it seems necessary to premise some General Observations about the Different Use and Pronunciation of Words; whence proceeds the Division of a Language into Dialects; which upon further Changes, growing unintelligible, become in Time distinct Languages.
>
> (Lhuyd 1707, 1)

He goes on to summarize and then detail the processes involved in such 'division':

> The Origin of Dialects which (as is before observ'd) become in time distinct Languages; happens
>
> I. *From the Alteration of the use of words, by applying them to signify different Notions from those already receiv'd.* [i.e. semantic shift]
>
> II. *From an Accidental Transposition of Letters or Syllables.*
>
> III. *From an Addition or subtraction of them; which is sometimes Casual, and sometimes Industrious, for Improvement.*

7.1. Facing page: title page of Edward Lhuyd's *Archæologia Britannica* (1707) with an engraving of the Sheldonian Theatre, Oxford (by permission of Llyfrgell Genedlaethol Cymru/National Library of Wales)

IV. *From using different prepositions in Compounds, or different Terminations.* [i.e. diachronic derivational morphology]

V. *From a Change of Letters on account of Mispronunciation.*

VI. *From the use of Foreign words, either Introduced by Conquest or borrow'd from those Nations with whom we have Trade and Commerce.* [i.e. adoption of loanwords]

(Lhuyd 1707, 3)

II, III and V represent in principle the essence of phonological change. The misformulation in terms of letters instead of sounds or, more accurately, phonological units, is to be excused as being understandable in pioneering work of that era. It does mean that there is no one-to-one relationship between Lhuyd's categories of change in these cases and modern theoretical categories. Nevertheless, with that reservation in mind, and with the addition of syntactic change, Lhuyd's categories of historical change by which languages acquire dialects and finally split into distinct languages exhaust the categories that would be seen to be relevant in the modern theory of historical language change. For all the terminological refinements necessary, essentially *this is* the modern theory of historical language change.

Darwin found these principles helpful by applying them analogically in his investigations into the evolution of species:

> But, in fact, a breed, like a dialect of a language, can hardly be said to have a definite origin. A man preserves and breeds from an individual with some slight deviation of structure, or takes more care than usual in matching his best animals and thus improves them, and the improved individuals slowly spread to the immediate neighbourhood . . . In semi-civilised countries, with little free communication, the spreading and knowledge of any new sub-breed will be a slow process. As soon as the points of value of the new sub-breed are once fully acknowledged, the principle, as I have called it, of unconscious selection will always tend—perhaps more at one period than at another, as the breed rises or falls in fashion—perhaps more in one district than in another, according to the state of civilisation of the inhabitants— slowly to add to the characteristic features of the breed, whatever they may be. But the chance will be infinitely small of any record having been preserved of such slow, varying, and insensible changes.
>
> (Darwin 2004, 50)

While the specifics of Darwin's account of the consciously guided development and propagation of an animal or plant breed do not cross from one term of the analogy to the other, most of the principles involved apply just as well, *mutatis mutandis*, to dialect groupings as to animal and plant breeds (e.g. for Darwin's 'points of value of the new sub-breed', read 'diagnostic features of an incipient dialect' more or less unconsciously selected by its speakers as functionally optimal for their communicative and discursive purposes). Darwin goes on to generalize from the principle of deliberate selection of features in animal and plant breeding to the principle of natural selection in evolution, giving rise to new species. This allows the extension of the analogy to the development of distinct languages out of originally dialectal variants of a single language. This extension has been enlightening in the conceptual development of comparative-historical linguistics. But the analogy is due to Darwin, and was originally formulated to elucidate the generation of biodiversity by analogy with a given conception of linguistic diversity, not vice versa.

The statements quoted capture what had been tacit knowledge in some quarters for a long time. For instance, there has never been a time in the historical period at which intellectuals amongst the Slavic-speaking peoples were not aware of the historical relationship between the individual Slavic languages (cf. Jakobson 1954, cited from Jakobson 1985, 65–85; it is quite a different question for what political ideological ends such awareness has been instrumentalized at different times). The same is probably true in respect of speakers of Romance, aware that their languages were descendants of Latin, or at least had very close historical affinities with each other. The insight that Romance is not descended from the Classical Latin of the familiar ancient sources but of an in principle unattested 'Vulgar Latin' is symptomatic of the refinement in theory and analysis, driven by brilliant conjectures and subject to rigorous testing, that characterizes all scientific progress. The principle that languages can be descended from, and traced by research to, unattested ancestral forms was perhaps most explicitly stated by William Jones:

> The *Sanscrit* language, whatever be its antiquity, is of a wonderful structure; more perfect than the *Greek*, more copious than the *Latin*, and more exquisitely refined than either, yet bearing to both of them a stronger affinity, both in the roots of verbs and in the forms of grammar, than could possibly be produced by accident; so strong indeed, that no philologer could examine all three, without believing them to have sprung from some common source, which, perhaps, no longer exists.
>
> (Jones 1786, cited from Fortson 2004, 8)

Jones's acceptance of the possibility that the common source of the languages in question might no longer be extant, as we would say, is a crucial methodological insight of the passage (not the only one), and led inexorably, both logically and historically, to the development of the methods of comparative-historical linguistics in particular connection with the reconstruction of such non-extant ancestral languages. Jones's explicit and concise statement of this principle (at least as a possibility) lends itself to easy citation in a historiographical context. But that principle too is, in fact, implicitly foreseen by Lhuyd:

> It's a very common Errour in Etymology, to endeavour the Deriving all the Radical words of our *Western European* Languages from the *Latin* or *Greek*; or indeed to

Derive constantly the Primitives of any one Language, from any particular Tongue. When we doe this; we seem to forget that all have been subject to Alterations; and that the Greater and more Polite any Nation is, the more subject they are, (partly for improvement, and partly out of a Luxurious Wantonness) to New model their Language.

We must therefore necessarily allow, that whatever Nations were of the Neighbour-hood, and of one common Origin with the *Greeks* and *Latins*, when they began to distinguish themselves for Politeness; must have preserv'd their Languages (which could differ from theirs but in Dialects) much better than them. And consequently no Absurdity to suppose a great many words of the Language spoken by the Old *Aborigines*, the *Osci*, the *Laestrigones*; the *Ausonians*, *Oenotrians*, *Umbrians* and *Sabins*, out of which the *Latin* was compos'd, to have been better preserv'd in the *Celtic* than in the *Roman*.

(Lhuyd 1707, 35)

It is appropriate to note Lhuyd's agenda of propagating a view of the Celtic languages as ancient, original and therefore worthy of notice and respect from the intellectuals (and aristocrats) of his time. But it is also important to note that principles of method are being stated here that are independent of that agenda. Ignoring Lhuyd's specific attack on the derivation from Latin or Greek, more generally: 'It's a very common Errour in Etymology . . . to Derive constantly the Primitives of any one Language, from any particular Tongue', which can only mean any particular *extant* language. The error arises when, 'we seem to forget that all have been subject to Alterations.' That is, we have no license to assume that any extant language is the same as it was in the distant, unattested past. On the contrary, we must assume that it is different, that extant languages are therefore reflexes of non-extant languages, and that that statement applies just as much to Latin and Greek as to any other language. One is prepared to take as given that Latin and Greek 'were of one common origin,' and that that origin was shared also by languages of 'whatever Nations were of the Neighbourhood,' which included the Gauls, whose language is 'retriev'd', in Lhuyd's term (1707, p. i of the Preface), in the comparative vocabulary of the extant 'Celtic Languages', as we would call them. Taken together, these statements constitute the founding principles of a theoretical programme of tracing the historical origins of languages in other prehistoric, that is, unattested, languages.

These principles continue to guide us in our research into the chronologically deeper historical connections between languages and the geographical correlate that, in the past, those unattested ancestral languages need not have been spoken in the areas where the extant descendant languages are spoken in historical times. It is essential to understand this in the investigation of the prehistory of any language or language group. The temptation is ever present to simplify the case by ignoring one or other of these principles, for instance by attempting to revive and perpetuate the myth of the autochthonous language. A shocking example of this myth-mongering is provided by the case of Hindu nationalist and/or fundamentalists (cf. Misra 1992, Talageri 1993, with willing supporters in the West, e.g. Frawley 1994) who react with horror to the suggestion that Vedic culture is anything other than an ancient autochthonous culture of the Subcontinent. The notion that Vedic culture is an element introduced to the north-west of the Subcontinent during the second millennium BC, with an ultimately European origin, is seen, understandably though not acceptably, as an affront to the integrity of the traditions of Hindu culture in India (with all their ideological, socio-political baggage). Such people, in their writings and teachings, pursue vigorously an agenda that might be termed 'Aryanization from the East'.

In contrast to such dogmatism, the theory of comparative-historical linguistics allows us to trace the prehistoric relations between languages and therefore between the prehistoric communities speaking those languages, independently of the contingencies of modern cultural and geographical politics. Consistent with the origins of the discipline in the Enlightenment programme of the liberation of epistemology from the oppression of locally and temporally specific authoritarian dogma, comparative-historical linguistics effectively frees us from the narrow perspective that our particular location and our particular culture impose on us. Our postulates on how our familiar languages came to be what they are, where they are, are constrained by the objectively given facts of how they are, and the comparative method will quickly root out the arbitrary ethnocentric presumption, in favour of the frequently surprising, sometimes, apparently, disturbing, true state of affairs of early relations between quite different cultures, in quite different geographical configurations. The discipline evolves, and must evolve, dependent on the quality and extent of the data available, as well as on the developing subtlety of analysis by which that data is elucidated by theory.

Apart from standing at the centre of the very beginnings of the discipline of comparative-historical linguistics in the late seventeeth and early eighteenth centuries, Celtic is still a fine example for the illustration of the principles I have just stated. The investigation of the prehistoric origins of the Celtic languages has been largely immune to the prejudices arising from the uncritical assimilation of the extant position of the Celtic languages in the far west of Europe and all the mythology of cultural autochthony. At the broadest level, the identification of Celtic as one of the branches of the Indo-European languages automatically shifts the origin of this linguistic culture far to the east, as no researcher has ever been so foolish as to posit the origins of Indo-European itself in western Europe. Far more important and interesting for our present purposes is the orientation of Celtic within Indo-European with respect to its prehistoric neighbours. Comparative-historical linguistics allows us to discover the chronologically deep features that Celtic shares with other Indo-European languages, and thus to align Celtic more closely with some than with others.

Thus, it turns out that, despite the western location of Celtic in historical times, it shares no significant innovative features with the other prominent languages of the Indo-European west, Italic and Germanic. There are commonalities with these groups, to be sure, but they are of a chronologically trivial nature. While there are many words that Celtic shares exclusively with Germanic or with Italic, the sharing of words with neighbours has no significance for prehistoric geographical configurations. Speakers of languages converse with neighbouring speakers of other languages in many social contexts. They exchange objects, ideas, practices and thus words. So for considerable time in their history and prehistory, Celtic, Germanic and Italic were neighbours. But that is not a significant result. We know they ended up as neighbours, because that is where we find them when they emerge into history. So of course they share many words with each other to the exclusion of other Indo-European languages.

For the comparative-historical linguist interested in the prehistoric relations and configurations of languages ancestral to extant ones, it is grammatical innovations that carry weight, as revealed in unusual alterations to the phonological and morphological systems of the language. This is where we find what we call the diagnostic features of prehistoric relations. For instance, Celtic shares the relative pronoun of the form Proto-Indo-European *ios, *ieh₂, *iod, with Greek, Slavic, Indo-Iranian, and Phrygian, to the exclusion of the western languages Italic and Germanic (and of others). Examples: Celtiberian nominative singular masculine ioś, accusative singular masculine iom, dative singular masculine/neuter iomui, accusative plural feminine iaś; Vedic yás, yā́, yát; Greek ὅς, ἥ, ὅ; Old Church Slavonic i-že; Phrygian ιος. The old assumption that that relative pronoun must be attributed to the undifferentiated Proto-Indo-European language itself has been undermined by the recognition of chronological layers of dialectal innovation within that protolanguage, and that Greek and Indo-Iranian in particular represent a particularly late form of that language, compared with the form represented by, say, Anatolian or Italic (and cf. Isaac 2007, 93). Of similar distribution are the forms of the future tense in the suffix *-sie-/*-sio-, found in Indo-Iranian, Greek, Baltic, Slavic, and Celtic. Examples: Gaulish pisíiumí 'I shall see'; Lithuanian dúosiu 'I shall give'; Vedic vakṣyáti 'he will speak'; Old Church Slavonic byšęšteje 'what will be'; Greek κείοντες 'those who will lie down'. Again, the reduplicated thematic sigmatic desiderative is an extraordinarily complex and innovative formation found only in Indo-Iranian and Celtic (in Old Irish future formations). Examples: Old Irish -silis 'he will fall' < *sisliǵ-s-e-t; Vedic cíkirṣati < *kʷíkʷrH-s-e-ti. For the grammatical features mentioned in this paragraph, cf. especially Schmidt (1996), also Isaac (2004, 52–3).

It should not be left unstated that criticisms of the position argued on the basis of the forms mentioned in the previous paragraph have been expressed most vigorously by Lindeman (1999) in a review of Schmidt (1996). Such criticisms are certainly to be answered, but the present summary paper does not appear to be the appropriate forum to do so in detail. I mention briefly three points: (i) Lindeman observes that we have no independent (my word, not his) corroboration of the prehistoric geographical configuration of the languages in question, and that therefore 'to determine which were the geographically "rather distant" early eastern contacts of Proto-Celtic is . . . impossible'; but the impossibility of 'determination' does not equate to the inadmissability of the explanatory postulate of contacts to account for a striking constellation of commonalities, especially given the concatenation of coincidences required in case the commonalities in question *are not* the result of contact, an issue which Lindeman does not address. (ii) Lindeman disagrees with Schmidt's analysis of the detail of the internal structure and combinatory behaviour of the future suffix *-*sie*-/*-*sio*-. Even if Schmidt's analysis of those details were incorrect (a point on which I state no position here), the evidential basis of the exclusive existence-in-that-function of the suffix in the languages in question (Indo-Iranian, Greek, Baltic, Slavic, and Celtic) is not compromised. (iii) The fact that the syncretism of plain-voiced (Proto-Indo-European *b, *d, *g, *ǵ) and 'voiced aspirated' (Proto-Indo-European *bʰ, *dʰ, *gʰ, *ǵʰ) stops is common to Celtic and *Iranian*, but not *Indo-Iranian*, as a whole, is indicative of differing dialectal contacts within Indo-Iranian—those of Iranian with Slavic and Baltic are hardly in question— and does not compromise the postulate that Celtic partook partially of the same areal configuration; this does not mean that the ancestors of Celtic and Iranian were in direct contact, merely that they were both—perhaps at opposite ends—parts of a contact continuum. This feature will be returned to below.

The common features mentioned and discussed in these and subsequent paragraphs are to be understood as constituting a corrective to arguments originating in the late nineteenth and early twentieth centuries, which focused on a limited set of features apparently common to Celtic and Italic, and which were taken as evidence of a special common 'Italo-Celtic' language, out of which differentiated Italic and Celtic developed (cf. summarily, Meillet 1967, 49–58). The selectivity applied to the features to justify this postulate will be returned to below. Additionally, many of the shared features originally adduced as the evidential basis of the 'Italo-Celtic' postulate have been shown to be spurious (by improved analysis of the historical phonology and/or morphology) or irrelevant (by discovery of similar or identical phenomena in other languages previously unknown). It must be admitted that the 'Italo-Celtic' postulate still has adherents (cf. Kortlandt 2007). But the counter-arguments are well documented and have not been adequately answered. For these counter-arguments, cf. especially Watkins (1966) and Schmidt (1991, 1996); summarily Isaac (2004). The most detailed attempt to counter the position of Watkins (1966) is that of Cowgill (1970). There, however, (i) the arguments are still based to some extent on analyses which, for reasons independent of the 'Italo-Celtic' question, have been *largely* (if not universally) abandoned by now (for instance the analysis of the Old Irish '*ā*-subjunctive', cf. McCone 1991, 85–113; Isaac 1996, 365–8; Schumacher 2004, 49–57), and (ii) even then, the statements in conclusion of close genetic ties between Italic and Celtic are tempered, with reference to the features chosen to illustrate this proximity, by the observation that they are 'hardly enough to establish a real subgroup' (Cowgill 1970, 143).

The two sigmatic formations previously mentioned, future and desiderative, are symptomatic of a general explosion in productivity of sigmatic verbal forms in general, represented also, and most strikingly, by the rise and generalization of the sigmatic aorist, as seen in Greek, Indo-Iranian, Slavic and Celtic. The formation is present incipiently in other languages, and indeed, attained a limited productivity in Italic also. But it is only in Greek, Indo-Iranian, Slavic and Celtic that the sigmatic aorist became the productive formation par excellence for all new verbs, as well as being generalized in many cases to old verbs whose inherited aorist formations were moribund. Given that one meets occasional misunderstanding of the significance of this point, it cannot be emphasized strongly enough that it is the expanded productivity of this formation that constitutes in this case the significant innovation common to Greek, Indo-Iranian, Slavic and Celtic, not merely the existence of the formation. Examples of possibly inherited formations (though all certainly re-formed in various ways in the individual branches): Old Irish *birt*, Vedic *ábhār* < Proto-Indo-European *$b^h\acute{e}r$-s-t* 'carried'; Old Irish *anais* 'remained', Vedic *prá ānīt* 'began to breathe' < Proto-Indo-European *$h_2\acute{e}nh_1$-s-t* 'breathed'; Old Irish *milt*, Old Church Slavonic *mlěchъ* < IE *$m\acute{e}lh_2$-s-t* 'ground'.

Distinctive morphological innovations such as these can only be shared by the language communities partaking of them when those communities are contiguous. Since it is recognized that Greek and Indo-Iranian in particular, Baltic and Slavic also, are representative of a very late dialectal configuration innovating many features not shared in common by other Indo-European languages which had already developed, 'split off', in other distinctive directions, it follows that Celtic too arose out of a section of that dialectal configuration. Much of what is distinctive, identifying, of the Celtic languages belongs therefore to this configuration, which geography and linguistic history force us to place in eastern Europe in the fourth to the third millennium BC.

These morphological features represent the chronologically deepest layers of innovation indicative of the dialectal and thus geographical configurations of the language communities out of which what became the Common Celtic language, and later the individual Celtic languages, developed. Phonological innovations give us further insight into, and further geographical and chronological information on, the course of the development of Celtic out of Proto-Indo-European. For instance, certain inherited clusters of consonants, a dental stop followed by a dorsal stop, underwent a metathesis to dorsal-dental in Celtic and in Greek, and, it now seems, nowhere else. So the Proto-Indo-European word for 'bear' *$h_2\acute{r}tk^os$* appears metathesized in Greek as ἄρκτος, and, through *arxtos*, became Common Celtic *artos*, giving our Welsh *arth*, Gaulish forms in *arto-* and the Old Irish *art*. And an adjectival derivation *$d^h\acute{g}^homio$-* of the Proto-Indo-European word for 'earth' appears in Greek as χθόνιος 'earthly' and in Celtic as *γ*donyos* in the sense of 'earthly being', that is 'human being', as seen in Welsh *dyn*, Irish *duine*, and, with the initial cluster still preserved, in the Gaulish form -XTONION. On the nature and implications of this metathesis, see Isaac (2007, 78–82).

TABLE I				
PIE	Greek	Latin	Celtic	Tocharian B
*$h_1$ndom	ἔνδον	(endo)	Old Irish and 'in it'	e(n)- 'in-' in compounds
*$h_1$rg^h-			*rig- > Old Irish rega 'will go'[1]	
*h_2ŕtk̂o- 'bear'	ἄρκτος	(ursus)	Old Irish art Welsh arth[2]	
*$h_2$mb^{h}í 'about'	ἀμφί	ambi-	Gaulish ambi- Welsh am	āmpi
*$h_3$mb^{h}el- 'navel'	ὄμφαλος	*ombel- > umbilicus	*ambel- > Old Irish imbliu	
*$h_3$mso- 'shoulder'	ὦμος	(umerus)		āntse

1 Compare Proto-Indo-European *b^{h}r̥ǵh- > Celtic *brig-, e.g. Celtiberian -brix, Gaul. -briga, Old Irish brí, Welsh bre.
2 Contrast Proto-Indo-European *prtu- > Celtic *ritu-, Welsh rhyd.

Languages always adopt various features from various of their neighbours, and the languages with which speakers are most in contact vary over time. So we find in the prehistory of any language that there are features shared in common with different languages consistent with those shifting orientations. Celtic shares an important characteristic feature of phonological development with Tocharian in the rule of the treatment of certain word-initial laryngeals. In original Proto-Indo-European word-initial clusters of laryngeal plus a sonant followed by another consonant, an anaptyctic or epenthetic vowel developed between the laryngeal and the following sonant. But the way this happened varied between languages. In Italic and Greek, the treatment was identical, with three different reflexes, dependent on the qualities of the three laryngeals: $*h_1RC- > *h_1eRC-$, $*h_2RC- > *h_2aRC-$, $*h_3RC- > *h_3oRC-$ (with R any sonant, $*m$, $*n$, $*l$, $*r$, syllabic or non-syllabic depending on phonological context; $C =$ any consonant). In Celtic and Tocharian on the other hand, only $*h_2$ and $*h_3$ developed such an anaptyctic vowel in this position, and the same vowel, $*h_2RC- > *h_2aRC-$, $*h_3RC- > *h_3aRC-$, followed by whatever specific additional changes apply to generate the forms in the extant languages, whereas $*h_1$ apparently disappeared in this position prior to anaptyxis, $*h_1RC- > *RC-$, whereby the resulting syllabic $*R$ underwent the usual preconsonantal developments for that language. The Celtic and Tocharian treatments are structurally identical. There are so many factors relevant in these processes that the identical Celtic and Tocharian outputs from the same inputs, contrasting with the Italic and Greek treatment, is diagnostic of this change taking place in common in contiguous languages or dialects. The developments and examples are tabulated in Table 1 (allowing that not all protoforms have reflexes in all the languages, and not all possible initial combinations are represented; bracketed examples are reflexes of the relevant protoforms but show interference from other factors that compromise their illustrative value in the present context).

This summary includes no implicit claim to have presented the arguments for this complex set of phenomena. I have here only stated and illustrated the case, and not exhaustively. The case for Greek and Latin was argued in a classic paper by Rix (1970), building on initial observations by Beekes (1969, 31–47), hence the designation of the phenomenon as 'Rix's Law'; for Latin, cf. also Schrijver (1991, 56–73). For the extension and implications of the law for Celtic, see McCone (1996, 52), Isaac (2007, 73, 82); and for Tocharian, Hackstein (1998).

A very striking way in which Celtic differs in its historical phonology from the other apparently western languages, Italic and Germanic, is that the original distinction between the plain-voiced stops and the so-called aspirated voiced stops was neutralized in Celtic, whereas they remained distinct in Italic and Germanic. Celtic shares this syncretism of the plain-voiced and aspirated voiced stops with Baltic, Slavic, Albanian and Iranian (all other Indo-European languages maintaining the distinction, even if altering the phonetics of its realization). Examples are given in Table 2.

TABLE 2

	*dᵇuór– 'door'	*duoh₁ '2'
PIE		
Latin	fores	duo
Greek	θύραι	δύο
English	door	two
Armenian	dowr̃n	erku

vs

Welsh	dôr	dau
Avestan	duuar–	dva
Old Church Slavonic	dvьri	dъva
Lithuanian	dùrys	dù
Albanian	derë	dy

It is noteworthy that the Celtic treatment is shared with specifically Iranian, not with Indo-Iranian as a whole (Indo-Aryan maintaining the distinction at all times). Our earliest extant Iranian, the language of the Avestas, the earliest portions of which are of the period 1000 to 800 BC, and our earliest extant Indo-Aryan, the language of the *Ṛgveda*, of the late second millennium BC, are grammatically so similar to each other that they cannot have been separated into distinct language communities for much more than the order of a thousand years before they are attested, if that. The loss of the distinction between the plain-voiced and the aspirated voiced stops is one of the most fundamental alterations to Iranian in comparison with Indo-Aryan and is part of the essence of the split of Indo-Iranian into its two branches. That places that change at around 2000 BC $\pm \leq c.$ 300. This means that the dialect or dialects that would, several centuries later, become Common Celtic, were part of a language-contact area about 2000 BC which encompassed also the ancestors of Baltic, Slavic, Albanian and Iranian. This gives us clear geographical and chronological parameters for the prehistoric position of the language that would become what we call Celtic. In Isaac (2007, 75–95), the early dialectal and areal relations of Celtic have been discussed in the light of a wide range of, mainly phonological, features.

A word of clarification on the nature of the argument is in order at this point. One could, for instance, simply reject, say, the significance of the treatments of the voiced aspirates as being a matter of coincidence, that it does not constitute significant evidence of prehistoric dialectal contacts. But one would have then to inquire as to why one would reject that set of facts in argument, while accepting some other set(s) of facts, say, on the assimilation of Proto-Indo-European $*penk^we > *k^wenk^we$, for instance, common to Italic, e.g. Latin *quinque*, and Celtic, e.g. MW *pymp* (without the assimilation, Proto-Indo-European $*penk^we$ would result in Middle Welsh $*ymp$, with loss of the initial $*p$). This assimilation had always played a role in arguments for a genetic 'Italic-Celtic'. But even in the narrow confines of this summary paper, we have seen that Celtic shares many innovatory features in common with many other languages. To single out one set as being exclusively diagnostic of a close genetic affinity with another language group, while rejecting the rest as coincidence—the rest, that is, of features which do not fit in with the preferred configuration—would of course be a typical case of arbitrary selectivity in the presentation of the empirical basis of an argument. Such arbitrariness is avoided in the approach favoured here, as we by no means reject or ignore such common features as the assimilation $*penk^we > *k^wenk^we$ (and many others, even if not mentioned explicitly here, for reasons of space). Rather we take such Italic-Celtic (not 'Italo-Celtic') features as clear evidence for a period of development in close proximity to each other of the dialects that were to become the Italic and Celtic languages—no surprise, as they are neighbours when they enter history, but no less worth stating for that. But then, for consistency, we are not at liberty to ignore the common innovations Celtic shares with other language groups, groups that are not neighbours of Celtic in historical times, and dismiss the chronological and prehistoric-geographical implications of the distributions of those innovations. The points of this paragraph are to be understood as applying to all features discussed in this paper, and indeed features not discussed here also.

In summary, the innovatory morphological characteristics of the Celtic languages place them in their earliest accessible phase of becoming what they are in a dialectal complex that includes also the ancestors of Indo-Iranian, Greek, Baltic and Slavic. Then, several distinctive phonological characteristics, symptomatic of shifting proximity to

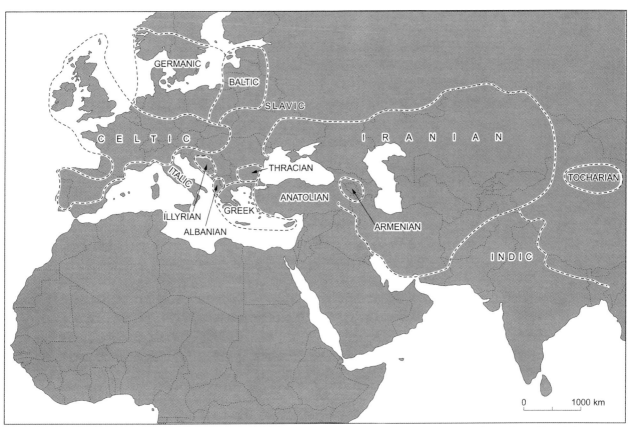

7.2. Approximate historical locations of the Indo-European languages

other languages over time, indicate further areal relations with the ancestors of Greek, Tocharian and around 2000 BC, Baltic and Slavic still, together with Albanian and Iranian. All this can only have been going on in eastern Europe. It makes no sense to think of Celtic becoming what it is on the late Neolithic and early Bronze-Age Atlantic seaboard while sharing striking grammatical innovations with Indo-Iranian, Baltic, Slavic, Greek, Tocharian and Albanian.

Since it has no meaning to speak of ancient or prehistoric 'Celts' independently of statements about the nature of the languages they spoke, there is no question of the origin of the Celts that is not by definition a question of the origins of the Celtic languages. Without language, there are no Celts, ancient or modern, but only populations bearing certain genetic markers or carriers of certain Bronze Age and Iron Age material cultures. The origin of the Celts therefore is the prehistory and protohistory of the Celtic languages. So questions surrounding that origin are by definition linguistic questions. And linguistic questions can only be given linguistic answers. And those answers are in eastern Europe. I look forward to the time when there is consensual recognition amongst representatives of all cognate disciplines of the need to confront their theories with the real results of linguistic research. The tendency to allow wishful thinking to creep into this interface on the part of non-linguists, the presumption that, for language prehistory, 'anything goes', is undoubtedly a hindrance to the insight that could be gained by cooperation informed by linguistically coherent argumentation.

BIBLIOGRAPHY

Beekes, R. S. P. 1969 *The Development of the Proto-Indo-European Laryngeals in Greek*. The Hague, Paris, Mouton.

Cowgill, W. 1970 'Italic and Celtic superlatives and the dialects of Indo-European.' *Indo-European and Indo-Europeans: Papers Presented at the Third Indo-European Conference at the University of Pennsylvania*, eds. G. Cardona, H. M. Hoenigswald and A. Senn, 113–53. Philadelphia, University of Pennsylvania Press.

Darwin, C. 2004 *The Origin of Species*. London, Collector's Library. [First edition, 1859 *The Origin of Species by Means of Natural Selection or, The Preservation of Favoured Races in the Struggle for Life*.]

Fortson IV, B. W. 2004 *Indo-European Language and Culture: An Introduction*. Oxford, Blackwell.

Frawley, D. 1994 *The Myth of the Aryan Invasion of India*. New Delhi, Voice of India.

Hackstein, O. 1998 'Tocharisch und Westindogermanisch: strukturell uneinheitliche Laryngalreflexe im Tocharischen (uridg. $*$-Ub_1C- vs. $*$-$Ub_{2,3}(C$-$)$ und $*\#h_1RC$- vs. $\#h_{2,3}RC$-$)$'. *Sprache und Kultur der Indogermanen: Akten der X. Fachtagung der Indogermanischen Gesellschaft Innsbruck, 22.–28. September 1996*, ed. W. Meid, 217–36. Innsbruck, Innsbrucker Beiträge zur Sprachwissenschaft.

Isaac, G. R. 1996 *The Verb in the Book of Aneirin: Studies in Syntax, Morphology and Etymology*. Tübingen, Max Niemeyer Verlag.

Isaac, G. R. 2004 'The Nature and Origins of the Celtic Languages: atlantic Seaways, Italo-Celtic and Other Paralinguistic Misapprehensions'. *Studia Celtica* 38, 49–58.

Isaac, G. R. 2007 *Studies in Celtic Sound Changes and their Chronology*. Innsbruck, Innsbrucker Beiträge zur Sprachwissenschaft.

Jakobson, R. 1954 'Slavism as a Topic for Comparative Studies'. *The Review of Politics* 16, 67–90. [Here cited from Jakobson 1985, 65–85.]

Jakobson, R. 1985 *Selected Writings. VI Early Slavic Paths and Crossroads*, ed. S. Rudy. Berlin, Mouton.

Jones, W. 1786 Address to the Asiatick Society. Calcutta.

Kortlandt, F. 2007 *Italo-Celtic Origins and Prehistoric Development of the Irish Language*. Amsterdam, New York, Rodopi.

Lhuyd, E. 1707 *Archaeologia Britannica, Giving some Account of the Languages, Histories and Customs of the Original Inhabitants of Great Britain: from Collections and Observations in Travels through Wales, Cornwal, Bas-Bretagne, Ireland and Scotland. Vol. I. Glossography*. Oxford, The Theater.

Lindeman, F. O. 1999 Review of Schmidt (1996). *Zeitschrift für celtische Philologie* 51, 234–6.

McCone, K. 1991 *The Indo-European Origins of the Old Irish Nasal Presents, Subjunctives and Futures*. Innsbruck, Innsbrucker Beiträge zur Sprachwissenschaft.

McCone, K. 1996 *Towards a Relative Chronology*

of Ancient and Medieval Celtic Sound Change.
Maynooth, Department of Old and Middle
Irish, St. Patrick's College, Maynooth.

Meillet, A. 1967 (trans. S. N. Rosenberg) *The
Indo-European Dialects*. Alabama, University
of Alabama Press. [Trans. of A. Meillet 1908
Les dialectes indo-européens. Paris, Edouard
Champion. 2nd printing 1922.]

Misra, S. S. 1992 *The Aryan Problem, a Linguistic
Approach*. New Delhi, Munshiram Manoharlal.

Rix, H. 1970 'Anlautender Laryngal vor Liquida
oder Nasalis sonans im Griechischen'. *Münchener
Studien zur Sprachwissenschaft* 27, 79–110.

Schmidt, K. H. 1991 'Latin and Celtic: genetic
relationship and areal contacts.' *Bulletin of the
Board of Celtic Studies* 38, 1–19.

Schmidt, K. H. 1996 *Celtic: A Western Indo-
European Language?* Innsbruck, Innsbrucker

Beiträge zur Sprachwissenschaft.

Schrijver, P. 1991 *The Reflexes of the Proto-Indo-
European Laryngeals in Latin*. Amsterdam, Atlanta,
Rodopi.

Schumacher, S. 2004 (in collaboration with
B. Schulze-Thulin and C. aan de Wiel)
*Die keltischen Primärverben: ein vergleichendes,
etymologisches und morphologisches Lexikon*.
Innsbruck, Innsbrucker Beiträge zur
Sprachwissenschaft.

Talageri, Sh. 1993 *Aryan Invasion Theory and Indian
Nationalism*. New Delhi, Voice of India.

Watkins, C. 1966 'Italo-Celtic revisited.' *Ancient
Indo-European Dialects*, eds. H. Birnbaum
and J. Puhvel, 29–50. Berkeley, Los Angeles,
University of California Press.

CHAPTER EIGHT

TRACKING THE COURSE OF THE SAVAGE TONGUE
PLACE-NAMES AND LINGUISTIC
DIFFUSION IN EARLY BRITAIN

David N. Parsons

M Y rather unwieldy title echoes a phrase from the thunderous invective of Gildas, the 6th-century British churchman. In an open letter to the politicians of his day he declaims that:

In just retribution for former crimes there spread from sea to sea a fire heaped up by the hand of the impious easterners. It devastated all the towns and countryside round about, and once alight did not subside until it had burned almost the whole surface of the island, and was licking the western ocean with its savage red tongue.[1]

The impious easterners, of course, are the Anglo-Saxons, sweeping across Britain from east to west. Gildas, I imagine, was not intending a pun with his *lingua trux*, 'savage tongue' (though the word-play would appear to work in Latin as in English), but it attracted me. For besides the devastation and political conquest, the Anglo-Saxons were bringing with them their ungodly Germanic language, which came, in relatively short order, to supplant British and Latin from east to west, and south to north, across most of what became England. Gildas is thus a contemporary witness to events that underlie a significant linguistic replacement in north-western Europe.

He is not an unproblematic witness, of course, and one should take with a pinch of salt many of the particulars of his testimony;[2] but in its simplest form, a spreading conquest of the island by Germanic-speaking incomers from the east, it is hardly controversial—apparently consistent with archaeological data, and supported by writers of the following centuries, and by linguistic geography.[3] For a plethora of reasons it is

---

1   This is the translation in Ireland 1996, 168. For the Latin text see Winterbottom 1978, 97. Winterbottom translates the key phrase 'fierce red tongue' (p. 27), which is unexceptionable, though 'savage' is time-honoured: see, e.g., Giles 1906, 311.

2   See, e.g., various contributions to Lapidge & Dumville 1984.

3   There is of course the ever-present controversy about how many Anglo-Saxons were involved in introducing

difficult to conceive of English as, in origin, anything other than a western salient of a language-group, Germanic, that is centred, and surely has its origins in the centre-north of the European continent.

To my knowledge no one has ever seriously suggested otherwise, and I am not about to entertain the idea now. But it is in the nature of examining 'Celticization from the West' that we should reflect hard on some of the things that we have previously assumed. The long-held view, at least until recent years, that Celtic language spread to the south-west and north-west of Europe from a core in the centre of the continent is one that we are invited to challenge (cf. Koch 2007, 9–17).

My work for some years has principally been in the field of place-name studies, and it is specifically the question of whether place-name distributions can throw any light on the direction of early Celtic diffusion that I want to consider. My first impulse in seeking an answer is to reach for parallels from the territory and period that is most familiar to me, Britain in the early Middle Ages. Hence the appeal to Gildas. For one of the results, of course, of the Germanicization of what became England, was the establishment of large numbers of English-language place-names across the country. The question I have to ask myself, before turning to early Celts, is this: if we did not know, from Gildas and the rest, which way Germanic language spread across England, could we deduce it from place-name evidence alone?

When put so bluntly, it must be conceded at once that this is a question difficult to answer satisfactorily. The problem homes in at once on the greatest weakness of place-names in historical investigation: a lack of chronological precision. Place-names, I would contend, have an enormous amount to offer in a variety of ways: above all, they tell us a great deal about where different languages have been spoken; in addition they often illustrate interaction between languages, and they tell us about aspects of society, administration, land-use, belief and perception. But they tend to resist enquiry into the ultimate date of their coinage. A place-name is at least as old as the date of the document that first records it (itself quite often difficult to establish with certainty), but how much older? A handful of Anglo-Saxon names are recorded around the end of the 7th century AD, two and a half centuries or so after the traditional date of arrival of the first Germanic-speaking settlers; the vast majority of Anglo-Saxon period names are first recorded hundreds of years later again, with the majority appearing for the first time in the Domesday Book, the late 11th-century survey compiled by the Norman conquerors. Yet reflected in these late, and later, sources, we assume, there are names that were given in the earliest decades of the invasions, no doubt rubbing shoulders with names that arose throughout the following centuries. If we are to understand the earliest phases—and that, of course, is fundamental to the question of where a language

---

the language (for recent assessments see various contributions to Higham 2007); and there is the new, and undoubtedly controversial, suggestion that Germanic language may have been established in eastern Britain before the arrival of the Romans (Oppenheimer 2006, 267–92). It does not seem to be disputed, even by Oppenheimer, that the language arrived from the European Continent (brought, he suggests, by the Belgae), and that the direction of diffusion in Britain was from east to west.

originally came from and in which direction it was travelling—we have to find ways of stratifying the name-types and distinguishing early from late.[4]

Now, it must be admitted that, in so far as this has seemed possible at all in English-language names, it has often depended, at least in part, on a comparison of name-distribution with the received historical narrative. Take that away and the implications of the distribution become much less clear. We might cite, for instance, the example of *throp*—the native English equivalent of the more familiar Scandinavian *thorp*, which in names like Scunthorpe and Grimethorpe is common in the east and north of the country, the so-called Danelaw. *Throp* and *thorp* both mean a 'hamlet' or 'outlying settlement'; the English cognate survives in village-names like Adlestrop and Hatherop in Gloucestershire. Its distribution in southern England is marked, for whilst it is found in a band down the middle of the country, it neither appears in the far south-east, Kent and Sussex, nor the far south-west, Devon and Cornwall. These circumstances have found a complex chronological explanation: on the one hand, the Anglo-Saxon settlers of Kent and Sussex came from a northerly region of the Continent—Danish Jutland—which had not, by the 5th and 6th centuries, yet adopted the *thorp*-term; on the other, its absence from Devon and Cornwall indicates that the term had passed into disuse among the southern English by, say, the 8th century, when Devon, at least, was settled by the advancing Anglo-Saxons.[5] Yet all this argumentation would collapse if we had no historical backbone against which to measure it. We would be left—as we are left in the case of many, many words—with a restricted distribution and a series of question marks as to why that should be. Chronology is always a possible factor, but dialectal 'preference', the apparent accident by which one region comes to promote one term above another, is another factor that is usually very hard to dismiss.[6]

Having said this, there are still a few important names and name-types which look relevant to the present problem. Above all, for the early Anglo-Saxons, there are the *-ingas* names: group- or clan-names denoting the descendants or followers, usually, of eponymous individuals. The *-ingas* groups give us names like Hastings (followers of Hæsta, Hæsta-people) and Reading (followers of Rēada, Rēada-people); combined with *hām* 'homestead' they give us the likes of Nottingham and Birmingham ('homestead of the Snot/Beorma-people'). On a range of measures this type of place-name looks significantly early. The overall distribution is heavily weighted towards the eastern half of the island, and, moreover, it complements extensive evidence for the same types of name in both Germany and Scandinavia. More than that, however, there is something

---

4 It is not appropriate here to give extensive references to discussions of chronology in English place-names. The most approachable overview is in Gelling 1988. I take up various general issues in Parsons forthcoming.

5 For the argument see Smith 1956, II, 216. But see also the following note.

6 In the case of *throp* I think that Smith's chronological explanation is unlikely: see Cullen et al. forthcoming. For a range of challenging distributions involving the topographical names drawn from the boundary-clauses of Anglo-Saxon charters see Kitson 1995. For most distributions a combination of date and dialect is likely: see in particular the discussion of Old English *burna* and *brōc*, competing words for 'stream', ibid. pp. 91–2.

in the semantics of the name-type which is at least suggestive. These clan-based groups, extended families if you like, are widespread and significant in the make-up of migration-age kingdoms, or proto-kingdoms. Yet when historical materials for Anglo-Saxon society become available, around about 700 AD, there are no more than weak echoes of *-ingas* groups in the social make-up: the place-names reflect a type of organization that is characteristic of the earliest centuries, but is generally otiose by the second half of the seventh.[7]

Something similar can be found in one particular element that, again, reflects early territorial arrangements. This is a word, *$g\bar{e}$ in Old English, equivalent to Modern German *gau* 'district'. In English the word did not survive to appear in literary texts—a notable point in itself—but it is to be identified in a small group of place-names in the south and east, most prominently in the county-name Surrey, originally the *$su\eth er\ g\bar{e}$, the 'southern district' (though of what is disputed). Various of the districts so named can be shown to be old—superseded by other arrangements that were in place later in the Anglo-Saxon period—which again, in combination with the distribution, is suggestive of early date and arguably, because of the geographical limitation, of the direction of travel.[8]

Another type of pointer, of more immediate interest in the present context, comes from the relationship of Anglo-Saxon names with those derived from earlier strata of language, and particularly Brittonic Celtic, or British, the ancestor of Modern Welsh. Anglo-Saxons found woods called, or referred to as, PrimWelsh *$c\bar{e}d$, Welsh *coed*, and thus we have names like Chetwood (literally 'wood-wood') and Lichfield (the *feld* or open land at Romano-British *Letocetum*, equivalent to Welsh *llwyd* + *coed* 'grey wood'); they found hills referred to as *Bre* (Welsh *bre*), and thus we have names like Bredon and Brill (both 'hill-hill'). Above all they found—or, rather, above all they adopted—river-names; and we have early, pre-English names for watercourses across the country. Kenneth Jackson's familiar map of the rivers (1953, 220; Figure 8.1 here), though by now in urgent need of revision, still makes the obvious distributional point very clearly. In essence, the further west you go in Britain, the more Celtic the surviving nomenclature. Take away our historical narrative and there are still enough clues here, I would have thought, to generate a story along the same lines. The structure of a name like Lichfield shows that the Germanic element is added to an earlier Celtic name, so we can deduce that we have English intruding on British, rather than vice versa.[9] It appears natural,

---

7   Most of the points suggestive of the names' antiquity are set out by Smith 1956, I, 298–301. It must be conceded that to stress these arguments is to swim against the tide of scholarship since the 1960s, which has left *-ingas* names rather uncomfortably belonging to a phase that, while it is relatively early, falls later than the period of accompanied pagan burial (5th–7th centuries). All of this is taken up in Parsons forthcoming.

8   Examples of *$g\bar{e}$, beside Surrey, include Eastry, Lyminge and Sturry, all Kent, Vange, Essex, and probably Ely, Cambridgeshire. On the element see Smith 1956, I, 196–7; Bailey 1998–9.

9   In this case and numerous others, of course, the point is anyway made by the chronology of attestation: Romano-British *Letocetum* is attested (albeit in two badly-copied forms) in sources from the Roman period, whereas Germanic names and additions (like *feld* in this case) only begin to appear in Anglo-Saxon sources.

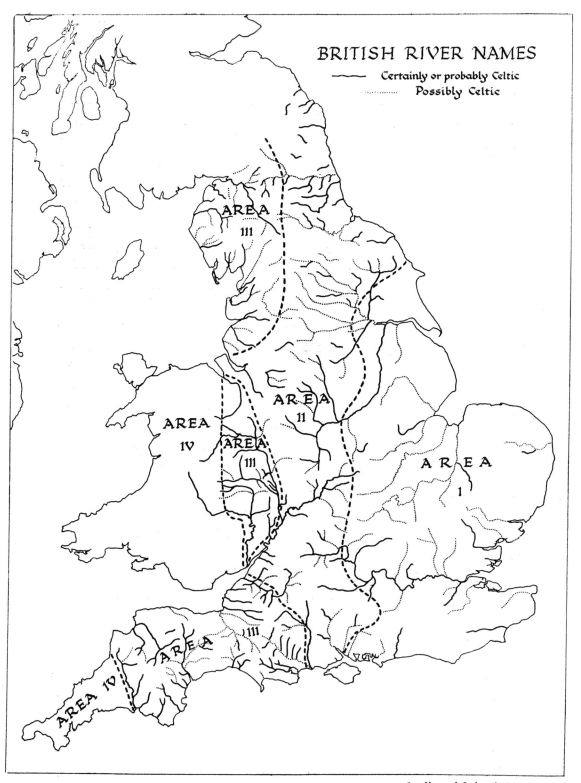

BRITISH RIVER NAMES

——— Certainly or probably Celtic
············ Possibly Celtic

AREA
111

AREA
11

AREA
1V

AREA
111

AREA
1

AREA
111

AREA
1V

AREA

8.1. Kenneth Jackson's river-name map
from *Language and History in Early Britain*

if it is not perhaps logical, to interpret the distributional pattern in terms of a major Germanic-speaking incursion, spreading but gradually thinning until giving way in the far west to surviving British language; an east to west movement that seems all the more secure given the concentration of Germanic language further east on the Continent. Perhaps it would be theoretically conceivable that our Germanic speakers made their way first to Ireland, entered from the west, but found the conditions or the reception too hostile until they had made their way across the mountains into the softer lowland zone. To counter this there are supplementary arguments (though I am not sure how watertight they would be) derived from the forms of British names encountered, and effectively fossilized, by the advancing English. Jackson found older sounds in the east of England and British innovations further west. Although, of course, he identifies them as innovations partly because he is using the historical framework of an Anglo-Saxon conquest in order to sequence them (Jackson 1953, 194–261 and Part II, *passim*; Sims-Williams 1990, 237–44). It really is very difficult to divorce ourselves entirely from the contextual information that we have.

Nonetheless, on the kinds of evidence that we have seen, I think it is clear that, in the case of English, we would have a reasonable chance of identifying the direction of the language's advance on the basis of place-name evidence alone, unguided by historical narrative. And, indeed, within Britain we have other instances of place-name patterns that suggest historical incursions for which there is little or no documentary record. Onomastic evidence has been frequently used to flesh out in great detail the briefest of historical references to Scandinavian settlement in eastern England. Although the conclusions drawn have sometimes stretched the evidence too far, there is no doubt that there is considerable historical potential encoded in the names (Abrams & Parsons 2004). In north-west England, indeed, there is extensive name-evidence for the presence of a community of mixed Scandinavians and Gaels, which would not be suspected at all from the written record (Ekwall 1918, 95–103). In such cases I do believe that place-name evidence can realistically suggest its own plausible narratives (albeit that those narratives are not as detailed, circumstantial or precisely dated as the general historian might wish).

But, in all the points that I have considered so far, I concede that I have not really shaken loose from one key piece of information. Behind all of my comments on the progress of Germanic language in England lurks the large block of Germanic speakers in north-central Europe. Behind the Gaels of the north-west are the established Gaels in Ireland, Man and western Scotland. However I dress them up, the best examples that I can find to a large extent distil down to a rather simplistic point about peripheraries and cores, and the inherent likelihood (by definition?) that the periphery derives from the

---

The absence of plausibly Germanic place-names from the records of Roman Britain does not help Oppenheimer's arguments (cf. 2006, 280–1, 292, where the discussion of toponyms that are not obviously Celtic should not be allowed to imply instead the presence of Germanic. This is a very well understood language-group, which would be recognized if it were present).

core, rather than vice versa. If what is core and what is periphery comes into question matters are going to be very difficult indeed.

Thus I turn, at last, to ancient Celtic names and some comments on their distribution. By way of introduction it must be said that this is, at least, a very propitious time to be thinking about this topic. The publication, within the last few years, of both John Koch's magisterial *Atlas for Celtic Studies* (2007) and Patrick Sims-Williams' *Ancient Celtic Place-Names in Europe and Asia Minor* (2006) have provided authoritative modern guides to a subject that was previously reliant on ancient and misleading reference works, like Holder's *Alt-celtischer sprachschatz*, and innumerable and very variable regional studies, published in many different lands and languages. The groundwork is at least now in place to begin to look: the questions are how to look, and what to look for.

As Koch (2007, 3–9) and Sims-Williams (2006, 3–4) agree, the general maximal extent of evidence for Celtic speech can best be established by analysis of the place-names and group- or people- or tribal-names recorded in the writings of ancient Europe, which means very predominantly those that come from 'Roman' sources, loosely defined. There is much more information, in many areas, to be gleaned from the records of place-names that are first recorded at a later date—the great majority of the Celtic river-names on the map of Britain fall into this category, for instance—and there remains very much to be done here, especially in works of synthesis; but the indications of classical sources are a good starting-point for the early distribution, and have the advantage—with this chronologically slippery material—of taking us back to at least the first half of the first millennium AD.[10]

The picture that thus emerges is, of course, a familiar one with Celtic language, as defined by its names, covering a great swathe of Europe from Britain and Ireland in the north-west, and much of the Iberian Peninsula in the south-west, through Gaul, with parts of the Low Countries in the north, much of the centre of the Continent, with in the south the Alpine regions, down to northern Italy; and east along the Danube to the Black Sea coast and beyond to Galatia. One of the extraordinary facts of the Celtic language-group as revealed by this earliest historical horizon is this huge dispersal, in place across nearly all of its extent by the very earliest records. (Of the major regions, only the extension to Galatia appears to be demonstrably secondary, as it is believed to be attributable to a recorded invasion of the 3rd century BC: Koch 2007, 13.) Another extraordinary feature is the apparent close similarity of the language across its dispersed regions. This is true for the varieties of language revealed by inscriptions, and it is particularly true with regard to the names (Koch 2007, 9). The point is most clearly made by examples like the nine instances of *Mediolanum*—'the middle plain (place)' or '(the place in) middle of the plain' (cf. De Bernardo Stempel 2000, 94)—stretching from the site which is now known as Whitchurch, in Shropshire, to northern Italy

---

10   The material used here is drawn from Sims-Williams's collections from the *Barrington Atlas*: as he discusses (2006, 16–21) this corpus has its drawbacks, but offers a huge, nearly comprehensive, dataset of early-recorded names.

and Milan, which, of course, is a direct development of the early Celtic name. Again, there are several places in Gaul called *Noviodunum*, 'the new fort', just as there is one in Dacia, near the western shore of the Black Sea. Such names, together with many other elements, appear in identical form in diffuse distributions encompassing huge distances. The closeness of correspondence is remarkable. But it is not as simple, of course, as everywhere sharing all the same vocabulary. Different patterns of correspondence are to be observed in different terms. And it is indeed these differences—the absence of a single obvious core which might be thought ancestral to the peripheries—which complicate the investigation.

The material mapped here is primarily drawn from Sims-Williams's detailed

8.2. The *-brigā* names of ancient Europe (dark yellow points indicate imprecisely located names).

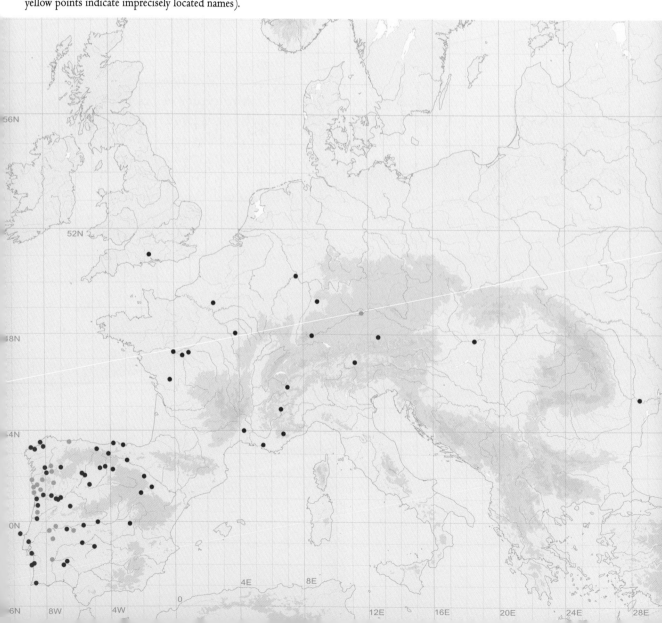

catalogue, with the occasional addition from Koch's *Atlas*. Sims-Williams himself provides distribution-maps, and these will be closely comparable with those produced here, save in one regard. His careful method was to include in his survey, and map, all instances of particular spellings and groups of spellings from the corpus of names known from classical sources. This made sure of including everything that could conceivably represent particular Celtic elements, but—as he discusses in detail throughout the work—a number of these are clearly 'false friends' which, in their local context, are not to be regarded as Celtic. The maps published here take into account these discussions and exclude, therefore, unlikely instances, principally from the edges of the main distributions.[11]

Figures 8.2–8.5 show the distributions of four widespread name-elements: *briga*, 'high place, hillfort', cf. Welsh *bre*, 'hill, highland'; *duno-*, 'enclosure, fort', cf. Welsh *din*, 'stronghold'; *duro-*, 'gated fort?, yard', cf. Welsh *dôr*, 'door, refuge'; *mag-*, 'field, plain', cf. Welsh *ma*, 'plain, place' and Welsh *maes*, 'open country, field'.

Now the question to be addressed in the present context is: what can be fairly concluded from such names and such distributions? Is there anything here that carries the sort of significance that was attributed to the *-ingas* distributions in Anglo-Saxon England? In that case socio-historical context suggested that the type was an early one, but it is hard to see with these, or with other early Celtic elements, that anything marks one word out as implicitly earlier than another. We would essentially be looking for social and semantic development within prehistoric centuries, and by definition that will be difficult to identify. Yet, if no geographical core is established from the independent indications of history or archaeology, it is difficult to see how else conclusions about the chronology of Celtic language-diffusion can be reached.

That is not to deny that the distributions are interesting and intriguing. But it is to observe that chronological explanations are not easy to sustain. One aspect of the problem is that the varied distributions of these elements—a variety that could be multiplied by reference to many more—are to some extent mutually opposed. Why argue on the basis of the distribution of *briga*, for instance, that it was an old element going out of use at the period when the Celts reached Britain, when one could equally make the opposite argument: that *duno-* may have belonged to the original period of British and Continental Celtic, and was going out of use when the language at last reached the Iberian Peninsula? These points, and others of similar significance, have been very effectively made by Sims-Williams (2006, 306–9).

The specific argument that *briga* is significantly early and predates the arrival of Celtic in Britain is the burden of a paper by Helmut Rix (1954), which was taken up and made more widely known by Stuart Piggott (1965, 172–4). For Piggott the hypothesis

---

11   It should be noted that a few such false friends from otherwise solidly Celtic areas may have slipped through since both Sims-Williams and I have been mainly concerned to investigate problematic cases on the edges of the distributions. Note also that I have followed the suggested identifications of sites accepted by Sims-Williams.

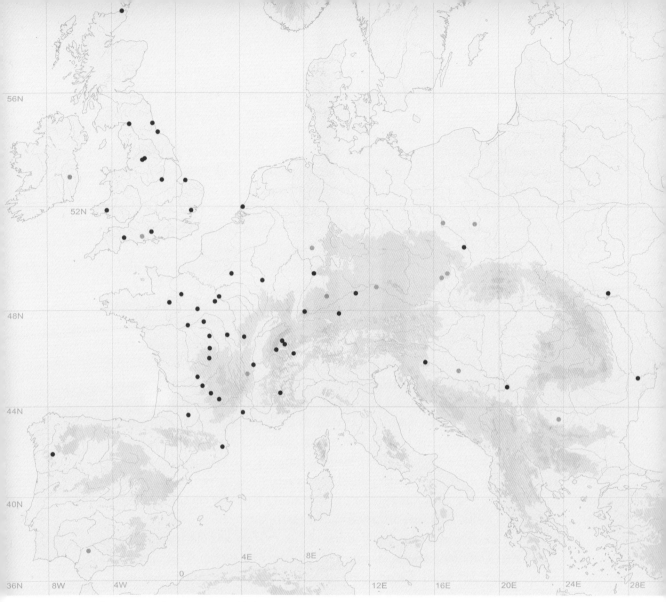

8.3. The -dūno- names of ancient Europe (dark
yellow points indicate imprecisely located names)

could be readily harmonized with the archaeological data of his Urnfield culture. It is
interesting to note, then, that archaeological assumptions play no part in Rix's original
reasoning: if there were something of substance in his argument, therefore, it would gain
great strength from clear correlations with archaeology. Yet in fact the basis of Rix's
argument—the reason that he suggests a chronological interpretation of his maps—is
very weak (1954, 105).[12] He first observes: (1) that *dūno- and *brigā mean much the same

12 Rix maps *dūno-, *brigā and *mag-. The outline distributions produced are certainly broadly comparable with
    those in the present maps, though there are many differences in detail: he missed many classical sources, now
    included, but he included an eclectic collection of later-recorded names, excluded here. See Sims-Williams

thing, 'fortress, hillfort', and (2) that their distribution overlaps in Gaul. From these observations he draws two conclusions: (1) that they cannot represent contemporary dialectal variation, because of the geographical overlap, and (2) that the difference between them must be a matter of chronology, because it is clearly not a question of semantics: 'es bleibt also nur die chronologische Differenz', 'thus there remains only chronological distinction'. Yet this is very shallow reasoning. On the one hand, contemporary dialectal usage often overlaps, so that it may be dangerous to exclude the possibility that the two words could be used synonymously in the same general area at the same time. On the other hand, and more worryingly, Rix's assertion that *brigā and *dūno- simply meant the same thing begs many questions. Although it is clear that the terms were applied, across much of their range, to strongholds and hillforts, it is unreasonable to assume that the usage was necessarily synonymous. To draw, once more, on parallel material from medieval England, it is now clear, after decades of work by Margaret Gelling, that many Old English terms once considered synonymous, as e.g. dūn, berg, hyll, all 'hill', are consistently applied to features of different forms, in this case hills of varying profiles, indicating that semantic distinctions could be fine and precise (Gelling 1984; Gelling & Cole 2000). In the pair of Celtic words under discussion there is certainly some reason to suspect a degree of semantic distinction, because both etymology and later Welsh usage tend to indicate that, although in some areas they could both be applied to a 'hillfort', *brigā is first and foremost the 'hill', while *dūno- is in origin the 'fort'. The possibility that in Gaul, where they overlap, some distinction in usage may have been at work can hardly be discounted. Progress could be made here: detailed observation and archaeological study of the places so named in central Gaul might suggest a semantic distinction; or might possibly reinstate, or reverse, Rix's proposed chronology. But, in their own terms, Rix's pioneering proposals are not convincing.[13]

Another attempt to read chronology into the distribution of early Celtic place-names was made by Rivet (1980, 13–15), who suggested that names in *Duro-, like Durovernum, Canterbury, might be characteristically Belgic in dialect, and belong to a later stratum of naming than many of the old Celtic toponyms. The appeal here is to Caesar's account of Belgic migration to Britain and, although it leaves some marginal details of distribution to be accounted for, there may be something to the idea (Sims-Williams 2006, 308–9). In fact, names that begin Duro-, as opposed to those in which the term appears in second position, look to form part of a pattern of correspondences linking Britain, and southern Britain in particular, with Gaul, and northern Gaul in particular. Another example, mapped in Figure 5, is *brīvā/*brīvo-, 'bridge' (as in two British instances

2006, 308.

13 Koch (2007, 4) notes the extraordinary pairing of Noviodunum and Aliobrix, 'the new fort' and 'the other hillfort', on opposite banks of the Danube near the Black Sea. He suggests that these tend to support Rix's chronology, by implying 'a degree of time depth', though since the names, as they stand, appear to be mutually dependent, this is not straightforward. It is notable that Falileyev (2007, 4) in effect reverses Rix's chronology by taking Aliobrix as '"the second/other high (fortified) settlement", the first being perhaps Noviodunum'.

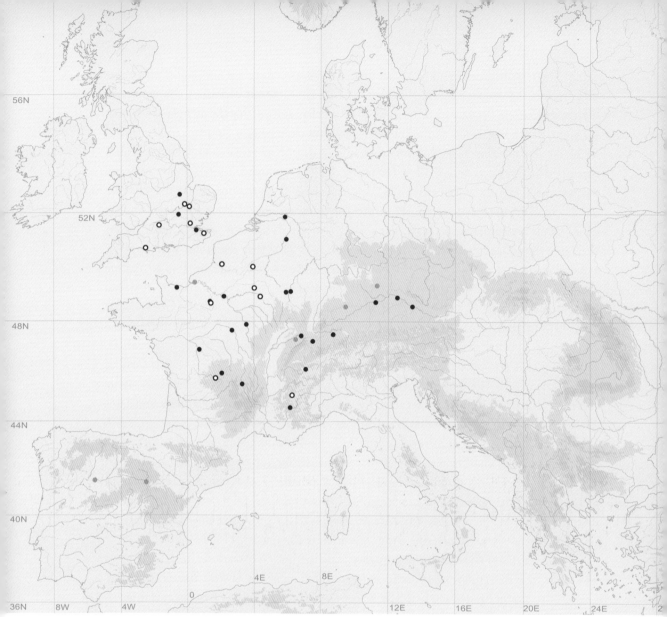

8.4. The *-duro-* names of ancient Europe, open points mark
Duro- as first element, solid points second element (dark
yellow indicates imprecisely located second-element names)

of *Durobrivae*, where it is combined with **Duro-*); others discussed and mapped by
Sims-Williams (2006, 310–11, mapped variously between 328–56) include **verno-*,
'alder, swamp', and **novio-*, 'new'. Together, these elements do tend to suggest dialectal
continuity across the sea, and they must raise the possibility of connections—contacts
and movements—between areas at some date before the names are recorded. They may
perhaps have something to do with Caesar's late Belgic migration, but presumably that
story, at the least, suggests the possibility or likelihood of linguistic influence, sometimes
as the result of population movement, within the Celtic speech-area in the centuries

before our names are recorded. The point to be made here is that linguistic movement and development within the larger Celtic area is bound to be a confusing factor in any attempt to deduce 'origins' and the 'earliest dispersal' from the patterns that survive for us. Indeed, it is worth noting that Rix himself, having proposed a chronology in which *brigā* did not survive late enough to enter Britain, conceded: 'Damit ist die Möglichkeit einer früheren Keltenwelle in England nicht ausgeschlossen; nur bietet das genannte Material keinen Anhalt dafür' 'this does not mean that the possibility of an earlier Celtic

8.5. The -*mag*- names of ancient Europe (dark yellow points indicate imprecisely located names)

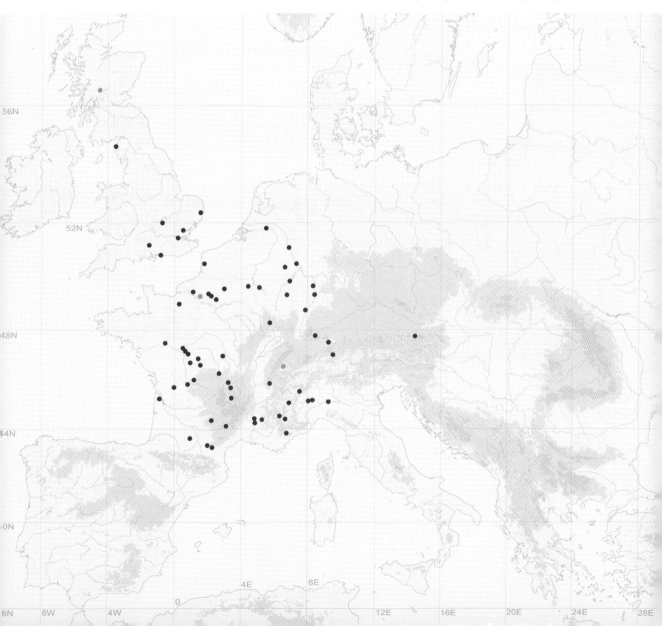

wave is excluded; but the material under discussion does not support it' (1954, 105 n. 20).

Another noteworthy point arises from the later attestation of some of the words discussed here. Thus whilst *verno- and *novio- survive intact in modern Welsh, as *gwern* and *newydd*, there is no clear trace of *brīvā 'bridge' in the insular Celtic languages. This may be thought to accord *brīvā a special place in our deliberations, and so it perhaps should, though its loss in Welsh is no mystery in the sense that it was the Latin loanword *pont* that took its place. The *brīvā names in England might therefore be regarded as typologically early, but in absolute terms that need put them no further back than the earlier, rather than the later, Roman period: hardly earlier, in fact, than they are first attested. These names serve as a reminder that the period of time-depth that we have to play with is a long one. When discussing Anglo-Saxon names, I remarked, in the case of *gē, 'district', that its absence from recorded Old English texts may be significant of its early date in place-names. Unfortunately, with Celtic languages this becomes a much more diluted criterion. The gap between place-names recorded in, say, the 1st and 2nd centuries AD and the first extensive written records of Celtic languages, such as might be expected to encompass a good deal of common terminology, is more than half a millennium. This is a very long time in which vocabulary could have been lost by quite usual processes. It will be very hard indeed to argue that terms in ancient place-names are likely to be genuinely early simply because they do not appear in the much later lexicon of Welsh or Irish.

To conclude, therefore, a comparison between the situation in early historic England with that in prehistoric Britain and Europe indicates some hugely significant differences. If there is no certainty as to the core Celtic area, place-name distributions are left floating, begging questions but providing precious few answers. And the problem of time-depth looms large. The enormous geographical spread of the Celtic language-group is largely securely attested by the later first millennium BC. How long could it have been there? If 500 years or more is a realistic suggestion, then we must question the chronological relevance of any patterns that we think we see in the distributions. If such patterns do have significance with regard to movement and linguistic influence, what is to stop them reflecting forces at work many centuries after the original Celticization? In fact this last point is the one to which I would attach some importance in future interdisciplinary research. For good reason it is no longer acceptable to associate some archaeological cultures with the original spread of Celtic language. Yet correlation between archaeological distribution and specific types of place-name continues to be well worth investigating, with the caveat that associations thus revealed may help us to identify some related communities, but by no means necessarily take us back to the original introduction of Celtic language to an area. Better yet, as I have suggested above, would be the focused archaeological investigation of similarly named places in an attempt to reveal what exactly associated them in the minds of early Celtic speakers.

A further point remains troubling. In his paper on 'Celtic names and Roman places' Rivet struggled with the observation that apparently Roman-built towns often acquired descriptive Celtic place-names (1980, 15). One of his suggested solutions was that sometimes, after the original troops had withdrawn, Roman administrators might have asked the locals what they called a place and then adopted it into official usage. Another was that since many auxiliary units of the Roman army 'were raised in Celtic-speaking areas' they may have had a hand in the naming. If this latter were a serious possibility it should cause us to think hard about the basis of our place-name distributions and indeed of our map of Celtic language-spread. Something it brings to my mind is the observation, briefly alluded to above, that the far-flung Celtic place-names are remarkably undifferentiated in the earliest records: 'the appearance', according to Koch (2007, 9), 'is one of an extensive and highly uniform lingua franca'. Would such a lingua franca—if that is an accurate characterization—have arisen in late pre-Roman Europe, representing connections and reconnections made across areas that were in many cases already Celtic-speaking? Or could it alternatively, following Rivet, be something inherent within the Roman Empire? If the names were not themselves being coined by Celtic-speaking legionaries, could there at least not have been a layer of administration, imposing—unconsciously perhaps—some consistency of form on names that one might have thought would show rather more variety in local pronunciation and representation from Portugal to the Black Sea. After all, as the maps appear so clearly to show, a vast tract of the Romans' territory was populated by Celtic speakers. Many must have found their way into the administration, and even those administrators who did not themselves speak the language would inevitably have become familiar with the toponymy of the major conquered provinces. The uncertain degree to which we are seeing early Celtic place-name distributions through the prism of Roman bureaucracy is yet another complicating factor in this challenging investigation.

BIBLIOGRAPHY

Abrams, L. & D. N. Parsons 2004 'Place-names and the history of Scandinavian settlement in England'. *Land, Sea and Home: proceedings of a conference on Viking-period settlement*, eds. J. Hines et al., 379–431. Leeds, Maney.

Bailey, K. 1998–9 'Some observations on *gē, gau* and *go*', *Journal of the English Place-Name Society* 31, 63–76.

Cullen, P., R. Jones & D. N. Parsons forthcoming *Thorps in a Changing Landscape*. Hatfield, University of Hertfordshire Press.

De Bernardo Stempel, P. 2000 'Ptolemy's Celtic Italy and Ireland: a linguistic analysis'. *Ptolemy: towards a linguistic atlas of the earliest Celtic place-names of Europe*, eds. D. N. Parsons & P. Sims-Williams, 83–112. Aberystwyth, CMCS.

Ekwall, E. 1918 *Scandinavians and Celts in the North-West of England*. Lund, Gleerup.

Falileyev, A. 2007 *Celtic Dacia: personal names, place-names and ethnic names of Celtic origin in Dacia and Scythia Minor*. Aberystwyth, CMCS.

Gelling, M. 1984 *Place-Names in the Landscape*. London, Dent.

Gelling, M. 1988 *Signposts to the Past*, 2nd ed. Chichester, Phillimore.

Gelling, M. & A. Cole 2000 *The Landscape of Place-Names*. Stamford, Shaun Tyas.

Giles, J. A. 1906 *Old English Chronicles*. London, George Bell.

Higham, N., ed., 2007 *Britons in Anglo-Saxon England*. Woodbridge, Boydell.

Ireland, S. 1996 *Roman Britain: a sourcebook*, 2nd ed. London & New York, Routledge.

Jackson, K. H. 1953 *Language and History in Early Britain*. Edinburgh, University Press.

Kitson, P. 1995 'The nature of Old English dialect distributions, mainly as exhibited in charter boundaries'. *Medieval Dialectology*, ed. J. Fisiak, 73–118. Berlin & New York, de Gruyter.

Koch, J. T. 2007 *An Atlas for Celtic Studies: archaeology and names in ancient Europe and early medieval Ireland, Britain, and Brittany*. Oxford, Oxbow.

Lapidge, M. & D. N. Dumville, eds., 1984 *Gildas: New Approaches*. Woodbridge, Boydell.

Oppenheimer, S. 2006 *The Origins of the British: a genetic detective story*. London, Constable.

Parsons, D. N. forthcoming *The Pre-Viking Place-Names of Northamptonshire*, 26th Brixworth Lecture.

Piggott, S. 1965 *Ancient Europe: from the beginnings of agriculture to classical antiquity*. Edinburgh, University Press.

Rivet, A. L. F. 1980 'Celtic names and Roman places'. *Britannia* 11, 1–19.

Rix, H. 1954 'Zur Verbreitung und Chronologie einiger keltischer Ortsnamentypen'. *Festschrift für Peter Goessler*, 99–107. Stuttgart, W. Kohlhammer.

Sims-Williams, P. 1990 'Dating the transition to neo-Brittonic: phonology and history'. *Britain 400–600: Language and History*, eds. A. Bammesberger & A. Wollmann, 217–61. Heidelberg, Carl Winter.

Sims-Williams, P. 2006 *Ancient Celtic Place-Names in Europe and Asia Minor*. Oxford, Blackwell.

Smith, A. H. 1956 *English Place-Name Elements*, 2 vols., EPNS 25–6. Cambridge, University Press.

Winterbottom, M., ed. and trans., 1978 *Gildas: The Ruin of Britain and other works*. London & Chichester, Phillimore.

CHAPTER NINE

PARADIGM SHIFT?
INTERPRETING TARTESSIAN AS CELTIC

John T. Koch

Keynote

T H E subject of this chapter is the Tartessian language, which is attested in south Portugal and south-west Spain, mostly as a corpus of inscriptions, dating to the mid 1st millennium BC, the number of which is now 95 and growing. This language is also sometimes called 'Sudlusitanian', i.e. '"South" Lusitanian', or merely 'South-western', which can be abbreviated in Spanish and Portuguese as 'SO'. The name 'Sudlusitanian' is potentially misleading, as there is a language of the Roman period for which the name 'Lusitanian' is already well established. The evidence of the Lusitanian language is discussed by Dagmar Wodtko in this volume. There is presently no reason to identify the Tartessian language or the kingdom of Tartessos with the language of the Lusitanian inscriptions. 'South-western' accurately describes the situation of Tartessian in the extreme south-west of the European continent, but the usual frame of reference is Peninsular, so that 'North-west' in this context means Galicia and parts nearby, rather than Ireland, Norway, or Brittany. 'Tartessian' is also a preferable name because the connection with the historically and archaeologically known kingdom of Tartessos appears increasingly certain.

In face of the rapid pace of discovery and interpretation (see Guerra above), the present publication provides an opportunity to re-present—in expanded and updated form—the texts and linguistic notes that appeared in my *Tartessian* (2009). Beyond this primary linguistic material, the study of Tartessian holds potentially decisive implications for the theme of this book. As shown below, much of the corpus can be interpreted as Indo-European and specifically as Celtic. Probably or possibly Celtic forms are of sufficient density to support the conclusion that Tartessian is simply a Celtic language, the oldest attested one, rather than a non-Celtic language containing a relatively small proportion of Celtic names and loanwords.

Paradigm Shift?

The Celts and Ancient Celtic speech are often closely identified with the Hallstatt and La Tène cultures. So, despite repeated debunkings and general signs of exhaustion (see, e.g., Sims-Williams 1998; James 2000), the standard narrative of the Celts still begins in Iron Age central Europe, much as it did half a century ago in T. G. E. Powell's *The Celts* (1958). Early mentions of Κελτοί *Keltoí* by the Greeks are often woven into this account. But if we look carefully at these texts, the Greeks do not clearly locate the Celts in the Hallstatt/La Tène zone. Barry Cunliffe cites the key evidence in his contribution to this volume, and John Collis (2003) has lately clarified in detail the south-western orientation of the early references to the Celts. Herodotus is the exception. He said the Keltoí lived at the source of the Danube.

§2.34. The Nile flows out of Libya, cutting through the middle of that country. And as I reason, calculating unknown things from known, it begins at the same distance as the Ister [Danube]. For the Ister, beginning in the land of the Celts and the city of Pyrene, flows through the middle of Europe. The Celts live beyond the Pillars of Hercules [Straits of Gibraltar] and border on the Cynetes [Κυνήσιοι], who are the westernmost inhabitants of Europe. The Ister then flows through all of Europe and empties into the Euxine [Black Sea] at Istria, which colonists from Miletus inhabit. (trans. Freeman in Koch & Carey 2003, 5)

§4.48. For the Ister [Danube] flows through all of Europe, rising among the Celts who are the westernmost inhabitants of Europe, except for the Cynetes [Κυνητες]. Flowing through all of Europe, it reaches its end along the borders of Scythia. (trans. Freeman 1996, 19)

Thus the upper Danube has been taken as the authoritative localization. References to Ἀλβιων *Albion* and Ἰερνη *Iernē*—Britain and Ireland—are nearly as early as Herodotus, maybe earlier, depending on what we make of the archaic sources used by Avienus in his *Ora Maritima* (cf. Freeman below). But Albion and Iernē tend to be relegated to a later chapter in 'The Story of the Celts'.

The evidence collected in this chapter implies that it might make more sense to begin the Story of the Celts in Tartessos, rather than on the Danube. Where and what is Tartessos? Most archaeologists and historians today put the centre of ancient Tartessos in or near Huelva on Spain's Atlantic coast, between Gibraltar and Portugal's border. Many ancient writers as well as modern experts also include Huelva's metal-rich hinterland. Tartessos can go down to the Straits, the ancient *Fretum Tartessium* (*Ora Maritima* line 54), and include the Kunētes of the Algarve (as in Justin's *Epitome* of the *Philippic Histories* of Trogus Pompeius, see Freeman below)—hence, the whole south-western quarter of the Iberian Peninsula. For the ancients, Tartessos could also explicitly include Gadir (Greek Γάδειρα, Latin *Gades*, now Cádiz in Spain) before the Phoenicians founded their colony there. Therefore, Tartessos was the earliest important native kingdom immediately beyond the Pillars of Hercules. (On the structure of this polity—often regarded a kingdom in ancient sources—and its probable extent in the south-western Peninsula, see further Almagro-Gorbea 1988; Gamito 1988; 1993.)

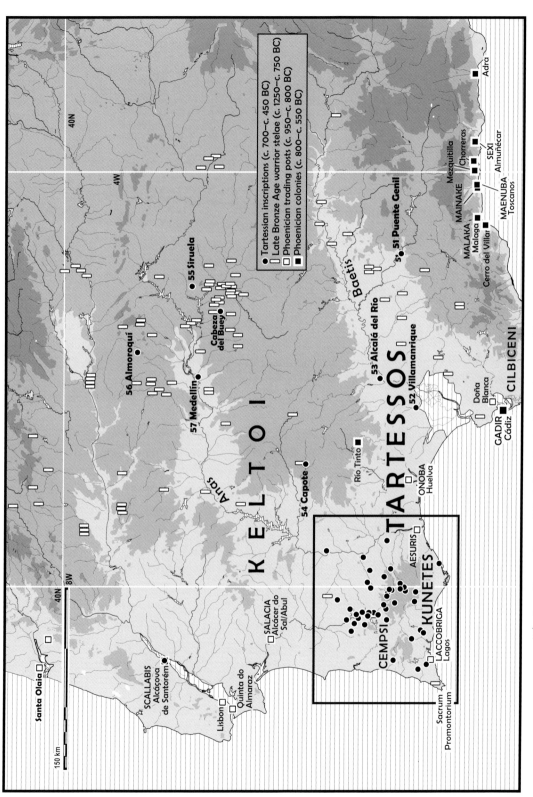

9.1. The Late Bronze Age and Early Iron Age in the south-western Iberian Peninsula: 'warrior' stelae, Phoenician colonies, and Tartessian inscriptions; for southern Portugal, see p. 79 above.

The classical sources show that Tartessos and the Tartessians occupied territory adjacent to, or overlapping with, that of the south-western Κελτοί or Κελτικοί *Celtici* (as in Strabo 3.5.5, Pliny, *Naturalis Historia* 3.1.13). Both are neighbours of the Kunētes and located near the rivers Anas and Baetis, today's Guadiana and Guadalquivir. But Tartessians and Celts are not often named together. For Herodotus the distinction appears to have been chronological. He used Ταρτησσος in relating events of the 7th and 6th centuries BC, but Κελτοί in describing the same region in his own day. The kingdom of Tartessos collapsed before 500 BC, but there is little evidence to show a new population moving in. In other words, Tartessians appear to have been replaced by Celts, in part at least, or simply to have become Celts. (It is possible that the long inscriptions of Bensafrim [J.1.1 'Fonte Velha 6'] and Mesas do Castelinho identify their honorands as 'Celt' and/or 'Gaul', if we read Tartessian kᵃaltᵉe as the dative singular corresponding to Greek nominative plural Γαλάται *Galátai* and/or Κέλται, Latin *Celtae*.)

Semitic sources tell of Tarshish, including Assyrian texts and the Phoenician inscription of Nora, Sardinia. Peckham's interpretation of the latter is relevant here:

> The Nora inscription . . . is evidence that around 850–825 BC a ship, with its captain and crew, dropped anchor in Sardinia, on its way from Tarshish [TRŠŠ] under adverse conditions, and that their safe arrival prompted them to offer thanks to the Cypriot God PMY and set up a stele recording the events . . . it has to be observed that either the ship carried a scribe, like the ship lost at Ulu Burun [off southern Turkey *c.* 1327 or 1305 BC], and a not unlikely feature of commercial travel, or that there was a resident Phoenician scribe in Nora. . . . it seems likely that Nora was a port of call on voyages between Cyprus and Spain . . . (1998, 352)

The Old Testament contains numerous mentions of 'ships of Tarshish' bringing metals and other luxuries from the outer ocean world (collected by Freeman, this volume). The earliest of these relates to the building of the Temple of Jerusalem at the time of the joint venture of Solomon (961–922 BC) and Hiram I (971–939 BC), the merchant king of Tyre. On the western terminus of this trade route the date of *c.* 950 BC is confirmed. That is the calibrated C14 date of the Huelva deposition (Ruiz-Gálvez Priego 1995; Kristiansen 1998, 126; Cunliffe 2001, 279). In it, objects from the eastern Mediterranean were found together with masses of Atlantic Late Bronze Age metalwork. So contact between Tartessos and the literate eastern Mediterranean goes back into the Late Bronze Age. First with the Mycenaean Greeks by *c.* 1340/30 cal BC (Mederos Martín 1997; 1999). In the period between the collapse of Aegean civilization *c.* 1200 BC and the beginnings of formal, archaeologically visible Phoenician colonies on the Peninsula's southern coast *c.* 850/800 BC, Tartessian links with Cyprus by way of Sardinia continued and grew (Mederos Martín 1996; Harrison 2004; Ruiz-Gálvez Priego 2008).

We can also trace a continuity of funerary tradition, with images of warriors on Late Bronze Age stelae evolving into—with some intermediate examples, such as

Cabeza del Buey IV below, p. 256—written inscriptions in Early Iron Age necropolises (Kristiansen 1998, 157–60). The 100 or so south-western stelae of Bronze Age Hispania include weapons that are clearly Atlantic Late Bronze Age types: leaf-shaped swords and Herzsprung or 'V-notched' shields (Celestino Pérez 2001; Harrison 2004). Examples of such shields in leather have been found preserved in Irish bogs. By 900 BC, the Iberian Peninsula had joined the Early Iron Age of the Mediterranean world, turning away from the Atlantic Bronze Age. A full-blown hybrid Orientalizing Period comes to the southern Peninsula by *c.* 800 BC with Phoenician colonies and literacy.

What were they exchanging? Wine, oil, cosmetics, jewellery, and figurines (many identifiable as gods) came from the east. From Tartessos came silver, copper, gold, and (transhipped) tin from Galicia and probably also Armorica and possibly even Cornwall. Finished Iberian Late Bronze Age metalwork (brooches, feasting equipment, swords) has been identified in Sardinia and Cyprus.

For us writing is the key import. The main concentration of Tartessian inscriptions is in southern Portugal with a much wider scatter over south-western Spain. New discoveries are coming from both regions—e.g. the inscriptions of Corte Pinheiro, Mesas do Castelinho, and Vale da Águia found in south Portugal in 2008 (Guerra above) and the inscription and warrior stela of Cabezo del Buey IV from near Badajoz (Correa 2008). The latter part of this chapter includes a catalogue of the Tartessian inscriptions and linguistic notes which show that much of this corpus can be interpreted as Celtic.

Even if the South-western inscriptions did not exist, or if we had no idea how to decode their script, there would be reason to think that Celtic was spoken in Tartessos. According to Herodotus (§1.163), a very rich king ruled Tartessos between about 625 and 545 BC. He was named Ἀργανθώνιος *Argantonios*. This name, or title, is clearly Celtic consisting of the word for silver and money *arganto-* (attested in all the Celtic languages), then the divine or mythological suffix found in Celtic divine names like *Maponos* and *Epona*, and then the agent suffix *-ios*. So 'agent of divine silver', which is closely comparable to the title ARGANTODANNOS found on Gaulish silver coinage. There could hardly be a more appropriate title than Ἀργανθώνιος for the ruler of the silver-based polity of Tartessos during the Orientalizing Period of the First Iron Age.

Numerous Greek and Roman references locate the Κυνητες in the Algarve, probably the same name as *Conii*, also located in the south-west. The name Κυνητες closely resembles the Ancient British place-name *Cunētio*, which corresponds to Medieval Welsh *Kynwydion* (British **Cunētiones*), the name of the war-band of Dark Age Strathclyde. The root of these names is apparently Celtic **kū*, **kuno-*, which literally means 'dog', but also metaphorically 'warrior, hero'. So I suggest that *Kunētes* in Tartessos means, like *Kynwydyon* in north Britain, 'band of warriors'.

When we come down to records of the Roman Period, there are Celtic names from the south-west of the Peninsula including names in Celtic *-brigā* meaning 'hillfort', also *sego-* 'strong', and *eburo-* 'yew-tree'.

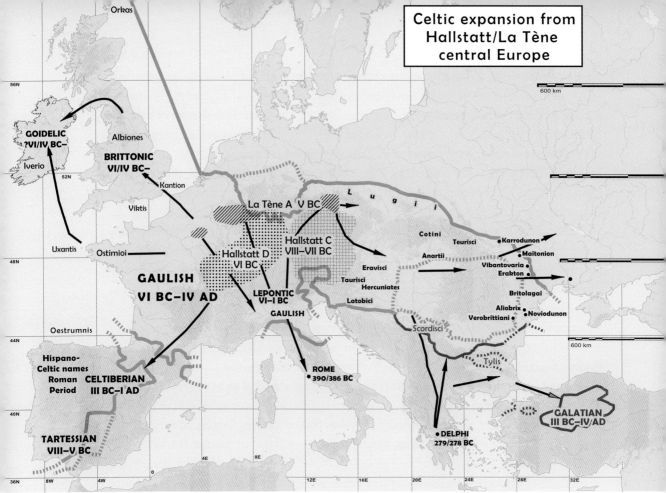

9.2. The traditional 'invasive' or diffusionist model for the expansion of the Celtic languages from Iron Age central Europe; the lavender outline shows the limits of Ancient Celtic linguistic evidence (mostly following place- and group names); areas in red indicate zones known to have been settled by Celtic groups after the attack on Delphi of 279/278 BC.

Is it a paradigm shift to recognize Tartessian as a Celtic language? Adding one more Ancient Celtic language to the list is *moderately* significant for Celtic studies overall. Tartessian doesn't change the extent of Ancient Celtic languages. We already knew about the *-brigā* names and so on in the south-west. The great sweep is still east-to-west and mostly inland, either side of the Danube. However, Tartessian is now the *oldest* of the attested languages, displacing Lepontic near Hallstatt central Europe. Even if we allow only that the Tartessian sources show some Celtic forms in the matrix of another, unidentified language, the implications are much the same: Celtic had come to the extreme south-west of Europe by *c.* 700 BC. So the east-west span now tilts westward.

Back when prehistoric invasions were favoured as an explanatory model, this great 4,000 kilometre overland span was explained by means of black arrows representing warlike Celts expanding east and west from Hallstatt/La Tène middle Europe. Tartessian unsettles this picture because it is in an area that Hallstatt and La Tène material never reached. It is also too early. Tartessos was all over before La Tène started. Even Hallstatt is too late. So back to the Bronze Age. There are two major candidates as Late Bronze Age cultural contexts for Proto-Celtic: the Urnfield Culture in the east and the Atlantic Bronze Age—in effect mirroring Herodotus's bilocation of the Κελτοί on the upper Danube and on the Atlantic near Gibraltar.

In favour of Urnfield. Urnfield burials spread from the Carpathian Basin into central Europe. Urnfield is the primary Late Bronze Age ancestor of Hallstatt and La Tène. So moving back to Urnfield does least to rock the boat of the established model. We can keep the arrows. Secondly, Iberian archaeologists recognize Urnfield influences in the eastern Peninsula by about 900 BC. So this is—or at least can be—their 'Coming of the Celts'.

On the other hand, we can start chipping away at the hypothesis Urnfield = Proto-Celtic. First, we know from historical sources that Galatia in Asia Minor (Mitchell 1993), Tylis in Thrace (Falileyev 2005), and the Scordisci in the upper Balkans (Gaspari 2006) all took shape after the Celtic attack on Delphi in 278 BC. So the whole south-eastern quarter of the Celtic world is known to be late, historical, post-classical, Hellenistic. The Urnfield homeland is nearby, but 1,000 years earlier and, therefore, explains nothing.

Moving north to the country of the first Urnfields, there are Celtic place-names all around the Carpathian Basin, but few in it. Falileyev's *Celtic Dacia* (2007) has now clarified this picture. There are La Tène burials in the area, but these are clearly an expansion from Bohemia and the west. They are Middle La Tène, 400 BC or later. Once again, the hypothesis Urnfield = Proto-Celtic does nothing to explain this material. We can understand the whole eastern half of the Celtic world as developments of Hellenistic times.

Redrawing the map to show the Ancient Celtic languages back in the days of Herodotus: Urnfield's Carpathian Basin home is now completely detached from Celtic Europe. The eastern Hallstatt area is in doubt. It was never completely Celtic speaking: the non-Celtic Rhaetian—possibly akin to Etruscan—was spoken in the central Alps.

So, with the great overland sweep cut in half, what now seems striking is the north–south, Orkney-to-Huelva dimension—the Atlantic Bronze zone + the countries reached by Atlantic-facing rivers.

Let's now ask the question, how did the Celtic languages spread, and consider two models. The tendency has been to see the expansion as primarily overland, Model 1. Of course, Hallstatt and La Tène are themselves landlocked. Also, the cultural and linguistic ancestors of the Celts, the Indo-Europeans had probably originally lived inland in western Asia and/or eastern Europe. There is Indo-European vocabulary for horses and wheeled vehicles (Mallory 1989; Mallory & Adams 2006), not so much for ships. However, some Indo-European languages became seaborne and then spread by sea—Greek, for example—thus, Model 2.

As well as being remote from the lands that spoke Celtic in Herodotus's day, another obstacle for supposing that Proto-Celts spread with the Urnfield rite is that their wagons must roll all the way to headlands, peninsulas, and (of course) islands—Sagres, Galicia,

Armorica, Ouessant, Cornwall, Anglesey, Dingle, Orkney. Celtic languages were both early established and held on tenaciously in places easily reached by sea and not easily reached by land.

Two further reasons against a Proto-Celtic-speaking Urnfield culture: (1) Where were Dacian, Pannonian, and Phrygian? There are non-Celtic languages for which good cases can be made for an Urnfield Late Bronze Age homeland (cf. Kristiansen 1998). The Carpathian Basin thus becomes rather crowded with Indo-European proto-languages in the later 2nd millennium BC—if Celtic was there too, that is. If Celtic had always been spoken by the Middle Danube, why then are Celtic and the indigenous Pannonian very different languages when we find them side by side there in Roman times in Tacitus's *Germania* (§43) and in the onomastic evidence of the languages themselves (Meid 2008)? (2) Herodotus knew the lower Danube, and there were no Keltoí or Celtic speakers there (as indicated by the dearth of Celtic proper names in the *Histories*) in the 5th century BC.

It is plain from the passages quoted above that Herodotus was confused about the Danube: it is not as long as the Nile and does not flow across the entire continent of Europe. He clearly thought it began in Spain. In the next century, when Aristotle reworked Herodotus's account (see Freeman this volume for the passage), he did not completely correct it. Πυρηνη *Purēnē* has ceased to be a city and become the more familiar mountain range. Ταρτησσος is for Aristotle a river (presumably the Guadalquivir) and Κελτοί significantly live nearby. The connection of the Κελτοί with the source of the Ister remains, but so does the mistaken idea that the Danube flowed from south-west Europe.

The evidence encapsulated above suggests an alternative hypothesis. A second group of Indo-Europeans became mariners like the Greeks. So, rather than walking or riding, they *sailed* west, to the outer ocean. Once based in the Atlantic zone, their Indo-European developed into Celtic, and that language came to dominate the Atlantic exchange networks. From the coast, Celtic spread up Atlantic-facing rivers.

Such a hypothesis is not a priori incompatible with the arguments for the eastern affinities of Celtic by Isaac (2004; 2007b; and this volume), Schmidt (1996), and De Bernardo Stempel (2006). That case pertains to an earlier stage, implying that the Late Indo-European background of Proto-Celtic was in proximity with that of eastern Indo-European languages including Greek and Indo-Iranian. The time of any such interaction would have to be some centuries before *c.* 1650 BC, at which time a fully developed Greek was already a written language in its historical Aegean homeland and no longer geographically in contact with Indo-Iranian, which as fully distinct Indic (Sanskrit) and Iranian was soon to be attested in writing as well. In other words, any old eastern unity would have to predate the Late Bronze Age significantly. A date of *c.* 2000 BC is within the range of possibility for this period of continued interaction, but towards its later edge. A horizon called 'Chalcolithic/Early Bronze Age (3rd millennium)' might fit more comfortably in back of the earliest written evidence (Hittite, Mycenaean Greek,

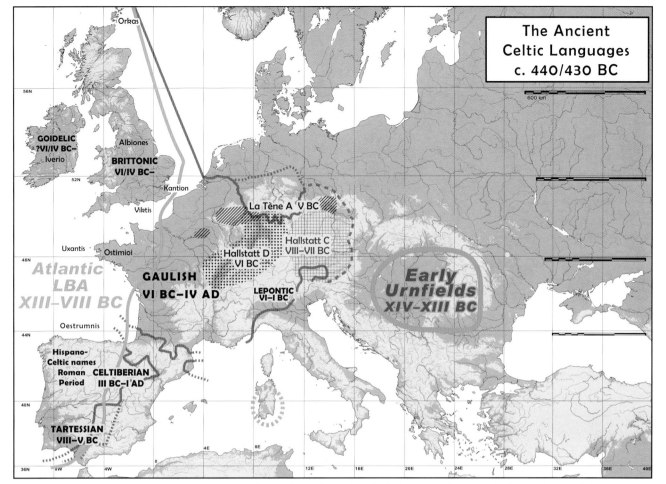

9.3. Some alternative archaeological contexts for Proto-Celtic: regions probably or certainly Celtic speaking when Herodotus wrote (outline in purple), shown together Hallstatt, Early La Tène core, Urnfield, and Atlantic Bronze Age core areas

&c.). But in considering progressively earlier horizons, other theories would eventually impose limits on when an eastern block of Late Indo-European, containing what became Celtic, could have existed—thus, probably not before the era of the domestic horse and wheeled vehicles. There is a common inherited vocabulary for these right across the Indo-European world (Mallory 1989). Renfrew's model (1987) would allow more time by envisioning Proto-Indo-European *Urheimat* in Anatolia in the 7th millennium, but brings what was destined to be Celtic to the west very early as well, with the First Neolithic 'wave of advance' *c.* 5000 BC.

That the territory of Tartessos had formed an integral part of the Atlantic Late Bronze Age can be seen abundantly in the archaeological evidence, such as the Huelva deposition of the 10th century BC (Ruiz-Gálvez Priego, ed., 1995). There is at least an inkling of textual confirmation in *Ora Maritima* of Avienus. Despite its remaining uncertainties and apparent confusions, this late 705-line poem (as extant) has unique value in its claims of detailed use of lost early Greek and Carthaginian sources, sometimes recording *their* view of *their* past. Avienus's statement concerning the Straits of Gibraltar, *hic Gadir urbs est dicta Tartessus prius* 'here is Cádiz formerly called Tartessos' (line 85) is intelligible as it stands as describing the Late Bronze Age state of affairs before Phoenician Gadir was founded. We need not assume confusion of two neighbouring Early Iron Age centres (Cádiz and Huelva), rather Tartessos and Gadir belong to earlier and later ages. *Ora Maritima* continues that the Tartessians had been wont to trade as far as the 'Oestrumnides' (*Tartessiisque in terminos Oestrumnidum negotiandi mos erat*), islands rich with tin and lead mines and situated two days sailing from the island thickly inhabited by the *gens Hiernorum* 'Irish people', which itself was near *insula Albionum*, i.e. Britain (lines 94–7, 110–16). (This passage sits alongside and is perhaps part of information derived from the Carthaginian navigator Himilco, who flourished in the 6th or earlier 5th century BC.)

Recognizing Celtic speech in Tartessos and that Herodotus's Keltoí were neighbours of the Kunētes of the Algarve reshapes the narrative. In short, we now have another set of data coming from another discipline for reconsidering some version of Cunliffe's (2001) theory of the expansionist ancient Celtic speech as the lingua franca of the Atlantic Bronze Age (note similar conclusions based on different evidence from Búa [2003, 156 n. 34]; also independently Brun 2006). Celtic names, Celtic inscriptions, and people called Keltoí—all make their first appearance in the south-west as part of a literate urban civilization often compared to that of the Etruscans. This subverts the stereotype of Celts as northern barbarians par excellence, antithesis to classical civilization. Standard introductions to the Celts have long included generalizations to the effect: 'The Celts never founded a great empire or centralized state'. However, it is likely that Arganthonios's Tartessos *was* a centralized state. Maybe not an empire, but being a non-empire was hardly the key defining attribute of the civilization of Tartessos.

Background and State of the Question

The idea that Tartessian is partly or wholly Celtic is not new. Interpreting several strings of signs in the inscriptions as Celtic names, Correa (1989 and especially 1992) proposed that Tartessian was a Celtic language. Correa has since revised his views, regarding the language as unclassified. Untermann in Ellis Evans's festschrift (1995) and in his imposing *Monumenta Linguarum Hispanicarum* 4 (1997) recognized the likelihood of several Indo-European and specifically Celtic elements in the Tartessian inscriptions, though viewing the language as a whole as still undeciphered. Thus, about twelve years ago, when the Tartessian corpus became available in an authoritative edition and amid preliminary indications of Celticity, the question might have received more attention from international Celtic studies and historical linguistics than it did. More recently, Ballester discusses the Celtic—and specifically Hispano-Celtic—affinities of the Tartessian personal name Ἀργανθωνιος and several forms in the inscriptions (2004, 118–21). In a lucid and densely informative survey, Villar (2004) has suggested the possibility that the Tartessian inscriptions contain items of 'ein frühes Gallisch' within a non-Celtic and probably non-Indo-European matrix language. Villar makes the important point—broadly consistent with the findings here—that the Celtic in the Tartessian inscriptions, like the Celtic theonyms found in Latin inscriptions of Galicia dating to the Roman period, shows some linguistic features more akin to what is found in Gaulish than in Celtiberian. Jordán Cólera provides a chart classifying the pre-Roman languages of the Hispanic Peninsula in which the 'South-west Language or Tartessian' is listed cautiously as 'Indo-European macrofamily? Celtic family?' (2007, 751)

On the other hand, Schulten, writing many years ago, saw connections with the poorly understood non-Indo-European Etruscan language. Mallory (1989) classes Tartessian as non-Indo-European; however, in view of the rapid and recent developments in the study of the ancient languages of Portugal and Spain in general and the analysis of the Tartessian alphabet in particular, this assessment must be attributed to a fundamentally earlier, and poorer, stage of knowledge of this language. Rodríguez Ramos (2002) forcefully concludes that the 'Sudlusitanian–Tartessian inscriptions' are 'definitely neither Celtic nor Anatolian, and probably also not Indo-European'. Regarding the Correa/ Untermann transcriptions of the Tartessian texts as 'unpronounceable', Sverdrup and Guardans (2002) present radically altered transliterations and conclude: 'The Tartessian language is morphologically and structurally different enough from Indoeuropean to exclude any genetic relationships'. Isaac (2004) calls Tartessian 'equally non-Indo-European' as/to 'Basque'. Salinas de Frías (2006, 26) recognizes the Tartessian name *Argantonios* as Indo-European but thinks that the Tartessian inscriptions look non-Indo-European, acknowledging this disparity as a problem. Similarly, De Bernardo Stempel implies that *Argantonios* and 'the *Ligustinus lacus* near Tartessos' were Celtic names 'too often disregarded . . . in order not to disrupt . . . a supposedly clean-cut division between a Celticized Iberian Peninsula and its allegedly Celtic-free counterpart' (2006, 47), but lists Tartessian as a 'non-Celtic language' in the same paper (2006, 43). The description of the Hesperia collaborative project on the pre-Roman languages of ancient Hispania (based at the Department of Greek Philology and Indo-European Linguistics of the Universidad Complutense de Madrid) views the language of 'south-western (or "Tartessian") inscriptions' as 'unidentified', thus making no claim either as to what Tartessian is nor what it is not.

The Corpus: Purpose, Scope, and Methods

As its first aim, the corpus gathered below makes the Tartessian inscriptions more widely available to an English-language readership. The tentative translations and the linguistic notes that follow present the case for Celticity, showing in detail resemblances to attested forms in the Ancient Celtic languages (Celtiberian and other varieties of Hispano-Celtic, Lepontic, Gaulish, and Galatian), Old Irish, Old Breton, Old and Middle Welsh. In the list of names (pp. 257–73) a few further proper names are included that occur in the region of Tartessos, recorded in Greek or Latin sources and surely or probably dating back to the mid 1st millennium BC. What I have generally not done is to seek out Indo-European words not attested in any (other) Celtic language and then run these through the requisite sound changes to see how these Indo-European preforms might have appeared in an ancient Celtic language, assuming that the root had once existed in Celtic, but had then either simply died out in all sub-branches except Tartessian, or somehow otherwise failed to be attested in all other Celtic languages. This procedure was not determined by an ethos of methodological purism—though etymological interpretations based solely on evidence from other branches of Indo-European are sometimes less persuasive—but rather the view that a more worthwhile contribution might result from keeping to my area of expertise in the Celtic languages.

The one glaring exception to this limitation of methodology was demanded by the most often repeated of the formulaic words of the Tartessian inscriptions: **naŕkᵉe** O)IꝶAꙎ (J.1.1, J.7.8, J.26.1, J.27.1, J.57.1), na]ŕkᵉeo-io* *‡ꝏ‡O)Iꝶ[(J.16.2), **naŕkᵉetⁱi** ꝏⴲO)IꝶAꙎ (J.56.1), **naŕkᵉeni** (J.1.3, J.1.2, J.7.2), **naŕkᵉenii** ꝏꝏꝏO)IꝶAꙎ (J.2.1, J.21.1), **n[aŕkᵉe]enii** (J.6.1), **naŕkᵉentⁱi** ꝏⴲꝏO)IꝶAꙎ (J.12.1, J.16.1, J.17.2, J.18.1, J.19.2), **[n]aŕkᵉeentii** (J.1.5), **na]ŕkᵉentⁱi[** (J.4.3), **n(a)ŕkᵉenii** ꝏꝏꝏO)IꝶꙎ (J.11.1), **n]aŕkᵉenii** ꙏ]AꙏKOꝏꙏ (J.11.3), **naŕ]kᵉenii** (J.19.1), **naŕrkᵉe:n:** Ꙏ | O)IꝶAꙎ (J.23.1), **naŕkᵉ[e]n** Ꙏ[O])IꝶAꙎ (Mesas do Castelinho). On the face of it, these forms appear, as Untermann has remarked (1995), to be inflected as an Indo-European verb, but no Celtic root immediately comes to mind. Nonetheless, so prevalent and pivotal is this **naŕkᵉentⁱi**, &c., that something had to be attempted. Therefore, in counter distinction to the approach usually followed and described above, the proposal is that the formation is the cognate of Greek ναρκάω 'grow stiff, numb, dead' (< Indo-European *[s]nerk- 'bind', cf. Old High German in-snerahan 'bind' [Rix 2001, 574])—both in the literal sense, suiting funerary inscriptions, but also more abstractly 'to bind, fix, make inalterable, carve in stone', hence 'so be it, amen'—an Indo-European formation which has otherwise died out or failed to be attested in Celtic. The formulaic word **naŕkᵉentⁱi**, &c., is often carved so as to turn around a bend as the text changes direction, possibly having to do with the symbolic binding of a permanent injunction.

The readings here generally follow Untermann (1997) as the authoritative starting point, based on both his roman transliterations and the accompanying photographs and line drawings. There is generally close agreement between the readings of Untermann and those of J. A. Correa, and for most points the Untermann/Correa transliterations agree also with those of Rodríguez Ramos. The roman transliteration system of V. H. Correia (1996, 50) differs somewhat more frequently; however, his catalogue is presented as standardized Tartessian letters, with palaeographical notes, rather than as romanizations, and so remain valuable. There are still some basic uncertainties in making out the signs on the stones, as well as interpreting those signs (see 'Script and Transliteration' below). (Working within the framework of the theory of Nostratic and other Eurasian linguistic 'macro families' dating back to the Palaeolithic, the Sverdrup/Guardans approach, and their divergent transcriptions of Tartessian, could not be usefully taken into consideration here.) In addition to using published sources, in March and July 2008, February and July/August 2009, I was able to examine (and was often permitted to photograph) the many Tartessian inscribed stones kept at the following museums: the new Museu da Scrita do Sudoeste (Almodôvar), Museu Regional (Beja), Museu Municipal (Faro), Museu Municipal (Lagos), Museu Nacional de Arqueologia (Lisboa), Museu Municipal (Loulé), Museu Municipal (Olhão), Museu Municipal (Silves), Museo Arqueológico (Sevilla), and Museo Arqueológico (Badajoz).

The procedure sketched above—essentially fishing for any further Celtic forms within a corpus of inscriptions in which a few promising examples had already been recognized—had the unexpected result of identifying a sufficient number of 'Celtic-looking' forms (often with *comparanda* in the core vocabulary of more than one Celtic language) as to call into question the hybrid positions taken by Untermann and Villar. Though significant, the Celtic-looking elements in Tartessian identified by earlier writers had remained small as an absolute number and as a relative proportion of the corpus. With a writing system that does not show word divisions or distinguish voiced from voiceless stops (along with the remaining uncertain details of the script), such a small number of resemblances might be coincidental. That is not to say that all elements in all the inscriptions have now fallen neatly into place as Celtic—far from it. But rather, there is no coherent residue of recurrent and systematic linguistic features that lack fairly obvious Indo-European (and most often Celtic) analogues. The inscriptions most devoid of Celtic-looking features are those that are generally of poorest quality— briefest, badly fragmented, poorly carved, badly worn, or using anomalous letter forms. In many of the inscriptions, especially the longer ones that are complete and unbroken, the Celtic-looking elements—names, common nouns, pronouns, preverbs, verbs, and inflexional terminations—accumulate to the point that the inscrutable forms that had implied the hypothetical non-Celtic matrix language are nearly, or wholly, absent. Consequently, it has been possible to offer here several original translations for words, for groups of words, and for some complete inscriptional texts.

Dating: Tartessian and the Orientalization

There is today a general consensus that the Tartessian is the earliest of the Palaeo-Hispanic *corpora*, predating Iberian, Celtiberian, and Lusitanian. The subsequent development was apparently that the Iberian scripts ('Meridional' and then 'Levantine') were adapted from the Tartessian 'abekatu', both before the end of the 5th century BC, and afterwards the Celtiberian scripts were developed from the Levantine (or north-eastern) Iberian script. The Iberian and Celtiberian scripts are semisyllabaries: some of the signs represent two phonemes (consonant+vowel), others a single vowel or consonant. Lusitanian and later Celtiberian were written in Roman letters, as are the mixed Latin–Hispano-Celtic inscriptions of the Roman Period.

Untermann (1995) has allowed 700–500 BC as the date range for the Tartessian inscriptions, likewise Villar (2004, 268), while Rodríguez Ramos (2002) dates them to certainly post-800 BC and probably belonging to the 6th and 5th centuries, adducing some archaeological finds, and Correia (2005) generally 7th–5th century. The origins of the 'south-western' or Tartessian script is discussed further in the next subsection. The fact that it is today widely agreed to be wholly or partly derived from the 27-letter Phoenician 'alephat' (Rodríguez Ramos 2000; Mederos Martín & Ruiz Carbrero 2001; Correa 2005) has general implications for the dating and cultural context. If we agree with Untermann's argument (1962) based on comparative letter forms, the Tartessian script was partly inspired by the Greek alphabet—as opposed to a 'monogenesis' from Phoenician—and the starting point is unlikely to predate *c.* 600 BC. However, a recently discovered graffito on a Phoenician sherd found at Doña Blanca near Cádiz has now been confidently identified as Tartessian and dated to the early to mid 7th century (Correa & Zamora 2008).

Tartessian literacy forms one facet of the broader subject of influences from the eastern Mediterranean reaching the Iberian Peninsula. Consequently, several thorny issues about the arrival of Phoenicians beyond the Straits of Gibraltar are revived. According to the chronology of the Roman historian Velleius Paterculus (1.2.3; 1.8.4; he lived *c.* 19 BC–post AD 30), Tyre's colony at Cádiz (Phoenician *Gadir*), near Tartessos and a short voyage north-west of the Straits, was founded 80 years after the fall of Troy. The date was, therefore, either 1110/1109 or 1104/3 BC depending on the reckoning used for the Trojan war. Though less exact, Strabo (1.3.2), Pliny (*Naturalis Historia* 19.216), and Pomponius Mela (3.6.46) were broadly in agreement with Velleius, writing that Gades was founded not long after the fall of Troy. If the ocean-going 'ships of Tarshish' mentioned in the Old Testament (e.g. Kings 1: 10.22, Ezekiel: 27.12) as bringing silver, gold, and other luxuries mean 'ships of Tartessos', as has long been believed (Blázquez 1993;

9.4. Swords of the 11th-/10th-century BC from the Huelva deposition, Museo Provincial de Huelva (photo: Jane Aaron)

though disputed by Aubet 2001), then major commercial links between the Phoenicians and Tartessians would date back to the time of Solomon and Hiram I of Tyre (see above).

In the archaeological record, we see that luxury manufactured Phoenician items—goldwork, armour, and bronze buckets—entered the Atlantic trading networks by the 10th century BC, the date of the Huelva hoard, a marine deposit of the Late Bronze Age, which contained 400 items (Ruiz-Gálvez Priego, ed., 1995; Kristiansen 1998, 126), more probably a ritual deposition than a shipwreck (Cunliffe 2001, 279). In the light of the recent analysis by Burgess and O'Connor (2008), intense influence from the eastern Mediterranean had catalysed a 'precocious' Iberian First Iron Age—and brought an end to the Atlantic Bronze Age in Iberia—as early as *c.* 950, contemporary with the Late Bronze Age carp's-tongue industries of Atlantic Gaul and Ewart Park Phase of LBA Britain. Brandherm (2008) interprets Phoenician pottery associated with calibrated radio-carbon dates of the late 10th to mid 9th century BC at Huelva and post-mid 9th century at Morro de Mezquitilla as evidence for early Phoenician emporia. Scientific dating is thus coming closer to validating classical ideas about the early presence of the Tyrians in the Atlantic west. This eastern influence confirms longstanding ideas about Phoenician 'pre-colonization' and a 'first orientalization' of Late Bronze Age Tartessos and Atlantic Hispania beyond. As well as the likelihood of direct links between the south-west and the mercantile towns of what is now Lebanon and Syria by 950/850 cal BC, there is evidence for a strong 'Cypriot connection' in the west operating during the period between the fall of Mycenae and the first clear-cut Phoenician colonies in southern Spain, i.e. *c.* 1200–850/800 BC (Mederos Martín 1996; Harrison 2004; cf. Ruiz-Gálvez Priego 2000; 2008; Peckham 1998). The possible Cypriot impact on literacy will be discussed in the next subsection. According to recent consensus, Phoenician colonies become archaeologically visible on the Mediterranean coast of the southern Iberian Peninsula by *c.* 800 BC, with datable Phoenician material at Cádiz/Gadir beginning *c.* 770. However, scientific dating now looks set to push some of the key finds back into the 9th century (Brandherm 2008).

According to Almagro-Gorbea (1988, 72), the highly 'orientalizing' proto-urban Tartessian archaeological culture reached its apogee in the second half of the 7th century BC. The Tartessian material culture was characterized in part by rich complex burials, and many of the inscriptions have been found in necropolises of the Early Iron Age, though the datable context has most often been only that of a given necropolis as a whole. The complete list of Tartessian inscriptions found in Iron Age necropolises or other Iron Age burial sites, as noted by Correia (1996), is as follows (using the Untermann's numbering system as in the catalogue below): J.1.1, J.1.2, J.1.3, J.1.4, J.1.5, J.4.1, J.4.2, J.4.3, J.4.4, J.6.1, J.7.1, J.7.2, J.7.3, J.7.10, J.11.1, J.11.2, J.12.1, J.12.4, J.15.1, J.15.2, J.15.3, J.16.2, J.16.3, J.18.1, J.18.2, J.18.3, J.19.1, J.19.2, J.19.3, J.22.1, J.22.2, J.26.1. The famous stela of Gomes Aires ('Abóboda 1', J.12.1), one of those found in a necropolis, was placed directly over a large jar filled with cremated remains; it is dated by Harrison (2004, 310) to the 7th century BC. The necropolis of Fonte Velha (Benasfrim) is the find site of inscriptions

9.5. Detail of a reconstruction of the La Joya funerary chariot, Museo Provincial de Huelva (photo: Jane Aaron)

J.1–6 and has been dated 8th–6th century BC (De Hoz 1989, 540). De Mello Beirão (1993) found 8th- and 7th-century associations in finds from the south Portuguese necropolis of Pardieiro where Tartessian inscribed stones were also discovered (J.15.1–3). In the case of the Mealha Nova stelae (J.18.1–2), the excavation of the two associated necropolises recovered an Egyptian scarab with the hieroglyph of Pharaoh Petubaste of the 23rd Dynasty (817–763 BC; Chamorro 1987, 229). Scarabs were common as imported antiquities, but had gone out of fashion by *c.* 400 BC (Harrison 1988, 135). For the necropolises in the district of Seville (the find sites of inscriptions J.52.1 and J.53.1), Catalán (1993) lists datable associations, the earliest of which is another scarab of Petubaste, followed by 7th-century pottery, and the latest are native annular fibulae of the 5th or 4th century BC. Almagro-Gorbea (2004) dates a Tartessian inscription (J.57.1) from the orientalizing necropolis at Medellín, Badajoz, Spain, to 650/625 BC, but Correa dates it to the second half of the 6th century on epigraphic grounds. Further dates for the Medellín necropolis include painted ceramics of the 7th–6th centuries (Ruiz 1989, 269), a Greek kylix of the first half of the 6th century, and a C_{14} date of the mid 6th century (uncalibrated) (Pereira 1989, 401). Harrison dates the inscriptions added to the Late Bronze Age warrior stela of Capote (J.54.1) to 700–600 BC (2004, 51, 79) and tells me that the Cabeza del Buey IV inscription is amongst the earliest.

As argued by Kristiansen (1998, 157–60), the funerary stones with Tartessian inscriptions probably form a continuum with these Late Bronze Age 'warrior stelae' of the south-western peninsula (on these pre-literate stelae in general, see further Pingel 1993; Celestino Pérez 1990; 2001; Harrison 2004; Celestino Pérez & López-Ruiz 2006). This archaeological interpretation is made stronger by one detail of the present study. Wheeled vehicles are a common motif in the LBA warrior stelae, and the Tartessian verbal noun **oret°o** (J.4.1.) 'to help, save, deliver', literally 'run under', and its perfect

3rd person singular form **kᵒtᵘuaratᵉe** 'has delivered', literally 'has run under (with)' (J.53.1), express the action of wheeled vehicles. Note that the Old Irish cognate *fod·rethat* 'that run under him' is used specifically of a king's chariot wheels in the 7th-century wisdom text *Audacht Morainn*. Harrison (2004, 147) collects a total of 24 examples of two-wheeled chariots from the warrior stelae. A more recent discovery is the well-carved chariot on the stela of Cabeza del Buey IV to which a Tartessian inscription was added (Correa 2008). The vehicles on the south-western stelae are now identified as a Mycenaean type, introduced to the Peninsula at Late Helladic IIIB, 1325–1185 BC (Mederos Martín 2008). It is likely, but not certain, that rings and buttons in the 11th-/10th-century BC Ría de Huelva hoard were harness fittings (Brandherm 2008/9). The rich Tartessian burial from tomb 17 at La Joya, Huelva (700–650 BC), included a luxurious two-wheeled chariot of walnut with lion-headed hub caps.

Chamorro (1987, 230) and Harrison (2004, 312) identified swords on the pre-literate stelae as specifically of the Atlantic 'carp's-tongue' type (more accurately the distinct and earlier 'Huelva' type), at least 84 examples of which were included in the Huelva deposition of *c.* 950 BC. In the discussion of Burgess and O'Connor (2008), the identifiable weapons types of these stelae belong to their Hío Phase of *c.* 1150–*c.* 950 BC.

In reviewing the pre-literate stelae, Almagro-Gorbea (2005) draws attention to a number of images of musical instruments, including lyres, which he argues show oral poetry flourishing at this stage, possibly a key prerequisite for the inception of written funerary texts. Harrison (2004, 146) notes six lyres on the stelae: Luna (Zaragoza) with 15 carefully carved strings (Harrison dates this stela as one of the earliest, at the 13th or 12th century BC), Herrera de Duque/Quinterías (Badajoz), and Capilla I, III, and IV (Badajoz). The stela from Capote, Higuera la Real (Badajoz), which shows both a lyre and a chariot, was reused for two short Tartessian inscriptions (J.54.1 below). As the lyres are generally shown together with shields and other items of the warrior's panoply that might imply that bards belonged to the class of the arms-bearing warrior élite. The instrument would therefore have been one of the status symbols of the deceased (cf. the suggestion of Harrison 1988, 32). Alternatively, the idea may be that a lyric elegy has been translated into pictures on the stone, in which case it was the bard, and not the lyre on its own, that was the status symbol.

According to Harrison (2004), the Late Bronze Age warrior stelae went out of favour rapidly in the period 800–750 BC. That period also saw a change of funerary rite, from a rarity or absence of burials—a general negative characteristic of Atlantic Late Bronze Age cultures—to burials with grave goods and tumuli. (The warrior stela of Solona de Cabañas, Logrosán, Cáceres, is thus exceptional in being placed above a warrior's burial.) This transition coincides with the opening of the Phoenician-catalysed 'Early Orientalizing Phase' of the Tartessian material culture *c.* 750–*c.* 650 (Chamorro 1987, 204; but beginning somewhat earlier in the scheme of Burgess and O'Connor). The revival of the burial rite at this stage, after a hiatus of several centuries, is probably itself of eastern Mediterranean inspiration, as the Early Iron Age burials of the region show less influence from the central-European Urnfield tradition.

There can be no obvious or predetermined answer to the question of whether the adoption of alphabetic writing necessarily came sooner or later—requiring a more or less intense, more or less prolonged Phoenician contact—than the other aspects of the revolutionary orientalization of the Tartessian material culture. It is inherently likely that a relatively abrupt transition to written funerary stones came as yet another facet of the sweeping 'orientalizing package' taking hold in the 8th century. But this is not certain.

Writing has not been found evenly distributed throughout the orientalizing area. Tartessian inscriptions are known from only a few of the orientalizing burial grounds of south-west Spain. As Rodríguez Ramos (2002) notes, the most intensive evidence of writing does not come from the Tartessian regions richest in imported luxuries. Future discoveries may alter this picture. The distribution of Ancient Celtic place-names in the peninsula suggests a possible explanation. They appear densely in southern Portugal and nearby parts of south-west Spain, while they progressively thin out and are intermixed with clearly non-Celtic place-names as one moves eastward across Andalucía (Sims-Williams 2006; Koch 2007). That probably means that, by the Roman period at least, the region about and west of the Guadiana was more heavily Celtic speaking than the basin of the Guadalquivir. As what now appears to be a literate tradition based in Celtic speech, the distribution of Tartessian inscriptions simply follows other indicators of Celtic in the southern peninsula.

On the later limit, Phoenician influence in Hispania slackened during and after Nebuchadnezzar of Babylon's siege of Tyre *c.* 586–*c.* 573 BC. The evident decline at the end of the 'Late Orientalizing Phase' of the Tartessian material culture *c.* 550 BC (Chamorro 1987, 204) might be a consequence of these disruptions in the east. Against this background, we can understand why Arganthonios, the ruler of Tartessos, was so eager, at about 550 BC, for the Phokaian Greeks to found a colony 'anywhere they liked' in his territory (Herodotus §1.163–5). The loss of most of the Phokaian fleet *c.* 539 BC off Alalia in eastern Corsica against a combined Etruscan/Carthaginian force, as well as the Persian conquest of Phokaia itself *c.* 540, precluded any such possibility, further constricting the Tartessian élite's economic lifeline to the eastern Mediterranean. However, the Tartessian inscriptions need not have stopped at that time, unless we suppose that stimulus from, or competition with, Phoenician and/or Greek literacy had been the sole *raison d'être* of the tradition.

The only apparent examples of the Tartessian script used in the Peninsular Later Iron Age (thus coeval with the Palaeo-Hispanic scripts derived from Tartessian) involves other media and other functions: for example, a graffito on a bowl dated to the later 4th or 3rd century BC from Garvão (Ourique, Beja, south Portugal) has been interpreted by Correa (2002) as a Tartessian personal name **aiot*i*ii.**

The Origins of the South-western Script

There is today consensus that the primary source was the Phoenician 'alephat' (e.g. De Hoz 1996; Correa 2005), though beyond this opinions differ. Untermann (1997b) sees the Palaeo-Hispanic scripts' addition of five vowel signs to the vowel-less Phoenician alphabet as undeniable evidence for influence from the Greek alphabet. The interpretation of Almagro-Gorbea (2005, 55) of the 6th-century BC graffito NIEΘΩI from Huelva as a Celtic theonym ('to [the wargod] Nētos') would show that Greek script was sometimes used to write Tartessian in the Later Orientalizing Period. Rodríguez Ramos (2000) has argued for a Phoenician-to-Tartessian monogenesis drawing special attention to the point that Tartessian and the Greek alphabet added vowels to the alephat according to different principles: for example, the symbol for the Phoenician laryngeal 'ayin' O is the source of Greek 'omicron' /o/, but Tartessian /e/. Apart from Λ a the south-western vowel signs do not resemble the corresponding Greek ones. The formulation of Rodríguez Ramos has an appealing clarity: the Phoenician script is the 'madre' of the Tartessian script (escritura sudlusitana), and south Iberian script (meridional) is its 'hija', or alternatively its 'sobrina'. The scheme of descent has obvious implications for absolute dating. Graffiti in the Phoenician script (the mother of the Tartessian script according to Rodríguez Ramos) found at the native sites of El Carambolo and Castillo de Doña Blanca (Cádiz) date back to the 8th and 9th centuries BC. The oldest known inscriptions in the south Iberian script (the daughter or niece) have an archaeological context of the 4th century BC.

The forms of the Tartessian signs are not similar to those attested for the Carthaginian or 'Punic' version of the Phoenician alphabet; therefore, the influence of Carthage in southern Hispania c. 539–208 BC cannot explain the phenomenon of Tartessian literacy. (A true Carthaginian military empire in the southern peninsula comes only at the end of this period, with Hamilcar in 237 BC.) Rodríguez Ramos (2000) has argued that some characters most closely resemble specific Phoenician letter forms found in inscriptions closely dated to c. 825 BC, or roughly the date of the Phoenician inscription from Nora, mentioned above. Ruiz-Gálvez Priego (2008) suggests that Tartessian writing might have developed a century or more before this through the agency of account-keeping traders (probably from Cyprus) employing an early Canaanite/Phoenician alphabet while resident in the south-western Peninsula; her evidence includes a probable stylus and writing board from Huelva.

The Cypriot connection of the Peninsular Bronze–Iron Transition raises interesting possibilities for the south-western (Tartessian) script. A perplexing feature shared by the various Palaeo-Hispanic scripts is their hybrid nature. They are not true alphabets, breeching the 'one sign = one phoneme' principle by incorporating 15 syllabic signs, each of which represents one of a series of three stop consonants plus one of the series of five vowels. As explained above, the key period for Cypriot initiative in the west was c. 1200–c. 850/800 BC. During this time, at least its latter half, both the Phoenician alephat and the Cypriot syllabary were in use in Cyprus. (The Greek alphabet, even if it existed yet, was not used there until the 4th century BC.) The Linear B script that had been used to write Mycenaean Greek in the Aegean was similarly syllabic. It went out of use in the 12th century BC. In its handling of the stop consonants, the Cypriot syllabary was more similar to the Palaeo-Hispanic scripts than was Linear B. Though using different graphemes, Cypriot and Palaeo-Hispanic represent the same inventory of 15 stop-consonant+vowel combinations: *ka ke ki ko ku, pa pe pi po pu* (= *ba be bi bo bu*), *ta te ti to tu*. On the other hand, Linear B, as well as containing these three series, has two more, representing: *da de di do du, qa qe qi qo qu*. Now, as both Iberian and the Indo-European languages of the Peninsula contrast /t/ and /d/, it would have been useful to adopt this feature had it existed in the Palaeo-Hispanic scripts' model. Celtiberian, and I believe Tartessian, also contrasted velars (e.g. /k/) with labiovelars (e.g. /kʷ/), so that series too would have been of use had it existed in the model. In other words, there is no compelling reason in the phonology of the indigenous languages of the Peninsula for the 15 stop-consonant+vowel inventory of the Cypriot system to have been independently selected there. The Cypriot syllabary was not ideally suited for Greek either: it did not distinguish voiced, voiceless, and voiceless aspirate consonants (e.g. δ, τ, θ). It was used to write Greek and the indigenous undeciphered 'Eteo-Cypriot' language. The Cypriot syllabary developed from the earlier 'Cypro-Minoan' syllabary, which resembles the 'Linear A' syllabaries of the Aegean Bronze Age. The Cypriot Syllabary possibly fit the sound system of Eteo-Cypriot like a glove, or it may merely have been an imperfect legacy. Unlike the rest of the Greek world, Cyprus did not relapse into illiteracy at the Bronze–Iron Transition.

Untermann (1962) emphatically ruled out Gómez-Moreno's (1949) derivation of the Palaeo-Hispanic scripts from the Cypriot syllabary. This rejection was based mostly on the forms of the individual signs, rather than the underlying structural principles considered here. With one possible exception, the sign forms are not the same: Tartessian **lakᵉentⁱi** ΓΑΙΚΟΥΦΝ (J.53.1) is probably a variant spelling for **lakⁱin↑i** ΓΑΦΝΥ↑Ν (J.12.4) and **nařkᵉen↑i** Ψ↑ΨΟ)ΙΚΑΥ (J.19.2) for **nařkᵉentⁱi** ΨΦΨΟ)ΙΚΑΥ (J.12.1, J.16.1, J.17.2, J.18.1), and the Cypriot sign for *ti* is ↑. In their forms (but not always their phonetic values), most of the south-western signs can be derived from Phoenician ones. In the light of the foregoing, it is worth considering the following likelihood. A person or persons who knew both writing systems then used in Cyprus, but not the Greek alphabet, saw the advantages of 27 or so easily written and distinguished symbols of the alephat, on the one hand, and of representing vowels and syllables as permitted by the syllabary, on the other. This Cypriot or Cypriot-trained scribe (or scribes) would thus have come up with a solution different from that of the Greek alphabet. The latter was devised in the Aegean after the example of the native Linear B syllabary had been abandoned.

The most striking feature of the Tartessian writing system is that a series of five different symbols are employed for each of the stop consonants (*b, k/g, t/d*) depending on the following vowel, even though the vowel itself is written. In the derivative systems of the Iberian and Celtiberian semisyllabaries, the redundant vowel is omitted. Thus ✕ is the Tartessian letter for /t/ or /d/ before **a** Λ, Δ for /t/ or /d/ before **o** ⧺, Δ for /t/ or /d/ before **u** Ч, Φ for /t/ or /d/ before **i** Ϻ, &c. This redundant system—considered alongside the absence of any graphic distinction between voiced and voicelesss stop consonants—may seem bizarre or intellectually deficient. However, in this respect, the Tartessian abekatu adheres to the 'one sign = one phoneme' principle where the later Palaeo-Hispanic scripts abandon it, an indication that the inventor(s) had deeply grasped the concept of alphabetic writing and had not set out to create a semisyllabary. The system of redundancy (and Tartessian's frequent doubling of vowels) arose during the period when the alephat and similar abekatu were in use side by side; the over-characterizing of vowels in the latter enhanced the differentiation, making the language of a text obvious at a glance to the literate.

In the explanation so far, nothing in the abekatu seems particularly well suited to representing any of the ancient indigenous languages of the Iberian Peninsula. Therefore, it might have been a purely Cypriot invention that never caught on in its homeland because its two models had strong traditions behind them (strong enough to keep the Greek alphabet out until the 4th century BC) and were kept studiously apart. However, there might be a slight suggestion of western influence favouring the 'redundancy principle'. Rather than being simply uneconomical, writing consonant+vowel graphemes in addition to vowels registers a phonetic reality true to varying degrees of most languages: a consonant anticipates the articulatory quality of the following vowel. It is possible, therefore, that as well as feeling a need to add vowels to the Phoenician system, the inventor(s) of the abekatu perceived variations in the phonetics or phonology for which the vowel-specific consonant signs were meaningful. As a fully grammaticalized principle, such consonant quality is one of the pervasive earmarks of the medieval and modern Gaelic languages. It is sometimes assumed that these contrasting consonant qualities would not have already existed (at a phonemic level) at the earliest stage of Primitive Irish written in the ogam script. But as ogam is closely based on the Latin alphabet, the script had no means to represent such a feature of the sound system had it already existed. Repetition of word-initial consonant+vowel sequences occurs in both early Welsh and early Irish poetry.

Transliteration

Untermann's edition in *Monumentum Linguarum Hispanicarum 4* is adopted here as the authoritative starting point, and his numbering system is followed in the present catalogue of inscriptions (pp. 210–56) and cross-references. Untermann's transliteration system of the Tartessian script is largely consistent with that developed in the work of Correa. Both build on Schmoll's breakthrough in the decoding, which recognized the 'principle of redundancy', that is, the agreement between the stop consonants and the following vowel signs. The version of the Untermann/Correa system used here follows.

a A	e O	i ⋎	o ‡	u 4
bᵃ }	bᵉ 9	?bⁱ	bᵒ □	bᵘ ⋈
kᵃ gᵃ ∧	kᵉ gᵉ)|	kⁱ gⁱ Φ ?↑	kᵒ gᵒ ⊗	kᵘ gᵘ 目
tᵃ dᵃ X	tᵉ dᵉ ⊨	tⁱ dⁱ ⦵ ↑	tᵒ dᵒ ∧⋁	tᵘ dᵘ △
1 ↑	m ⋔ ⋔	n ⋎	r 9⟨	ŕ ⋏
s ‡	s′ M	?Hᵃ ⋶	:		

The system of Rodríguez Ramos diverges from Correa/Untermann over a few key details. Where his published transcriptions differ from the texts adopted here, these variants are given at the end of entries on the individual inscriptions below. I have accepted Rodríguez Ramos' and Correa's interpretation of Φ as kⁱ/gⁱ, but retain the Untermann/Correa transliteration of ⋈ as bᵘ (notionally also pᵘ), rather than as Rodríguez Ramos' kᵘ/gᵘ. (It should be remembered, in considering these alternative proposals for Tartessian ⋈, that the allophonic alternation of [kʷ] and [p] was a characteristic tendency of the Ancient Celtic sound systems.) ↑ clearly represents a stop consonant before the vowel ⋎ i; its appearance in the verbal endings in recurrent formulaic language favours a transcription tⁱ (as a variant of the grapheme ⦵ tⁱ), rather than bⁱ as proposed by Rodríguez Ramos. (A similar sign occurs for *ti* in North-eastern Iberian script.) Along with the Greek spelling Ἀργανθώνιος (for etymological *Argantonios*), the orthographic variation -ntⁱi, -nii, -n↑i seen in the Tartessian inscriptions may reflect a general instability in clusters of nasal + stop consonants (as in Insular Celtic) and in the combination *-nt-* in particular. There is also uncertainty over the value of some other (mostly infrequently occurring) signs. The current state of our knowledge of the Tartessian script and language is thus relatively less advanced than that of the North-eastern Iberian and Celtiberian scripts and languages. Against this background, the Tartessian script is sometimes still termed 'undeciphered'. It is more accurate to say 'not wholly decoded' (cf. Villar 2004). There are broad areas of agreement among the experts concerning the values of most of the frequently occurring Tartessian signs. There is thus consensus concerning most of the readings that first suggested Celticity and compelling motivation for widening comparisons with the early Celtic languages on the basis of those preliminary findings.

Two copies of an inscribed Tartessian, or closely related, alphabet occur on the inscription from Espanca, Castro Verde, within the zone in south Portugal where most of the extant Tartessian inscriptions have been found (Correa 1993; De Hoz 1996; Untermann, MHL 4.327–9, J.25.1). The opening sequence of letters is obviously related to that of the Phoenician alephat: aleph, beth, gimel, daleth, &c.

In Espanca, as in most of the Tartessian inscriptions, we are to read from right to

9.6. The Espanca stone (J.25.1), with two complete 27-sign sequences of the Tartessian abekatu, or a closely related archaic Palaeo-Hispanic signary [Câmara Municipal, Castro Verde; Museu da Escrita do Sudoeste, Almodôvar]; 25 signs are transcribed below with the names of corresponding Phoenician and Greek letters noted.

A a	9 b^e	Λ k^a	Δ t^u	ᙏ i	)| k^e	٦l	} b^a	Ɣ n
ALEPH	BETH	GIMEL	DALETH	YODH	KAPH	LAMEDH		NUN
ALPHA	BETA	GAMMA	DELTA	IOTA	KAPPA	LAMBDA		NU

ᙏ m	)) ?r	ᙏ ś	X t^a	Ɣ u	٩ r	⫰ ?H^a	◑ t^i
MEM		SHIN	TAW	WAW	RESH	HE	TETH
MU		SIGMA	TAU	UPSILON	RHO	EPSILON	THETA

日 k^u	▢ b^o	Ψ ?	↑ ?t^i	‡ o	Ζ ?	≡0 ?	⋈ k^o
HETH	PE						
ETA	PI						

left, though left to right and boustrophedon (alternating lines, right-to-left and left-to-right) also occur. The more common shape of the letters is most often reversed (as a mirror image) in lines to be read left to right, leaving little doubt over the intended direction. In the edited inscriptions below, arrows are inserted at the beginning of lines to clarify the direction of the reading. The romanized transcriptions are all written left-to-right here. Undivided *scripta continua* is usual in Tartessian. Line breaks do not systematically correspond to word divisions, and vertical lines | infrequently carved between letters and transcribed as colons [:] in the diplomatic romanizations do not consistently mark word divisions.

Unlike the Palaeo-Hispanic scripts derived from the Tartessian abekatu, Tartessian itself can be considered a true alphabet, in that each character represents a single phoneme. There are, however, two extraordinary features of the Tartessian script which might be thought to raise the possibility that the alphabet was originally devised for a language which differed phonetically from Tartessian—such as Iberian, which is likely for geographic reasons to have come into contact with Phoenician at an early date. First, whereas the language clearly distinguished voiceless from voiced stops as phonemes— /t/ vs. /d/, /k/ vs. /g/—these opposed series were not distinguished in writing. The phoneme /p/ quite possibly did not exist in Tartessian. There are signs that can be read as /m/— M and W and possibly D—but these are rare in the inscriptions, and it seems that /m/ can also be represented by the letters ꟼ n and Ꝑ bᵃ.

The Tartessian writing system had no consistent way to write the sound /w/ (or /u̯/) and most often writes nothing in this sound's etymological position. It could be that it had lost /w/ as had Old Irish and most dialects of ancient Greek. But /w/ is in some examples apparently written as o ⧺ or u ꟼ, though in these examples the vowel signs could in fact mean that the old glide /w/ had become a vowel. (It is possible that in some examples like eertᵃaune O ꟼꟼAX꟡OO [J.55.1] = Celtiberian uertaunei, the apparently unnecessary doubling of the vowel is meant to represent the glide /w/ before the vowel.) It is possible, therefore, having re-used Phoenician 'waw' ꟼ /w/ as the vowel /u/, Tartessian retained no unambiguous way of writing the corresponding consonant.

The 'Hamito-Semitic' Hypothesis: Linguistic Orientalization?

This study takes an essentially agnostic attitude towards the recurrently formulated hypothesis that syntactic similarities between the medieval and modern Goidelic and Brittonic languages, on the one hand, and various non-Indo-European languages of Middle East and north Africa, on the other, reflect a substratum effect or some other situation of contact in antiquity between Celtic and a language of the Afro-Asiatic group (Gensler 1993; Jongeling 2000). Conversely, the present conclusions are relevant to that hypothesis, whose chief weakness heretofore has been the absence of any documented historical mechanism for contact between the relevant language families (Isaac 2007). In the light of the present interpretations, it appears that an ancient Celtic language was directly and profoundly interacting with a Semitic language (one very similar to Hebrew, which has often been invoked in the Hamito-Semitic argument) and at the same time participating in innovations shared with the Celtic of Gaul, Britain, and Ireland. In the notes on words below, I allow that Tartessian had possibly borrowed the Phoenician divine names *Astarte* (J.7.1, J.11.4) and *El* (J.23.1) and that the Tartessian personal name **uarbᵒoiir saruneea** 'noble consort of the star goddess' (J.22.1) was an early 'inversion compound' modelled on the highly common Semitic name type: titular office + genitive divine name. The Tartessian name **iubᵃa** (J.7.8), **iobᵃa[** (J.16.2) may be the same as the Numidian king's name *Iuba*, 'Ιουβας and thus reflect a language akin to ancient Berber in use in the area. After the faltering of Tyrian independence *c.* 573 BC, south-west Hispania remained within the Semitic influence of Tyre's daughter cities Gadir and Qart-hadašt (Carthage) until Rome captured Punic Gadir in 208 BC. According to Strabo (1.3.2, 2.13–14), Phoenician/Punic was still spoken in Turdetania in south-west Hispania (that region's name at least is probably the successor of Tartessos) in his own time about the turn of the 1st centuries BC/AD. But it would be the earlier 'Pre-Colonial' or 'Proto-Orientalizing' period (about 1300–900 BC) that could be relevant to the formation of the Insular Celtic languages. After *c.* 900 BC the western Iberian Peninsula appears no longer to have been an integral part of the Atlantic Bronze Age, sharing in the same types of weapons, feasting equipment, and so on (Cunliffe 2008, 299–300).

In an earlier paper (Koch 1991), I proposed that Celtic speech had reached Ireland primarily through the agency of the peripatetic professional classes (*aes dáno* 'people of skill', to use the Old Irish term, for which Tartessian **kᵉertᵒo[**-] probably expressed a similar concept), rather than a conquering warrior aristocracy. I also suggested that the key chronological horizon had been the Late Bronze Age, or about 1200–600 BC in calendar years. As far as I can see, nothing in the present study excludes that scenario concerning the Celticization of Ireland. I continue to see the extratribal professional/artisan class(es) as key figures in this process: the *aes dáno*/**kᵉertᵒo[**i] with the pan-Celtic god, the outsider Lugus [J.1.1], as the divine genius of their class. Where the evidence of Tartessos and Tartessian changes the picture is in showing that one of the most dynamic regions influencing Ireland and Britain during the period *c.* 1300–*c.* 900 BC was probably itself Celtic speaking and also in contact with, and receiving influences from, non-Indo-European partners in the eastern Mediterranean and north Africa.

TARTESSIAN INSCRIPTIONS

¶NOTE. Where variant readings are given below, for convenience of comparison, the superficial differences in the varying transcription conventions of individual scholars are not replicated here. At the time of writing the Museu da Escrita do Sudoeste, Almodôvar (MESA), displays many inscribed stones belonging to the permanent collections of other museums in Portugal; as a rule, both institutions will be noted here.

J.1.1 'Fonte Velha 6' Bemsafrim, Lagos, south Portugal [Museu Municipal Figueira de Foz; MESA] (Correia no. 15) 136 x 73 x 15cm

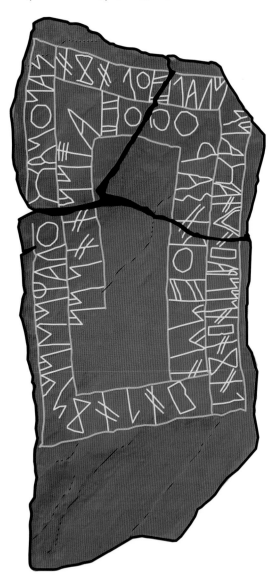

J.1.1. 'Fonte Velha 6' (photo: Jane Aaron)

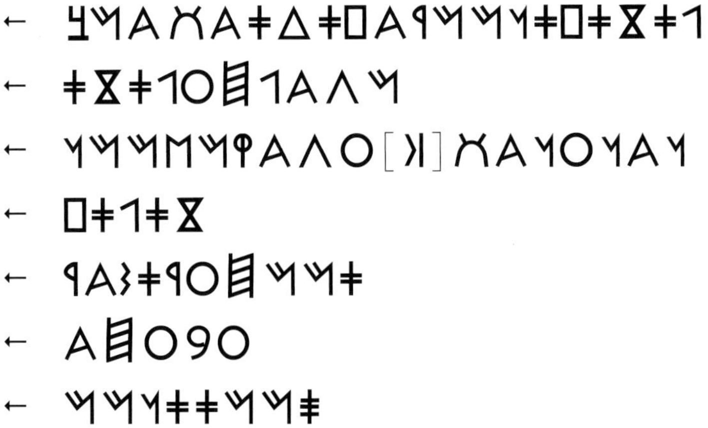

← ᚼᛗᴀᚼᴀᛩᛆᛩ�□ᚫᚹᛗᛗᛩᛩᛆᛩ□ᛩ☒ᛩ1   lokᵒobᵒo niirabᵒo tᵒo aŕaiạ

← ᛩ☒ᛩ1ᛆ□ᛇ1ᴀᴧᛗ   i kᵃaltᵉe lokᵒo

← ᛗᛗᛗᛗᛗᚿᴀᴧᛆ[ᛩᛁ]ᚼᴀᛜᛆᚼᴀᛗ   n ane naŕkᵉe kᵃakⁱiśiin

← □ᛩ1ᛩ☒   kᵒolobᵒ

← ᚹᴀᛇᛩᚹᛆᛇᛗᛗᛩ   o ii tᶜ’-e·ro-bᵃar

← ᴀᛇᛆᛆᛆ   e(bᶜ)e tᶜa

← ᛗᛗᛗᛩᛩᛗᛗᛩ   siioonii

LOGOBO NERABO DO AŔAIAI KALTE LOGON AN(D)E-NAŔKE

Kᵛ̄ĀKᵛ’-IŚIINGOLOBO II T’E·RO-BARE-(B)E TASEO(V)ONII

'Invoking the divine Lugoves of the Neri (tribe), this funerary monument for a noble [aŕaios *or* aŕaia] 'Celt/Gaul'. It/he remains fixed, unaltered within. Invoking all the heroes (Eśkingolī group) [the necropolis] has received, [the grave] of Ta[χ]seovonos.'

Celtiberian ·TO LVGVEI | ARAIANOM· 'for Lugus "*araianom*"' (Peñalba de Villastar, K.3.3) provides a striking parallel for Tartessian lokᵒobᵒo niirabᵒo tᵒo aŕaia | i, indicating closely related Celtic languages with a shared formulaic religious vocabulary and Lugus cult.
Masculine aŕaiu | i is a possible alternative reading.

J.1.2 'Fonte Velha 3' Bemsafrim, Lagos, south Portugal [Museu Nacional de Arqueologia, Lisbon] (Correia no. 11) 117 X 51 X 15cm

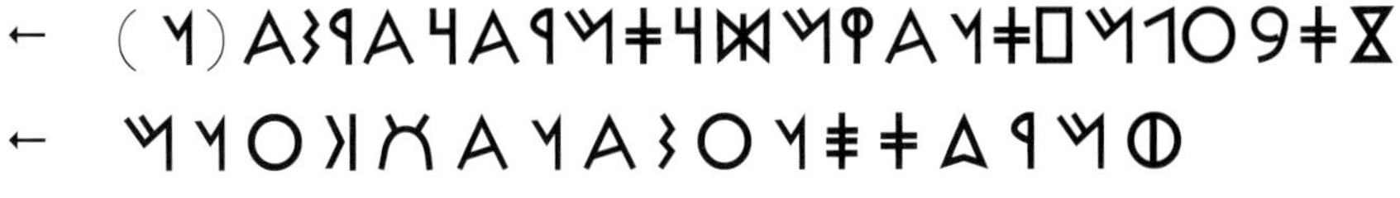

← (ᛗ)ᴀᛆᚹᴀᚼᴀᚹᛗᛩᛩᛩᛗᛗᚿᴀᛗᛩ□ᛗ1ᛆᚹᛩ☒

← ᛗᛗᛆᚼᛁᚼᴀᴧᛗᴀᚼᴀᛆᛆᛆᛗᛩᛩᴀᚹᛗᛆ

kᵒo-bᶜelibᵒo na-kⁱi·bᵘu oira uarbᵃan

tⁱirtᵒos ne-bᵃa naŕkᵉeni

KOᴺ-BELIBO NA-Kᵛ I·BU OIRA UVARMAN TIRTOS NE-BA NAŔKENI

'In the company of the Belīs ("the strong ones"), if no man was supreme, Tirtos ("Third") was not there.' They [the elements of the burial/these words] remain fixed unaltered.'

[Ramos: kobelibona*kikuoirauarban tirtosnebanaŕrkeni]

The name **Tⁱirtos** was probably in origin the Celtic ordinal number 'third' (Gaulish *tritos*, Latin *Tertius*, which was used as a man's name) or was similar enough in form to have been felt to mean that. Therefore, the poetry of the epitaph plays on the name, to say that 'Third' was foremost, i.e. the first. The syntax juxtaposes the playfully contrasting **uarb^aan** and **tⁱirt^oos**.

Dative plural **b^eelib^oo** could be either a group name or a common noun 'strong ones'.

J.1.2 'Fonte Velha 3' Bemsafrim

J.1.3 'Fonte Velha 1' Bemsafrim, Lagos, south Portugal [Museu Nacional de Arqueologia, Lisbon] (Correia no. 9) 67 × 53 × 9cm

→] ᚲᚨᕼᕵᏚᛘᛞᛟᛊᚨ

Ꮢᛟᛟᚨ

ᚲᛊᛟᚻᛟ

→ ᚪᚥ**ᚥᏔᕵᛟᛟᚪᛟᚨ[

1)]ŕak^uurś t^e'-e·b^aare naŕk^eeni
2) ak^a<u>a</u>**iriona

'. . . [the grave] has received him/it. He/she/it rests unmoved. . . [?who has been entombed].'

Compare line 2 **ak^a<u>a</u>**iriona** with J.7.2 **k^aaŕner-ion** 'who has been entombed', thus we may consider reading likewise here **a k^a<u>a</u>[ŕn] ir-ion a[**.

J.1.4 'Fonte Velha 2' Bemsafrim, Lagos, south Portugal [Museu Nacional de Arqueologia, Lisbon] (Correia no. 10) 43 × 68 × 12cm

←] * ᚼᚨᚾᚴᛟᛘᚻᛟᚲᛁᚦᚦᛘᚦᚺᛟᚩ[   ]s̲ek^uui uurk^ee ot^eerk^aa ŕ*[

←]ᚨᚩᚨᚨᛟᚱᚦᛟᚼᛁᛟᚨ[   ]aeHaeol̲eaala[

]-s̲ek(v)ūi uurge voderka ŕ-['. . . has made the grave(s) for (-)Segos . . .' *or* '. . . for -(s)-ekvos, Tegos'

J.1.5 'Fonte Velha 5' Bemsafrim, Lagos, south Portugal [Museu Nacional de Arqueologia, Lisbon] (Correia no. 13) 115 × 43 × 12cm

←]ᚩᚨᛉᚨᛟᚱᛘᚻᚨᚦᛘ

← ᛘᛟᛉᛟᚲᛁᚼᚨ[

→ ᚨ*ᛗᚺᚻᚻᚲᛟᚻᛁᚲᛁ

1) **mut^uuirea b^aar[e n]aŕk^ent^i i**
   (*or* **śut^uuirea**)
2) **a(a/m)m̲u̲s̲ok^eeonii**

'[This grave] of Mutura has received; they remain fixed in place, of the divine Amusogeonos.'

It is possible alternatively to segment an initial masculine dative singular **mut^uui** (*or* **śut^uui**), with **r'-ea·b^aar[e** as a preverb+infixed pronoun+verb 'for Mutos, [this grave] has received him/it. . .'; cf. the spelling of the infixed pronoun in (J.6.1) t^e'-] **ea·b^aare**.

[Rodríguez Ramos: **śut^uuirea . . .**]

J.1.6 Fonte Velha, Bemsafrim, Lagos, south Portugal [Museu Nacional de Arqueologia, Lisbon] 8.4 × 6.0 × 1.3cm

→ XAƷA*   1) t^aab^aa*

→ ᕼᑭ   2) ur

J.2.1 Corte de Pére Jaques, Aljezur, south Portugal [Museu Municipal, Lagos] (Correia no. 24) 97 × 42 × 5cm

→] □ / ‡A9AᙏKO / ᙏ௭ᙏ

]b^ooara nar̓k^eenii

'I [the grave] have received ... They rest unmoving.'

J.3.1 Dobra, Monchique, south Portugal [Museu Municipal Lagos] (Correia no. 25) 124 × 82 × 10cm

←]‡ᙏ9ᕼᙏᙏ   aib^uuris[

← ᙏ⊤ᙏAƷᙏᙏФA[ ]<u>a</u> kⁱinb^aai⊤ⁱi

← AᕤA⤙‡9   ro-la🬀a

←]ᙏᙏᙏAƷ9Aᙏ   uarb^aanub^u[u

  ᙏ[   ]i

AIBURIS[ ]]A KIMBAI(T)I RO·LA(H)A UVARMAN( )UBU[ ]I

'I, Aiburis, a tributary (Cempsian) to the supreme men, have lain down.'

or

'(For) Aiburis, a tributary (Cempsian) to the supreme men, I [the grave] have lain down.'

The basic word order is uncertain, and thus the suggested translation is especially so. The reading is given here following the text anticlockwise from the lower right-hand corner, as occurs in J.1.1 and several other inscriptions. But that may not have been the intended order. The inscription has been carefully laid out. It is unusual in that each 'panel' seems to represent a discrete word or phrase. It is therefore probably intentional that the name **aib^uuris** is physically parallel to, and centred above, the title **uarb^aan** 'the one who is uppermost'. One key issue of interpretation is whether **kⁱinb^aai⊤ⁱi** is related to the name *Cempsi* used for a group near Tartessos to the north-west in the *Ora Maritima* of Avienus, otherwise *Cimbii*. Alternatively, compare **kⁱinb^aai⊤ⁱi** to Old Irish *cimbid* 'captive, condemned man' (probably based on Old Irish *cimb* 'tribute'), or possibly related to both *Cempsi* and *cimbid* (cf. Vendryes 1960– , C99–100). As Hawkes argued (1977), Avienus's Cempsi lived in the western Algarve, thus their territory included Dobra where this inscription was found, strengthening the identification. It is likely enough that the Cimbii/Cempsi, as inhabitants of this marginal region, were a tributary people of Tartessos and that their name reflected their subordinate status. If **uarbᵃanubᵘ**[u is read as one word, that might represent dative/ablative plural *uuarᵃmobo* 'for/from the supreme men'. If the verb **ro-la卋a** means 'I have lain down' or 'he has lain down' (cf. **lakintⁱi**, &c.), the statement could have a double meaning: as a tributary in life Aiburis submitted to overlords; he now lies down in death. Formally, the verb in ~a appears to be a 1st singular perfect. The single **i** 𐌖 inside the central panel of the stone has perhaps been added to make the name of the honorand dative singular, as most common in the inscriptions, thus **aibᵘuris-i** 'for Aiburīs', cf. **ariariśe** ΟΜ𐌖ꟼΑΜꟼΑ 'for Ariarīs' (J.10.1).

J.4.1 'Benaciate 2', S. Bartolomeu de Messines (Concelho de Silves), south Portugal [lost] (Correia no. 51)
120 × 60 × 12cm

←]**ΑꟼΑ϶ꟼΑ϶‡Ο𐌖Μ𐌗ꟼ⊟ΟꟼΑ϶ꟼΑꟺΟ𐌖϶‡Α𐌖‡Μꟺ⊟𐌖
← [-------]‡△Ο϶‡ΑΧ**[/ ?

ibᵒo-iion asune uarbᵃan ekᵘuŕine obᵃar bᵃara[** (or ibᵒonion...)
]****tᵃa oretᵒo / ?

IBO-IION ASUNE UVARMAN EKⱽUŔI(G)NE (V)OBAR BARA**[   ]**TA VORETO

'For the ones whom I [this grave] carry, for Asuna, the supreme one, for Ekurini (Ekvorīgnī "Horse Queen")
... deliverance (lit. running under).'

The script continues along a continuous rectangle with round corners, beginning and ending with an incised box at the lower right corner containing a hapax sign resembling a dollar symbol. The signs are arranged carefully between two incised lines. There is a large section broken away and missing in the lower left of the stone between b^aara**[and]**t^aa oret^oo, which presumably contained several letters. It is conceivable that b^aara 'I have received, have carried' refers not to the remains in the grave, but to the image of the horsewoman (Ekurini herself?) carved on stone J.4.2 from the same site (see next item).

J.4.2 'Benaciate 1', S. Bartolomeu de Messines (Concelho de Silves), south Portugal [Museu Municipal, Silves] (Correia no. 50) 42.5 x 41 x 12cm

←]*ᴹWO[   ]eṡi*[

photo: Jane Aaron

Though the remains of the fragmentary inscription are too short to be interpreted, it is accompanied on the stela with a figure of a relief of a broad-hipped female figure brandishing a long wand, sceptre, weapon, or possibly thick reins and riding a horse side-saddle. She appears to wear a helmet with noseguard, which is comparable to the Corinthian helmet of the earlier 7th century BC found in the river Guadelete, up-river from Cádiz (Olmos 1989, figure 1). What appears to be a circle carved near her chin may represent a neckring shown from a turned perspective. This female rider is reminiscent of some images of the goddess Epona in Gaul and may be related to the form **ekⁿuṟine** 'to the horse-queen', which occurs on inscription J.4.1. above from the same site carved on the same type and thickness of stone. Inscription J.4.1 ends with the verbal noun **oret°o** 'running under, deliver', signifying the action of a vehicle or steed. Several of the images from the 'horse sanctuary' at Marchena, Sevilla, Spain (6th–4th century BC, now held in the Museo Arqueológico de Sevilla) are reminiscent of the Benaciate 1 figure, especially the gracefully curving back and neck of the galloping horse carved on an altar-shaped stele (below right). Another significant comparison is that some of the Marchena horse carvings, grouped in pairs, clearly continue the tradition of the stick-figure chariot teams that appear on 25 of the Late Bronze Age warrior stelae. These points suggest that the figure called **ekⁿuṟine** on J.4.1 had a deep and widespread basis in myth and cult of the south-western Peninsula.

9.7–8. Sculpture from the horse cult centre at Marchena, south-west Spain, 5th–4th century BC, Museo Arqueológico, Sevilla (photos: Jane Aaron)

J.4.3 'Cômoros de Portela 2', S. Bartolomeu de Messines, south Portugal [Museu Municipal, Silves] (Correia no. 24) 64 x 53 x 15cm

J.4.4 'A e B de Cômores da Portela', S. Bartolomeu de Messines, south Portugal [Museu Municipal, Silves] (Correia no. 14) 27 x 25 x 12.5cm; 24 x 18 x 12.5cm

←   ] A ⟨ ⟩ Ψ ≠ Ϻ Α Ο Η Ϙ * [

]*r tᵉeaion(kᵃ)a[

←   ] Ϻ Ο Ϡ Ο) Ϻ * [

. . . na]ŕkᵉentⁱi[

]*ʀ ᴅᴇɪᴠᴏɴᴀ[. . . ɴᴀ]ŕᴋᴇɴᴛɪ[

' . . . the goddess (Deiu̯ona) . . .
They remain bound.'

Examination of the stone favours the reading tᵉeaiona[over Untermann's tᵉeaionkᵃa[. The find site is very near to Benaciate (J.4.1 and J.4.2); therefore, tᵉeaiona['goddess' may reflect a form of the same goddess cult as seen in the dedication to ekᵘuŕine (J.4.1) and the equestrian figure (J.4.1).

←   ] Ψ Ψ Ψ ≠ Ο Ϙ * [

]*ʳeonuu[

←   ] * ≷ * Ϙ Ψ [

]u[a]rbᵃa[an . . .

←   ] Ϻ Ϻ Ϻ Ο) Ϻ Α Ψ

. . narˊ ᵏᵉ]enii[

' . . . who is the highest one . . .
They remain fixed . . .'

J.5.1 Barradas, Benafim (Concelho de Loulé), south Portugal [Museu da Escrita do Sudoeste, Almodôvar; Museu Municipal, Loulé] (On the text, see also Correa 2002.) 114 × 73 × 13cm

← ✕‡ᛘ | ᛘ‡�

saboi : ist͟aa

→ ᛘ⊟‡ᛈᛟᛘ‡�⊟‡

iboo rinoe͟boo

← ᛟ | ᚕᛆᛎᛟᚕᛆᛎᛆ

anakᵉenakᵉ : e

← ᛎᛎᛟᛈᛆᕗᛎ ᛆ ᕗᛎᛎ‡⊟ᛎ

iboo iibᵃa͟n bᵃare͟ii

SABOI : ISTA͟IBO RI(G)NOEBO
AN(N)AGENAK͟:EIBO IIBA͟N BARE͟II

'[The grave] for Samos (or Sabos) . . . has received [him], invoking those queens of the indigenous people.'

The interpretation above is based on the assumption that this is a funerary inscription and the text commences with a dative singular of the name of the deceased, as in J.7.6, J.10.1, J.11.1, J.12.1. Thus, **sabᵒoi** would be an o-stem dative singular, with a variant of the same ending otherwise spelled **-ui** and **-u**, cf. NIEΘΩI 'for Nētos'.

Alternatively, Untermann (1997, 167) has suggested that **sabᵒoi** is a locative singular. Herodotus wrote that Kolaios of Samos received a massive cargo of silver in Tartessos in the mid 7th century BC, and objects of Samian type have been found amongst the orientalizing goods of the Tartessian culture (Chamorro 1987).

Therefore, we might consider whether this inscription commemorates a voyage or seeks divine protection for a voyage to that Samos, i.e. the large Greek island near Ephesos. If so, the locative of the destination provides the topic of the inscription.

The sequence **ist^{a}aib^{o}o rinoeb^{o}o anak^{e}enak^{e}:eib^{o}o** consists of three datives/ablatives plural in concord: a demonstrative followed by a plural noun followed by a Hispano-Celtic group adjective Annagenāk-. As in J.19.1 and J.26.1, a group adjective formed with the suffix *-ak-* is used to identify otherwise unnamed women. In the present inscription, these women are 'queens', possibly a divine group (cf. **ek^{u}uŕine** [J.4.1]). In these three forms, the characteristic final syllable **-b^{o}o** is in each instance preceded by what appears to be a diphthong. It is possible that rather than true diphthongs these spellings reflect hesitation over the quality of unaccented vowels. In **muŕb^{o}** from S. Martinho the syllable is apparently lost altogether.

J.6.2 'Alagoas 2', Salir, Loulé, south Portugal [Museu Nacional de Arqueologia , Lisbon] (Correia no. 34) 20.5 x 23.5 x 4cm

←] O9A◻ [ ]**b^{o}ab^{e}**[

J.6.3 'Viameiro', Salir, Loulé, south Portugal (Correia no. 72) 50 x 26 x 6.5cm

←] 1ǂǂΥǂ [ ]**onsol**[

J.6.1 'Alagoas 1', Salir, south Portugal [Museu Municipal, Loulé] (Correia no. 16) 6.2–9.0 x 3.6cm

←]ΥO9AƷAO[t^{e}'-]**ea·b^{a}are n**[a

← ΥΥΥ[ŕk^{e}e[**enii**

'. . . [this grave] has received it . . . they remain fixed, unmoved.'

J.7.1 Ameixial (Concelho de Loulé) 'Vale dos Vemelhos 3', south Portugal [Museu Nacional de Arqueologia, Lisbon] (Correia no. 23) 144 × 58 × 12cm

← ᛘᚨᛉᛟᛘᚲᚨᛉᛈᛘᛏ⧫▢ᚨᛈᛘᚨ

← ᛉ⧫ᛏ⧫▢ᚨᛉᚨᛈᛘᚨ

aśtᵃa bᵒo(tⁱ)ir naŕkᶜenai
aśtᵃa na·bᵒolon

Aśᴛᴀ ʙᴏᴛɪʀ ɴᴀŕᴋᴇɴᴀɪ | Aśᴛᴀ ɴᴀ·ʙᴏʟᴏɴ

'[The divinities] ?Aśta(rte) have been awakened.
They keep themselves [so].
[The divinities] Aśta(rte) do not die.'

The text, which is complete, appears to be poetic and/or proverbial in which the repeated noun is followed by alliterating verbs, one affirmative and one negative. Both verbs are plural in form, suggesting that **aśtᵃa** should be understood as nominative plural, such as a pluralized divinity like the Lugoues invoked in the opening of J.1.1. The cult of the Phoenician goddess Astarte was practised at the important Phoenician colony of Gadir (Cádiz), west of Gibraltar, and numerous images of the goddess have been found in southern Spain, therefore in and around Tartessos and near the land of the Kunētes in south Portugal. She was the consort of Melqart, the leading male god of Tyre and its colony Gadir, whose annual spring festival celebrated the god's death and 'awakening'. A bronze statuette of a seated nude Astarte datable to the 7th century BC was found at El Carambolo near Seville, i.e. within the zone of easterly outlying Tartessian inscriptions. But the identification here is highly tentative.

[Rodríguez Ramos: **aśtabobir naŕken-ai** / **aśtanabolon**]
[Correia: **abⁱtᵉoa bᵒobⁱirnaŕkᶜenai** / **aśtᵉanabᵒolin**]

J.7.2 'Vale dos Vemelhos 2', south Portugal [Museu Municipal, Loulé] (Correia no. 19) 58 × 41 × 9cm

J.7.3 'Vale dos Vermelhos 1', Ameixial, Loulé, south Portugal [Museu Municipal, Faro] (Correia no. 19) 12 × 8 × 4cm

← —| ٩A‡Δ |—]t°oar[

J.7.4 'Vale dos Vemelhos 4', Ameixial, Loulé, south Portugal [Câmara Municipal, Almodôvar] 97 × 21 × 20cm

← ٩A⧣‡Δ‡⫟

← O٩ꟿꟻ‡ꟿꟼOꟼꟼⵀΛΛAA*[

b°ot°o⧻ar

]*aa kᵃaŕner-ion ire

BOD(V)O(H)AR . . . KAŔNER-ION VIRE

'Bōdo- (< Boudo-) *or* Boduo- . . . of the man whose stone funerary monuments have been built.'

← [ꟼ] Δꟿꟻ iśtᵘ[u

← Λ]A kᵃ[a

'For this man . . .'

J.7.5 'Ameixial 3', Loulé, south Portugal [Museu Nacional de Arqueologia, Lisbon] (Correia no. 28) 33 × 19 × 5cm

←]ᗰᔔ‡ロ9Aᖶ   uarbᵒoᔔi[

← ᖶOIᛝAᖶ   naŕken

'. . . the supreme man. They remain unmoving.'

On **uarbᵒoᔔi**[, cf. **uarbᵒoiir** Ᏹᗰᔔ‡目9Aᖶ (J.22.1) 'lord' < *u(p)ermᵐo-uiros* 'highest man/ hero/ husband'. The symbol ᔔ is of uncertain value, but **uarbᵒoiir** suggests that it could be a variant of the similar ᖶ **u** and represent the inherited labial glide [w] (in Celtic *uiros* 'man') that is usually not written in Tartessian. It is alternatively possible that **uarbᵒoᔔi** is to be read **uarbᵒoii** ᗰᔔ‡目9Aᖶ, the dative singular of the Tartessian formula word **uarbᵃan** 'supreme one'.

[Correia: . . . **uartᵉoli**. . . **naŕkᵉen** . . .]

J.7.6 'Ameixial 2', Loulé, south Portugal Museu Nacional de Arqueologia, Lisbon] (Correia no. 27) 99 × 53 × 4cm

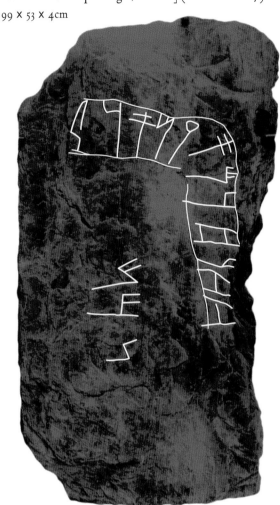

← ᖶIA◁(Φ)ᖶᗰᏱ‡ᗰᖺ⊦9AA

← 9AO9ᖺ1O |—

aarkᵘui oriou⟨tⁱ⟩bᵉa:i   **elurear**[

← ᖶᖺᖶ   **uii**

AARKUI VOR-IOUBA:I ELU-REA**R**[   ]**U**II

'For Argos/Arkvos, for Iouba's ?successor, numerous . . . for . . .'

[Correia: **aartᵉuiolour**]

J.7.7 'Ameixial 4', Loulé, south Portugal [Museu Nacional de Arqueologia, Lisbon] (Correia no. 29) 34 × 22 × 3.5cm

←] ‡ꟼ⋈‡ꟼꟼꟼ [   ]ninok°oro[

←]⋈ꟼA ꟼ[   ]iark°[o-

k°o-ro- could be a series of the preverbs: Indo-European *kom and *pro. ark°[o- is possibly the nominative or accusative *Arkuos/Argos* or *Arkuon/ Argon* (a more archaic spelling of the dative as aark°oi is also possible) of the same personal name occurring in the dative aark^uui on an inscribed stone also from Ameixial (J.7.6).

J.7.8 'Ameixial 1', south Portugal [Museu Municipal, Loulé] (Correia no. 26) 115 × 24 × 13cm

←]*O)A ꟼꟼO)**[

← O)⋈AꟼOꟼOℨO⊟⧺⊡O[

← AℨꟼꟼAOꟼꟼ△ꟼꟼꟼOꟼ

* *k^euuak^e*[
]eb°o t^e'-e·b^aere nařk^e
nemun t^uurea iub^aa

**]KEUUAKE* [   ]EBO T'-E·BERE NAŔKE
NEMUN TUREA IUBA

'Invoking the group of [?Se]keuuos, the grave received him/it, he remains unmoved—Iuba son of Tura(s) of the ?Nemi group.'

[Correia: . . .]et^e?t^eb^aarenařk^ee / neśun?ureaiob^aa. . .

J.7.9 'Azinhal dos Mouros', Loulé, south Portugal [Museu Nacional de Arqueologia, Lisbon] (Correia no. 30) 69.5 x 18 x 7.5cm

→ **ᴎᑭᚺᔕᎪᑭᚺᎪᴎ╪ᛁᔕᎪ[**

iru bᵃarua-ion bᵃ**a**[

VIRU BAR⟨U⟩A-ION B**A**[

'For the man/hero whom I [the grave] have received . . .'

The **u** of bᵃarua is possibly erratic, influenced either by the ending of the preceding dative noun or the present-stem of this verb, Celtic *berū* 'I bear'.

J.7.10 'Touril', Castro Verde, south Portugal [Museu Nacional de Arqueologia, Lisbon] (Correia no. 33) 97 x 26 x 9cm

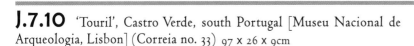

← **OᑭᎪᔕᎩOᗰᎪᑑᎷᎷᎩOꓘᎷᎪᎩ****[**

]****naŕkᵉeni iraś-en bᵃare

'. . . they are bound [i.e. remain unmoving]: the man/hero has received it.'

alternatively '. . . [the grave] has received this man/hero', with accusative ira-śen < *ụiron-sin.

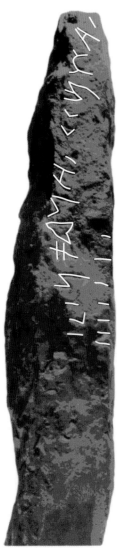

J.8.1 Fuzeta (Concelho de Tavira, 'Cerro do Castelo da Fuzeta'), south Portugal [Departamento de Arqueologia, University of Lisbon] (Correia no. 62) 141 x 16.5 x 19.5cm

←]*‡□Ч‡АЧА***ЧХА*[   ]*aŕi***ant°onb°**o** *[

← *******[

'. . . invoking the deities _____antonas *or* _____antoni.'

J.9.1 Alcoutim, south Portugal [Museu Nacional de Arqueologia, Lisbon] (Correia no. 32) 97.5 x 52 x 19.5cm

← Оꓘ]ꓘАЧОⴹОЧАꙄꝎАЧЧАЧАꓥ[

]k͟ᵃanan uar͟bᵃan(-)e͟bᵉe naŕ[ke. . .

'. . . a supreme one: it remains (*or* they remain) with them' *or* '. . . she/he remains with the highest ones.'

J.10.1 'Mestras' (Martin Longo, Alcoutim), south Portugal [Museu Municipal, Olhão] (Correia no. 32) 128 × 62 × 8.5cm

← ᴎ‡│OⳘᴎᲑᴀ ᴎᲑᴀ

  ariariśe : o-n-

← Ⳡᴀᴧᴀ↑ᴎ

  i-↑akᵃatⁱ

← OᑕᲑO↑‡│OⳘᴎ

  i-śe : o(?t̲ⁱ)er-b̲ᵉe /

← ᴀOᴎᴎ‡O↑│ᴎᴋ

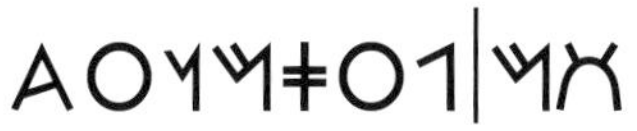

  ŕi : leoine a /

← ᴎᲑᴀᲞᲑ

  r-bᵃar⟨i⟩ /

← OᲑOᵻᴎO↑ᴎ(?)O

  e (??) i(?t̲ⁱ)ensere /

→   ⧻ᴀ�4

  (?tᵃ)au

ARIARIŚE : VO-NI-L̲AGATI-ŚE : VO-ER-BERI:
LEVOINE AR-BARE . . .

'For Ariariś (Arioríχs), he ?lies down under here . . . afterwards it/he carries . . .
invoking the goddess [of beauty] Līvonā, [the grave] has received . . .'

The sign ↑ usually precedes i ᴎ but apparently has a different value in ↑akᵃatⁱi; therefore, 1↑, which has a similar form and occurs in similar sequences, is considered. There is possibly a poetic device in the contrast er-bᵉeri 'carries after' : ar-bᵃare 'has carried before'. Both preverbs are unique in collocation with this verb, which is otherwise very common in the formulaic language of the Tartes- sian inscriptions. The second alliteratively echoes the name of the deceased, *Arioríχs* 'foremost leader', as keynote of the epitaph. The error bᵃar⟨i⟩e for the usual and correct 3rd singular perfect bᵃare is probably due to the influence of the preceding paradigmatic form of the same verb bᵉeri.

J.11.1 Almodôvar, 'Tavilhão 2', south Portugal [Museu da Escrita do Sudoeste, Almodôvar; Museu Nacional de Arqueologia, Lisbon] (Correia no. 32) 82 × 39 × 13cm

← |O✝A1OⱵ⏀

← ⱵⱮⱮO)IⱵⱮOA϶✝⑁OⱵA϶AⱵAⱵⱵ

k^{i}ielaoe | oiśaH^{a}a b^{a}ane ro·b^{a}a(r)e n(a)ŕk^{e}enii

KELAVE : VIŚA⧅A BANE RO·BA(R)E N(A)ŔKENII

'For Kēlavā, wife of Oiśas (?"the leader"), [this grave] has received : they remain unmoving.'

[Correia: k^{i}ielao k^{v}orśat^{e}ab^{a}aneb^{a}aeler̂k^{e}enii]

J.11.2 Almodôvar, 'Tavilhão 1', south Portugal [Museu da Escrita do Sudoeste, Almodôvar; Museu Municipal, Faro] (Correia no. 21) 105 × 28 × 10cm

←]A϶ⱮAO⑁Ⱶ✝☐ⱮⱮ1⅄✝[   ]onlinb^{o}o ire anb^{a}a[t^{e}e

] ONLINBO VIRE AMB<u>A</u>[(χ)TE

'Invoking the divine group (?water spirits) . . . [the grave stone] of a man sent as an overlord's representative. . .'

[Correia:]onlin b^{o}oirea b^{a}a(?)[ ]

J.11.3

J.11.3 Almodôvar, 'Cerca do Curralão', south Portugal [Museu da Escrita do Sudoeste, Almodôvar; Museu Municipal, Setúbal] (Correia no. 63) 73 × 38 × 8cm

→ ‡‡ſ‡ℵPҺAP⟨A̱ℕ̱ [ ]ℕℲA ‡*[

→ ℲA̱ℵⱩOſℵℕ

    soloir uarb^aan [ ]ina o*[
    n]aŕk^eenii

SOVLIVIR UVAR<u>MA</u>N . . . [N]AŔKENII

'Sovlivir(os), who was chief man . . . they remain bound unmoving.'

J.11.4

J.11.4 Almodôvar, 'Vale de Ourique', south Portugal (Correia no. 2)

←]**Ⅎ‡ℲAA3ℲℲℲAꝒ‡ℵ‡‡ℲA

← ℲℲℲOⱩℵAℲℲOꝒA3Ⅎ‡AO

← OℲℲℲ1A

← AХ*AХ*MA⇑ℳ

    aioo̱ŕo̱rainnb^aaanon**[
    a ro-n·b^aaren naŕk^eenii
    aliśne
    ś<u>t</u>ⁱaś*t^aa*<u>t</u>^aa

. . . BAANON RO-N·BAREN NAŔKENII ALIŚNE ŚTI-AŚ*TA(R)TA

'. . . of the women, [the stones of the grave] have received him/it: they remain unmoving in [the place called] Alisna, invoking this goddess ?Astarte.'

The inscription is known only from the generally excellent drawing in the 'Album' of Frei Manuel do Cenáculo Vilas-Boas, Bishop of Beja 1770–1802. Some letter forms are uncertain.

J.11.5 Almodôvar, 'Canafexal', south Portugal [Museu da Escrita do Sudoeste, Almodôvar; Câmara Municipal, Almodôvar] (Correia no. 74) 58 × 54 × 5cm

← ⟨glyphs⟩ [

a]nb^eik^i[i

←]⟨glyphs⟩ [

]arsk^eeirn̲*[

← ⟨glyphs⟩ [

naŕk^ee]nt^ii

. . . A]MBIK̲I̲ . . .   NAŔKENTI

'. . . they remain unmoving.'

J.12.1 Gomes Aires (Concelho de Almodôvar) 'Abóboda 1', south Portugal [Museu da Escrita do Sudoeste, Almodôvar; Museu Regional, Beja] (Correia no. 48) 83 × 51 × 11cm

← ⟨glyphs⟩

→ ⟨glyphs⟩

iru alk^uu sie: naŕk^ent^ii mub^aa t^e'-
e·ro-b^aare H^at^aneat^ee

VIRU (V)ALKU SIE NAŔKENTI MUBA T'-E·RO-BARE (H)ATANEA̲T̲E

'For the man/hero Alkos (*or* Valkos): they are bound unmoving . . . [this grave] has borne him, for the winged one (*or* invoking Ataniatis).'

[Rodríguez Ramos: irualb^uusielnaŕk^eent^iiQub^aa . . .]

If the name of the deceased is to be read as *Valkos* 'hawk, falcon', Welsh *gwalch* (Jenkins 1990; Delamarre 2003, 327), a winged divinity is appropriately invoked to close the epitaph. Alternatively, **iru alk^uu** 'hawk/wolf man', i.e. 'freelance warrior' might merely have been a description of the occupation of the deceased, and does not contain the proper name in its usual position, and *Ataniatis* 'winged' was the man's name. If **H^at^aneat^ee** 'winged' is taken as a detached epithet referring to **iru alk^uu**, that

epithet might describe the accompanying relief image of an armoured warrior waving weapons in both hands, thus resembling a 'winged hawk-man'; see note on H^aat^aane<u>at</u>^ee below. Numerous small bronze spear heads and spear butts of the 11th/10th century BC were found as part of the great deposition of Huelva and have been reconstructed as throwing javelins similar to those shown on the Abóboda stone. It is also noteworthy in this connection that the second element of the double tribal name *Volcae Tectosages*—who lived about Tolosa/Toulouse in south-west Gaul, also in the silva Hercynia of central Europe according to Caesar, and as simply Tectosages in central Asia Minor—meant 'migratory'.

9.9. Late Bronze Age throwing spears from the Ría de Huelva deposition, Museo Provincial de Huelva (photos: Jane Aaron)

J.12.2 Gomes Aires (Concelho de Almodôvar) 'Abóboda 2', south Portugal [Museu da Escrita do Sudoeste, Almodôvar; Museu Nacional de Arqueologia, Lisbon] (Correia no. 49) 38 x 40.5 x 2.5cm

→　]ОΔФᴎ[　　　　　]etᵘtⁱi[

J.12.3 San Sebastião de Gomes Aires (Concelho de Almodôvar) 'Corte do Freixo', south Portugal [Museu da Escrita do Sudoeste, Almodôvar; Museu Regional, Beja] (Correia no. 36)　154.5 x 62 x 12cm

]uultⁱina ar-bᵉ⟨i⟩erĩitᵘu la[k. . .　　*or*　　]uultⁱina ar-bᵉ⟨i⟩erĩi tᵘula[

'Ultina: ʔhenceforth [this grave] bore/bears [? lie down]. . .'

We might segment the compound verb either as **ar-bᵉ⟨i⟩erĩitᵘu** 'carried onward', a preterite comparable to Gaulish ΚΑΡΝΙΤΟΥ *karnitu* (Saignon) 'built a cairn', or as present or imperfect **ar-bᵉ⟨i⟩erĩi** < Celtic **are-beret(i)*.

J.12.4 Gomes Aires (Concelho de Almodôvar) 'Corte Azinheira 1', south Portugal [Museu da Escrita do Sudoeste, Almodôvar; Museu Nacional de Arqueologia, Lisbon] (Correia no. 64) 39 × 31.5 × 6cm

photo: Jane Aaron

→ ‡ΑΓ‡ΑΓ‡ΜΊ[salsaloi t^i[

→]ƷΟƷΑΓΑΦΜΥΊΜ   ]b^{a}eb^{a}a lak^{i}int^{i}i

. . . L A G I N T I

'For Salsalos: . . . [the grave contents] lie down.'
or 'The Salsaloi [group] . . . lie [here].'

J.12.5 south Portugal   18 × 25.5 × 6.5cm

→]**Δ ΚΟ[   ]** t^u k^{e}e[

J.14.1 Alcoforado, São Teotonio, Aljezur (Concelho de Odemira), south Portugal [Câmara Municipal, Castro Verde] (Correia no. 71) 102.5 × 39 × 5cm

←]9‡ℳ4ℬ0ᛡ4△4‡4ℳ△1△ᚷ /

[ ] * [ ]

t^aalainon t^uuŕek^uui or

[ ]*[ ]

←]4‡ℳᚷᛡ△4ᛡ9△ᛒ0△ᚷℳ‡4[

4

noś t^aa-e·b^aare naŕk^e e

n

TALAVIN(D)ON TUŔEKVUI (V)OR[ ]*[

'The country of the blessed headland (*Sacrum promontorium*) for Turekvos . . . . . [this grave] received it/him. They remain bound.'

Several of the inscriptions (J.5.1, J.7.6, J.10.1, J.11.1, J.12.1) commence with the name of the deceased in the dative singular. We understand this to be a burial/tumulus/inscription 'for' the deceased. Here something more is explicit: accusative or nominative/accusative neuter **t^aalainon** 'country of the *Sacrum promontorium*', literally the extreme south-western end of Europe, today Ponta de Sagres, but figuratively, invoking the land of and beyond the setting sun, the afterworld.

J.15.1 São Martinho das Amoreiras (Concelho de Odemira) 'Pardieiro 1', south Portugal [Museu da Escrita do Sudoeste, Almodôvar; Museu Regional Beja] (Correia no. 67) 104 × 58 × 9.5cm

← ⵉ[ ]*OAYOAⰨ //OAMO1OⵠAᑫ𐤍ⵉ ⵉAⰨ

Hᵃaitᵘura meleśae*: : bᵃaenae*(*)   n
(H)AVITURA MELEŚ AE BANAE . . . N [

'Ⱘᵃaitura: for Meleśa, the woman/wife . . .' *or* '. . . for the wife of Meleśos . . .'

One characteristic of this inscription is the frequent occurrence of the double vowel **ae**. As **bᵃaenae** probably corresponds to **bᵃane** 'to the wife, woman' elsewhere, the usage appears to be idiosyncratic, possibly triggered by uncertainty over the *a*-stem dative singular ending **-e** < earlier **-ai** and/or the paradigmatic changes of the vowel of the root in nominative ***bᵉena**, dative **bᵃane**.

J.15.3 São Martinho das Amoreiras (Concelho de Odemira) 'Pardieiro 3', south Portugal [Museu Regional, Beja] (Correia no. 69) 60 × 32 × 6cm

←]O𐤍ⵉⵉOA1AA

aalaein ŕe̲[

← ⵉⵉOⵊ[𐤍Aⵉ

naŕ]k̲ᶜeni

'. . . they are bound unmoving.'

aalaein ŕe̲ probably contains the name of the deceased, but the segmentation, gender, and case are uncertain: nominative **aala**, dative **aalae(i)**, or accusative **aalaein**.

J.15.2 São Martinho das Amoreiras (Concelho de Odemira) 'Pardieiro 2', south Portugal [Museu Regional, Beja] (Correia no. 68) 112 × 40 × 7cm

← ⵉ[
←]𐤍A

]n̲ / aŕ̲[kᶜe(n) . . .

J.16.1 'Nobres', San Salvador, Ourique, south Portugal [Museu da Escrita do Sudoeste, Almodôvar; Museu Nacional de Arqueologia, Lisbon] (Correia no. 47) 110 x 58.5 x 7.5cm

uursaau *arbᵃan tᵉ'-e·bar[e] bᵃa naŕkᵉentⁱi

'For Uursaos who was a supreme man, this grave has received him. They are bound unmoving.'

J.16.2 'Fonte Santa 2', San Salvador, Ourique, south Portugal [Museu Nacional de Arqueologia, Lisbon] (Correia no. 55)

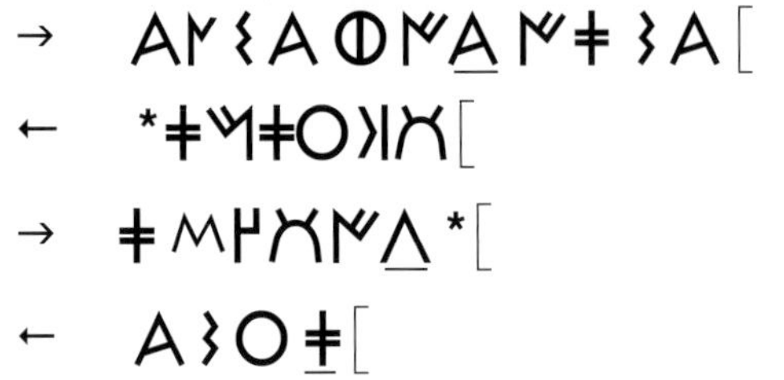

anb^{a}at^{i}ia iob^{a}a[

na]**ŕk^{e}eo-io***

omuŕik^{a}a[

]**oeb^{a}a**

AMBATIA IOBA[NA]ŔKEO-IO*
VOMUŔIKA[ ]OEBA

'As the representative of Ioba, I who lie unmoving under the sea . . .'

Gaulish *Ambaχtos* usually signifies a person 'sent about' on behalf of someone more powerful. In a funerary inscription, and accompanied by the word *u̯omurika* 'realms below the sea' (cf. *Aremorica* 'country by/before the sea'), *ambatia* may refer to a cenotaph, a funerary monument standing in for a body lost at sea. It is likely that this inscription uses the recognized oral formulaic language used by the usual human *Ambaχtos*: 'As representation for [GENITIVE OF NAME OF SUPERIOR]', then in order to switch to the voice of the superior, 'I who . . .' and the rest of the message.

J.16.3 'Fonte Santa 1', San Salvador, Ourique, south Portugal [Museu Nacional de Arqueologia, Lisbon] (Correia no. 54) 75 x 55 x 10cm

→ ᛘⴲᛘ∀ᗞ᛭ⴲᗞ∀ᛘᴀᴧᴀ

→ Ρ⧻ⴿAⴽΟϚAᛘAᛀ⧼[Ο]ᛀⴲᛘ

it·iab^eŕ eb^e an<u>ak</u>^aa
ro·b^aak^ee b^aa naŕk^e[e]ntⁱi [?r. ro·b^aare]

. . . AN<u>AK</u>A . . . RO·BA[R]E BA NAŔKENTI

'. . . [this grave] has received. They are bound.'

ro·b^aa⟨k^e⟩e is probably an aberrant scribal anticipation of ⴿ k^e in the continuing formula in naŕk^eentⁱi. The chief problem with the text is the value of the symbol D, transcribed here as b^e, but followed by the expected O in neither instance and, therefore, probably having some other value. In neither instance is there room for another sign following D. A possible alternative transliteration is Ρ r with no stem line. That an<u>ak</u>^aa is an ā-stem feminine adjective, or final part of a feminine adjective, is likely. A connection with the name of the major river Anas (now the Guadiana at the border of Spain and Portugal) is conceivable.

J.16.5 'Penedo', San Salvador, Ourique, south Portugal [Museu Nacional de Arqueologia, Lisbon] (Correia no. 44) 45 × 21 × 3cm

←]Οᛘ | ᛘAⱻA⌆

uab^aan : ne[

'The supreme one . . .'

J.16.4 'Fonte Santa 3', San Salvador, Ourique, south Portugal [Museu Nacional de Arqueologia, Lisbon] (Correia no. 56) 38 × 8.5 × 7.5cm

→ AᛘᛉΟ⧻ⵝAΙ AⵝA [

ainest^aa : at^a<u>a</u>[

→ AᛘᛉΟ⧻ⵝAΙ A*[

a<u>inest</u>^aa : a*[

J.16.6 Carapetal, San Salvador, Ourique, south Portugal [Museu Nacional de Arqueologia, Lisbon] (Correia no. 45) 14 × 10.5 × 1.5cm

←]Ο⊲A [   ]<u>a</u>re[

'. . .?[this grave] has received . . .'

J.17.1 'Ourique 2', south Portugal (Correia no. 4; on the reading, see also Correa 2006.)
198 x 53 x 24cm

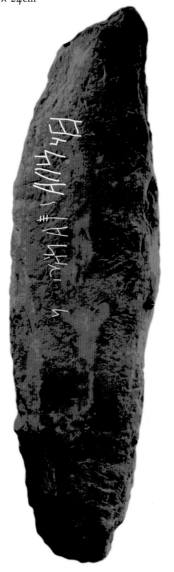

←]***ᚼᎪᎩᎪ‡ᎪᎷᎩᎯᏴ

k^uuik^aa<u>o</u>sa naŕ[k^eeni

'Kuika*sa: they are bound, unmoving.'

J.17.2 'Ourique 4', south Portugal (Correia no. 6)

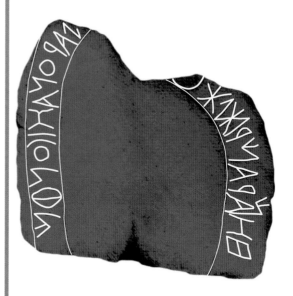

←]*ᚼᎱᎩᎷᎪᎡᎪᎩᎯᏴ

← ᎩᏅᎩᎾᏆᎪᎩᎾᎯᎪᏚ[

k^uuiarairb^ub^u[u   ]b^aare naŕk^eentⁱi

'For the (divine) ?Kuiaraires . . . [the grave] has received. They are bound, unmoving.'

J.17.3 'Ourique 3', south Portugal (Correia no. 5)

←]ᎾᏆᎪᎩᎾ*[

b^aar]e naŕk^ee[

'. . . [the grave] has received. They are bound, unmoving (. . .)'

J.17.4 'Ourique 1', south Portugal (Correia no. 3)

← ᚳᛗᛈ⊓(*)Λ⊓ᛗᛗᛟᛘ | : kᵉenila(*)<u>rin</u>

← |Oᛈᛈ| ⚭ᚦᛟᛗᛗᒷ|O⊙   bᵉe:lin en<u>bᵉ·k</u>ᵃarne :

GENILARIN BELIN EMBE·KARNE

'[This grave] has ʔentombed in stone ʔGenilaris, a member of the Beli- group (*or* the strong one, hero).'

or

KENILARINBE LINEMBE KARNE

'With the queens (i.e. goddesses) of the people of ʔLinem-, [ ] has built the cairn.'

The stone is lost, and the transliteration is based on the later 18th-century 'Album Cenaculo'. Some of the signs are therefore doubtful, especially the second group of underlined letters. They appear to overlap in the surviving drawing, so that the crossed strokes resemble ✕ tᵃ, though that would make the flanking strokes meaningless. If one reads the first line continuously into the second up to the vertical stroke (transcribed as :), kᵉenila-<u>rin</u>bᵉe could be understood as an instrumental plural 'by/with the queens of the kindred' /kenetlo-riɡnʼbi/, Old Irish *cenél* + *rígnaib*.

J.18.1 'Mealha Nova 1', Aldeia de Palheiros (Concelho de Ourique), south Portugal [Museu Regional, Beja] (Correia no. 38) 107 × 45 × 7cm

← ▢◻‡Φ𐤛⋈Λ𐤰Λ𐤰⋈Α⋇⋈Φ‡◻

← [𐤛]ΟΗΛ‡‡

← 𐤰ΟⵣⵘΛ𐤰Λ𐤰ⵣΟ𐤰Λ

← ⋈Φ

b°ot'i⋇ana k°ert°o r̲ /
o-bᵃa t̲ᵉ'-e·b̲ᵃ /
are -bᵃa naŕkᵉen /
t'i /

BŌDIANA KERDO RO-BA T'-E·BARE -BA
NAŔKENTI

'Bōdiana daughter of the artisan has been – [this grave] has received it [her remains] –: they are bound unmoving.'

The sign ⋇ is interpreted here as a solar or astral symbol rather than having the value of a letter. Such an unusual embellishment may have been the work of the father of the deceased, the *kerdos* 'artisan'.

J.18.2 'Mealha Nova 2', Aldeia de Palheiros (Concelho de Ourique), south Portugal [Museu Regional, Beja] (Correia no. 39) 67 × 38 × 9cm

← ·· | Λ𐤰ΟⵘΛ‡𐤛ΟΟΗ𐤰Λ | ··

]an tᵉ'-ee·ro-bᵃare na[ŕkᵉent'i

' . . . [this grave] has received him/her. May they stay unmoved.'

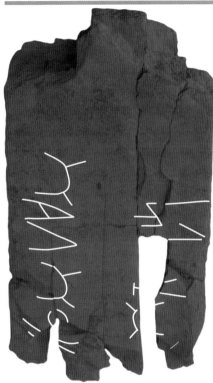

J.18.3 'Mealha Nova 3', Aldeia de Palheiros (Concelho de Ourique), south Portugal [Museu Regional, Beja] (Correia no. 40) 73 × 39 × 6cm

← . . .]ᚺᚦ*ᚾᛝ[   ]ᛔᚤᚾᛞᚤᛔ

k^eer̂ k^aar̂[   ]i↙*o̲r̂[

J.19.1 Herdade do Pêgo, Santana da Serra (Concelho de Ourique), 'Pêgo 1', south Portugal [Museu Regional, Beja] (Correia no. 41) 37 × 45 × 5cm

← ᛝᛉᛉᛔᛞᛟ. . . .A̲|ᛉᛟᛕᛉᚦᚺᚦᚦᛔᛉᛉᛝᛈᚤᚢᚦᛟᛉᛉᛉᛉᛉ

]l̲iirnest^aak^uun b^aane oor̂oire b^a̲[re nar̂]k^enii

L]IIRNESTAKUN BANE VOŔVIRE BA[RE NAŔ]KENII

'For the wife of Oor̂oir (Vorviros), of the people of [?L]ir-ned-s- (?"those dwelling nearer the sea"). [This grave] has received [her]. They remain unmoving.'

This is the epitaph of the wife (dative singular b^aane) of the man commemorated in J.19.2.

[Rodríguez Ramos:]iirnest^a b^uun-b^aane. . .]

J.19.2 Herdade do Pêgo, Santana da Serra (Concelho de Ourique), 'Pêgo 2', south Portugal [Museu da Escrita do Sudoeste, Almodôvar; Museu Nacional de Arqueologia, Lisbon] (Correia no. 42) 39 × 36.5 × 5cm

← ‖‡ⵏⵏ⌐ⴰⵏ⌐ⵎ⊙ⵏ⊙ⵏⵏ

ooŕoir naŕkᵉentⁱi

'Ooŕoir (Vorviros): they [the components of the burial] are bound unmoved.'

This is the epitaph of the husband of the woman commemorated in J.19.1.

[Rodríguez Ramos: . . . naŕkᵉenbⁱi]

J.19.3 Herdade do Pêgo, Santana da Serra (Concelho de Ourique), 'Pêgo 3', south Portugal [Museu Nacional de Arqueologia, Lisbon] (Correia no. 43) 12 × 14 × 9.5cm

]* ‡1‡ [   ]olo*[

J.20.1 Bastos, Santa Luzia (Concelho de Ourique), south Portugal [Museu Regional, Beja] (Correia no. 37) 15 × 32 × 15cm

← ⵎ⊙ⴰⵏⵏ‡ⵎⵏ1⊙ⵒⵎⵏⵏⵎ[

]uŕni bᵉelis̱o̱n uarn

←]⊙⌐ⵏⴰⵏⵏⵒⴰⵏ*⊙ⵏⴰⵏ

bᵃane * bᵃar(e)n naŕkᵉe̱n̲[. .

'For Urnī of the Beli- group (or of the strong ones), for a woman of the highest rank. [This grave] has received [her]. They [the components of the burial] are bound unmoved.'

J.20.1

J.21.1 Arzil, Garvão (Concelho de Ourique), south Portugal [Museu da Escrita do Sudoeste, Almodôvar; Museu Regional Beja] (Correia no. 61)
109.5 × 46.5 × 11cm

← ꟼꟼꓵ꘎ꓘꓵ꙼ꓵꓤ[
   ]ꂦ⊢ꟼꓵꓘꓵꟼ[

]uarbᵃan t̲ᵉ'-e[·ᵇᵃ]a̲r̲e[   ]naŕkᵉenii

'. . . a supreme man. [This grave] has received him. They [the components of the burial] are bound unmoved.'

J.22.1 'Cerro dos Enforcados 1', Panóias (Concelho de Ourique), south Portugal [Museu da Escrita do Sudoeste, Almodôvar; Museu Nacional de Arqueologia, Lisbon] (Correia no. 17) 144 × 67 × 13cm

← ᐱᕼᕚᗝᗝᎧᎧᔦᐱᕼᕙᒣᗰᏔᎧᏔᗣᓭᕼᐱᕙᎧ

uarbᵒoiir saruneea bᵃa

← ᐱᕼᎧᕙᏔᗣ   re naŕ

← ᎧᎧᕙᏔᏔᗝᏔ   kᵉenii

UVARMOVIIR SARUNEEA BARE NAŔKENII

'Uarboiir Saruneea ("the Noble Consort of Saruna [< *Sterunā]"). [This grave] received [him]. They [the components of the burial] are fixed, unmoving.'

J.22.2 'Cerro dos Enforcados 2' Panóias (Concelho de Ourique), south Portugal [Museu Nacional de Arqueologia, Lisbon] (Correia no. 18) 69 × 60 × 5cm

←]ᕙᐱᒣᐱᗝᗝᎧᎧᔦᐱᕙᒣ[

]saruneea oar['. . . Saruneea Oar[?boiir] . . .'

J.23.1 Monte Nova do Visconde, Casével (Concelho de Castro Verde), south Portugal [Câmara Municipal, Ourique] 95 × 34 × 22cm

← 𐤔𐤉𐤌𐤌𐤨𐤀𐤖𐤀𐤔𐤀𐤁𐤀���8𐤄𐤌𐤀𐤅𐤌𐤀𐤀9

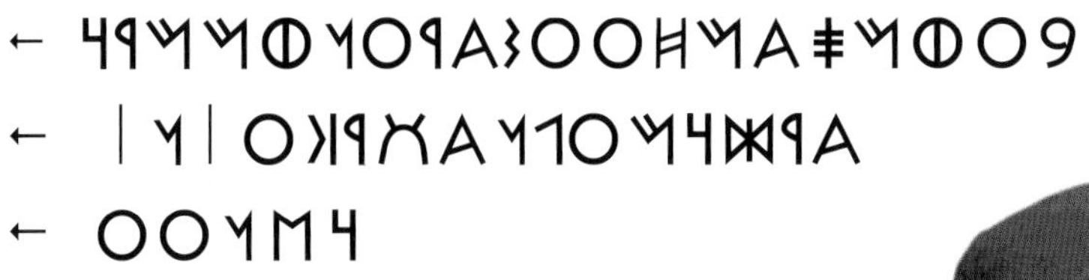

← |𐤌|𐤀𐤉𐤔𐤊𐤀𐤖𐤌𐤌𐤀𐤅𐤌𐤔𐤉𐤀

← 𐤀𐤀𐤖𐤌𐤔

b^cet^isai t^e'-ee·b^aarent^i iru

arb^uui-EL naŕrk^ee:n:
uśnee

BETISAI T'-EE·BARENTI VIRU[I
U]VARBUI-EL NAŔRKENI UŚNEE

'For Betisa: they [?the components of this grave] have received it, invoking the lord god; they are bound unmoving in Uxama.'

J.24.1 Neves, Castro Verde, south Portugal [Mining Museum, Neves-Corvo] (Correia no. 70) 25 X 39 X 2.5cm

J.26.1 Herdade do Gavião, Aljustrel, south Portugal [Museu da Escrita do Sudoeste, Almodôvar; Museu Regional, Beja] (Correia no. 59) 115 X 46 X 12cm

← OꟼAƐꟼꟼˠHOꟼꟼAX[

→]ƐAPOꟼAꟼK[

]tᵃarnekᵘun bᵃane

*bᵃare naŕkᵉ[e . . .

'For a woman of the group/family of Tarnos: [this grave] has received [her]; they are bound unmoving.'

←]Ɛ***A1[

←]ꟼ‡ꟼ‡□1AO*[

←]ⱵXAO‡A△A‡ꟼ

← Oꟼ‡AA[

←]OAA∧[

]laᵃ***bᵃ[

]*ealb̲ᵒoroi[

isak̲ᵃaoeaŕt̲ᵉ[

]atᵒore/

]kᵃaae̲[

'. . . For Alburos ʔthe leader: . . . ʔstone . . .'

J.27.1 Góis, São Miguel do Pinheiro (Concelho de Mértola), south Portugal

J.28.1 Mértola (Marques de Faria), south Portugal [Museu Municipal, Mértola]
79 × 39 × 8–12cm

←]ΧΚΟΜΑ⋎ΟϼΑϞ⋎ΟΑΜΟϞΙ⋎[

]ukᵉe śaen bᵃare naŕkᵉe

→ ϤΟΜ**⋎[

bᵉeś**n[

'. . . ?for -uka, [the grave] has received this; it is bound unmoving . . .'

]**[   ]**[

→]ΑΟϤΑΗ≠*[   ]aetᵉabᵒo*[

←]⋎⋎≠⋎ϞϼϤ⋎[   ]norⳠioni[

← ≠口⋎Α[   ]aibᵒo

In the second and third lines of the text as printed above, it is likely that there are dative/ablative plural forms in -bᵒo.

J.51.1 Los Castellares, Puente Genil, Córdoba, Spain [Museo Arqueológico Provincial, Málaga] (Correia no. 76) 96 x 48 x 15cm

J.52.1 Villamanrique de la Condesa, Sevilla, Spain [Museo Arqueológico, Sevilla] (Correia no. 79) 61 x 61 x 28cm

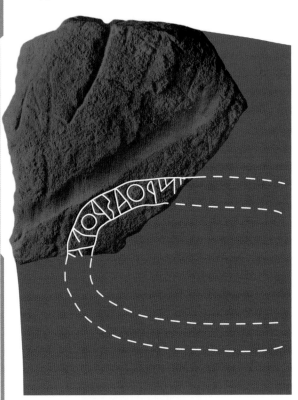

←] A10PᴮAO9Ϻ [←

]ire abᵃre la[

read]ire bᵃare la[k-

'. . . [the tomb] of the man has received; lies down . . .'

The arc of text is a fragment of a very thick stone (see below), which had probably been part of a large stela with a long inscription in a complete circuit. **abᵃre** for the very common formulaic **bᵃare** is an obvious error and—since Tartessian could also be written left to right—easily explained.

← ꟼ[   ]k̲ⁱu

← A⌐**[   ]**bᵃa

→]Δꟼ𐊣ΛAϺ‡[   ]t̲ᵘurkᵃaio[

J.53.1 Alcalá del Río, Sevilla, Spain [now lost] [Correia no. 75; on the reading, see further Correa 2005, 138.]

→ ⋈ΔⱵΑΡΑΗΟΔⱮⱢⱮΗ‡ƷΑⱮ‡ΡƷΑ‡ΟΧΑ

→ ΓΑΚΟⱮⱰⱮΡΑⱫΑΛΑΜΟΧΑⱮΑ

← ΗΟꟼΑΊ‡ꓷⱵ‡⋈

kᵒtᵘuaratᵉe tᵘntⁱitᵉsbᵃan orbᵃa setᵃa   [r. tᵘn(ʔkⁱ)itᵉsbᵃan]

lakᵉentⁱi raⱫa kᵃaśetᵃana

kᵒoŕbᵉo b̠ᵃarleⱵ

KOTUVARATE TUN<u>K</u>ITESMAN ORBA-SEDA LAGENTI RA<u>H</u>A KAŚEDAN(N)A KORŃB⟨E⟩O B̠ARLE<u>H</u>

'The inherited resting place that is most ?auspicious has safely conveyed [her]. They [the components of this burial] lie down. RaⱫa, the priestess/tin-magistrate, daughter of Korbos ...'

The first words **kᵒtᵘuaratᵉe tᵘntⁱitᵉsbᵃan** contain three instances of symbols for stop consonant + inherent vowel (**kᵒ, tᵘ, tᵉ**) without the usual redundant vowel. As one of the more easterly Tartessian inscriptions, it is interesting to note this tendency in the direction of the principles of the Iberian and Celtiberian semisyllabaries.

The statement appears to begin with a finite verb compounded with three preverbs, a common enough syntagm in the Insular Neo-Celtic languages but rare, or even otherwise unknown, in the extant corpus of Continental Celtic.

The disagreement of consonant and vowel quality in **kᵒoŕbᵉo** may reflect two competing o-stem genitive singular endings, Gaulish-type *korbī* versus Hispano-Celtic-type *korbo*.

There are internal harmonies linking the key words *ko-tu-ṷa-rāte* 'has delivered, gone under' with the name of the deceased *RaHᵃa*, and the father's name *Korbos* with *orba* 'inheritance, &c.' She had probably inherited the office from him.

If Tartessian had Celtic vocabulary for wheeled vehicles similar to the Belgic *assedon* 'war-chariot' (Caesar's Latinized *essedum*, also seen in the British king's name AΘΘEDOMAROS 'great in chariots') <

ad-sedo- 'seat' and Old Irish *aire* 'chariot driver' < *are-sed-s* 'the one seated in front', the use of the Tartessian verb -*u̯a-rāte* 'has run under' together with the noun *seda* probably echoes the traditional poetic vocabulary of high status wheeled vehicles, including traditional funerary vehicles.

The Alcalá inscription is not the only evidence for women of important social and economic rank in Tartessian society. The famous wealthy orientalizing burial of Aliseda, Cáceres (*c.* 625 BC), was that of a woman who has been interpreted as a priestess.

Alcalá del Río was also the find spot of a Late Bronze Age sword of a type with parallel sides and an elongated point.

J.54.1 Capote, Higuera la Real, Badajoz ('La losa de Capote'), Spain [Museo Arqueológico Provincial, Badajoz] (Correia no. 80) 95 × 60 × 16cm

←]4AX909‡‡‡4*[   ]**MO)M*[

]*ikᵉei**[   ]*uosor ertᵃau[ne

The iconcogarphy of the Late Bronze Age 'warrior stelae' is orinetated downwards from the perspective of the inscription and includes schematic images of chariot with two horses and what appears to be large lyre at the bottom.

J.55.1 near Siruela, Badajoz, Spain [Museo Arqueológico Provincial, Badajoz] (Correia no. 78)
120 X 52 X 25cm

← OYAAꟼOOYⱢ Y1ⱢꟼⱢ1

→ XAꟼYOᒧᒧⱢY |

→ ᒪYↃYYOYOYAꟼKOYAY

ro- kᵒoli̱o̱n eertᵃaune (*or* aokᵒoli̱o̱n eertᵃaune)
tᵃarielnon :
lifniene nafkᵉenai

RO- KOLION VEERTAUNE
DARIVELNON : LIŔNIENE NAŔKENAI

'For the exchanging of Darivelnos of/in Liŕ-ne(d)- (the land by the ocean) for Kolios. They [these words, marking stones] remain.'

This inscription diverges from the usual formulae and thus may not be a funerary monument, but rather possibly marks a succession of rulers or the exchange of high-status hostages. It is perhaps significant that the stone is one of the easternmost of the Tartessian inscriptions, far from the Atlantic and the densest concentration of inscriptions in south Portugal. The stone may therefore mark an extension of power and/or cultural influence. The Kolios named here may be the same man as the Akoḻios whose funerary monument (J.56.1) was not far away. The similarity of the name to that of Kolaios of Samos who visited Tartessos about 650 X 638 BC is intriguing, but probably coincidental.

The basic syntax is a verbal noun /u̯ertaune/ taking two accusative nouns, thus 'to exchange' is proposed as a suitable sense.

If the alternative reading **aokᵒolion** is preferred, then it is more likely that this is precisely the **akᵒolioś** of J.56.1.

[Rodríguez Ramos: **aokᵒolion** . . .]

J.56.1 Almoroquí, Madroñera, Cáceres, Spain [Museo Arqueológico Provincial, Cáceres] (Correia no. 77) 160 x 65cm

← ꟿΦ◯)|ꓘꓯꓨꟿ‡ꟿ(ꓒ)‡ꓮ   akᵒo(l)ioś naŕkᵉetⁱi

AKOLIOŚ NAŔKETI   'Akolios remains here.'   [Rodríguez Ramos: akᵒolion: . . .]

J.57.1 Medellín, Badajoz, Spain (On the reading, see also Correa 2006, 297.]

←)|ꓘꓯꓩꓯ ꟿ‡ꓒ◯)ꟿ‡ꓧ ‡ꓒ[   ]lokᵒon kᵉₑloia naŕkᵉ[e .

←] ꟿꓒ   li[

←] ꓮ}   bᵃa[re

'. . . the grave of [Kē]lova: it is bound/remains . . . it has received . . .'

Monte Novo do Castelinho, Almodôvar, south Portugal [Museu da Escrita do Sudoeste, Almodôvar] (Guerra et al. 1999; Correa 2002, 409)

← ꟿΦꓩꓗ[ ]‡ꓲꓥ[ ]ꓒ⅁ꓯ‡ꓒ‡ꓧ:ꟿ‡ꟿ‡ꓒ‡ꓧ[

]kᵒoloion : kᵒoloar[ ]ŕ[.]s[?kᵉ]ntⁱi

The inscription appears to end in a plural verb, and the surviving text begins with an accusative singular noun or nominative/accusative neuter.

Corte Freixo 2 (Concelho de Almodôvar), south Portugal, [Museu da Escrita do Sudoeste, Almodôvar] (text from Guerra 2002, cf. Correa 2004)

←]ꟿꟿ◯)|ꓘꓯꟿ[   ]naŕkᵉeuu['. . . I rest unmoving . . .'

S. Martinho, south Portugal [Museu da Escrita do Sudoeste, Almodôvar] (text from Guerra 2002; cf. Correa 2004) 133 × 95 × 11–13cm

[text in a continuous anticlockwise circle printed here as three lines]

bᵃasteᵉbᵘuŕoi onunaio tᵉʔe   'in the yew wood of death ...
[...]i[...]o*reiar*nio
ebᵘu alakⁱimuŕboʔ a na͇ŕkᵉe bᵃa͇*   ʔinvoking the seas ... rests unmoving ...'

← AⵁAꟻYAO   ea<u>n</u>b^aara   '?I have carried around'

← ?▢   b^o?

Though the inscription survives complete, the carving is shallow and hard to read in places. The sequence o*reiar*nio|eb^uu alakⁱimuŕb^o appears to be two datives/ablatives plural in concord, probably invoking a divine group. If we read r(i)nioeb^uu alakⁱimuŕb^o, that could be something like 'to the queenly ones *alaki* of the sea'.

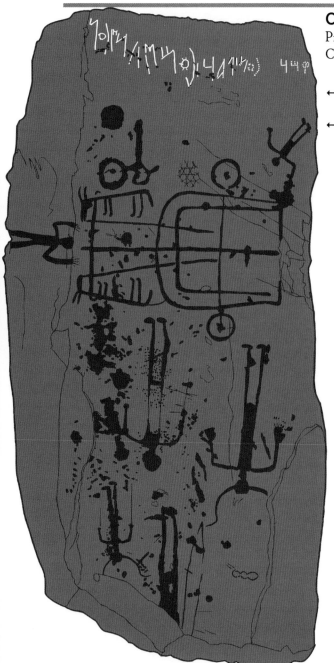

Cabeza del Buey IV [Museo Arqueológico Provincial de Badajoz] (De Hoz et al. undated, 52–4; Correa 2008) 100 x 40 x 20cm

←]*ꝐYꝐ [

←] YOꖾꓘYAMꟿOꖾꓨA⸀YOꖾ

]kⁱiu [---] k^eeilau k^ee iśa n[a]ŕk^en

'. . . they remain . . .'

redrawn after Tera, S.L. L.

¶NOTE. For the recently discovered inscriptions from **Mesas do Castelinho**, **Corte Pinheiro**, and **Vale Águia**, see Guerra above.

TARTESSIAN LINGUISTIC ELEMENTS

¶NOTE. The term 'Hispano-Celtic' is used in the citations and compared forms below for more than one degree of Celticity. (1) For forms which have recognized Celtic parallels outside the Iberian Peninsula, or where there is a distinctively Celtic sound change, such as loss of Indo-European *p* or **g*^{u} > *b*, then Celticity is more certain. The relevant comparanda and/or sound changes are given in the entries below. (2) Other forms labelled 'Hispano-Celtic' are probably but not certainly Celtic. These occur in the zone of Celtic names in the north, west, and centre of the Peninsula. They appear to be Indo-European (rather than Iberian or Basque) but are not Latin. They do not show preserved Indo-European *p*. The label 'Lusitanian' is applied only to forms from the five Lusitanian inscriptions discussed by Wodtko (this volume). No attempt has been made to identify Celtic borrowings in the Lusitanian inscriptions.

NAMES

SUMMARY

(1) PERSONAL NAMES. (A) MASCULINE: **aark^{u}ui** (dative), ?**ark^{o}**[o- (nominative or accusative), **aib^{u}uris**[(nominative or dative); **ak^{o}olioś** (nominative), **alb^{o}oroi** (dative), **alk^{u}u** (dative), **aŕaiui** (dative), 'Αργανθωνιος, **ariariśe** (dative), **b^{o}ot^{o}o-**, **t^{a}arielnon** (accusative), *Gargoris* (nominative), **iob^{a}a**[, **iub^{a}a** (nominative), ?**k^{e}enila**(*)**rin** (accusative), **k^{o}olion** (accusative), **k^{o}oloion** (accusative), Νωραξ, **saboi** (dative), -**sek^{u}ui** (dative), **soloir** (nominative), **t^{e}asiioonii** (genitive), **t^{i}ilek^{u}urk^{u}u** (dative), **t^{i}irt^{o}os** (nominative), **t^{u}uŕek^{u}ui** (dative), **oiśaHa** (genitive), **ooŕoir** (nominative), **ooŕoire** (genitive), **leb^{o}o-iire** (genitive), **uursaau** (dative), **uarb^{o}oiir saruneea** (nominative+genitive);

(B) FEMININE: **asune** (dative), **b^{e}et^{i}isai** (dative), **b^{o}ot^{i}i☼ana** (nominative), **H^{a}ait^{u}ura** (nominative), **k^{i}ielaoe** (dative), ?**meleśae** (dative), **mut^{u}uirea** (genitive), **t^{u}urea** (genitive); **isak^{a}aoe** (?dative),] **uult^{i}ina** (nominative).

(2) GROUP NAMES: **b^{e}e:lin** (accusative singular), **b^{e}elib^{o}o** (dative plural), **b^{e}eliśon** (genitive plural), **iśiink^{o}olob^{o}o** (dative plural), probably **k^{a}alt^{e}e** (dative singular) also the compound **nira-k^{a}alt^{e}e**, **k^{i}inb^{a}ai↑^{i}i** (singular) = *Cempsi/Cimbii* (plural), Κυνητες/Κυνησιοι, **liirnest^{a}ak^{u}un** (genitive plural), possibly **nemun** (genitive plural), **niirab^{o}o** (dative plural), ?[Si]**k^{e}euuak^{e}e***[ ] **eb^{o}o** (dative plural), **t^{a}arnek^{u}un** (genitive plural).

(3) DIVINE NAMES. (A) MASCULINE: **lok^{o}ob^{o}o** (dative plural), ΝΙΕΘΩΙ (dative), **iru**[i u]**arb^{u}ui-EL** 'the lord god' (dative);

(B) FEMININE: ?**aśt^{a}a** ?'Astarte', **aś*t^{a}a*t^{a}a** 'Astarte', **t^{e}eaiona**['Goddess', **ek^{u}uŕine** 'Horse-Queen' (dative), possibly **H^{a}at^{a}aneat^{e}e** 'the Winged One' (dative), (?) instrumental/associative plural **k^{e}enila-rinb^{e}e** ?'queens of the kindred', **leoine** 'the Beautiful One' (dative), **rinoebo anak^{e}enak^{e}:eibo** 'the Queens of the Indigenous People' (dative plural), **saruneea** 'Star Goddess' (genitive),]**uŕni**;

(C) UNCERTAIN GENDER: **k^{u}uiarairb^{u}b^{u}**[u (dative plural); **ark^{a}ast^{a}ab^{u}u** (dative plural).

(4) PLACE-NAMES: **aliśne** (locative), **b^{a}ast^{e}eb^{u}uŕoi** (locative), **t^{a}ala-inon** (accusative or nominative neuter), **omuŕik^{a}***[, **uśnee** (locative).

ALPHABETICAL LIST OF NAMES

]**eb^{o}o** ⫩□O[(J.7.8) incomplete form, dative/ablative plural ending, probably divine name, less probably personal pronoun 'to/from them', similarly]**aib^{o}o** ⫩□ΜA[(J.28.1).

aalaein ΥΜOA1AA (J.15.3) possibly the same root as in Celtiberian *alaboi* and/or the family name

Alaskum. Untermann (1997, 168) cites *Alainus* and *Alaius* from Yecla de Yeltes, Spain.

aarkᵘui ᙏᔨᖰ᙭AA (J.7.6) 'for Argos' or 'for Arkʷos' masculine dative singular *o*-stem, cf. ARCO · MANCI F · commemorated at Oliveira do Hospital, Coimbra, Portugal (Búa 2000, 481), ARC[O] | NI AMB | ATI F at Villar Pedroso, Cáceres, Spain (Sánchez Moreno 1996, 124), ARCIVS EPEICI BRACARVS on an altar from Vila da Feira, Aveiro, Portugal (Búa 2007, 26), ARCVIVS at Barcelos, Braga, Portugal (Búa 2000, 359), the Western Hispano-Celtic divine epithets in NAVIAE ARCONNVNIECAE (*L'Année épigraphique* 1955, 78, Lugo) and LVGVBO ARQVIENOBO (Sober, Lugo), LVCOVBV[?s] ARQVIENI[s] (Outeiro do Rei, Lugo; Búa 2000, 266–7), Celtiberian *Arkailikos*, genitive singular place-name ARGAILO (Untermann, MLH 4.407), Gaulish personal name *Com-argus*, Old Irish *arg* 'warrior, hero', Greek ἀρχός 'guide, leader'. Untermann (1997, 168) cites the personal name *Arquius* attested in Celtiberia, Lusitania, and southern Extremadura (e.g. CAMALA ARQVI F. TALABRIGENSIS [*L'Année épigraphique* 1952, 27, Viano do Castelo]). Note also the Hispano-Celtic place-name *Arcobriga.* **arkᵒ**[o- ᙭ᔨAᙏ (J.7.7), also from Ameixial, is possibly the nominative or accusative of this same name. Note also the first element of the dative plural compound **arkᵃastᵃabᵘu** ᔨᙈA᙭ᖱAᙡᔨA (Mesas do Castelinho).

]**aetᵉabᵒo***[   ]AOᖱAᖻ ᖱ*[(J.28.1) ?dative/ablative plural.

aibᵘuris[   ]ᖱᙏᔨ᙭ᙏᙏA (J.3.1) possibly a name in *-ris* from Celtic *-rīχs* (< Indo-European **h₃rēg-s*), or dative singular **-ris**[e. For the first element, compare Western Hispano-Celtic AEB(VRVS) (*Hispania epigraphica* 1994, 133–4, A Coruña) and CRISSVS TALABVRI F. AEBOSOCELENSIS (*L'Année épigraphique* 1952, 42–3, Cáceres). *Aebarus* and *Aebicus* occur as personal names in Lusitania (Untermann 1992, 392). Alternatively, cf. the Gaulish personal names *Eburia, Eburius, Eburo,* ᾿Εβουρωνος, ᾿Εβουρος, *Eburus,* and the recurrent Hispano-Celtic place-name *Ebura* 'yew-tree(s)'. This tree-name is the base of the name of the Celtiberian *gens,* the *Eburanci,* cf. the Gaulish group names *Eburones* and *Eburovices* (Marco Simón 2005, 297). One place named *Aipora/ Ebora* near Gadir/ Cádiz was the find site of a spectacularly wealthy hoard or burial of the Tartessian culture, which included 93 manufactured gold items and 43 carnelians (Cunliffe 2001, 271). Another *Aebura* is known at the important Early Iron Age silver mining site at Ríotinto, Huelva. There was also an *Epora* near Seville and another *Ebora* in south central Portugal. See further **bᵃastᵉebᵘuroi** below.

akᵒoḷios ᙏᖱᙏ(ᔨ)ᖱᙈA (J.56.1) nominative singular masculine *o*-stem, possibly the same individual named in (J.55.1) **kᵒolion** or his relative (see below). If they are not merely graphic variants of the same name—the latter with elision following **ro- -akᵒoḷios** might include the preposition **ad** prefixed to **kᵒolios**. Cf. Celtiberian and North-west Hispano-Celtic personal name ACCA (Albertos 1985, 261).

albᵒoroi ᙏᖱᔨᖱᦺᒷA (J.24.1) ?dative singular 'to Alburos' /*alburūi*/ or nominative plural group name 'the Alburoi' or locative singular 'in Alburo-' (cf. Untermann, MLH 4.327), cf. North-west Hispano-Celtic ALBVRVS, ALBVRA (Albertos 1985, 263; Luján 2007, 248).

alkᵘu ᔨᖻᔨA (J.12.1) /*alkūi*/ or /*u̯alkūi*/ 'for Alkos' or 'for Valkos', dative singular masculine *o*-stem, cf. Lepontic *Alko-uinos,* Gaulish *Alco-uindos, Alcus, Alcius,* and the place-names *Alcena, Alciacum,* Αλχι-μοντς, Hispano-Celtic *Alce* (Delamarre 2003, 38). Tacitus (*Germania* 43) mentions central-European divine twins called *Alci,* worshipped by the Naharvali, subtribe of the extensive Lugii (whose name is probably related to the divine name **lokᵒobᵒo** in J.1.1). Alternatively, compare the widely distributed Gaulish group name *Volcae* and the personal names *Uolcius, Uolcenius, Uolcenia, Uolcinius, Uolcacius,* &c., ogamic Primitive Irish ULCAGNI; cf. the second element of the compound that might be read **tⁱilekᵘuḷkᵘu** ᔨᖻᔨᖻᖱᒷᒪᙏᒷ (Mesas do Castelinho) below. The vowel agrees with the treatment in Welsh *gwalch* 'hawk' also 'rogue' (the same treatment of Celtic *u̯o- > u̯a-* is also found in Tartessian (**u)aratᵉe** ᖾAᒷAᖻO [J.53.1] = Early Welsh *gwarawt* 'saved' < Celtic **u̯u̯o rāte*). The original meaning of Celtic *u̯olko- was probably 'wolf, beast of prey' (Indo-European *u̯lku̯o-), by transferred sense 'warrior, hero' (Jenkins 1990). On the semantics, cf. Old Irish *cú glas*, literally 'wolf', but figuratively 'landless, extra-tribal mercenary warrior'. That the deceased was a warrior is strongly implied by the stela which shows an armed man brandishing weapons—short throwing spears and a shield—surrounded by the inscribed text. Rodríguez Ramos's reading **albᵘu** could also be paralleled in Celtic.

aliśne ΟϒϺϺ1Α (J.11.5.) locative singular place-name 'in Alisno-, Alisnā', cf. Latin *alnus* 'alder' < *alisnos*, Celtiberian *alizos* (K.0.2), and the family name *Alizokum* (K.0.1, genitive plural), Northern Hispano-Celtic ALISSIEGINI (genitive, Latinized?) (Untermann 1980, 376), Gaulish place-names *Alesia*, IN ALISIIA, IN ALIXIE, *Alisicum*, also ALISANV 'to the god of Alesia' (Indo-European *h₂éliso- 'alder').

a(a/m)musokᵉeonii

Α*ϺΗ‡‡ΚΟ‡ϒϚϺϺ (J.1.5) possibly with the divine suffix and locative singular of a -*i̯o*-stem; cf. Ἀργανθωνιος, **tᵉasiioonii** (J.1.1).

anakᵉenak͟ᵉ:eibᵒo ‡ΗϺΟ|ΙΑϒΟΙΑϒΑ (J.5.1) /annagenākabo/ < *Andogenākabo dative/ablative plural group adjective 'indwelling, belonging to the indigenous people', cf. Gaulish forms from Larzac *andogna[* 'indigenous', feminine accusative singular *andognam*, negatived *anandognam*, Middle Welsh *annyan* 'nature, inborn quality' < *andoganā, Latin *indigena* 'native, &c.' < Indo-European *(e)ndo-g´enh₁ 'born inside' (Delamarre 2003, 48), possibly also the comparable British *andagin-* collocated with an invocation of an unnamed local goddess on the Bath pendant ADIXOVI | DEVINA | DEVEDA | ANDAGIN | VINDIORIX | CVAMIIN | AI 'Vindiorix ardently entreats the indwelling holy goddess for Cuamena (the dear woman)' (cf. Welsh *dihew-yd* 'ardent desire', but other meanings are possible, for example, if this pendant is another Bath curse inscription, 'Vindiorix ardently entreats the holy goddess: something bad (*an-+daga-) for Cuamena' (published interpretations vary: Tomlin 1988, 133; Lambert 1994, 174; Schrijver 2004, 16–17;

2005, 57–9; Sims-Williams 2007, 16–17). The vowel or diphthong written -ei- in the declensional ending has probably been influenced by the dative/ablative plural pronoun **eibᵒo** 'for them' and/or the dative/ablative plural noun **rinoebo**, historically an *i*-stem, with which **anakᵉenak͟ᵉ:eibo** agrees. To invoke the indigenous queens, probably meaning goddesses, reflects the fact that in the Orientalizing Period (*c.* 750–*c.* 550 BC) the cult of the Phoenician goddess Astarte flourished in the south-western Iberian Peninsula. **ekᵘuŕine** was probably one of these native 'queens' competing with Astarte (see below).

Anas is the ancient name of a great river of the south-western Iberian Peninsula, which reaches the Atlantic at the modern border of Portugal and Spain. It is now called *Guadiana* (with Arabic *wadi* 'river' prefixed). *Anas* is probably related to Gaulish *anam* glossed 'paludem' ('swamp') in Endlicher's Glossary, cf. also Old Irish *an* 'water, urine'. If this is the correct etymology, the name shows loss of Indo-European *p* in the root *pen-* 'swamp, dirty water', cf. Sanskrit *pánka-* 'swamp', Prussian *pannean* 'swamp', English *fen* (Delamarre 2003, 43–4). Citing archaic sources, Avienus (*Ora Maritima*, line 202) wrote that the Anas flowed through the land of Cynetes.

]antᵒonbᵒo ‡Οϒ‡ΑϒΑ[(J.8.1) dative/ablative plural ??= /argantonbo/ 'invoking the gods of silver', cf. Ἀργανθωνιος below.

aŕaiui ϺϒϺϒΑΧΑ or **aŕaiai** ϺΑϒΑΧΑ (J.1.1) /araiūi//araiāi/ dative singular personal name '(to) Aŕaius, Aŕaios, Aŕaia', corresponding exactly to the Celtiberian genitive plural family name *Araiokum* 'of the people of Araios', cf. also the accusative singular ARAIANOM, which is possibly distinct from the Western Hispano-Celtic personal name and family name occurring in an inscription from Ávila ARAV(VS) | ARAV | IAQ(VM) TVRANI F(ILIVS) (Sánchez Moreno 1996, 121) and the theonym ARABO COROBE|LICOBO TALVSICO·BO (Arroyomolinas de la Vera, Cáceres, Spain [Búa 2000, 526]). If both the Tartessian and Celtiberian reflect a development of an epenthetic vowel in an older *ario- 'one who is in front' (alternatively 'man of the native group', Indo-European *$h_4eri̯ós$ [cf. **ariaríse** below]), that would be a significant shared innovation betokening a close relationship between Tartessian and Celtiberian. Note also that the *Ora Maritima* of Avienus mentions a promontory called *Aryium* (line 157) a few days journey by sea beyond Tartessos. That name, deriving from sources as old as the 6th century BC, would mean simply 'promontory, projecting point' in the Celtic of west Hispania.

Ἀργανθώνιος (Herodotus 1.163–5) /*argantonios*/ masculine *o*-stem, 'pertaining to the god **Argantonos, -ā*, or gods, of "silver" **arganton*', cf. Celtiberian *arkanta*, *Arganda*, Old Irish *arggat*, *airget* 'silver', Middle Welsh *aryant* 'silver', Breton *arc'hant*, *argant-* 'silver', Latin *argentum*, Sanskrit *rajatám* 'silver' < Indo-European *$h_2erǵntom$ 'silver' (< *$h_2erǵ-$ 'white'). Note also the Western Hispano-Celtic ARGANTO MED-VTICA MELMANIQ[VM] (Riba de Saelices [Vallejo Ruiz 2005, 186–7]), the divine epithet in LVGGONI ARGANTICAENI (Villaviciosa, Oviedo [Búa 2000, 274]), the family name of [T]OVTONI ARGANTIOQ[VM] AMBATI F[ILIVS] (Palencia [(González Rodríguez 1986, 123; Vallejo Ruiz 2005, 186–7]). Ἀργανθώνιος was the name of the king of Tartessos who hosted a party of Phokaian Greeks *c.* 550 BC and gave them 30 talents of silver (about 780 kg) with which they paid for a defensive wall to protect their home city against the Medes. Ἀργανθώνιος is the only Celtic personal appellation in the Histories of Herodotus. Remarkable details of the story—that Arganthonios ruled for 80 years and died at the age of 120, soon after the visit of the Phokaians—are explicable if we understand that the king of Tartessos who welcomed the ship's captain Kolaios of Samos in the period 650 × 638 BC (Herodotus 4.152) was also named Arganthonios and was assumed to be the same ruler (cf. Harrison 1988, 54). Writing about a century before Herodotus, the poet Anakreon, a contemporary of Arganthonios, also mentioned a fabulously long-lived ruler of Tartessos, surely the same man or men. Given his function, which included making massive diplomatic exchanges of silver, it is likely that 'Arganthonios'

designated the office of the most powerful man of Tartessos (inexactly understood as 'king' by the Greeks), rather than being the man's name. Compare Cisalpine ARKATOKO⟨K⟩MATEREKOS/ ARGANTOCOMATERECVS 'magistrate related to silver or coinage' (De Hoz 2007b, 192), Gaulish ARGANTODANNOS/ARCANTODANNOS 'moneyer' on the coins of the Lexovii and Meldi (De Hoz 2007b, 192–3), Tartessian kᵃaśetᵃana 'tin-/bronze-minister' below. As well as the episodes recorded by Herodotus, Greek contacts with Tartessos are indicated by an abundance of Greek material, mostly pottery, recovered from Tartessian sites and datable to the Orientalizing Period (*c.* 750–*c.* 550 BC), including material from Cyprus and Attica, as well as Samos and Phokaia. An Attic krater found at Huelva dates to 800–760 (Harrison 1988, 69). This Greek material is explicable partly as redistribution by the Phoenicians and partly the result of direct contact. A gravestone for FLACCVS | ARGANTONI [filius] | MAGILANICVM | MIROBRIG | ENSIS in Vettonian territory (Alconétar, Cáceres) shows *Argantonios* in use as a personal name during the Roman Period (Sánchez Moreno 1996, 127; Vallejo Ruiz 2005, 186–7, cf. Luján 2007, 253). It is possible that this later individual was named after the famous Tartessian king as known through classical literature; however, continuous survival as a Hispano-Celtic name in the western Peninsula seems likely, especially in light of the apparent Celticity of *Magilo-* and *Mirobrigā*. During the Hellenistic period, a similar name, Ἀργανθώνειον *Arganthoneion*, was in use for a mountain on the north-west coast of Asia Minor near Byzantium. It is not impossible that that name was old and known to Herodotus and thus might have influenced how he wrote the king's name (cf. Moret 2006), such as the ϑ for the expected τ. Nonetheless, Herodotus would hardly have thought in this connection of the name of a Bithynian mountain (which happened to be homophonous with the Celtic word for the principal export of Tartessos), unless the king of Tartessos had been known by a very similar name. The references to mount Arganthoneion by Apollonius of Rhodes and Strabo post-date Herodotus by centuries, so any hypothetical assimilation more probably ran in the opposite direction, from the famous king to the landmark. It is also worth noting that the Celtic Aigosages were settled in the Troad very near the mountain during the 3rd century BC.

ariariśe OMꟿꟼAꟿꟼA (J.10.1) 'For Ariorīχs ("Foremost leader")', dative singular, cf. North-west Hispano-Celtic ARIOVNIS MINCOSEGAEIGIS (A Porqueira, Ourense [Búa 2000, 303–4]); Gaulish *Ario-manus* (attested five times in Roman inscriptions from Austria [Raybould & Sims-Williams 2007, 37]), *Ario-uistus*, *Ario-gaisus*, simplex *Ariíos* (St-Germaine-Source-Seine), *Arius*, *Ariola*, the coin legend ARIVOS SANTONOS, the central-European *Harii* named as a subgroup of the Lugii (Tacitus, *Germania* §43), Old Irish nominative singular *aire* 'lord, freeman, noble', genitive *airech* < *arik-s, -os (De Hoz 2007b 192). If Tartessian **aria-** is based on Indo-European *peri* 'over', it shows characteristically Celtic loss of Indo-European *p*. Alternatively, Indo-European *$h_4$eriós* 'member of one's own group' has been reconstructed as the source of the now infamous Indo-Iranian self-designation *árya-* 'Aryan' (Pokorny 2002, 1.67; Mayrhofer 1992–2001, vol 1.3, 174–5; Mallory & Adams 2006, 266). In the second element (Celtic *rīχs* 'king', dative singular *rīgi*), the sign śM may reflect phonetic palatalization [ri:g´i] or, less probably, the spread of the ś from the nominative singular.

arkᵃastᵃabᵘu ꟼAꟼ∀X‡∀ꟼᗅꟼA (Mesas do Castelinho) dative plural compound name. For the first element, cf. **aarkᵘui** above. For the second element, see **aśtᵃa** below.

aśtᵃa AꟸMA (J.7.1, twice) nominative plural noun, ?a borrowing of the Phoenician Astarte worshipped as a group of goddesses, **aś*tᵃa*tᵃa** AX*AX*MA (J.11.4). Her cult was strong among the Tyrians and was established in their colony at Cádiz/Gadir near Tartessos. The same form may occur as the second element of the dative plural group name in **arkᵃastᵃabᵘu** ꟼAꟼ∀X‡∀ꟼᗅꟼA (Mesas do Castelinho) above.

asune Oꟼꟼ‡A (J.4.1) dative singular of feminine personal name *As(s)unā*, cf. Gaulish *Assuna*, *Assonius*.

bᵃastᵉ- ⱶ‡A⟩ (S. Martinho) 'death' = Celtic *bāsto-m* < *g^uōsto-m* (Indo-European *g^ues-* 'extinguish') showing the characteristically Celtic treatment of Indo-European *g^u* and *ō*, see next item. Cf. Celtiberian *bastoniam* (though explained differently by Prósper 2007, 26–7).

bᵃastᵉebᵘuŕoi ꟼ‡ꟼꟼOⱵ‡A⟩ (S. Martinho) ?'in the yew-wood of death' locative singular of an o-stem compound necropolis name or epithet, comprising the cognate of Old Irish *bás* 'death' + the common Old Celtic place-name element *Eburo-*, *Ebura* 'yew wood' (there was an *Ebora* near Cádiz, also *Ebora* now *Évora* and *Eburobrittium* on the Atlantic coast north of Lisbon), cf. also the North-west Hispano-Celtic personal names EBVRA, EBVRVS (Albertos 1985, 283). The Old Irish cognate *ibar* has strong mythological associations, especially with death and the otherworld. Catuvolcus, chief of the Eburones of Gaul, committed suicide, by means of the poisonous yew (Caesar, *De Bello Gallico* 6.31). *Eburianus* is attested as a Hispano-Celtic divine name on a tombstone from Duratón, Segovia (Marco Simón 2005, 297). As Welsh *efwr* means 'cow parsnip' and Breton *evor* 'hellebore', it is possible that Proto-Celtic *eburo-* could refer to a variety of plants. See also **aibᵘuris**[above.

bᵉe:lin ꟼꟼ1|O9 (J.17.4) i-stem accusative singular, **bᵉeliboo** ‡◻ꟼ109 (J.1.2) dative/ablative plural, **bᵉeliśon** ꟼ‡Mꟼ109 (J.20.1) genitive plural showing case inflexion similar to the Celtiberian, cf. Western Hispano-Celtic dative plural divine name COROBELICOBO (Arroyomolinos de la Vera, Cáceres), Celtiberian group names *Belisonae*, *Belloi*, the accusative personal name *Belikiom*, the genitive plural family name *Belaiocum*, Gaulish and British divine names *Belisama*, *Belenos*; possibly either a group name or simple noun in these examples, if the latter, 'the strong one(s)' or similar. For the root, compare the second element of Welsh *rhyfel*, Latin *proelium* 'war'. John Carey reminds me that, in the absence of a certain Celtic etymology, the Phoenician theonym *Baal* should not be overlooked as a possible source.

bᵉetⁱisai ꟼA‡ⵙO9 (J.23.1) 'For Betisa', ā-stem dative singular, cf. the Celtiberian family name

Betikum.

bᵒotⁱ✡ana ΑΥΑ ✭ΜΦ⸸□ (J.18.1) /*boudi̯anā*/
nominative singular feminine *ā*-stem name, based
on the common Celtic word *boudo-, boudi-* 'victory,
benefit, &c.', Old Irish *búaid*, Early Welsh *buð* cf.
Western Hispano-Celtic names BOVTIVS (several
examples, genitive BOVTI), BOTILLA, BOVTILA
(or BOVTII̯A [Búa 2000, 564]), BODIVS,
BOVDICA, BODECIVS (Albertos 1985, 271) and
the family name B | OVTIE[CVM] from Yecla de
Yeltes, Salamanca (Sánchez Moreno 1996, 122).
The symbol ✡ has been taken as a unique variant
letter form for *e* Ο; however, as the woman's father
was a professional artisan and therefore probably
carved the stone (see the inscription above), it is
likely that he lovingly inserted the image of the
sun or a star into the middle of his dead daughter's name between the stem and the suffix. On the
symbol, see the discussion and photograph pp.
61–2 above. Astral symbols on Hispano-Roman
funerary inscriptions are discussed by Marco Simón
(2005, 331).

bᵒotᵒo- ⸸Δ⸸□ (J.7.2) /*bodu̯o-*/, cf. the Hispano-
Celtic place-name *Budua* (south-west Spain),
Gaulish personal names *Boduos, Boduus, Bodua,
Boduo-genus, Boduo-gnatus, Maro-boduus,* &c., British
BODVOC, Old Irish *bodb*, later also *badb* 'crow,
war goddess', Old Breton *Boduuan*, &c., Old Welsh
Bodug.

tᵃarielnon Χ ΑΡṀΟΓΥ⸸Ṁ (J.55.1) accusative
singular of two-element compound man's name
Dari-u̯elnos. Dari(o)- is very common in Gaulish
proper names: *Dari-bitus, Dario-ritum* 'Vannes', &c.
Delamarre (2003, 136) suggests a meaning 'furious'
as in Welsh *cyn-ddar-edd* 'rabies', cf. also the British genitive man's name DAARI. *u̯elno-* would be
the older form of the common Old Celtic name
element *u̯ello-* and probably means 'ruler'.

tᵉeaiona[ΑΥ⸸ṀΑΟH̱ /*dei̯u̯onā*/ 'goddess' or
tᵉeaionkᵃa[ΑΛΥ⸸ṀΑΟH̱ (J.4.3) /*dei̯u̯onka-*/
'of the group pertaining to the divinity', feminine *a*-
stem or neuter *o*-stem nominative/accusative plural,
cf. Celtiberian family name *Teiu̯antikum* (interpreted
as 'who swears'? by De Hoz 2007b, 203), personal
name *Teiu̯oreikis* /*dẹ̄u̯orīχs*/, Gaulish *Deuonia* (Dela-

marre 2003, 142–3), goddess name *Diiona* (Jufer &
Luginbühl 2001, 37): Indo-European **dei̯u̯o-* 'god'
+ Gallo-Brittonic divine suffix *-onā/-ono-* (+
adjectival *-ko-/-kā* suffix used in formation of
Hispano-Celtic family names). On the *-onā/-ono-*
suffix, cf. ᾽Αργανθωνιος. **tᵉeaionkᵃa[** is
Untermann's reading. After examining the stone, the
more basic formation **tᵉeaiona[** ΑΥⱮΑΟH̱ is
what seems to be there. The etymologically surplus
vowel **a** may reflect mere difficulty in 'sounding out'
the sequence of three or four vowels or alternatively
phonetic epenthesis of a neutral glide before /u̯/
[deiᵃwona:] in anticipation of the low back vowel
in the following syllable.

ebᵘuṟoi Ψ⸸ṄΨⵅΟ (S. Martinho) ?'in the
yew-wood', see **bᵃastᵉebᵘuṟoi** above.

ekᵘuṟine ΟⱮⱮⵅⱢⱭΟ (J.4.1) dative singular
of a feminine personal or divine name *Ekurinā* or
Ekurini with an initial element *Ekᵘo-* 'horse' (Indo-
European **h₁ek´u̯os* [Wodtko et al. 2008, 230–3]),
cf. the consecration to DEIS EQVEVNV(BO(S))
'equine gods' on a tombstone of the Roman period
from north-west Spain and most significantly the
epithet of the goddess Arentia at Sabugal (Guarda)
EQVOTVLLAICENSI (Marco Simón 2005,
299–300). In Vettonian territory in the western
Peninsula, Luján (2007, 255ff.) lists two names
apparently based on 'horse': EQVAESVS, with
the velar retained, and EPONEILVS, with *p* <
Indo-European *k´u̯*. Cf. also Celtiberian *ekualakoś,
ekualaku*? (Wodtko 2000, 104–5), possibly meaning
'warrior, knight' < 'horseman' (De Hoz 2007b,
200), cf. Middle Welsh *ebawl* 'foal'. The second element of **ekᵘuṟine** is probably Celtic **rīgnī* 'queen',
a reflex of Indo-European **h₃rḗǵnih₂* (cf. Sanskrit
rā́jñī 'queen'), a byform of the attested Gaulish
rigani, Cisalpine genitive *rikanas*, Old Irish *rígain*
from an Indo-European **h₃rēǵ´nⁿih₂* with a syllabic
nasal. It would be a common phonetic development
if Celtic **rigni* had developed as Tartessian /*rīnī*/
with loss of *g* before *n*. Alternatively, the Tartessian
writing system made it impossible to represent a
g (or any other stop consonant) at the end of a
syllable. Therefore, we cannot be certain that the
spelling here does not mean *i*-stem /*rīgni*/ or

ā-stem /*rigne*/ with inherited *g* preserved. The same element probably occurs also as a simplex dative/ablative plural **rinoeb°o** РⵕᎩⵖ⧾Oᘓ⧾ (J.5.1). The complete compound name **ek^uuṛine** is reminiscent of the Gaulish and British divine name *Epona* 'Horse goddess', and note again EPONEILVS from Roman Vettonia, which appears to be a man's name based on *Epona*. The Middle Welsh *Riannon* of the Welsh Mabinogi has often been interpreted as the functional equivalent of Epona in the light of her numerous equine associations. The accompanying image on stone J.4.2 is comparable to representations of Epona of the Roman Period. In the Roman dedications, the recurrent collocation EPONAE REGINAE 'to queen Epona [Horse-goddess]' (Jufer & Luginbühl 2001, 39–40) suggests that Eponā and the equestrian Rhiannon < *Rīgantonā* may both continue the function and myth of an earlier *Ekuo-rīg(a)nī*. It is possible that Tartessian **rin-** 'queen' recurs in J.17.4 as instrumental plural in a compound **k^eenila-(*)ṛinb^ee** OᎡᎩ⧾Ꭹ(ᐧ) ᎯᎢᎩᎩOᛟ 'with/by the queens of the kindred'. Welsh *Rhiannon* and РIᒤᎯΝTIΚ on Gaulish coin legends point to the existence of a form *rigant-* in both Gaulish and British.

Ἐλιβύργη, πόλις Ταρτησσοῦ 'Eliburgē, a city of Tartessos' is attributed to Hekataios (*c.* 500 BC) by Stephanus of Byzantium (see Freeman, this volume). The place-name appears to combine the well-attested Iberian word for town, *il(l)i*, *ilti* with a second element. Untermann (forthcoming) proposes that -βύργη is an Iberianization (explaining *b* < *m*) of the Tartessian element -*murga* as found in the ancient place-name *Lacimurga* near Badajoz. An alternative possibility is the tautological Celtic *briga* 'hillfort, town' < *b^hrgā*, common in Ancient Celtic place-names, most especially in the Atlantic zone and interior of the Iberian Peninsula (see Parsons, this volume). In this connection, it is worth considering the possibility that the place-names *Lacimurga* and *Lacobriga* reflect dialect variants of the same compound, both attested within the zone of the Tartessian inscriptions.

Gargoris 'Savage king': in an excellent example of a myth of cultural origins, Justin's epitome of the Philippic Histories of Trogus Pompeius (44.4) tells of the pre-agricultural honey collector Gargoris, first king of the Cunetes (see Κυνητες below) who dwelt in the forest of the Tartessians (*saltus uero Tartessiorum, in quibus Titanas bellum aduersus deos gessisse proditur, incoluere Cunetes, quorum rex uetustissimus Gargoris mellis colligendi usum primus inuenit*). It is widely recognized that *Gargoris* reflects Celtic *Gargo-rixs*. For the first element, cf. Old Irish *garg* 'fierce, savage' and the Gallo-Roman place-name *Gargarius* (Delamarre 2003, 175–6). Compare also the woman's name *Gargenna*/*Gergenna* from Abertura, Cáceres (Luján 2007, 256). Probably not the form **k^eerk^aaṛ[ ]iᐱ** in J.18.3.

H^aait^uura ᎯᎩᎯᎽᎯᎽᎯᐳ (J.15.1) feminine nominative singular *ā*-stem. Possibly compare Western Hispano-Celtic AVITVS (Montehermoso, Cáceres [Búa 2000, 552–3]), genitive AVITI from Ávila (Sánchez Moreno 1996, 133), the genitive plural group name AVITA[E]CON from Cantabria (Untermann 1980, 375) and the woman's name to ogam Irish AVITTORIGES, Late Romano-British AVITORIA on the stone from Eglwys Gymyn, Carmarthenshire.

H^aat^aaneat^ee ᛲᎯΧᎯᎽOᎯᕼO (J.12.1) 'to the winged one (Ataniatis)', as a personal name, divine name, or epithet, *i*-stem dative singular, cf. Old Breton *attanoc* 'winged creature', plural *atanocion*, Old Welsh *hataneð* 'wings', Early Welsh *edein*, plural *adaneð* 'wings' < Indo-European *ptn-* : *pet(e)r-* 'wing, feather', with characteristically Celtic loss of Indo-European *p*, and Celtic agent suffix -*iatis*. The dative singular of a feminine *ā*-stem *Ataniatā* 'winged goddess' is also possible. Almagro-Gorbea (1988, 73) mentions Tartessian images of the 'Dea Mater' type (reminiscent of the Phoenician Astarte), some of which have wings. The image on this stone shows a warrior in bulky armour with straps crossing his chest. His arms are extended symmetrically with a throwing spear pointing outward from his right hand and another short spear and small shield in his left. This image is reminiscent of an intriguing description of a hero in the *Gododdin* as *aer seirchyawc | aer edenawc* 'harnessed [armoured] in battle, winged in battle'

< *(φ)ataniako-. Like the Abóboda warrior, short throwing spears were the principal weapon of the Gododdin heroes.

iubᵃa A͜3͜4͜M (J.7.8) ?nominative singular ā-stem, cf. **iou⟨tⁱ⟩bᵉa:i** M | A͜d(Φ)͜4͜‡͜M (J.7.6) dative, nominative, or genitive, **iobᵃa[** N‡3A[(J.16.2) with case ending possibly lost. There were two well-known native Numidian kings, father and son, named *Iuba* (Ιόβας, Ιουβας in Greek sources) in the period *c.* 60 BC–AD 23. The younger king was re-located westward to Mauretania as a Roman client. Their name is therefore presumably Numidian (Palaeo-Berber) and suited an aristocratic male. Tartessian **iubᵃa** thus suggests that a language related to Numidian was either indigenous in the south-western Iberian Peninsula—where the Numidian place-name *Hippo* has numerous parallels—or that individuals of such a linguistic background had come in during the Orientalizing Period from Phoenician colonies in north Africa. Iuba I's kingdom was not far from Utica and Carthage. Note also that *Corduba*, the ancient name of Córdoba, is sometimes derived from Punic *Qart-Iuba* 'Iuba's city'. **iubᵃa** and **ioubᵉa:i** from Ameixial (J.7.8 and J.7.6) may well refer to the same individual, his own gravestone and that of his successor, respectively. In the proposed interpretation of J.16.2, that Ioba was lost at sea, which is consistent with the idea that the family was of north African origin and had developed links with south Portugal in the context of intense Phoenician maritime activity.

(kᵃakⁱ)iśiinkᵒolobᵒo ‡□‡1‡X͜M͜M͜M͜M͜Φ͜ΛΛ (J.1.1) dative plural group name *Eχs-kingo-lo-bos*, cf. Gaulish personal name Εσκεγγολατι (genitive, Les Pennes-Mirabeau), also ESCENCOLATIS in Roman script (Aubagne) for EXCINGOLATIS (Raybould & Sims-Williams 2007, 59). The preceding element may represent Celtic pronominal *kᵘāḵᵘo-* 'all, everyone' < *kʷōkʷo-*, Gaulish inflected forms *papon, papi, pape, papu*, Old Irish *cách*, Old Welsh *paup*, Old Breton *pop*, hence 'invoking all the heroes'.

kᵃaltᵉe O͜H͜1͜ΛΛ (J.1.1) possibly a dative singular of an ā-stem group name in concord with dative singular o-stem or u-stem **araiu̱i**, notional

nominative singular *kᵃaltᵃa* or *kᵃaltᵃas*. It would thus correspond to the ā-stem plural group names Greek Γαλάται *Galátai* and/or Latin *Celtae*. Note that some modern writers consider these often-interchangeable Greek and Latin names to be of common origin (cf. Sims-Williams 1998, 22). McCone (2006) rejects that possibility. However, he suggests that another Latin synonym *Gallus* comes immediately from Etruscan **Kalde*—thus similar phonetically to *Celta* and any possible Etruscan version of that—though ultimately, and plausibly, he derives both *Gallus* and Γαλάτης from a Celtic **galatis*, meaning essentially 'fighter'. Cf. the Celtiberian family name *kaltaikikos* on a tessera from Osma, Soria (González Rodríguez 1986, 126). During the Roman Period, *Celtius* occurred frequently as a personal name in the western Iberian Peninsula and mostly in context with other Hispano-Celtic names, making the possibility of a learned borrowing from Latin unlikely. Strabo (4.1.14) considered Κέλται, rather than Herodotus's Κελτοί, to be the oldest form of the name, agreeing with the Latin *Celtae* and Tartessian **kᵃaltᵉe** (if dative singular); he used the form Γαλάται himself. Note that, in the passages cited above (p. 186; cf. p. 128), Herodotus locates the Κελτοί *Keltoí* 'Celts' beyond the Pillars of Hercules as neighbours of the Kunētes and that writers of the Roman Period name peoples in the western Iberian Peninsula as belonging to the Κελτικοί *Celtici*. **nira-kᵃaltᵉe** O͜H͜1͜Λ͜Λ͜Λ͜9͜M͜M (Mesas do Castelinho) is possibly a compound, ?'for the Nerian Celt', in which the group names **nira-** and **kᵃaltᵉe** are again juxtaposed as in J.1.1. Alternatively, **kᵃaltᵉe** can be compared with a Cisalpine Celtic past-tense verb *kalite* (see below).

]kᵃanan M͜4͜M͜A(Λ)[(J.9.1) /-ganan/ or /-kanan/ fragmentary feminine a-stem or ā-stem accusative singular, possibly with the common Ancient Celtic name element *-ganā* 'born of' (Indo-European *ǵenh₁-* 'beget a child, be born' [Wodtko et al. 2008, 136–9]).

kᵉenila(*)r̲i̲n̲ M͜M͜9͜(*)A͜1͜M͜M͜O͜)͜| (J.17.4) /genilarin/ or /-lārin/ i-stem accusative singular of a Celtic two-element compound name, Indo-European *ǵenh₃-* 'to be born' as the first element, cf. Celtiberian *kenis*, *eśkeninum* (Botorrita). The second element may correspond to Old Irish *lár*, Welsh *llawr* 'floor, flat open area', Indo-European **pleḫₐro-*, showing characteristically Celtic loss of Indo-European *p*. Alternatively, the Tartessian writing system (which could not accurately represent *tl*) allows that **kᵉenila** could stand for Celtic **kenetlā* 'kindreds' (neuter nominative accusative plural) or **kenetlo-*, a composition form of the same, cf. Old Irish *cenél*, Old Welsh *cenetl*: Indo-European **ken-* 'fresh'.

kⁱielaoe ꝑꝑꝑꝑꝑ (J.11.1) 'for Kīlaụā, Kēlaụā' dative singular feminine *ā*-stem, possibly the same name as genitive singular k̲ᵉ̲**eloia** ꝑꝑꝑꝑ (J.57.1), also k̲ᵉ̲**eilau** ꝑꝑꝑꝑꝑ Cabeza del Buey IV, cf. Gaulish *cele* 'companion' (Château-bleau; Delamarre 2003, 112), Old Irish *céile* 'fellow, client, spouse'; Middle Welsh *kilyð* shows a different vowel, agreeing with Western Hispano-Celtic CILEA, CILEIOVI, CILIVS, CILO, CILSVS, MORICIL**O** (Albertos 1985, 278; Vallejo Ruiz 2005, 278ff.; cf. Búa 2000, 530–6), also the group name *Cileni* attested in the north-west of the Peninsula in Roman times. If **kⁱielaoe** means, essentially, 'dear companion, wife', this woman's status apparently depended on that of her husband.

kⁱinbᵃaiꝑi ꝑꝑꝑꝑꝑ (J.3.1) ?= /kimbaiti(s)/ ?'a man of the Cempsi', ?*i*-stem nominative singular, a people residing west of the Anas (river Guadiana) near Tartessos and the Cynetes (see Κυνητες below) according to the *Ora Maritima* of Avienus (lines 179, 192–8, 251–5, 297–8), probably the same name and people as the *Cimbii* noted near Gadir during the Roman period. Compare Old Irish *i*-stem *cimbid* 'captive' (< Celtic **kimbiatis*), probably with an earlier sense 'giver of tribute' (Old Irish *cimb*). If this is the correct etymology, the Cempsi were probably the collective clients of Tartessos and/or the Κυνητες.

kᵒolion ꝑꝑꝑꝑ (J.55.1) accusative singular or genitive plural of the name *Kolịos*, the same or similar occurs as k̲ᵒ̲**oloion** (Monte Novo de Castelinho, possibly with an epenthetic vowel developing before the glide *ị*), cf. Celtiberian *Kueliokos* (probably an adjective derived from a

proper name). The Western Hispano-Celtic family name COILIONICV[M] from Yecla de Yeltes, Salamanca (Sánchez Moreno 1996, 124) may derive from earlier **kolịo-*. *Kolịos* possibly means 'chariot-' or 'cart-driver, -warrior', as an agent noun corresponding to Old Irish *cul* 'chariot' < Proto-Celtic **kᵘol-* : Indo-European **kᵘel-* 'turn'. Alternatively, *Kolịos* could correspond to the second element of Old Irish *búachaill*, Old Welsh *buceil* 'cowherd' < Indo-European **gᵘou-kᵘolịos*, hence *Kolịos* 'leader, guide, protector' (ultimately also Indo-European **kᵘel-* 'turn').

kᵒoŕbᵉo ꝑꝑꝑꝑꝑ (J.53.1) 'of Korbos', genitive singular masculine *o*-stem, cf. the common Old Irish man's name *Corb*, ogam genitives CORBBI, CORBAGNI, also the common Old Irish man's names *Cormac* < older *Corb-macc* and *Coirpre*. The apparent disagreement of quality between the consonant and the following vowel (-bᵉo) may reflect uncertainty between competing *o*-stem genitives singular: *-i* and *-o*.

kᵘuiarairbᵘb̲ᵘ̲[u] *ꝑꝑꝑꝑꝑꝑꝑ (J.17.2) The position of this form at the beginning of the inscription and what survives of the form's ending suggests a dative/ablative plural as an invocation of a group of deities. The two opening letters have unusual forms (Untermann, MLH 4.298).

kᵘuikᵃa̲o̲sa ꝑꝑꝑꝑꝑ (J.17.1) Opening a fragmentary and badly worn inscription (Untermann, MLH 4.295–6), this form is probably the name of the deceased, resembling a nominative singular feminine *ā*-stem. A name built on the Celtic number '5' **kᵘinkᵘe* (Indo-European **pénkᵘe*), Old Irish *cóic*, is one possibility, in which case, compare Celtiberian *Kuintitaku* (an adjective from a man's name **Kuintitos*). If Celtiberian *kuekuetikui* does mean 'to whomever' (Wodtko 2000 s.n.), that or a similar sense would suit the opening of an inscription. Alternatively, cf. Gaulish personal names *Peccia*, *Peccio*, ogamic Primitive Irish (genitive) QECIA, QECEA (Delamarre 2003, 247).

Κυνητες, Κυνησιοι *Kunētes, Kunēsioi* Speaking of his own time (the mid 5th century BC), Herodotus (4.50) calls the Kunētes the westernmost people of Europe (i.e. in what is now southern Portugal, the area of densest concentration of Tartessian inscriptions) with the Κελτοί as their immediate neighbours to the east. Compare the Romano-British place-name *Cunētio* and Old Welsh *Cinuit*, the eponym of the *Kynwydyon* < Brittonic *Cunētiones* (probably a recharacterized plural from older *Kunētes*), the principal dynasty of Dumbarton in the early Middle Ages, also the Old Welsh place-name *arx Cynuit* in Asser's Life of Alfred. These names are based on Celtic *kuno-* 'hound, wolf' and commonly in metaphoric extension 'warrior, hero': Indo-European *ḱ'(u)u̯on* 'dog' (Wodtko et al. 2008, 436–40). In the 12th-century Welsh genealogical source *Bonedd Gwŷr y Gogledd* ('Pedigree of the Men of the North'), the *Kyn[n]wydyon* figure specifically as a warband (cf. Charles-Edwards 1978, 66–8), so it may be that the ancestor *Cinuit* was a legendary eponym extracted from a name that was primarily a plural group name. The name *Kunētes* likewise implies a society of warriors. According to the myth preserved by Trogus/Justin, the first king of Tartessos ruled the Cunetes, and it implies that the wooded territory inhabited by the Cunetes was an integral part of Tartessos (see *Gargoris* above). In the *Ora Maritima* of Avienus, the Cynetes are mentioned five times, they figure there as neighbours of the Tartessians, and the river Anas (Guadiana) was their common boundary.

lebᵒo-iire ᴼ⟨Ϙ⟩ᳵ⟨ᳵ⟩‡☐Ο**1**(Mesas do Castelinho) a compound noun, possibly a proper name; the second element *-iire* is probably genitive 'man' (see below). On the first element, compare the Gaulish group name *Lemouices* and the *Lemaui* of central Galicia. This latter group is attested, for example, in an inscription of the Roman Period from Astorga, León: FABIA EBVRI F LEMAVA ... VIRIVS CAESSI F LEMAVS ... (Búa 2004, 387).

Ligustinus lacus (Avienus, *Ora Maritima*, lines 284–5; see Freeman, below) is the ancient name for the broad shallow estuary of the Guadalquivir, the river Avienus calls 'Tartessus'. This body of water, between the city of Seville and the Atlantic, is today low and marshy land. De Bernardo Stempel (2006, 47, 49) takes *Ligustinus* to be a Celtic name,

based on the population name *Ligues* 'the strikers' < Indo-European *pleh₂g-*, thus with characteristic Celtic loss of Indo-European *p*. Even if we accept this etymology and the implication that *Ligustinus* is a Celtic name, it would not necessarily follow that all groups called 'Ligurians' and the like in ancient sources spoke Celtic. There is, however, an early and recurrent connection between the names: Stephanus of Byzantium quotes Hekataios of Miletos (*c.* 500 BC) calling Massalia a 'Ligurian city' (πόλις τῆς Λιγυστικῆς) near Keltikē.

liirnestᵃakᵘun ᳵᴴ⟨⟩ᴀ᙭‡Ο⟨Ϙ⟩ᳵᳵᳵ**1** (J.19.1) genitive plural Hispano-Celtic 'family-name' or 'gentilic-name' formation (using an adjectival *k*-suffix) 'people near(er) the ocean' with Tartessian *-un* < Indo-European *-ōm*. For group names of this type, cf. Tartessian **tᵃarnekᵘun** (below), Celtiberian *Alizokum* and from Cantabria AVITA | [E]CON (Untermann 1980). In inscriptions of the Roman Period, endings with *-on* and *-um* are well attested, but also *-velar+un* as in the Tartessian examples: ALONGVN, AVLGIGVN, BALATVSCVN, BODDEGVN 'of the clan of Bōdios', CA | DDECVN, CANTABREQVN, CELTIGVN 'of the clan of Celtius', VIR[ONI] CVN (González Rodríguez 1986, 145–6). It is likely in any event that the articulation of the final nasal assimilated to the following consonant. For the first element of the compound (examination of the stone supports the reading with l̲-), compare Old Irish *ler*, Middle Welsh *llyr* 'sea' < Celtic *lir-o-*, perhaps related to Latin *plērus* < *pleiro-* 'very many' (Indo-European *pelh₁-* 'fill') showing characteristically Celtic loss of Indo-European *p*; cf. also the 'family name' LER | AN[I]QV | M on a funerary inscription from Segovia (González Rodríguez 1994, 172) and the place-name *Lerabriga* in west-central Portugal, overlooking the Tagus estuary, though the variant *Ierabriga* is probable. For the second element, compare Gaulish *neððamon* 'of the nearest ones', Old Irish *nessam* 'nearest' < *ned-smᵐo-*. The corresponding place-name in a locative singular occurs as **liŕniene** ᴦᴹᴴ⟨ᴹᴺ⟩ᴼᴹᴼ (J.55.1) 'in the land by the ocean' = *lir-(o-)ned-nā-i*. As the place was mentioned in an inscription far from J.19.1,

Lirnena was evidently a sizeable important country and the Lirnestākī a numerous people, rather than an extended family (cf. De Hoz 1992).

leoine ΟΨΜ≠Ο꜒ (J.10.1) dative singular, feminine a-stem /liu̯ine/ or /liu̯oi̯ne/ 'to Līvonā [the goddess of beauty]': Gaulish *Liona, Liuoni* (in Noricum), *Lioni,* the by-forms *Llion* and *Lliwan* in south Wales as river names. Cf. Gaulish *Lio-mari* (genitive), Welsh *lliw,* Old Cornish *liu* 'colour', Old Irish *lí* 'colour, beauty', Latin *līuidus* 'livid' (Delamarre 2003, 205). On the suffix, see cf. Ἀργανθώνιος, t^ceaiona[above. The **i** in **leoine** may be understood as the result of difficulty in spelling the complex sequence of vowels and semi-vowels, or, more probably, reflecting phonetic epenthesis or palatalization of the [ⁱn´] before a front vowel. On the comparable feature in Lusitanian LOIMINNA/LOEMINA, see below.

lok°ob°o ≠□≠Ⅹ≠꜒ (J.1.1) /lugubo/ dative plural divine name, 'to/for the divine Lugoues', corresponding exactly to the north-western Hispano-Celtic dative plural theonym LVCVBO ARQVIENOBO (Sober, Lugo), LVCOVBV[S] ARQVIENI[S] (Outeiro do Rei, Lugo; Búa 2000, 266–7), and DIBVS M[.] LVCVBO from Peña Amaya, north of Burgos (Búa 2003, 153–4; Marco Simón 2005, 301), LVCOBO AROVSA[-] (Lugo); cf. Gaulish dative plural in *-bo,* Celtiberian *-bos* (Untermann 1985, 358). Note also Celtiberian dative singular LVGVEI 'to [the god] Lugus' (Peñalba de Villastar, K.3.3). A Latin inscription from Uxama in Celtiberia records a dedication to LVGOVIBVS 'to the divine Lugoues' by a guild of shoemakers, which is intriguing in view of the shoemaking episode in the story of Lleu (< Celtic *Lugus)* in the Mabinogi. Cf. Gaulish *Lugoues* (nominative plural) from Avenches, Switzerland, Old Irish *Lug,* Welsh *Lleu.* Hispano-Celtic LVGVA CA│DDEGVN is a personal name (inscription from La Remolina, León; Untermann 1980, 386) like Gaulish ΛΟΥΓΟΥΣ, also commonly as an element in compound personal and place-names in Gaulish (e.g. LVGVSELVA [Raybould & Sims-Williams 2007, 65]), Goidelic (e.g. Ogamic LUGUQRIT, LUGUVECCA, LUGUDECCAS, &c., cf. Hispano-

Celtic genitive LVGVADICI from Segovia), Brittonic (e.g. Late British *Louocatus,* Old Breton and Old Welsh *Loumarch),* as well as the simplex ΛΥγοι group name of north Britain, the extensive *Lugii* of central Europe, also the *Luggoni* in Asturias, northern Spain (LVGGONI ARGANTICAENI [Villaviciosa, Oviedo, Búa 2000, 274]). *Lugunae* are attested as a group of goddesses at Atapuerca (Burgos) (Marco Simón 2005, 302), and it is possible that in Tartessian **lok°ob°o niirab°o** the qualifying adjective is feminine.

meleśae ΟΔΜΟ꜒ΟΨ (J.15.1) /meliˢsai/ ā-stem dative singular 'for Meliśā', alternatively a less accurate spelling for genitive singular o-stem /meliˢsī/ 'of Meliśos', cf. Gaulish personal name *Meliððus,* Old Irish *milis,* Welsh *melys* 'sweet' (< 'honey-flavoured', an epithet of mead) < Indo-European **melit-ti-.* Ψ is a common form for /m/ in Phoenician scripts.

mut^uuirea ΔΟꟼΨ꜕ΔꟼΜ (J.1.5) cf. the Celtiberian personal names *Muturiskum* (family name < **Muturos), Muturrae, Mutorke.* If not a nominative iā-stem, the case form could be a genitive singular *-ā,* like the ogamic Primitive Irish -EAS. **śut^uuirea** is a possible reading. The **i** before the **r** apparently represents phonetic epenthesis or palatalization of the consonant reminiscent of the varying consonant qualities of Goidelic. Note also **leoine** above. On Lusitanian LOIMINNA/LOEMINA, see above.

ʔnemun ꟽꟽꟼΟꟼ (J.7.8) 'of the Nemī' genitive plural, a group name possibly related to the tribe called Hispano-Celtic Νεμετατοι *Nemetatoi* of ancient western Iberia, cf. also Western Hispano-Celtic dative plural goddess name DEIBA̱ḆO NEMVCE̱ḺA̱I̱G̱A̱ḆO (Aguas Frías, Chaves, Vila Real, Portugal [Búa 2000, 396]), the Celtiberian personal name (?) NEMAIOS, Cisalpine NEMETALVI (Davesco 4th/3rd century BC [Morandi 2004, 530–40]), NEMUŚVS (Zignago end of the 4th century BC [Morandi 2004, 696–7]), Gaulish, British, and Galatian *nemeton* 'sacred place', Old Irish *nemeth* 'thing or person of special privilege', Early Welsh *niuet (Gododdin),* also Old Irish *nem* 'heaven', genitive *nime,* Welsh *nef,* plural *nefoedd* < Celtic **nemos, *nemesos.* **nemun** might also be a common noun 'of the privileged persons, of the sacred things'. Alternatively, the initial **n-** might belong to the preceding word, in which case **emun** could be read as a masculine genitive plural pronoun 'of the men', constructed as **em** + the genitive plural ending Tartessian **-un** < Indo-European *-ōm.

NIEΘΩΙ occurs as a graffito in archaic Ionic Greek script on a Greek bowl (probably Milesian) found at Huelva and dated by Almagro-Gorbea (2005, 55) to 590–560 BC. He identifies this linguistic form with the name of the Hispano-Celtic divinity Nētos (accusative Nēton), who is described by Macrobius (Saturnalia I.19.5) as a solar, ray-adorned manifestation of the war god, i.e. Mars. Incidentally, Macrobius's description of Netos as simulacrum Martiis radiis ornatum may illuminate the enigmatic imagery of the numerous so-called 'diademed' Bronze Age stelae of the western peninsula. Harrison (2004) lists four 'diademadas', which are likely to predate significantly the stelae with weapons. Note also the probable etymological connection with Old Irish níam 'radiance, beauty' (Vendryes 1960, N-16). For the name, Marco Simón (2005, 292) compares Nēton with Celtiberian Neito (Botorrita) and the Hispano-Celtic divine epithets of the Roman period—Cossue Nedoledio, Nidanlua-, Reva Nitaecus, and the Netaci Veilebricae named on an altar from Padrón. Cf. also NETONI DEO on an altar, now lost, from Trujillo, Cáceres (Búa 2000, 571–2). F. Beltrán (2002) has registered doubts about this reading, as well as some of the other evidence which has been adduced for a Hispano-Celtic god Neito-/Nēto-. Almagro-Gorbea compares Νιεθωι and Neton with Irish forms such as Old Irish nía, genitive níath, ogam NETTA, NETA 'champion, hero': e.g. NETTASLOGI, NETASEGAMONAS, NET(T)ACUNAS. That word could also be related to Old Irish nioth (genitive), ogam NIOTA 'nephew, sister's son' < Indo-European *nepot-s, genitive *nepotos (McManus 1991, 109–10). Νιεθωι and Neton would imply a Hispano-Celtic o-stem, dative and accusative respectively. If Νιεθωι is indeed derived from Indo-European *nepot-, it shows that characteristic Celtic loss of Indo-European p between vowels was complete in Tartessian by the earlier 6th-century BC. However, the sequence

ιε more probably represents an attempt to write a palatal consonant and long close vowel in N´ētūi (from an earlier *Neitōi, with a diphthong) and thus unconnected with 'nephew' and Indo-European p.

niirabᵒo ╪◻Α٩ᛉᛉᛁ (J.1.1) /nerabo/ dative/ ablative plural, 'belonging to the Neri', cf. Welsh ner 'lord', Sanskrit nárya- 'masculine, virile, heroic', Indo-European *hₐnér- 'man' (Búa 2004, 382; Wodtko et al. 2008, 332–8), Hispano-Celtic group name Neri and the place-name promontorium Nerium situated in the north-west in early historical times, alternatively possibly as a common noun 'to men, heroes'. In classical times the Nerii or Neri lived in coastal Galicia (ancient Callaecia/Gallaecia). The Tartessian example, therefore, raises the possibility that they had moved north in the meantime, or that there were two branches of the group, or that the inhabitants of Galicia had been very involved in the cultural life of the south-west during the Early Iron Age. The fact that Strabo (3.3.5) and Pliny (Naturalis Historia 4.111) classed the Νεριοι Neri of Galicia as Κελτικοί Celtici, an over-arching group name also used in south-west Hispania, is certainly relevant to this problem and points towards a general shared 'Celtic' identity across the western Peninsula (cf. Villar 2004, 247). In this connection, note the compound **nira-kᵃaltᵉe** ОᚺᛁΛΛΑ٩ᛉᛁ (Guerra, 73 above) ?'for the Nerian Celt' in the Mesas do Castelinho inscription. In a Roman-period inscription from Briteiros, north Portugal—CORONERI CAMALI DOMVS 'a casa de Coronerus Camali' (Búa 2007, 28)—Nero- occurs in a compound name, where it could signify either 'of the Neri' or 'man, hero (of the warband)' or both.

Oestrymnin (accusative promontory name: prominentis iugi caput), (insulae) Oestrymnides, Oestrumnides, Oestryminicae, (sinus) Oestrymnicus, Oestrymnis, Oestryminicis (Latin ablative plural). These names are amongst the archaic forms in Avienus's Ora Maritima (lines 90, 94, 95, 112, 129, 152, 153). They include references to 'islands' and inhabitants in a region rich in lead and tin, which had once been an important terminus of Tartessian maritime exchange (112–13: Tartessiisque in terminos Oestrumnidum nego-

tiandi mos erat). Therefore, while the name may or may not itself be Tartessian, it has probably come to us through Tartessian. The references to the *Oestrymnides/Oestrumnides* as islands (95, 112) are very closely linked to mentions of 'the sacred isle' (probably Greek word play for ʾΙερνη 'Ireland'), the populous *gens Hiernorum* 'Irish people', and the nearby *insula Albionum* 'island of the Britons'. Therefore, in that passage at least, the most straightforward interpretation is that *(insulae) Oestrumnides* mean Ireland and Britain. It is likely that Avienus has elided part of the Atlantic coastline owing to the similarity of this name and the early group name applied to westernmost Armorica, i.e. ʾΟστιμιοι in Strabo (4.1) going back to Pytheas in the later 4th century BC, corresponding to Caesar's *Osismii* (*De Bello Gallico* 2.34, 3.9, 7.75). ʾΟστιμιοι/*Osismii* is clearly a Celtic superlative, cognate with Latin *postumus* 'last' and showing characteristically Celtic loss of Indo-European *p-*. It designates the 'last people', inhabiting the end of Gaul's long Atlantic peninsula (Delamarre 2003, 244–5). Though superficially similar to ʾΟστιμιοι, *Oestrymnis* is more probably connected with Indo-European *$*u̯ésperos$*, *$*u̯ékeros$* 'evening', hence 'place of the setting sun, west' and resembles closely formations underlying Germanic as in Old English *westerna*, Old High German *westrôni*, Old Norse *vestránn* 'dwelling in the west, &c.' If this is the correct etymology, *Oestrymnis* is Indo-European. *Oest-* < Indo-European *$*u̯est$*- parallels the development of Tartessian *-oir* < Indo-European $u̯ih_xrós$ 'man, hero' (Wodtko et al. 2008, 726–9) in the name *ooŕoir* (J.19.2), similarly Welsh *ucher* 'evening' < *$*oiχseros$* < Indo-European *$*u̯ék(s)eros$* or *$*u̯épseros$* alongside Welsh *gosber* < Latin *vesper(-)* (*ps* < Indo-European *sp* is also found in Celtic words for 'wasp'). Jordán Cólera (2002) explains *Oestrumnides* as the *o*-grade of an Old European root *$*eis$*- 'to move fast, with impetus' compounded with the well-attested hydronymic element *-umni-/-umna-* < *$*up-n$*-, *$*ub-n$*-. The *-tr-* is more easily explained if the first element is understood as 'west' < 'evening', thus *Oestrumni-* 'the Atlantic' < *$*u̯estr-ubn$*- 'western stream(s)'. As an ancient Indo-European name for the western ocean, '*$*u̯estr-ubn$*-' possibly contributed to the erroneous idea of Herodotus (§§2.34, 4.48) that the Danube, which had the similar name ʾΙστρος, flowed all the way from the west, i.e. from the Atlantic.

]on**l**inb°o ‡◻ᚤᚋ⅃ᚤ‡[(J.11.2) dative/ablative plural, probably a divine group name.

Νωραξ According to mythology recorded by Solinus (§4.1, cf. Pausanias *Description of Greece* 10.17.5; Freeman below), Nōrax of Tartessos was the founder of the town Nora in southern Sardinia, the site of a Phoenician presence of the 9th/8th century BC. These names are probably linked with the Sardinian term *nuraghe* for the prominent Late Bronze Age fortified sites of the island, Palaeo-Sardinian *nurake*, which possibly contains the Celtic adjectival suffix *-āko-/-ā*. The Νυραξ *Nurax* (or Νυρακη) mentioned by Hekataios of Meletos, writing *c.* 500 BC (Fragment 54), as a *polis* of the *Keltoí* is more often identified with Noricum, the historical kingdom of the last centuries BC in the eastern Alps, but the fragments of Hekataios say nothing about Nurax being in central Europe. Therefore, a link with *nurake*, Nora, and Norax of Tartessos is possible. There were in fact intense trade links between southern Hispania and southern Sardinia *c.* 1200–*c.* 750 BC: for example, numerous Huelva swords (similar to the Armorican carp's-tongue type) have been found at both Huelva (with 84 examples) and Monte Sa Idda in Sardinia near Nora.

rinoeb°o ᚱᚤᚤ‡O日‡ (J.5.1) 'for the queens', see **ekᵘurine** above.

sab°oi ᚤ‡日A‡ (J.5.1) /samūi/ or /sabūi/ dative singular 'for Samos, Sabos', or /samoi/, /saboi/ 'in Samos, Sabos'; cf. Celtiberian family name *Samikum* (K.1.3, III–15) 'of the family of Samos', Gaulish personal names *Sama, Samo, Samus*, &c. (Delamarre 2003, 266). If Celtic, the basic sense is 'summer', Old Irish *sam*, Old Welsh and Old Breton *ham*, Gaulish month name SAMONI < Indo-European *$*sem$*- 'summer'. **m** is infrequent in Tartessian inscriptions and the Tartessian character ᚄ **b** is derived from Phoenician *mem* /m/, cf. *ŕatubaŕ* in an Iberian inscription from Ensérune, France, for Celtic *Rātumāros*. If, however, we consider the less well paralleled *Sabos*, compare Welsh *saf-af* 'I stand' and/or the ?Hispano-Celtic place-names *Sabetanum*, *Sabora*. A reference to the Greek island of Samos (which was in direct contact with Tartessos) is not impossible; see further note on J.5.1 above.

salsaḻoi ‡ΑΓ‡ΑΓ‡Ν or possibly **salsanoi** ‡ΑΓ‡ΑΥ‡Ν (J.12.4) ?cf. Gaulish *salico-* 'willow'. In the absence of any closely similar Celtic names, we should possibly consider the Numidian (Palaeo-Berber) names *Zelalsen* (a king of the 3rd century BC) and *Salsa* (a Christian martyr of the 4th century AD). However, **salsaloi** appears to be inflected as Indo-European, ?dative singular 'for Salsalos' or locative, alternatively nominative plural as subject of the plural verb.

saruneea ΑΟΟΥϞϞΑ‡ (J.22.1, J.22.2) *ā*-stem genitive singular < **Sterunā* ?'Star-goddess', probably accusative singular in **saru(-?-)an** ‡ΑΡϞ-Ö-ΑΥ (Mesas do Castelinho; see Guerra, 71–3 above), cf. the well-attested Gaulish goddess *Sirona*/*Đirona* probably from a similar preform with a long vowel in the root (Indo-European **h₂stēr* 'star' [Wodtko et al. 2008, 348–54]), but also *Serona* and *Serana* (Jufer & Luginbühl 62) with a short vowel in the root as in Old Welsh *ser-enn*. Almagro-Gorbea (1988, 73) mentions Tartessian images of the 'Dea Mater' type (reminiscent of the Phoenician Astarte) sometimes featuring 'éléments astraux'.

-seḵᵘui ΥϞΗΟ‡[(J.1.4) o-stem dative singular, as the second element of a compound or a complete simplex name with the widely attested Celtic *segos* 'strong, bold, &c.', as found in the Hispano-Celtic place-names *Segontia*, *Segovia*, *Segida*, *Segumaros* (in the territory of the Celtici of the south-west [Vallejo Ruiz 2005, 471]), SEGIDIAECO (*L'Année épigraphique* 1967, 76, León), cf. Gaulish *Sego-dumnus*, ΣΕΓΟΜΑΡΟϹ, superlative *Segisami* = Hispano-Celtic *Segisama*, Old Irish *seg* 'force, vigour', Welsh *hy* 'audacious': Indo-European **segʰ-h-* 'conquer, victory' (Wodtko et al. 2008, 600–4). Alternatively, the form could be the latter part of an incomplete personal name in which Celtic **ekᵘos* 'horse', dative **ekᵘūi* is the final element.

<u>si</u>]kᵉeuuakᵉe*[ ]ebᵒo (dative plural), ‡□□[ ]*ΟΙΑϞϞΟΧ[(J.7.8) /segeṵākebo/ 'in-

voking the people of ?Segevos' dative plural; see previous.

soloir ‡‡Γ‡ΝP (J.11.3) ?/soḻiṵir(as)/ nominative singular masculine o-stem, with final syllable not written or lost as in Latin *vir*, cf. the Hispano-Celtic 'family name' SOLICVM on a funerary inscription from Navas de Estena, Ciudad Real (González Rodríguez 1994, 172), Gaulish SOLIBODVVS, SOLICVRVS (2 attestations in Latin inscriptions), SOLIMARIVS (4 attestations), SOLIMARVS (12 attestations), SOLIRIX (2 attestations), SOLISETIVS, SOLORIX (Delamarre 2003, 287; Raybould & Sims-Williams 2007, 74–6). The first element would correspond to Old Irish *súil* 'eye', Old Welsh *houl* 'sun', probably also the Romano-British divine name *Sūlis*, as worshipped at Bath/Aquae Sulis: Indo-European **séh₂ul* 'sun' (Wodtko et al. 2008, 606–11). There was a Hispano-Celtic place-name *Solia* in the south-west, between the sites of inscriptions J.51.1 and J.55.1.

tᵃala-inon ΥϞΥΜΑΊΑΧ (J.14.1) ?/talṵin(d)on/ o-stem accusative singular or nominative-accusative neuter or, less probably, genitive plural 'having a fair front/brow', as a place-name 'country with a fair/blessed headland', thus the Celtic form underlying *sacrum Promontorium* or *cautes sacra* 'the sacred crag' in the *Ora Maritima* (line 212), today Sagres point, the ultimate extremity of south-west Europe; cf. the Celtiberian family name *Talukokum* (genitive plural, Botorrita), Western Hispano-Celtic dative plural divine name ARABO COROBELICOBO TALVSICO·BO (Arroyomolinas de la Vera, Cáceres, Spain [Búa 2000, 526]) and the personal name CRISSVS TALABVRI F. AEBOSOCELENSIS (*L'Année épigraphique* 1952, 42–3, Cáceres), the place-name *Tala-briga* (northern Portugal), and the personal names TALAIVS, TALAVIVS, TALAVI, TALAVICA, TALABARIVS (Albertos 1985, 295–7), SEGONTIVS TALAVI F(ILIVS) TALABONICVM on an inscription from Yecla de Yeltes, Salamanca (González Rodríguez 1986, 133; Vallejo Ruiz 2005, 406ff), Gaulish *Argio-talus*, *Dubno-talus*, *Cassi-talos*, *Orbio-talus* &c. (Delamarre 2003, 288–9), Old Welsh *Talhaern*, Old Breton *Talhoiarn* 'Iron-brow'. The Old Irish common noun *tul*, *taul*, and Welsh *tal* < Celtic **talu-* have meanings including 'front, brow, headland, protuberance, shield boss'. A borrowing from Semitic *tel* 'hill, &c.' has been suggested (Vendryes 1960–, T-180–2). The second element is interpreted as Celtic **u̯indo-* 'white, fair, blessed', Gaulish *vindo-*, Lepontic *-uino-*, &c.: Indo-European **u̯eid-* 'see' (Wodtko et al. 2008, 717–22). The find spot of the inscription, Alcoforado, is in the far west of the zone with Tartessian inscriptions, but north of the cape and not immediately near Sagres. As to why the extreme south-western headland of Europe was called 'the sacred headland', the place beyond the horizon of the setting sun, is universally associated with the otherworld/ afterlife, as is the case in medieval Celtic legend with the Irish Tech Duinn and Gwales in the Welsh Mabinogi.

tᵃarnekᵘun ᗉᏌᎳᎻᎾᎾᎳᎳᎪᚷ (J.26.1) Hispano-Celtic family name formed by adding an adjectival suffix -*ko*- and genitive plural ending to a personal name: 'of the family of Tarnos'. As with **ḷiirnestᵃakᵘun** (J.19.1) a family name formed in this way is used to identify a woman, dative singular **bᵃane**. Is *Tarnos* the Tartessian equivalent of the Gaulish god's name *Taranos* (cf. Welsh *taran*), the thunder god? Note also the Celtiberian family name *Turanikum* (genitive plural) compared to Old Irish *torann* 'thunder' (Wodtko 2000, 422).

Ταρτησσος, *Tartessus*, *Tartessii*, &c. In Semitic sources the name usually occurs as *Taršiš*, hence *Tarshish* in the Old Testament, which figures in the List of Nations in Genesis 10:4 as the name of a child of Javan, son of Japhet, thus connected with the Greeks and peoples of the Mediterranean. Tartessos is probably the meaning of Phoenician *tršš* on the stela from Nora, Sardinia, *c.* 850/750 BC. In the terms of the second treaty between Rome and Carthage of 348 BC cited by Polybius (III.24), Roman activities were curtailed beyond a place called Μαστια Ταρσηιον *Mastia Tarsēion*, i.e. 'Mastia in the country of the *Tarsēioi*', which probably identifies a place near Cartagena in south-eastern Spain. It appears, therefore, that a population name based on Semitic *Taršiš* (*Tarsēioi* in Greco-Punic form, with a possible Old Latin intermediary) had come to designate for the Carthag-

inians much of the southern Iberian Peninsula, including the non-Indo-European east (De Hoz 1989b, 25–40). On the Semitic forms, see further Lipinski (2004, 248–52), who does not seem to regard the name as of Semitic origin. Villar (1995) reconstructs early byforms **Turta* and **Tartis*, going back at least to the 8th century BC or (if Semitic *Taršiš* does mean Tartessos) the later 2nd millennium. He connects these forms with numerous river-names in the Iberian Peninsula and regards them as Indo-European in origin (from **ter-* 'rub, bore, penetrate, &c.'; but contrast Untermann 2004, 207 n. 40). In *Ora Maritima* (line 54), *Fretum Tartessium* clearly means the Straits of Gibraltar, the gap where *nostrum mare* (the Mediterranean) meets the outer ocean. This usage suggests an Indo-European and possibly Celtic etymology from **ter* 'through' or the derived verb **terh₂-* 'cross over, overcome, pass through', cf. Old Irish *tar* 'across, over' (Celtic **tares*), Welsh *tra* 'beyond', *trwy* 'through' (Old Welsh *trui*), Latin *trāns*, Sanskrit *tiráḥ*, Avestan *tarō* 'across', Sanskrit *tárati* 'crosses over, overcomes', Hittite *tarḫuzzi* 'overcomes, is able' (Rix 2001, 633–4). Thus, the original primary sense of the name, highlighting the region's most significant feature for travellers, would have been 'where one passes through, crosses over, the place beyond, the region of transit' between the countries around the great inland sea and those of the outer ocean. Originally, the reference might have been to the world of the outer ocean in general—which would help to explain some apparent contradictions in the usages of *Tarshish* in the Old Testament—then secondarily focusing more specifically on the first important country immediately beyond the single maritime channel leading from the inner world to the outer. After the non-Indo-European Phoenicians increasingly dominated commerce through the straits and founded a great commercial town with the new name *Gadir*, the names *Taršiš*, *Tartessii*, and *Tartessos* came understandably to designate mainly the pre-Phoenician native population and their leading polity, still wealthy and influential about Huelva and the northern hinterland of the straits. According to *Ora Maritima* (line 85), Gadir was (?part of) what had formerly been called *Tartessus*.

Another Celtic etymology, from 'dryness' (Old Irish *tart* 'thirst') was offered by Sims-Williams, albeit with apparent disbelief (2006, 226).

t^casiioonii ꓬꓬꓨ++ꓬꓨ‡ꓯꓮ (J.1.1) masculine personal name, genitive singular, possibly identical to British *Tasciovanos* < *Tasgiog^uonos*, Gaulish *Tascouanos*. If the Tartessian is this same name, Indo-European *g^ub* in *g^uben-* 'strike, kill' has become /u/ in Tartessian, as in British and Gaulish. An alternative possibility is suggested by the similar ending of inscription J.1.5 a(a/m)musok^eeonii (note also J.7.6). The king's name *Argantonios* 'agent/devotee of the divine silver' shows that Tartessian had this type of meaningful high-status occupational name. It is therefore possible that J.1.1 and J.1.5 name a priest or some other similarly styled (with the double suffix -(i)on-io-) ruler or presiding official as their final statement. If so, the case ending is probably genitive singular. Another possibility is that the ending is locative (cf. Celtiberian *Lutiak-ei*) and that the final statement identifies the precinct (possibly of the god or priesthood) in which the grave is located, thus *Ta(χ)seon̦iei* 'in the precinct of Ta(χ)seonos/-ā'.

t^ilek^uurk^uu ꓬꓴꓯꓬꓮꓳꓹꓭꓳ or t^ilek^uulk^uu ꓬꓴꓯꓬꓮꓳꓹꓭꓳ (Mesas do Castelinho; see Guerra, 67–73 above) man's compound name, dative singular, opening the inscription and probably naming the deceased. For the first element, cf. an inscription of AD 28 from Caurel, Lugo, Galicia: TILLEGVS AMBATI F SVSARRVS | AIOB[R]IGIAECO (Búa 2004, 387) with *Tillegus* probably reflecting an earlier *Tillekos*. For the second element, if the reading is -urk^uu, cf. Celtiberian *urkala* and the Hispano-Celtic names *Urcala*, *Urcalonis*, *Urcalocus*, and *Urcico*, also the Iberian name element *urke* (Wodtko 2000, 461–2). If it is -ulk^uu, cf. alk^uu (J.12.1). Here, this could be Indo-European *ulk^uo-* 'wolf', Sanskrit *vŕkah*, Avestan *vəhrka-*, Lithuanian *vilkas*, Gothic *wulfs*, common in Germanic compound personal names, also Celtic *Catuvolcus*. Compare Ogam Irish (genitive) ULCAGNI, ULCCAGNI = Romano-British VLCAGNI, nominative VLCAGNVS (McCone 1985). The indigenous second element of the Roman-

period north-western place-name *Octaviolca* is not likely here, as it appears to be confined to place-names, for which suitable etymologies have been proposed (Búa 2007, 23–4).

t^iirt^oos ‡‡ꓯꓯꓳ (J.1.2) man's name, nominative singular, cf. Celtiberian *Tirtouios*, *Tirtunos*, *Tirtano*, *Tirtu*, family names *Tirtanikum* and *Tirtalicum*, *tirtotulu* 'triple' (Prósper 2007, 24–6), North-west Hispano-Celtic personal names TRITIA, TRITIVS, TRITEVS (Albertos 1985, 298), the divine epithet TRITIAECIO (Torremenga, Cáceres [Untermann 1985, 360; Búa 2000, 567]), TRITIAEGIO (Navaconcejo, Cáceres [Búa 2000, 563]), Gaulish personal names *Trito[s]*, *Tritus*, *Triti*, cf. Old Welsh *triti(d)* 'third', Latin *tertius* (Wodtko 2000, 297).

t^uurea ꓯꓳꓯꓯꓮ (J.7.8) personal name, genitive singular (cf. ogam Irish -IAS, -EAS, -EA), signifying an ancestor, cf. Celtiberian *Turaios*, *Tureibo*, *Turenta*, *Tures*, *Turo*, *Turaesos*, *Turanus*, *Turos* family names *Turaku*, *Turanikum*, TVRIASICA, *Turikum*, *Turumokum*, *Turanicus*, North-west Hispano-Celtic personal names TVRAIVS, TVREVS, TVREIVS and the divine epithet TVRIACO (Untermann 1985, 360; Búa 2000, 447), the place-name TVROBRIGA, TVRVBRIGA (attested also in Beja and Faro, south Portugal), TVRIVBRIGA attested in the region of Badajoz, Spain (Búa 2000, 90–1, 641, 645).

t^uu͗rek^uui ꓬꓯꓮꓳꓬꓯꓯ (J.14.1) o-stem dative singular, cf. Celtiberian *Tureka*, *Turaku*, and the Celtiberian family names *Turikum* and *Turanikum*; the second element may be Indo-European *h₁ek ´uo-s* 'horse'. Cf. also]t^uurk^aaio[ ]ꓯꓯꓯꓯꓯꓮꓬꓯ‡[(J.51.1). See previous entry.

uarb^ooiir saruneea ꓯꓳꓳꓬꓯꓯꓯꓮ‡ꓯꓬꓬ‡ꓭꓯꓬꓬꓯ (J.22.1), nominative+genitive 'lord consort of Saruna [the ?star goddess]', is of a type otherwise unknown in the ancient Celtic languages, but common by the early medieval period: e.g. Old Irish *Mael-Brigte* 'Servant of St Brigit', Cumbric *Gos-Patric* 'Servant of St Patrick', &c. The present example was probably based on the pattern of Phoenician *Abd-Astarte* 'Servant of [the goddess] Astarte', *Abd-Tanit*, *Gel-Melqart* 'Client of [the god] Melqart', &c. Though Saruna might herself be an *interpretatio phoenica* of Astarte, the name is thoroughly Celticized, not only using Celtic elements rather than Semitic, but defining the relationship of mortal rulers to gods on the basis of a different mythology, not as priestly servants of the gods, but rather as royal consorts linked to the tribal goddess by the *hieros gamos* (sacred marriage) of the characteristically Celtic dynastic foundation legend. **uarbᵒoiir saruneea** is the earliest attested Celtic name of the characteristically Insular Neo-Celtic 'inversion compound' type, and this example can be traced directly to contact (intellectual and literate) with Semitic. **uarbᵒoiir** is analysed as a compound with a superlative first element Celtic **u(p)ermᵐo-uiros* 'highest man/hero/ husband', cf. Old Welsh *Guorthemir* < **u̯ertamo-rīχs* 'highest king'.

iru[i u]**arbᵘui-EL** ꓩOᛉꓧ𐌇ꟼ9A[ ]ꟼꟼꓴ /u̯irūi uu̯armūi el/ 'invoking the lord god' (J.23.1) uses the dative singulars of the Celtic noun and superlative attributive adjective in concord, followed by an uninflected Semitic loanword, Phoenician *el* signifying the highest god.

oiśaHa ꓒHAꓳᛉꟷ (J.11.1) /u̯iˈsā_ə(s)/ ?genitive singular, cf. Celtiberian *ueizos, ueizui, ueiziai* (Wodtko 2000, 437–9), possibly meaning 'inspector, witness' (De Hoz 2007b, 202), Primitive Irish and British TO-VISACI 'of the leader' = Old Irish *toísech*, Middle Welsh *tywyssawc*: Indo-European **u̯eid-* 'see, know (a fact)'.

isakᵃaoe O𐌗AꓥA𐌸ᛉ (J.24.1) /u̯iˈsākau̯ē/ feminine dative singular or masculine /u̯iˈsākau̯ōi/ ?'the leader', see previous item.

ooŕoir 9ᛉꟷꓵꟷꟷ (J.19.2) /u̯u̯or u̯ir(əs)/ nominative singular, most probably naming the same man as **ooŕoire** Oꟼᛉꟷꓵꟷꟷ (J.19.1) /u̯u̯oru̯iri/ genitive singular, compound of Indo-European **(s)h₄upér* 'over' (with characteristically Celtic loss of Indo-European *p*) + **u̯ihₓrós* 'man, hero'; both elements are extremely common in the name formation of all the ancient and medieval Celtic languages. Note especially the parallel Celtiberian collocation VERAMOS VIROS 'supreme man' (Peñalba de Villastar). /u̯or/ rather than /u̯er/ is reminiscent of Brittonic and Goidelic, but also occurs sometimes in Gaulish, e.g. DIVORTOMV alongside

DIVORTOMV on the Coligny Calendar and the compound verb *de-uor-buet-id* (Lezoux). Celtiberian has VORAMOS and, as well as VERAMOS, accusative VERAMOM, so the development is obviously Hispano-Celtic too and occurs in this particular word, 'over'. Another probable example is the well-attested divine epithet VORTEAECIO which occurs in Lusitania.

]**uŕni** ᛉꟼꟷꓧ (J.20.1) nominative or dative singular feminine *ī*-stem, cf. the goddess name *Urnia* (Nîmes, Jufer & Luginbühl 2001, 67).

uśnee OOᛉᛉꓧ (J.23.1) /uχsᵃmai/ 'in Uxama, the highest place', a common Hispano-Celtic place-name (e.g. Pliny, *Naturalis Historia* 3.27, Ptolemy 2.6.55 Οὔξαμα Ἀργαιλα, 2.6.52 Οὔξαμα Βαρκα), Celtiberian *Usama*, Old Breton *Ossam* 'Ouessant', &c., though possibly in this inscription figuratively for the home of the celestial god(s), locative singular. This etymology for **uśnee** implies the Celtic treatment of *p* in earlier **upsᵐmā-i*. The name form *Ossonoba* (possibly an Iberianized or Punicized form of Hispano-Celtic *Uxama, Usama*) occurs for towns at Faro and Huelva in the former Tartessian region during the classical period. As the urban centre of Tartessos, Huelva would have been 'highest' in either the sense of 'most important' or the dry land above the morass at the Río Tinto and Odiel estuaries. However, neither Ossonoba is very close to the find spot of inscription J.23.1.

]**uultⁱina** Aᛉ𐌏ꟷꓧ[(J.12.3) individual name, feminine *ā*-stem nominative singular, cf. Celtiberian personal names *Ultinos* (Botorrita), *Ultia, Ultu, Ultatunos*, Lepontic dative/ablative plural UVL̲TIAUIOPOS (Prestino). *Ulti-* also occurs as an Iberian name element.

uursaau ꓴAA𐌸9ꟷꟷ (J.16.1) dative singular 'for Uursaos', possibly < Indo-European **(s)h₄uper-steh₂-* 'stands above', with a sense opposite to Gaulish *uossos, uassos*, Old Irish *foss*, Old Welsh and Old Breton *guas* 'servant, lad' (also 'land, surface of the earth') < Celtic **u̯u̯ost(a)o-* 'one who stands below' < Indo-European **(s)h₄upo-steh₂-*. Untermann (1997, 168) compares the gentilic name *Ursius* from Lisbon and the (clearly Celtic) personal name *Ursacius* from Conimbriga.

NOUNS (SUBSTANTIVES)

anbᵃa̲[(χ)te]A꜒MA (J.11.2) literally 'of a man sent
in service of a chief', genitive singular, cf. Gaulish
ambactus (e.g. Caesar, *De Bello Gallico* 6.15), *ambaxtus*
'servant of high rank, envoy, representative' (De
Hoz 2007b, 191), as a personal name Celtiberian
and North-west Hispano-Celtic and Lusitanian
AMBATVS, based on the past passive particle
of a Celtic compound verb **ambi-ag-tó-s* 'one
sent around', Indo-European **hₐentbʰi-* 'around'
+ **hₐeg´-* 'drive, send', also North-west Hispano-
Celtic AMBATIO (Albertos 1985, 264). anbᵃat̲ⁱia
AMꜱAⱯ̃N̲A (J.16.2) /amba(χ)tia/ could be either
an instrumental singular or an abstract nominative
singular noun 'representation, a stand in', hence
'cenotaph' (see note on inscription), possibly a
formation identical to Gaulish *ambascia* 'embassy' <
*ambi-aχtia (De Hoz 2007b, 191). AMBACTHIVS
and AMBAXIVS occur as names in Latin inscriptions of the Roman Period from the Netherlands
and Germany respectively, and AMBACTVS is
found as a name in Germany and Serbia (Raybould
& Sims-Williams 2007, 34). If Tartessian anbᵃat̲ⁱia
is a personal name, it is probably a feminine nominative. A corresponding woman's name occurs in
Celtiberia: AMBATA PAESICA ARGAMONICA
(CIL II 2856, Lara de los Infantes [Untermann
1992, 391]).

a]nbᵉik̲ⁱ or a]nbᵉit̲ⁱ ⱯMⱭⱱ[(J.11.5) ?cf. Gaulish
ambito (Lezoux) of uncertain meaning (Delamarre
2003, 42) based on the Celtic preposition *ambi*
'around' < Indo-European **hₐentbʰi-*, Celtiberian
and Gaulish *ambi*, Old Irish *imb, imm*.

ar̃tᵉ[ ]⊢ᴋA (J.24.1) ?'stone', cf. Cisalpine Gaulish
ARTVAŚ (accusative plural) used for the stones
of a funerary monument at Todi, Old Irish *art*
'stone'.

bᵃane OMA꜒ (J.11.1, J.19.1, J.26.1) 'for the woman,
wife' dative singular, feminine *a*-stem < Celtic
*bnⁿai (Indo-European **gʷénhₐ* 'woman' [Wodtko
et al. 2008, 177–85], showing characteristically
Celtic *b* < Indo-European voiced labio-velar *gʷ*);
bᵃaenae OAMOA꜒ (J.15.1) is probably a variant
of bᵃane and may reflect an earlier vocalism **benai*
= early Old Irish *bein*; genitive plural bᵃaanon

M╪MAA꜒ (J.11.4), cf. Gaulish ?accusative singular
beni (Châteaubleau), genitive plural *bnanom* (Larzac),
accusative plural *mnas* (Larzac) < Celtic **bnam-s*
(see further Delamarre 2003, 72), personal names
Seno-bena, Uitu-bena, Old Irish nominative singular
ben 'woman, wife' < Celtic **bena* < Indo-European
*gʷénhₐ, dative singular archaic *bein* < Celtic **bene*,
later Old Irish *mnái*, genitive plural *ban* < Celtic
*banom, compositional form *ban-* < Celtic **bano-*.
In J.19.1, bᵃane is preceded by the genitive plural
of a group name liirnestᵃak̲ᵘun and followed by
the genitive of the husband's name oor̃oire for
identification. In J.26.1 bᵃane is preceded by the
genitive group name tᵃarnek̲ᵘun.

ek̲ᵘu- 'horse' (Indo-European **hₐek´uos*) in the
names ek̲ᵘur̃ine OMMⱯ4EO (J.4.1), possibly
o-stem datives singular in -sek̲ᵘui M4HO*[(J.1.4)
and t̲ᵘur̃ek̲ᵘui M4EOⱧⱯⱭ (J.14.1). These
forms indicate that Tartessian was not a *p*-Celtic
language.

elu- 41O (J.7.5) 'many, numerous', cf. Celtiberian
Elu (Botorrita), family name *Elokum*, Gaulish
personal names *Eluontiu, Eluadius, Eluo-rix* group
names *Elu-sates, Helvetii, Helve-cones* (a subtribe of
the Lugii in central Europe), Old Irish *il-* 'many,
poly-', Welsh *elw-* 'profit, gain' (Delamarre 2003,
162): Indo-European **pélh₁us* 'much'. elu- shows
characteristically Celtic loss of Indo-European *p-*.

iibᵃau̲ 4A꜒MM (J.5.1) If read iibᵃan /eban/,
this could be equivalent to the form *eban* in
Iberian inscriptions indicating the builder of a
monument.

kᵃaśetᵃana ᴧAMOXAⱯA (J.53.1) /kassi-
dannā/ 'priestess, specifically female minister
in charge of the distribution of tin or bronze',
feminine *ā*-stem nominative singular, cf. inflected
variants of the masculine Gaulish *casidani, casidan(n)*
o, &c., repeatedly in the graffiti of La Graufesenque,
translated once as Latin 'flamen' and directly comparable to the Gaulish term ARGANTODANNOS
'moneyer' (< 'silver-minister') occurring on Gaulish
coinage (Delamarre 2003, 108, citing De Bernardo
Stempel 1998), also *platiodanni* 'overseers of metal'
or 'overseers of streets' (De Hoz 2007b, 193, 196).
Cf. also the personal names Celtiberian *Kasilos*,

Gaulish *Cassi-talos*, British *Cassi-vellaunos*, &c. Greek κασσίτερος 'tin' is of uncertain origin and probably a trade word going back to the Bronze Age. The name Κασσιτερίδες 'tin islands', mentioned repeatedly in the Greek sources (e.g. Herodotus III.115), is of course related. Modern writers have located these islands variously in Galicia, Armorica, Scilly, and Cornwall, perhaps all of these.

k^ert°o ✳ΔꟼΟꟾ (J.18.1) /kerdo/ 'of the artisan' genitive singular *o*-stem, cf. Gaulish personal name *Cerdo*, Old Irish *cerd* 'artisan' or specifically 'bronze smith', Early Welsh *kerδawr* 'artisan' or specifically 'musician, poet': Indo-European **kérdos* 'craft'. It is noteworthy that the formulaic closing of the inscription is longer and more complex than usual, containing several words alliterating with the name of the deceased, the daughter of the *kerdos*.

lok°on Ϻ✳Ʂ✳ꟾ (J.1.1), **l̲o̲k°on** (J.57.1) /logon/ 'grave, funerary monument', accusative singular; cf. Cisalpine *lokan* /logan/ 'grave, funerary monument' (Todi), Early Welsh *golo* 'burial' (< **u̯o-log-*): Indo-European root **legʰ-* 'lie down'.

muŕi- 'sea', see **omuŕik̲ª*[** above.

orbªa ✳ꟼꞫΔ (J.53.1) 'heiress, inheritance, inherited', cf. the Hispano-Celtic family name [o]ʀʙɪᴇɴɪᴄ[ᴠᴍ] on an inscription from León (González Rodríguez 1986, 132), Old Irish *orbae, orb(b)* 'heir, inheritance', Early Welsh *wrvyδ* < Celtic **orbi̯om*, Gaulish personal names *Orbius, Orbia*, &c. (Delamarre 2003, 243), the Gaulish and British compound name ᴏʀʙɪᴏᴛᴀʟᴠs (Raybould & Sims-Williams 2007, 69) < Indo-European **h₂/₃orbʰos* 'orphan' (De Hoz 2007b, 197).

rinoeb°o ꟼϺϻ✳Οꟺ✳ (J.5.1) dative/ablative plural, possibly invoking a group of deities, probably the feminine of the following item (Celtic **rīχs* 'king, leader'), thus *rignoebo* 'to the queens', cf. feminine dative singular **r̲i̲ne** ΟϺϻꟾ /rignē/ 'queen' in the divine or personal name **ek^ur̲i̲ne** ΟϺϻꟼꟼꟷΟ (J.4.1). Alternatively, compare Gaulish *Rēnos* 'Rhine' < 'river' (Delamarre 2003, 257), Old Irish *rían* 'sea': Indo-European **rei-* 'flow'. See **anak^e** above.

ris ✳Ϻꟼ nominative singular 'leader, king', in the personal names **aib^uris** (J.3.1), *Gargoris*, dative singular **risé** ΟϺϻꟼ in **ariarisé** (J.10.1), cf.

Gaulish *Ambiorix, Biturix, Coticorix, Dumnorix, Secorix, Vercingetorix*, probably Celtiberian *-rés* in *kombalkokores* (De Hoz 2007b, 197–8, 201; Wodtko 2000, 188–9), but *-ris* in Celtiberian *Caturis* (De Hoz 2007b, 203) < Indo-European **h₃rḗǵ's* 'king, ruler'.

set^a ✳Ο✕Δ (J.53.1) 'resting place', cf. Early Welsh *seδ* 'seat', *gorseδ* 'burial mound, &c.', also Gallo-Brittonic ᴀꝹꝹᴇꝺᴏ- 'war chariot' (cf. North-west Hispano-Celtic ɴɪᴍᴍᴇᴅᴏ ᴀsᴇꝺꝺɪᴀɢᴏ [Mieres, Oviedo, Búa 2000, 270–1]) and Old Irish *aire* 'chariot driver' < **are-sed-s*: Indo-European **sedes-, *sed-* 'seat' (Wodtko et al. 2008, 590–600). Old Irish *síd* 'tumulus, fairy mound', also 'peace' (Welsh *hedd*) goes back to the same root with a long vowel (see further Ó Cathasaigh 1977/8).

t^uⁿ¹it^esbaan [*r.* **t^uⁿ(?k̲i̲)it^esbaan**] Δϻꟷϻϻ✳Ꝫ Δϻ (J.53.1) 'that is most fortunate' /tunketis^(a)mən/, neuter singular nominative/accusative, cf. the North-west Hispano-Celtic personal or divine name ᴛᴏɴᴄᴇᴛᴀᴍᴠs, ᴛᴏɴɢᴇᴛᴀᴍᴠs 'most fortunate' ([both attested at Fundão, Castelo Branco, Portugal; Búa 2000, 490–1] with a different but related superlative suffix [Albertos 1985, 298], connected with 'oath' by De Hoz 2007b, 203), Old Irish *tocad* 'fate, destiny', Middle Welsh *tynghet* 'destiny', Breton *tonket* 'luck', and the British personal name ᴛᴠɴᴄᴄᴇᴛᴀᴄᴇ 'Fortunatae' (genitive). On Tartessian superlatives, see also **uarbªan** below.

(o)ira Δꟼϻ✳ (J.1.2) /u̯irə(s)/ 'man, hero, husband' nominative singular = Proto-Celtic **wiros* < Indo-European **u̯ihₓrós* 'man, hero', Celtiberian ᴠɪʀᴏs, Gaulish *uiros* in names, Old Irish *fer*, Old Welsh *g(u)ur*, cf. Lusitanian/North-west Hispano-Celtic personal names ᴠɪʀɪᴀᴛɪs, ᴠɪʀɪᴀᴛᴠs, ᴠɪʀᴏɴᴠs (Albertos 1985, 302), genitive singular **(o)ire** Οꟼϻ✳ /u̯irī/ (J.11.2), dative singular **iru** Ϻꟼꟶ and ꟺꟼϻ /u̯irū(i)/ (J.7.9, J.12.1), plural nominative (or genitive singular) **ire** /u̯irī/ (J.7.2, J.52.1). The letters **ire** also occur on a fragment of a vessel from the 5th or 4th century BC from Córdoba (De Hoz 1989, 555). In **iraś-en** ϻΟϺΔꟼϻ (J.7.10), the final *s* of the nominative singular **u̯iros* may be preserved by the following enclitic pronoun 'him, it'. The nominative singular also occurs (with lost final syllable) in the personal name **ooŕoir** ᚁᚋᚆᚐᚐ (J.19.2) and the compound **uarbᵒoiir** ᚁᚋᚋᚆᚉᚃᚐᚄ (J.22.1), and the genitive singular in <u>leb</u>ᵒ**o-iire** ᚑᚃᚋᚋᚆᚐᚁᚑᚁ (Mesas do Castelinho; Guerra, 67–73 above) and **ooŕoire** ᚑᚃᚋᚆᚆᚐᚐ (J.19.1).

uarbᵃan ᚄᚐᚌᚆᚐᚄ (J.1.2, J.3.1, J.4.1, J.21.1) /ṷṷarmən/, **uarbᵃan** ᚄᚐᚄᚆᚐᚄ (J.9.1), **uarb<u>ᵃan</u>** ᚆᚐᚐ⟨ᚐᚔ (J.11.3),]<u>u</u>[a]rbᵃ[an (J.4.1), ***arbᵃan** ᚄᚐᚌᚆᚐ* (J.16.1) 'the highest one', cf. Celtiberian masculine nominative singular VERAMOS, VORAMOS, accusative VERAMOM. Note also VRAMVS in Roman Lusitania (Vallejo Ruiz 2005, 695). Unlike Celtiberian, Indo-European *$(s)h_4upermᵐom$ > Tartessian **uarbᵃan** does not develop as /-am-/ from syllabic /m̥/ before a vowel, similarly the Armorican name *Osismii* 'furthest ones', also Tartessian **-ŕine** < Indo-European *$h_3rēg'n^nih_2$ 'queen', contrasting with Old Irish *rígain*, Gaulish *rigani* with *an* < n̥. Tartessian **-bᵃan** instead of ***-man** is unsurprising given the rarity of **m** in Tartessian and similar limitations in the cognate Iberian script, e.g. Gaulish *Ratumāros* written as Iberian *ŕatubaŕ*. **uarbᵃan** is the most common form of one of the recurrent formulaic words of the Tartessian inscriptions. As such, it appears to be an inflexible neuter, unlike VORAMOS, but like the Old Irish equative, comparative, and superlative degrees of the adjective, which are not attributive adjectives agreeing with their nouns, but inflexible predicate nouns, e.g. '[the person who is] the better one, the best one', &c. (Thurneysen, GOI §363). Generally applied to individuals, the transferred meaning must be 'chief, foremost man/woman'. Though the syntax is different in J.1.2 **(o)ira uarbᵃan**, the social concepts and institutions, as well as the words, are as in the Celtiberian VIROS VERAMOS (Peñalba de Villastar; Wodtko 2000, 444; De Hoz 2007b, 202). **uarbᵃanub**ᵘ[(J.3.1) possibly shows a reanalysis in which the dative/ablative plural ending has been added to the inflexible form, but the inscription breaks off here and other interpretations are possible. **uabᵃan** ᚄᚐᚄᚐᚄ (J.16.5) may simply be an error for **uarbᵃan**, but the ancient place-name *Uama* in south-west Spain

and the Lepontic personal name UVAMO-KOZIS (Prestino) show that there had also been a superlative without the *r* < Indo-European *$(s)h_4upmᵐo$- 'highest'. That these inscriptions use **uarbᵃan**, but Celtic *rīχs* 'king' apparently not at all as a common noun, may reflect that important social innovations had occurred between the Proto-Celtic and Common Hispano-Celtic horizons.

uarbᵒoiir ᚁᚋᚋᚆᚉᚃᚐᚄ (J.22.1) nominative singular, **uarbᵒoŝi**[r- (J.7.5) /ṷṷarmoṷir-/ 'supreme man, lord', a compound of the previous, incorporating the same elements as **(o)ira uarbᵃan** (J.1.2) < notional Indo-European *$(s)h_4upermᵐo$ + *ṷih_xro*- (cf. J.22.2). The corresponding feminine compound probably occurs as the dative singular **uarn/bᵃane** ᚑᚄᚐᚌᚄᚆᚐᚄ (J.20.1) 'for a woman of highest rank' < Celtic *ṷṷermᵐa-bn̥nā-i.

otᵉerkᵃa ᚐᚈᚃᚆᚑᚅᚆ (J.1.4) /ṷoderka/, /ṷoderkə(n)/ ?'tomb(s)' < 'under-cavity', cf. Gaulish *uodercos*, *uoderce* (Larzac) 'tomb' according to Delamarre (2003, 326) citing Fleuriot: Indo-European *derk´- 'glance at, see'. Old Irish *derc*, also *deirc*, does commonly mean 'cavity' as well as 'eye'. This development is a semantic universal. The final syllable, written **-a**, may represent a reduced form /-ə/ for the accusative singular /-on/ or /-an/, alternatively o-stem neuter nominative/accusative plural -a. Cf. the personal name *Adercus* < Celtic *ad-derkos in Vettonian territory (Luján 2007, 253, 256), and the Gaulish personal names INDERCILLVS, INDERCINIVS, INDERCVS (Raybould & Sims-Williams 2007, 63). The word possibly occurs again as **ot<u>i</u>erb<u>ᵉ</u>e** ᚑᚉᚃᚑᚈᚆ (J.10.1).

omuŕik<u>ᵃ</u>*[ᚆᚋᚆᚐᚅᚃᚌᚆ*[(J.16.2) /ṷomurika/ or /ṷomorika/ 'the under-sea world', see note on inscription. John Carey has suggested to me a possible link with the demonic Fomoire of Irish mythology, who might originally have had a more benign function in connection with the otherworld and afterlife. This word for 'sea' may occur also in the dative/ablative plural compound **alak<u>i</u>-muŕb**ᵒ? ?ᚑᚆᚋᚋᚌᚄᚐᚌᚐ (S. Martinho): Indo-European *móri 'sea'.

PRONOUNS

-e (J.1.1, J.1.3) accusative infixed pronoun, 'him' or 'it', supported by the preverb t^uu as t^e'-e, t^e'-ee preceding b^aare and ro·b^aare ᴏ৭А⋝⧫৭ᴏᴏн (J.18.2), also 3rd plural t^e'-ee·b^arent^ii ᴎ⊕ᴎᴏ৭А⋝ᴏᴏн (J.23.1): t^e'-]ea·b^aare (J.6.1); t^e'-e·b^aere (J.7.8), t^e'-e·bare ᴏ৭А⋝ᴏн (Vale de Águia; Guerra, above 77), t^e'-e·bar[e] ৭А⋝ᴏн (J.16.1), t̲^e̲'-e̲·b̲^aare ᴏ৭А[⋝]ᴏн (J.18.1), t^e'-e[·b^a]are ᴏ৭А[ ]ᴏн (J.21.1); cf. Old Irish -a, Archaic Old Irish -e < Celtic masculine singular enclitic pronoun -em, neuter -e(d).

eb^ee ᴏᗡᴏ (J.9.1), **eb^e** ᴏᗡ (J.16.3) '?by/with them' personal pronoun, instrumental plural, cf. Gaulish instrumental plural eiabi (Larzac), and the instrumental plural or dual Gaulish noun SVIOREBE 'with/by the sisters'.

eib^oo ⧫ᗒᴎᴏ (J.5.1) could be a dative/ablative plural personal pronoun 'for/ from them', but is more probably the case ending of the adjective anak̲^e̲:eib^oo (see above). Another possible instance of a dative/ablative plural personal pronoun is **eb^uu alak^iimuŕb^o?** ?▢ᴋᴧᴎᴎᴧ৭А1Аᴧᴈᴏ (S. Martinho) showing agreement with the following dative/ablative plural noun, cf. Gaulish instrumental plural eiabi (Larzac).

?emun ᴧᴧᴎᴏ (J.7.8) masculine genitive plural, see **nemun** above.

?en ᴎᴏ (J.7.10) masculine accusative singular enclitic pronoun.

ib^ooiion ᴎⵜᴎᴎⵜ冒ᴎ or **ib^oonion** (J.4.1) personal pronoun dative/ablative plural **ib^oo** + suffixed relative **-iion** or ?masculine/neuter genitive plural; cf. the Gaulish personal pronouns of the Larzac inscription: eianom 3rd feminine genitive plural, 3rd singular nominative feminine eia, 3rd plural feminine instrumental plural eiabi, possibly genitive singular esias (Delamarre 2003, 161).

ii (J.1.1) relative pronoun? possibly the same element found suffixed to the verb: if we adopt the reading naŕk^eii for J.1.3; n[aŕk^e]enii (J.6.1).

-ion enclitic relative pronoun accusative singular 'that, which, whom', cf. Celtiberian iom, Gaulish uninflected io: ?relative 1st singular perfect b^ar⟨u⟩

a-ion ⟨АРᕼАᴎⵜᴍ /bāra-ion/ 'whom I [the grave] have received' (J.7.9); ?suffixed relative in **k̲^a̲aŕner-ion** 'to whom funerary monuments have been built' (J.7.2), possibly again in k̲^a̲a̲[ŕn]ir-ion (J.1.3). See also **ib^ooiion** (J.4.1) above.

ist̲^u̲[u (J.7.4) /istūi/ 'to this one' masculine singular, **ist̲^a̲[a]ib^oo** (J.5.1) 'to those/these', demonstrative pronoun dative/ablative plural, possibly also **s̲t̲^i̲** ↑ᴍ (J.11.4), cf. Celtiberian demonstrative pronoun accusative singular feminine stam, also iste (for which there are various interpretations, see MLH 4.506), Lepontic iśos, Latin iste.

k̲^a̲ak̲^i̲ (J.1.1) ?*k^uāk^uo- 'all, everyone', Old Irish cách, Old Welsh paup, Gaulish inflected forms pape, papon, papi, papu; followed by dative plural group name **iśiink^oolob^oo**.

śaen ᴎᴏАᴍ (J.27.1) accusative demonstrative pronoun, cf. Celtiberian stam.

sieś ᴍᴏᴎ⧫ or **sie** ᴏᴎ⧫ (J.12.1) /sie(s)/ 'they' nominative plural ?feminine, cf. Gaulish sies 'they' (Larzac); the reading **sien** ᴎᴏᴎ⧫ is also possible.

NUMERALS

t^iirt^oos ⧫⧫А৭ᴎ⊕ (J.1.2) is a nominative singular masculine name probably derived from the ordinal 'third'; see above.

PREPOSITIONS

ambi 'around', see **anb^a̲a̲[(χ)te** and **a]n̲b̲^e̲it̲^i̲** above, **enb̲^e̲** below.

ane ᴏᴎА (J.1.1) ?cf. the Gaulish and British preposition ande. With the sequence lok^oo | n ane naŕk^ee, one might consider the Gaulish compound preserved in the 9th-century *Andelagum monasterium* (De Hoz 2007b, 195), possibly with a basic sense of 'lying down within'. An intensive force is often attributed to Gaulish and British compounds with initial ande-, e.g. *Ande-roudos* 'very red', similarly Welsh *annwyl* 'dear' : *gŵyl* 'humble', cf. also Sanskrit *adhi-deva-* 'greatest god', *adhi-rāj-a-* 'over-king' (Búa

2005, 119–20).

k^{o}o ǂ⧗ (J.1.2) *ko*^{N} 'together with' followed by the dative, Old Irish *co* nasalizing with dative 'with', Latin *cum* with ablative, Indo-European **kom*.

t^{o}o ǂ△ (J.1.1) /*do*/ 'to, for' with dative = Old Irish and Old Breton *do*, &c. In J.1.1, **t^{o}o** functions to distinguish the dative personal name of the deceased for whom the grave was made from the names of gods who are invoked in the opening of the statement. Celtiberian TO prefixed to the dative divine name LVGVEI (ARAIANOM) in the inscription from Peñalba de Villastar (K.3.3) closely recalls the diction of Tartessian J.1.1: **lok^{o}ob^{o}o niirab^{o}o t^{o}o aŕaiu̯i**.

o- /*u̯o-*/, **ua-** 'under', this word is discussed as a preverb below.

or- /*u̯or-*/ 'over' (Celtiberian *uer* and *uor*, Gaulish *uer* sometimes *uor*, Old Irish *for*, Old Welsh *guar, guor*: Indo-European **(s-)h$_4$upér*) may indicate succession in the example **ori̯ou⟨t^{i}⟩b^{e}a:i** ꟽ|Aᗡ(Φ) ᛋǂꟽᑫǂ /*u̯or ioubai*/ 'successor of Iuba' (J.7.6), cf. Old Welsh *Cein map Guorcein map Doli map Guordoli map Dumn map Gurdumn* in the prehistoric section of the Old Welsh genealogy of Gwynedd, in which *map* 'son' has presumably been inserted in making an archaic king list conform to the pattern of a pedigree. **uarb^{a}an** is a superlative based on this preposition (see above).

PREVERBS

ar- ᑫA < Celtic **are* (cf. Gaulish *Armorica/Aremorica*), Indo-European **peri* 'over', in the compound verb **ar-b^{e}⟨i⟩eŕi** ꟽᛋ∧Oꟽᗡᑫ A (J.12.3) 'carries/carried forward (henceforth)' 3rd singular ?present or imperfect < **are-beret(i)* (alternatively segment as preterite **ar-b^{e}⟨i⟩eŕit^{u}u** ᛋ△ꟽᛋ∧Oꟽᗡᑫ A 'carried onward'), perfect **ar-b^{a}ar⟨i⟩e** Oꟽᑫ A⟅ᑫ A (J.10.1), 'has borne (forward)'.

k^{o}o ǂ⧗, **k^{o}** ⧗ /*ko*^{N}/ < Indo-European **kom* possibly has perfective force (expressing the completed nature of past action), as is often the case with the Old Irish preverb *con* and probably *ko* in Cisalpine Celtic *to-śo·ko-te* 'has given these' (Vercelli), in Tartessian **k^{o}t^{u}uarat^{e}e** ⋈△ᛁAPA⊟O 'has delivered, has run under' (J.53.1).

t^{e}e· O⊟ (Mesas do Castelinho) is interpreted as *dē* 'out of, away from' (with Celtic *ī* < *ē* not yet completed) or the shortened variant *dĕ*; see the verb **t^{e}e·b^{a}ant^{i}i** below.

en<u>b</u>^{e} ᗡꟽO (J.17.4) /*embi*/ or /*ambi*/, cf. Celtiberian preverb *ambi-*, Gaulish *ambi-*, Old Irish *imb·*, *imm·*, Welsh *am-* and reflexive *ym-* < Indo-European **en-b^{h}i*, **n̥-b^{h}i*. The sense of the preverb is that the action of the verb encompasses the direct object of the verb, hence **en<u>b</u>^{e}·<u>k^{a}a</u> | rne** 'has entombed'. **ea<u>n</u>b^{a}ara** Aᑫ A⟅ꟽAO (S. Martinho) probably contains this preverb/preposition; see the verb **b^{a}ara** below.

er- ᑫO 'after, afterwards, henceforth' in **er-b^{e}eŕi** (J.10.1), cf. Old Irish *íar, er* 'after(wards)'.

na-k^{i}i (J.1.2) /*nak^{w}e*/ 'and not' corresponding to Celtiberian *ne-kue* 'and not', Old Irish *na·*, *nach·*, Welsh *na, nac* 'that not, and not, than' < Indo-European **ne-k$^{u̯}$e* 'and not'.

na· (J.7.1), **ne·** (J.1.2) 'not' corresponding to Celtiberian *ne*, Gaulish *ne* < Indo-European **ne* 'not'.

-ni- ꟽᛋ 'down' < Indo-European **ni* in **o-ni-[l]ak^{a}at^{i}i-śe** OMꟽΦAΛΛAᛏꟽᛋǂ (J.10.1) 'lies down under here', cf. Old Welsh *ni-tanam* 'down under me [the memorial stone]' (Tywyn inscription).

ro ǂᑫ (J.1.1, J.3.1, J.11.4, J.12.1. J.16.3) with functions including expressing or reinforcing perfect action in the past (e.g. J.18.2 **t^{e}'-ee·ro-b^{a}are** OᑫA⟅ǂᑫOO⊟, **ro·b^{a}are** OᑫA⟅ǂᑫ (Mesas do Castelinho), **ro·b^{a}a(r)e** O A⟅ǂᑫ (J.11.1), **ro-laH^{a}a** A⊟Aᛚǂᑫ (J.3.1), corresponding exactly to Celtiberian (in *ro·biseti*), Gaulish, Old Irish, Old Breton *ro*, Old Welsh *ri* < Indo-European **pro* 'forward, ahead, &c.', showing loss of Indo-European *p* in Tartessian, a defining feature of Celtic. In J.11.5, the preverb supports an infixed pronoun, 3rd singular masculine or neuter singular **ro-n** ᛋǂᑫ. In J.18.1, the preverb appears to support an enclitic form of the verb 'to be', strongly reminiscent of Old Irish: **ro-ba** A⟅ǂᑫ. In J.55.1 **ro-** probably begins a statement concerning 'exchanging' **eert^{a}aune**, and the preverb may be understood in more than one way: possibly the meaning is that Dariuelnos is exchanged *for* (**ro**) Kolios, or **ro** may convey the completion of the action ('for having exchanged'), or **ro** may add special force to the finite verb at the ending of the statement (**ro- -naŕk^eenai** 'let them remain so').

t^uu ⵝ⊦ (J.53.1) = Cisalpine Celtic *to* used to support an infixed pronoun at Vercelli in the form *to-śo·ko-de* 'has given them/these', Old Irish *do*, Archaic Old Irish *tu*, Old Breton *do*, Old Welsh *di*. As in Old Irish, Tartessian *tu* often functions to support an infixed object pronoun. In the Tartessian examples with infix, there is elision of vowel, thus written **t^ee**, e.g. **t^e·ro-b^aare** ⵂOⴲⵌAⵀO (J.1.1, J.12.1) = **t'e·ro-bāre*, **t^e·b^aare** OⵋAⵘOⵂ (J.1.3), **t^e'-e·bar[e]** (J.16.1), **t^e'-]ea·b^aare** (J.6.1), **t^e'-e·b^aare** OⵋA[ⵌ]Oⵂ (J.18.1), **t^e'-e·b^aere** (J.7.8), **t^e'-e·[·b^a]are** OⵋA[␣]Oⵂ (J.21.1), 3rd plural **t^e'-ee·b^aaren-t^i** ⵝOⵝOⵋAⵘOOⵂ (J.23.1), and with a different 3rd plural verb in **t^e'-e·b^aant^i** ⵝOⵝAⵘOⵂ (Mesas do Castelinho). The several examples written **t^ee** may mean that *tu* + infixed pronoun *e* could be pronounced as two syllables or reflect the underlying feeling that the form comprised two words, e.g. **t^e'-ee·ro-b^aare** OⵋAⵘ‡ⵊOOⵂ (J.18.2).

o- /u̯o~/, **ua-** 'under' < Indo-European **(s)h₄upó* in **o-ni-[l]ak^at^i-śe** OⵝⵝⵝAⵋⵝⵝⵝⵘ (J.10.1) /u̯o ni lagati ᵗse/ 'lies down under here', cf. **ot^erk^a** and **omuŕik^a*[** above. The phonological variant /u̯a/, common in Brittonic, occurs in **k^ot^uaratᵉe** 'has gone under, has delivered/rescued' (J.53.1).

VERBS

-b^aa (J.1.2) ?unaccented enclitic form of **b^uu(o)** 'was, has been' below; cf. Old Irish enclitic *-b*: **ro-b^aa** Aⵌ‡ⵊ (J.18.1) 'has been': Indo-European **bʰu̯eh₂-* 'be' (Rix 2001, 98–101; Wodtko et al. 2008, 46–58).

b^aa- 'dies' < Indo-European **gʷeh₂-* 'steps, goes' (Rix 2001, 205) in the 3rd plural compound verb **t^e·b^aant^i** /de-banti/ ⵝOⵝAⵘOⵂ (Mesas do Castelinho), compare the Old Irish simplex *baïd* 'dies', *bath* 'died' < **gʷh₂-tó-*, *bath* 'death', and the

compound *dí-ba-* 'becomes extinct' (< 'goes away from'), *-dibatur* 'they became extinct' (Lewis & Pedersen 1989, §500), *dibad* 'destruction, extinction', possibly likewise Gaulish *dib(ato-)* 'end, extinction' (Delamarre 2003, 144). The common Early Welsh *difa* 'destruction, devastation, killing' is compared to the Middle Irish verb *dí-baigim* 'I destroy' by GPC, but a connection with Old Irish *dí-ba-* could also explain the phonology and meaning. **t^e·b^aant^i** immediately follows the dative proper names (**t^ilek^uurk^uu ark^aast^ab^uu**) that open the inscription and probably name the deceased. Therefore, the sense 'they pass away' suits the context. The proposed etymology implies characteristically Celtic sound change of *b* < Indo-European *gᵘ*. The position of the verb on the stone directly opposite the opening of the text and the first name **t^ilek^uurk^uu**, turning at a right angle in the middle of the suitably distorted character **n** ⵝ, may have intentional significance.

ar-b^e⟨i⟩eŕi ⵝⵝⵝOⵝOⵋA (J.12.3) compound verb 'carries forward (henceforth)' 3rd singular ?present < Celtic *are-beret, **er-b^eeŕi** ⵝⵝⵝOⵋO (J.10.1) '[this grave] carries, bears henceforth/afterwards/later' < Indo-European **bʰeret(i)*; **b^aara**** (J.4.1) probably 1st singular perfect 'I [the tomb] have carried, borne, received' < Indo-European root **bʰer-* 'carry, bear' (Wodtko et al. 2008, 15–30), ?relative 1st singular perfect **b^ar⟨u⟩a-ion** ⟨AⵝⵝAⵝ‡ⵝ 'whom I [the grave] have received' (J.7.9 [the erroneous **u** may be due to the influence of the preceding word **iru** or confusion with the present *berū 'I bear'])—simplex 3rd singular perfect **b^ar[e]** (J.1.5), **b^are** OⵋAⵌ (J.7.10, J.26.1, J.27.1), **]b^are** (J.17.2), **ab^are** OⵌA (J.52.1) with transposition of letters, **b^a[re** (J.57.1) 'has borne, carried received', **b^a(r)e** OAⵌ (J.11.1), cf. also J.16.6—compound verb perfect 3rd singular **ar-b^ar⟨i⟩e** OⵝⵌAⵌA (J.10.1) 'has borne (forward)'—compound verb 3rd singular perfect **ro·b^aare** OⵋAⵌ‡ⵊ (Mesas do Castelinho), **ro·b^aa(r)e** OAⵌ‡ⵊ (J.11.1), **ro·ba[r]e** ⵝ‡ⵌAⵝO (J.16.3), **t^e'-e·ro-b^aare** OⵝⵌAPO (J.1.1, J.12.1) and **t^e'-ee·ro-b^aare** OⵋAⵌ‡ⵊOOⵂ (J.18.2) = **t'e·ro-bāre* 'has received it/him' with preverbs *ro* and *tu*, the former supporting an infixed object pronoun, masculine singular *en* or neuter *e(d)*, **tᵉe·bᵃare** ᴏ9ᴀƷᴏᴇ (J.1.3), **tᵉe·bar[e]** (J.16.1), **t̲ᵉ̲'-e·bᵃare** ᴏ9ᴀ[Ʒ]ᴏᴇ(J.18.1), **t̲ᵉ̲'-e·[bᵃ]are** ᴏ9ᴀ[ ]ᴏᴇ (J.21.1), (cf. tᵉ'-]ea·bᵃare [J.6.1]) = **t̲ᵉ̲-e bāre* 'has borne, received it/him'; cf. Old Irish *da beir* 'gives it' < Celtic **t̲ᵉ̲-e beret(i)*. **tᵉ'-e·bᵃere** 'has received it' (J.7.8) shows the vocalism of the present stem *ber-*, though the consonant grapheme **bᵃ** anticipates the usual vowel of the perfect *bāre*; possibly this form can be read as imperfect (with the present stem and ending *-e* < Indo-European **bʰeret*) rather than perfect. **tᵃa-e·bᵃare** ᴏ9ᴀƷᴏᴀх (J.14.1) may show that the preverb and infixed pronoun could be pronounced, or at least carefully sounded out, as two syllables with differing qualities. The 3rd plural perfect occurs as **bᵃar(e)n** (J.20.1), **tᵉ'-ee· bᵃarentⁱi** ᴍᴏʏᴏ9ᴀƷᴏᴏᴇ (J.23.1), and as **ro-n·baren** ʏᴏ9ᴀʏᵻ9 (J.11.4), in which the perfective preverb supports an accusative infixed pronoun. Cf. Old Irish *beirid* 'bears, carries, takes, &c.', *da beir* 'gives it' < Celtic **t̲ᵉ̲-e beret(i)*. Tartessian **bᵃare** may show *a* < Proto-Celtic *e* (**beret*) or more probably **bāre* using an Indo-European perfect formation with Celtic *ā* < *ō* as in **kᵒtᵘuaratᵉe** ᴍ ∆ʰᴀᴘᴀʜᴏ (J.53.1) 'has saved, delivered' below, cf. also the Vedic Sanskrit perfect *ja-bhāra* 'has brought' (Rix 2001, 77). The uncertainty over the vowel in first singular **bᵒoara** ▢/ᵻᴀ9ᴀ (J.2.1) may reflect older *bōra*, before Indo-European /ō/ had fully changed to Celtic /ā/. **eanbᵃara** ᴀ9ᴀʒʏᴀᴏ (S. Martinho) is possibly a compound of this verb, if from **ambi-bāra*, meaning 'I have carried around' (this form is inscribed within a long text written in a complete anticlockwise circle), cf. Old Irish *imm beir* 'operates, wields, plays', literally 'carries around' < Celtic **ambi beret(i)*.

bᵒotⁱir 9ʏᴛᵻ▢ (J.7.1) /bōdir/ or /boudir/ 3rd plural middle perfect verb 'they have been awakened', cf. Old Irish *ro-bud*, Middle Welsh *ry-bub* 'warning', *bob* 'awareness, free will, &c.' < Celtic **budā*, Sanskrit *bōdhati* 'is awake, is aware of' (Lewis & Pedersen 347), Indo-European **bʰeudʰ-* 'make aware, pay attention, be observant' (Rix 2001, 82–3).

bᵒolon ʏᵻᴛ▢ (J.7.1) 3rd plural active verb, ?present or imperfect indicative 'they are/were dead'. If the former, the absence of -tⁱi may reflect a development like that of the 'Insular Celtic' conjunct verbal endings, in which a shorter form of the verb is used where there are one or more preverbal elements, here **na** 'not' as well as the subject noun. The -*o*- in the root syllable might alternatively indicate a perfect formation, 'they have not died'. Cf. Old Irish *at baill* 'dies', Early Welsh *aballaf* 'I (shall) perish' (Marwnad Cunedda), Sanskrit *galati* 'drops, disappears', Old English *cwelan* 'to die' (Lewis & Pedersen §502), Lithuanian *gālas* 'end, death': Indo-European root **gʷelH-* (Rix 2001, 207–8). Tartessian **bᵒolon** shows diagnostically Celtic *b* from Indo-European *gʷ*.

bᵘu(o) (J.1.2) 'was, has been' < Celtic **bou(e)* corresponding to Old Irish substantive verb *boí* 'there was', Old Welsh *bu* 'was', Indo-European root **bʰueh₂-* 'be' (Rix 2001, 98–101).

ibᵒoiion ʏᵻʏʏᵻᴇʏ (J.4.1) resembles a verb with a suffixed relative, like **kᵃafner-ion** (J.7.2), but the sense 'that I drink' is difficult to construe in the context.

(to-)kᵃaltᵉe ᴏᴇᴧᴧ (J.1.1)   cf. Lepontic *kalite* (Vergiate) ?'has made a funerary monument', possibly with Celtic preverb/'sentence connective' *tu/to* (see above). More probably, a dative singular *ā*-stem group name, see above.

kᵃafner-ion ᴧᴀᴋʏᴏ9ᴍᵻʏ (J.7.2) 'to whom funerary monuments that have been built', perfect middle 3rd plural with suffixed relative (possibly again in **kᵃa[fn]ir-ion** [J.1.3]); cf. Cisalpine Gaulish KARNITU (Todi) 'built a stone funerary monument', plural KARNITUS 'they built a stone funerary monument' (Briona); compound verb, perfect active 3rd singular **enbᵉ· kᵉa | rne** ᴏʏ9 | ᴀʏᴅᴍᴏ (J.17.4) /embi karne/ 'has entombed' (but this reading is doubtful). It is widely thought that KARNITU, &c., are verbs derived from a noun, Celtic **karnom* 'stone funerary monument'. However, in the light of the early attestation of the verbal forms, the reverse development is worth considering, that is, Celtic **karn-* in the first instance being a verb ('to build a stone funerary monument') and the noun being derived from that.

ro-laɃa ΑɃΑ˥‡٩ (J.3.1) ?= ro-laHᵃa *or* ro-lakᵘa /*ro lāga*/ 1st singular perfect 'I have lain down', possibly 1st singular present l̲a̲k̲ⁱiuu ٨٨ϻφΑ˥ 'I [this stone/grave/the deceased] lie down' (Mesas do Castelinho; see Guerra, above 73): Indo-European **legᵇ-* 'lie'; cf. Old Irish suppletive perfect *ro-laa, ro-lá* 'has placed' 3rd singular; 3rd singular compound verb **o-ni-[l]akᵃatⁱi-śe** ΟϻϻΦΑΛΑ⇑ϻϻ‡ (J.10.1) /*u̯o ni lagăti 'se*/ 'lies down under here', 3rd plural **lakⁱintⁱi** ΓΑφΝΥ⇑Ν (J.12.4), **lakᵉentⁱi** ΓΑΚΟϻΦΝ (J.53.1) /*lāginti*/ 'they have lain' or /*laginti*/ 'they lie down'. **la[**]Α˥ (J.52.1) probably belongs here. As Dagmar Wodtko suggests to me, the latter three forms may reflect *ā*-stem formation, with raising of *ā* before *nt* in the 3rd plural. Such a stem could be either present indicative or subjunctive. The same root is reflected in Old Irish *laigid* 'lies down', which may show that the stem **lag-* existed in Common Celtic. The Gaulish verbs LEGASIT (Bourges) and LOGITOE (Néris-les-Bains) also belong to this root. In context, both require a past tense transitive meaning, 'caused to lie down, placed, offered'. LEGASIT appears to be based on an Indo-European *s*-aorist. It is less clear what historical tense LOGITOE belongs to, but the ending is reminiscent of Cisalpine KARNITU 'built a stone funerary monument', also clearly past tense.

naŕkᵉe ΟϳΚΑΥ (J.1.1, J.7.8, J.26.1, J.27.1, J.57.1, S. Martinho, ?Corte Freixo) 3rd singular ?imperfect or present ('… which remain[s] fixed, unmoving; rests in peace'); possibly 1st singular present at Corte Freixo **]naŕkᵉeuu[**]٨٨ΟϳΚΑΥ[, 1st singular present relative **na]ŕkᵉeo-io*** *‡ϻ‡ΟϳΚ[(J.16.2) ?'I who lie still/dead'; 3rd singular present tense with primary ending **naŕkᵉetⁱi** ϻΦΟϳΚΑΥ (J.56.1). **naŕkᵉentⁱi** ϻΦϻΟϳΚΑΥ (J.12.1, J.16.1, J.17.2, J.18.1, J.19.2), **[n]aŕkᵉentⁱi** (J.1.5), **na]ŕkᵉentⁱi[** (J.4.3), **naŕkᵉe]ntⁱi** ϻΦϻ̲Ο̲ϳΚΑΥ (J.11.5); note also **naŕkᵉeni** (J.1.2, J.1.3, J.7.2), **naŕkᵉenii** (J.2.1), **n[aŕkᵉe]enii** (J.6.1)), probably identical to naŕkᵉ[e̲n̲i̲ ϻϻΟ*]ϳΚΑΥ (J.15.3), **naŕkᵉenii** ϻϻϻΟϳΚΑΥ (J.2.1), **n(a)ŕkᵉenii** ϻϻϻΟϳΚΥ (J.11.1), **n]aŕkᵉenii** ΝΑϷΚΟϻΝΝ (J.11.3), **naŕ]kᵉenii** (J.19.1), **naŕkᵉenii** ϻϻϻΟϳΚΑΥ

(J.21.1), **naŕrkᵉe:n:** Υ|ΟϳφΚΑΥ (J.23.1), and probably **naŕ[kᵉenii** (J.17.1) are 3rd plural and appear to have the Indo-European active primary ending *-nti*; 3rd plural middle **naŕkᵉenai** (J.7.1, J.55.1), 3rd plural with active secondary ending and no suffix **naŕkᵉen** (J.7.5), **naŕk̲e̲[en]** [ΥΟ]ϳΚΑΥ (Mesas do Castelinho). (J.7.8) could also be read as 3rd plural **naŕken** with **n-** from the following line. There is also a line break in J.14.1 **naŕkᵉe | n** Υ|ΟϳΚΑΥ. Note also the fragmentary **naŕ[ke** Οϳ]ΚΑΥ (J.9.1). Note also **]n/aŕ[kᵉen . . .** (J.15.2), **naŕkᵉe[**]ΟϳΚΑΥ (J.17.3; Vale de Águia); **naŕkᵉe̲n̲** ΥΟϳΚΑΥ (J.20.1).

On the root and meaning, in the absence of obvious Celtic parallels, cf. Greek ναρκάω 'grow stiff, numb, dead' < Indo-European **(s)ner-* 'bind, fasten with thread or cord'. In the recurring formulaic words of the Tartessian inscriptions, various forms of the verb **naŕkᵉentⁱi**, &c., most usually occur at the end of the inscription, where they may express, as an injunction, the permanence of the resting place of the deceased, the stone, and words of the inscription itself, as 'bound, fixed, permanent (carved in stone)'. The most usual orientation of the inscriptions, as an anticlockwise circle or spiral, may likewise be meant to affect the closing or binding of the inscriptional statement. In these, **naŕkᵉe** (&c.) often occurs at the final turning of the direction of the anticlockwise written text. Functionally, as a near-obligatory liturgical element, the force would be much like 'so be it, amen'. However, the sense of the similar Greek verb ('stiffen, die') would also suit funerary inscriptions in its literal meaning, or as an artful interplay of the literal and metaphoric. As *-e-* appears consistently through the paradigm an original Indo-European *-ei̯e/o-* stem is possible, as Dagmar Wodtko has suggested to me. That could explain why *-e-* occurs in all attested forms of the paradigm, thus contrasting with the verb **bᵒolon** (J.7.1), which shows that *o* of the Indo-European thematic 3rd plural *-ont* survived in Tartessian. A suffixed formation like that found in Old Irish *arcu* 'I entreat, ask' < Indo-European **pr̥k'-sk'e/o-* is also possible (thus zero-grade **nr̥(k)-sk'e/o-*), though that is not necessary to explain Tartessian /*nark-*/, as the predicted Celtic **nrik-* < Indo-European zero-grade **nr̥-k-* was probably impossible (see below). A less probable alternative is that naŕk[e]- results from a metathesis of k[a]arn- '(builds) a stone funerary monument' above.

t[e]e·b[a]ant[i]i /*de-banti*/ 'they pass away', see b[a]a- 'dies' above and t[e]e for the preverb.

eert[a]aune ΟΥΉΑΧ9ΟΟ (J.55.1), ert[a]au[ne] ΉΑΧ9Ο (J.54.1) = Celtiberian *uertaunei* (Botorrita; cf. Ballester 2004, 119), usually interpreted as the dative of a verbal noun, though various meanings and etymologies have been proposed (see Untermann, MLH 4.529). The most suitable of these meanings here would be 'to exchange, sell', Welsh *gwerthu* < Indo-European **u̯ert-* 'turn' (Rix 2001, 691–2).

(t[a]a-)oret[o]o ‡ΔΟ9‡(ΑΧ) (J.4.1.) /*(tə) u̯o reto-*/ verbal noun, *o*-stem 'to help, save, deliver', literally 'to run under' (Indo-European **reth₂-* 'run'), Gaulish *uoreto-* in names (?cf. the North-western Hispano-Celtic personal name VRETA [Albertos 1985, 302]), Old Irish *fo·reith*, Old Welsh *guoret*, Middle Welsh *gwaret*, *dywaret*, &c.; perfect singular k[o]t[u]uarat[e]e ⋈ΔΡΑΡΑΗΟ (J.53.1) /*ko(n) tu u̯a rāte*/ 'has saved, delivered'; cf. Old Irish *fu·rráith* = Old Welsh *guo-raut* 'he saved, helped' < 'has run under' < Celtic **(u)u̯o-rāte*.

uurk[e]e Ο)Ι944 (J.1.4) 'has made', perfect 3rd singular of the Indo-European root **u̯erǵ-* 'make, work'. The Early Welsh *guoreu* and Middle Breton *gueureu* 'did, made' reflect a reduplicated perfect **u̯e-u̯rāge* based on a variant form of the root **u̯reǵ-* found throughout the Brittonic paradigm. The Brittonic past tense forms, Middle Breton 3rd singular *greaz*, Welsh *gwnaeth*, show that British had a *t*-preterite formation **wraχt-* or **wreχt-* from the Indo-European aorist alongside the Indo-European perfect (whence *guoreu*, &c.). The spelling uurk[e]e may or may not represent reduplication in Tartessian, thus /*(u̯a)u̯orge*/, cf. Greek perfect 3rd singular ἔοργε, Avestan *vauuarəza* (Rix 2001, 686–7). Alternatively, *Uŕke-* occurs as an Iberian name element.

INFLEXIONAL CATEGORIES

NOUNS AND PRONOUNS

nominative singular

(1) *o-stem*: ak[o]olio**ś** Μ‡Μ(↑)‡⋈Α (J.56.1), soloir ‡‡Γ‡ΜP (J.11.3), t[i]irt[o]os ‡‡Α9ΜΟ (J.1.2), ooŕoir 9Μ‡Λ‡‡ (J.19.2), (o)ira Α9Μ‡ (J.1.2) /*u̯irə(s)*/, uarb[o]oiir 9ΜΜ‡θ9ΑΥ (J.22.1). (Note: the apparent weakening and loss of the nominative singular termination, Indo-European *-os*, is not general, but limited to *u̯iros* 'man, &c.' and compounds ending in *-u̯iros*, as in Latin.)

(2) *ā-stem*: b[o]ot[i]i☆ana ΑΥΑ☆ΜΟ‡□ (J.18.1), **‡**ait[u]ura Α9ΥΛΥΑ**‡** (J.15.1), iub[a]a Α3ΥΜ (J.7.8), k[u]uik[a]aosa Α‡*ΑΛΥΥ**θ** (J.17.1),]uult[i]ina ΑΥΜΟ1ΥΥ[(J.12.3), k[a]aset[a]ana ΛΑΜΟΧΑ**Υ**Α (J.53.1), orb[a]a ‡P**‡**Α (J.53.1), set[a]a ‡ΟΧΑ (J.53.1), omuŕik[a]*[‡ΜΡΝ**Υ**Λ*[(J.16.2).

(3) *i-stem*: ?k[i]inb[a]ai↑i ΥΤΥΑ**3**ΥΜΡ (J.3.1).

(4) *consonant-stem*: aib[u]uris[   ]‡Μ94**⋈**ΥΑ (J.3.1).

genitive singular

(1) *o-stem* (a. Hispano-Celtic type): k[o]oŕb[e]o ‡**d**Ν‡⋈ (J.53.1), k[e]ert[o]o ‡Α9Ο)Ι (J.18.1).

(b. Gaulish/Goidelic type): ooŕoire Ο9Μ‡Λ‡‡ (J.19.1) /*u̯oru̯irī*/, leb[o]o-iire Ο9ΜΜ‡□Ο1 / *lemou̯irī*/ (Mesas do Castelinho).

(2) *ā-stem*: mut[u]uirea ΑΟ9ΜΥΔΥΜ (J.1.5), saruneea ΑΟΟΥΥ9Α‡ (J.22.1, J.22.2), t[u]urea ΑΟ9ΥΔ (J.7.8), cf. ogamic Primitive Irish -IAS < *[-*iiās*], later also -EAS, -EA (McManus 1991, 115).

dative singular

(1) *o-stem* /*-ūi*/ > /*-u*/: aark[u]ui ΥΥΗ9ΑΑ (J.7.6), alb[o]oroi Υ‡9‡□1Α (J.24.1), -sek[u]ui ΥΥΗΟ‡[(J.1.4), sab[o]oi Υ‡θΑ‡ (J.5.1), salsaloi ‡ΑΓ‡ΑΓ‡Ν (J.12.4), t[u]uŕek[u]ui ΥΥθΟΛΥΑ (J.14.1), ΝΙΕΘΩΙ, alk[u]u ΥΗ1Α (J.12.1), isak[a]aoe Ο‡ΑΛΑ‡Μ (J.24.1), uuŕsaau̱ ΥΑΑ‡9ΥΥ (J.16.1), t[i]ilek[u]uŕk[u]u Υθ94θΟ1ΜΟ (Mesas do Castelinho).

(2) *ā-stem* /-āi/ > /-e/: **asune** ΟႸႿ‡Ⴈ (J.4.1), **bᵉetⁱisai** ႸႴ‡ⴹ09 (J.23.1), **kⁱielaoe** Ο‡Ⴈ10ႸႵ (J.11.1) *or masculine o-stem dative of* *Kelau̯os*, **leoine** ΟႸႿ‡Ο1 (J.10.1), **meleśae** ΟႴႿΟ10Ⴍ (J.15), si]kᵉeuuakᵉe ΟႨႴႸႸΟ)((J.7.8), **bᵃane** ΟႸႴჃ (J.11.1, J.19.1, J.26.1), **bᵃaenae** ΟႴႸΟႴჃ (J.15.1), *probably* **kᵃaltᵉe** ΟႨ1ႴႱ (J.1.1) *and* **nira-kᵃaltᵉe** ΟႨ1ႴႱႱႴႸႸ (Mesas do Castelinho).

(3) *i-stem*: **Ɛatᵃaneatᵉe** ƐႴႾႴႿΟႴႾΟ (J.12.1).

(4) *u-stem*: *possibly* **aŕaiui** ႸჄႴΡႴ (J.1.1).

(5) *consonant-stem*: **ariariśe** ΟႿႸ9ႴႸ9Ⴈ (J.10.1).

accusative singular

(1) *o-stem*: **kᵒolion** Ⴘ‡Ⴘ1‡ⴻ (J.55.1),]kᵒoloion (Monte Novo do Castelinho), **tᵃarielnon** ႶႴΡႸႭ1Ⴘ+Ⴘ (J.55.1), lokᵒon (J.57.1), **lokᵒon** Ⴘ‡ⴼ‡1 (J.1.1), **tᵃalainon** ⴸ‡ႸႿႴ1ႴႶ (J.14.1, *or neuter*).

(2) *ā-stem*:]kᵃanan ႸႴႸႴ(Ⴅ)[(J.9.1).

(3) *i-stem*: **bᵉe:lin** ႸႸ1|09 (J.17.4), **kᵉenilarin** ႸႸ9Ⴈ1ႸႭ0)((J.17.4).

-iion, -ion (suffixed relative), **śaen** ႸΟႴႿ (J.27.1 demonstrative pronoun), **-e** (J.1.1, J.1.3 enclitic pronoun).

locative singular

(1) *o-stem/io-stem*: **bᵃastᵉebᵘuŕoi** ⴸ‡ⴻႸႾⴼΟႵ‡ႴჃ (S. Martinho), *less probably* **sabᵒoi** ⴸ‡ⴲႴ‡ (J.5.1), **kⁱinbᵃai(tⁱ)i** ႸⴹႸႴჃႸႸႵ (J.3.1), ?a(a/m)musokᵉeonii Ⴈ*ⴍⴲ‡‡)(Ο‡ႸႴჄ (J.1.5), ?tᵉasiioonii ႸႸႵ‡‡Ⴘ‡Ⴔⴲ (J.1.1).

(2) *ā-stem*: **aliśne** ΟႸႿႸ1Ⴈ (J.11.5.), **uśnee** ΟΟႸႸ (J.23.1).

instrumental singular, ā-stem:

?anbᵃatⁱia ⴈႾ‡ⴈ0ႴႴ (J.16.2) ?'as a stand-in grave, with a cenotaph'.

nominative plural: **sieś** ⴹ0ⴸ‡ (J.12.1. pronoun).

nominative/accusative neuter plural o-stem: **otᵉerkᵃa** ႴႱ9ОႵ‡ (J.1.4).

genitive plural

(1) *o-stem*: <u>l</u>iirnestᵃakᵘun ႸႴႲႴႾ‡ΟႸႸႸ1 (J.19.1), **nemun** ႸႸⴍΟႸ (J.7.8), **tᵃarnekᵘun** ႸႸႸⴵΟႸ9ႴႾ (J.26.1), *less probably* **tᵃalainon** ⴸ‡ႸႸႴ1ႴႾ (J.14.1).

(2) *i-stem*: <u>b</u>ᵉeliśon Ⴈ‡ⴍႸ109 (J.20.1).

dative/ablative plural

]ebᵒo ‡ⴲО[(J.7.8),]aibᵒo ‡ⴲႸႴ[(J.28.1),]aetᵉabᵒo*[ ]ႴО‡Ⴔⴹ‡[(J.28.1),]antᵒonbᵒ<u>o</u> ‡ⴲ‡Ⴔ9Ⴈ[(J.8.1), **bᵉelibᵒo** ‡ⴲႸ109 (J.1.2), (kᵃakⁱ)iśiinkᵒolobᵒo ‡ⴲ‡1‡ⴷႸႸႸႸႸ9ႴႱ (J.1.1), **lokᵒobᵒo** ‡ⴲ‡ⴷ‡1 (J.1.1), **niirabᵒo** ‡ⴲႴ9ႸႸ (J.1.1),]onlinbᵒo ‡ⴲႸႸ1Ⴥ‡ (J.11.2), **rinoebᵒo** ΡႸႸ‡Οⴲ‡ (J.5.1), istᵃ[a]ibᵒo (J.5.1 demonstrative pronoun), anakᵉenak<u>e</u>:eibᵒo ‡ⴱႴО|)(ႴႸႴ)(ႴႸႴ (J.5.1 group adjective), **ebᵘu alakⁱimuŕbᵒ** ?ⴲ)(ႸႸႸ9ႴႲႴ)(ⴼО (S. Martinho), **arkᵃastᵃab<u>u</u>u** ႸⴺႴX‡ႴႱ9Ⴈ (Mesas do Castelinho).

instrumental plural (pronoun)

ebᵉe ОႨО (J.9.1), **ebᵉ** ОႨ (J.16.3).

neuter superlative singular nouns

tᵘnkⁱitᵉsbᵃan ⴈႶႸ)(ⴹ‡ⴲႴႸ (J.53.1), **uarbᵃan** ႸႴⴲ9ႴႸ (J.1.2, J.3.1, J.4.1, J.21.1), **uabᵃan** ႸႴⴲႴႸ (J.16.5).

VERBS

?present 1st singular

]naŕkᵉeuu[ ]ႸႸΟ)(ⴺႴႸ[(Corte Freixo) 'I lie still', <u>l</u>akⁱiuu ႸႸⴹ9Ⴈ1 (Mesas do Castelinho) 'I lie down'.

?present 1st singular relative

na]ŕkᵉeo-io* *‡ႸႸ‡О)(ⴺ[(J.16.2) ?'I who rests/ lies dead . . .' (J.16.2 with suffixed relative). This form may show that the older ō in the verbal ending was preserved before the relative suffix, but **o** here might be purely orthographic: note that this same inscription has **iob^aa**, contrasting with **iub^aa** in J.7.8.

present 3rd singular

ar-b^e⟨i⟩eŕi ꓬꓘOꓬꓷꟼA (J.12.3), **er-b^eŕi** ꓬꓘOꓷꟼO (J.10.1), **o-ni-[l]ak^aat^i-śe** OꟽꟽⴹＡＬＡＴꓬꓬꟽ≠ (J.10.1) /u̯o ni lagati ˈse/ 'lies down under here', **naŕk^ee** OꓘꟽＡꓬ (J.1.1, J.7.8, J.26.1, J.27.1, J.57.1), possibly **naŕk^eei̲i** (J.1.3), **naŕk^eet^i** ꓬⴹOꓘꟽＡꓬ (J.56.1).

present 3rd plural active

naŕk^eeni (J.1.2, J.7.2), **naŕk^eent^i** ꓬⴹOꓬOꓘꟽＡꓬ (J.12.1, J.16.1, J.17.2, J.18.1, J.19.2), **naŕk^eenii** (J.2.1), **naŕken** (J.7.5). (J.7.8), **lak^iint^i** ꙆＡꟼꓬꙏꙆꓬ (J.12.4), **lak^eent^i** ꙆＡꓘOꓬⴹꓜ (J.53.1), cf. Lusitanian DOENTI 'they give' < *dōnti (Schmidt 1985, 337). Note also]nt^i at the end of the fragmentary inscription from Monte Novo do Castelinho.

3rd plural middle

naŕk^eenai (J.7.1, J.55.1).

[NOTE. In the past tenses, the type known in comparative Celtic grammar as the 'suffixless preterite' or 'ā-preterite', which is derived from the Indo-European perfect, is well represented in Tartessian. These forms are classified and translated here as perfect (expressing completed action) rather than as a simple past tense (preterite). However, the fact that the 'perfectivizing' Celtic preverbs **ro** (repeatedly) and **k^o** (once) are used with such etymologically perfect verbal forms suggests that Indo-European perfect might already have given rise to—or was merging into—a simple Celtic past tense in Tartessian, so that an additional marker was required to clarify the perfect aspect, as in early medieval Goidelic and Brittonic.]

perfect 1st singular

b^aara** (J.4.1), **b^aar⟨u⟩a-ion** (J.7.9 with suffixed relative), **ro-la(?k^u)a** AⴹＢＡꙏ≠ꟼ (J.3.1).

imperfect 3rd singular

?t^e'-e·b^aere 'received it' (J.7.8), very probably a spelling error for common formulaic **t^e'-e·(ro-)b^aare**,

under the analogical influence of the vowel of the present-stem.

imperfect 3rd plural

?na·b^oolon ꓬ≠ꓕ≠□ (J.7.1).

perfect 3rd singular

-b^aa (J.1.2 enclitic), **ro-b^aa** Aꓜ≠ꟼ (J.18.1), **b^aare** OꟼAꓜ (J.7.10, J.26.1, J.27.1), **ro-b^aare** OꟼAꓜ≠ꟼ (Mesas do Castelinho), **ro-b^aa(r)e** O Aꓜ≠ꟼ (J.11.1), **t^e'-e·ro-b^aare** ꟼOꟼ≠ＡꟼO (J.1.1, J.12.1), and **t^e'-ee·ro-b^aare** OꟼAꓜ≠ꟼOOꓭ (J.18.2), **k^ot^uuarat^e·e** ꓚⴹ ＾ＡꟼＡꓭO (J.53.1), **b^uu(o)** (J.1.2), possibly **k^aalt^e·e** OꓛꙆＡＬ (J.1.1), **enb_e·k_ea|rne** Oꟼꟼ|AꓘⴹꓬO (J.17.4), **uurk^ee** Oꓘꟽꓭꓭ (J.1.4).

[NOTE: Villar (1997, 931–2) interprets Celtiberian *kombalkez* and *terturez* as 3rd singular perfects in which the Indo-European secondary ending *-t* (whence Celtiberian *-z*) has been added to the inherited 3rd-person singular perfect ending *-e*. Although we do not see such an innovation in Tartessian **b^aare, -rat^e·e, k^aalt^e·e, -k_ea|rne**, and **uurk^ee**, the writing system did not permit the representation of word-final stops, so it is not impossible that the spellings mean /bāret, rātet/, &c.]

perfect 3rd plural active

b^aar(e)n[(J.20.1), **ro-n·baren** ꓬOꟼAꓜꓬ≠ꟼ (J.11.4), **t^e'-ee·b^aarent^i** ꓬⴹOꓬOꟼAꓜOOꓭ (J.23.1).

perfect 3rd plural medio-passive

b^oot^i̲r ꟼꓬ＾≠□ (J.7.1), **k^aaŕner-ion** ＬＡꓘꓬOꟼ-ꓬ≠ꓬ (J.7.2 with suffixed relative), possibly also **k^aa̲[ŕn]ir-ion** (J.1.3).

3rd plural uncertain mood and tense, possibly present indicative

t^e·b^aant^i ꓬⴹꓬAꓜOꓭ (Mesas do Castelinho).

verbal nouns

eert^aaune OꓬꓬAꓮꟼOO (J.55.1 dative), **(t^aa-)oret^oo** ≠ⴹOꟼ≠(Aꓮ) (J.4.1. nominative).

NOTES ON SYNTAX AND WORD ORDER

There are a number of obvious obstacles preventing a straightforward recovery of Tartessian syntax: the small size of the extant corpus, outstanding uncertainties of interpretation, the high proportion of fragmentary texts, the elliptical and probably formulaic ordering of elements demanded by the funerary context. Owing to the last consideration, the corpus might be more accurately taken as reflecting the Tartessian 'funerary inscriptional statement', rather than the Tartessian sentence. Nonetheless, there are few noteworthy recurrent patterns, and some examples show ordering of elements strikingly similar to patterns known from better-attested Celtic languages.

THE POSITION OF THE VERB

The finite verb **naŕkᵉeni**, &c., which occurs frequently in the formulaic language of the inscriptions, often appears at or near the ending of the statement (for example J.1.2, J.1.3, J.1.5, J.2.1, J.7.5, J.11.1, J.14.1, J.16.1, J.16.3, J.17.2, J.18.1, J.19.1, J.19.2, J.21.1, J.22.1, J.23.1, J.26.1, J.55.1; cf. J.7.1, J.11.4, J.11.5). J.56.1 **akᵒolioś naŕkᵉetⁱi** has been recognized as a simple sentence comprising a nominative singular name as subject of a 3rd singular verb, in that order. The fragmentary inscription from Monte Novo do Castelinho seems to end with a 3rd plural verb. These examples could favour the possibility that Tartessian, like Celtiberian and several other Ancient Indo-European languages, had a basic verb-final word order. However, this placement may also have had a semantic or logical factor behind it, if, as proposed here, the sense of **naŕkᵉeni**, &c., is basically 'remain fixed unmoving'. That would be the final thought in the funerary statement: the grave has been constructed, it has received (**bᵃare**) the remains and grave goods, then finally it all remains unaltered (in perpetuity). Cf. J.1.3 **tᵉ'-e·bᵃare naŕkᵉeni** '[this grave] has received him; they remain unmoving', **]bᵒoara naŕkᵉenii** 'I [the grave] have received . . . They rest unmoving' (J.2.1). **sieś naŕkᵉentⁱi** (J.12.1) is unusual in this respect, with **naŕkᵉentⁱi** preceding the **tᵉ'-e·ro-bᵃare** formula, as well as being a unique example of what appears to be a nominative pronoun or demonstrative preceding the verb as its subject. J.12.1's final segment **Hᵃatᵃaneatᵉe**, a dative singular?, appears unusual both syntactically and as regards the physical layout of letters on the stone, turning outwards, rather than spiralling inwards, as demanded by the image of the warrior at the centre. In J.12.4, the verb **lakⁱintⁱi** 'they lie down, they have lain down' ends the statement.

    iraś-en bᵃare (J.7.10) is interpreted as 'the man has received it': nominative subject + enclitic object pronoun + verb.

    Examples of possible verb-medial statements include: . . . s̲ekᵘui uurkᵉe otᵉerkᵃa . . . '. . . [X] has made a grave for [S]egos . . .' (J.1.4), where the verb is simplex without preverbs or enclitics; **aibᵘuris[| kⁱinbᵃai↑ⁱi | ro-la⊟ᵃa | uarbᵃanubᵘ[u |]i** (J.3.1).

    With J.53.1 **kᵒ-tᵘ-ua-ratᵉe** . . . 'has run under', a past-tense verb compounded with three preverbs, but no infixed pronouns, begins the statement, a pattern that anticipates a common pattern in Old Irish syntax.

    A possible example of a preverb detached from the verb (tmesis) is J.55.1 **r̲o- kᵒolion eertᵃaune**.

THE VERBAL COMPLEX

In the formulaic t^e'-e·ro-b^{a}are 'has received it/him' (J.1.1, J.1.3, and t^e'-ee·ro-b^{a}are J.18.2), the sequence of elements is preverb + enclitic accusative pronoun + perfective preverb ro + verb. In a variant of the formula, the preverb and infix are present without the perfective ro: t^e'-e· b^{a}are (J.1.3, J.7.8, J.16.1, J.18.1, J.21.1), t^{a}a-e·b^{a}are (J.14.1), 3rd plural t^e'-ee·b^{a}arent^{i}i (J.23.1). It is possible that the Indo-European perfect had, without ro < *pro, already lost its perfective sense in Tartessian, as in Goidelic and Brittonic, so that t^e'-e·b^{a}are meant 'received it/him', as a simple past tense. These syntactic structures (preverb+infix[+preverb. . .] +verb) are common to the early Celtic languages and abundantly attested in Old Irish. In J.11.1 ro·b^{a}a(r)e, ro and the past perfect verb occur without the first preverb or infix, a structure also well attested in Old Irish and (with ry < ro < pro) in Early Welsh. In J.11.4 ro-n·b^{a}aren there appears to be an infixed element between ro and the verb, such as an elided form of the 3rd singular accusative masculine pronoun *en 'him'. In J.10.1, o(?t^i)er-b^{c}e/ŕi and ar-b^{a}ar⟨i⟩e are probably also examples of preverbs compounded with the verb ber- 'carry', likewise ar-b^c⟨i⟩eŕi (J.12.3). Simplex b^{a}are occurs in the same formulaic context in J.22.1, J.26.1, and J.27.1, cf. J.52.1. J.7.1 . . . na·b^{o}olon can be read as a statement-final 3rd-plural verb preceded by the negative particle, and J.17.4 . . . enb^c·k^{a}arne as a statement-final compound verb, 'has entombed'. J.10.1 o-ni-↑ak^{a}at^{i}i-s′e is interpreted as 'he lies down under here', a 3rd singular verb with two preverbal particles and a pronominal or demonstrative suffix, a structure found in other Celtic languages, especially common in Old Irish. The proliferation of preverbs, so characteristic of the word-formation patterns of the Insular Neo-Celtic languages, is anticipated in J.53.1 k^o-t^u-ua-rat^{e}e. In this formation k^o- possibly reinforces the perfective aspect of the verb rat^{e}e—a function also attested for Old Irish com/con· and probably also in Cisalpine Celtic to-so·ko-te 'has given these' (Vercelli)—but it could also have semantic force, i.e. 'has run under together with'.

NOUN PHRASES WITHIN THE STATEMENT

In J.1.1, the statement begins with the dative divine name lok^{o}ob^{o}o niirab^{o}o, probably modified by a following adjectival group name, 'invoking the Lugoues of the Neri'. J.5.1 ist^a[a] | ib^{o}o rinoeb^{o}o | anak^{e}enak^e:e | ib^{o}o similarly shows datives plural in concord. Like J.1.1, J.17.2 seems to begin with a dative/ablative plural k^{u}uiarairb^{u}b^u[u . . . In J.3.1 aib^{u}uris[is possibly the name of the deceased as a detached nominative noun phrase at the beginning of the statement. In J.11.3 soloir uarb^{a}an . . . is interpreted as an initial nominative, naming the deceased, accompanied by a predicative epithet ('who is of the highest rank'). J.19.2, J.22.1 apparently begin with the name of the deceased in the nominative, ooŕoir < *ueruiros and uarb^{o}oiir *uermo-uiros. The surviving fragmentary text of J.12.3 begins with the apparent nominative name]uult^{i}ina.

J.7.5 aark^{u}ui . . . and J.10.1 ariariśe . . . begin with dative singular masculine names, probably naming the deceased, similarly J.11.1 k^{i}ielaoe . . . (or the full noun phrase k^{i}ielaoe | oiśaH^{a}a b^{a}ane . . .), probably also J.16.1 uuŗsaau . . . The statement begins with a dative singular noun in J.7.9, iru 'for the man/hero/husband', once more probably referring to the deceased. J.12.1 iru alk^{u}u . . . again begins with 'for the man' followed by another masculine o-stem dative singular probably referring to the deceased. J.5.1 sab^{o}oi . . . can be read as an initial locative singular ('in Samos') or as a further example of an initial dative singular, naming the deceased ('for Sabos, Samos'). The opening of the long San Martinho inscription bᵃastᶜebᵘuŕoi . . . could also be locative singular. J.14.1 begins tᵃalainon tᵘuŕekᵘui, in which a noun in another case (accusative or nominative/accusative neuter) precedes what is probably the name of the deceased in the dative; this initial noun is interpreted as expressing what the deceased is to receive, 'the place of the fair/blessed headland, i.e. Sacrum Promontorium, Sagres'. A noun in another case also appears to precede a phrase in the dative singular in J.15.1, Hᵃaitᵘura Meleśae*: : bᵃaenae* 'H. for the woman Meliśa'. J.18.1 begins with a nominative singular personal name bᵒotⁱi⚹ana, presumably the name of the deceased.

THE SYNTAX OF THE NOUN PHRASE

In two examples of a dative plural divine name accompanied by a defining adjective of place or group, the adjective follows and is also inflected as a dative plural: lokᵒobᵒo niirabᵒo 'invoking the Lugoues of the Neri' (J.1.1), istᵃaibᵒo rinoebᵒo anakᶜenak̲ᶜ̲:eibᵒo 'for these indigenous queens' demonstrative + noun + adjective (J.5.1). Similarly, araiu|i kᵃaltᶜe, if understood as 'for the Celtic/Galatic nobleman' (J.1.1), shows the group label following the title, or personal name, *Araios*. In J.17.4, kᶜenila(*)rin / bᶜe:lin can be interpreted as accusatives singular in concord. In J.18.1 bᵒotⁱi⚹ana kᶜertᵒo, the nominative singular name is followed by a 'Celtiberian-type' *o*-stem genitive singular, presumably used as a patronym, 'Bōdianā daughter of the artisan'. The noun phrase ra⨎a kᵃaśetᵃana kᵒoŕbᶜo (J.53.1) is interpreted as name+title+genitive patronym, 'RaHa, the tin/bronze-minister, [daughter] of Korbos'. In J.19.1,]l̲iirnestᵃakᵘun bᵃane ooŕoire, the genitive plural group name precedes the dative of 'woman/wife' and a 'Gaulish-type' *o*-stem genitive singular follows; note likewise the position of the genitive plural group name in]tᵃarnekᵘun bᵃane (J.26.1). uarbᵒoiir saruneea (J.22.1) is interpreted as an 'inversion compound', that is a name comprising a noun phrase with a first element susceptible to case inflexion followed by a stereotyped genitive, 'noble consort of the star goddess', the type is common in Insular Neo-Celtic, e.g. *Mael-brigte* 'tonsured devotee of St Brigit'. In J.23.1 iru[| arbᵘui-EL 'invoking the lord god', the first element is interpreted as Celtic dative singular phrase *u̯irūi u̯erm̥ūi 'to the highest man', the second element as an inflexible divine name borrowed from Semitic.

THE SYNTAX OF THE SUPERLATIVE

Though they occur in other syntactic functions as well, the superlatives, such as the formulaic uarbᵃan 'uppermost one' (J.1.2, J.4.1, J.16.1, J.21.1), often appear as stereotyped predicate neuter 'the one who is highest', which is the usual syntax of the Old Irish superlative. Note also tᵘn(?kⁱ)itᶜsbᵃan (J.53.1) ?'that is most fortunate'. However, inflected forms also occur, for example, dative/ablative plural uarbᵃanubᵘ[u (J.3.1), also the possibly instrumental or associative plural uar̲bᵃan(-)ebe (J.9.1), dative singular in the phrase iru[| arbᵘui 'to the highest man' (J.23.1), and the first element in a compound in uarbᵒoiir 'highest man' (J.22.1). The use of the superlative suffix with prepositions and nouns occurs in the other Celtic languages: e.g. Celtiberian VORAMOS, Welsh *pennaf* from *pen(n)* 'head'.

PREPOSITIONAL PHRASES are few in the Tartessian inscriptions in keeping with the syntactic possibilities of a fully inflected Ancient Indo-European language. **tᵒo araiu̯ | i kᵃaltᶜe** 'for the Celtic/Galatic nobleman' (J.1.1) shows the preposition 'to' before a noun phrase in the dative, probably designating the deceased, which usually requires no preposition in the inscriptions, but in this case **tᵒo** apparently functions to separate the dative plural divine name **lokᵒobᵒo niirabᵒo** which precedes the dative name of the deceased. In **kᵒo-bᵉelibᵒo** 'together with the Belīs, the strong ones' (J.1.2), **kᵒo** 'together with' is used with the dative, where the sense of an independent dative would be different ('for/to/invoking the Belīs').

THE RELATIVE

In J.4.1., **ibᵒo-iion** can be read as relative particle suffixed to a statement-initial element (dative/ablative plural personal pronoun). In J.7.2, . . . **kᵃařner-ion ire** is read as simple verb with relative + genitive noun 'of the man whose funerary monuments have been built', with the verb beginning the relative clause. The relative is again suffixed to an uncompounded verb at the head of its clause in J.7.9 **bᵃar⟨u⟩a-ion** 'that I have received'.

DIALECT AFFILIATION

The interpretations put forward in this study include two Semitic (Phoenician) divine names—*Astarte* (J.7.1, J.11.4) and *El* (J.23.1)—, one possible Iberian loanword, **iibᵃan** /*eban*/ (J.5.1), and a recurring Numidian personal name **iubᵃa** (J.7.8), **iobᵃa[** (J.16.2). Although it is suggested that Tartessian **nařkᶜentⁱi**, &c., is equivalent to Greek ναρκάω 'grow stiff, numb, dead' in form and sense, it is not necessarily, nor even possibly, a borrowing from Greek, rather the proposal is that it is a native Tartessian inheritance from Indo-European with a similar form and meaning to its Greek cognate due to their common source. In all other instances, the *comparanda* given here for Tartessian forms are not only wholly Indo-European, but in the first place specifically Celtic. In many instances the phonology of the words excludes the possibility of assigning them to any branch of Indo-European other than Celtic; the Tartessian forms show sound shifts that are the defining features of Celtic, as itemized in the following list.

INDO-EUROPEAN > COMMON CELTIC INNOVATIONS IN TARTESSIAN

(2) Loss of Indo-European *p*, initially before vowels and between vowels: **(s)upermᵐom* > predicative superlative **uarbᵃan** /*u̯arᵃmən*/ 'supreme one', preverb **pro* > Tartessian **ro**, Indo-European **(s)upo-* 'under' > Tartessian **o-** /*u̯o-*/, Indo-European **(s)b₄upér* or **(s)b₄upor* 'over' > Tartessian **ooř-** /*u̯u̯or-*/, Indo-European **ptn̥-*: **pet(e)r-* 'wing, feather' > Tartessian **atᵃan-**, Indo-European **pleir-o-* 'very many' > Tartessian **liir-** 'ocean'.

(3) Indo-European *-ps-* > Common Celtic *-χs-* > Tartessian **ś** (heavy *s*): **upsmᵐā-i* > Common Celtic **uχsᵃmāi* 'at the highest place' > Tartessian **uśnee**.

(4) Indo-European *gᵘ* > Common Celtic *b*: Indo-European **gᵘn̥ⁿa-* 'woman' > Tartessian dative singular

b^{a}ane, genitive plural **b^{a}aanon.**

(5) Later Indo-European *ō* in final syllables to Common Celtic *ū*: dative singular *o*-stem ending *-ōi* > Tartessian **-ui, -u** in **aŕaiui, alk^{u}u**, &c., genitive plural *o*-stem ending *-ōm* > Tartessian **-un**, in **l̲iirnest^{a}ak^{u}un, nemun**, &c., possibly also in the thematic present 1st singular ending in]**naŕk^{e}euu**['I lie still'. In other examples, Tartessian **o** is found in this position (**sab^{o}oi** 'for Samos' [J.5.1, if this is not locative 'in Samos' (Untermann 1997, 167)], na]**ŕk^{e}eo-io** 'I who lie still' [J.16.2]), which might be either purely orthographic variants or evidence that the older sound was sometimes preserved. (The position immediately before the enclitic might not have evolved as a true final syllable.) If **t^{a}alainon** (J.14.1) is a genitive plural, rather than an accusative singular, it would indicate either that the change *ō* > *ū* in the final syllables was not altogether complete at the date of the Tartessian inscriptions or that there was also an *o*-stem genitive plural ending with a short *o*.

(6) Later Indo-European *ō* in non-final syllables to Common Celtic *ā*: Tartessian perfect **-rat^{e}e** /*rāte*/ 'has run' < */*rōte*/, **b^{a}are** 'has borne' < */*bōre*/. The change is possibly not complete in]**b^{o}oara** ▯ / ǂA9A 'I have borne' (J.2.1) from older *bōra*.

(7) Later Indo-European *ē* > Common Celtic *ī*: **h_3rēg´-s* 'king' in Tartessian *Gargo-ris* and probably **aiburis**.

TARTESSIAN IMPLIES A REVISED RECONSTRUCTION OF COMMON CELTIC in one phonological feature only.

Indo-European syllabic nasals */*m̥ n̥*/ show the usual Celtic treatment in Tartessian ᾿Αργανθωνιος /*argantonios*/ with 'silver', Indo-European **$h_2$erǵn̥tom* 'silver'. However, in **ek^{u}uŕ̲i̲ne** OYMMY4日O (J.4.1), probably also dative plural **rinoeb^{o}o** PᛗᛉǂO日ǂ (J.5.1), Celtic **rīgnī* 'queen' < Indo-European **h_3rēg´nih$_2$* (cf. Sanskrit *rājñī* 'queen') has not developed like Gaulish *rigani*, Cisalpine genitive *rikanas*, Old Irish *rígain* from Celtic **rīganī* < a notional Indo-European **h_3rēg´n̥^{n}ih$_2$* with a syllabic nasal. Similarly, *m* in the 'Italo-Celtic' superlative ending did not develop as *m̥* > *am* in Tartessian as in the other Celtic languages, for example: **uarb^{a}an** ЧAᛋ9AЧ (J.1.2, J.3.1, J.4.1, J.21.1) 'the highest one' < Indo-European **(s)$h_4$uperm̥^{m}om* vs. Celtiberian masculine nominative singular VERAMOS, VORAMOS, accusative VERAMOM; **t^{u}n↑^{i}it^{e}sb^{a}an** ΔᛉᛏᛗHǂᛋAᛉ (J.53.1) 'that is most fortunate', vs. North-west Hispano-Celtic TONGETAMVS (Albertos 1985, 298). In these examples, the syllabic nasal either never developed in the first place in Tartessian or ceased to be syllabic when a vowel followed.

POST-COMMON CELTIC INNOVATIONS IN TARTESSIAN

Despite its early date, the Tartessian linguistic evidence does not reflect an undifferentiated Proto-Celtic, i.e. a pre-dialectal state of affairs, but rather shows various points of agreement with the distinguishing innovations of sometimes Celtiberian, sometimes Gaulish, and also the 'Insular Celtic' languages, Goidelic, and Brittonic (this last, for present purposes may be treated as a Gallo-Brittonic unity).

(1) Tartessian agrees with Celtiberian: *o*-stem genitive singular in *-o*, e.g. Tartessian k°oŕb°o ‡ᐁᒍ‡ᐊ (J.53.1) 'of Korbos', k°ert°o ‡Aꟼ⊙)((J.18.1) 'of the artisan', Celtiberian *Aualo* 'of Aualos' (Froehner Tessera) (see further (8) below); *i*-stem genitive plural < *-isōm*, e.g. Tartessian b°eliśon ꟼ‡Mꟼꟼꟼⵋ9 (J.20.1), Celtiberian *kentisum* 'of the sons' (Villar 1997, 918, citing Untermann); group affiliation expressed with genitive plural < *-kōm*, e.g. Tartessian liirnest°ak°un ꟼꟼᗺAX‡⊙ꟼꟼMꟼꟼⵋ (J.19.1), t°arnek°un ꟼꟼꟼᗺ⊙ꟼꟼAX (J.26.1); Proto-Celtic *χt* > *t*, e.g. Tartessian anb°at'i°a AMⵓA⊙ℕ_A (J.16.2) < **ambaχtia*, Celtiberian [*R*]*etukenos* < *Reχtugenos*; the Tartessian superlative uarb°an = Celtiberian VORAMOS 'most high, supreme' (cf. also uab°an corresponding to the Hispano-Celtic place-name *Uama* and the Lepontic name UVAMO-KOZIS), contrasting with Gaulish *uertamos* = Old Welsh *guartham* 'highest, summit'. Like Celtiberian and unlike Goidelic, Gaulish, and probably British, the Tartessian relative particle/pronoun is inflected: e.g. na]ŕk°eo-io* *‡ꟼ⊙)(ꟼ[(J.16.2) 'I who lie still', k°aŕner-ion ΛAꟼꟼⵋ⊙ꟼꟼ‡ꟼ (J.7.2) 'to whom funerary monuments that have been built', i.e. 'who has been entombed', vs. Gaulish DVGIIONTI-IO 'who serve'. The Tartessian verbal noun eert°aune ⊙ꟼꟼAXꟼⵋ⊙ (J.55.1) and Celtiberian *uertaunei* (Botorrita) are probably identical formations. Celtic final *-ks* (> *-χs*) became Tartessian *-s* in *Gargoris*, cf. Celtiberian SEGOBRIS < *Segobriks* (Villar 1997, 912).

(2) Tartessian shows a tendency paralleled elsewhere in Western Hispano-Celtic: historical *g* is represented as a sibilant before a front vowel in ariariśe ⊙MꟼꟼAꟼꟼA (J.10.1) < **ario-rīgi*, cf. MEDUSINUS otherwise written *Medugenos* (Villar 1997, 905–6). Another possible example in this dialectal category is loss of an etymological *g* in ek°uŕine ⊙ꟼꟼ)(ꟼᗺ⊙ (J.4.1) < **Ekuo-rīgni*, cf. *Augustabria*, Βρουτοβρια, *Calabria*, *Conimbriensis*, *Segobriensis*, *Meduenos* (Villar 1997, 905–6); however, the Tartessian writing system had no means of representing /*gn*/, which could therefore be how n must be read here. Note also Celtiberian *Toutinokum* (Iniesta), possibly from Celtic **Toutigno-*.

(3) Tartessian agrees with Gaulish (and, in the first example below, Western Hispano-Celtic): ablative/dative plural in *-bo*: Tartessian]eb°o ‡⊓⊙[(J.7.8),]aib°o ‡⊓MA[(J.28.1),]aet°ab°o*[ ]A⊙‡Aᕼ‡[(J.28.1),]ant°onb°o ‡⊓Mꟼ‡AꟼA (J.8.1), b°elib°o ‡⊓Mⵋ⊙9 (J.1.2), (k°ak')iśiink°olob°o ‡⊓‡ⵋXꟼMꟼMMꟼꟼAΛ (J.1.1), lok°ob°o ‡⊓‡Xⵓⵋ (J.1.1), niirab°o ‡⊓ꟼMꟼꟼ (J.1.1),]onlinb°o ‡⊓MMⵓꟼ‡ (J.11.2), rinoeb°o ꟼꟼꟼ‡⊙ᗺ‡ (J.5.1), istaib°o (J.5.1 demonstrative pronoun), cf. Gaulish ATREBO 'to the fathers' (Plumergad), contrast Celtiberian *Arekoratikubos*, *Loukaiteitubos*, Lepontic UVLTIAUIOPOS, ARIVONEPOS (both Prestino). Old Irish *-aib* must reflect a different preform, with *-bis*. The Tartessian personal pronoun's nominative plural sieś ꟼⵋMꟼ‡ or sie ⊙Mꟼ‡ (J.12.1) and instrumental plural eb°e ⊙ⵓ⊙ (J.9.1), eb° ⊙⊓ (J.16.3) are closely comparable to the Gaulish series occurring in the Larzac inscription, including nominative plural *sies* and instrumental plural *eiabi*.

(4) Tartessian agrees with Gaulish and British in the tendency for *u̯o-* or *u̯e-* to become *u̯a-* (see Koch 1992): Tartessian k°t°uarat°e 'has gone under, has rescued' (J.53.1) /*-u̯a rāte*/ < Common Celtic **/(u̯)u̯o rāte*/; probably Tartessian alk°u ꟼᕼⵓA (J.12.1) /*u̯alkū(i)*/ 'for Valkos' < Common Celtic **/u̯olkūi/*, cf. Welsh *gwalch*; probably also uarb°an 'the supreme one', but this could

be an analogical reformation of **uabᵃan** ᕼᎪ ⧫ Ꭺᕼ (J.16.5) /uṵᵃmom/ (cf. the south-western Hispano-Celtic place-name *Uama*), in which the *-r-* has been inserted into *am* < *m̥*, and /uṵa/, thus not from earlier /uṵo/. However, Celtiberian may have shared this *u̯e- > u̯a-* tendency: Celtiberian *uarakos* has been derived from a Proto-Celtic **u̯erákos* (Wodtko 2000, 434). Tartessian also shows affinities with Gaulish and British with the name Ἀργανθωνιος /*argantonios*/, which appears to show both a divine suffix *-ono/ā* and an agent suffix *-i̯o-* better paralleled in those Celtic languages. For the former, cf. also probably Tartessian **saruneea** ᎪᎾᎾᕼᕼᎪ ⧧ (J.22.1, J.22.2) ?'of the star goddess'.

(5) Tartessian appears to agree with Gaulish and Primitive Irish (probably British as well) in replacing a final *-m* with *-n*; however, the infrequency of the Tartessian character **m** ᛗ suggests that **n** ᕼ is sometimes to be read as /*m*/, or as a general nasal whose specific phonetic realization was determined by context.

(6) Tartessian appears to agree with Gaulish, Primitive Irish, and British in the simplification of the diphthong *ei > ē* in the example **eertᵃaune** ᎾᕼᕼᎪ᙭ᎰᎾᎾ (J.55.1) vs. Celtiberian *uertaunei* (Botorrita).

(7) Tartessian agrees with Goidelic if **saruneea** ᎪᎾᎾᕼᕼᎪ⧧ (J.22.1, J.22.2) is correctly interpreted as the genitive singular of an *ā*-stem **ᵗSarunā* ?'star goddess' with the ending found as ogamic Primitive Irish -EAS, -EA < -*ii̯ās*. The Tartessian system of writing the stop consonants (᙭ **tᵃ**, ⊧ **tᵉ**, ⊕ **tⁱ**, △ **tᵒ**, ▲ **tᵘ**, &c.) itself implies that consonants were perceived to have distinct qualities conditioned by the following vowel. As Tartessian shows significant fluctuation in the representation of *i* and *e* (e.g. **niirabᵒo** [J.1.1] = *Nerᵃbo*), and *u* and *o* (e.g. **lokᵒobᵒo** [J.1.1] = *Lugubo*, **-muri-** [J.15.2] = *-mori-*), a threefold system, like that of Old Irish, is possibly indicated: *i/e*-quality versus *a*-quality versus *u/o*-quality. Similarly, Tartessian **leoine** (J.10.1) resembles palatalization or *i*-epenthesis of a consonant (**n**) preceding a front vowel, cf. Lusitanian LOIMINNA/LOEMINA < **lōmena* < **louksmena* 'shining, brilliant' (Schmidt 1985, 335). The system of phonemic consonant quality of Old Irish is not represented in the Primitive Irish ogam inscriptions. However, the fact that the ogam script is most probably derived from the Roman alphabet and that the bilingual ogams of Britain show a close, almost letter-for-letter, system of transliteration probably means that Irish consonant quality (as a system wholly alien to Latin and its alphabet) would have been impossible to represent in the earliest written Irish, even if it was then already fully phonemic by that period. In fact, consonant quality is not represented consistently even in Old Irish, though there is no doubt of its phonemic status at that stage.

Tartessian anticipates Old Breton and Old Welsh in the fluctuation of original *-nti*, with *-n(i)* in the terminations of 3rd-person plural verbs: for example, **naŕkᵉeni** (J.1.2, J.7.2), **naŕkᵉentⁱi** ᕼ⊕ᎾᎾᕼᕼᎪᕼ (J.12.1, J.16.1, J.17.2, J.18.1), **naŕkᵉenTi** ᕼᎱᎾᎾᕼᕼᎪᕼ (J.19.2), **naŕkᵉenii** (J.2.1), **naŕken** (J.7.5). (J.7.8), **n[a]ŕken** ᎾᎾᕼᕼᕼ (Cabeza del Buey IV). The ϑ in Herodotus's spelling Ἀργανθωνιος may also be significant in this regard: cf. Old Welsh *hanter* 'half', also *hanther*, Middle and Modern Welsh *hanner*. That instability of inherited *nt* may have been incipient within Hispano-Celtic generally is suggested by Celtiberian *arkanta* 'silver' alongside *Arganda* and *turtunta/Tortonda* (Villar 1997, 904).

(8) In one important respect, Tartessian appears to show a sporadic but recurrent anticipation of one defining feature of the Insular Neo-Celtic languages, namely the weakening of some final and internal syllables, with the result that etymological *o* is sometimes written *a* (possibly for the central unrounded vowel /ə/). In the nominative of Celtic u̯iros 'man, hero, husband', the final seems sometimes to be reduced (e.g. **(o)ira** [J.1.2] /u̯irə(s)/), or simply lost (e.g. **ooŕoir** [J.19.2] < *u̯eru̯iros, **uarbᵒoiir** [J.22.1] < *u̯ermᵐo-u̯iros), cf. also Latin *vir*; alternatively, this common word may have been abbreviated. In inscriptions so old, this apparent precocity is surprising, though sporadic examples also occur in Gaulish, Galatian, and British, as well as systematically in Primitive Irish. It should be remembered that most of the evidence for the Ancient Celtic languages survives mediated through the writing systems of Greek and Latin. This circumstance is likely to have contributed to an impression that Ancient Celtic had a sound system more like those of Greek and Latin and less like Neo-Celtic than was actually the case. With a literacy based mainly or wholly on Phoenician (a Non-Indo-European language that didn't write vowels at all), the writing of Tartessian would not have been influenced by grammatical ideas derived from a cognate Old Indo-European language. In other words, it is unlikely that the language of the Tartessian inscriptions has been misleadingly 're-Indo-Europeanized'.

(9) According to De Hoz (1992; cf. 2007, 6), Lepontic shows two *o*-stem genitive singular forms, both derived from Proto-Celtic: (i) -*u*, corresponding to Celtiberian -*o*, and (ii) -*i* as in Gaulish and Primitive Irish. Tartessian apparently has both forms as well: **kᵒoŕbᵉo** ‡ꓷꓘ‡ꓮ '[daughter] of Korbos' (J.53.1), **kᵉertᵒo** ‡Δꟼꓳꓫ '[daughter] of the artisan'(J.18.1), contrasting with **ooŕoire** ꓳꟼꓴ‡ꓵ‡‡ '[wife] of Uoru̯iros' /u̯oru̯iri/. As both of the Tartessian examples of the Celtiberian-type genitive can be interpreted as expressing parentage, this suggests that the Tartessian genitives differed functionally and that the -*o* form derives from the ablative -*ōd*, thus perhaps still preserving the older sense 'issuing from Korbos', 'from the artisan'. This explanation of the Celtiberian genitive in -*o* was advanced by Schmidt (1976, 388), but has since been mostly abandoned.

(10) If it is not purely an orthographic feature, Tartessian shows a strong tendency to lose /w/ in all positions, like Greek, but unlike the other Ancient Celtic languages. The fact that Goidelic completely lost lenis *w* before the earliest written Old Irish suggests a common inherited basis not unique to Tartessian. A plausible starting-point for this development would be for *w* to be lost when articulated weakly in some phonetic environments—a situation then systematized in the Goidelic mutational system—but extended more widely in Tartessian.

In sum, then, Tartessian is well within the limits defining a Celtic language and not within the dialectically grey area of its more recently attested Indo-European neighbour to the north, Lusitanian. In other words, there is no need to expand the usual linguistic parameters of Celtic to include Tartessian in the family. Tartessian shares with Celtiberian a sufficient core of distinctive and probably innovative features to justify 'Hispano-Celtic' as a term for a linguistic sub-family as opposed to a purely geographical classification.

It is also worth noting in this connection Pliny's statement (*Naturalis Historia* 3.13) that the

Celtici (of south-west Hispania) and Celtiberians shared common religions, languages, and names for their fortified settlements (*Celticos a Celtiberis . . . aduenisse manifestum est sacris, lingua, oppidum uocabulis . . .*). On the other hand, innovations shared by Tartessian and British, and Goidelic, and most especially Gaulish, show that Tartessian's position in south-west coastal Hispania and within the Phoenician sphere of influence was—rather than being isolated and marginal—well placed for participating at an early date in linguistic innovations taking place in various parts of the wider Celtic-speaking world. The rapid economic and social development of the 10th–6th centuries BC could naturally have led to a 'gold-rush' situation favouring the mixing of dialects and acceptance of some innovative features within the resulting *koine*.

It appears, therefore, that Hispania had at least two, closely related, ancient Celtic languages: (1) a more easterly, inland Celtic language attested at a somewhat later date in the far more extensive corpus of Celtiberian, and (2) a more westerly Celtic of the Atlantic zone, more meagrely attested, but to which the earlier inscriptional corpus of Tartessian may be assigned. In addition to these two, and in addition to the two non-Indo-European languages of Hispania—Iberian and Aquitanian/Palaeo-Basque—there are traces of a complex matrix of other pre-Roman Indo-European languages in the Hispanic Peninsula. Lusitanian is an Indo-European language found in five inscriptions from east-central Portugal and adjacent parts of Spain, which are written in Roman letters and date to the early centuries AD (see Wodtko this volume). In Lusitanian the word for 'pig' is the Indo-European PORCOM, which preserves Indo-European *p*. The loss of *p* is often considered a defining feature of the emergence of Celtic from Indo-European, often *the* pre-eminent defining sound change. Lusitanian thus lacks a key innovation and would require a rethinking of Celtic to accommodate it within the definition of that language family. As well as retained Indo-European *p* in PORCOM, Lusitanian also possibly shows *p* from Indo-European k^w in PVMPI and the pronominal PVPPID < $*k^uodk^uid$ (Búa 2007, 27; Wodtko this volume).

The term 'Hispano-Celtic' can be extended and further validated by the numerous parallels between Tartessian and the indigenous proper names from the west and central north of the Peninsula occurring in inscriptions and other sources of the Roman Period. In some features— such as the inventory of names and name elements, the dative plural in *-bo*, and the genitive plural in *-un*—Tartessian appears to agree closely with the indigenous Indo-European names found mixed with Latin in brief inscriptions widely distributed in areas north and west of the Celt-iberian area and north and east of the Lusitanian. One might conclude that this uncategorized Hispano-Celtic represents the later stage of the same language. However, this widespread mater-ial is likely to represent more than one dialect. We find in it, for example, numerous examples of genitives plural in *-um* and *-on*, as well as *-un*, and there is at least one inscription with datives plural in *-bor*. Owing to the fragmentary and mixed nature of the evidence, attempts to distinguish 'Vettonian', 'Callaecian', 'Cantabrian', and so on, present a formidable challenge (cf. the approach of Untermann 1996), but one result of such an effort might be to reveal a dialect continuum embracing the Celtiberian, Tartessian, and Lusitanian *corpora*.

In Roman times, in the Indo-European zone of the Iberian Peninsula (the north, west, and centre), names beginning with *p-*, and themselves having an Indo-European appearance, occur in all major regions—Celtiberia, Vettonia, Callaecia, Cantabria, and Lusitania (Untermann

1985/6). In numerous examples, it is not immediately plain whether these have preserved Indo-European *p* or *p* from Indo-European *kᵘ* as in P-Celtic and some Italic dialects: for example, in CASTELLANOS PAEMEIOBRIGENSES and CASTELLANIS PAEMEIO-BRIGENSIBVS which occur on a bronze from Bembibre, León, the etymology of the first element of the ethnonym, compounded with Celtic *-brigā*, is uncertain (Búa 2007, 20), and note that *p-* is continued by *b-* in the modern name. Similarly, the Lusitanian divine epithet PETRANIOI could contain Indo-European **kᵘetr-* '4' (thus showing *kᵘ* to *p*) or **petr-* 'feather, wing' with *p* preserved (contrast Old Welsh *eterin* 'bird') (Búa 2007, 26). The ancient place-name *Bletisama* occurs in the north-central Peninsula, where it is today *Ledesma*, clearly cognate with Celtiberian *Letaisama*, all from **pletismᵐā* 'broadest', showing a superlative suffix limited to the Celtic and Italic branches of Indo-European. *Bletisama* can be explained by a two-stage transformation: first, the place-name **Pletismᵐā* was rendered pronounceable by speakers of *p*-less dialects by substituting /b/ as the closest possible approximation for the absent phoneme /p/; then, the name was simply replaced by its obvious *p*-less Hispano-Celtic cognate *Letaisama*, whence modern *Ledesma* (see further Villar 2004; Búa 2007, 20, 33).

One hypothesis worth considering in the context of the study of Tartessian is that Celtic first emerged in Hispania. In *Bletisama/Letaisama* we have a doublet in which a *p*-less Celtic appears to be emerging from an Indo-European with *p* before our eyes. We might call the variety of Indo-European in which the name **Pletismᵐā* was coined, 'Hispanic' (or 'Peninsular'), to avoid 'Iberian' (which already designates a non-Indo-European language). This 'Hispanic' would be the common ancestor of Celtic (which lost Indo-European *p* in most positions) and Lusitanian (which did not). To refer to both branches as 'Celtic' strikes many historical linguists as a confusing self-contradiction, because, as explained above, loss of Indo-European *p* has been used to define Celtic. However, we could redefine Celtic on the basis of a different phonological change, such as Indo-European syllabic *ḷ* and *ṛ* becoming Celtic *li* and *ri* (as Dagmar Wodtko suggests to me). We could thus retain the old name 'Celtic', while expanding its definition to include Lusitanian and other evidence of the **Pletisamā* type. With the loss of Indo-European /p/ in one dialect of this proto-language (whether we call that 'Celtic with Indo-European *p*' or 'Hispanic'), the *p*-less ancestor of most of the Celtic languages emerged. The conserving dialect or dialects did not participate in loss of Indo-European *p*, as reflected in the Lusitanian inscriptions and some of the pre-Roman Indo-European names of the Peninsula.

The fact that the non-Indo-European language of the Iberian inscriptions of the eastern Peninsula also lacks *p* raises the possibility that it was prolonged exposure to the Iberian sound system that led to the loss of Indo-European *p* in Celtic. Celtiberian and Tartessian are both *p*-less Celtic languages. They were also both situated alongside the territory of the Iberians with whom they came to share a writing system. (From the Roman Period in the south-west, place-names in *-ippo* are recorded: these have neither an Indo-European nor an Iberian appearance, nor do they resemble forms in the Tartessian inscriptions, but rather suggest comparison with the repeated *Hippo* in north Africa and hence an explanation in the Carthaginian period.) Across the Pyrenees, *p*-less Celtic was to find itself in contact with Italic and Germanic and other languages with *p*. It was here that Celtic developed, or restored, a sound system more like those of its central-European neighbours: inherited *k*ᵘ came to be articulated as *p*, the defining criterion of the 'P-Celtic'.

The Gaulish (and Goidelic and British) affinities of Tartessian contrast with the conservative and relatively isolated character of Celtiberian. But, if one views the Atlantic maritime routes as the primary avenue of Celticization and subsequent innovations within Celtic, this is hardly surprising. Land-locked and wedged between non-Indo-European Iberian, non-Indo-European Aquitanian/palaeo-Basque, and the Pyrenees, Celtiberian was ideally placed to be insulated from innovations affecting the other Celtic languages. No one has taken the possibility of Celtic coming from Hispania to the other Celtic countries seriously since we stopped taking *Lebar Gabála Érenn* (the 11th-century Irish 'Book of Invasions') seriously, but it is now at least worth pausing to review what it is that we think we know that makes that impossible.

BIBLIOGRAPHY

Albertos Firmat, M. L. 1985 'La onomástica personal indígena del noroeste peninsular (astures y galaicos)', *Actas del III Coloquio sobre Lenguas y Culturas Paleohispánicas*, ed. J. de Hoz, 255–310. Salamanca, Universidad de Salamanca.

Almagro-Gorbea, M. 1988 'Société et commerce dans la péninsule Ibérique aux VII–Vᵉ siécles', *Les princes celtes et la Méditerranée*, 71–9. Paris, La Documentation Française.

Almagro-Gorbea, M. 2004 'Inscripciones y grafitos tartesicos de la necrópolis orientalizante de Medellín', *Palaeohispanica* 4.13–44.

Almagro-Gorbea, M. 2005 'La literatura tartésica. Fuentes históricas e iconográficas', *Gerión* 23/1.39–80.

Anthony, D. W. 2007 *The Horse, the Wheel, and Language: How Bronze-Age Riders from the Eurasian Steppes Shaped the Modern World*. Princeton, Princeton University Press.

Aubet, M. E. 2001 *The Phoenicians and the West: Politics, Colonies, and Trade*, trans. M. Turton. 2nd edn. Cambridge, Cambridge University Press. 1st English edition, 1993.

Ballester, X. 2004 'Hablas indoeuropeas y anindoeuropeas en *Hispania prerromana*', *Estudios de lenguas y epigrafía* 6.107–38.

Beltrán Lloris, F. 2002 'Les dieux des celtibères orientaux et les inscriptions: quelques remarques critiques', *Dieux des celtes (Études luxembourgoises d'Histoire & de Sciences des religions 1*, 39–66. Luxembourg.

Blázquez, J. M. 1993 'El enigma de Tarteso en los escritores antiguos y en la investigación moderna', *Los enigmas de Tarteso*, eds. J. Alvar & J. M. Blázquez, 11–30. Madrid, Cátedra.

Brandherm, D. 2008 'Greek and Phoenician Potsherds between East and West: A Chronological Dilemma?', *A New Dawn for the Dark Age? Shifting Paradigms in Mediterranean Iron Age Chronology / L'âge obscur se fait-il jour de nouveau? Les paradigmes changeants de la chronologie de l'âge du Fer en Méditerranée*, BAR International Series 1871, eds. D. Brandherm & M. Trachsel, 149–74.

Brandherm, D. 2008/9 'Sobre los supuestos arreos

de caballo y piezas de carro de la Ria de Huelva', *Boletín de la Asociación Española de Amigos de la Arqueología* 45, 27–34.

Bromwich, R. (ed. & trans.) 2006 *Trioedd Ynys Prydein / The Welsh Triads.* 3rd edn. Cardiff, University of Wales Press. First published, 1961.

Brun, P. 2006 'L'origine des Celtes: Communautés linguistiques et réseaux sociaux', *Celtes et Gaulois, l'Archéologie face à l'Histoire, 2: la Préhistoire des Celtes*, dir. D. Vitali. Bibracte 12/2, 29–44.

Búa Carballo, J. C. 2000 'Estudio lingüístico de la teonima lusitano-gallega', Tesis Doctoral, Salamanca.

Búa Carballo, J. C. 2003 *Cosus. Una exemplo da epigrafía e relixíon*, Boletín Avriense.

Búa Carballo, J. C. 2004 'Tres cuestións relacionadas coa toponimia antiga en -*bris*, moderna -*bre*', *Novi te ex nomine: Estudios filolóxicos ofrecidos ao Prof. Dr. D. Kremer*, ed. A. I. Boullón Angelo, 381–99. Instituto da Lingua Galega, A Coruña.

Búa Carballo, J. C. 2005 'Zur Etymologie der deutschen Konjunktion *und*', *Sprachwissenschaft* 30/2, 111–25.

Búa Carballo, J. C. 2007 'O *Thesaurus Palaeocallaecus*, un proxecto que quere botar a andar', *Onomástica galega con especial consideración da situación prerromana. Actas do primeiro Coloquio de Trier 19 e 20 de maio 2006*, ed. D. Kremer, 15–40. Verba, Anuario Galega de Filoloxía, Anexo 58. Universidade de Santiago de Compostela.

Burgess, C. & B. O'Connor 2008 'Iberia, the Atlantic Bronze Age and the Mediterranean', *Contacto cultural entre el Mediterráneo y el Atlántico (siglos XII–VIII ANE), La precolonización a debate*, Serie Arqueológica 11, eds. S. Celestino, N. Rafel & X-L. Armada, 41–58. Madrid, Escuela Española de Historia y Arqueología en Roma-CSIC.

Catalán, M. P. 1993 'Crítica analítica de la arqueología tartesia y turdetana', *Lengua y cultura en la Hispania prerromana, Actas del V Coloquio sobre Lenguas y Culturas Prerromanas de la Península Ibérica*, eds. J. Untermann & F. Villar, 189–207. Salamanca, Ediciones Universidad de Salamanca.

Celestino Pérez, S. 1990 'Las estelas decoradas del s.w. peninsular', *La cultura tartesica y Extremadura*, 45–62. Cuadernos Emeritenses 2. Mérida, Museo Nacional de Arte Romano.

Celestino Pérez, S. 2001 *Estelas de guerrero y stelas diademadas: La precolonización y formación del mundo tartésico.* Barcelona, Edicions Bellaterra.

Celestino Pérez, S., & C. López-Ruiz 2006 'New light on the warrior stelae from Tartessos (Spain)', *Antiquity* 80.89–101.

Chamorro, J. G. 1987 'Survey of Archaeological research on Tartessos', *American Journal of Archaeology* 91/2.197–232.

Charles-Edwards, T. M. 1978 'The Authenticity of the *Gododdin*: An Historian's View', *Astudiaethau ar yr Hengerdd: Studies in Old Welsh Poetry*, eds. Rachel Bromwich & R. Brinley Jones, 44–71. Caerdydd, Gwasg Prifysgol Cymru.

Collis J. 2003 *The Celts: Origins, Myths & Inventions.* Stroud, Tempus.

Correa, J. A. 1985 'Consideraciones sobre las inscripciones tartesias', *Actas del III Coloquio sobre Lenguas y Culturas Paleohispánicas*, ed. J. de Hoz, 377–95. Salamanca, Universidad de Salamanca.

Correa, J. A. 1989 'Posibles antropónimos en las inscripciones en escritura del SO. (o tartesia)', *Veleia* 6.243–52.

Correa, J. A. 1992 'La epigrafía tartesia', *Andalusien zwischen Vorgeschichte und Mittelalter*, eds. D. Hertel & J. Untermann, 75–114. Cologne, Böhlau.

Correa, J. A. 1993 'El signario de Espanca (Castro Verde) y la escritura tartesia', *Lengua y cultura en la Hispania prerromana, Actas del V Coloquio sobre Lenguas y Culturas Prerromanas de la Península Ibérica*, eds. J. Untermann & F. Villar, 521–62. Salamanca, Ediciones Universidad de Salamanca.

Correa, J. A. 1996 'La epigrafía del Sudoeste: Estado de la cuestión', *La Hispania Prerromana, Actas del VI Coloquio sobre Lenguas y Culturas Prerromanas de la Península Ibérica*, eds. F. Villar & J. d'Encarnação, 65–75. Salamanca, Ediciones Universidad de Salamanca.

Correa, J. A. 2002 'Crónica epigráfica del sudoeste', *Palaeohispanica* 2.407–9.

Correa, J. A. 2004 'Crónica epigráfica del sudoeste', *Palaeohispanica* 4.283–4.

Correa, J. A. 2005 'Del alfabeto fenicio al semisilabario paleohispánico', *Palaeohispanica* 5.137–54.

Correa, J. A. 2006 'Crónica epigráfica del sudoeste', *Palaeohispanica* 6.295–8.

Correa, J. A. 2008 'Crónica epigráfica del sudoeste IV', *Palaeohispanica* 8.295.

Correa, J. A. & J. Á. Zamora 2008 'Un graffito tartesio hallado en el yacimiento del Castillo de Doña Blanca', *Palaeohispanica* 8.179–96.

Correia, V. H. 1996 *A epigrafia da Idade do Ferro do Sudoeste da Península Ibérica*. Porto, Etnos.

Correia, V. H. 2005 'The Collection of Pre-Latin Writing in the Museum of Faro', *Paths of the Roman Algarve*, 14–19. Faro, Câmara Municipal de Faro.

Cunliffe, B. 1997 *The Ancient Celts*. Oxford, Oxford University Press.

Cunliffe, B. 2001 *Facing the Ocean: The Atlantic and its Peoples 8000 BC–AD 1500*. Oxford, Oxford University Press.

Cunliffe, B. 2008 *Europe between the Oceans, 9000 BC–AD 1000*. New Haven, Yale University Press.

De Bernardo Stempel, P. 1998 'Minima Celtica zwischen Sprach- und Kultur-geschichte', *Man and the Animal World: Studies . . . in memoriam Sándor Bökönyi*, eds. P. Anreiter, L. Bartosiewucz, E . Jerem, W. Meid, 601–10. Arquaeolingua, Budapest.

De Bernardo Stempel, P. 2006 'Language and Historiography of Celtic-speaking Peoples', *Celtes et Gaulois, l'Archéologie face à l'Histoire: Celtes et Gaulois dans l'Histoire, l'historiographie et l'idéologie moderne*, ed. S. Rieckhoff, Bibracte 12/1, 33–56.

De Hoz, J. 1989 'El desarrollo de la escritura y las lenguas de la zona meridional', *Tartessos: Arqueología Protohistórica del Bajo Guadalquivir*, ed. M. E. Aubet Semmler, 523–87. Barcelona, Sabadell.

De Hoz, J. 1989b 'Las fuentes escritas sobre Tartessos', *Tartessos: Arqueología Protohistórica del Bajo Guadalquivir*, ed. M. E. Aubet Semmler, 25–43. Barcelona, Sabadell.

De Hoz, J. 1992 'The Celts of the Iberian Peninsula'. *Zeitschrift für celtische Philologie* 45.1–37.

De Hoz, J. 1996 'El origen de las escrituras paleohispánicas quince años después', *La Hispania Prerromana, Actas del VI Coloquio sobre Lenguas y Culturas Prerromanas de la Península Ibérica*, eds. F. Villar & J. d'Encarnação, 171–204. Salamanca, Ediciones Universidad de Salamanca.

De Hoz, J. 2007 'The Mediterranean Frontier of the Celts and the Advent of Celtic Writing'. *Crossing Boundaries / Croesi Ffiniau: Proc. XII International Congress of Celtic Studies 24–30 August 2003*, eds. P. Sims-Williams & G. A. Williams. *Cambrian Medieval Celtic Studies* 53/54.1–22.

De Hoz, J. 2007b 'The Institutional Vocabulary of the Continental Celts', *Gaulois et Celtique continental*, eds. P.-Y. Lambert & G.-J. Pinault, 189–214. Genève. Librairie Droz.

De Hoz, J., et al. undated *Catálogo de estelas decoradas del Museo Arqueológico Provincial de Badajoz*.

De Mello Beirão, C. 1993 'Novos dados arqueológicos sobre a epigrafia da I Idade do Ferro do sudoeste da Península Ibérica', *Lengua y cultura en la Hispania prerromana, Actas del V Coloquio sobre Lenguas y Culturas Prerromanas de la Península Ibérica*, eds. J. Untermann & F. Villar, 683–96. Salamanca, Ediciones Universidad de Salamanca.

Delamarre, Xavier 2003 *Dictionnaire de la langue gauloise: une approche linguistique du vieux-celtique continental*. Collection des Hespérides. Paris, Errance. First published, 2001.

Falileyev, A. 2005 'In Search of Celtic Tylis: Onomastic Evidence', *New Approaches to the Celtic Place-names in Ptolemy's Geography*, eds. J. de Hoz, E. R. Luján, P. Sims-Williams, 107–33. Madrid, Ediciones Clásicas.

Falileyev, A. 2007 *Celtic Dacia: Personal Names, Place-names and Ethnic Names of Celtic Origin in Dacia and Scythia Minor*. Aberystwyth, CMCS.

Freeman, P. 1996 'The Earliest Greek Sources on the Celts', *Études Celtiques* 32, 11–48.

Gamito, T. Júdice 1988 *Social Complexity in Southwest Iberia 800–300 BC—The Case of Tartessos*, BAR, Oxford.

Gamito, T. Júdice 1993 'The Internal and External Dynamics of the Development and Collapse of Tartessos. A Possible Explanatory Model', *Lengua y Cultura en la Hispania Prerromana: Actas del V Coloquio sobre lenguas y culturas prerromanas de la Península Ibérica* (Colonia, 25–28 de Novembre de 1989), ed. J. Untermann, F. Villar, 127–42.

Gaspari, A. 2006 'Scordisci', *Celtic Culture: A Historical Encyclopedia*, ed. J. T. Koch, 1569–71. Santa Barbara, ABC–Clio.

Gensler, Orin David 1993 'A Typological Evaluation of Celtic/Hamito-Semitic Syntactic Parallels'. Ph.D., University of California.

Godley, A. D. (trans.) 1920 *Herodotus: The Persian Wars, Books I-II*. Loeb Classical Library. Cambridge Massachusetts, Harvard University Press.

Gómez-Moreno, M. 1949 *Misceláneas. Historia, Arte, Arqueología. Primera serie: la antigüedad*. Madrid.

González Rodríguez, Mª. C. 1986 *Las unidades organizativas indígenas del área indoeuropea de Hispania*, Veleia Anejo 2. Vitoria/Gasteiz.

González Rodríguez, Mª. C. 1994 'Las unidades organizativas indígenas II: *addenda et corrigenda*', *Veleia* 11, 169–75.

Guerra, A. 2002 'Novos monumentos epigrafados com escrita do Sudoeste de vertente setentrional da Serra do Caldeirão', *Revista Portuguesa Arqueologia* 5/2.219–31.

Guerra, A., A. C. Ramos, S. Melro, I. A. Pires 1999 'Uma estela epigrafada da Idade do Ferro, proviente do Monte Novo do Castelinho (Almodôvar)', *Revista Portuguesa de Arquelogia* 2/1, 143–52.

Harrison, R. J. 1988 *Spain at the Dawn of History: Iberians, Phoenicians and Greeks*. London, Thames and Hudson.

Harrison, R. J. 2004 *Symbols and Warriors: Images of the European Bronze Age*. Bristol, Western Academic & Specialist Press.

Hawkes, C. F. C. 1977 *Pytheas: Europe and the Greek Explorers. A Lecture Delivered at New College, Oxford on 20th May 1975*. J. L. Myres Memorial Lecture 8. Oxford, Blackwell.

Isaac, G. R. 2004 'The Nature and Origins of the Celtic Languages: Atlantic Seaways, Italo-Celtic and Other Paralinguistic Misapprehensions', *Studia Celtica* 38.49–58.

Isaac, G. R. 2007 'Celtic and Afro-Asiatic'. *The Celtic Languages in Contact: Papers from the Workshop within the Framework of the XIII International Conference of Celtic Studies. Bonn 26–27 July, 2007*, ed. H. L. C. Tristram, 25–80. Potsdam, Potsdam University Press. (e-book: http://opus.kobv.de/volltext/2007/1568)

Isaac, G. R. 2007b *Studies in Celtic Sound Changes and their Chronology*. Innsbruck, Innsbrucker Beiträge zur Sprachwissenschaft.

James, S. 2000 *The Atlantic Celts: Ancient People or Modern Invention?* London, British Museum Press.

Jenkins, D. 1990 'Gwalch: Welsh', *Cambridge Medieval Celtic Studies* 19.55–67.

Jongeling, Karel 2000 *Comparing Welsh and Hebrew*. CNWS Publications 81. Leiden, Research School of Asian, African and Amerindian Studies, Universiteit Leiden.

Jordán Cólera, C. 2002 'De las *Oestryminides*, la *Garumna* e de hidrotopónimos relacionados', *Emerita, Revista de Lingüística y Filología Clásica* 70/2, 213–30.

Jordán Cólera, C. 2007 'Celtiberian', *e-Keltoi* 6: The Celts in the Iberian Peninsula, 749–850.

Jufer, N., & Th. Luginbühl 2001 *Les dieux gaulois: répertoire des noms de divinités celtiques connus par l'épigraphie, les textes antiques et la toponymie*. Paris, Errance.

Koch, J. T. 1991 'Ériu, Alba, and Letha: When was a Language Ancestral to Gaelic First Spoken in Ireland?', *Emania* 9.17–27.

Koch, J. T. 1992 '"Gallo-Brittonic" vs. "Insular Celtic": The Inter-relationships of the Celtic Languages Reconsidered'. *Bretagne et pays celtiques—langues, histoire, civilisation: Mélanges offerts à la mémoire de Léon Fleuriot*, eds. G. Le Menn & J.-Y. Le Moing, 471–95. Saint-Brieuc, Skol Uhel ar Vro.

Koch, J. T., et al. 2007 *An Atlas for Celtic Studies: Archaeology and Names in Ancient Europe and Early Medieval Ireland, Britain, and Brittany*. Celtic Studies Publications 12. Oxford, Oxbow Books.

Koch, J. T. 2009 *Tartessian: Celtic in the South-west at the Dawn of History*, Celtic Studies Publications 13. Aberystwyth.

Koch, J. T., & J. Carey, eds. 2003 *The Celtic Heroic Age: Literary Sources for Ancient Celtic Europe & Early Ireland & Wales*. 4th ed. Celtic Studies 1. Aberystwyth.

Kristiansen, K. 1998 *Europe Before History*. New Studies in Archaeology. Cambridge, Cambridge University Press.

Kristiansen, K., & T. Larsson 2005 *The Rise of the Bronze Age: Travels, Transmissions, and Transformations*. Cambridge, Cambridge University Press.

Lambert, P.-Y. 1994 *La langue gauloise*, Collection des Hesperides. Paris, Editions Errance.

Lewis, H., & H. Pedersen 1989 *A Concise Comparative Celtic Grammar*. 3rd edn. Göttingen, Vandenhoeck and Ruprecht. First published, 1937.

Lipinski, E. 2004 *Itineraria Phoenicia*. Studia Phoenicia 18, Orientalia Lovaniensia Analecta. Leuven, Peeters.

Luján, E. 2007 'L'onomastique des Vettons: analyse linguistique', *Gaulois et celtique continental*, eds. P.-Y. Lambert & G.-J. Pinault, 245–75. Genève,

Librairie Droz.

McCone, K. R. 1985 'Varia II', *Ériu* 36.169–76.

McCone, K. R. 2006 'Greek Κελτός and Γαλάτης, Latin *Gallus* "Gaul"', *Die Sprache* 46, 94–111.

McManus, D. 1991 *A Guide to Ogam*. Maynooth Monographs 4. Maynooth, An Sagart.

Mallory, J. P. 1989 *In Search of the Indo-Europeans: Language, Archaeology and Myth*. London, Thames and Hudson.

Mallory, J. P., & D. Q. Adams 2006 *The Oxford Introduction to Proto-Indo-European and the Proto-Indo-European World*. Oxford, Oxford University Press.

Marco Simón, F. 2005 'Religion and Religious Practices of the Ancient Celts of the Iberian Peninsula', *e-Keltoi 6: The Celts in the Iberian Peninsula*, 287–345.

Mayrhofer, M. 1992–2001 *Etymologisches Wörterbuch des Altindoarischen*. Heidelberg, Carl Winter Universitätsverlag.

Mederos Martín, A. 1996 'La connexión Levantino-Chipriota. Indícios de comercio atlántico con el Mediterráneo Oriental durante el Bronce Final' (1150–950 AC), *Trabajos de Prehistoria* 53(2), 95–115.

Mederos Martín, A. 1997 'Cambio de rumbo. Interacción comercial ente el Bronce Final Atlántico ibérico y el micénico en el Mediterráneo Central (1425–1050 AC)', *Trabajos de Prehistoria*, 54(2), 113–34.

Mederos Martín, A. 1999 'Ex occidente lux. El comercio micénico en el mediterráneo central y occidental (1625–1100 AC)', *Complutum* 10, 229–66.

Mederos Martín, A. 2008 'Carros micénicos del Heládico Final III en las estelas decoradas del Bronce Final II–IIIA del suroeste de la Península Ibérica', *Contacto cultural entre el Mediterráneo y el Atlántico (siglos XII–VIII ane). La precolonización a debate*, ed. S. Celestino, N. Rafel, X.-L. Armada, 437–63. Madrid, Escuela Española de Historia y Arqueología en Roma.

Mederos Martín, A., & L. A. Ruiz Carbrero 2001 'Los inicios de la scritura en la Península Ibérica: grafitos en cerámicas del Bronce Final III y Fenicias', *Complutum* 12, 97–112.

Meid, W. 2008 'Celtic Origins, the Western and the Eastern Celts', Sir John Rhŷs Memorial Lecture, *Proceedings of the British Academy* 154, 177–99.

Mitchell, S. 1993 *Anatolia: Land, Men and Gods in Asia Minor*. 2 vols. Oxford, Clarendon.

Morandi, A. 2004 *Celti d'Italia. Tomo II. Epigrafia e lingua*. Roma, Spazio Tre.

Moret, P. 2006 'La formation d'une toponymie et d'une etnonymie grecque de l'Ibérie: étapes et acteurs', *La invención de una geografía de la Península Ibérica. 1. La época republicana*, eds. G. Cruz Andreotti, P. Le Roux, P. Moret, 39–76. Madrid.

Ó Cathasaigh, T. 1977–8 'The Semantics of "Síd"', *Éigse* 17, 137–55.

Olmos, R. 1989 'Los griegos en Tartessos: una nueva contrastación entre las fuentes arqueológicas y las literarias', *Tartessos: Arqueología Protohistórica del Bajo Guadalquivir*, ed. M. E. Aubet Semmler, 497–521. Barcelona, Sabadell.

Peckham, B. 1998 'Phoenicians in Sardinia: Tyrians or Sidonians?', *Sardinian and Aegean Chronology*, eds. M. S. Balmuth, R. H. Tykot, 347–54. Studies in Sardinian Archaeology 5. Oxford, Oxbow.

Pereira Sieso, J. 1989 'Nuevos datos para la valoración del hinterland tartésico. El enterramiento de la Casa del Carpio (Belvis de la Jara, Toledo)', *Tartessos: Arqueología Protohistórica del Bajo Guadalquivir*, ed. M. E. Aubet Semmler, 395–409. Barcelona, Sabadell.

Pingel, V. 1993 'Bemerkungen zu den ritzverzierten Stelen im Südwesten der Iberischen Halbinsel', *Lengua y cultura en la Hispania prerromana, Actas del V Coloquio sobre Lenguas y Culturas Prerromanas de la Península Ibérica*, eds. J. Untermann & F. Villar, 209–31. Salamanca, Ediciones Universidad de Salamanca.

Pokorny, J. 2002 *Indogermanisches etymologisches Wörterbuch*. 4th edn. 2 vols. Tübingen, A. Francke.

Prósper, B. M. 2007 *Estudio lingüístico del plomo celtibérico de Iniesta*. Acta Salmanticensia, Estudios Filológicos 319. Salamanca, Ediciones Universidad de Salamanca.

Raybould, M. E. & P. Sims-Williams 2007 *The Geography of Celtic Personal Names in the Latin Inscriptions of the Roman Empire*. Aberystwyth, CMCS.

Renfrew, C. 1987 *Archaeology and Language: The Puzzle of Indo-European Origins*. London, Pimlico, 1998. First published, London, Cape.

Rix, H. 2001 *Lexikon der indogermanischen Verben*.

Wiesbaden, Ludwig Reichert.

Rodríguez Ramos, J. 2000 'La lectura de las inscripciones sudlusitano-tartesias', *Faventia* 22/1.21–48.

Rodríguez Ramos, J. 2002 'Las inscripciones sudlusitano-tartesias: su función, lengua y contexto socio-económico', *Complutum* 13.85–95.

Ruiz, M. M. 1989 'Las necrópolis tartésicas: prestigio, poder y jerarquás', *Tartessos: Arqueología Protohistórica del Bajo Guadalquivir*, ed. M. E. Aubet Semmler, 247–86. Barcelona, Sabadell.

Ruiz-Gálvez Priego, M. 1995 'Cronología de la Ría de Huelva en el marco del Bronce Final de Europa occidental', *Ritos de paso y puntos de paso. La Ría de Huelva en el mundo del Bronce Final europeo*, ed. M. Ruiz-Gálvez, 79–83. Madrid, Editorial Complutense.

Ruiz-Gálvez Priego, M. 2000 'Weight Systems and Exchange Networks in Bronze Age Europe', *Metals Make the World Go Round: Supply and Circulation of Metals in Bronze Age Europe*, ed. C. F. E. Pare, 267–79. Oxford, Oxbow.

Ruiz-Gálvez Priego, M. 2008 'Writing, Counting, Self-Awareness, Experiencing Distant Worlds. Identity Processes and Free-lance Trade in the Bronze Age/Iron Age Transition', *Contacto cultural entre el Mediterráneo y el Atlántico (siglos XII–VII ane). La precolonización a debate*, eds. S. Celestino, N. Rafel, X.-L. Armada, 27–40. Madrid, Escuela Española de Historia y Arqueología en Roma.

Salinas de Frías, M. 2006 *Los pueblos prerromanos de la península Ibérica*. Madrid, Ediciones Akal.

Sánchez Moreno, E. 1996 'A proposito de las *gentilitates*: los grupos familiares del área vetona y su adecuación para la interpretación de la organización social prerromana', *Veleia* 13, 115–42.

Schmidt, K. H. 1976 'Zur keltiberischen Inschrift von Botorrita', *Bulletin of the Board of Celtic Studies* 26/4.375–94.

Schmidt, K. H. 1985 'Contribution to the Identification of Lusitanian', *Actas del III Coloquio sobre Lenguas y Culturas Paleohispánicas*, ed. J. de Hoz, 319–41. Salamanca, Universidad de Salamanca.

Schmidt, K. H. 1996 *Celtic: A Western Indo-European Language?* Innsbruck, Innsbrucker Beiträge zur Sprachwissenschaft.

Schmoll, U. 1961 *Die südlusitanischen Inschriften.*

Wiesbaden, Harrassowitz.

Schrijver, P. 2004 'Der Tod des Festlandkeltischen und die Geburt des Französischen, Niederländischen un Hochdeutschen', *Sprachtod und Sprachgenurt*, eds. P. Schrijver & P.-A. Mumm, 1–20. Bremen, Hempen Verlag.

Schrijver, P. 2005 'Early Celtic Diphthongization and the Celtic–Latin Interface', *New Approaches to Celtic Place-names in Ptolemy's Geography*', eds. J. de Hoz, E. R. Luján, P. Sims-Williams, 55–67. Madrid, Ediciones Clásicas.

Schulten, A. 1945 *Tartessos*. Madrid, Espasa-Calpe.

Sims-Williams, P. 1998 'Celtomania and Celtoscepticism', CMCS 36 (1998) 1–35.

Sims-Williams, P. 2006 *Ancient Celtic Place-names in Europe and Asia Minor*. Publications of the Philological Society 39. Oxford, Blackwell.

Sims-Williams, P. 2007 *Studies on Celtic Languages before the Year 1000*. Aberystwyth, CMCS.

Sverdrup, H., & R. Guardans 2002 'A Study of the Tartessian Script and Language', *Languages and their Speakers in Ancient Eurasia: Studies in Linguistics and Cultura; Language Reconstruction Presented in Honour of Prof. Aharon Dolgopolsky*, eds. V. Shevoroshkin & P. Sidwell, 115–48. Association for the History of Language Monographs and Serials 4. Canberra, Association for the History of Language.

Thurneysen, R. 1975 *A Grammar of Old Irish*, trans. D. A. Binchy & O. Bergin. Rev. and enlarged edn. Dublin, Dublin Institute for Advanced Studies. First published, 1946.

Tomlin, R. S. O. 1988 'The Curse Tablets', *The Temple of Sulis Minerva at Bath: Volume 2 The Finds from the Sacred Spring*, ed. B. Cunliffe, 59–277. Oxford, Oxford University Committee for Archaeology, Monograph 16.

Untermann, J. 1962 'Das silbenschriftliche Element in der iberischen Schrift', *Emerita* 30, 281–94.

Untermann, J. 1980 'Namenkundliche Anmerkungen zu lateinischen Inschriften aus Kantabrien', *Beiträge zur Namenforschung* 15, 367–92.

Untermann, J. 1985 'Los teónimos de la región lusitano-gallega como fuente de las lenguas indígenas', *Actas del III Coloquio sobre Lenguas y Culturas Paleohispánicas*, ed. J. de Hoz, 343–63. Salamanca, Universidad de Salamanca.

Untermann, J. 1985/6 'Lusitanisch, Keltiberisch,

Keltisch', *Veleia* 2/3, 57–76.

Untermann, J. 1992 'Anotaciones al estudio de las lenguas prerromanas del noroeste de la Península Ibérica (1)', *Galicia: da romanidade á xermanización, Problemas históricos e culturais. Actas do encontro científico en homenaxe a Fermín Bouza Brey (1901–1973)*, 369–97. Santiago de Compostela.

Untermann, J. 1995 'Zum Stand der Deutung der "tartessischen" Inschriften'. *Hispano-Gallo-Brittonica: Essays in Honour of Professor D. Ellis Evans on the Occasion of his Sixty-Fifth Birthday*, eds. J. F. Eska et al., 244–59. Cardiff, University of Wales Press.

Untermann, J. 1996 'VII. La onomástica de Botorrita 3 en le contexto de la Hispanica indoeuropea', *El tercer bronce de Botorrita (Contrebia Belaisca)*, ed. F. Beltrán, Collección Arqueología 19, 167–80. Zaragoza, Gobierno de Aragon.

Untermann, J. (ed.) (with D. S. Wodtko) 1997 *Monumenta Linguarum Hispanicarum 4*. Wiesbaden, Ludwig Reichert.

Untermann, J. 1997b 'Neue Überlegungen und eine neue Quelle zur Entstehung der althispanischen Schriften', *Madrider Mitteilungen* 38, 49–66. *Deutsches Archäologisches Institut Abteilung Madrid. Mainz, Verlag Philipp von Zabern*.

Untermann, J. 2004 'Célticos y Túrdulos', *Palaeohispanica* 4.199–214.

Untermann, J. forthcoming 'La aportación de la toponimia a la definición de las lenguas ibérica y tartesia'.

Vallejo Ruiz, J. M. 2005 *Antroponimia indígena de la Lusitania romana*. Vitoria/Gasteiz, Anejos de Veleia, Series Minor 23.

Vendryes, J. 1960– *Lexique étymologique de l'Irlandais ancien*. Dublin, Dublin Institute for Advanced Studies/Paris, CNRS.

Villar, F. 1995 'Los nombres de Tartesos', *Habis* 26, 243–70.

Villar, F. 1997 'The Celtiberian Language', *Zeitschrift für celtische Philologie* 49/50.898–949.

Villar, F. 2004 'The Celtic Language of the Iberian Peninsula', *Studies in Baltic and Indo-European Linguistics in Honor of William R. Schmalstieg*, eds. P. Baldi & P. U. Dini, 243–74. Amsterdam, John Benjamins.

Wodtko, D. S. 2000 *Monumenta Linguarum Hispanicarum 5.1, Wörterbuch der keltiberischen Inschriften*, ed. J. Untermann. Wiesbaden, Ludwig Reichert.

Wodtko, D. S., B. Irslinger, & C. Schneider 2008 *Nomina im Indogermanischen Lexikon*. Heidelberg, Universitätsverlag Winter.

ANCIENT REFERENCES TO TARTESSOS

Philip M. Freeman

TARTESSOS appears in ancient sources from Greece and the Near East beginning in the middle of the first millennium BC as merchants from these regions sailed beyond the fabled Pillars of Hercules in search of new business opportunities. Over the next thousand years, Greeks, Assyrians, Hebrews, and Romans considered Tartessos as the frontier of civilization, an exotic land of rivers rich in silver and gold, an exceptionally long-lived king, and dangerous ferrets. To many classical authors Tartessos is notable primarily as the setting of the deadly mythological contest between the hero Hercules and the three-headed monster Geryon. The passages below include all significant references to Tartessos until the collapse of the Roman Empire in the west. I have taken as my starting-point the comprehensive list of references to Tartessos in Alvar and Blázquez *Los Enigmos de Tarteso* (pages 204–14). It should be noted that the question of whether Semitic *Taršiš* (*Tarshish* in the Old Testament) invariably refers to Tartessos is not altogether settled; however, that this is what it does mean in many of its occurrences is a long-standing view and accepted by many scholars today.

CLASSICAL REFERENCES

Aelian (*c.* AD 170–235)

Varia Historia 14.4:

ὅτι Ἀριστείδης ὁ Λοκρὸς ὑπὸ Ταρτησσίας γαλῆς δηχθεὶς καὶ ἀποθνήσκων εἶπεν ὅτι πολὺ ἂν ἥδιον ἦν αὐτῷ δηχθέντι ὑπὸ λέοντος ἢ παρδάλεως ἀποθανεῖν, εἴπερ οὖν ἔδει τινὸς τῷ θανάτῳ προφάσεως, ἢ ὑπὸ θηρίου τοιούτου, τὴν ἀδοξίαν, ἐμοὶ δοκεῖν, ἐκεῖνος τοῦ δήγματος πολλῷ βαρύτερον φέρων ἢ τὸν θάνατον αὐτόν.

When Aristides of Locris was bitten by a Tartessian ferret, his dying words were that, if he had to die, he would have preferred to have been perished from the bite of a lion or leopard than such a lowly beast. It seems to me he felt the indignity of the bite much more than death itself.

NOTE: γαλέη (contr. γαλῆ) is a term for various animals, including the ferret, marten, polecat, and weasel.

Anacreon (sixth century BC)

s.v. Strabo, *Geography* 3.2.14:

> ἐγωγ᾽ οὔτ᾽ ἂν ᾿Αμαλθίης
> βουλοίμην κέρας οὔτ᾽ ἔτεα
> πεντήκοντα τε καὶ ἑκατόν
> Ταρτησσοῦ βασιλεῦσαι.

> I myself would not wish
> for the horn of Amaltheia,
> nor to rule Tartessos
> for one hundred and fifty years.

Appian (second century AD)

Hispanica 6.2:

οἵ τινες δ᾽ αὐτὴν οἰκῆσαι πρῶτοι νομίζονται καὶ οἱ μετ᾽ ἐκείνους κατέσχον, οὐ πάνυ μοι ταῦτα φροντίζειν ἀρέσκει, μόνα τὰ ῾Ρωμαίων συγγράφοντι, πλὴν ὅτι Κελτοί μοι δοκοῦσί ποτε, τὴν Πυρήνην ὑπερβάντες αὐτοῖς συνοικῆσαι, ὅθεν ἄρα καὶ τὸ Κελτιβήρων ὄνομα ἐρρύη. δοκοῦσι δέ μοι καὶ Φοίνικες, ἐς ᾿Ιβηρίαν ἐκ πολλοῦ θαμινὰ ἐπ᾽ ἐμπορίᾳ διαπλέοντες, οἰκῆσαί τινα τῆς ᾿Ιβηρίας, ῞Ελληνές τε ὁμοίως, ἐς Ταρτησσὸν καὶ ᾿Αργανθώνιον Ταρτησσοῦ βασιλέα πλέοντες, ἐμμεῖναι καὶ τῶνδέ τινες ἐν ᾿Ιβηρίᾳ· ἡ γὰρ ᾿Αργανθωνίου βασιλεία ἐν ῎Ιβηρσιν ἦν. καὶ Ταρτησσός μοι δοκεῖ τότε εἶναι πόλις ἐπὶ θαλάσσης, ἣ νῦν Καρπησσὸς ὀνομάζεται. τό τε τοῦ ῾Ηρακλέους ἱερὸν τὸ ἐν στήλαις Φοίνικές μοι δοκοῦσιν ἱδρύσασθαι· καὶ θρησκεύεται νῦν ἔτι φοινικικῶς, ὅ τε θεὸς αὐτοῖς οὐχ ὁ Θηβαῖός ἐστιν ἀλλ᾽ ὁ Τυρίων. ταῦτα μὲν δὴ τοῖς παλαιολογοῦσι μεθείσθω.

I do not intend to investigate fully who first came there and who came later since I am writing only Roman history. But I do believe that some Celts once crossed the Pyrenees mountains and mixed with the local population, hence the name Celtiberia. I also believe that from early times the Phoenicians sailed to Spain and established trading posts there. Likewise the Greeks visited Tartessos with its king Arganthonios and some remained there, for the kingdom of Arganthonios was in Spain. I believe that Tartessos was the city on the sea now called Karpessos. I also think the Phoenicians built the temple of Hercules which stands on the straits. The rituals there are still of a Phoenician type and their Hercules is of Tyre, not Thebes. But I leave these matters to other historians.

Hispanica 6.63:

Ῥωμαίων δὲ μόλις ἐκ μυρίων ἑξακισχίλοι διέδρασαν ἐς Καρπησσόν, ἐπὶ θαλάσσῃ· πόλιν, ἣν ἐγὼ νομίζω πρὸς Ἑλλήνων πάλαι Ταρτησσὸν ὀνομάζεσθαι, καὶ Ἀργανθώνιον αὐτῆς βασιλεῦσαι, ὃν ἐς πεντήκοντα καὶ ἑκατὸν ἔτη ἀφικέσθαι φασίν.

Only six thousand of the ten thousand Romans struggled alive to the city of Karpessos on the sea. I believe the town was once called Tartessos by the Greeks and was ruled by King Arganthonios, who is said to have lived one hundred and fifty years.

Aristophanes (*c.* 445–*c.* 385 BC)

Frogs 474–5:

> πλευμόνων τ᾽ ἀνθάψεται
> Ταρτησσία μύραινα.

> A Tartessian sea-eel
> will attack your lungs!

Aristotle (384–322 BC)

Meteorologica 350b:

ἐκ δὲ τῆς Πυρήνης (τοῦτο δ᾽ ἐστὶν ὄρος πρὸς δυσμὴν ἰσημερινὴν ἐν τῇ Κελτικῇ) ῥέουσιν ὅ τε Ἴστρος καὶ ὁ Ταρτησσός. οὗτος μὴν οὖν ἔξω στηλῶν, ὁ δ᾽ Ἴστρος δι᾽ ὅλης τῆς Εὐρώπης εἰς τὸν Εὔξεινον πόντον.

From Pyrene (this is a mountain towards the equinoctial sunset in Celtica) the Ister and Tartessos rivers flow. The latter enters the sea outside the Pillars of Hercules, while the Ister flows across Europe into the Euxine.

(Pseudo-Aristotle) *De mirabilibus auscultationibus* 844a:

τοὺς πρώτους τῶν Φοινίκων ἐπὶ Ταρτησσὸν πλεύσαντας λέγεται τοσοῦτον
ἀργύριον ἀντιφορτίσασθαι, ἔλαιον καὶ ἄλλον ναυτικὸν ῥῶπον εἰσαγαγόντας,
ὥστε μηκέτι ἔχειν δύνασθαι μήτε ἐπιδέξασθαι τὸν ἄργυρον.

They say that the first Phoenicians sailing to Tartessos traded olive oil and other goods
for so much silver that no one could keep or receive it.

Arrian (second century AD)

Anabasis of Alexander 2.16:

ὡς τόν γε ἐν Ταρτησσῷ πρὸς Ἰβήρων τιμώμενον Ἡρακλέα, ἵνα καὶ στῆλαί
τινες Ἡρακλέους ὠνομασμέναι εἰσί, δοκῶ ἐγὼ τὸν Τύριον εἶναι Ἡρακλέα,
ὅτι Φοινίκων κτίσμα ἡ Ταρτησσὸς καὶ τῷ Φοινίκων νόμῳ ὅ τε νεὼς
πεποίηται τῷ Ἡρακλεῖ τῷ ἐκεῖ καὶ αἱ θυσίαι θύονται.

So also I believe that the Hercules honoured at Tartessos by the Iberians (where the
pillars are named for Hercules) is the Hercules of Tyre. This is because Tartessos is a
Phoenician town, with the temple of Hercules built in the Phoenician style and worship
conducted according to Phoenician custom.

Ausonius (fourth century AD)

Epistle 6:

> *Si qua fides falsis umquam est adhibenda poetis*
> *   nec plasma semper adlinunt,*
> *Paule, Camenarum celeberrime Castaliarum*
> *   alumne quondam, nunc pater,*
> *aut avus, aut proavis antiquor, ut fuit olim*
> *   Tartesiorum regulus:*
> *intemerata tibi maneant promissa, memento.*

> If any faith is to be placed in the false words of poets,
>   if they are not forever writing fiction,
> Paulus—once the most famous offspring of Castalian Camenae,
>   now father or grandfather
> or more ancient than a great-grandfather,

as once they said of the king of Tartessus—
remember to keep your promises true.

Epistle 23:

Condiderat iam Solis equos Tartesia Calpe
stridebatque freto Titan iam segnis Hibero.

Now Tartessian Calpe has hidden the chariot horses of the sun
and sluggish Titan sinks groaning beneath the Spanish wave.

Avienus (fourth century AD)

Ora maritima 51–6:

Hic porro habebis, pars mei cordis Probe,
quicquid per aequor insularum attollitur
—per aequor illud scilicet, quod post cava
hiantis orbis a freto Tartessio
Atlanticisque fluctibus procul sitam
in usque glaebam proruit nostrum mare.

Here, Probus, dear to my heart, you will have
whatever islands rise up from the waters
—the waters from which our sea stretches
after the gaping recesses of the Tartessian sea
and the Atlantic waves.

85–7:

hic Gadir urbs est, dicta Tartessus prius,
hic sunt columnae pertinacis Herculis,
Abila atque Calpe.

Here is the city Gadir, once called Tartessus,
here the pillars of unyielding Hercules,
Abila and Calpe.

108–19:

> *ast hinc duobus in sacram, sic insulam*
> *dixere prisci, solibus cursus rati est.*
> *haec inter undas multam caespitem iacet,*
> *eamque late gens Hiernorum colit.*
> *propinqua rursus insula Albionum patet.*
> *Tartessiisque in terminos Oestrumnidum*
> *negotiandi mos erat. Carthaginis*
> *etiam colonis et vulgus inter Herculis*
> *agitans columnas haec adhibant aequora.*
> *quae Himilco Poenus mensibus vix quattuor,*
> *ut ipse semet rem probasse rettulit*
> *enavigantem, posse transmitti adserit.*

> But from here there is a two-day journey to the sacred isle,
> as the ancients called it, a great land among the waves.
> The Hierni dwell throughout the island.
> Nearby is the island of the Albiones,
> and the Tartessians used to sail to the end of the Oestrumnides.
> The Carthaginian colonists and the common people
> around the Pillars of Hercules also visited these waters.
> Himilco of Carthage says that he himself dared the voyage
> and that the journey was scarcely less than four months.

NOTE: *Sacra insula* 'sacred isle' is probably based on a connection or confusion between Ἰερνη, or some similar early Greek form of *Iveriō* 'Ireland', and ἱερή 'holy, sacred'.
Himilco of Carthage lived in the later sixth or early fifth century BC.

178–80:

> *et rusus inde si petat quisquam pede*
> *Tartessiorum litus, exuperet viam*
> *vix luce quarta.*

> And again if someone sought
> the Tartessian shore from there by foot,
> he would scarcely complete the journey in four days.

223–5:

genti et Cynetum hic terminus. Tartessius
ager his adhaeret adluitque caespitem
Tartessus amnis.

This is the border of the Cynetian people.
The Tartessian land borders them
and the Tartessian river washes the land.

250–5:

at Hiberus inde manat amnis et locos
fecundat unda. plurimi ex ipso ferunt
dictos Hiberos, non ab illo flumine
quod inquietos Vascones praelabitur.
nam quicquid amnem gentis huius adiacet
occiduum ad axem, Hiberiam cognominant.
pars porro eoa continet Tartessios
et Cilbicenos.

But the Hiberus river flows from here
and its water nourishes the land. Many say
the Hiberi are named from this river, not from
that which flows past the hostile Vascones.
For whoever dwells to the west of the river
they call Hiberi. But to the east
live the Tartessians and the Cilbiceni.

265–70:

hic ora late sunt sinus Tartessii.
dictoque ab amni in haec locorum puppibus
via est diei. Gadir hic est oppidum,
nam Punicorum lingua consaeptum locum
Gadir vocabat. ipsa Tartessus prius
cognominata est.

Here is the wide shore of the Tartessian bay.
To here from the river mentioned above, the journey
for boats is one day. Here is the town of Gadir,
for in the Punic language Gadir means enclosed.
Once it was called Tartessus.

284–5:

Tartessus amnis ex Ligustino lacu
per aperta fusus undique adlapsu ligat.

The Tartessian river spilling out from the Ligustine lake
laps the shore on all sides.

308–9:

Tartessiorum mons dehinc attollitur
silvis opacus.

From there the Tartessian mountain rises,
dark with forests.

331–2:

nec respuendus testis est Dionysius,
Libyae esse finem, qui docet Tartessium.

Nor is the testimony of Dionysius to be rejected,
Who claims that the boundary of Africa is Tartessus.

425–30:

hos propter autem mox iugum Barbetium est
Malachaeque flumen urbe cum cognomine.
Menace priore quae vocata est saeculo.
Tartessiorum iuris illic insula
antistat urbem, Noctilucae ab incolis
sacrata pridem.

Near these is soon the Barbetian ridge
and the river Malacha with a city bearing the same name.
In an earlier age it was called Menace.
An island once ruled by Tartessus lies opposite the city,
long ago made sacred to Noctiluca by those who dwelt there.

460–3:

> *rursus hinc se litoris*
> *fundunt harenae et litus hoc tres insulae*
> *cinxere late. hic terminus quondam stetit*
> *Tartessiorum, hic Herna civitas fuit.*

> Again from here the sands of the shore extend
> and three islands bind the shore over a great distance.
> Here was once the border of the Tartessians,
> here was the city Herna.

Cicero (106–43 BC)

Epistulae ad Atticum 7.3.11:

puto enim, in senatu si quando praeclare pro re publica dixero, Tartessium istum tuum mihi exeunti, 'iube sodes nummos curari'.

For I think that if I ever make a speech in favour of the state before the Senate, your friend from Tartessus will say to me on the way out: 'Pay up, if you please.'

De senectute 69:

Da enim supremum tempus, expectemus Tartessiorum regis aetatem—fuit enim ut scriptum video Arganthonius quidam Gadibus qui octoginta regnaverat annos, centum viginti vixerat.

Grant that we might live as long as possible, hoping to reach the age of the Tartessian king—for I have read of a certain Arganthonius at Gades who reigned eighty years and lived to be one hundred and twenty.

Claudian (fourth/fifth centuries AD)

Epithalamium 159–61:

> *nec non et variis vectae Nereides ibant*
> *audito rumore feris (hanc pisce voluto*
> *sublevat Oceani monstrum Tartesia tigris).*

> When they heard the story, the Nereids came
> mounted on various beasts (a monstrous sea-tiger
> of Tartessus carried one).

Columela (first century AD)

De re rustica 8.16:

sola ex pretiosis piscibus muraena, quamuis Tartesii Carpathiique pelagi, quod est ultimum, vernacula, quovis hospes freto peregrinum mare sustinet.

Of valuable fish, only the sea-eel found in Tartessian waters and the distant Carpathian Sea can survive in whatever sea it finds itself.

10.185–6, 192:

> *Et mea, quam generant Tartesi litore Gades,*
> *Candida vibrato discrimine, candida thyrso est...*
> *Tuque tuis, Mavors, Tartesida pange calendis.*

> And my own lettuce, which Gades produces on the Tartessian shore,
> with pale curved leaf and white stalk...
> On your calends, Mars, plant the Tartessian lettuce.

NOTE: Columela was a native of Gades.

10.370–1:

> *Sed iam prototomos tempus decidere caules*
> *Et Tartesiacos Paphiosque revellere thyrsos.*

> But now is the time to cut the early stalks,
> with Tartessian and Paphian stems.

Ephorus (fourth century BC)

FGrH 2a, 70, F 1:

ἀλλὰ μὴν καὶ ἄλλην τινὰ ἱστορίαν εἴρηκεν παλαιὰν Ἔφορος, ᾗ οὐκ ἄλογον ἐντυχεῖν καὶ Ὅμηρον. λέγεσθαι γὰρ φησιν ὑπὸ τῶν Ταρτησσίων Αἰθίοπας τὴν Λιβύην ἐπελθόντας μέχρι δύρεως τοὺς μὲν αὐτοῦ μεῖναι, τοὺς δὲ καὶ τῆς παραίας κατασχεῖν πολλήν.

But Ephorus relates another ancient story, which it is reasonable that Homer knew. He says that it is reported by the Tartessians that the Ethiopians advanced into Africa as far as the Atlas Mountains and that some remained there, while others settled on the lands around the sea.

FGrH 2a, 70, F 129b:

μετὰ ταῦτα δ' ἐστιν ἡμερῶν δυοῖν τελέσαντι πλοῦν ἐμπόριον εὐτυχέστατον ἡ λεγομένη Ταρτησσός, ἐπιφανὴς πόλις, ποταμόρρυτον κασσίτερον ἐκ τῆς Κελτικῆς χρυσόν τε καὶ χαλκὸν φέρουσα πλείονα.

After this it is a two-day sail to a very prosperous market called Tartessos, a famous city, with much tin carried by river, as well as gold and copper from Celtic lands.

Hecataeus (*c.* 500 BC)

s.v. Stephanus of Byzantium Ἐλιβύργη·

Ἐλιβύργη, πόλις Ταρτησσοῦ, Ἑκαταῖος Εὐρώπῃ.

Elibyrge: A city of Tartessos, according to Hecataeus in his *Europa*.

Herodian (second century AD)

De prosidia catholica 3.1, page 210:

Ταρτησσός· πόλις Ἰβηρίας ἀπὸ ποταμοῦ τοῦ ἀπὸ τοῦ Ἀργυροῦ ὄρους ῥέοντος.

Tartessos: an Iberian city by the river running from the Silver Mountain.

De prosidia catholica 3.1, page 255:

Ἴβυλλα· πόλις Ταρτησσίας.

Ibylla: a Tartessian city.

De prosidia catholica 3.1, page 334:

Λιγυστίνη· πόλις Λιγύων τῆς δυτικῆς Ἰβηρίας ἐγγὺς καὶ τῆς Ταρτησσοῦ πλησίον.

Ligystine: a city of the Ligurians near western Spain and Tartessos.

Herodotus (*c.* 490–*c.* 425 BC)

1.163:

οἱ δὲ Φωκαιέες οὗτοι ναυτιλίῃσι μακρῇσι πρῶτοι Ἑλλήνων ἐχρήσαντο,
καὶ τόν τε Ἀδρίην καὶ τὴν Τυρσηνίην καὶ τὴν Ἰβηρίην καὶ τὸν Ταρτησσὸν
οὗτοι εἰσι οἱ καταδέξαντες· ἐναυτίλλοντο δὲ οὐ στρογγύλῃσι νηυσὶ ἀλλὰ
πεντηκοντέροισι. ἀπικόμενοι δὲ ἐς τὸν Ταρτησσὸν προσφιλέες ἐγένοντο τῷ
βασιλέι τῶν Ταρτησσίων, τῷ οὔνομα μὲν ἦν Ἀργανθώνιος, ἐτυράννευσε
δὲ Ταρτησσοῦ ὀγδώκοντα ἔτεα, ἐβίωσε δὲ πάντα εἴκοσι καὶ ἑκατόν.
τούτῳ δὴ τῷ ἀνδρὶ προσφιλέες οἱ Φωκαιέες οὕτω δή τι ἐγένοντο ὡς τὰ μὲν
πρῶτα σφέας ἐκλιπόντας Ἰωνίην ἐκέλευε τῆς ἑωυτοῦ χώρης οἰκῆσαι ὅκου
βούλονται· μετὰ δέ, ὡς τοῦτο γε οὐκ ἔπειθε τοὺς Φωκαιέας, ὁ δὲ πυθόμενος
τὸν Μῆδον παρ' αὐτῶν ὡς αὔξοιτο, ἐδίδου σφι χρήματα τεῖχος περιβαλέσθαι
τὴν πόλιν, ἐδίδου δὲ ἀφειδέως· καὶ γὰρ καὶ ἡ περίοδος τοῦ τείχος οὐκ ὀλί
γοι στάδιοι εἰσί, τοῦτο δὲ πᾶν λίθων μεγάλων καὶ εὖ συναρμοσμένων.

These Phocaeans were the first Greeks to make long sea voyages, discovering the Adriatic
and Tyrrhenia and Iberia and Tartessos. They did not sail in cargo ships but in vessels
with fifty oars. When they arrived at Tartessos they made friends with the king of the
Tartessians named Arganthonios. He ruled Tartessos for eighty years and lived to be one
hundred and twenty. They were so friendly to the king that he tried to persuade them to
leave their own country and settle anywhere in his land they might wish. But when he was
not able to persuade them, having learned how the power of the Medes was increasing,
he gave them money to build a wall around their city. He gave this money generously,
for the circuit of the wall is many stades long, all made of large stones fitted closely
together.

1.165:

πρὸς ταῦτα οἱ Φωκαιέες ἐστέλλοντο ἐς Κύρνον· ἐν γὰρ τῇ Κύρνῳ εἴκοσι
ἔτεσι πρότερον τούτων ἐκ θεοπροπίου ἀνεστήσαντο πόλιν, τῇ οὔνομα ἦν
Ἀλαλίη. Ἀργανθώνιος δὲ ἐπὶ τηνικαῦτα ἤδη τετελευτήκεε.

Because of these things the Phocaeans prepared to sail to Kyrnos [Corsica], where
they had built the city of Alalia twenty years earlier at the command of an oracle.
Arganthonios by this time had already died.

4.152:

αὐτοὶ δὲ ἀναχθέντες ἐκ τῆς νήσου καὶ γλιχόμενοι Αἰγύπτου ἔπλεον,
ἀποφερόμενοι ἀπηλιώτῃ ἀνέμῳ· καὶ οὐ γὰρ ἀνίει τὸ πνεῦμα, Ἡρακλέας

στήλας διεκπερήσαντες ἀπίκοντο ἐς Ταρτησσόν, θείη πομπῇ χρεώμενοι. τὸ
δὲ ἐμπόριον τοῦτο ἦν ἀκήρατον τοῦτον τὸν χρόνον, ὥστε ἀπονοστήσαντες
οὗτοι ὀπίσω μέγιστα δὴ Ἑλλήνων πάντων τῶν ἡμεῖς ἀτρεκείην ἴδμεν ἐκ
φορτίων ἐκέρδησαν.

These men from Samos with their captain Kolaios then sailed from the island planning
to voyage to Egypt, but a wind from the east drove them off course. The wind did not
stop until it had blown them through the Straits of Hercules to Tartessos, by the will
of the gods. This port at that time was still virgin territory, so that the Samians brought
back from there a greater profit than any Greek merchants we have ever known.

4.192:

εἰσὶ δὲ καὶ γαλαῖ ἐν τῷ σιλφίῳ γινόμεναι τῇσι Ταρτησσίῃσι ὁμοιόταται.

[In Africa] there are also ferrets in the silphium plants very much like those in
Tartessos.

Hesychius (fifth century AD)

Letter T (213):

Ταρτησσίαις· γαλαῖς.

Tartessians: ferrets

Letter T (214):

Ταρτησσός· πόλις περὶ τὰς Ἡρακλείους στήλας.

Tartessos: a city near the pillars of Hercules

Himerius (c. AD 310–c. 390)

Orationes 10:

πόλεις ἐγειρομένας, δήμους ἀκμάζοντας, Ταρτησσοῦ βίον, Ἀρμαλθείας
κέρας, πᾶν ὅσον εὐδαιμονίας κεφάλαιον.

Cities raised up, flourishing people, the life of Tartessos, the horn of Armaltheia,
everything which brings happiness!

Jerome (c. 347–420)

Commentariorum in Epistulam ad Galatas 2.3:

et oppidum Tartesson, quod nunc vocatur Carteia.

The city is Tartesson, which is now called Carteia.

Josephus (first century AD)

Antiquitates Judaicae 1.127:

Ἰαυάνου δὲ τοῦ Ἰάφθου τριῶν καὶ αὐτοῦ παίδων γενομένων Ἀλισᾶς μὲν Ἀλισαίους ἐκάλεσεν ὧν ἦρχεν, Αἰολεῖς δὲ νῦν εἰσι, Θάρσος δὲ Θαρσεῖς· οὕτως γὰρ ἐκαλεῖτο τὸ παλαιὸν ἡ Κιλικία.

Javan son of Japhet had three sons. Of these Halisas gave his name to those he ruled, the Halisaeans (now called Aeolians) and Tharsos (the ancient name for Cilicia) gave his name to the Tharsians.

NOTE: Josephus identifies Tharsos with Tarsus on the south-east coast of Asia Minor.

8.181:

πολλαὶ γὰρ ἦσαν νῆες ἃς ὁ βασιλεὺς ἐν τῇ Ταρσικῇ λεγομένῃ θαλάττῃ καταστήσας παραγαγεῖν εἰς τὰ ἐνδοτέρω τῶν ἐθνῶν παντοίαν ἐμπορίαν προσέταξεν, ὧν ἐξεμπολουμένων ἄργυρός τε καὶ χρυσὸς ἐκομίζετο τῷ βασιλεῖ καὶ πολὺς ἐλέφας Αἰθίοπές τε καὶ πίθηκοι. τὸν δὲ πλοῦν ἀπιοῦσαί τε καὶ ἐπανερχόμεναι τρισὶν ἔτεσιν ἤνυον.

King Solomon had many ships in the Sea of Tarshish, as it was called, and he ordered to carry various goods to inland peoples. In return, the king received much silver, gold, ivory, Ethiopians, and apes. The voyage there and back again took a total of three years.

Justin (second or third century AD):

Epitome 44.4:

Saltus vero Tartessiorum, in quibus Titanas bellum adversus deos gessisse proditur, incoluere Curetes [read Cunetes], quorum rex vetustissimus Gargoris mellis colligendi usum primus invenit. Huic cum ex filiae stupro nepos provenisset, pudore flagitii variis generibus extingui parvulum voluit; sed per omnes casus fortuna quadam servatus ad postremum ad regnum tot periculorum miseratione pervenit. *Primum omnium cum eum exponi iussisset et post dies ad corpus expositi requirendum misisset, inventus est vario ferarum lacte nutritus. Deinde relatum domum in tramite angusto, per quem armenta commeare consueverant, proici iubet, crudelis prosus, qui proculcari nepotem, quam simplici morte interfici maluit. Ibi quoque cum inviolatus esset nec alimentis egeret, canibus primo ieiunis et multorum dierum abstentia cruciatis, mox etiam suibus obiecit. Itaque cum non solum non noceretur, verum etiam quarundam uberibus aleretur, ad ultimum in Oceanum abici iussit. Tum plane manifesto quodam numine inter furentes aestus reciprocantes undas, velut nave, non fluctu veheretur, leni salo in litore exponitur, nec multo post cerva adfuit, quae ubera parvulo offerret. Inde denique conversatione nutricis eximia puero pernicitas fuit; inter cervorum greges diu montes saltusque haud inferior velocitate peragravit. Ad postremum laqueo captus regi dono datus est. Tunc et liniamentorum similitudine et notis corporis, quae inustae parvulo fuerant, nepos agnitus. Admiratione deinde tot casuum periculorumque ab eodem successor regni destinatur. Nomen illi inpositum Habidis, qui ut regnum accepit, tantae magnitudinis fuit, ut non frustra deorum maiestate tot periculis ereptus videretur. Quippe et barbarum populum legibus vinxit et boves primus aratro domare frumentaque sulco quaerere docuit et ex agresti cibo mitiora vesci odio eorum, quae ipse passus fuerat, homines coegit. Huius casus fabulosi viderentur, ni et Romanorum conditores lupa nutriti et Cyrus, rex Persarum, cane alitus proderetur. Ab hoc et ministeria servilia populo interdicta et plebs in septem urbes divisa. Murtuo Habide regnum per multa saecula ab successoribus eius retentum.*

The forests of the Tartessians, in which they say the Titans waged war on the gods, were once inhabited by the Cunetes, whose king, Gargoris, first discovered how to collect honey. After his daughter had a son born of an illicit affair, Gargoris was ashamed and tried to have the boy killed in various ways. But with the help of fortune, when the child survived all these attempts and his grandfather felt pity because of all he had put him through, the boy became king in his place. The first attempt of Gargoris to kill him was through exposure. After a few days, the king sent someone to see the body of the child, but he discovered that he had been nourished by the milk of wild animals. The boy was brought home and Gargoris ordered him to be placed in the middle of a narrow path frequently used by cattle. This was the act of a cruel man who instead of a swift death preferred that his own grandson be trampled. But the boy was unharmed here as well. Then Gargoris commanded that he be given to starving dogs who had been kept without food for several days, even garbage thrown to pigs. The boy was not only safe, but some of the animals nursed him. Finally, the king ordered him to be thrown into the ocean. By now it was clear that he was divinely protected, since he floated on the waves as if on a ship and was brought by a gentle current to shore. Soon after a deer arrived and nursed him, then the boy joined the herd of deer and learned to run as fast as them over the mountains and through the forests. At last he was trapped in a snare and brought before the king who recognized him because of his features and the marks of a brand given him as an infant. The boy then was named as heir to the throne by his grandfather who was amazed at all the dangers he had survived. The boy was named Habis. When he became king, it was clear that the gods had rescued him from all his trials. He gave laws to a barbarian people and taught them how to plow with oxen and grow grain. He hated the wild foods he had been forced to eat as a boy, and so forced the people to abandon their rough diet and live as civilized men. His would seem like a myth except for the stories that the founders of Rome were suckled by a wolf as Cyrus, king of the Persians, was nourished by a dog. Habis also forced the people to work at servile tasks and organized them into seven cities. After his death, the kingdom remained in the hands of the descendants of Habis for many generations.

Livy (59 BC–AD 17)

Ab urbe condita 23.26:

Fecerant hi transfugae motum in Tartesiorum gente, desciverantque his auctoribus urbes aliquot; una etiam ab ipsis vi capta fuerat. In eam gentem versum ab Romanis bellum est, infestoque exercitu Hasdrubal ingressus agrum hostium pro captae ante dies paucos urbis moenibus Chalbum, nobilem Tartesiorum ducem, cum valido exercitu castris se tenentem, adgredi statuit.

These deserters stirred up trouble among the Tartessians, causing a few cities to rebel. One city they even stormed. Against this people the war now turned instead of the Romans. Hasdrubal entered this hostile territory and decided to attack a Tartessian nobleman named Chalbus, who was camped before the walls of a city he had taken a few days before.

Lucian (c. AD 115–after 180)

Macrobii 10:

Ἀργανθώνιος μὲν οὖν Ταρτησσίων βασιλεὺς πεντήκοντα καὶ ἑκατὸν ἔτη βιῶναι λέγεται.

It is said that Arganthonios, the king of the Tartessians, lived for one hundred and fifty years.

Martial (c. AD 40–103/4)

Epigrammata 7.28:

> *Sic Tiburtinae crescat tibi silva Dianae*
> *et properet caesum saepe redire nemus,*
> *nec Tartesiacis Pallas tua, Fusce, trapetis.*

Fuscus, may the forest of Tiburtine Diana grow for you
and the grove, often cut, hasten to return,
and your olives not yield to Tartessian presses.

Epigrammata 8.28:

> *an Tartesiacus stabuli nutritor Hiberi*
> > *Baetis in Hesperia te quoque lavit ove?*

Did Baetis, the Tartessian nourisher of the Iberian flock,
wash you also on the back of a Hesperian ewe?

Epigrammata 9.61:

> *In Tartesiacis domus est notissima terris,*
> > *qua dives placidum Corduba Baetin amat,*
> *vellera nativo pallent ubi flava metallo*
> > *et linit Hesperium brattea viva pecus.*

In the Tartessian lands there is a famous house,
where wealthy Cordoba loves placid Baetis,
where yellow fleece are pale with native ore
and living foil covers the Hesperian flock.

Epigrammata 11.16:

> > *urbanae scripsimus ista togae;*
> *iam mea Lampsacio lascivit pagina versu*
> *et Tartesiaca concrepat aera manu.*

> I wrote those poems for city taste,
but now my page frolics with verse of Lampsacus
and clashes with Tartessian cymbals.

Ovid (43 BC–AD 17)

Metamorphoses 14.416–18:

> *Sparserat occiduus Tartessia litora Phoebus,*
> *et frustra coniunx oculis animoque Canentis*
> *exspectatus erat.*

Now the setting sun had bathed the Tartessian shores,
and in vain Canens had looked with her eyes and heart
for the return of her husband.

Pausanius (second century AD)

Graeciae descriptio 6.19:

εἰ δὲ καὶ Ταρτήσσιος χαλκὸς λόγῳ τῷ Ἠλείων ἐστίν, οὐκ οἶδα. Ταρτήσσιον
δὲ εἶναι ποταμὸν ἐν χώρᾳ τῇ Ἰβήρων λέγουσι στόμασιν ἐς θάλασσαν
κατεχόμενον δυσὶ καὶ ὁμώνυμον αὐτῷ πόλιν ἐν μέσῳ τοῦ ποταμοῦ τῶν
ἐκβολῶν κειμένην· τὸν δὲ ποταμὸν μέγιστόν τε ὄντα τῶν ἐν Ἰβηρίᾳ καὶ
ἄμπωτιν παρεχόμενον Βαῖτιν ὠνόμασαν οἱ ὕστερον, εἰσὶ δ᾽ οἳ Καρπίαν
Ἰβήρων πόλιν καλεῖσθαι νομίζουσι τὰ ἀρχαιότερα Ταρτησσόν.

Whether the bronze of the treasury is Tartessian, I do not know. They say that Tartessos
is a river in the land of the Iberians that flows to the sea in two mouths and that between
these mouths is a city of the same name. The river is tidal, the largest in Iberia, and later
called Baetis. Some think that Tartessos was the ancient name of Karpia, an Iberian
city.

Pherecydes of Athens (fifth century BC)

Histories (Fragment 33):

ἀφικόμενος δὲ εἰς Ταρτησσόν, πορεύεται εἰς Λιβύην, ἔνθα ἀναιρεῖ Ἀνταῖον
τὸν Ποσειδῶνος, ὑβριστὴν ὄντα.

Having journeyed to Tartessos, Hercules went to Africa, where he defeated Antaios, the
proud son of Poseidon.

Pliny the Elder (AD 23/24–79)

Naturalis historia 3.7:

Mellaria, fretum ex Atlantico mari, Carteia, Tartesos a Graecis dicta, mons Calpe.

Next is Mellaria, the strait from the Atlantic, Carteia, called by the Greeks Tartesos, and
Gibraltar.

Naturalis historia 4.120:

maiorem Timaeus Potimusam a puteis vocitatam ait, nostri Tarteson appellant, Poeni Gadir, ita Punica lingua saepem significante.

According to Timaeus the larger island is called Potimusa because of its wells, but we call it Tartesos. The Punic name is Gadir, which in their language means fence.

Naturalis historia 7.154:

Anacreon poeta Arganthonio Tartesiorum regi CL tribuit annos.

The poet Anacreon says that Arganthonius king of the Tartessians lived one hundred and fifty years.

Pollux (second century AD)

Onomasticon 6.63:

μύραινα Ταρτησσία, καὶ θύννος Τύριος, καὶ κεστρεὺς ἐκ Σκιάθου.

Tartessian sea-eel, tuna from Tyre, mullet from Skiathos.

Pomponius Mela (first century AD)

De chorographia 2.96:

Et sinus ultra est in eoque Carteia, ut quidam putant aliquando Tartesos.

And the gulf beyond is now Carteia, but some say that it was once called Tartesos.

Pseudo-Apollodorus (first or second century AD)

Bibliotheca 2.5.10:

πορευόμενος οὖν ἐπὶ τὰς Γηρυόνου βόας διὰ τῆς Εὐρώπης, ἄγρια πολλὰ ζῷα ἀνελὼν Λιβύης ἐπέβαινε, καὶ παρελθὼν Ταρτησσὸν ἔστησε σημεῖα τῆς πορείας ἐπὶ τῶν ὅρων Εὐρώπης καὶ Λιβύης ἀντιστοίχους δύο στήλας . . . Ἡρακλῆς δὲ ἐνθέμενος τὰς βόας εἰς τὸ δέπας καὶ διαπλεύσας εἰς Ταρτησσὸν Ἡλίῳ πάλιν ἀπέδωκε τὸ δέπας.

Journeying through Europe to capture the cattle of Geryon, Hercules killed many wild beasts and crossed to Africa. Having gone to Tartessos, he then erected as a memorial of his travels two pillars opposite each other on the boundaries of Europe and Africa... And Hercules, sailing with the cattle in the golden bowl, reached Tartessos and returned the bowl to the sun god.

Pseudo-Lycophron (second century BC)

Alexandra 641–2:

> καὶ τοὶ μὲν ἀκτὰς ἐμβατήσονται λεπρὰς
> Ἰβηροβοσκοὺς ἄγχι Ταρτησοῦ πύλης.

And these will land on the rough shores
that nourish the Iberians near the gate of Tartesos.

Pytheas (fourth century BC)

s.v. Strabo *Geography* 3.2.11:

ἐοίκασι δ’ οἱ παλαιοὶ καλεῖν τὸν Βαῖνιν Ταρτησσόν, τὰ δὲ Γάδειρα καὶ τὰς πρὸς αὐτὴν νήσους Ἐρύθειαν ... δυεῖν δὲ οὐσῶν ἐκβολῶν τοῦ ποταμοῦ, πόλιν ἐν τῷ μεταξὺ χώρῳ κατοικεῖσθαι πρότερον φασιν, ἣν καλεῖσθαι Ταρτησσόν, ὁμώνυμον τῷ ποταμῷ, καὶ τὴν χώραν Ταρτησσίδα, ἣν νῦν Τουρδοῦλοι νέμονται. καὶ Ἐρατοσθένης δὲ τὴν συνεχῆ τῇ Κάλπῃ Ταρτησσίδα καλεῖσθαί φησι, καὶ Ἐρύθειαν νῆσον εὐδαίμονα ... καὶ ὅσα δὴ ἄλλα εἴρηκε Πυθέᾳ πιστεύσας δι’ ἀλαζονείαν.

Those in ancient times seemed to have called the Baetis River Tartessos, while they called Gades and the nearby islands Erytheia... The river has two mouths and thus it is said that a city was founded on the land between which was called Tartessos after the river. The country, which is now occupied by the Turdulians, was called Tartessis. Eratosthenes says that the country next to Calpe is called Tartessis and that Erytheia is called the Blessed Isle... Also in many other statements he has mistakenly relied on Pytheas.

Sallust (86–35 BC)

Historiae 2.5:

Ut alii tradiderunt Tartessum, Hispaniae civitatem, quam nunc Tyrii mutato nomine Gaddir habent.

Others record that the people of Tyre have changed the name of Tartessus, a city of Spain, to Gaddir.

Seneca (*c.* 4 BC–AD 65)

Hercules 231–3:

> *inter remotos gentis Hesperiae greges*
> *pastor triformis litoris Tartesii*
> *peremptus, acta est praeda ab occasu ultimo.*

> Among his distant herds in the land of the Hesperians,
> the three-formed shepherd of the Tartessian shore
> was slain, his cattle led as spoils from the farthest west.

Servius (fifth century AD)

In Vergilii Aeneidos 7.662:

hunc Geryonem alii Tartessiorum regem dicunt fuisse et habuisse armenta pulcherrima, quae Hercules occiso eo abduxit.

Others say that Geryon was king of the Tartessians and had very fine cattle, which Hercules led away after he killed him.

Sidonius Apollinaris (fifth century AD)

Carmina 2.362–5:

> *simil et reminiscitur illud*
> *quod Tartesiacis avus huius Vallia terris*
> *Vandalicas turmas et iuncti Martis Halanos*
> *stravit et occiduam texere cadavera Calpen.*

> He also remembers this,
> that Wallia, grandson of Ricimer, destroyed
> on Tartessian soil the Vandals and their allies the Alans
> and their bodies covered Calpe in the west.

Carmina 5.285–6:

> *si bibit Hispanus Gangen tepidisque ab Erythris*
> *ad Tartesiacum venit Indus aquator Hiberum.*

> If a Spaniard drinks from the Ganges and an Indian
> comes from warm Erythrae to draw water at the Tartessian Ebro.

Carmina 15.154–5:

> *texuerat tamen et chlamydes, quibus ille magister*
> *per Tartesiacas conspectus splenduit urbes.*

> She wove the clothing which he her master
> wore splendidly through all the Tartessian cities.

Silius Italicus (*c.* AD 26–102)

Punica 3.399–400:

> *armat Tartessos stabulanti conscia Phoebo*
> *et Munda Emathios Italis paritura labores.*

> Thus armed Tartessos, which sees the setting sun,
> and Munda, giving birth to the pain of Pharsalia for Italy.

5.398–9:

> *fractasque in rupibus undas*
> *audit Tartessus latis distermina terris.*

> The crashing waves on the shores is heard
> by Tartessos, parted by broad lands.

6.1–3:

> *Iam, Tartessiaco quos solverat aequore Titan*
> *in noctem diffusus, equos iungebat Eois*
> *litoribus.*

> Now on eastern shores the Titan was yoking the horses
> he had freed in Tartessian waters.

10.537–8:

> *donec anhelantis stagna in Tartessia Phoebus*
> *mersit equos.*

> Until Phoebus drove his weary steeds
> into Tartessian waters.

13.671–4:

> *octava terebat*
> *arentem culmis messem crepitantibus aestas,*
> *ex quo cuncta mihi calcata meoque subibat*
> *germano devicta iugum Tartessia tellus.*

> Eight years had passed
> since I tamed the Tartessian land
> and my brother conquered it,
> making it pass beneath the yoke.

15.5–6:

> *hinc metus, in Tyrias ne iam Tartessia leges*
> *concedat tellus proprioraque bella pavescat.*

> Thus they dreaded that the Tartessian land would fall
> to the rule of Carthage, fearing a closer war.

16.112–14:

> *rapido certamina linquit*
> *in latebras evectus equo noctisque per umbram*
> *ad Tartessiacos tendit per litora portus.*

> Fearing a fight, he fled rapidly on horseback
> to a hiding place and then at night along the coast
> to the port of Tartessos.

16.465–6:

> *Fulgentes pueri Tartessos et Hesperos ora*
> *ostendere simul vulgi clamore secundo.*

Two splendid boys, Tartessos and Hesperus,
stood forth together before the applauding crowds.

16.509:

> *Tartessos fratrem medio Therone premebat.*

Tartessos followed his brother, with Theron between them.

16.646–7:

> *cum tota subisset*
> *Sidonium possessa iugum Tartessia tellus.*

When all the Tartessian land
fell under the yoke of Carthage.

17.590:

> *ac Tartessiacas profugi sparguntur in oras.*

Some fled as far as the Tartessian shores.

Solinus (third century AD)

Collectanea Rerum Memorabilium 4.1

*Sardinia quoque, quam apud Timaeum Sandaliotin legimus, Ichnusam apud Crispum, in quo mari
sita sit, quos incolarum auctores habeat, satis celebre est. nihil ergo attinet dicere [ut] Sardus Hercule,
Norax Mercurio procreati cum alter a Libya, alter ab usque Tartesso Hispaniae in hosce fines
permeavissent, a Sardo terrae, a Norace Norae oppido nomen datum.*

Sardinia and its inhabitants are also well known. Timaeus calls the island Sandaliotis and
Crispus calls it Ichnusa. We know that Sardus the son of Hercules and Norax the son of
Mercury both came to that land, one from Africa and the other from Tartessus in Spain.
The island is named from Sardus and the city of Nora from Norax.

Stephanus of Byzantium (sixth century AD)

Ταρτησσος· πόλις Ἰβηρίας, ἀπὸ ποταμοῦ τοῦ ἀπὸ τοῦ Ἀργυροῦ ὄρους. ὅστις ποταμὸς καὶ κασσίτερον ἐν Ταρτησσῷ καταφέρει.

Tartessos: An Iberian city near the river flowing from the Silver Mountain. This river also carries tin to Tartessos.

Stesichorus (sixth century BC)

s.v. Strabo *Geography* 3.2.11:

διόπερ οὕτως εἰπεῖν ὑπολαμβάνουσι Στησίχορον περὶ τοῦ Γηρυόνος βουκόλου, διότι γεννηθείη

σχεδὸν ἀντιπέρας κλεινᾶς Ἐρυθείας
Ταρτησσοῦ ποταμοῦ παρὰ ἀπείρονας ἀργυρορίζου
ἐν κευθμῶι πέτρας.

This is why Stesichorus spoke thus about the herdsman of Geryon born:

opposite famous Erytheia,
beside the endless silver-bearing waters of Tartessos
in a cave of a cliff.

Strabo (c. 64 BC–after AD 24)

Geography 3.2.12:

ὁ δὲ ποιητὴς πολύφωνός τις ὢν οὐδὲ τούτων πολυΐστωρ, δίδωσιν ἀφορμὰς ὡς οὐδὲ τούτων ἀνήκοός ἐστι τῶν τόπων, εἴ τις ὀρθῶς συλλογίζεσθαι βούλοιτο ἀπ᾽ ἀμφοῖν, τῶν τε χεῖρον λεγομένων περὶ αὐτῶν, καὶ τῶν ἄμεινον καὶ ἀληθέστερον. χεῖρον μέν, ὅτι πρὸς δύσιν ἐσχάτη ἤκουεν αὕτη, ὅπου, καθάπερ αὐτός φησιν, εἰς τὸν ὠκεανὸν ἐμπίπτει·

λαμπρὸν φάος ἠελίοιο,
ἕλκον νύκτα μέλαιναν ἐπὶ ζείδωρον ἄρουραν.

ἡ δὲ νὺξ ὅτι δύσφημον καὶ τῷ ἅδης τῷ Ταρτάρῳ. εἰκάζοι οὖν ἄν τις ἀκούντα περὶ Ταρτησσοῦ τὸν Τάρταρον ἐκεῖθεν παρονομάσαι τὸν ἔσχατον τῶν ὑποχθονίων τόπων, προσθεῖναι δὲ καὶ μῦθον, τὸ ποιητικὸν σώζοντα. . .

πρὸς μὲν δὴ τὸ χεῖρον ἀπὸ τῆς τοῦ Ταρτάρου μυθοποιίας αἰνίττοιτό τις ἄν τὴν τῶν τόπων μνήμην τῶν περὶ Ταρτησσόν.

The poet Homer, a man of many voices as they say and widely-learned, gives evidence that even these western regions were known to him, if one wishes to argue logically from not only worse statements made about these regions but also from those better and more truthful. A worse statement is that Tartessus was known to him indirectly as the farthest place in the west where, as the poet himself says, there falls into the ocean:

> the bright light of the sun
> drawing with it black night on earth the giver of grain.

It is obvious enough that night is considered an evil thing associated with Hades, as Hades is with Tartarus. So one could argue that because he had heard of Tartessos, he named the farthest regions Tartarus after Tartessis, with a slight variation of the letters, adding a mythical and poetic quality...As for the worse statement, one could suppose that Homer had in mind the region around Tartessos from the mythical creation of Tartarus.

Geography 3.2.14:

ἔνιοι δὲ Ταρτησσὸν τὴν νῦν Καρτηίαν προσαγορεύουσι.

But some call Tartessos the modern Carteia.

Suda (tenth century AD)

Letter Γ (29):

Γαλῆ· τὸ ζῷον . . . καὶ Γαλῆ Ταρτησσία· ἡ Ταρτησσὸς πόλις ἔξω τῶν Ἡρακλείων στηλῶν πρὸς τῷ ὠκεανῷ, ἔνθα μέγισται γίνονται γαλαῖ.

Gale: Animal...The Tartessian ferret. Tartessos was a city beyond the Pillars of Hercules facing the ocean. In that place are large ferrets.

Letter T (136):

Ταρτησία μύραινα· ὡς ἐκεῖ γινομένων μεγίστων.

Tartessian sea-eel: There they grow large.

Letter T (137):

Ταρτησσός· Ἰβηρικὴ πόλις πρὸς τῷ ὠκεανῷ. ἐκτετοπισμένη παρὰ τὴν
Ἄορνον λίμνην. τῆς δὲ Ταρτησσοῦ Ἀγαθώνιος ἐβασίλευσεν. Ἀριστοφάνης
Ταρτησίαν μύραιναν λέγει. καὶ οὐδετέρως Ταρτήσιον.

Tartessos: An Iberian city facing the ocean. A remote place near Lake Avernus. Agathonius
ruled over Tartessos. Aristophanes writes Tartesian sea-eel. In the neuter it is Tartesion.

NOTE: The *Suda* is a Byzantine lexicon that preserves grammatical and historical information from
many Greek authors whose works are now lost.

Thallus (first or second century AD)

s.v. Theophilus *Ad Autolycum* 3.29:

καὶ Ὤγυγος ἡττηθεὶς ἔφυγεν εἰς Ταρτησσόν [. . .] τότε μὲν τῆς χώρας
ἐκείνης Ἀκτῆς κληθείσης, νῦν δὲ Ἀττικῆς προσαγορευομένης, ἧς Ὤγυγος
τότε ἦρξε.

Ogygus, having been defeated, fled to Tartessos [...] the region was then called Akte,
but is now called Attica, which Ogygus ruled then.

NOTE: Ogygus was a primeval king, variously of Greece, Asia, Egypt, or the Titans. The passage is
corrupt.

Theopompus (fourth century BC)

s.v. Stephanus of Byzantium Μασσία:

Μασσία, χώρα παρακειμένη τοῖς Ταρτησσίοις. τὸ ἐθνικὸν Μασσιανός.
Θεόπομπος τεσσαρακοστῷ τρίτῳ.

Massia: a country near the Tartessians. The ethnic name is Massianos. Theopompus
Book 43.

s.v. Stephanus of Byzantium Τλῆτες:

Τλῆτες, ἔθνος Ἰβηρικὸν περιοικοῦν τοὺς Ταρτησσίους. Θεόπομπος
τεσσαρακοστῷ πέμπτῳ.

Tletes: an Iberian people living near the Tartessians. Theopompus Book 45.

Varro (116–27 BC)

s.v. Aulus Gellius *Noctes Atticae* 6.16:

genera autem nominaque edulium et domicilia ciborum omnibus aliis praestantia, quae profunda
ingluvies vestigavit, quae Varro obprobrans exsecutus est, haec sunt ferme, quantum nobis memoriae
est: pavus e Samo, Phrygia attagena, grues Melicae, haedus ex Ambracia, pelamys Chalcedonia,
muraena Tartesia, aselli Pessinuntii, ostrea Tarenti,
petunculus Siculus, helops Rhodius, scari Cilices, nuces Thasiae, palma Aegyptia, glans Hiberica.

As far as I can remember, these are the types and names of foods surpassing all others
which a shameless glutton seeks and Varro mentions in his satire: peacock from Samos,
partridge from Phrygia, crane from Media, young goat from Ambracia, tuna from
Chalcedon, sea-eel from Tartessus, cod from Pessinus, oysters from Tarentum, scallops
from Sicily, swordfish from Rhodes, parrotfish from Cilicia, nuts from Thasos, dates
from Egypt, and acorns from Spain.

NEAR EASTERN REFERENCES

Inscription of Esarhaddon (Pritchard 290)

All the kings from the islands in the midst of the sea, from Cyprus as far as Tar-si-si, bowed to my feet and I received heavy tribute from them.

NOTE: Esarhaddon reigned over Assyria from 681–669 BC.

BIBLICAL REFERENCES

All biblical passages are from the New Revised Standard Version.

Genesis 10.4:

The descendants of Javan: Elishah, Tarshish, Kittim, and Rodanim.

1 Kings 10.22:

For the king had a fleet of ships of Tarshish at sea with the fleet of Hiram. Once every three years the fleet of ships of Tarshish used to come bringing gold, silver, ivory, apes, and peacocks.

22.48:

Jehoshaphat made ships of the Tarshish type to go to Ophir for gold; but they did not go, for the ships were wrecked at Ezion-geber.

1 Chronicles 1.7:

The descendants of Javan: Elishah, Tarshish, Kittim, and Rodanim.

7.10:

The sons of Jediael: Bilhan. And the sons of Bilhan: Jeush, Benjamin, Ehud, Chenaanah, Zethan, Tarshish, and Ahishahar.

2 Chronicles 9.21:

For the king's ships went to Tarshish with the servants of Huram; once every three years the ships of Tarshish used to come bringing gold, silver, ivory, apes, and peacocks.

20.36–7:

He joined him in building ships to go to Tarshish; they built the ships in Ezion-geber. Then Eliezer son of Dodavahu of Mareshah prophesied against Jehoshaphat, saying, 'Because you have joined with Ahaziah, the Lord will destroy what you have made.' And the ships were wrecked and were not able to go to Tarshish.

Psalm 48.7:

…as when an east wind shatters the ships of Tarshish.

72.10:

May the kings of Tarshish and of the isles render him tribute.

Isaiah 2.16:

…against all the ships of Tarshish, and against all the beautiful craft.

23.1 (23.14):

Wail, O ships of Tarshish, for your fortress is destroyed.

23.6:

Cross over to Tarshish—wail, O inhabitants of the coast!

23.10:

Cross over to your own land, O ships of Tarshish. This is a harbour no more.

60.9:

For the coastlands shall wait for me, the ships of Tarshish first, to bring your children from far away, their silver and gold with them.

66.19:

From them I will send survivors to the nations, to Tarshish, Put, and Lud—which draw the bow—to Tubal and Javan, to the coastlands far away that have not heard of my fame or seen my glory; and they shall declare my glory among the nations.

Jeremiah 10.9:

Beaten silver is brought from Tarshish, and gold from Uphaz.

Ezekiel 27.12:

Tarshish did business with you out of the abundance of your great wealth; silver, iron, tin, and lead they exchanged for your wares.

27.25:

The ships of Tarshish travelled for you in your trade.

38.13:

Sheba and Dedan and the merchants of Tarshish and all its young warriors will say to you, 'Have you come to seize spoil? Have you assembled your horde to carry off plunder, to carry away silver and gold, to take away cattle and goods, to seize a great amount of booty?'

Jonah 1.3:

But Jonah set out to flee to Tarshish from the presence of the Lord. He went down to Joppa and found a ship going to Tarshish; so he paid his fare and went on board, to go with them to Tarshish, away from the presence of the Lord.

4.2:

He prayed to the Lord and said, 'O Lord! Is not this what I said while I was still in my own country? That is why I fled to Tarshish at the beginning...'

BIBLIOGRAPHY

Most of the Greek and Latin authors can be found with English translations in the Loeb Classical Library series published by Harvard University Press. More obscure texts and secondary sources are noted below.

Alvar, J., and Blázquez, J. 1999 *Los Enigmas de Tarteso*. Madrid, Cátedra.

Apollodorus (trans. P. Dräger) 2005 *Bibliotheke*. Düsseldorf, Artemis & Winkler.

Avienus, Rufus Festus (trans. J. P. Murphy) 1977 *Ora maritima*. Chicago, Ares Publishers.

FGrH = Jacoby, F. 1957–1999 *Fragmente der griechischen Historiker*. Leiden, Brill.

Hesychius (ed. M. Schmidt) 2009 *Lexicon*. Whitefish, Montana, Kessinger Publishing.

Kassel, R., and Austin, C. 1983, 1991 *Poetae Comici Graeci*. Berlin, De Gruyter.

Lycophron (ed. A. Hurst) 2008 *Alexandra*. Paris, Belles lettres.

Penella, Robert J. 2007 *Man and the Word: The Orations of Himerius*. Berkeley, University of California Press.

Pollux, Julius (ed. E. Bethe) 1967 *Pollucis Onomasticon*. Stuttgart, Teubner.

Pomponius Mela (trans. Paul Berry) 1997 *Geography*. Lewiston, New York, Mellen Press.

Pritchard, J., ed., 1955 *Ancient Near Eastern Texts Relating to the Old Testament*. Princeton, Princeton University Press.

Pytheas (trans. C. Roseman) 1994 *On the Ocean*. Chicago, Ares Publishers.

Servius (ed. G. Thilo and H. Hagen) 1961 *In Vergilii Carmina commentarii*. Hildesheim, Olms.

Stephanus of Byzantium (ed. A. Meineke) 1992 *Ethnikon*. Chicago, Ares Publishers.

Stesichorus (ed. F. Pontani) 1968 *Alcmane, Stesícoro, Íbico. Frammenti*. Turin, G. Einaudi.

THE PROBLEM OF LUSITANIAN

Dagmar S. Wodtko

§ 1 Lusitanian is a pre-Roman Indo-European language that was spoken in an area within the Roman province of *Lusitania* at the beginning of our era. It is fragmentarily attested in five indigenous inscriptions, by indigenous names in Latin inscriptions, and to a lesser extent by names in works of the classical writers.

The core region inhabited by Lusitanians seems to have comprised the lands between the Douro and the Tejo in the modern Portuguese provinces of Viseu and Guarda, the eastern parts of Coimbra and Castelo Branco, and the west of Cáceres in Spain, although establishing concrete language boundaries is not easy, and three of the five inscriptions have been found south of the Tejo. Neighbours of the Lusitanians were the *Vettones* in the East and the *Celtici* in the south; the western seaboard south of the Douro was inhabited by the *Turduli Veteres*.[1] In the north many peoples are named in ancient sources as inhabiting *Gallaecia*, and some of them are explicitly referred to as *Celtici*.[2] However, Strabo tells us that 'now most of the Lusitanians are called Callaicans' and that *Lusitania* 'the greatest of the Iberian nations' extended from the *Tagus* to the ocean in the west and in the north, with the Gallaecians as their eastern neighbours in the northern part.[3] The river *Baenis* or *Minius* (mod. Minho) is named as 'the greatest of the rivers in *Lusitania*'.[4] This suggests that, in Strabo's conception, the northern provinces of Portugal and the western provinces of modern Galicia, Pontevedra and the greatest part of A Coruña was Lusitanian territory. Still, he remarks (Geography 3.3.5) that *Celtici*, akin to the *Celtici* on the *Anas* (Guadiana), as the result of an expedition they made jointly with the *Turduli*, came to inhabit the area around Cape *Nerium*, next to the *Artabri*, who are 'now' called *Arrotrebae*.[5] He speaks of thirty different tribes living between the *Tagus* and the *Artabri* (Geography 3.3.5), and alludes to a former habit of extending the name 'Lusitanians' to

---

1 Cf. Pliny, *Naturalis Historia* 4.113; their presence is confirmed by two *tesserae hospitalis*. For the *Celtici* in the south see Berrocal Rangel (1993).

2 Cf. Pliny, *Naturalis Historia* 4.111: . . . *promunturium Celticum, amnes Florius, Nelo; Celtici cognomine Nerii et Supertamarci . . ., Capori, oppidum Noega, Celtici cognomine Praestamarci, Cileni.* For *Celtici* and *Turduli* cf. Untermann (2004).

3 Cf. Strabo, Geography 3.3.2f.: καὶ νῦν ἤδη τοὺς πλείστους τῶν Λυσιτανῶν Καλλαϊκοὺς καλεῖσθαι . . . μέγιστον τῶν Ἰβηρικῶν ἐθνῶν . . . περιέχει δὲ τῆς χώρας ταύτης τὸ μὲν νότιον πλευρὸν ὁ Τάγος, τὸ δ' ἑσπέριον καὶ τὸ ἀρκτικὸν ὁ ὠκεανός . . . .

4 Cf. Strabo, Geography 3.3.4: . . . Βαῖνις (οἱ δὲ Μινιόν φασι) πολὺ μέγιστος τῶν ἐν Λυσιτανίᾳ ποταμῶν . . . 'Baenis (others say Minius) by far the greatest of the rivers in Lusitania'.

5 Cf. Strabo, Geography 3.3.5: οἱ δὲ νῦν τοὺς Ἀρτάβρους Ἀροτρέβας καλοῦσιν 'But the people of today call the Artabri 'Arrotrebae''.

their northern and eastern neighbours (Geography 3.3.3), and to a comparable lifestyle of all the peoples on the north coast of the peninsula, *Gallaeci*, *Astures*, *Cantabri* and *Vascones* (Geography 3.3.7). *Asturia* to the north-east is generally regarded as a Hispano-Celtic area, which, like *Gallaecia*, shows some affinities to *Lusitania*.

The Celtic nature of the Lusitanian language is still debated and is rejected by most scholars at present. Yet the Lusitanians seem to have been in close contact with Celts at least in the north and south, and possibly on all sides.[6] In the north and south some people are known as *Celtici*, as noted above. However, the question remains whether all of the neighbours of the Lusitanians were Celtic speaking, even those groups who were not part of the population groups designated as *Celtici* (or Celtiberians), and if not, whether they spoke a language identical with or closely related to Lusitanian, or, alternatively, yet another Indo-European dialect which has not been positively identified so far in the purely onomastic remains. The problem is therefore how Lusitanian can be integrated into a linguistic map of the Pre-Roman Iberian Peninsula.

§ 2   Apart from Lusitanian itself, languages known to have been spoken in antiquity in the Iberian Peninsula are Iberian on the east and south coast, Celtiberian in the north-eastern central region, Tartessian in the south-west, and probably Basque in the north-east.[7] Of these, Iberian and Basque are clearly non-Indo-European, and Tartessian has usually been so classified likewise. However, attempts have been made to detect Indo-European and specifically Celtic elements in Tartessian inscriptions, and Koch (this volume) now argues for an overall Celtic character of Tartessian. This would reduce the number of languages epigraphically attested to three, non-Indo-European Iberian along the Mediterranean coast, Lusitanian in a comparatively small area in the west, and Celtic everywhere else. On the other hand, this does not mean that no further languages, Indo-European or otherwise, existed; for if Basque is not attested in epigraphic sources from

---

6   The Celticity of the *Vettones* is regarded as doubtful by, e.g., Luján (2007), cf. below.
7   Villar (2005, 510ff.) doubts the presence of Basque in ancient Hispania.

11.1. The find spots of the Lusitanian inscriptions in the ancient Iberian Peninsula (base map from Koch et al. [2007] *An Atlas for Celtic Studies*, map §16.2).

surely or probably CELTIC name
possibly CELTIC name
surely or probably NON-CELTIC
modern name
□   Phoenician settlements, 9th–6th centuries BC
north-western zone of densely distributed 'castros'
o   individual castros
≈≈   *chevaux de frise* defensive works
carp's-tongue/Huelva swords
antenna-hilted swords
LBA warrior steles
later Iron Age warrior steles

gold torcs
LBA Irish cauldrons
flesh hooks & articulated spits
south-western 'Tartessian' inscriptions
☆ Lusitanian inscriptions
– – – limits of Cogotas I LBA culture
Ⓑ *-briga* names
Ⓔ *Eburo-* names
Ⓜ *-magos* names
Ⓝ *nemeton* names
Ⓢ *Sego-* names

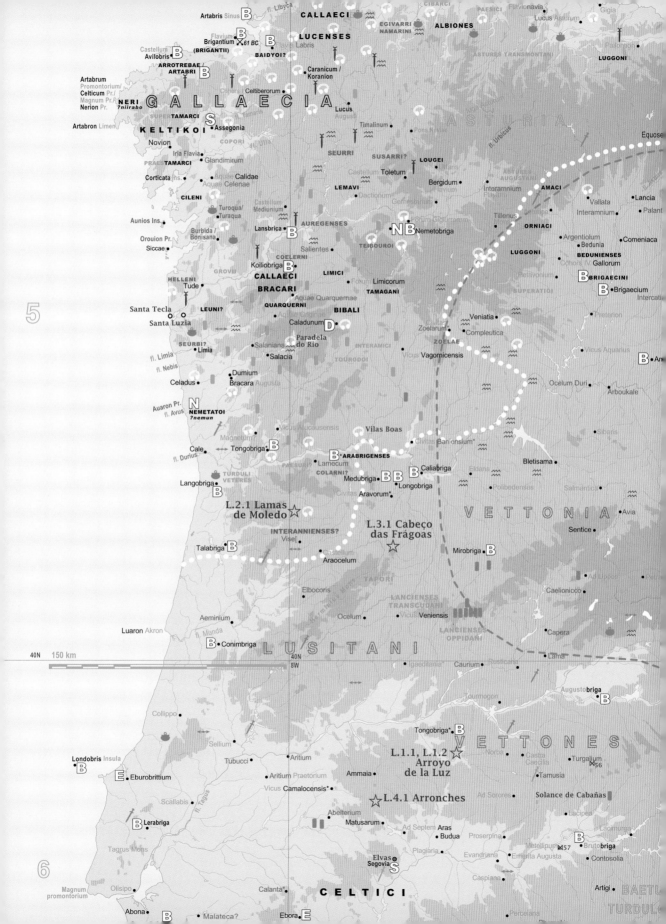

Antiquity, the same may apply to other languages as well. Their linguistic characteristics would then only be detectable in indirect sources, i.e. in names attested in the context of another language, such as personal names in Latin inscriptions or place-names (in the wide sense) in classical writers. This, after all, is also the fate of the Hispano-Celtic languages in *Gallaecia* and generally beyond Celtiberia. In fact, the presence of a number of Indo-European languages, such as Illyrian and Ligurian, has been postulated for the Iberian Peninsula in the past, and more recently Villar (e.g. 1990, 367ff.) has argued for at least one more Indo-European layer, Old European (*Alteuropäisch*) preserved in river names, but confined—like, presumably, elsewhere—to this hydronymic substratum, and with no immediate relationship to Lusitanian.[8]

§ 3 The five Lusitanian inscriptions were found in four places with a considerable distance between them; all are written on stone in the Latin alphabet. Three of them have been published in MLH IV and all will be numbered here according to the system of that edition.

L.1.1, found in Arroyo de la Luz (Cáceres), is known only from a sketch published in 1800 (MLH IV, 747ff.). It consists of two parts written on two separate stones, but has usually been treated as one text.[9] If it is one text, it is the longest Lusitanian inscription known so far. It begins with the Latin introduction *Ambatus scripsi*. Word boundaries are mostly marked by a dot in the surviving transcript, but not at the end of lines.

An inscription found at the same place without archaeological context was published by Almagro-Gorbea et al. (1999) and again by Villar & Pedrero (2001 and 2001a). This text is apparently incomplete at the beginning. It can be labelled L.1.2. Word boundaries are marked by a dot.

L.2.1 is a rock inscription from Lamas de Moledo (Viseu), first mentioned in 1630 (MLH IV, 751ff.). Like L.1.1 it begins with the Latin introduction of the scribes, *Rufinus et Tiro scripserunt*. It shows a number of ligatures and marks word boundaries by a dot, but not at the end of lines.

L.3.1 is written on a natural rock on the mountain top known as Cabeço das Frágoas, Guarda (MLH IV, 755ff.). It uses a few ligatures and marks word boundaries by a dot, including at the end of most lines. The new inscription found at Arronches (Portalegre) can be labelled L.4.1. (see Carneiro, Encarnação et al. 2008). Again, words are separated by a dot.

Dating is difficult for all these texts, but while L.1.1, L.2.1 and L.3.1 are usually held to date from imperial times, it has been argued on palaeographic grounds that L.1.2 can be placed in the second century BC, after which time the 'open' shape of the letter P fell out of use (Villar & Pedrero 2001, 667ff.). For L.4.1 the editors suggest a date at the beginning of the first century AD.

---

8   'Old European' place-names are nevertheless sometimes assumed as the basis of Lusitanian onomastic material. For a criticism of 'Old European' see Untermann (1999), De Hoz (2001, 122–8).

9   With caveats expressed in MLH IV, 747 and Villar & Pedrero (2001, 663f. and 2001a, 235ff.).

The five texts read as follows:[10]

L.1.1: AMBATVS
     SCRIP̱SI
CARLAE PRAISOM
SECIAS . ERBA . MVITIE
AS . ARIMO . PRAESO
NDO . SINGEIE*O
INDI . AVA . INDI . VEA
VN[11] . INDI . *EDAGA
ROM . TEVCAECOM
INDI . NVRIM . I**
VDE *EC . RVRSE*CO
AMPILVA
INDI

G̱OEMINA (or ḺOEMINA) . INDI . ENV
PETANIM . INDI . AR
IMOM . SINTAMO
M . INDI . TEVCOM
SINTAMO

L.1.2: -----------
ISAICCID . RVETI . [
PVPPID . CARLAE . EM
]TOM . INDI . NAC[
---]IOM .

L.2.1 RVFINVS . ET
     TIROSCRIP
SERVNT
VEAM̱ṈICORI (or VEAM̱I̱ṈICORI)
DOENTI
ANGOM LAM̱ATICOM (or LAM̱M̱ATICOM)
CROVCEAIMAGA
REAICOI . PETRAṈIOI (or PETRAV̱IOI) . Ṯ
ADOM . PORGOMIOVEA. (or IOVEAI̱)
CAELOBRIGOI

10   Letters are underlined when only partly preserved or of uncertain reading, * denotes a letter preserved only in traces and therefore not identified;] and [indicate missing text.

11   VEAVN in the transcript may be misread for VEAM, cf. MLH IV, 750.

11.2. L.4.1, the
Lusitanian inscription
of Arronches
(Portalegre)

L.3.1: OILAM . TREBOPALA .
INDI . PORCOM . LABBO .
COMAIAM . ICCONA . LOIM
INNA . OILAM . VSSEAM .
TREBARVNE . INDI . TAVROM
IFADE<u>M</u>[
REVE . *<u>RE</u>[

L.4.1 -----] OILAM . ERBAM
HARASE OILA . X . BROENEIAE . H
---]OIIA[12] . X . REVE . AHARACVI . T . AV[
IEATE . X . BANDI HARACVI . AV[---
MVNITIE . CARLA[13] CANTIBIDONE

APINVS . VENDICVS . ERIACAINV[-
OVOVIANI (?)
ICCINVI . PANDIT . I . ATTEDIA . M . TR
PVMPI . CANTI . AILATIO

---

12   Carneiro, Encarnação et al. (2008, 167) read OILA, which is quite probably intended.
13   Carneiro, Encarnação et al. (2008, 167) read CARIA, but L is certain.

§ 4 These texts together provide *c.* 90 words.[14] Some of them appear several times, in the same text or in more than one text. Some seem to show a paradigmatic or derivational relationship, thus

words with a probable paradigmatic relationship:

ARIMO	L 1.1	:	ARIMOM	L 1.1
CARLAE	L 1.1, L 1.2	:	CARLA	L 4.1
ERBA	L 1.1	:	ERBAM	L 4.1
OILA	L 4.1	:	OILAM	L 3.1 (2x), L 4.1
SINTAMO	L 1.1	:	SINTAMOM	L 1.1

words with a probable derivative relationship:

HARACVI	L 4.1	:	AHARACVI	L 4.1 if prefix *a-*
ICCINVI	L 4.1	:	ICCONA	L 3.1 if root *icc-* with suffix *-ino-*, *-ona*
PRAISOM	L 1.1	:	PRAESONDO	L 1.1 if root/base *prais-*
TEVCOM	L 1.1	:	TEVCAECOM	L 1.1
? VEAM*	L 1.1	:	VEA<u>MN</u>ICORI	L 2.1 if VEAVN stands for VEAM

words attested more than once (including all the presumably paradigmatically related forms)

ARIMO	L 1.1	:	ARIMOM	L 1.1
CARLAE	L 1.1, L 1.2	:	CARLA	L 4.1
ERBA	L 1.1	:	ERBAM	L 4.1
INDI	L 1.1 (8x), L 3.1 (2x), L 1.2			
OILA	L 4.1			
OILAM	L 3.1 (2x), L 4.1			
REVE	L 3.1, L 4.1			
SINTAMO	L 1.1	:	SINTAMOM	L 1.1
? AV[	L 4.1	:	AVA	L 1.1 quite uncertain
? IEATE	L 4.1	:	IFADEM[	L 3.1 if E or F wrong spelling
? MVNITIE	L 4.1	:	MVITIEAS	L1.1 if misread for MVNITIEAS[15]
? PORGOM	L 2.1	:	PORCOM	L 3.1 quite probable

---

14 The number depends on the acceptance of unindicated word boundaries and on the counting of apparent abbreviations like M, TR in L.4.1.

15 J. Untermann, p.c.

words attested in more than one indigenous inscription

ERBA	L 1.1	:	ERBAM	L 4.1
CARLAE	L 1.1, L 1.2	:	CARLA	L 4.1
INDI	L 1.1 (8x), L 3.1 (2x), L 1.2			
OILAM	L 3.1 (2x), L 4.1			
REVE	L 3.1, L 4.1			

less certain (cf. above)

? AV[	L 4.1	:	AVA	L 1.1
? IEATE	L 4.1	:	IFADEM[	L 3.1
? MVNITIE	L 4.1	:	MVITIEAS	L 1.1
? PORGOM	L 2.1	:	PORCOM	L 3.1

with a derivative relationship perhaps

ICCINVI	L 4.1	:	ICCONA	L 3.1 if root icc- with suffix -ino-, -ona
? VEAM*	L 1.1	:	VEAMNICORI	L 2.1 if VEAVN stands for VEAM*

The words certainly attested as recurring in inscriptions of different provenance are few in number, but they suffice to testify to the unity of the Lusitanian language in space and (apparently) time.

Most of the words attested in indigenous texts are nouns and adjectives, as is usually the case with languages of fragmentary attestation; these lexical classes are enriched by material from secondary sources, see below. Probable finite verbal forms are DOENTI (L 2.1), PANDIT (L 4.1), RVETI (L 1.2) and perhaps SINGEIE*O (L 1.1). The word INDI which is most frequently attested and occurs in three of the five texts is unanimously interpreted as a conjunction 'and'.[16]

§ 5 The texts reveal structural characteristics immediately reminiscent of other early Indo-European languages, but the morphosyntactic value of a number of forms is far from clear.

The words with a probable paradigmatic relationship ERBA : ERBAM, OILA : OILAM, ARIMO : ARIMOM and SINTAMO : SINTAMOM contrast endings in -m, readily identifiable as accusative singular, with endings in pure vowels, -a and -o respectively. For -a the interpretation as ā-stem nominative singular, Proto-Indo-European *-ah_2 would be straightforward, but classifications as dative singular or ablative singular have also been suggested for words in -a.[17] If -o continues *-ō (< *-oh_1), this would point to

---

16 This has mostly been compared to Germanic words like English *and*, German *und*, cf. e.g. Tovar (1966–7, 250ff.). But as Lühr (1979) has shown, the Germanic forms can be traced back to *$h_2(a)nt$- 'frontside', which means that Lusitanian ind- would likewise reflect older *ant-. While perhaps not impossible, there is no further indication of a change *an > in in the language and Prósper (2002, 355f.) now prefers a comparison with Latin *inde* 'thence'.

17 Cf. MLH IV, 732; Villar & Pedrero (2001, 673ff.), Búa (1999, 323ff.); -a can be a nominative/accusative plural neuter ending, a paradigmatic relation with -am would then be possible for adjectives.

an instrumental singular; Untermann, MLH IV, 732f. and n. 26, on the other hand, suggested a genitive singular qualifying the preceding word. The ending would then be comparable to the Celtiberian genitive singular of *o*-stems in *-o*. A nominative singular in *-os* is not yet attested; the names VENDICVS and APINVS in L.4.1 must be *o*-stems, since suffixes *-iku-* and *-inu-* are highly improbable; however, while they are indigenous names,[18] they show a Latinized form of the ending.

Other nominal endings are *-ai*, *-ae* and *-ui*,[19] which are most easily understandable as dative singular of *ā*- and *o*-stems respectively. The ending *-oi* could be the nominative plural of *o*-stems, or alternatively a locative singular, but a dative value has also been assumed; possibly some forms in *-i* show a Latinized form of the nominative plural. The difference between *-ai* and *-ae* can be variously explained as merely orthographic,[20] as Latin influence, or as a reflex of the inherited dative singular $*-ah_2-ay$ and locative singular $*-ah_2-i$ respectively. For *-as*, genitive singular, nominative plural or accusative plural seem possible.

L.1.1 attests two words in *-im*, NVRIM and ENVPETANIM, which could be accusative singular forms of *i*-stems; however, a development from *-yo-* has also been suggested (MLH IV 732, Prósper 2002, 78, 82). ISAICCID and PVPPID in L.1.2 show the remarkable ending *-id*, that may point to the analogical spread of the ablative singular ending *-d* of the *o*-stems to other stem classes, as in Celtiberian, Latin and Young Avestan; but PVPPID at least has been alternatively explained as a pronoun $*k^wod k^wid$.[21]

Of the words in *-e*, REVE and TREBARVNE are divine names, attested in this form also in Latin inscriptions where they can be clearly identified as datives. If *-e* is monophthongized < *-ey*, they are consonantal stems, and REVE must be classified as a root noun or alternatively as an original *u*-stem.[22] TREBARVNE would seem to belong to a *n*-stem *trebarō*, and CANTIBIDONE could be explained along similar lines. *-un-* and *-on-* in the suffix may reflect different *ablaut* grades, but Latin influence can perhaps not be ruled out. However, TREBARVNE has been alternatively taken as an *i*-stem or as yet another variant of the *ā*-stem dative singular.[23] If LABBO and AILATIO are *n*-stems, they show nominative singular *-o* < *-ō*, coinciding with the Latin ending, and the same applies if they are seen as variant forms of the dative singular. HARASE and IEATE are

---

18 Cf. Untermann (1965, 187), Vallejo Ruiz (2005, 159f.).

19 Confined to L.4.1 so far, but with correspondences in Latin texts, see below.

20 Cf. the spelling PRAESONDO next to PRAISOM in L.1.1.

21 Cf. Villar & Pedrero (2001, 682), Prósper (2002, 84ff.), see below on further implications of this classification; Prósper ibid. takes ISAICCID as an adverb originating from a particle chain. As Villar & Pedrero point out, *-id* could be a verbal ending, but this would suggest an unexpected sequence of three possible verbs.

22 Búa (1997, 8off.) assumes REVE < *dyéwey*, Villar (1996, 199) opts for a *u*-stem *Hr-ew-*.

23 See MLH IV 732, 742f. with references; Prósper (2002, 48f.) suggests a direct connection of *-arun-* with the heteroclitic stem $*h_2arh_3-wr/n-$ in Old Irish *arbe* etc. (cf. NIL 322); while the connection of *treb-* 'place of human habitation' and $*h_2arh_3-$ 'to plough' seems attractive enough semantically, it is questionable whether the neuter *r/n*-stem as such, rather than a derivative, should be regarded as the second member of the compound. Possibly Old Irish *trebar* shows a similar formation.

even less clear.

Another divine name also known from Latin inscriptions is BANDI, apparently in the dative singular, which appears alternatively as *Bandu, Bandue, Bandei, Bande* in Latin context, cf. below.

§ 6 This short survey draws attention to some of the many remaining uncertainties in our understanding of the Lusitanian nominal system. While most endings are comparable to what is found in other Indo-European languages, their grammatical value often remains ambiguous and variant forms for the same function are frequently assumed; moreover, Latin interference must sometimes be taken into account.

The situation gets even more complex when Lusitanian forms from Latin inscriptions are added to the picture. While indigenous personal names usually adopt Latin inflectional endings in Latin contexts, Lusitania shares with Galicia a very characteristic epigraphy of votive texts addressed to indigenous divinities (see Untermann 1988). Divine names like REVE, CROVCEAI and BANDI appear to the north and the south of the Douro and the same is true for e.g. *Nauia* and *Cossue*. These names alone may serve to identify the divinity to whom the dedication is addressed, but they are more commonly accompanied by epithets, mostly derived with a *ko*-suffix, just as REVE AHARACVI, BANDI HARACVI and CROVCEAI MAGAREAICOI in Lusitanian texts. The derivational basis of the epithets is often identifiable as a place-name. In other cases the epithet alone takes the place of the divine name or specifies a Latin designation like *deus* 'god'.

The following examples may illustrate this type of text:[24]

Reue in Latin texts
(1) *D(eo) Reue Larauc(.) Valliu(s) Aper ex uoto* (cf. HAE 1966–9, 2723, Ourense)
cf. the epithet alone in
(2) *Larauco D. Max(uminus) p(ro) f(ilio). D Maxumo u.(l.)a.s.* (cf. AE 1980, 148, Vila Real)
(3) *Larocu Ama Pitili filia libe(ns) animo uotum retuli(t) pro marito su(o)* (cf. AE 1973, 86f., Vila Real)
(4) . . . *]nis f. Meducenus Uxsamensis Reo Bormanico u.s.l.* (etc., cf. CIL II 2403, 5558, Braga)
cf. the epithet alone in
(5) *Medamus Camali Bormanico u.s.l.m.* (cf. CIL II 2402, Braga)
(6) *Reo Paramaeco Aidi(. . .) Pothinus et Prud(ens) f. u.s.l.m.* (cf. Ares 1965–6, 10, Lugo)
(7) *Rectus Rufi f. Reue Langanidaeigui u.s.* (cf. AE 1961, 89, Castelo Branco)

---

24 The reading of many of these texts is highly controversial and the various proposals will not be discussed here; I have adopted the readings of Búa (2000) and added one reference for every text, which, however, may prefer a different reading. Cf. Prósper (2002) for an extensive discussion of this material, based in many cases on alternative readings of the texts.

Reue is attested in some 20 inscriptions from *Lusitania* and *Gallaecia*. It appears as *Reue* in all the Lusitanian texts—both in Latin and in the indigenous language—and this is also the most common form in *Gallaecia*, but here an alternative dative singular *Reo*, as in no. 6, is also attested. The epithet *Langanidaeigui* shows a dative singular in *-ui* which is not Latin, and must therefore belong to the native language of the dedicants as an example of the Lusitanian dative singular of o-stems in *-ui*.

Crouciai in Latin texts:
(8) *Crougiai Toudadigoe Rufonia Seuer(a)* (cf. CIL II 2565, Ourense)
(9) *Arcuius aram pos(u)it pro uo(t)o domin(i) Corougia Vesucoi seruis d(e)i ubicu(e) terraru(m)* (cf. AE 1983, 156, Braga)
(10) *Croucae Ni[.]aicui Clementinus Gei[. . .] a.l.u.s.* (cf. AE 1985, 133, Viseu)
Corougia apparently shows epenthesis in the word initial cluster and the ending is merely *-a*.[25] The epithets show dative singular endings in *-oe*, *-oi* and *-ui*, where the latter, again, is the Lusitanian form, and the former must be indigenous variants. *Croucae* seems to point to a stem **Crouca* beside **Croucia* in all other forms, but is now generally seen as a mere graphic variant of **Croucia*. *Crougiai* in the first text is based on an emendation suggested by Gorrochategui (1985–6, 87); the form on the lost inscription was formerly read *Crougin*, which caused comparisons of the *ā*-stem paradigm nominative singular **krowkā*, accusative singular **krowkin* with the Old Irish type of inflection *crúach*, accusative singular *crúaich* and some Gaulish forms.[26] As in L.2.1, the epithets of the *ā*-stem **Crougia* are apparently o-stems, which means that either **Crougia* is a masculine *ā*-stem of the type Latin *agricola*, or there were o-stem adjectives that could be used for the masculine and feminine alike, as in Greek φρόνιμος etc. The regular *ā*-stem forms of the *ko*-adjectives used as epithets with *Nauia* (cf. below) point to a normal feminine inflection for the epithets and therefore to the first alternative.[27]

Bandi in Latin texts:
(11) *Bandue Cad[..]go Tere(nti)a Rufina u.l.m.s.* (cf. HAE 1950–2, 354, Ourense)
(12) *u.s.l.m. Bandue Veigebreaego M. Silonius Gal(eria tribu) Silanus sig(nifer) coh(ortis) I Gall(icae) C(iuium) R(omanorum)* (cf. HAE 1957–60, 1687, Ourense)
(13) *Bandu Alanobrigue Aemilius Reburrinus* (cf. HAE 1966–9, 38, Ourense)
(14) *Bandu Vordeaeco sacrum Sulpicius Paternus u(o)tum solui(t)* (cf. AE 1991, 272f., Bragança)
(15) *Reburrus Tangini Bandi Vorteaeceo u.s.* (cf. AE 1967, 51, Castelo Branco)

25 Assuming that the word is complete and *-i* has not been left out by a scribal mistake.
26 Cf. e.g. Gaulish accusative singular *Seuerim* in Larzac; see Prosdocimi (1989).
27 But see MLH IV, 734, where the possibility of separating *-coi* and variants as an enclitic conjunction is raised. For masculine *ā*-stems cf. Búa (1997, 74), Prósper (2002, 185f.), Villar & Pedrero (2001, 688ff.), who note, however, that an unmarked feminine remains possible for compounds like CAELOBRIGOI. By this reasoning BANDI (cf. below) must be a male god, notwithstanding the depiction as Fortuna in a dedication from Badajoz (cf. AE 1960, 76). For gender in personal names see Vallejo Ruiz (2008).

cf. the epithet alone:

(16) . . .]*turius Felix Vortiaeci(o) u.s.* (cf. AE 1985, 136f., Castelo Branco)

(17) *Vorteaecio Auitus [Aui]tici Au[it]ici Tong(i) f. patris sui u.s.a.l.* (HE 1994, 100, Cáceres)

(18) *G. Iulius Montanus eq(ues) leg(ionis) VII (Geminae F)elicis Bandi Langobricu u.s.l.a.* (cf. AE 1985, 135, Guarda)

(19) *Bandei Brialeacui Seuerus Abruni f. u.s.* (cf. AE 1967, 50, Castelo Branco)

(20) *Bandi Isibraiegui Cilius Camali f. u.s.* (cf. AE 1067, 50, Castelo Branco)

(21) *Duatius Apini f. Bandi Tatibeaicui uocto solui* (cf. AE 1961, 87, Viseu)

(22) *Bandi Oilienaico* [. . . (cf. Hübner 1913, 24, Viseu)

(23) *Bande Velugo Toiraeco L. Lattius Blaes(u)s u.l.a.s.* (cf. AE 1954, 29, Aveiro)

Some 40 dedications to *Bandi* are known from *Gallaecia* and *Lusitania*. As these examples show, the name appears with the ending *-i* in Latin texts from *Lusitania* just as in L.4.1; there are variant forms in *-e* and *-ei*, as well as *-u* and *-ue* prevailing in the north, but also attested in two dedications to *Bandu Roudaico* from Cáceres (AE 1977, 109; M. Beltrán (1975–6, 89f.).

TREBARVNE is not yet attested north of the Douro or indeed the Mondego; the same is true for the divinities *Arantia, Arantio, Quangeio, Ataecina* and *Endouellicus*, well represented in the southern areas; dedications to *Lugubo* are only found in *Gallaecia* and *Celtiberia* and do not extend to *Lusitania*. But other divine names attested in *Lusitania* and *Gallaecia* are *Cosu* and *Nauia*, which so far have not appeared in indigenous Lusitanian texts.

Dedications to *Cosu*:

(24) *Coso Vdauiniago Q. V C ex uoto* (cf. HAE 1950–2, 464, A Coruña)

(25) *Coso Oenaego G. Iul(ius) Nepos ex uot(o)* (cf. HAE 1957–60, 1703, A Coruña)

(26) *Deo Domeno Cusu Nemedeco ex uoto Seuerus posuit* (cf. CIL II 2325, 5552, Porto)

(27) *Cosei Va(c)oaico* (cf. AE 1989, 117, Viseu)

(28) *Cusei Baeteaco Boutius Turami a.l.p.* (cf. AE 1986, 76, Aveiro)

(29) *Cuhue Berralogegu ex uoto Flauius Valeria(n)u[* (cf. AE 1957, 93, Lugo)

(30) *Cohue Ten[. . .] E(. . .) R(. . .) N(. . .)* (cf. AE 1950, 13, Lugo)

Only two dedications for *Cosu* come from *Lusitania*, both with a dative singular in *-ei*. Forms in *-o* appear in the extreme north-western corner of *Gallaecia*; further to the east, the remarkable forms *Cuhue, Cohue* are attested.

Dedications to *Nauia*:

(31) *Nauiae Sesmacae V Anniu* (cf. CIL II 2602, Galicia)

(32) *Nauiae Arconnuniecae Sulp(icius) Max(imus) ex uoto* (cf. AE 1955, 78, Lugo)

(33) *(N)abiae Elaesurraega sacrum (p)ositum cura Vicci Silon(is)* (cf. CIL II 2524,

Ourense)

This name often appears without epithets, cf. e.g.:

(34) *Nabiae Rufina u.s.l.m.* (HAE 1950–2, 473, Braga)

(35) *Cicero Manci Nabiae l.u.s.* (cf. CIL II 5623, Castelo Branco)

(36) *Boutius Antubel(i) f. d(eae) Naui u.s.l.m.* (cf. CIL II 756, Cáceres)

The forms show variation between *nau-* and *nab-* and dative singular forms in *-i* in addition to *-iae*, which may not in all cases be intended as abbreviations. *Nauia* is better attested in *Gallaecia*, in *Lusitania* it is found only in no. 35 quoted above and in six texts from Cáceres, south of the Tajo, where *Naui* and *Nabi* occur twice respectively.

§ 7 The examples demonstrate that indigenous forms in Latin texts can offer some additional information for native case endings. The dative singular in *-ui* is well attested here and was thus known before the new discovery of L.4.1 provided confirmation in a Lusitanian inscription. The dative plural ending is still unattested in the small corpus of indigenous texts, but there is at least one indication that it was *-bo* in the Latin dedication from Arroyomolinos de la Vera:

(37) *Arabo Corobelicobo Talusicobo* (cf. AE 1977, 108, Cáceres).

Dative plurals in *-bo* appear also in two Gallaecian dedications, the famous

(38) *Lugubo Arquienobo C. Iulius Hispanus u.s.l.m.* (cf. HAE 1957–60, 1718, Lugo)

and

(39) *Deibabo Nemucelaigabo Fuscinus Fusci f. u.l.a.s.* (cf. AE 1987, 159, Vila Real).[28]

Forms like *lokᵒobᵒo niirabᵒo* in Tartessian inscriptions have likewise been interpreted as dative plural in *-bo*, cf. MLH IV, 166f., Villar (2004, 262f., 267), Koch (2009, 125).

While the Latin texts often offer confirmation for Lusitanian forms, the formal variety of case endings increases when they are taken into account, and doublets cannot always be resolved by paying close attention to the geographical distribution of the attestations.[29] Thus, while datives like *Bandu* and *Bandue* are unattested in the Lusitanian heartland, *Bande* and *Bandei* must be added to BANDI as indigenous possibilities. There was, therefore, certainly dialectal diversity in the area considered, but no clear language boundary emerges.

§ 8 The dedications also illustrate that *Gallaecia* and *Lusitania* shared the cult of gods with the same name and the habit of providing them with adjectival derivatives as epithets, formed most frequently, although not exclusively, with the suffix *-ko-* added to various bases among which *-aico-* with its variants *-aeco-*, *-aeico-*, *-eco-*, *-aego-*, *-ego-* prevails, cf. e.g. *Paramaeco, Langanidaeigui, Oilienaico* (no. 6, 7, 22 above).[30] Adjectival *ko*-suffixes are

---

28   The reading follows Búa (1997, 60). Prósper (2002, 49) reads *Debaroni Muceaicaeco* and takes *Debaroni* as a corrupt form of *Trebarune*, which would then be the only attestation of this name outside of *Lusitania* and the only example for an epithet with *Trebarune*.

29   Cf. distribution maps for dative endings in Búa (1997, 91, 94), Prósper (2002, 515f.). As dating is quite difficult, no thorough diachronic approach seems to have been carried out as yet.

30   The suffix has been explained as resulting from 'infection' of earlier *-akyo-*, but also as a *ko*-derivative from

frequent in various IE languages including Celtic.[31] In Celtiberian -*aiko*- is rare, most common are -*ako*-, which derives adjectives from place-names, and -*iko*- and -*oko*- which, among other things, are frequent in the formation of family names. It may be added here that Lusitanians and Gallaecians, as well as the *Celtici* in the south, do not share the name formula involving family names, which is found regularly in Celtiberia and beyond.[32] A typical name formula of the north-west, extending to Asturias, but not into the Lusitanian heartland, is the expression of origin by means of an inverted C, which, as Albertos (1975) has shown, refers to a *castellum* 'a small fortified place, a hillfort', as in the following examples:

(40) *Eburia Calueni f. Celtica Sup(ertamarca)* Ɔ *Lubri an. XXVI h.s.e.* (cf. AE 1997, 873, León)

(41) *Reburrus Ari Seurus* Ɔ *Narelia an. LXII* (cf. CIL II, 6290, Bragança)

(42) *Bassus Medami f. Crou(i)us* Ɔ **Verio** *an. XXV h.s.e. s.t.t.l.* (cf. CIL II 774, Cáceres)

(43) *Caeleo Cadroiolonis f. Cilenus* Ɔ **Berisamo** *an. LX et Caesarus Caeleonis f. an. XV h.s.s.* (cf. CIRG I 52, A Coruña)

(44) *Celer Erbuti f. Limicus* [Ɔ ?] *Borea Cantibedonie(n)si muneris tesera(m) dedit anno M. Licino cos* (cf. CIL II 6246, Huelva)

(45) *Apana Ambolli f. Celtica Supertam(arca)* Ɔ **Miobri** *an. XXV h.s.e. Apanus fr(ater) f. c.* (cf. HE 1997, 397, Lugo)

These and similar texts have recently been discussed by Luján (2008), who interprets many, but by no means all, names of such *castella* and of the persons relating to them as Celtic. If, then, there were Celts as well as other peoples, including presumably Lusitanians, in the north-west, they shared an onomastic formula, that might be connected to the *castro* system, but is not continued in the southern part of *Lusitania*, nor, apparently, is it confined to the inhabitants of *Gallaecia* known as *Celtici*.

If, as the dedications show, inhabitants of *Gallaecia* and *Lusitania* worshipped the same deities, then the question arises whether these deities originally belonged to the Lusitanians, and, if so, whether they and their names were then borrowed by northern peoples of Celtic speech, or, alternatively, whether Celtic gods were integrated into the Lusitanian pantheon. An answer can be attempted by looking at the names of the dedicants, but the latter rarely state their Celticity or their provenance otherwise in the dedication.[33] The cases where the dedicants identify themselves more explicitly than just by their names and father's names are usually confined to soldiers or liberated slaves.[34] In some instances statements of origin are found, e.g.

(46) *Caro cons(?) Q. P(. . .) Matucenus Lusit(anus) V(. . .) f. a(ram) m(erito) l(ibens) l(aetus)*

---

a base in -*ayo*-, see Luján (2007, 26off.), Prósper (2002, 403ff.), Vallejo Ruiz (2005, 69off.).

31 See Russell (1990); for Celtiberian see Villar (1995, 126ff.), MLH IV, 417f., Rubio Orecilla (2001).

32 Cf. the map in MLH IV, 436; see a collection of family names in González Rodríguez (1986).

33 But it may be mentioned in their epitaphs, cf. *Eburia . . . Celtica* no. 40 above. In the case of *Apana* (no. 45) this may have been all the more desirable as both she and her brother have good Lusitanian names.

34 Cf. no. 12 above; also e.g. *Ara(m) pos(uit) Toncius Toncetami f. Icaedit(anus) milis Trebarune l.m.u.s.* (cf. ILER 941, Castelo Branco).

d(edit) (cf. AE 1965, 32, Viana do Castelo)

(47) *Maxum[u]s Vlat[i]ci f. Ta[p]orus [N]a[b]iae [s]acrum* [. . . (cf. AE 1984, 131f., Cáceres)

(48) *Camala Arqui f. Talabrigensis Genio Tiauranceaico u.s.l.m.* (cf. AE 1952, 27, Viano do Castelo)

(49) *Nauia Ancetolu[s] [..]RI exs Ɔ Sesm. uotum possit q... e... c...* (cf. CIL II 2601, Galicia, exact location unknown)[35]

(50) *Coso domino Aeb(urus) Ati Cil(enus) exs uoto p(osuit)* (cf. HE 1994, 133f., A Coruña)

(51) *Aegiamunniaego Antistius Placidus Cili filius Alterniaicinus u.s.l.m.* (cf. CIL II 2523, Ourense)

(52) *[Ce]licus Fronto Arcobrigensis Ambimogidus fecit. Tongoe Nabiagoi* (cf. CIL II 2419, Braga)

(53) *. . .]nis f. Meducenus Uxsamensis Reo Bormanico u.s.l.* etc. (cf. CIL II 2403, 5558, Braga; = no. 4)

(54) *Crissus Talaburi f. Aebosocelensis T[r]ebaroni u.s.l.m.* (cf. AE 1952, 42f., Cáceres)

In the first example the dedicant is specified as *Lusitanus*, in the second as *Taporus*, a people of *Lusitania* mentioned by Pliny (*Naturalis Historia* 4.118) and in the third as a citizen of *Talabriga*, a Lusitanian town.[36] The next example mentions the *castellum* to which the dedicant belongs, but this is unidentified.[37] *Alterniaicinus* may be related to the Carpetanian town Ἀλτέρνια (Ptolemy 2.6.56) of uncertain location, cf. García Alonso (2003, 324). The *Cileni*, a member of whom may be mentioned in the next example (if the abbreviation is extended correctly), are a small tribe mentioned by Pliny (*Naturalis Historia* 4.111) after the *Celtici Praestamarci* and regarded as *Celtici* themselves by, e.g., Luján (2008, 69); however, García Alonso (2003, 452) classifies their tribal name at least as non-Celtic. *Arcobriga* and *Uxama* (or **Uxamom*) are names occurring more than once in the Iberian Peninsula (see MLH V.1, 33, 463), and it remains unclear to which—if any—of the known towns of these names they refer here. Finally, the location of **Aebosocelom*, probably a compound in **okelom*, is unidentified (cf. Guerra 2005, 811).

§ 9 Indications of the origin of dedicants, even when they occur, are thus not necessarily helpful in determining their ethnic or linguistic provenance, or more specifically, their Celticity as opposed to their Lusitanian identity. In many cases they rather refer to places whose location must be considered as either far away from the place of the dedication (as possibly *Alterniaicinus* and perhaps *Uxamensis*) or simply as unidentified. Even when the location is fairly clear, as in the case of the *Cileni*, doubts on the Celtic character of the inhabitants may remain, and this is all the more true if one assumes a linguistic

---

35 Cf. on this text Luján (2008, 76f.) with a different reading; for the extension of *Sesm.* to *Sesmaca* cf. no. 31 above.

36 Cf. Pliny, *Naturalis Historia* 4.113, see Guerra (2005, 805) and García Alonso (2003, 111f.) for further references and suggested identifications.

37 According to Prósper (2002, 190) *Sesmaca* is a north-western Celtic development of **segisamā*, but Luján (2008, 77) remains sceptical.

and cultural mix of Lusitanians and *Celtici* in the western part of the Iberian Peninsula. None of the dedicants is explicitly named as *Celticus, -a*, but some have *Celt-* as a personal name element, cf.

(55) *Besen(. . .) C. Lae(lius) Docquirus Celti u.a.l.* (cf. AE 1989, 119, Viseu)

(56) *Band(. . .) Oge(. . .) uotum Camali Ulpini f. Celtius filius soluit* (cf. HE 1994, 399, Viseu)

(57) *Celtienus Canapi (or Cauapi) f. Laribus Cailie(n)sibus u.l.a.s.* (cf. ILER 673, Castelo Branco)[38]

(58) *Tritiaegio Gaius Celti a(m)pliauit fines* (cf. Blázquez 1962, 215, Cáceres)

(59) *Clemens Cel[t]i Arpaniceo u.a.l.s.* (cf. AE 1972, 75, Badajoz)

Such names are expected to be preferred in areas where they might distinguish a *Celtius* from other people, who might not designate themselves in such a way. They are frequent in *Lusitania* and extend along the north of the Peninsula, but are lacking in Celtiberia, the south and the east.[39] Yet it is not immediately apparent what made a person a *Celtius*, when others were not. *Celtius* does not in itself seem to be an ethnic name, as opposed to *Celtica* or *Celtiber*.[40] Was a *Celtius* a person felt to be a Celt, and was he so regarded because he spoke a Celtic language which his neighbours did not, or did the distinction rest in some other characteristic or cultural property?

§ 10   If, then, the presumed mixture of *Celtici* (and possibly other Celts) and non-Celtic Lusitanians cannot be disentangled with the help of direct references to the Celticity of the protagonists in the attestations, the argument must be based on a strictly linguistic basis. Since the Celtic languages of the north-west are not preserved in indigenous texts, their presence and extension can only be deduced from indigenous names in Latin inscriptions and in classical sources; thus the onomastic record is the only source of linguistic information. The characteristics of these names may then be compared to the Lusitanian inscriptions on the one hand, and to Celtic features elsewhere on the other.

An examination of the evidence has been carried out for divine names and their epithets by Prósper (2002), for place-names by García Alonso (2003) and Luján (2008), and for personal names by Vallejo Ruiz (2005) and Luján (2007), among others. The results are not always consistent among the various authors.

In a comprehensive survey of the personal names of the Roman province of *Lusitania* (with the Douro as its northern boundary), Vallejo Ruiz (2005) has shown how a number of names belong to this province exclusively, while others show noticeable extensions to the north or north-east (cf. Untermann (1965, 19ff.), Albertos (1985)).

Examples of the typical Lusitanian personal names include: *Tanginus*, with its variant *Tancinus* well represented in Vettonian territory (Vallejo Ruiz 2005, 411ff.); *Aranta* and

---

38   On *Celtienus*, attested only here, see Vallejo Ruiz (2005, 277 n.104), who argues against a derivation from **Celti-genus*.

39   Cf. the maps in Vallejo Ruiz (2005, 274f.).

40   And no feminine **Celtia* seems to be attested, as opposed to *Celtica* and *Celtibera*. For a discussion of the evidence for **kelt-* in the Iberian Peninsula and elsewhere see Untermann (2001, 204ff.).

Arantonius (ibid. 175ff.), *Docquirus* (ibid. 302), *Sunua* (ibid. 400ff.), *Bouius, -ia* (ibid. 214ff.), *Maelo* (ibid. 341ff.), *Tongeta* and *Tongetamus* with *Tonceta* and *Toncetamus* (ibid. 417ff.), *Tureus, -a* (ibid. 441),[41] *Camira* (ibid. 254) and *Leurius* (ibid. 332).

Names extending northwards into *Gallaecia* and eastwards into the territory of the *Astures* are much more frequent, e.g. *Reburrus*, one of the most frequent indigenous Palaeohispanic names also well represented further to the north-east (ibid. 384ff.), *Caturo* (ibid. 267f.), *Talabus* with its variant *Talaus* (ibid. 406ff.),[42] *Cilius* (ibid. 278ff.), *Louesius* (ibid. 332ff.), *Camalus* (ibid. 249ff.), *Caino* (ibid. 238ff.), *Medamus* (ibid. 355f.), *Boutius, -ia* (ibid. 216ff.), *Caburus, -a* (ibid. 228ff.), and names derived from *Pent-, Pint-* (ibid. 370ff.).

§ 11 It is quite difficult to draw a distinction between names belonging to the Lusitanians proper and names of the *Vettones*. In his attempt to differentiate the personal names of the *Vettones*, Luján (2007) has given a description of this onomastic material including the following remarks on historical phonology (pp. 255ff.):[43]

$*\bar{o} > \bar{a}$ occurs in *Enimarus*, which is Celtic.

$*\bar{o} > \bar{u}$ in final syllables is indicated by the suffix of e.g. *Abrunus, Caurunius*.

$*\bar{e} > \bar{i}$ is attested in genitive singular *Riuei*.

$*\underset{\circ}{n} > an$ appears in *Argantonius*, and $*\underset{\circ}{m} > am$ in names with *Amb-*, but the development of $*\underset{\circ}{r}$ and $*\underset{\circ}{l}$ before stops is not clearly represented.

$*g^w > b$ is attested in names like *Bouius*, derived from $*g^wow$- 'cow'.

$*k^w$ appears in a lenited form in the name *Erguena* < $*perk^wos$ 'oak', which, moreover, shows $*p > \emptyset$ word-initially before a vowel; however, $*k'w$ seems to be preserved in *Equaesus*, but developed > p in *Eponeilus*, if both are derived from Proto-Indo-European $*h_1ek'wo$- 'horse'. This indicates that the names of the *Vettones* reflect more than one language or dialect.

$*p > \emptyset$ is also exemplified by *Laboina* < root $*plab$-, and between vowels by *Uralus, Urocius* with *ur-* < $*uper$-; yet *Cupiena*, a Vettonian name not attested in *Lusitania*, shows intervocalic $*p$ preserved, and the same is true for names like *Pinara* with word-initial p. $*-pl-$ probably developed into $-bl-$ in names like *Ableca*.

Indo-European voiced aspirates have merged with plain voiced stops, as e.g. in *Boutila* < $*b^howd^hi$- 'victory', where $-t-$ is written for $-d-$; however, the spelling $-u-$ for $-b-$ < $*b^h$ is also found as in *Lobesius* and *Lubacus*, both < $*lub^h$- 'to love', and in *Douitena, Douiterus* < $*dub^h$-, cf. Old Irish *dub* 'black'. Intervocalic $-g-$ has disappeared in names like *Catuenus* < $*Catu-genus$.

Luján concludes that some of the names of the *Vettones* show clearly Celtic features, such as the development of $*\bar{o}$ and the loss of $*p$, but the double reflex of $*k'w$ suggests

---

41 Names in *tur-* with various other suffixes are widespread throughout the Peninsula, and not confined to Indo-European speaking areas, cf. MLH V.1, 428f. with references.

42 The latter more frequent in *Asturia* and also found elsewhere in the north.

43 The following short summaries cannot do full justice to the works of the respective authors, only some points important for the discussion here have been selected.

that there may be more than one Celtic dialect involved and, moreover, preservation of *p* in names like *Pinara* makes it clear that a non-Celtic language is also represented, and no clear linguistic boundary can be established.

§ 12   Vallejo Ruiz (2005) in his extensive discussion of the personal names attested in the Roman province of *Lusitania* agrees with Luján on this last point, but is often led to different evaluations in other cases. According to him (p. 736) the anthroponymy offers no indication that the Lusitanians and the *Vettones* spoke different languages. Both areas rather constitute a unitary onomastic zone without tangible trace of linguistic diversity. The language of the personal names can be identified in many particular points with the language of the Lusitanian inscriptions, which is not Celtic. Accordingly, a number of characteristically Celtic sound changes adduced by Luján are questioned by Vallejo Ruiz. Here belong *$\bar{e}$ > i, as the evidence is based on the name *Riuei* alone, but this is of uncertain reading (p. 505); the corpus does not provide conclusive evidence for the development of *$\bar{e}$ (p. 693), and the same is true for *$\bar{o}$, since *Enimarus*, a hapax, may well be a Gaulish name (p. 471), and while suffixes like *-un(i)us* exist, *-on(i)us* is much more frequent (p. 694).

Regarding the treatment of *-p-*, *Cupiena* has to be excluded, as it might be Latin, even if the reading is correct, which is uncertain (p. 489); however, the connection of *Uramus* with *uper-* is also doubtful, and there is therefore no evidence for intervocalic loss of *-p-* (p. 695); rather it appears preserved, for instance, in the well-attested name *Apana* < *h_2ap- 'water'. Initial *p-* is preserved throughout, for Luján's connection of *Erguena* with *$perk^wus$ is to be rejected in favour of a comparison with names like *Elgueni*, *Elguisteri* etc.,[44] and *Laboina* besides *Lapoena* rather reflects a root *lap-* (pp. 319, 701 n.268).

The development of *$k'w$ > p cannot be substantiated by the doubtful hapax *Epo[n]eilus* (p. 322), rather names like *Equalius* point to the preservation of the group, and the frequent occurrence of *-q-* in well-attested names like *Allucquius*, *Docquirus*, *Arquius* suggests that *k^w remained likewise unchanged, although here the onomastic evidence seems to be in contrast to the language of the Lusitanian inscriptions, where PETRANIOI (L.2.1) has been derived from *k^wetwor- 'four' with *$k^w > p$, and this is the most likely explanation for PVPPID (L.1.2) < *k^wodk^wid (p. 703 with n.269, following Villar & Pedrero (2001, 682).

Another such contrast shows up in the treatment of intervocalic *-w-*, which must have been lost in the language of the inscriptions if the unanimously accepted interpretation of OILA < *$h_2owi-lah_2$ 'sheep' is correct. The personal names, on the other hand, show *-w-* preserved or developed into a sound written *-b-*, notably in the amply attested forms *Douiterus / Dobiterus*, *Douiteina / Dobiteina*, which have variant forms in *Doi-* only outside of *Lusitania*, in *Lobessa / Louessa*, where *b*-forms are confined to *Lusitania*, and in

---

44   For *-r-* in interchange with *-l-* cf. *Mermandi* vs. the well-attested base *melm-* in names like *Melmandus*, cf. Vallejo Ruiz (2005, 360f).

Talabus vs. *Talauius*, which must be the older form (pp. 304ff., 406ff., 695).[45]

A further widely assumed development in the language of the Lusitanian inscriptions is $*b^h > f$, evidenced only by the alleged connection of IFADEM (L.3.1)—of unclear word formation—with the root $*yeb^h$- 'to penetrate, have sexual intercourse'.[46] The personal names add no supporting examples to this suggested sound change, the outcome of $*b^h$ seems to be *b* in well-attested names like *Boudica* ($*b^howd^hi$- 'victory') and *Albonius* ($*Halb^h$- 'white'), and *f* plays no noticeable role in the anthroponymy (pp. 708f.). It may be added here that the same is true for *h* which is now attested several times in L.4.1.[47]

Like Luján, Vallejo Ruiz assumes $*g^w > b$ for names like *Bouius* (p. 708), and the loss of intervocalic -*g*- in names like *Catuenus, Meduenus* < $*$-*genos*, which are directly comparable to Old Irish *Caithgen, Midgen* (p. 707).

A last important point is his suggestion that $*\underset{.}{r}, *\underset{.}{l}$ developed into *ar, al* before stops, based above all on *Malgeinus*, which could then represent a zero grade $*ml\underset{.}{g}$- to e.g. $*h_2mel\underset{.}{g}'$- 'to milk' (pp. 346, 710).[48]

§ 13 As opposed to Luján's and Vallejo Ruiz's treatments, which focused on personal names and on a possible distinction of Lusitanians and *Vettones*, Prósper (2002) concentrates on the evidence of the divine names and their epithets, and on the distinction of Lusitanian from the surrounding Celtic languages, particularly in *Gallaecia*, which shares the Lusitanian theonyms. She draws the following conclusions regarding Lusitanian historical phonology:

$*p$ is preserved in many examples of which only very few, e.g. the epithet *Toudopalandaigae*, can be explained as belonging to another language, in this case Old European (pp. 395f., 46.).

$*k^w > p$, but $*kw$ appears as *q* in names like *Alluquius* (< $*ad$-*luk*-*wo*-) and *Doquirus* ($*dok$-*wo*-) and in the purely Lusitanian theonym *Quangeio* ($*k'w\underset{.}{n}$-*k*-*eyo*-, p. 310); ICCONA (L.3.1) is the Lusitanian form of the divine name *Epona*, the Celtic character of which is doubtful. Exceptions are rare, and *Erguena* may be a Celtic name < $*perk^wu$-*genā* or $*perk^wunyā$, cf. Caesar's *Hercynia* (*silua*) (pp. 396ff., 51f., 422).

$*p...k^w > k^w...k^w$ as seen in the Galician tribal name *Querquerni*, likewise derived from $*perk^wus$ with a suffix -*erno*-. The development is comparable to Latin rather than Celtic.[49]

$*g^w > b$, e.g. in *Bandue* < $*g^wm$-*tu*-, cf. $*g^wem$- 'to come' (p. 398).

---

45 *Talabus* < $*talawos$ may be a straightforward derivation $**tlth_2$-*aw*-*o*- from the full grade suffix of a *u*-stem adjective; it may alternatively be a backformation if the starting point was an adjective $* tlh_2$-*u*- > $*talu$-, feminine *talawī*, genitive singular *talawyās* (< $* tlh_2$-*aw*-*yah_2$-) with a transfer from the oblique feminine cases to *yā*-stems which then triggered a masculine *yo*-stem $*Talauios$.

46 The etymology was suggested by Tovar (1966/67, 257f.); Prósper (2004, 176ff.) suggest $*en$-b^hat-*yom*.

47 On the attestations of *f* and *h* in Latin context see also Albertos (1985–6), Búa (1997, 76ff.).

48 Evidence for $*\underset{.}{r} > ar$ is less cogent, for while a zero grade seems to be the most likely basis for names in *arg*-, the development $*h_2r\underset{.}{g}'$- > *arg*- can be exemplified for a number of languages, including Celtic (cf. NIL 317ff. with notes 1 and 16).

49 Although the same can perhaps not be said of the suffix.

$*\underset{\circ}{N} > aN$, but $*\underset{\circ}{R} > uR$ (p. 399)

$*w$ between vowels is preserved, it disappears in northern forms like *Reo* for REVE, but the name is a loanword in these areas. Intervocalic $*\text{-}w\text{-}$ is sometimes lost, thus in OILAM and DOENTI, where the conditions are not very clear. The personal names *Douiterus, Douitena* and *Douidona* are Celtic and came as loans into Lusitanian, where, as foreign names, they are often written with -*b*-. They are based on Celtic $*dubwo\text{-}$ and are to be compared to Ogam-forms in DOV-. The same holds for names like *Duatius, Duanna*, which belong to the southern *Celtici* and likewise have close cognates in the Ogam DOV-forms (pp. 406ff.).[50] Of the other names showing w/b-interchange *Louessa / Lobessa* are probably illusionary because etymologically distinct.

The divine name *Cossue* appears as *Cohue, Cuhue* in two inscriptions from the region of the *Seurri*, whose tribal name is Celtic (Prósper 2008, 40f.), and *Laho* is found in the same area. -*h*- for -*s*- (< a group of two dentals) here may then be a dialectal development in the Celtic speech of the area (pp. 246f.).

§ 14 The only agreement emerging so far from the different studies seems to concern the preservation of $*p$ in Lusitanian, the development of $*\underset{\circ}{n}, *\underset{\circ}{m} > an, am, *g^w > b$ and the possibility of $*k^w > p$ at least in some cases. The treatment of $*\underset{\circ}{r}, *\underset{\circ}{l}$ remains disputed, as all the clear examples involve -*brig*-, which is regarded as a Celtic loan. For the development of $*\bar{o}$ the evidence is inconclusive. Lusitanian f and h are unexplained.

Still the lingering suspicion that $*k^w$ may develop into p in Lusitanian opens the way to a number of new etymological possibilities. Thus the second element of TREBOPALA has usually been compared to the epithet *Toudopalandaigae* in

(60) *Munidie Berobrigae Toudopalandaigae Ammaia Boutila* (cf. AE 1916, 8, Cáceres)[51]

It might now be connected with $*k^welh_1\text{-}$ 'to turn' rather than with a root beginning in $*p\text{-}$.[52] PANDIT could belong to the root $*k^wendh\text{-}$ 'to experience, bear' and ENVPETANIM

---

50   Names in *Dou*- are discussed at length ibid. 417ff. on the assumption that they are Celtic and based on a thematic variant $*d^hub^h\text{-}w\text{-}o\text{-}$ of the *u*-stem adjective $*d^hub^h\text{-}u\text{-}$ preserved in Old Irish *dub* 'black'. Open questions are the etymology of *dub* < $*d^hub^h\text{-}u\text{-}$ rather than $*d^hub\text{-}u\text{-}$ and the occurrence of a thematicized variant only in Ogam Irish, when the *u*-stem alone seems to survive in later Irish. For the Hispanic names *Douiterus, Douitena* a derivation from compounds in $*h_1i\text{-}ter/n\text{-}$ 'way, path' remains attractive (cf. Vallejo Ruiz 2005, 309). The first member could be e.g. $*d^howo\text{-}$ from $*d^hew\text{-}$ 'to run', cf. Greek θοός 'fast', and the meaning 'having a fast course, whose course is fast'.

51   The reading follows Fariña Busto & Suárez Otero (2002, 34); the first two words have previously been interpreted as *Munidi Eberobrigae*, but as *Munidie* can be compared to MVNITIE (L.4.1) and *Berobrigae* to *Lari Berobreo, castello Berisamo* etc. the alternative word division is very attractive.

52   Cf. $*k^welh_1\text{-}$ as the second member of compounds in forms like Old Irish *búachaill* 'cowherd', Lat. *agricola* 'farmer', Young Avestan *ātarəcar*- 'having the movement of fire', which, like *trebo*- and $*touto\text{-}$, refer to interactions of man with his domestic environment. -*pala* in TREBOPALA could be the root noun $*k^w\underset{\circ}{l}h_1\text{-}$, perhaps remodelled as an *ā*-stem. Prósper (2002, 81f.) derives AMPILVA from $*k^welh_1\text{-}$ and compares Greek ἀμφίπολος and Old Irish *caile* 'female servant'. The second member of *Toudopalandaigae* is usually connected with river names in *Palant*-, ascribed to the Old European hydronymic substratum. As Prósper (2002, 45ff.) points out, this would make the word a hybrid compound with an Old European loanword as a second member.

might be a secondary derivative of an *en-uk^w-$et(o)$-, containing the root *wek^w- 'to say' in the zero grade. For some personal names containing *p*, alternative etymologies involving *k^w might be envisaged, e.g. *Apana* < *h_2ak^w- 'water', *Pisirus* < *k^weys- 'to notice'.

§ 15 The problem of distinguishing Lusitanian linguistic material from Celtic forms is thus quite pronounced not only at the eastern border, but also in Galicia, where *Celtici* seem to be enmeshed in a close cultural relationship with *Lusitania* regarding the religious sphere as well as personal names and toponyms. The presence of Celtic speakers in the north of *Lusitania* is clear not only from the reports of classical authors and the affiliation *Celtica* in Latin inscriptions from the area, but also from a number of obviously Celtic indigenous names.

As for place-names, it is well known that compounds in -*brig*- abound in the west of the Iberian Peninsula, both in *Lusitania* and *Gallaecia*, and some are found among the southern *Celtici*; for a recent collection of the evidence cf. Guerra (2005, 812ff. and the map p. 822). Derivatives of *brig*-names are found in epithets of divine names like *Alanobrigue*, *Langobricu* (cf. no. 13, 18) and in CAELOBRIGOI (L.2.1). Another well-attested place-name element is *Ocelum*, which appears alone or as the second member of compounds as in *Aebosocelensis* (cf. no. 54) and as the basis of divine epithets, cf. e.g.
(61) *Rufus Peicani f. Arant[i]a Ocela[e]ca et A[r]antio [O]celaeco [...* (Encarnação 1987, 17, Castelo Branco; see a collection in Guerra 2005, 810ff.). The Celtiberian coin legend *okalakom* (A.85) has now been reread **okelakom** (Rodríguez Ramos 2001–2) and thus refers to another place of that name in Celtiberia. The Celtic character of *Ocelum* has been doubted, but while the word is well attested in place-names and as epithet of Mars in Britain, no clear connections of extra-Celtic provenance have been adduced; although the presumed root *h_2ak'- 'sharp, pointed' is widely attested in Indo-European languages, the combination of o-grade and -*elo*-suffix is unparalleled.

The Galician town named Κονπλούτικα in Ptol. 2.6.38 shares the basis with **konbouto** in Celtiberian coins (A.74), Φλαούιον Βριγάντιον on the north coast matches the southern Irish and northern British *Brigantes* and the southern Gaulish people who minted coins with the legend **biṙikatio** in Iberian script (A.3). Among tribal names, the *Albiones* in the north and the *Nerii* in the north-west may well have Celtic names, and this is certainly so for the *Nemetates* on the western coast north of the Douro. The suffix -*at*- in this form recurs in the epithet *Toudadigoe* of *Crougia* (no. 8),[53] that can be traced to earlier *$teutatiko$- sharing the base with Gaulish *Teutates*.

nemeto- seems to be named directly in the dedication
(62) *Nimmedo Aseddiago G. Sulpicius Africanus u.s.l.m.* (cf. HAE 1957–60, 1660, Ovideo) and twice in Celtiberia:

---

53   And perhaps in IFADEM (L.3.1), if the word is complete.

(63) *Nemedo Augusto* and *Nemedo V* (cf. HE 5, 1995, 196, Segovia).

In Porto it is attested in

(64) *Nimidi Fiduenearum hic*

on the same stone as the dedication: *Cosu Ne.* AE(. . .) F(. . .) *s(acrauit)* (cf. CIL II 5607, Porto), where, with Búa (1999, 315ff.), *Ne.* may be an abbreviated epithet, perhaps identical to the epithet *Nemedeco* in the same area, which qualifies *Cosu* in *Deo Domeno Cusu Nemedeco* etc. (no. 26) and

(65) *Dom(ino) Deo Nemedec[o] Seueru[s S]aturni f. ex uoto posuit Homullus Catur[* (cf. Búa 1997, 75; Porto).

Fiduenearum is a rare form with *f.* If it represents an older **widu-gen-yā-* it may be compared to the personal name Old Irish *Fidgen*, Welsh *Guidgen*;[54] a further possible example for **w* spelled *f* is found in the epithet of the *Lares*:

(66) *Albinus Balesini Laribus Findene[a]icis libens posui[t]* (cf. CIL II 2471, Vila Real), if this is related to Celtic **windo-* 'white, bright'.

An inscription to the *Lugubo* has already been mentioned (no. 38), a second, more Latinized text reads:

(67) *Lucoubu[s] Arquieni[s] Silonius Silo ex uoto* (cf. AE 1957, 93, Lugo).

The third example from the Iberian Peninsula is the well-known

(68) *Lugouibus scarum L. L. Urcico(m) collegio sutorum d. d.* (cf. CIL II 2818, Osma, Soria) from Uxama in Celtiberia, and the forms LUGUEI, LUGUES in the Celtiberian inscription from Peñalba de Villastar (K.3.3) are usually identified with the divine name.[55]

A single dedication is addressed to *Suleis*, female divinities also known from Britain, Gaul and the neighbouring provinces of *Germania*:

(69) *Suleis [.]antugaicis Flauinus Flaui u.s.l.m.* (cf. HAE 1966–9, 2724, Ourense).

Further 'Celtic-looking' forms are the epithets *Segidiaeco* of *Cossue* (cf. AE 1967, 76, León) and *Bormanico* (no. 4, 5), usually compared to the Gaulish divine name *Bormanus, Bormana*, a *genius Brocci* from León (cf. CIL II 2694, 5726), reminiscent of Old Irish *brocc*, Welsh *broch* 'badger', the dedication to *Deae Deganto[* (cf. CIL II 5672, León) possibly from the same base as the British tribal name *Decantae* and the Irish *Maicc Dechet* (Búa 1997, 70), and another one to *Senaico* (cf. AE 1973, 85, Braga). Yet the last example could of course belong to Lusitanian or another ancient Indo-European language, and, like the tribal name *Albiones* above, will only be considered Celtic if one assumes that there were no speakers of another such language in the area. A morphological indication of Celtic speech is the superlative-formation in **-isamo-* in the name of the *castellum Berisamo* (no. 43).[56]

---

54   Búa (2007, 18 n.3) compares *Nimidi Fiduenearum* to Old Irish *fidnemed* 'sacred grove'.

55   These forms have recently been the victims of an attempted theocide by Jordán (2006); however, as gods are notoriously hard to kill, it would not be surprising to see *Lugus* rise again in Peñalba de Villastar.

56   Cf. a discussion in Untermann (2007, 68f.), Luján (2008, 70ff.).

Finally it must be stressed that none of the Celtic elements just listed is defined by loss of *p. But rather, the personal names in *Pent-* and *Pint-* are well represented in the north-western region of the Peninsula, the tribe of the *Copori* inhabited an area between the rivers *Tamaris* (mod. Tambre) and Ulla, and among epithets are found *Pemaneieco* (Ourense), *Paraliomego* (Lugo) and *Paramaeco* (Lugo). Before returning to a further phonological characterization of the Celtic languages in the north-west, the coherence of the lexicon in the Indo-European dialects of these areas shall be briefly considered.

§ 16 As has become clear in the preceding discussion the linguistic evidence for common nouns is severely limited. Apart from the words attested in the Lusitanian inscriptions—many of which are names or can be names—only *Nimmedo, Nimidi* (no. 62, 64) can be interpreted as probably common nouns. The lexicon is therefore predominantly visible in proper names. The lexical elements of several onomastic types overlap. As noted above, epithets are usually derived from place-names, which, in their turn, can be associated with personal or tribal names, cf. e.g. *Arquienobo* (no. 38) with the well-attested personal name *Arquius*, *Elaesurraega* (no. 33) and the personal name *Elaesus*, *Arantoniceo* (cf. CIL II 4991, Lisboa) and the personal name *Arantonius*, the divine name *Arantia* and the personal name *Aranta* (cf. Vallejo Ruiz 2005, 180f., 315f., 175f. for the attestation of the personal names). The names of the divinity *Collouesei Caielonico* (cf. AE 1986, 80, Guarda), if read correctly, seem comparable to the personal names *Louesius, Louessa* and *Caelioniga* (CIL II 5736, Oviedo) respectively, and the latter, again, may be related to CAELOBRIGOI (L.2.1).

The first member of CAELOBRIGOI (L.2.1) can further be compared to the epithet *Cailie(n)sibus* of *Lares* in Castelo Branco (no. 57).[57] The element *treb-* in TREBOPALA and TREBARVNE (L.3.1) seems to find parallels in a dedication to *Ambidrebi*[. . . (cf. AE 1973, 85, Braga), perhaps in the name of the *Arrotrebae*, and moreover in the well-known Celtiberian towns *Contrebia*.[58] ERBA and ERBAM (L.1.1 resp. L.4.1) may well be connected to the divine name *Erbine* and to the personal name *Erbutus* (no. 44). *Erbine* is attested in connection with *Cantibidone*, the exact match of CANTIBIDONE in L.4.1, in a Latin context, cf.

(70) *Andercius Allucqui f. Erbine Iaedi Cantibidone u.l.a.s.* (cf. HE 1994, 380f., Castelo Branco)

(71) *Capito Pisiri f. Erbine Iaidi Cantibidone l.a.u.s.* (cf. HE 1994, 381, Castelo Branco; Carneiro, Encarnação et al. 2008, 171).

The derivative *Cantibedonie(n)si* may refer to the *castellum* of *Erbutus'* son, a *Limicus* from *Gallaecia*, if the text is interpreted correctly.

OILA apparently shares the base with the epithet of *Bandi Oilienaico* (no. 22) and perhaps with Celtiberian OILOBOS (K.3.11) and the place-name **oilaunu** (A.56). As noted above (§ 12) OILA is usually understood as *$h_2owilah_2$-* 'sheep' or 'lamb' which

---

57   For the personal name *Caelius, Caelia* see Vallejo Ruiz (2005, 235ff.).
58   One might, of course, postulate that *treb-*, just like *-brig-*, is yet another Celtic loanword in Lusitanian.

fits the context of divine names in the dative, as it could be an offering, and this is further strengthened by its correlation to PORCOM and TAVROM in L.3.1, which have unanimously been translated 'pig' (cf. Lat. *porcus*) and 'bull' (cf. Lat. *taurus*), following Tovar's (1966–7) comparison with the Roman *suouetaurilium*. The implied loss of **-w-* is hard to explain, and the same would hold for the Celtiberian words if they are derived from the same base.[59]

The *Celtici* called *Praestamarci* may show a *praes-* in their epithet related to Lusitanian PRAISOM and PRAESONDO (L.1.1, cf. Untermann forthcoming). VEAMNICORI may contain a second element related to the epithets *Corobelicobo* (no. 37), *Coronae* (of *Nabiae*, cf. AE 1973, 88f., Porto), *Corono* (alone, cf. CIL II 5562, Braga) and the personal names (all genitive singular) *Coroneri* (Braga), *Corocaudi* (Viana do Castelo), *Corogeni* (Bragança), *Coropoti* (Cáceres), which have been connected with **kor(y)o-* 'war; army' (Vallejo Ruiz 2005, 293f.).

The typical Lusitanian personal names *Mailo* and *Toncetamus* only find plausible etymological connections in Celtic **maylo-* 'shorn, bald' (Old Irish *maíl*, Middle Welsh *moel*) and **tonketo-* 'fate' (Old Irish *tocad*, Middle Welsh *tynghet*) respectively. Since both forms are lacking plausible extra-Celtic parallels, one would have to postulate loanwords in either of the two languages.

While compound personal names are well attested in Iberian, they are rare in the Indo-European languages of the Peninsula, but Celtic and Lusitanian seem to share a certain predilection for names in **-genos*.[60]

This short survey indicates a number of lexical relations between Lusitanian words and names from *Lusitania* and *Gallaecia*, which point to a shared lexicon. As far as the words in question are regarded as Celtic, they will usually be claimed to be loans in Lusitanian. Since this is the case for many of them, Schmidt (1985, 330) went so far as to speak of 'the hybrid character of Lusitan[ian] i[n]s[cription]s', in which '[t]he Lusitan[ian] elements are especially difficult to identify'; he adds a list of no less than twelve Celtic loanwords in the three indigenous texts known at the time.

§ 17 A description of the phonological characteristics of the Celtic languages in the west of the Iberian Peninsula has been attempted by Prósper (2002, 422ff.). It can be summarized as follows:

$*\underset{\circ}{R} > Ri$ and $*\underset{\circ}{N} > aN$

$*\bar{o} > \bar{a}$ cannot be demonstrated for the north-west, but is exemplified by the personal

---

59　Prósper (2002, 263) suggests an etymological connection of *Oilienaico* with **h₁ey-* 'to go', but does not consider OILAM in this context. Note that L.4.1, with three attestations of OILA(M), also seems to contain OVOVIANI with a sequence -OVI-.

60　For Iberian compound names cf. MLH III.1, 195ff., for Celtic and Lusitanian see Vallejo Ruiz (2005a). See Uhlich (1993, 129f.) for the Common Celtic inflection of those names as o-stems, where other Indo-European languages would preserve the s-stem as second members of compound names, cf. e.g. Greek Διο-γένης.

names *Enimarus* and *Segumarus* for the southern *Celtici*.[61]

*ey > *ē*

*ow > *ō* as in the personal names *Bodius* vs. *Boudica*, *Totonus* vs. *Toutonus*

The suffix *-iko-* becomes *-eko-* in Asturias when unstressed, cf. e.g. the personal name *Ableca*.

Examples of Joseph's rule may be seen e.g. in the river name *Tamaris* and perhaps in personal names like *Talauia*.

*-mnV- > *-unV-*[62]

Celtic **g* > Ø next to palatal vowels, in particular *i*.

*kʷ and **kw* > *p*, although examples are rare. The epithet of the *Lugubo Arquienobo* is not Celtic but a Lusitanian reflex of **arkw-*.[63]

*p > Ø, but this change occurs retarded in some contexts, notably in *anlaut* before *-l-*, thus the place-name *Bletisam(a)* (modern *Ledesma* in Salamanca) seems to be an attempt to write **φletisamā* in the Latin alphabet; likewise *Blaniobrensi*, the name of the *castellum* of a *Celtica Supertamarca*, reflects **φlān-yo-bri-* (p. 427).

§ 18 As Prósper stresses (p. 426), the conservative character of marginal areas as opposed to central areas—in this case Celtiberia with its place-name **letaisama** (A.68), showing **φ* > Ø—is well known, and a reflex of Celtic **φ* has also been postulated by Eska (1998) for Lepontic **uvamokozis** and **uvitiauiopos**.[64]

Recent work on historical Celtic phonology has made clear that the complete loss of **p* between vowels and word initially before a vowel must have been a comparatively late development, preceded e.g. by **R̥* > *Ri* and other changes (cf. McCone 1996, 43f., KP 129ff., Matasović 2009, 15). Sims-Williams (2007, 310) therefore rightly doubts that **p* > Ø should be regarded as a *conditio sine qua non* for the classification of a language as Celtic, and Schumacher, KP 133f., mostly on the strength of the Lepontic evidence, argues for the possibility that **φ* was preserved in all positions in Proto-Celtic.[65] The Hispano-Celtic forms would seem to be a rather stronger indication for a late persistence of **φ* in some Celtic dialects, as they are attested in the Latin alphabet so much later than the Lepontic inscription of Prestino. It may be mentioned here that Schrijver (1997, following Pedersen 1909, 410f.) has attempted to establish *h* as a possible reflex of Proto-Celtic **φ* in the Würzburg glosses.

---

61 On *Enimarus* see Vallejo Ruiz (2005, 471, cf. § 12 above). *māro-* 'great' now seems to be attested in **maromiðom** on the Celtiberian lead inscription from Cuenca (Lorrio & Velaza 2005, 1040), and would thus prove the change for Celtiberian, where clear examples were previously lacking.

62 A development also envisaged by Prósper for Celtiberian and discussed at length p. 426 with respect to Celtiberian **launi**.

63 It is not clear whether that is to imply that the Lusitanians borrowed the Celtic cult of the *Lugoues* and provided them with epithets in their own language, or whether north-western Celts themselves are thought of as using Lusitanian epithets for their gods.

64 And further e.g. for the divine name *Pritona* next to *Ritona* (a goddess of the ford) in the area of the *Treueri* (cf. Jungandreas 1981, 7f.).

65 Note, however, the criticism of Isaac (2007, 11f.).

If it is correct, then, that Hispano-Celtic languages, with the exception of Celtiberian, are at least in part *p*-Celtic and, moreover, preserve reflexes of Proto-Indo-European *p > Proto-Celtic *φ word initially before *-l-*, this again has consequences for the assessment of Lusitanian forms.[66] Accepting that Hispano-Celtic dialects preserved a reflex of Proto-Celtic *φ, which could be spelled *b-* in the Latin alphabet, one might wonder whether *p-* should be allowed as an alternative spelling. On the hypothesis that *φ was preserved in *φr- as well as *φl-, the *Celtici Praestamarci* might thus have had a purely Celtic epithet after all. If *praes-* is further identified with the base of Lusitanian PRAISOM and PRAESONDO, these again would have to be regarded as Celtic loans, or perhaps as indigenous equivalents of the Celtic form, just as ENVPETANIM might be a Lusitanian or *p*-Celtic word to be compared with *Ucuete* in *p*-Celtic Gaul.

The assumption that Western Hispano-Celtic shares with Lusitanian (and with the rest of Celtic) the development *g^w > *b*, but also, at least in some cases, *k^w > *p*, implies that the development of the labiovelars cannot be used as a distinguishing criterion for words of Lusitanian or Hispano-Celtic provenance. A distinction is supposedly found in the treatment of *kw, where Celtic has *p*, but Lusitanian *q* (or *-kk-* in ICCONA according to Prósper). However, the probative value of examples with *q* must remain doubtful, as they tend to rely on ad hoc etymologies invoking *wo*-formations, and the possibility of *q*-Celtic dialect forms in the area cannot be ruled out. While for some Hispano-Celtic forms with *p-*, such as the tribal name of the *Pelendones* in Celtiberia, etymologies starting from *kw may be envisaged more confidently, if the presence of *p*-Celtic speakers in the Peninsula is admitted, the sound change *kw > *p* loses its force in separating Lusitanian from Celtic.

There is no clear example proving that the western Celts shared the development *$p...kw$ > *$kw...kw$ (> *$p...p$), but as the sound change is usually regarded as Proto-Celtic, it seems quite probable that they did. This would be another isogloss with Lusitanian then, and while Prósper stresses (p. 397) that the chronology might be different for the two languages, the chronology is not established with absolute certainty for Celtic (McCone 1996, 44). Still, the possibility that north-western Celtic had a numeral *$pempe$ 'five' (< *k^wenk^we < *$penk^we$, cf. Gaulish *pempe*, Old Welsh *pimp*), identical with the presumed Lusitanian form *$pempe$ (< *$penk^we$), would make the presence of widely attested names in *Pent-* and *Pint-* in their territory easier to understand, as the similarity to their cardinal number may have been observed (cf. Prósper 2002, 398).[67]

§ 19 The number of etymological possibilities and the presumed phonological

---

66   *p*-Celtic forms in the Iberian Peninsula, a reflex of *φ in *Bletisam(a)* and, moreover, the presence of 'Gaulish-looking' forms like the dative plurals in *-bo* have also been recently acknowledged by Villar (2004).

67   Villar (1994) has doubted the Celtic character of these names on morphological grounds, as one might expect an ordinal formation in *-eto-* (cf. Gaulish *pinpetos*, Old Welsh *pimphet*). Yet Gaulish *suexos* vs. Middle Welsh *chweched* and Old Irish *tris* vs. Old Welsh *tritid* vs. Gaulish *tritos* indicate that Celtic ordinal formation was not completely immune to suffix variation.

isoglosses shared by Lusitanian and Western Hispano-Celtic thus leads to a more and more impenetrable mix of linguistic material, particularly when one allows for the massive interchange of loanwords in the onomastic systems of these languages, the only well-attested linguistic subsystems for both. There is an obvious danger here of ignoring the philological evidence, which points to a fairly unitary lusitano-gallaecian linguistic continuum (while allowing for dialectal diversities), and opting for a purely etymological assessment of relevant forms. This is all the more problematic because the 'one form–one meaning' relationship required for sound etymologies is necessarily lacking, as the meanings of the solely onomastically attested forms, as well as of most of the probable common nouns in the indigenous Lusitanian inscriptions, are unknown. This approach can therefore easily lead to a vicious circle, when a preconceived etymological 'knowledge' is superimposed on linguistic material of unknown semantics to establish 'sound laws', which in turn will be the only proof of linguistic affiliation. The high number of loanwords which have to be assumed on both sides, but especially on the Lusitanian side, partly results from the contradiction between etymological assumptions and the inscriptional context. This contradiction is reflected e.g. in De Hoz' (2005, 88f.) suggestion to see in 'el masivo uso de elementos célticos que encontramos en lusitano' an indication of language death, when Lusitanian had come under pressure by Celtic and Latin, and in Schmidt's desperate statement on the problem of 'identifying Lusitanian' in Lusitanian texts (above § 16).

§ 20 It is this range of problems in telling the Celtic and Lusitanian forms apart which has led some scholars to the conclusion that Lusitanian and the Western Hispano-Celtic of *Gallaecia* are in fact one language, with merely dialectal diversity. Corominas (1972, 206), Untermann (1985–6) and Ballester (2004) risked the proposal that, given the archaic character of Hispano-Celtic, the languages of the west might be an early form of Celtic with Proto-Indo-European *p preserved.[68]

A hypothesis for a historical scenario concerning the position of Lusitanian has been developed by Almagro-Gorbea (1993, 125, 128, 144), who suggests that Lusitanian might be regarded as a pre-Celtic language, which formed the basis for the development of Celtic in the west of the Iberian Peninsula. In accordance with archaeological data, the Celtic culture of Celtiberia is here understood as emerging from an older cultural and linguistic stratum of which Lusitanian is the remnant in Roman times.[69] In this model the genetic relationship of Celtiberian with the Celtic languages outside of the Iberian Peninsula needs to be more clearly defined.[70]

---

68 Ballester (2004, 53f.) draws attention to the lack of p in Iberian and Aquitanian, which may have accelerated its complete loss in neighbouring languages like Celtiberian; cf. also McCone (1996, 43), Koch (2009, 129).

69 By contrast, Ruiz-Gálvez (1991) thinks of Lusitanian as a trade language of the Atlantic zone in the Late Bronze Age; Alarcão (2001, 322ff.), on the basis of an interpretation of the *Ora Maritima*, argues for a mass invasion of Lusitanians from the western coasts of Gaul by the end of the second millennium BC.

70 The same is true for alleged similarities between Lusitanian and Italic on the one hand, and Celtic and

The assessment of the linguistically Celtic and non-Celtic features in western Spain, Galicia and Portugal depends crucially on the interpretation of the evidence, specifically the etymologies accepted and the conclusions drawn from them regarding historical phonology and thereby linguistic affiliation. As has become clear above, interpretations suggested so far are by no means unanimously accepted. Contrasting opinions on individual words could be multiplied. For a number of forms, as e.g. for many names containing -q-, etymologies are quite arbitrary, and while the development $*k^w > p$ at least in some of the dialects spoken in the western Peninsula has long been used as an explanatory device, it usually remains disputable for individual forms. The problem of Lusitanian is therefore its demarcation from Celtic in the west of the Iberian Peninsula and the justification for the assumption of an extensive body of loanwords on both the Lusitanian and Celtic sides. The case may be argued for every individual word, but etymological arguments based on purely formal grounds are hardly sufficient as the only criterion.

BIBLIOGRAPHY

AE: *L'Année épigraphique*. Paris, 1888–.

Alarcão, J. de 2001 'Novas perspectivas sobre os Lusitanos (e outros mundos)', *Revista Portuguesa de Arqueologia* 4, 293–349.

Albertos, M. L. 1975 'Organizaciones suprafamiliares en la Hispania antigua', *Studia Archaeologica* 37, Valladolid = *Boletín del Seminario de Estudios de Arte y Arqueología* 40–1, 5–66.

Albertos, M. L. 1985 'La onomástica personal indígena del noroeste peninsular (astures y galaicos)'. *Actas del III Coloquio sobre lenguas y culturas paleohispánicas (Lisboa, 5–8 noviembre 1980)*, ed. J. de Hoz, 255–310. Salamanca, Ediciones Universidad Salamanca.

Albertos, M. L. 1985–6 'Las aspiradas en las lenguas paleohispánicas: la F y la H', *Studia Palaeohispanica. Actas del IV Coloquio sobre lenguas y culturas paleohispánicas*, Vitoria-Gasteiz 1985 = *Veleia* 2–3, 139–43.

Almagro-Gorbea, M. 1993 'Los Celtas en la Península Ibérica: origen y personalidad cultural'. *Los Celtas: Hispania y Europa*, eds. M. Almagro-Gorbea & G. Ruiz Zapatero, 121–73. Madrid, Actas de El Escorial, Universidad Complutense.

Almagro-Gorbea, M., et al. 1999 'Una nueva inscripción lusitana: Arroyo de la Luz III', *Complutum* 10, 167–73.

Ares Vázquez, N. 1965–6 'Ara dedicada a Reo Paramaeco Aidi', *Boletín de la Comisión Provincial de Monumentos Históricos y Artísticos de Lugo* 8, 10–14.

Ballester, X. 2004 "Páramo' o del problema de la */p/ en celtoide', *Studi Celtici* 3, 45–56.

Beltrán Lloris, M. 1975–6 'Aportaciones a la epigrafía y arqueología romanas de Cáceres', *Caesaraugusta* 39–40, 19–101.

Berrocal Rangel, L. 1993 *Los pueblos célticos del suroeste de la Península Ibérica*. Madrid, Editorial Complutense.

Blázquez, J. M. 1962 *Religiones primitivas de Hispania I*. Roma, Consejo Superior de Investigaciones Científicas, Delegación de Roma.

Búa, C. 1997 'Dialectos indoeuropeos na franxa occidental hispánica'. *Galicia fai dous mil anos. O feito diferencial galego, vol. I*, ed. G. Pereira Menaut, 51–99. Santiago de Compostela, Museo do Pobo Galego.

Búa, C. 1999 'Hipótesis para algunas inscripciones rupestres del occidente

Italic on the other. Such similarities have been discussed at length by Prósper (2002, 429ff. and 2007, 103ff.), but consequences for the linguistic geography of these languages still have to be made explicit.

peninsular'. *Pueblos, lenguas y escrituras en la Hispania Prerromana, Actas del VII coloquio sobre lenguas y culturas paleohispánicas, Zaragoza 12 a 15 Marzo 1997*, eds. F. Villar & F. Beltrán, 309–27. Salamanca, Ediciones Universidad Salamanca.

Búa, C. 2000 *Estudio lingüistico de la teonimia lusitano-gallega*. Tesis doctoral, Universidad de Salamanca.

Carneiro, André, José d'Encarnação, et al. 2008 'Uma inscriçao votiva em língua lusitana', *Palaeohispanica* 8, 167–78.

CIL II: *Corpus Inscriptionum Latinarum. Vol. II*, ed. E. Hübner. Berlin, Akademie der Wissenschaften, 1869–92.

CIRG I: *Corpus de inscricións romanas de Galicia, Vol. I*, ed. G. Pereira Menaut. Santiago de Compostela, 1991.

Corominas, J. 1972 *Tópica Hespérica*. Madrid, Gredos.

De Hoz, J. 2001 'Sobre algunos problemas del estudio de las lenguas paleohispánicas', *Palaeohispanica* 1, 113–49.

De Hoz, J. 2005 'Epigrafías y lenguas en contacto en la Hispania antigua', *Palaeohispanica* 5, 57–98.

Encarnação, J. d' 1987 'Divindades indígenas da Lusitânia', *Conimbriga* 26, 5–37.

Eska, J. F. 1998 '*p > Ø in Proto-Celtic', *Münchener Studien zur Sprachwissenschaft* 58, 63–80.

Fariña Busto, F., & J. Suárez Otero 2002 'El santuario galaico-romano de O Facho (O Hío, Pontevedra)', *Boletín Auriense* 32, 25–52.

García Alonso, J. L. 2003 *La Península Ibérica en la Geografía de Claudio Ptolomeo*. Vitoria-Gasteiz, Anejos de Veleia, Series Minor 19.

González Rodríguez, M. C. 1986 *Las unidades organizativas indígenas del área indoeuropea de Hispania*. Vitoria-Gasteiz, Anejos de Veleia 2.

Gorrochategui, J. 1985–6 'En torno a la clasificación de Lusitano'. *Studia Palaeohispanica. Actas del IV Coloquio sobre lenguas y culturas paleohispánicas*, Vitoria-Gasteiz 1985 = *Veleia* 2–3, 77–91.

Guerra, A. 2005 'Povos, cultura e língua no ocidente peninsular: uma perspectiva, a partir da toponomástica', *Palaeohispanica* 5, 793–822.

HAE: *Hispania antiqua epigraphica*. Madrid.

HE: *Hispania epigraphica*. Madrid.

Hübner, E. 1913 'Additamenta nova ad corporis vol. II', *Ephemeris epigraphica* 9, 12–185.

ILER: J. Vives, *Inscripciones latinas de la España romana*. Barcelona, Universidad de Barcelona, 1971–2.

Isaac, G. R. 2007 *Studies in Celtic Sound Changes and their Chronology*. Innsbruck, Innsbrucker Beiträge zur Sprachwissenschaft.

Jordán, C. 2006 '[K.3.3]: Crónica de un teicidio anunciado', *Estudios de lenguas y epigrafía antiguas* 7, 37–72.

Jungandreas, W. 1981 *Sprachliche Studien zur germanischen Altertumskunde*. Wiesbaden, Franz Steiner Verlag.

Koch, J. T. 2009 *Tartessian: Celtic in the South-west at the Dawn of History*. Aberystwyth, Celtic Studies Publications.

KP: St. Schumacher unter Mitarbeit von Britta Schulze-Thulin und Caroline aan de Wiel, *Die keltischen Primärverben*. Innsbruck, Innsbrucker Beiträge zur Sprachwissenschaft, 2004.

Lorrio, A. J. & J. Velaza, 2005 'La primera inscripción celtibérica sobre plomo', *Palaeohispanica* 5, 1031–48.

Lühr, R. 1979 'Das Wort "und" im Westgermanischen', *Münchener Studien zur Sprachwissenschaft* 38, 117–54.

Luján, E. 2007 'L'onomastique des Vettons: analyse linguistique'. *Gaulois et celtique continental*, eds. P.-Y. Lambert & G.-J. Pinault, 245–75. Genève, Librairie Droz.

Luján, E. 2008 'Galician place-names attested epigraphically'. *Celtic and Other Languages in Ancient Europe*, ed. J. L. García Alonso, 65–82. Salamanca, Ediciones Universidad de Salamanca.

McCone, K. 1996 *Towards a Relative Chronology of Ancient and Medieval Celtic Sound Change*. Maynooth, Maynooth Studies in Celtic Linguistics I.

Matasović, R. 2009 *Etymological Dictionary of Proto-Celtic*. Leiden, Brill.

MLH III.1: J. Untermann, *Monumenta Linguarum Hispanicarum, vol. III.1. Die iberischen Inschriften aus Spanien. Literaturverzeichnis, Einleitung, Indices*. Wiesbaden, 1990.

MLH IV: J. Untermann in collaboration with D. S. Wodtko, *Monumenta Linguarum Hispanicarum, vol. IV. Die tartessischen, kelt-*

iberischen und lusitanischen Inschriften. Wiesbaden, 1997.

MLH V.1: D. S. Wodtko, *Monumenta Linguarum Hispanicarum, vol. V.1. Wörterbuch der keltiberischen Inschriften*. Wiesbaden, 2000.

NIL: D. S. Wodtko, B. Irslinger, & C. Schneider, *Nomina im indogermanischen Lexikon*. Heidelberg, 2008.

Pedersen, H. 1909 *Vergleichende Grammatik der keltischen Sprachen. Vol. I*. Göttingen, Vandenhoeck und Ruprecht.

Prosdocimi, A. L. 1989 'L'iscrizione gallica del Larzac e la flessione dei temi in -*a*, -*i*, -*ja*. Con un "excursus" sulla morfologia del lusitano: acc. *crougin*, dat. *crougeai*', *Indogermanische Forschungen* 94, 190–206.

Prósper, B. M. 2002 *Lenguas y religiones prerromanas del occidente de la Península Ibérica*. Salamanca, Ediciones Universidad Salamanca.

Prósper, B. M. 2004 'Varia palaeohispanica occidentalia', *Palaeohispanica* 4, 169–94.

Prósper, B. M. 2007 *Estudio lingüístico del plomo celtibérico de Iniesta*. Salamanca, Ediciones Universidad de Salamanca.

Prósper, B. M. 2008 'En los márgenes de la lingüística celta: los etnónimos del noroeste de la Península Ibérica y una ley fonética del hispano-celta occidental', *Palaeohispanica* 8, 35–54.

Rodríguez Ramos, J. 2001–2 'Okelakom, Sekeida, Bolsken', *Kalathos* 20–21, 429–34.

Rubio Orecilla, F. 2001 'Las formaciones secundarias en -*ko*- del celtibérico'. *Religión, lengua y cultura prerromanas de Hispania*, eds. F. Villar & M. P. Fernández Álvarez, 581–94. Salamanca, Ediciones Universidad de Salamanca.

Ruiz-Gálvez, M. 1991 'Songs of a Wayfaring Lad: Late Bronze Age Atlantic Exchange and the Building of the Regional Identity in the West Iberian Peninsula', *Oxford Journal of Archaeology* 10, 277–306.

Russell, P. 1990 *Celtic Word Formation: The Velar Suffixes*. Dublin, Dublin Institute for Advanced Studies.

Schmidt, K. H. 1985 'A Contribution to the Identification of Lusitanian'. *Actas del III coloquio sobre lenguas y culturas paleohispánicas*,

ed. J. de Hoz, 319–41. Salamanca, Ediciones Universidad de Salamanca.

Schrijver, P. 1997 'On the nature and origin of word-initial *h*- in the Würzburg Glosses', *Ériu* 48, 205–27.

Sims-Williams, P. 2007 'Common Celtic, Gallo-Brittonic and Insular Celtic'. *Gaulois et celtique continental*, eds. P.-Y. Lambert & G.-J. Pinault, 309–54. Genève, Librairie Droz.

Tovar, A. 1966–7 'L'inscription du Cabeço das Fraguas et la langue des Lusitaniens', *Études Celtiques* 11, 237–68.

Uhlich, J. 1993 *Die Morphologie der komponierten Personennamen des Altirischen*. Witterschlick/Bonn, M. Wehle.

Untermann, J. 1965 *Elementos de un Atlas Antroponímico de la Hispania Antigua*. Madrid, Consejo Superior de Investigaciones Scientíficas, Universidad de Madrid.

Untermann, J. 1985–6 'Lusitanisch, Keltiberisch, Keltisch'. *Studia Palaeohispanica. Actas del IV Coloquio sobre lenguas y culturas paleohispánicas*, Vitoria-Gasteiz 1985 = *Veleia* 2–3, 57–76.

Untermann, J. 1988 'Zur Morphologie der lusitanischen Götternamen'. *Homenagem a Joseph M. Piel por ocasião do seu 85.⁰ aniversário*, ed. D. Kremer, 123–38. Tübingen, Max Niemeyer.

Untermann, J. 1999 '"Alteuropäisch" in Hispanien'. *Florilegium linguisticum. Festschrift für Wolfgang P. Schmid zum 70. Geburtstag*, eds. E. Eggers, J. Becker, et al., 509–18. Frankfurt am Main, Peter Lang.

Untermann, J. 2001 'La toponimia antigua como fuente de las lenguas hispano-celtas', *Palaeohispanica* 1, 187–218.

Untermann, J. 2004 'Célticos y Túrdulos', *Palaeohispanica* 4, 199–214.

Untermann, J. 2007 'Topónimos y apelativos de la lengua lusitano-galaica'. *Onomástica galega: con especial considerción da situación prerromana*, ed. D. Kremer, 57–73. Santiago de Compostela, Verba Anexo 58.

Untermann, J. forthcoming 'Galicia y Celtiberia: rasgos comunes y diferentes'. *Anexos Verba*, ed. D. Kremer. Santiago de Compostela.

Vallejo Ruiz, J. M. 2005 *Antroponimia indígena de la Lusitania romana*. Vitoria-Gasteiz, Anejos de

Veleia, Series Minor 23.

Vallejo Ruiz, J. M. 2005a 'La composición en la antroponimia antigua de la Península Ibérica', *Palaeohispanica* 5, 99–134.

Vallejo Ruiz, J. M. 2008 'El género en la antroponimia antigua: algunas consideraciones galas e hispanas', *Palaeohispanica* 8, 143–63.

Villar, F. 1990 'Indo-Européens et Pré-Indo-Européens dans la Péninsule Ibérique'. *When Worlds Collide: Indo-Europeans and Pre-Indo-Europeans*, eds. T. L. Markey & J. A. C. Greppin, 363–94. Ann Arbor, Michigan, Karoma.

Villar, F. 1994 'Los antropónimos en *Pent-*, *Pint-* y las lenguas indoeuropeas prerromanas de la Península Ibérica'. *Indogermanica et Caucasica, Festschrift für Karl Horst Schmidt zum 65. Geburtstag*, eds. R. Bielmeier & R. Stempel, 234–64. Berlin/New York, de Gruyter.

Villar, F. 1995 *Estudios de celtibérico y de toponimia prerromana*. Salamanca, Ediciones Universidad Salamanca.

Villar, F. 1996 'El teónimo lusitano Reve y sus epítetos'. *Die grö\u0301weren altkeltischen Sprachdenkmäler*, eds. W. Meid & P. Anreiter, 160–211. Innsbruck, Innsbrucker Beiträge zur Sprachwissenschaft.

Villar, F. 2004 'The Celtic Language of the Iberian Peninsula'. *Studies in Baltic and Indo-European Linguistics in honor of William R. Schmalstieg*, eds. P. Baldi & P. U. Dini, 243–74. Amsterdam, John Benjamins.

Villar, F., & R. Pedrero 2001 'La nueva inscripción lusitana: Arroyo de la Luz III'. *Religión, lengua y cultura prerromanas de Hispania*, eds. F. Villar & M. P. Fernández Álvarez, 663–98. Salamanca, Ediciones Universidad de Salamanca.

Villar F., & R. Pedrero 2001a 'Arroyo de la Luz III', *Palaeohispanica* 1, 235–74.

Villar, F., & B. M. Prósper 2005 *Vascos, celtas e indoeuropeos: genes y lenguas*. Salamanca, Ediciones Universidad Salamanca.

APPENDIX
Vocabulary of Lusitanian inscriptions

*EC	L 1.1		CAELOBRIGOI	L 2.1
*EDAGAROM	L 1.1		CANTI	L 4.1
]IOM	L 1.2		CANTIBIDONE	L 4.1
*RE[	L 3.1		CARLA	L 4.1
]TOM	L 1.2		CARLAE	L 1.1
				L 1.2
AHARACVI	L 4.1		COMAIAM	L 3.1
AILATIO	L 4.1		CROVCEAI	L 2.1
AMPILVA	L 1.1			
ANGOM	L 2.1		DOENTI	L 2.1
APINVS	L 4.1			
ARIMO	L 1.1		EM[	L 1.2
ARIMOM	L 1.1		ENVPETANIM	L 1.1
ATTEDIA	L 4.1		ERBA	L 1.1
AV[	L 4.1		ERBAM	L 4.1
AVA	L 1.1		ERIACAINV[S	L 4.1
BANDI	L 4.1		GOEMINNA	L.1.1
BROENEIAE	L 4.1			
			H	L 4.1
			HARACVI	L 4.1
			HARASE	L 4.1

I	L 4.1	PETRANIOI	L 2.1
I**	L 1.1	PORCOM	L 3.1
ICCINVI	L 4.1	PORGOM	L 2.1
ICCONA	L 3.1	PRAESONDO	L 1.1
IEATE	L 4.1	PRAISOM	L 1.1
IFADEM[(?)	L 3.1	PVMPI	L 4.1
INDI	L 1.1 (8x)	PVPPID	L 1.2
	L 1.2		
	L 3.1 (2x)	REVE	L 3.1
IOVEA.	L 2.1		L 4.1
ISAICCID	L 1.2	RVETI	L 1.2
		RVRSE*CO	L 1.1
LABBO	L 3.1		
LAMATICOM	L 2.1	SECIAS	L 1.1
LOEMINA	L 3.1	SINGEIE*O	L 1.1
		SINTAMO	L 1.1
M.	L 4.1	SINTAMOM	L 1.1
MAGAREAICOI	L 2.1		
MVITIEAS	L 1.1	T.	L 4.1
MVNITIE	L 4.1	TADOM	L 2.1
		TAVROM	L 3.1
NAC[	L 1.2	TEVCAECOM	L 1.1
NVRIM	L 1.1	TEVCOM	L 1.1
		TR.	L 4.1
OIIA	L.4.1	TREBARVNE	L 3.1
OILA	L 4.1	TREBOPALA	L 3.1
OILAM	L 3.1 (2x), L.4.1		
	L 4.1	VDE	L 1.1
OVOVIANI[(?)	L 4.1	VEAMNICORI	L 2.1
		VEAVN	L 1.1
PANDIT	L 4.1	VENDICVS	L 4.1
		VSSEAM	L 3.1

Reverse index of words attested on Lusitanian inscriptions

I**	L.1.1	ERBA	L 1.1
NAC[	L.1.2	IOVEA. (?)	L 2.1
*RE[	L.3.1	ATTEDIA	L 4.1
EM[	L.1.2	OIIA	L.4.1
AV[	L 4.1	TREBOPALA	L 3.1
		OILA	L 4.1

CARLA L 4.1
LOEMINA L 3.1
ICCONA L 3.1
AVA L 1.1
AMPILVA L 1.1

*EC L 1.1

ISAICCID L 1.2
PVPPID L 1.2

BROENEIAE L 4.1
CARLAE L 1.1
MVNITIE L 4.1
CANTIBIDONE L 4.1
TREBARVNE L 3.1
HARASE L 4.1
IEATE L 4.1
REVE L 3.1
L 4.1

H L 4.1

I L 4.1
CROVCEAI L 2.1
BANDI L 4.1
INDI L 1.1 (8x)
L 1.2
L 3.1 (2x)
OVOVIANI[(?)L 4.1
MAGAREAICOI L 2.1
CAELOBRIGOI L 2.1
PETRANIOI L 2.1
PVMPI L 4.1
VEAMNICORI L 2.1
RVETI L 1.2
CANTI L 4.1
DOENTI L 2.1
HARACVI L 4.1
AHARACVI L 4.1
ICCINVI L 4.1

M. L 4.1
ERBAM L 4.1
VSSEAM L 3.1
COMAIAM L 3.1
OILAM L 3.1 (2x)
L 4.1
IFADEM[(?) L 3.1
ENVPETANIM L 1.1
NVRIM L 1.1
TEVCAECOM L 1.1
LAMATICOM L 2.1
PORCOM L 3.1
TEVCOM L 1.1
TADOM L 2.1
ANGOM L 2.1
PORGOM L 2.1
]IOM L 1.2
SINTAMOM L 1.1
ARIMOM L 1.1
*EDAGAROM L 1.1
TAVROM L 3.1
PRAISOM L 1.1
]TOM L 1.2

VEAVN L 1.1

SINGEIE*O L 1.1
LABBO L 3.1
RVRSE*CO L 1.1
PRAESONDO L 1.1
AILATIO L 4.1
SINTAMO L 1.1
ARIMO L 1.1

TR. L 4.1

MVITIEAS L 1.1
SECIAS L 1.1
VENDICVS L 4.1
ERIACAINV[S L 4.1
APINVS L 4.1

PANDIT L 4.1

ABBREVIATED LANGUAGE NAMES USED IN THE INDEX

Av	Avestan
B	Breton
Brit	(Old) British
Britt	Brittonic
C	Cornish
Celt	Celtic
Cis	Cisalpine Gaulish/Celtic
Ctb	Celtiberian
Cumb	Cumbric
E	English
EW	Early Welsh
Galat	Galatian
Gall.Lat.	Gallo-Latin
Gaul	Gaulish
Gk	Greek
Goth	Gothic
HC/Lus	Hispano-Celtic or Lusitanian (pre-Roman from the Indo-European zone of the Iberian Peninsula)
Hitt	Hittite
Ib	Iberian
IE	(Proto-)Indo-European
Ir	Irish
Lat	Latin
Lpt	Lepontic
Lus	Lusitanian
MB	Middle Breton
MC	Middle Cornish
MIr	Middle Irish
MW	Middle Welsh
Myc	Mycenaean Greek
Num	Numidian (Old Berber)
OB	Old Breton
OC	Old Cornish
OCS	Old Church Slavonic
OE	Old English
Og	Ogamic Primitive Irish
OHG	Old High German
OIr	Old Irish
ON	Old Norse
OW	Old Welsh
Phoen	Phoenician/Punic
Pict	Pictish
PrW	Primitive Welsh
Scand	Scandinavian (Norse)
ScG	Scottish Gaelic
Sem	Semitic
Skt	Sanskrit (incl. Vedic)
T	Tartessian
W	Welsh

INDEX